ATTENTION À LA MARCHE MIND THE GAP

ÉQUIPE DE DIRECTION

Bertrand Gervais, UQAM, directeur / Chair
Caitlin Fisher, Université York, co-directrice / Co-Chair
Joanne Lalonde, UQAM, direction du comité artistique / Artistic Committee Chair
Sophie Marcotte, Université Concordia, direction du comité scientifique / Scientific Committee Chair
Marcello Vitali-Rosati, Université de Montréal, direction du comité francophone / French Committee Chair
Dene Grigar, WSUV, présidente de ELO / ELO President
Ariane Savoie, UQAM, NT2, chargée de projet / Project Manager
Gina Cortopassi, UQAM, NT2, coordination générale / Event Coordinator
Élaine Després, UQAM, centre Figura, coordination générale / Event Coordinator
Michaël Trahan, Figura-NT2-Concordia, coordination Concordia / Concordia Coordinator
Lisa Tronca, UQAM, NT2, Exposition *Uchronia* | *What If?* Exhibition
Jean-Michel Berthiaume, UQAM, NT2, assistant à la coordination / Coordination Assistant
Robin Varenas, UQAM, NT2, équipe médiatique / Media Team
Sylvain Aubé, UQAM, NT2, équipe médiatique / Media Team
Sophie Julien, direction artistique / Artistic Director
Hugo Marchand, coordination, direction artistique / Artistic Director Coordinator
Kevin Nicolas, direction technique / Technical Director
Marc-Antoine Goyette, assistant / Assistant
Vanessa Duval, graphisme / Graphic Designer
Sarah Grenier-Millette, Benoit Bordeleau, Charles Marsolais-Ricard, UQAM, NT2

ÉQUIPE ÉDITORIALE

Bertrand Gervais et Sophie Marcotte, directeurs de la publication / Editors
Gina Cortopassi, chargée de projet / Project Manager
Emmanuelle Lescouët, éditrice / Publisher
Gwénaël Graindorge, éditeur / Publisher
Alexandra Martin, réviseure et traductrice / Copy editor and Translator
Anastasia Llewellyn, traductrice / Translator

TECHNIQUE

Emmanuelle Lescouët, édition sémantique et mise en page sous Stylo / Semantic editing and layout in Stylo
Emmanuelle Lescouët & Gwénaël Graindorge, créations des publications numérique et papier / Creators of digital and paper publications
Polices de caratères utilisées / fonts used : Garamond MD Std, Georgia, Roboto, Sofia, Open Dyslexic

Dépôt légal : novembre 2020
ISSN : en cours – ISBN : 979-10-384-0004-7

Fonds de recherche Société et culture Québec
Canada Research Chairs / Chaires de recherche du Canada
Canada
figura Centre de recherche sur le texte et l'imaginaire
Conseil de recherches en sciences humaines du Canada / Social Sciences and Humanities Research Council of Canada
Canada

Attention à la marche! / Mind The Gap!

THINKING ELECTRONIC LITERATURE
IN A DIGITAL CULTURE

*PENSER LA LITTÉRATURE ÉLECTRONIQUE
EN CULTURE NUMÉRIQUE*

sous la direction de / edited by
BERTRAND GERVAIS
& SOPHIE MARCOTTE

LES PRESSES *DE* L'ÉCUREUIL

Table des matières
Table of contents

PARTIE 2

LE LANGAGE COMME INTERFACE
LANGUAGE AS INTERFACE

PARTIE 3

PLATEFORMES ET NARRATIONS
PLATFORMS AND NARRATIVES

PARTIE 4

ESTHÉTIQUES NUMÉRIQUES
DIGITAL AESTHETICS

PARTIE 5

LIRE ET ÉCRIRE EN CULTURE NUMÉRIQUE
READING AND WRITING IN A DIGITAL CULTURE

PARTIE 6

PERSPECTIVES DIACHRONIQUES SUR LA LITTÉRATURE ÉLECTRONIQUE
READING E-LIT ACROSS TIME

BERTRAND GERVAIS
SOPHIE MARCOTTE

Attention à la marche!

Penser la littérature électronique en culture numérique

Mind The Gap!

Thinking Electronic Literature in a Digital Culture

Comme un train entré en gare, la littérature électronique s'est arrêtée en 2018, le temps d'une escale, dans ce vaste immeuble tout neuf que représente la culture numérique. Le train avait déjà un certain âge, tandis que la gare était récente. Il apparaissait évident que la rencontre entre les deux n'était pas parfaite. À tout moment, on risquait de trébucher, surtout si on ne faisait pas attention où l'on mettait les pieds. Il y avait un écart, une faible distance, entre le marchepied et le quai. Faible, de sorte que de loin, on ne le remarquait guère, mais assez marqué pour provoquer des faux pas.

Le congrès de l'Electronic Literature Organization, *Attention à la marche!*, tenu à Montréal à la fin de l'été 2018, entendait questionner de façon explicite la place de la littérature électronique dans la culture numérique. Quelle est la nature de la relation entre les deux? Comment une forme déjà vieille de cinquante ans parvient-elle à rester pertinente dans un environnement culturel fortement marqué par le numérique? Comment une pratique d'avant-garde développée en culture du livre réussit-elle à s'ajuster aux principes d'une culture de l'écran?

Les expressions « littérature électronique » et « culture numérique » viennent d'être employées comme s'il s'agissait de pratiques ou de champs homogènes aisés à définir. Il en va évidemment tout autrement. En effet, la littérature électronique n'a pas connu un développement homogène, elle n'a pas suivi une progression linéaire; et on en serait même rendu, comme le dit Leonardo Flores (**2019**), à une troisième génération. Les deux premières générations, définies par N. Katherine Hayles, permettaient de distinguer, d'une part, une littérature pré-web, fondée sur des formes complexes de textualité, axées notamment sur les fonctionnalités de l'hypertextualité, mais respectant globalement les conventions de la culture de l'imprimé et du livre; et d'autre part, à partir de 1995, un ensemble de pratiques basées sur le web et intégrant le multimédia et l'interactivité (Hayles **2008**). La troisième génération est celle de la littérature numérique en tant que telle, une littérature qui se sert de l'ensemble des dispositifs et des plateformes de diffusion rendus disponibles par les développements informatiques récents, notamment les développements de l'infrastructure technologique qu'est Internet. Cette dernière génération englobe les deux premières qui continuent à avoir leurs adeptes et épigones.

Like a train entering the station, electronic literature stopped in 2018 in the vast new building that is digital culture. The train was already a certain age, while the station was brand new. It was obvious that the meeting between the two was not perfect. At any time, there was a risk of stumbling, especially if you weren't careful where you set foot. There was a gap, a small distance, between the step and the platform. It was small, so that from a distance you could hardly notice it, but it was marked enough to cause you to stumble.

The Electronic Literature Organization's conference *Mind the Gap!*, held in Montreal in late summer 2018, was intended to explicitly question the place of electronic literature in digital culture. What is the nature of the relationship between the two? How does a form that was already fifty years old manage to remain relevant in a cultural environment strongly marked by digital technology? How does an avant-garde practice developed in the context of book culture succeed in adjusting to the principles of a culture heavily engaged in screens, networks and mobile devices.

We've just used the terms "electronic literature" and "digital culture" as if they were practices or homogeneous fields that are easy to define. This is obviously false. Indeed, electronic literature has not developed homogeneously, it has not followed a linear progression; and we are even in the presence, as Leonardo Flores (**2019**) says, of a third generation. The first two generations, as defined by N. Katherine Hayles, made it possible to distinguish, on the one hand, a pre-web literature based on complex forms of textuality, focusing in particular on the functionalities of hypertextuality but generally respecting the conventions of print and book culture; and on the other hand, from 1995 onwards, a set of web-based practices integrating multimedia and interactivity (Hayles **2008**). The third generation is that of digital literature as such, a form that makes use of all the devices and platforms made available by recent computer developments, particularly developments in the technological infrastructure that is the Internet. This last generation encompasses the first two which continue to have their followers and epigones.

De la même façon, il n'y a pas une seule culture numérique, mais un ensemble de pratiques culturelles, artistiques et textuelles, diverses et non conventionnelles, pour ne pas dire divergentes, en marge bien souvent des institutions (quoique celles-ci cherchent de plus en plus à les intégrer), qui se servent de ces dispositifs et plateformes de diffusion ou de l'infrastructure d'Internet. Comprendre les manifestations et la logique sous-jacente des cultures numériques exige des formes de recherche et de recherche-création innovantes, ainsi que des approches à la croisée des disciplines, telles que l'herméneutique, l'esthétique ou l'ethnographie numériques (Miller **2011**), l'archéologie des médias, les humanités numériques, etc.

Le principal objectif du congrès ELO 2018, duquel découle la publication que ce texte introduit, était d'ailleurs de chercher à multiplier les perspectives critiques sur les formes de communication et d'imbrication, mais aussi de résistance entre littérature électronique et culture numérique, en réunissant un très grand nombre de chercheurs et d'artistes préoccupés par leur développement. La rencontre a ainsi servi à favoriser le renouvellement des perspectives de recherche et de recherche-création en littérature électronique, à mieux définir les zones de recoupement entre cette forme littéraire et les humanités numériques, à prendre en compte les technologies mobiles, de plus en plus présentes au quotidien, dans leur impact sur les habitudes d'écriture et de lecture et à investiguer la dimension politique du numérique, dans ses liens à l'art, à la littérature et à la culture. Parmi les autres thèmes abordés, on a pu noter un intérêt accru pour les principes de réalité augmentée et de réalité virtuelle, pour les formes et enjeux de la traduction (en termes de codes, de langues ou de médias), pour les spécificités langagières et culturelles de la littérature électronique, pour les liens entre le numérique et la culture urbaine, ainsi que pour les pratiques éditoriales destinées aux jeunes (les lecteurs de demain).

*

* *

Il est difficile de résumer une rencontre où une plus de cent cinquante communications et conférences ont été prononcées, un congrès accompagné d'une importante exposition de 60 œuvres numériques, ainsi que d'un festival de performances échelonné sur 3 soirées. Il est tout aussi difficile de structurer

Similarly, there is not a single digital culture, but a set of diverse and unconventional–not to say divergent–cultural, artistic and textual practices, often at the margins of institutions (although these are increasingly seeking to integrate them), which use these devices and platforms or the internet infrastructure. Understanding the manifestations and underlying logic of digital cultures requires innovative forms of research and research-creation, as well as cross-disciplinary approaches, such as hermeneutics, digital aesthetics or ethnography, media archaeology, digital humanities, etc. (Miller **2011**).

The main objective of the ELO 2018 conference, the origin this publication, was moreover to multiply critical perspectives on forms of communication and interaction, but also of resistance between electronic literature and digital culture, by bringing together a large number of researchers and artists concerned about their development. The meeting thus served to encourage research and research-creation perspectives in electronic literature, to better define the intersections between this literary form and digital humanities, to take into account mobile technologies which are increasingly present in everyday life, their impact on writing and reading habits, and to investigate the political dimension of digital technology, in its links to art, literature and culture. Other themes addressed during the four days of the conference included an increased interest in the principles of augmented and virtual reality, the forms and challenges of translation (in terms of codes, languages or media), the linguistic and cultural specificities of electronic literature, the links between digital and urban culture, and editorial practices aimed at young people, that is, the readers of tomorrow.

*

* *

It is difficult to summarize a meeting where some one hundred and fifty papers and conferences were delivered, a congress accompanied by a major exhibition of 60 digital works, as well as a festival of performances spread over three evenings. It is just as difficult to structure the 35 texts that have been proposed for publication and that are gathered here. The

les 35 textes qui ont été proposés pour publication et qui sont réunis ici. Le congrès ayant été bilingue, les textes publiés sont ainsi en français et en anglais. Nous n'avons pas choisi de les regrouper en fonction de la langue de rédaction, mais plutôt en regard des enjeux abordés.

L'ouvrage est composé de six sections. La première, intitulée « **Des sons, des bruits et des voix** », explore la dimension acoustique de notre relation à la littérature électronique. On ne fait pas que lire lorsque confrontés à de telles œuvres, on regarde des vidéos, on explore une architecture virtuelle et, dimension trop souvent oubliée, on écoute toute sortes de bruits et de sons. La deuxième section, « **Le langage comme interface** », suit de près cette première exploration, en portant l'attention cette fois sur la programmation et le code, dans leur capacité à structurer une expérience et à l'orienter de manière précise. Les pratiques numériques reposent sur du langage qui renouvelle notre rapport aux œuvres.

La troisième section, « **Plateformes et narrations** », examine diverses plateformes, allant des jeux vidéo aux dispositifs de Réalité Virtuelle, utilisées, voire détournées, afin de générer des œuvres inattendues, qui renouvellent notre compréhension des arts numériques. Sous le titre très large des « **Esthétiques numériques** », la quatrième section s'arrête sur quelques œuvres récentes, présentées bien souvent par les artistes qui les ont produites. Cette section permet de donner un aperçu des projets qui ont été exhibés dans le cadre du congrès et de son exposition.

La cinquième section « **Lire et écrire en culture numérique** » s'interroge sur nos stratégies de production et de réception des œuvres de littérature électronique, y compris dans les salles de classe. Cette interrogation permet de revenir de façon importante sur les enjeux pédagogiques de notre passage à la culture numérique, dimension qui devient de plus en plus importante.

Finalement, la sixième et dernière section s'arrête sur des « **Perspectives diachroniques sur la littérature électronique** ». Cette section est l'occasion d'approfondir notre connaissance des développements de la littérature numérique, depuis les 50 dernières années. L'hypothèse des trois générations de cette littérature, discutée d'entrée de jeu, y trouve un écho explicite.

conference was bilingual, thus the texts published are in French and English. We have not chosen to group them according to the language of writing, but rather according to the themes addressed.

The book is divided into six sections. The first, entitled "**Sounds, Noises and Voices**," explores the acoustic dimension of our relationship to electronic literature. We don't just read when confronted with such works, we watch videos, explore a virtual architecture and, a dimension too often forgotten, listen to all sorts of noises and sounds. The second section, "**Language as Interface**," follows closely on from this first exploration, this time focusing on programming and code, in their capacity to structure an experience and orient it in a precise manner. Digital practices are based on language that renews our relationship to works.

The third section, "**Platforms and Narratives**," examines various platforms, from video games to Virtual Reality devices, which are used, or even hijacked, to generate unexpected works that renew our understanding of digital art. Under the broad title of "**Digital Aesthetics**," the fourth section focuses on some recent works, often presented by the artists who produced them. This section provides an overview of the projects that were exhibited at the conference and its exhibition.

The fifth section, "**Reading and Writing in Digital Culture**," looks at the strategies used for producing and consuming electronic literature, including in the classroom. This questioning allows us to return in a significant way to the pedagogical stakes of our transition to digital culture, a dimension that is becoming increasingly important.

Finally, the sixth and last section focuses on "**Reading E-Lit across Time**." This section is an opportunity to deepen our knowledge of developments in digital literature over the last 50 years. The hypothesis of three generations of e-Lit, mentioned earlier, is explicitly echoed here.

This diachronic view closes the loop, as it were. The sections have followed one another in a centrifugal spiral, starting as close as possible to the text and its experience, from the acoustic or coding point of view, and gradually opening up to the platforms and devices exploited, the

Ce regard diachronique vient en quelque sorte boucler la boucle. Les sections se sont enchainées en fonction d'une spirale centrifuge, commençant au plus proche du texte et de son expérience, du point de vue acoustique ou du code, et s'ouvrant peu à peu aux plateformes et dispositifs exploités, aux principes esthétiques qui ont servi à la production et à la réception des œuvres, aux stratégies de lecture et d'écriture, abordées de façon analytique et, ultimement, aux transformations historiquement datées que cette pratique littéraire et artistique a connues.

aesthetic principles that have served for the production and reception of the works, the reading and writing strategies, approached analytically and, ultimately, the historically dated transformations that this literary and artistic practice has undergone.

Did we succeed in closing the gap? Mind you... We barely managed to look at the space itself and figure its form! But in doing so, we continued to explore a literary form that still evolves and questions our ability to represent our world.

Centre de Design, vue de l'exposition.

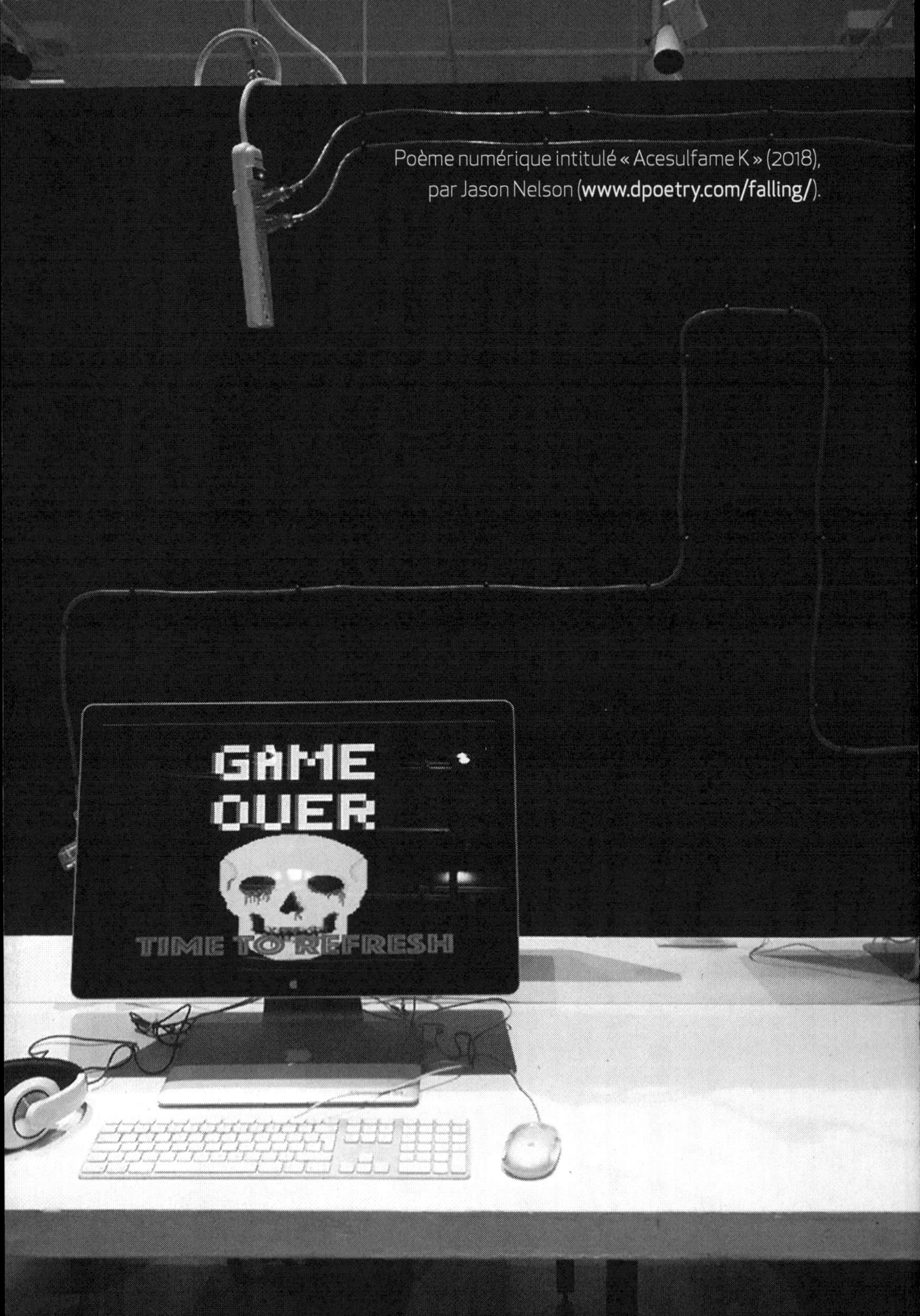

Poème numérique intitulé « Acesulfame K » (2018),
par Jason Nelson (**www.dpoetry.com/falling/**).

Centre de Design de l'UQAM,
vue de l'extérieur.

« It Must Have Been Dark By Then » (2017), par Duncan Speakman, présentée dans le cadre de l'exposition.

Flores, Leonardo. 2019. « Third Generation Electronic Literature ». *Electronic Book Review*. Link: https://doi.org/10.7273/axyj-3574

Hayles, Katherine N. 2008. *Electronic Literature. New Horizons for the Literary*. Indiana : Notre Dame University Press.

Miller, Vincent. 2011. *Understanding Digital Culture*. London : Sage.

Partie / Part 1

DES SONS, DES BRUITS ET DES VOIX

SOUNDS, NOISES AND VOICES

PART 1

DES SONS, DES BRUITS ET DES VOIX
SOUNDS, NOISES AND VOICES

Listening to Electronic Literature: Sounds At The Heart Of Works By Jeremy Hight, Stuart Moulthdrop, And Mohamed Habibi

JOHN F. BARBER

Abstract

This essay argues that sound(s) in electronic literature, experienced through listening, prompt(s) readers to re-think their relational experiences with literary worlds, real or imagined, with others in these spaces and places, and with themselves. This centrality of sound(s) is examined through discussions of works of electronic literature by Jeremy Hight et al., Stuart Moulthrop, and Mohamed Habibi. Each has something to say about listening to electronic literature.

Résumé

Cet article démontre que le(s) son(s) dont on fait l'expérience dans la littérature électronique poussent les lecteurs à repenser leurs expériences avec le monde littéraire, réel ou imaginé, avec les autres qui sont présents dans ces espaces et ces lieux, ainsi qu'avec eux-mêmes. La centralité des sons est examinée à travers l'analyse des œuvres de littérature électronique de Jeremy Hight et al., de Stuart Moulthrop et de Mohamed Habibi. Chacune de ces oeuvres nous dit quelque chose sur le son et l'écoute de la littérature électronique.

INTRODUCTION

Electronic literature, as a field of research and creative practice evolving from electronic and digital computing technologies, displays its artifacts primarily on screens of various devices. And, given its iterative and experimental evolution, one might suggest what one sees when considering electronic literature depends upon the perspective from which one looks. This essay suggests another way of considering electronic literature: by listening.

Printed text–literature or poetry, print or pixels–has long afforded readers opportunities to create immersive virtual worlds using their memories and imaginations. Sound(s) make(s) these worlds believable. Listening is the portal. To explore these ideas, this essay first defines sound as the experience of acoustic energy that conveys information. Listening promotes the understanding of this information. Next, the centrality of sound, especially the speaker's voice, and its forward inclusion through print and pixels is outlined. To examine these ideas, pioneering works of electronic literature by Jeremy Hight et al., Stuart Moulthrop, and three contemporary video poems by Mohamed Habibi are considered. As will be suggested, these works of electronic literature each promote our engagement through their effective use of sound. This essay concludes by considering the significance of this alliance.

CONCEPTUAL FRAMEWORK

The term "sound," as used here, signifies vibrations of acoustic energy that travel through air, or some other medium. These vibrations are experienced (heard) when they reach one's ears and register in one's brain as sound(s).

According to Walter Murch, hearing is one of the first human senses to develop, and for approximately 4.5 months before birth one is bathed in a rich soup of sounds heard within the womb. After birth, a baby reacts immediately to sound, before its vision fully develops (Murch **2005**).

Different from hearing, listening is the active processing of auditory stimuli, a carefully and purposefully conducted activity, involving conscious effort and attention. French critic and composer Michel Chion, in his discussion of aural relationships to sound in cinema, suggests one listens to obtain information about a sound source, to appreciate the sound itself, and to learn what is communicated by the sound (Chion **1994**). Nicole Brittingham Furlonge calls listening "a physiological form of reception," a practice that is at once "interpretive, situated, and reflective." Listening to sound, as analytic "storyhearers" says Furlonge, prompts engagement that is participatory, interactive, and experiential (Furlonge **2018**, 60, 83).

With Murch's positioning of awareness of sound(s) as primary, Chion's suggestion of listening to learn, and Furlonge's notion of engagement as storyhearers, Bruce R. Smith posits that knowing the world through active listening is fundamentally different from knowing the world through passive viewing (Smith 2003). Michael Bull and Les Back echo this idea when they say sound is primary for knowing and being in the world. One hears a sound and it provides immediate clues about one's location, and what to expect. If the sound is acousmatic, originating from an unseen source, one can use experience, memory, or imagination to discern its source and meaning (Bull and Back **2003**).

At the risk of oversimplifying the work of Walter Ong and others regarding orality (both primary and secondary) and literacy, one might consider speech as expressing and sharing abstract ideas, histories, memories, and cultures, as spoken narratives for understanding external and internal worlds (Ong **1982**). With the advent of writing, sounds of speech were graphically transcribed. Thus, writing provides scripts for reproducing the sounds of the spoken voice, whether internally, as part of silent reading, or externally, as the result of reading aloud. In either case, the dynamics of voice are transmitted to the reader, despite its remediation.

Although speech and writing are fundamentally different—speech being based upon hearing and writing upon seeing—at the heart of each is the sound(s) of the speaker's voice. Listening to these sounds directly engages our memories and imaginations, helps us rethink our relational experiences with others, with ourselves, and the spaces and places we inhabit. Listening to sound(s) provides a way of knowing and being in a world, whether real or imagined.

DISCUSSION

To examine these ideas, we can consider two pioneering works of electronic literature–*34 North 118 West* by Jeremy Hight et al. (2003), and *Under Language* by Stuart Moulthrop (2007) (2020)–as well as three contemporary video poems by Mohamed Habibi–*Just Words, Matchbox*, and *Mug*. These examples are chosen for their strong emphasis on sound.

34 NORTH 118 WEST

Jeremy Hight, with Jeff Knowlton and Naomi Spellman, created and released *34 North 118 West* in 2002-2003. This pioneering work of locative electronic literature combined multiple media and Global Positioning System (GPS) technology to create an interactive series of narratives about a once thriving railroad depot situated at 34 North latitude, 118 West longitude in downtown Los Angeles, California, during the first half of the twentieth century (Hight, Knowlton, and Spellman 2003).

Participants walked through the four-block area formerly occupied by the railroad station and other businesses with a laptop computer, a GPS device, and headphones. GPS tracked and overlaid their position on a map displayed on the computer screen. Easily identifiable locations were also displayed. Approaching these "hot spots," participants triggered recorded narratives and soundscapes created from historical, ethnographic, and architectural information about the area.

Other sound effects–squeaking wooden cart wheels and musicians entertaining on busy street corners, for example–were triggered by hidden GPS locations, each waiting to be discovered by wandering participants. These sounds were purposely designed to connect physical locations with events, activities, narratives, and lives of a past dismissed by urban change. Signs, displays, and other physical artifacts or details at each location augmented the narratives, providing metaphors and information for interaction(s) with the characters and history of the area defined by the geographic coordinates 34 North 118 West.

Hight, Knowlton, and Spellman investigated the half-square mile area around the former railroad freight station for more than a year, digging through the histories of the buildings to learn about people who worked and lived there. They crafted narratives from the hidden or lost information they recovered.

For example, at the site of a former tire factory, a worker describes how bits of rubber rained down on Los Angeles after the factory caught fire. A waitress at the train station restaurant talks about the harried passengers she serves. A railroad worker recounts cleaning the tracks after people committed suicide by stepping in front of trains. A cook, the station clock inspector, and others provide additional narratives.

As participants moved throughout the area, triggering multiple sound-based narratives, they uncovered the hidden history of this once thriving part of downtown Los Angeles, and developed a sense of the work's larger scope and concept. These narratives of forgotten or faded histories, lost buildings, tensions still present of past persons, all buried in memory, could, Hight contends, return with sufficient ability to sustain listeners simultaneously in two separate realities at the same location, one present, the other past (Hight **2013**).

Hight contends this approach helps organize forgotten historical and cultural information into meaningful narratives about a place, a time, and people. Hight calls these narratives "sonic archaeology in the urban landscape," or "narrative archaeology" (Hight **2013**).

NOTE 1

Under Language shared the 3rd International Digital Literature Award Ciutat de Vinarós Prize for Digital Narrative with Isaias Herrero Florensa's *Universo Molecula*. In his artist statement, Moulthrop describes the origin of the term "textual instrument."
[Textual instruments is] a term I borrowed from John Cayley many years ago to describe things that might look like literature, but also like structures for play, though not necessarily what we would call games. In fact, this one lies pretty close to game space, having rules, a scoring system (albeit invisible), and even a simple agon in which you compete against the perversity of the puzzle-maker, and constraints of the clock (Moulthrop **2020**).

UNDER LANGUAGE

Pioneering electronic literature author Stuart Moulthrop released *Under Langua-ge* in 2007. Moulthrop calls this work a "textual instrument," an artifact akin to literature but structured like a game (Moulthrop **2020**). Few instructions are pro-vided for interaction, however, leaving the reader and/or player to learn the rules for the work. Using a game-like screen display interface that responds to mouse clicks, users select ten lines of text for a poem. These ten lines of text are displayed on screen, along with a closing graphic, chosen by Moulthrop's textual instrument to reflect the quality of the final poem. Repeat as many times as desired for different poems.[1]

Moulthrop uses the term "under language" in two ways. First, the title, Under Language, speaks to the underlying computer code that drives the work. Under language, the concept, speaks to both the necessity to notice how writing intersects code, and the consequences of a collision (collusion?) when poetry meets code.[2]

So, under language, the concept, underlies and infuses *Under Language*, the work, which is, fundamentally, a generative textual work, meant to be experienced visually, on a screen. But the brilliance of this work is Moulthrop's sonification of the underlying five layers of computer code. The first is a series of computer-voiced renditions of ActionScripts programmed by Moulthrop that operate the work. The second layer is a series of ambient recorded collages of tunings across radio broadcasts. The third level consists of pseudo-code, again voiced by text-to-speech technology. Comments and summaries, ostensibly voiced by the ten-line poem at the heart of this work, constitute the fourth level. The fifth level is an audio collage, where the poem's ten lines are each vocalized, as well as comments seemingly from the poem's self awareness of its creation.

These vocalized narratives of the under language for Moulthrop's work are not specifically ordered, but rather assembled from user choices of lines of text for a generated poem. Still, the result provides unprecedented access to the interactive affordances beyond the program's screen-based visual displays.

Moulthrop's point is that under language (the underlying code) is the language of computer programming, and is inseparable from the work titled *Under Language*. With *Under Language*, the work, Moulthrop argues that to experience electronic literature one must appreciate the underlying code, which is vocalized as part of the work.

NOTE 2

Moulthrop maintains an archival webpage for *Under Language* (**http://www.smoulthrop.com/lit/ul/**), where he provides information and listening opportunities. In the "About" section of this website he describes the inspiration for the term *under language*. The phrase "under-language" was invented by the comics artist Alan Moore in an interview he gave in the early 1980s. He used it to describe the essence of comics art, which is neither verbal nor visual, but something that underlies and infuses both modes. The term gets at the essence behind Moore's great genius for irony and verbal-visual puns. It also provides a convenient reminder that everything, these days, tends to mean more than it seems (Moulthrop **2020**). The author maintains an archival webpage for a remix he created using original sound files supplied by Moulthrop (Barber **2020c**).

One might extend Moulthrop's point by arguing that *Under Language* is an example of sound-based electronic literature. Hearing the under language vocalized, one understands the presence of hidden narratives concurrently creating and commenting upon one's experience of the work's visualization, and, indeed, writing the larger context for its experience. Rather than visuals augmented by sound, *Under Language* is a work of electronic literature where sound is augmented by visuals, where sound is at the heart of the literary experience.[3]

MOHAMED HABIBI

Contemporary examples of Arabic electronic literature by Mohamed Habibi extend the idea of sound-based electronic literature. Habibi, a Saudi scholar and poet working in the genre of video poetry, has for the past decade shared his work through his YouTube channel (Habibi **2018**). This essay examines three of Habibi's video poems: *Just Words*, *Matchbox*, and *Mug*.[4]

JUST WORDS

Just Words (2:11) begins with a flashlight beam illuminating what appears to be a blank wall. All else is black, and silent. The focus changes and the beam illuminates Arabic writing on a piece of paper. Sound begins–insects and rhythmic clicking. Text appears superimposed on the screen, below the image of the paper, reading,

We dream

Almost unseen, a hand turns the paper to expose another, again with Arabic writing,

dream

NOTE 3

Similar to *Under Language*, Moulthrop's *Radio Salience* (2007) is an interactive image-text-sound instrument with a game-like interface that explores indeterminacy, accident, and resonance, taking as its muse the breathless voice of the airwaves and radio. The author maintains an archival webpage for a remix he created using original sound files supplied by Moulthrop (Barber **2020a**).

NOTE 4

The author met Saudi poet and scholar Mohammed Habibi and was introduced to his video poetry at the Arabic Electronic Literature: New Horizons and Global Perspectives conference. Perhaps the first focusing on Arabic electronic literature, this conference was convened at Rochester Institute of Technology, in Dubai, United Arab Emirates, Feb. 25-27, 2018. Organization website: **https://www.arabic-elit.org/** / Conference program: **https://www.arabic-elit.org/schedule**.

The sound continues. One now has the sense of discovering this text in a darkened room, at night. Turning the paper–might one say "pages" now?–reveals another, again with writing. The superimposed translation reads,

in the morning

The rhythmic clicking becomes more rapid, intense, almost insistent. Another page flip...

We carry our dreams

page flip...

to dry it out.

Another page flip...

it won't fly away;

Two page flips...

as we'll clasp them.

At 1:35 the scene changes to ten white "pages," each inscribed with Arabic writing, secured on a line by clothespins–three groups of two pages, one of three pages, and one of one page–near a window. Daylight illuminates the room, and the pages.

One has the sense that these pages represent the dream portrayed in the first scene of Habibi's video poem, and that these parts of the dream are drying in the morning light. At first this tableau is silent, but the sound of these pages rustling fades in as they are seen moving in an air current from the nearby window.

A dissolve at 1:58 returns us to the first scene: a piece of paper illuminated by a flashlight beam, the rest of the room in darkness.

the clasps

The night insects and rhythmic clicking sounds begin. The page is turned ...

are... Just words

Fade to black, and end (Habibi **2018**).

MATCHBOX

Matchbox (1:52) begins with a black screen. Sounds are quickly heard–footsteps running, dogs barking, some vocalizations that hint at physical effort. Memories of similar sounds suggest this is perhaps someone running.

At 0:30 the running stops, the runner seems to take a breath, and one hears a series of sliding, scratching sounds. Silence as Arabic writing appears on the screen, from top right across, then back to the right margin before beginning a new line. The screen fills with writing.

The soundtrack begins anew–breathing, running, dogs, the same sliding, scratching sound. More Arabic writing appears on the screen, right to left, appearing to be written as one watches.

More scratching, sliding sounds until a match lights in the darkness, briefly illuminating a person's face.

Four seconds of silence and blackness passes until the soundtrack–running feet, breathing, dogs barking–returns. English writing appears on the screen, left to right, as if being typed in real time.

The child
–who runs out of the door
like a pullet
who gets up to glance at his injured
elbow
who walks by anyone to reassure
himself
is you.

They send you out
to the neighborhood
along the dark street,
where the walls are painted with ghosts
to get a matchbox.

A match is lit, again briefly illuminating the face of a young person. End (Habibi 2018).

MUG

Like *Matchbox* and *Just Words*, *Mug* (3:59) begins with a black screen. The rhythmic clicking, heard in *Just Words*, begins the soundtrack and is quickly followed by sounds of birds, geese, and a crowing rooster. Night sounds follow immediately–insect sounds and human vocalizations in the background.

At 0:46 a small circle of white light appears in the lower right quadrant of the otherwise black screen. It begins to gyrate, seemingly synchronically with the background insect sounds.

At 1:20 the insect sounds stop. Silence until 1:26 when the sound of liquid being poured onto some surface is heard. Suddenly, the white light is interrupted by small, circular waves. Immediately it is clear: the liquid heard is being poured into a container. The white light is a reflection in that container.

Silence as the white light, now tiny and surrounded by a ring, like an orbiting moon, moves on the surface of what is now understood as liquid.

At 2:00 the sounds of ducks and geese return. Arabic writing appears on an entirely black screen. Sounds of ducks and geese and rhythmic clicking continue. A rooster crows. Sounds, seemingly of something walking, slowly, carefully, on gravel. Slow zoom into text overlaid on the screen.

At 2:25 a second screen of Arabic writing appears. The sound changes to nighttime insects. Slow zoom into another, different text.

The white light, now understood as a reflection in liquid, reappears. Night insect sounds continue as a third screen of Arabic text overlays the visual. The reflected light dances behind and in the center of the text filling the screen.

The text disappears. More liquid is poured into the container. The reflected light is disturbed. The sound fades out as a final screen of Arabic text appears, as if being written onto the screen.

Translation of the text to English speaks to images and sounds.

It is not surprising that the ear depends upon imagination
surrounded by sounds.
A rooster crows for the time of prayer.
Frogs croaking foretell the smell of rain.
A dog passes nearby, pauses, continues on his way.
Your eyes, staring up for a long time,
suddenly look down to the mug into which you are pouring water.
You were in the mug where the water reflected the moon.

The reflected light of the moon dances in the mug at the bottom of the screen. Fade to black. End (Habibi **2018**).

SIGNIFICANCE

These works of electronic literature by Hight et al., Moulthrop, and Habibi each promote engagement through their effective use of sound, vocal, environmental, or mechanical.

For example, the sounds of *34 North 118 West*, according to Hight, positioned one in both past and present at specific locations comprising the work.

The original *34 North 118 West* is no longer available as an in situ experience. But, the sound files are available, and several were given to the author by Hight, along with permission to remix them so as to portray a sense of the original, larger work. For all practical purposes, these sounds–a train crossing, a street band, a street salesperson, narratives of individuals living in the area–are all that remain of the work.

In a 13:00 recombination of these sounds, the author utilized an Aristotelian, linear narrative structure of beginning, middle, and end, bookended by the sound of a passing train. Other approaches would be equally valid. The result from any approach is for the sound-based narratives of *34 North 118 West* to provide effective access to this work–no longer available–a facsimile for the intent and content of the original work (Hight, Knowlton and Spellman **2018**).[5]

NOTE 5

The author maintains an archival webpage providing information and listening opportunities.

Under Language is still available in its original context thanks to a website maintained by the author, Stuart Moulthrop. Like Hight, Moulthrop was generous in providing the author with sound files from this work, as well as permission to create experimental remixes.

NOTE 6

The author maintains an archival webpage providing information and listening opportunities.

Using sound files provided by Moulthrop, the author created a 14:20 audio narrative by arranging individual sound files following their numbering from Moulthrop's original content database to create a serendipitous narrative. Other methodologies could easily be used. As with the original work, there are five layers (as described previously) to this re-conceptualized narrative. The reader and/or player is responsible for making sense of the artifact (Moulthrop **2020**).[6]

Missing in this effort is the direct interaction the user/reader/player/participant has with choosing the lines of the poem. But, remaining is the direct experience with the under language, the vocalization(s) of the computer programming underlying, supporting, creating the original work.

The three works by Habibi, while each an example of video poetry, incorporate strong, and one might argue essential, sound elements. In *Just Words*, one sees a hand turning individual pieces of paper on which are inscribed Arabic words and/or phrases. But it is the *sound* of these pages turning that sparks one's imagination, encouraging one to ask for more perspective on this literary experience. What are these pages? How do they relate to one another? Who is turning the pages? What is the reader and/or viewer to think of these words and their display?

In another scene one sees these individual pages hanging from a line, like fish or dried fruits, evidence of their collection and display outside their native element. But again, it is the *sound* of these pages, this time rustling in the air moving through a nearby window, that makes clear what one sees is a context, a place, a space in which these words might be experienced. Taken out of context, do these words still convey the same meaning(s) as when bound with others into the form of a book? Again, what is the reader and/or viewer to think of these words and their display?

In *Matchbox*, one sees nothing but blackness. Only at the end of this video poem, when a match is struck and thus illuminates the face of a young person, does one understand what is seen is the darkness of night. Only with the appearance of the text superimposed at the end of the video does one have full context for the poem. Again, it is *sound*, this time the striking of a match, that provides a sense of presence in a particular place and brings the visual elements together, providing an interface with which one can engage the essential nature of the poem.

At the heart of *Mug*, is, one might argue, an acoustic listening experience, where one does not know the source of the sound(s) heard. One might also argue that the substance of the visual experience is unknown, too. Beyond the text, it is the sound of liquid being poured into a container of more liquid that provides the crucial key for understanding this video poem and its examination–interrogation?–of what is, ultimately, a reflection. At this point, as noted in the text of the poem, one is present in the mug. That space, created by sound, defines one's interaction with the poem.

What does all this mean? Why is it important? A first response might be to note that sound provides a fundamental sensory input and communication channel for human culture. Sound is the phoneme for speech (verbalization of abstract thought). Sound can be a central component of narrative (the re-counting of a sequence of events and their meaning) and storytelling (the addition of setting, plot, characters, logical unfolding of events, a climax).

Allan Moore describes how motifs that remind of and return lyrical references provide embedded meaning in popular music (Moore **2012**). This same connection is demonstrated in the examples of electronic literature and poetry discussed in this essay. Each uses sound to connect and surround readers with multiple, concurrent aspects of their storytelling. If readers are fully engaged with the imaginative situation—whether musical or literary—the result can be quite powerful, according to Tim Crook, who says sound effectively prompts life from little details seen in the listeners' mind's eye (Crook **1999**).

Alan Hall describes how this phenomenon works. Listening carefully and purposefully to sound(s) offers, according to Hall, "a portal through which a deeper, often inarticulate, consciousness can be glimpsed... The intention is to find deeper and wider resonances within—and without—the listener" (Hall **2010**, 99, 104).

Michael Bull and Les Back say sound provides a place in which embodied social and cultural traces can be carried, often without the awareness of their bearers. Therefore, it is good to actively and deeply listen to the sounds of the world in which one lives. In this way, according to Bull and Back, one opens new approaches to thinking about and appreciating the social experience, memory, time, and place—the auditory culture—of sound (Bull and Back **2003**).

The works by Hight et al., Moulthrop, and Habibi considered in this essay encourage consideration of how different aesthetic conceptualizations and material practices of voice and other sound(s) inform literary expression. For example, sound and poetry might be considered an exchange between language and code, and thus at the center of our understanding of language arts. The desired outcome is to expand understanding of literature and textuality as vehicles for exchanges in and across media, languages, and cultures.

Finally, this focus foregrounds an approach to literature characterized by what Edmund Carpenter calls the verbal, musical, and poetic traces and fragments (figures) of oral culture (Carpenter **1970**). The works by Hight et al., Moulthrop, and Habibi discussed in this essay show how sound provides a way of knowing and being in a literary world, real or imagined. In this regard, sound is the basis for literature (written works considered to possess lasting artistic merit) and the various practices and cultures associated with its production and consumption (reading, writing, and listening). Listening, as real and concrete participatory practice, evokes aural experiences across a wide range of theory and practice through which listeners can derive information about the world they inhabit. This suggests a way forward for electronic literature, through careful listening.

Patterned after the first video game, *Pong*, Moulthrop's *Sc4nda1 in New Media* (2012) converges philosophical meditation with a retro video game. The sounds provide context(s) in this new space. The author maintains an archival web-page for a remix he created using original sound files supplied by Mouthop (Barber **2020b**).

Barber, John. 2020a. "Radio Salience." 2020.
Link: http://www.nouspace.net/john/archive/radioelo/moulthrop/radiosalience/radio-salience.html.

Barber, John. 2020b. "Sc4nda1 in New Media. radioELO." 2020.
Link: http://www.nouspace.net/john/archive/radioelo/moulthrop/sc4nda1/sc4nda1.html.

Barber, John. 2020c. "Under Language." 2020.
Link: http://www.nouspace.net/john/archive/radioelo/moulthrop/underlanguage/under-language.html.

Bull, Michael, and Les Back, ed. 2003. *The Auditory Culture Reader.* Oxford: Berg.

Carpenter, Edmund. 1970. *They Became What They Beheld.* New York: Outerbridge & Dienstfrey.

Chion, Michel. 1994. *Audio-Vision Sound on Screen.* Translated and edited by Claudia Gorbman. New York: Columbia University Press.

Crook, Tim. 1999. *Radio Drama Theory and Practice.* Abingdon, UK: Routledge.

Furlonge, Nicole Brittingham. 2018. *Race Sounds: The Art of Listening in African American Literature.* Iowa City: University of Iowa Press.

Habibi, Mohamed. 2018. "habibi1366." YouTube. 2018.
Link: http://www.youtube.com/user/habibi1366/videos.

Hall, Alan. 2010. "Cigarettes and Dance Steps." In *Reality Radio: Telling True Stories in Sound*, ed. by John Biewen and Alexa Dilworth, 96-107. Chapel Hill: University of North Carolina Press.

Hight, Jeremy. 2013. "Narrative Archaeology." In *NeMe.* March 25.
Link: http://www.neme.org/texts/narrative-archaeology.
Also available here: http://www.academia.edu/203311/narrative_archaeology.

Hight, Jeremy, Jeff Knowlton, and Naomi Spellman. 2003. "34 North 118 West." In *radioELO.* Link: http://www.nouspace.net/john/archive/radioelo/34n118w/34n118w.html.

Moore, Alan. 2012. *Song Means: Analyzing and Interpreting Recorded Popular Song.* Farnham, NY: Ashgate.

Moulthrop, Stuart. 2020. *Under Language.* 2020.
Link: http://www.smoulthrop.com/lit/ul/about.htm.

Murch, Walter. 2005. "Womb Tone." *Transom Review* 5 (1).
Link: http://transom.org/2005/walter-murch-part-1/.

Ong, Walter J. 1982. *Orality and Literacy: The Technologizing of the Word.* York: Methuen.

Smith, Bruce R. 2003. "Tuning into London c. 1600." In *The Auditory Culture Reader*, ed. by Michael Bull and Les Back, 127-35. Oxford: Berg.

PART 1

DES SONS, DES BRUITS ET DES VOIX
SOUNDS, NOISES AND VOICES

SIMON BIGGS

Speech To Text: Between The Real And The Unreal

Abstract

This article discusses the Augmented Reality (AR) language-based artwork *Mnemo*, developed by the author in 2018. *Mnemo* employs multiple Microsoft Hololens head-mounted AR headsets to immerse participants, or the preferred term interactors, within an interactive environment where what interactors say appears inscribed, or written, in the environment around them. All interactors within the environment can see what the others can see, from their own point of view, including the written texts captured from the speech of the interactors that are virtually co-located with the object an interactor was looking at when they spoke.

Mnemo is discussed in the context of the ancient practice of the "art of memory," known as memory theatre, from which the work took its initial inspiration. Memory theatre, the practice of mentally annotating a physical location, often an architectural environment, with mnemonic elements (usually short phrases or terms, known as "imagines"), that can be employed to recollect a narrative or argument as a practitioner physically navigates a space and the objects within it. Whereas in memory theatre such mnemonic devices are imaginary, in *Mnemo* uttered phrases visually appear virtually co-located with the objects and places where they were first deposited, or written, by an interactor, visible to themselves and anybody else wearing the Hololens AR head-unit. The practice of memory theatre is also considered in relation to the 20th century psycho-geographic practice of Dérive, where multiple participants in a site-specific action interpret and critically engage place as they move through it.

The work is further discussed in the context of a number of works by other artists who engage location and context dependent practices, including Janet Cardiff and George Bures Miller and the performance groups Anatomical Theatres of Mixed Realities and Stationhouse Opera. Earlier works by the author, that explore place, memory, history and the inter-subjectivity of interactive systems, are also discussed, critically contextualizing the work *Mnemo*. The focus of the discussion is upon processes of collaborative-reading and collaborative-writing, where the binary aspects of the practice function as a generative hermeneutic cycle that can shift our perception of place and ourselves within it.

Résumé

Cet article est consacré à *Mnemo*, une œuvre artistique de Réalité Augmentée (RA) fondée sur la langue et développée par l'auteur en 2018. *Mnemo* emploie de multiples casques de RA de Microsoft Hololens afin d'immerger les participant·e·s, ou l'interacteur/interactrice, dans un environnement interactif où leurs paroles apparaissent gravées, ou écrites, dans l'environnement qui les entoure. Tous les interacteurs dans l'environnement peuvent voir ce que voient les autres, de leur propre point de vue, y compris les textes écrits saisis à partir des énoncés des interacteurs/interactrices qui sont virtuellement co-localisé·e·s avec l'objet que regardait un·e interacteur/interactrice lorsqu'iels prenaient la parole.

Mnemo est abordée dans le contexte de la pratique antique de la « mnémotechnique », connue sous le nom de mémoire théâtre, dont l'œuvre s'est inspirée au départ. La mnémotechnique, la pratique de l'annotation mentale d'un lieu physique, souvent un environnement architectural, avec des éléments mnémoniques (généralement des phrases ou des termes courts, appelés « imaginés »), qui peuvent être utilisés pour se souvenir d'un récit ou d'un argument alors qu'un·e praticien·ne navigue physiquement un espace et les objets qui s'y trouvent. Tandis que dans la mnémotechnique les dispositifs mnémotechniques sont imaginaires, dans *Mnemo* les phrases prononcées apparaissent visuellement virtuellement co-localisées au même endroit que les objets et les lieux où ils ont été déposés ou écrits par un·e interacteur·e, visibles à ceux qui portent un casque Hololens de RA. La mnémotechnique est également considérée en relation à la pratique psycho-géographique du XXe siècle de la Dérive, où plusieurs participant·e·s à une action spécifique à un site interprètent et engagent de manière critique le lieu alors qu'ils s'y déplacent.

L'œuvre est examinée plus en détail dans le contexte d'un certain nombre d'œuvres d'autres artistes qui engagent des pratiques dépendantes du lieu et du contexte, notamment Janet Cardiff et George Bures Miller et les groupes de performance Anatomical Theatres of Mixed Realities et Stationhouse Opera. Des œuvres précédentes de l'auteur qui explorent le lieu la mémoire, l'histoire et l'inter-subjectivité des systèmes interactifs sont également abordées, en contextualisant Mnemo de manière critique. La discussion porte essentiellement sur le processus de lecture et d'écriture en collaboration où les aspects binaires de la pratique fonctionnent comme un cycle herméneutique générateur qui peut modifier notre perception du lieu et de nous-même en son sein.

INTRODUCTION

Context aware technologies (Augmented Reality, or AR) allow for novel forms of interaction with physical environments, including performance environments. These technologies feature properties that allow information to be situated in the environment in a context aware manner.

There are diverse ways in which information can be integrated into the environment by such means. Augmented reality technologies allow the placing of virtual information in locations that are congruent with physically tangible objects and environmental elements. However, the main concepts behind the technology have been around for a long time. The Greek pre-Socratic rhetoricians of classical antiquity developed the discipline of mnemonics, employing a system correlating real places (*loci*) and imagined images (*imagines*) (Yates 1966, 18) as an aid to the public presentation of their theories.

Where conventional augmented reality devices, such as AR apps on mobile phones, allow you to co-locate information with real world objects, head-up displays, such as the Microsoft Hololens, allow this as an immersive experience, so the user (interactor) is fully engaged with the AR merged environment. Interactors can place virtual images or other elements (*imagines*) onto physical walls or objects (*loci*). This can include altering visual aspects of the physical environment around them, such as creating virtual portals through actual walls or floors to reveal other virtual spaces, or placing a virtual ball on a physical table so that when the physical table is tilted the ball rolls along its surface and drops onto the physical floor, bouncing on impact. The virtual object and the physically tangible space the virtual object has been placed in are, within the logic of the system, of the same ilk. The imaginary and the tangible are merged in a novel manner.

PSYCHOGEOGRAPHY AND *DÉRIVE*

Artists have been developing context specific creative interventions for some time, where the imaginary is sited in particular places. Such works have often drawn on the psychogeographical theories of French Situationist Guy Debord, who proposed

> ... the *dérive*, a technique of rapid passage through varied ambiences. *Dérives* involve playful-constructive behaviour and awareness of psychogeographical effects, and are thus quite different from the classic notions of journey or stroll. (Debord 2006)

Psychogeographic works tend to be site responsive, the artist developing an acute close reading of a site that they can employ in the construction of their intervention in that place. For this reason, few such works are developed for the blank space of the art gallery or museum, except where the site might have characteristics of interest to the artist.

Janet Cardiff's work employing recorded spoken narrative for pre-determined walks (psychogeographies) are an exemplar. Cardiff carefully crafts the recording of her voice to create a sense of co-location not only with the physical and visual environment the walkers encounter, as they listen on headphones to the narrative, but also the aural characteristics of the location; Cardiff states,

> On the CD you hear my voice giving directions, like "turn left here" or "go through this gateway," layered on a background of sounds: the sound of my footsteps, traffic, birds and miscellaneous sound effects that have been pre-recorded on the same site as where they are being heard. (Gibbons 2007)

In the more recent collaborative work, such as *Alter Bahnhof Video Walk* (Cardiff and Miller **2012**), the artists have extended their use of technology to create augmented psychogeographic experiences to include video and mobile technologies. This work exploits the capacity of the geolocating technologies incorporated into contemporary mobile devices, such as mobile phones, along with such device's audio-visual capabilities.

Figure 1. Janet Cardiff and George Bures Miller, *Alter Bahnof Video Walk*, 2012, 26-minute walk produced for dOCUMENTA 13, Kassel, Germany.

Similar to wearing the Hololens, a Cardiff psychogeographic experience employs technology to mediate the experience of place, the user of a work such as *Alter Bahnhof Video Walk* wearing an audio headset attached to a mobile phone. By these means information is co-located with real world objects and experiences. Although this work does not employ technology as immersive and total as augmented or virtual reality headsets, the merging of real and virtual is compelling, due in large part to the great care Cardiff takes in designing the audio-visual environment and correlating it to the actual environment the interactor is in.

THE ART OF MEMORY

The merging of now and then, here and there, the constructed and the experiential, in works such as those by Janet Cardiff allows the creation of hybrid places that exist in the physical now and the artistic imaginary. Whilst characterised as a psychogeography, this could also be considered a form of memory theatre. In the *Art of Memory*, the art historian Frances Yates recounts how early Greek rhetoricians developed the art of the memory theatre; where memories, as images (*imagines*), could be associated with places (*loci*) in order to create a mnemonic system that could be used to create an "artificial memory"–a system of mnemonics that exists not in the mind (what is described as "natural memory") but in *loci*. Thus the rhetoricians could recount their memorised narrative simply by revisiting the loci in the correct order and reconstruct their argument from the associated *imagines*. Such an approach offers a model for how augmented reality might be used to create 1:1 mappings as a memory theatre.

Yates's recounting of various examples of memory theatres, sometimes known as memory palaces, is a widely known and outstanding example of historical research, drawn from numerous texts, many archaic. Yates identifies three classical sources for the art of memory, the first being a story associated with Simonides of Ceos. To quote:

> persons desiring to train this faculty [of memory] must select places and form mental images of the things they wish to remember and store those images in the places, so that the order of places will preserve the order of the things, and the images of the things will denote the

things themselves, and we shall employ the places and images respectively as a wax writing-tablet and the letters written on it.[1] (Yates 1966, 17)

Yates provides a further source for the invention of the memory theatre, a classical text on rhetorical technique by an unknown author, the *Ad Herennium*[2] (circa 86-82 BCE), where it is written:

"Now let us turn to the treasure-house of inventions, the custodian of all the parts of rhetoric, memory." There are two kinds of memory, he continues, one natural, the other artificial. The natural memory is that which is engrafted in our minds, born simultaneously with thought. The artificial memory is a memory strengthened or confirmed by training. (Yates 1966, 20)

Continuing:

The artificial memory is established from places and images... a *locus* is a place easily grasped by the memory, such as a house, an intercolumnar space, a corner, an arch, or the like. Images are forms, marks or simulacra... of what we wish to remember... The art of memory is like an inner writing. (Yates 1966, 22)

These texts from antiquity suggest to us that rhetoricians and philosophers were well versed in the arts of memory they illustrate. However, as Yates identifies in Cicero, "Themistocles refused to learn the art of memory 'which was then being introduced for the first time' saying that he preferred the science of forgetting to that of remembering." Cicero wrote (in Yates):

Memory for words, which for us is essential, is given distinctness by a greater variety of images; ... for there are many words which serve as joints connecting the limbs of a sentence, and these cannot be formed by any use of similitudes–of these we have to model images for constant employment; but a memory for things is the special property of the orator–this we can imprint on our minds by a skilful arrangement of several masks... that represent them, so that we may grasp ideas by means of images and their order by means of places. (Yates 1966, 33-34)

NOTE 1

Originally in Cicero, *De Oratore*, II, lxxxvi, 351-4, 55 BCE, translated by E.W. Sutton and H. Rackham as *De Oratore* of Cicero (1942), Loeb Classical Library, London : Heinemann.

NOTE 2

Available in English as *Rhetorica ad Herennium*, translated by Harry Caplan (1954), Loeb Classical Library, London: Heinemann, available at this link: **https://archive.org/details/adcherenniumdera00capluoft** (accessed March 19, 2018).

The reference to masks is noted by Yates who, recognizing the use of the Latin terminology of *Persona*, suggests that the rhetorician's application of the art of memory was akin to an actor wearing a mask upon the stage, enabling a kind of theatrical experience.

ATOM-R AND STATIONHOUSE OPERA

The concept of memory theatre can be observed deployed explicitly in recent work by the Anatomical Theatres of Mixed Realities (a Chicago-based ensemble composed of Mark Jeffery, Judd Morrissey and others, shortened to ATOM-r), including The Operature.[3] ATOM-r explore the dramaturgies of augmented reality in a manner directly evocative of the memory theatre described by Yates. The work of the ATOM-r collective merges digital, literary, and performance practices employing augmented reality systems such as custom mobile AR apps, immersive digital projection and various sensing technologies.

NOTE 3

For a discussion of this and related works, see Engberg (2017).

Figure 2. ATOM-r, *Kjell Theory*, 2015. Performed in installation by Sarah FitzSimmons, for Chicago Architecture Biennial 2018, USA.

In the recent ATOM-r project *Kjell Theory* (2015) the collective developed a narrative around the life of computing pioneer Alan Turing, employing eye-tracking technology and high precision projection systems, to create, amongst other things, projected augmented reality tattoos upon the bodies of performers and interactors. The stated intent of such work is to investigate how technology can be queered through its blending with the human body. ATOM-r performed *Kjell Theory* in the physical context of a schematic, but tangibly real, house-like architectural structure (by architect Sarah FitzSimmons) as part of the 2018 Chicago Architecture Biennial. In this version of the work the performers enact the work within an architectural schema reminiscent of that described in *Ad Herennium*.

Such work evokes earlier projects by the London-based performance group Stationhouse Opera, including *Split Seconds of Paradise* (1985), *The Bastille Dances* (1988) and *Dedesnn nn rrr* (Stationhouse Opera 1996), where the performers not only interact with architectural scale constructions but, through their actions, over a period of hours, construct and then deconstruct the environment around them, in a form of performative architectural speculation.

In works such as these, by ATOM-r and Stationhouse Opera, as well as that of Janet Cardiff and George Miller, we can see how co-located information in real world contexts (*loci*) can elicit a kind of intertextual folding between a physical experience and a recollected or imagined association (*imagine*). Narratives and stories become closely associated not only with place but with the objects within it, the structure of the information deployed throughout the environment via its association with specific objects, including human subjects, or sites within it.

Figure 3. Stationhouse Opera, *Dedesnn nn rrr*, 1996. Performance at the Frauenkirche, Dresden. Commissioned for Theater der Welt, Dresden, Germany.

THE WAITING ROOM AND *LONDON DIG*

The author has developed a number of previous works that employed augmented technological systems in site-specific contexts, in the form of interactive digital projections that employed full body motion-tracking of visitors to envelop them in augmented environments integrated into sites of specific interest. An example of this is *The Waiting Room* (Biggs **1998**), developed by the author (choreographed by Sue Hawksley and with sound by Stuart Jones), which was located in a railway station waiting room that was built to be used by Queen Victoria when she visited the city of Sheffield in 1897. The room, approximately 100 square metres in area and with lofty 5-metre ceilings, was notable for being entirely lined with cream coloured tiles, with relief details of lions' heads, and on each side of the room full-length mirrors, creating a space of unique quality and power.

Figure 4. Simon Biggs, *Waiting Room*, 1998. Installation view. Commissioned by Site Gallery, Sheffield, UK.

The author found this space in a semi-derelict state, unused for decades, and developed a work (commissioned by Sheffield's Site Gallery) for the site, transforming it into a mixed-reality dance hall, where virtual and real people could mingle in the same environment. The virtual figures, all dancers, were equally distributed female and male (three of each) and, surrounding the people who entered the space, waited to be engaged by the visitors (employing low-light video-based motion-tracking sensors), upon which they would invite another virtual dancer to dance a tango with them (choreography by Sue Hawksley). The space was interactively zoned, with a relatively fine granularity, so that visitors to the space could physically interact with the virtual dancers in various ways but also contribute to the composition of a live-generated interactive soundtrack played by a virtual, but not visible, tango ensemble (composed and programmed by Stuart Jones). The virtual dancers continued to use the room to wait–but rather than waiting for a train, as the British monarch once did, they waited to be invited to dance, either by a visitor to the space or by another of the virtual dancers. The work sought to function as a speculative archeological dig, an oneiric re-imagining, of the site, revealing aspects of the waiting room that were both historically factual and an artistic re-imagining of place (not unlike Debord's *dérive*).

London Dig (Biggs **2006**) is another work by the author that explores the specificity of a space through temporal re-imagining. This is an explicitly topographic work, comprised of numerous aerial images of the City of London, many of them in the form of maps, or fragments thereof. *London Dig* is composed of four 42-inch 16:9 plasma screens arranged in a rectangular array of two-by-two screens, creating a single image. The imagery displayed on the screens derives from numerous bird's eye views of the City of London, centered on the site of the building in which the work is located, Allen & Overy LLB's world headquarters in Spitalfields, City of London. The site of the building is an historically loaded one, located adjacent to the site of one of the original Roman gates to the City of London, and over the plague pits where those that died during the Great Plague were buried *en masse*. The location is also within the extent of the Great Fire of London, the previous buildings destroyed, and what ultimately became Spitalfields Market, much of which remains a trade and cultural site today. The building, designed by Norman Foster and Partners, is also located at the site of the birthplace of Jeremy Bentham, Utilitarianist philosopher and penal reformer. To say the site is loaded with historical associations is something of an understatement.

Figure 5. Simon Biggs, *London Dig*, 2006. Installation view. Commissioned by Allen & Overy LLB, London, UK.

In *London Dig*, imagery documenting the 2,000-year history of the site is presented on the plasma screen array, including maps from the Roman period through to contemporary images including data visualisations of the City in various forms, flight data from local airports (including radar visualisations), and photographs from space. The work was the result of extensive archival research, exploring both public and private image libraries, museum collections, and other organisations (including the Bodleian Library, Museum of London, NASA, European Space Agency, Science and Society Picture Library, etc.).

Located in a rather featureless anteroom, leading to the main auditorium of the building, *London Dig* functions as an imaginary interactive portal revealing the history of the site. A video camera located above the plasma array tracks all physical activity in the room in which the work is installed. This acquired data is employed to manipulate the imagery displayed on the screens. People passing by or standing before the screens cause the surface of the imagery to ripple, buckle and distort, depending on their movement. The effect is akin to an earthquake disrupting an overhead scene, fragmenting the visualisations of the city. Most of the time the tessellated and disrupted view of the city is composed of a field of rectangular fragments of many different simultaneous visualisations, collaged together in response to interactor activity. Sometimes, due to a randomly assigned time-out, the imagery is prompted to evolve so as to converge on a single coherent target image, randomly selected from the image library, before this image is again lost in the visual complexity of the ongoing temporal re-mix. In this work the body of the viewer acts as the excavator, 'digging' into the imagery of the site through disrupting the digital surface of the imagery. Viewers do not pass through the geographical space of the site, but they do pass through a spatio-temporal simulation of place that would otherwise not be possible.

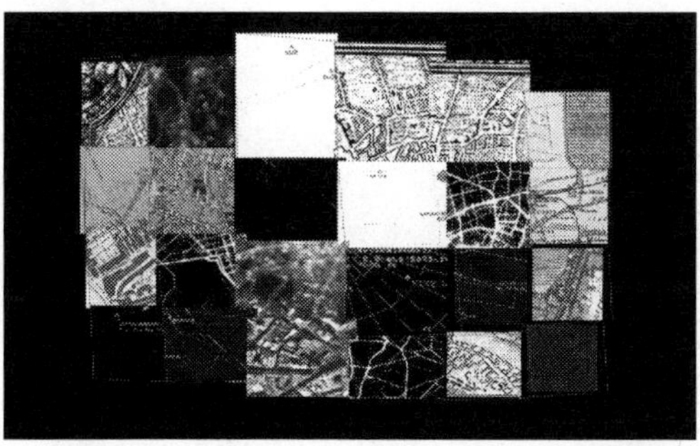

Figure 6. Simon Biggs, *London Dig*, 2006. Studio screenshot. Commissioned by Allen & Overy LLB, London, UK.

MNEMO

Partly informed by these earlier site-specific interactive works, and developing out of more recent work by the author exploring the interactive and dynamic spatialisation and temporalisation of spoken language (in works such as *Bodytext, Tower, Crosstalk and Dark Matter*), current research by the author is exploring how people can encode textual information, similar to the imagines discussed by Yates, into the environment around them. The aim is to allow interactors, or others, to recover and read information at a later time from the *loci* where the *imagines* were placed. The research, leading to the development of the AR project *Mnemo*, sought insights into how place might be explored as an active mnemonic, a site of literary and artistic expression, or topopoetics (Cresswell and Janz **2017**), in the form of inter-subjective perception represented at a 1:1 scale in physical space.

Mnemo employs the Microsoft Hololens to co-locate information on objects and places in specific sites. The Hololens is a lightweight untethered wearable Augmented Reality headset. Physically it resembles a hybrid of a pair of wrap-around sunglasses and the sort of head-up display you might expect a fighter-pilot to wear. The Hololens is effectively a stand-alone computer. It does not need to be connected to any other device, with or without wires, to be fully functional. The user simply puts it on, adjusts the headset for comfort and turns it on. The Hololens launches immediately into Microsoft Windows and its familiar tiled interface, where various applications can be launched, including *Mnemo*.

Application development was undertaken using the Unity 3D games engine, with software written in C#, exported to Visual Studio and then to the Hololens. The process is similar to developing apps for an Android, Windows, or iOS mobile device.

Figure 7. Simon Biggs, *Mnemo*, 2018. Studio screenshot. Creative Computing Studio, University of South Australia.

The Microsoft Hololens has a number of unique key interaction identifiers. These include hand gestures (Microsoft a), such as the snapping of the index finger down and then back up, called an *air tap*, which allows the interactor to select a function. Holding the index finger down to hold or engage an object allows the interactor to hold or move a virtual element. *Blooming*–a gesture involving the whole hand moving in an upward flowering-like gesture–evokes the system menu. Most of these gestures are reliant in part on another key interaction identifier, known as *gaze* (Microsoft b). This is where the interactor fixes their gaze on a specific physical or virtual location or object and the system determines the direction and focus of the gaze (a process known as *ray-casting*). Together these interaction identifiers allow a full range of interactions, as we are familiar with from point-and-click operating systems, such as in Windows or MacOS. The sensors embedded in the headset are able to determine the angle and depth of view of the wearer's orientation and co-relate this with data from other sensors determining the position of real and virtual objects in the space around the interactor. This allows the headset to accurately identify physical objects and surfaces around the wearer.

The *Mnemo* software employs the gaze interaction and voice recognition capabilities of the Hololens to allow a wearer of the headset to directly inscribe, or write, texts upon objects in the real world around them by simply fixing their gaze upon an object and speaking. Once a text (an *imagine*) is attached to an object or place it will remain visibly co-located with the associated *loci* indefinitely. The interactor can remove the AR headset, leave the room for an hour, a day or a month, and on returning and donning the headset they will see the *imagine* they created remains where they placed it. In many ways this resembles the memory theatre, recounted by Yates and described in *Ad Herennium*, and as practiced by the Pre-Socratic rhetoricians.

Figure 8. Simon Biggs, *Mnemo*, 2018. Studio screenshot. Cherryville, Australia.

When the wearer of the Hololens, using the Mnemo application, first speaks they see the words they have spoken floating in the space immediately in front of where they are looking, through the Hololens lenses, written in a red-coloured sans-serif font. The floating text moves with the interactor's head movements and gaze. When the interactor fixes their gaze upon a specific location, for a second or two, the text becomes fixed, changing colour and becoming an *imagine*, at the location of whatever object occupies the *loci*. This might be a wall, a floor, a piece of furniture—even another person in the space. The orientation of the text is also fixed at this time, with the text facing the interactor for ease of legibility.

Once the *imagine* is fixed at a locus, it remains there indefinitely. When the interactor moves, the position and orientation of the *imagine* remain fixed. Thus the interactor can walk around the imagine, viewing it from various angles, or turn away from it, to return their gaze and see the *imagine* still at its *locus*. If the interactor removes the Hololens headset, and another person puts it on, this second interactor will see the same *imagines*, at the same *loci*, as the first interactor. If they speak, they will create a new *imagine* which will be located at the *locus* they gazed at, at that time. This new *imagine* will be added to the virtual environment that is mapped, at a scale of 1:1, onto the physical environment around the interactors.

Interactors can save "spaces" composed of their *imagines* and loci, including assigning them a name, by simple voice command.[4] Similarly, the interactor can load saved textual datasets (*imagine spaces*), which then appear all around the interactor just as they were saved. There are also voice commands available for clearing all the *imagines*, browsing and loading saved datasets, displaying and hiding the command menu, enabling or disabling spatial mapping, and accessing information on the development of the project.

NOTE 4

The Microsoft Hololens incorporates the speech recognition software Cortana that is available across much of the Windows 10 environment. In *Mnemo*, Cortana functionality is used to acquire both the speech to be written into the space around the interactor and for voice command control of the software.

Figure 9. Simon Biggs, *Mnemo*, 2018. Studio screenshot. Cherryville, Australia.

Ultimately what an interactor or interactors might say, and thus inscribe into the environment around them, is arbitrary. The system will only work as a geo-located mnemonic system if it is consciously employed to do so. On its own the system is primarily of technical and conceptual interest, a platform of potentials. For the interactor the question is what to do with it? The *Mnemo* project could be seen as an instrument to be used for creating *imagines* in specific *loci* or as a provocative system designed to enable Situationist-like *dérive*. In a more quotidian context, the system could be used by site construction engineers to leave notes for their colleagues, associated with the item they wish to have noted.

SHARING

When proposing the concept of *dérive*, Guy Debord suggested that the activity was most effectively undertaken not by individuals but small groups of people, ideally of no more than two or three members. His view was that a small number of such participants would provoke one another in the exploration of place and their reaction to it, leading to the more likely occurrence of interesting situations. Responding to this, we developed *Mnemo* so that two (or more) wearers of separate Hololens headsets who occupy the same space can share the augmented reality environment together. Each interactor can write *imagines* at *loci* in the space and both can see these *imagines*, at their specific locations, simultaneously. Together they can speak *imagines* into the space all around them, creating an externalised manifestation of their speech which can, if they choose, function as a dialogue—or not.

Figure 10. Simon Biggs, *Mnemo*, 2018. Studio screenshot. Cherryville, Australia.

Once an *imagine* is fixed at its *locus*, it becomes shared between the wearers of the Hololens running the *Mnemo* software. Each interactor's texts are written in a different colour, so it is possible to differentiate between who said what. The intention is to create a discursive environment that fosters conversation and engagement with place through speech, evoking Debord's preferred collective approach to *dérive*.

The shared experience *Mnemo* provides is distinct from the memory theatre composed of personal memories, as proposed in *Ad Herennium* and discussed by Yates. The *Mnemo* application, when in shared mode, is less a platform for the solo rhetorician and more an enabler of shared discourse, dialogue and conversation between multiple users, inscribed upon place. The *Mnemo* software exploits the Hololens's built-in capability for shared augmented reality to enable the co-creation and co-reading of information and can be used as the wearer of the device determines.

Figure 11. Simon Biggs, *Mnemo*, 2018. Studio screenshot. Cherryville, Australia.

Mnemo was developed using the Unity 3D platform by Simon Biggs and Research Assistant Puzhi Yao, whose contribution was instrumental in the technical realisation of the work. The application source code and assets are accessible to other developers under share-alike terms via Github (https://github.com/CreativeComputingStudio/Mnemo) on the Creative Computing Studio's repository.

Please feel free to download the source code and play with or further develop the system. Keep us in the loop.

"ATOM-r". **2015.** http://atom-r.com/, published October 25, 2015. Consulted October 20, 2017.

Biggs, Simon. 1998. "The Waiting Room." Consulted March 3, 2018.
Link: http://littlepig.org.uk/installations/waiting/waiting.htm.

Biggs, Simon. 2006. "London Dig." Consulted March 10, 2018.
Link: http://littlepig.org.uk/installations/london/index.htm.

Cardiff, Janet, and George Miller. 2012. "Alter Bahnhof Video Walk." *Commissioned for DOCUMENTA 13*, Kassel, Germany. Consulted March 20, 2018.
Link: http://www.cardiffmiller.com/artworks/walks/bahnhof.html.

Cresswell, Tim, and Bruno Janz. 2017. "Towards Topopoetics: Space, Place and the Poem." In *Place, Space and Hermeneutics*. Cham: Springer.

Debord, Guy. 2006. "Theory of the Dérive." In *The Situationist International Anthology*, translated by Ken Knabb. Berkeley: Bureau of Public Secrets. (First published in Les Lèvres Nues #9, November 1956).

Engberg, Maria. 2017. "Augmented and Mixed Reality Design for Contested and Challenging Histories." Published January 30, 2017. In *MW17: MW 2017*. Consulted September 4, 2017.
Link: https://mw17.mwconf.org/paper/augmented-and-mixed-reality-design-for-contested-and-challenging-histories-postcolonial-approaches-to-site-specific-storytelling/.

Gibbons, Joan. 2007. *Contemporary Art and Memory: Images of Recollection and Remembrance*. London: I.B. Taurus.

"Microsoft (a)." **2017.** Consulted November 2, 2017.
Link: https://developer.microsoft.com/en-us/windows/mixed-reality/gestures#hand_recognition.

"Microsoft (b)." **2017.** Consulted November 2, 2017.
Link: https://developer.microsoft.com/en-us/windows/mixed-reality/gestures#gaze-and-commit.

Stationhouse Opera. 1996. "Dedesnn nn rrr." *Commissioned for Theater der Welt, Dresden, Germany*. Consulted March 20, 2018.
Link: http://www.stationhouseopera.com/project/6042/.

Yates, Frances. 1966. *The Art of Memory*. London: Routledge & Kegan Paul.

Clic-Clang-Cornelius: Digital Sound Poetry As Embodied Posthumanism

CHRISTOPHE COLLARD

ABSTRACT

Starting from the problematic gap between the unicity of the human voice and the socio-cultural variables that are unavoidably attached to her expressions, this article proposes the phenomenon of "sound poetry" as a paradigmatic bridge between a biological reality and its posthuman condition. The underlying reasoning harks back to media artist and philosopher Norie Neumark's remark that sound poetry like no other mode of artistic expression "stimulates reflection on the uncanny and complicated relation between embodiment, alterity, and signification" (**2010**).
Most notably the appropriation and–literal–embodiment of electronic technologies in *digital sound* poetry has recently yielded a new dynamic to the *performativity* of poetic composition. With today's technical possibility to sample and mediate minimal acoustic nuances in the here-and-now we are allowed a glimpse into the supplement of meaning generated by the meeting between text/script and voice/sound. Such post-human amplification of an intrinsically arch-human act accordingly finds its broader relevance broadside conventional aesthetic standards.
The "meta-pop" of Japanese musician/sound poet Cornelius marks a case in point by weaving together digital samples and loopings of "live" vocalizations into a musical-seeming texture from which nonetheless no melodies seem discernable–or at least no recognizable ones. The result however is not entirely estranging, and this not in the least because the artist putatively plays on a continual cognitive oscillation between the referential frames "music," "performance," "text," and "technology." Bearing in mind Neumark's aforementioned relational model, Cornelius's sound poetry with its idiosyncratic explorations of digital signification arguably generates a genuine soundtrack for a posthuman condition.

RÉSUMÉ

Partant de l'écart problématique entre l'unicité de la voix humaine et les variables socioculturelles qui sont inévitablement liées à son expression, cet article propose de la « poésie sonore » comme un pont paradigmatique entre une réalité biologique et sa condition post-humaine. Le raisonnement sous-jacent renvoie à la remarque de l'artiste médiatique et philosophe Norie Neumark que la poésie sonore, comme aucun autre mode d'expression artistique, « stimule la réflexion sur la relation étrange et compliquée entre l'incarnation, l'altérité et la signification » (**2010**).
Plus particulièrement, l'appropriation et – littéralement – l'incarnation des technologies électroniques dans la poésie sonore numérique a récemment donné une nouvelle dynamique à la performativité de la composition poétique. Grâce aux possibilités techniques actuelles d'échantillonnage et de médiation de nuances acoustiques minimales dans l'ici et maintenant, nous avons un aperçu du supplément de sens généré par la rencontre entre le texte/script et la voix/son. Une telle amplification post-humaine d'un acte intrinsèquement archi-humain trouve par conséquent sa pertinence plus large à côté des normes esthétiques conventionnelles.
La « méta-pop » du musicien/poète sonore japonais Cornelius en est un bon exemple. Il tisse des échantillons numériques et des boucles de vocalisations « live » dans une texture musicale dont aucune mélodie ne semble discernable – ou du moins reconnaissable. Le résultat n'est cependant pas totalement étranger, et ce d'autant plus que l'artiste joue putativement sur une oscillation cognitive continue entre les cadres référentiels « musique », « performance », « texte » et « technologique ». En gardant à l'esprit le modèle relationnel de Neumark mentionné ci-dessus, la poésie sonore de Cornelius, avec ses explorations idiosyncratiques de la signification numérique, génère sans doute une véritable bande sonore pour une condition post-humaine.

"He's really just cobbling sounds together" (Spin magazine qtd. in Hadfield **2016**)–such was the tenor of most of the specialized press upon the release of *Fantasma* (1997) two decades ago. More forthcoming outlets called the album's "melodic blending [...] *addictive*" (Santiago **2008**–emphasis added) or insipidly "layered." Better still, some critics even noted that the videos accompanying this music by Japanese one-man-band Cornelius constituted some of "the best visual representations of sound [...] ever seen" (LaBelle **2010**). Almost as if this artist, somehow, was *not* "just cobbling sounds together," but actual strata of signification.

Sidestepping speculation, the next album *Point* (**2001**) made a point of ostensibly disassembling and reconfiguring vocals so as to shift emphasis away from melodic progression to a form of poly-sensorial modularity–a move confirmed with *Sensuous* (**2006**) five years later. Now, if one combines these introductory elements in as simple a proposition as possible, one is left with three dimensions: a) the materiality of commercialized recordings; b) a digital composition method; and c) the elusive principle of "sound" here straddling both material and digital dimensions while evoking a sense of reflexive layeredness but being reducible to neither. That said, the element of reflexivity is paradoxical in this regard: after all, even the elusive principle of "sound" does not automatically stimulate thinking about its ontological status. Another element all three aforementioned albums share, however, does: *voice*.

One decade ago, renowned *Québécois* artist Robert Lepage hammered this "point" home during his 9-hour production *Lipsynch* (**2008**), which explored voice's "many manifestations, declensions, and implications through different procedures that convey and reproduce it" (qtd. in Neumark **2010a** XV). By thus stressing the mediated and embodied character of vocal expression, Lepage effectively echoed a formula proffered by fellow Canadian luminary Marshall McLuhan of voice as "extension of man." And, as leading voice-scholar Norie Neumark posits, the related concepts, mediation and embodiment, are precisely what cause that paradox of reflexivity, as the human voice is unique but invariably attached to socio-economic, technological, and physical variables: "Voice is paradoxically, ambiguously, and uncannily at the intersection of subjectivity, intersubjectivity, and signification. In one way, we could hear voice as a hinge, holding the sonorous and signifying together and apart–preventing them from collapsing into a unity" (Neumark **2010a**, XXI).

Philip Brophy in the same collection summarizes Neumark's point even more succinctly when he states that "The voice is corrupted by being human" as it "readily becomes its Other through vocalization" (Brophy **2010**, 361). With voice, indeed, mediation and embodiment are one and the same phenomenon, and thus infinitely irreducible to any sense of essence. And as mediation serves communication, which happens in a social context, any vocal expression is potentially subject to scrutiny, negotiation, and manipulation. Inherently intimate, once released the voice thus becomes a vehicle for reflexivity–not least about how human meaning making comes into being.

Still, this is all too speculative and tinged with idealism. Especially so since reflexivity must be triggered as the result of communicative 'uptake' rooted in a mutually shared "code." And, as specified by anthropologist Marcel Mauss, communicative uptake in a socialized context requires *technique*–the locus where man, machine, and culture intersect (qtd. in Neumark **2010a**, XXI). Vocal technique, in turn, relies *on breath*, itself a nexus between convention, intention, and our body–the 'ground zero' where concepts are embodied whilst maximally elusive. Therefore, with compromise and convention present at every level of (vocal) signification, and cognition itself rooted in recognition (see also Defays and Hofstadter **1997**, 131), there is indeed ample room to stimulate reflexivity through vocalized sound art.

As this paper deals with a layered subject ostensibly stimulating reflexivity through an elusive interface, I propose to sidestep momentarily the material dimension of Cornelius's commercialized recordings and introduce the paradigm of "sound poetry" as referential framework. As Steve McCaffery posits, sound poetry's primal goal is "the liberation and promotion of phonetic and sub-phonetic features to language to the state of a *materia prima* for creative, subversive endeavors" (McCaffery **1998**, 163). As such, as with Cornelius's "music," it thrives on an embodied conflict between expectation and interpretation as it allows communicative "uptake" while problematizing the communicative "relationship." Or, as Brandon LaBelle pointedly put it: "sound poetry yearns for language by rupturing the very coherence of it" (LaBelle **2010**, 150). The "techniques" thereby employed vary widely: mounting idiosyncratic language and notational systems, performing spontaneous and improvised poetical oralities, fooling with the performer's body to rupture the ordered movements of vocality, or indeed by appropriating new technologies and digital devices in order to disassemble, reconfigure, and "cobble together" personal and/or imported sounds and utterances.

In the communicative "situation" of a sound poetry-performance–whether live or recorded–sender and receiver alike interpret the "volumetric text at a visceral embodied level" (Johnston **2016**, 43). Sound, as such, takes shape without becoming permanently materialized. It does not alter the experiencer's physical integrity yet makes us physically conscious of the impact of technique–a posthuman "extension," indeed, but slippery all the same. From an analytical angle, pairing sound poetry and posthumanism thus makes methodological sense when investigating the reflexive qualities of Cornelius's meta-pop. For, according to Ralf Remshardt's lucid formulation, the principle of 'posthumanism' "designates an evolutionary or morphological step towards a synthesis of the organic and mechanical/digital" (Remshardt **2010**, 135). Presented as such it evokes primarily a signifying *potential* by means of technological *extension*. Moreover, the appropriation and–literal–embodiment of techniques and technologies in *digital* sound poetry has recently yielded a new dynamic to the *performativity* of poetic composition itself. With today's technical possibility of sampling and mediating minimal acoustic nuances in the here-and-now we are allowed a glimpse into the supplement of meaning generated by the meeting between text/script and voice/sound. Such posthuman amplification of an intrinsically arch-human act accordingly finds its broader relevance broadside conventional aesthetic standards as a *bona fide* heuristic device to address the challenges of our contemporary culture.

Modernity brought us radios, telephones, and phonautographs, which seamlessly led to a spectrum of voice-centered and electronically amplified poetics by pioneering sound poets like Hugo Ball, F.T. Marinetti, Giacomo Balla, V. Klebnikov, Arthur Pétronio, Hans Arp, I.K. Bonset/Theo Van Doesburg, Richard Huelsenbeck, Tristan Tzara, as well as collectives like Lettrism, the Vienna Group, Ultra-Lettrism or Text-Sound in Sweden. Almost immediately, artistic experimentation with sound gave rise to early multimedia hybrids that integrated avant-garde trends into a poetics uncannily prescient of cyber-cultural and transverbal conditions (LaBelle **2010**, 149)–not least because of shared structuring principles. Most notable, in this regard, is their overt *performativity*. In early electronic mediations, just as in today's omnipresent and hence barely noticeable recordings of disembodied voices, performance and absence co-occur.

And even if the Montreal Metro's "Mind the Gap" warning does not automatically stimulate meta-artistic reflexivity at the best of times, the signifying potential of this ontological hybrid keeps circulating. Especially considering that the digital age is virtually characterized by a relentless renegotiation and remediation of communicative platforms and parameters.

Intrinsically revolutionary by virtue of their synergetic design and rhizomatic interconnection, digital technologies are at the same time deeply conventional as every new development marks an evolution or an integration of extant techniques: reading, writing, listening, telecommunicating, or indeed programming. Whilst dauntingly complex, the digital nevertheless still pulsates with human energy: its development is unpredictable, and it requires human input in order to function. In its most basic form, digital technology is hence performative because it is animated by an agent to perform a task. Incidentally, a key tenet from performance studies stipulates that "There is nothing more illusory in performance than the illusion of the unmediated" (Blau **1987**, 164-5). The "common language" of coding is thus not the ontological endpoint that Charlie Gere termed a "seamless digital mediascape" (Gere **2002**, 8) where all signifying systems come to converge, but rather, like breath to the human voice, a "ground zero" where concepts, conventions, and cultural distinctions can *potentially* meet and morph. The distinction is subtle, yet since "Performance [...] provides a frame that invites critical reflection on communicative processes" (Baumann and Briggs **1990**, 60), this perspective shift takes us from assessing a certain state or a derivative product, to engaging with the signifying process. Cue Cornelius.

Because digital poetics relies on century-old tenets of poetry like animism, agency, and consciousness (Johnston **2016**, 3) coupled with the computer's hypermedia capacity of integrating an infinite amount of different media, provoking reflexivity on creative processes *Cornelius-style* automatically becomes a meta-poetic act. Moreover, as David Jhave Johnston stipulates, code, poetry, and Cornelius's acoustic collages rely at once on structure and agency–hence allowing for communicative "uptake" while subverting illusions of transparency by virtue of human "corruption," just as, indeed, the human voice is inevitably corrupted by being human. In short, focusing on performativity highlights the active role of the experiencer and releases heuristic potential. As stated by Jacques Derrida in *La voix et le phénomène* (**2009**):

> Le s'entendre parler n'est pas l'intériorité d'un dedans clos sur soi, il est l'ouverture irréductible dans le dedans, l'œil et le monde dans la parole. *La réduction phénoménologique est une scène* (Derrida **2009**, 102–original emphasis).

Reflexivity, revealed as such, becomes a matter of *design*–design that stages itself to engage the experiencer and remind them that signification is a matter of mediation through posthuman extensions. As such, meta-poetic creations *à la Cornelius* effectively constitute a soundtrack to our posthuman condition.

The *poeticity*–i.e., the deliberate opacity of an artistic creation intended to stimulate aesthetic consideration of formal features–according to Tartu-school semiotician Iurii Lotman involves the experiencer–/–reader by means of condensation and semantic over-saturation (see Lotman **1977**). Contrary to the dictum of mainstream media theory that "more information leads to less communication," poetic creations communicate self-reflexively: a minimal amount of components suffices to channel perception towards the creation's structuring principles. Sound poetry in particular cannot be reduced to "just" its scripted dimension or its sonic constituents, but rather communicates as a *Gestalt*–effect and affect are greater than the sum of the work's individual parts (Bobillot **2013**, 11). Words, sounds, text, typography, didascalia, technology, performance, amplification, scenography, production, ... In the case of Cornelius, all these elements weave together into "a dense polychromatic meta-pop" (Hadfield **2016**) which for the album *Sensuous* even developed into a multimedia performance entitled the "Sensuous Synchronized Show."

Another case in point is "Point," title track from the 2001 album which music critics have aligned with The Beatles' *Sergeant Pepper's Lonely Hearts Club Band* (1968), Brian Eno's *Taking Tiger Mountain By Strategy* (1974), and ABC's *The Lexicon of Love* (1982) (see Hadfield **2016**, Labelle **2010**, and Santiago **2008**). On a surface level, that alleged lineage is a plausible one as it is rife with samples and choice intertextual references. However, "Point" takes the audience "uptake" a step further by quickly shifting the tension between recognition and subversion into a domain of wordless vocals and paralinguistic experimentation. A key compositional device hereby is once again digital sampling, but also the insertion of looping effects on a held vocal pitch used to generate the effect of the voice singing for impossibly long durations without dynamic variance. The same operation is then repeated with several other voices and subsequently multitracked. The end result is a slightly estranging choir singing fixed chord clusters heavy with second, fourth, fifth, and sixth harmonic intervals without any melodic lines being articulated whatsoever. The experiencer, accordingly, has to reconcile the recognizability of the human voices with their ghostly performance before key changes gradually usher perception towards the technical manipulations. It is, in the words of sound poet and scholar Philip Brophy, an instance of "the human voice [...] textured into an apparition of itself" (Brophy **2010**, 364)—an *apparition*, mind, not a stable materialization; just like the digital world from which it oh so elusively sprang.

Indeed, Cornelius's sound sculptures simultaneously create a sense of instability out of a seemingly ordered system while these superficially simplistic synthetic compositions quickly unfold into complex poly-sensorial environments that directly affect us yet categorically resist interpretative transparency. In this sensorium where meaning is at once found and distorted, the experiencer becomes acutely aware of the embodied quality of interpretation. But whereas absolute "meaning" remains beyond our grasp, a limited time lapse allows us to align our thoughts with the evident insight that this has never been possible with "traditional" music either. Perhaps, then, the poly-sensorial quality of Cornelius-style digital sound poetry allows us to step away from unproductive essentialisms towards a better understanding of the convergence between man and machine. Machines, after all, need to be animated, just as humans cannot communicate without "extensions." And once again the digital represents a helpful parallel. Discussing its typical tension between materiality and immateriality, Harris and Taylor insist that these are "not contradictory qualities but rather essential, mutually constituting elements" (Harris and Taylor **2005**, 18). If anything, it implies that interrelated elements and phenomena can coexist, and that we navigate these hybrids as a matter of course in our contemporary culture. This, of course, makes for what Agamben calls a generalized "technological signification" (Agamben **2014**, 19), and thus it becomes crucial to gain a better grasp of *how* posthuman meaning making actually occurs. If anything, it allows us to remain active agents in an ever more complex environment, yet a better understanding is also an *ethical* imperative—an incentive to keep making better choices and respond to perceived abuses.

With machine cognition now a dominant cultural force, standardized categorization could credibly lead to a general obsolescence of critical thinking—disregarding the obvious exception of protocol programmers and designers. With a sonic composition dramatizing at once the materiality and immateriality, as well as the humanism and posthumanism, of digital signification, on the other hand, Cornelius forces their experiencers to reinstate, each individually, human cognition as prime cultural mover. Precisely because all thinking is embodied, poetics still plays a pivotal role in puncturing the charisma of the machine. For, as Montreal-based artist/scholar Chris Salter so convincingly claims, human agency "seeps across the stuff of the world, unbounded, not subjected to containment within rigidly defined categories such as subject or object, human or animal" (Salter **2015**, 40). Adopting a poetic posture as proverbial "soundtrack" to our posthuman condition thereby *transversally* engages with a world perennially in the making by investigating the *interface* between "material agency" and "experiential affects"—a "voice" of reason, as it were, helping us to focus on *how* things and experiences emerge in a technically saturated world while gauging the *quality* of our own actions.

Agamben, Giorgio. 2014. *Qu'est-ce qu'un dispositif?* Translated by Martin Rueff. Paris: Payot & Rivages.

Baumann, Richard, and Charles L. Briggs. 1990. "Poetics and Performance as Critical Perspectives on Language and Social life." *Annual Review of Anthropology* 19:59-88.

Blau, Herbert. 1987. *The Eye of Prey: Subversions of the Postmodern*. Bloomington: Indiana University Press.

Bobillot, Jean-Pierre. 2013. "Poésie sonore, aujourd'hui? L'exemple d'Anne-James Chaton et de Sébasten Lespinasse." Poésie autre 114:10-13.

Brophy, Philip. 2010. "Vocalizing the Posthuman." In *Vocal Aesthetics in Digital Arts and Media*, ed. by Norie Neumark, Ross Gibson, and Van LeeuwenTheo, 361-82. Cambridge: MIT Press.

Cornelius. 2006. *Sensuous.* Warner Music Japan.

Defays, Daniel, and Douglas Hofstadter. 1997. "Numbo: A Study in Cognition and Recognition." In *Fluid Concepts and Creative Analogies: Computer Models of the Fundamental Mechanisms of Thought*, 131-54. London: Penguin.

Derrida, Jacques. 2009. *La voix et le phénomène : Introduction au problème du signe dans la phénoménologie de Husserl.* Paris: Presses Universitaires de France. [1967]

Gere, Charlie. 2002. *Digital Culture.* London: Reaktion Books.

Hadfield, James. 2016. "Keigo Oyamada sees U.S. 'Fantasma' tour as a good warm-up to new Cornelius material." *Japan Times*, July 24.

Harris, Jan L, and Paul A. Taylor. 2005. *Digital Matters: Theory and Culture of the Matrix.* London: Routledge.

Johnston, David Jhave. 2016. *Aesthetic Animism: Digital Poetry's Ontological Implications.* Cambridge: MIT Press.

LaBelle, Brandon. 2010. "Raw Orality: Sound Poetry and Live Bodies." In *Vocal Aesthetics in Digital Arts and Media*, ed. by Norie Neumark, Ross Gibson, and Van LeeuwenTheo, 147-71. Cambridge: MIT Press.

LaBenne, Luke. 2018. "A Natural Process – An Interview with Keigo Oyamada of Cornelius." *Ghettoblaster Magazine*, January 17.

Lotman, Iurii. 1977. *The Structure of the Artistic Text.* Translated by Gail Lenhoff and Ronald Vroon. Ann Arbor: University of Michigan Press.

McCaffery, Steve. 1998. "Voice in Extremis." In *Close Listening: Poetry and the Performed Word*, ed. by Charles Bernstein, 162-77. Oxford: Oxford University Press.

Neumark, Norie. 2010a. "The Paradox of Voice." In *Vocal Aesthetics in Digital Arts and Media*, ed. by Norie Neumark, Ross Gibson, Van LeeuwenTheo, and XV-XXXIII. Cambridge: MIT Press.

Neumark, Norie. 2010b. "The Paradox of Voice." In *Voice: Vocal Aesthetics in Digital Arts and Media*, ed. by Norie Neumark, Ross Gibson, and Theo van Leeuwen. Cambridge: MIT Press.

Remshardt, Ralf. 2010. "Posthumanism." In *Mapping Intermediality in Performance*, ed. by Sarah Bay-Cheng, Chiel Kattenbelt, Andy Lavender, and Robin Nelson, 135-39. Amsterdam: Amsterdam University Press.

Salter, Chris. 2015. *Alien Agency: Experimental Encounters with Art in the Making.* Cambridge: MIT Press.

Santiago, Manny. 2008. "This Is Cornelius – Interview with Oyamada Keigo." *HESO Magazine*, July 1.

Demagogic Speech And Rhetorical Emptiness

VERÓNICA PAULA GÓMEZ

Abstract

The third volume of the Electronic Literature Collection (ELC3) is home to *Radikal Karaoke*, by Argentine-Spanish artist Belén Gache. This work offers a criticism of the political speech by transforming it into a karaoke and, consequently, raising the question about the decreasing "value" of this locus (Grossberg **2012**). *Radikal Karaoke* is an interactive online device that displays a video in loop while the user/reader speaks/shouts using a microphone and pressing the keyboard randomly. The video shows people applauding, explosions, spectators watching a show, aliens, slaves, etc., and at the same time, the user/reader is pressing the keyboard following instructions and reading a written text that scrolls along the bottom of the screen. Depending on the volume of the voice and the use of the keyboard, the video will produce different images, colors and sounds. The author clearly marks a position related to the need for intervention from those who consume her technopoetic (Kozak **2015**). Gache's work interrogates us about the indiscriminate consumption of nonsense political speeches and aims to implicate us as part of this parody. What is the relationship to current political practices and social reception? Regarding this question, this paper analyses the way Gache focuses on the rhetorical emptiness of hegemonic discourses renewing the debate over the relation between demagogic politics and automated society (Berardi **2014**). The objective is to identify the strategic use of this device to make people take on an active role in the execution of poetry through karaoke and to denounce the political use of propaganda through an excess of linguistic nonsense and over-saturation of media space.

Résumé

Dans le troisième volume de l'Electronic Literature Collection (ELC3), *Radikal Karaoke* de l'artiste argentine-espagnol Belén Gache offre une critique du discours politique en le transformant en karaoké et, par conséquent, en soulevant la question de la chute de la « valeur » de ce type de discours. *Radikal Karaoke* est un dispositif interactif en ligne qui affiche une vidéo en boucle pendant que l'utilisateur/lecteur parle ou crie dans le microphone et tape au hasard sur le clavier. La vidéo montre des individus qui applaudissent, des explosions, des spectateurs regardant une émission, des extraterrestres, des esclaves, etc.; en même temps, l'utilisateur/lecteur tape sur le clavier d'après des instructions et lit un texte qui défile au bas de l'écran. En fonction du volume de la voix et de l'usage du clavier, la vidéo présente des images, des couleurs et des sons différents. Gache se positionne clairement par rapport au besoin d'intervention de la part de ceux qui consomment sa technopoétique (Kozak **2015**). Son œuvre nous interroge au sujet de la consommation sans discernement du discours politique absurde et cherche à nous impliquer dans cette parodie. Quel est le rapport aux pratiques politiques actuelles et à leur réception sociale? L'article analyse la manière par laquelle Gache centre notre attention sur le vide rhétorique des discours hégémoniques, renouvelant le débat sur le rapport de la politique démagogique et de la société automatisée (Berardi **2014**). L'objectif est d'identifier l'usage stratégique de ce dispositif afin d'encourager un rôle actif dans l'actualisation du texte poétique à travers le karaoké et de dénoncer la propagande politique par le biais d'un excès de non-sens linguistique et d'une saturation de l'espace médiatique.

INTRODUCTION

The third volume of the Electronic Literature Collection (ELC3) is home to *Radikal Karaoke*[1] by Argentine-Spanish artist Belén Gache, originally made in 2011. This work offers a criticism of political speech by transforming it into a karaoke, consequently posing a question about the decreasing "value" of this locus (Grossberg **2012**).

Radikal Karaoke is an interactive online device that displays a video in loop while the user/reader speaks/shouts using a microphone and randomly pressing the keyboard. Specifically, the video shows people applauding, explosions, spectators watching a show, aliens, slaves, etc., and at the same time, the user/reader is pressing the keyboard following some instructions and reading a written text passing along the bottom of the screen. Depending on the volume of the voice and the use of the keyboard, the video will produce different images, colors and sounds. We can observe performative aspects of the users who, when interacting with the machine, reveal "the monolingualism of the other" (Derrida **1967**).

NOTE 1

Available here: **http://belengache.net/rk/**. Also on this web page there are videos where Belén Gache performs her work herself. The work is part of the third volume of the Electronic Literature Collection (ELC): Link: **http://collection.eliterature.org/3/work.html?work=radikal-karaoke.**

Figure 1:
Radikal Karaoke screenshot: Controls

The author clearly marks a position related to the need for intervention of those who consume this technopoetic (Kozak **2015**). As part of an artistic program, Gache restores its specific place for political action in a world overrun by automated discourses that function mechanically as machines (Groys **2016**). Gache's work poses the question about the indiscriminate consumption of nonsensical political speeches and aims to involve us as part of this parody

(Hutcheon 1988). What is the relationship between current political practices and their social reception? Regarding this question, this paper analyses the way Gache focuses on the rhetorical emptiness of hegemonic discourses renewing the debate about the connection between demagogic politics and automated society (Berardi 2014). The objective is to identify the strategic use of this device to make people take on an active role in the execution of poetry through karaoke and to denounce the political use of propaganda through an excess of linguistic nonsense and over-saturation of media space.

THE CONVERSION: FROM DEMAGOGIC POLITICAL PRACTICES TO RADIKAL

Here we will first develop what we call "the conversion" of demagogic political practices into radikal karaoke. In regard to this idea, *Radikal Karaoke* is a technopoetic (Kozak 2015) that poses a question: what does somebody do when speaking as part of the political class? The work suggests that it is all built into demagogic political practices that focus on keywords and images leading to a passive reception: "Speeches are structured on emphatic and demagogic formulae and linguistic clichés reproducing themselves as viruses" (Gache 2011). This is why the work aims to awaken the audience into a karaoke.

A karaoke is a popular form of entertainment, offered typically by bars and clubs, in which people take turns singing popular songs into a microphone over pre-recorded backing tracks. In addition, Gache expanded the functions of regular karaoke–a vintage technology that had its heyday in the entertainment industry in the 70s, although it is still reverting as a practice–using other tools of present times such as the computer itself.

Based on this reproduction device, Gache offers a Derridean idea: to reach the difference (*la différance*) in the repetition of texts–songs, discourses, poems. The fact that the author chooses to use a "k" in 'radikal'–instead of following the regular spelling "radical" with a "c"–could be related to the dual "k" of karaoke, which seems the most visible cause for this choice. But also, this device of repetition always has moments of discourse deviation that are very productive in their excess, as we could see with the "a" introduced by Derrida (1967)–difference / différance.

Figure 2:
A user performing *Radikal Karaoke*

A deviation radically converts the political proposal by means of its stereotyped discourse: to make people drowsy with repeated demagogic "songs" that everybody seems to remember but nobody analyzes deeply. Through this operation that seeks to plunge people into drowsiness, politicians and governments satisfy their main objective: to bring about lack of sense and hinder critical thinking in the audience. That is why karaoke seems both–a way to focus on the spectacularity of politics and the device to give the opportunity to people to have a voice in this decreasing *locus*: "En la era del teleprompter el discurso político es más karaoke que teatro y por más gravitas que el andamiaje del gobierno le otorgue, sería más honesto ver este espectáculo en un bar"[2] (Flores **2017**).

NOTE 2

"In a teleprompter era, the political discourse is more karaoke than theatre and no matter how much gravitas the government scaffolding, it would be more honest to watch this spectacle in a bar." (Our translation)

Reshaping the textual past through a postmodern parody (Hutcheon **1988**), which entails an ironic rupture with the awareness of that past, Gache proposes three transcriptions–in Spanish [Figure 3] or in English–that we could perform to shake off drowsiness: SPEECH 1 "We are the charming gardeners" (in English); "Ex Africa semper aliquid novi" (in Spanish). SPEECH 2: "Things that you will never see in Australia" (in English); "Mirad cómo Kate presume de su anillo" (in Spanish). SPEECH 3: "We have no past, you have no present" (in English); "Es tiempo de escuchar a los guacamayos" (in Spanish). With these speeches Gache's work seeks to denaturalize clichés and stereotyped phrases that circulate as meaningless slogans, while being uncritically received (Gache **2014**).

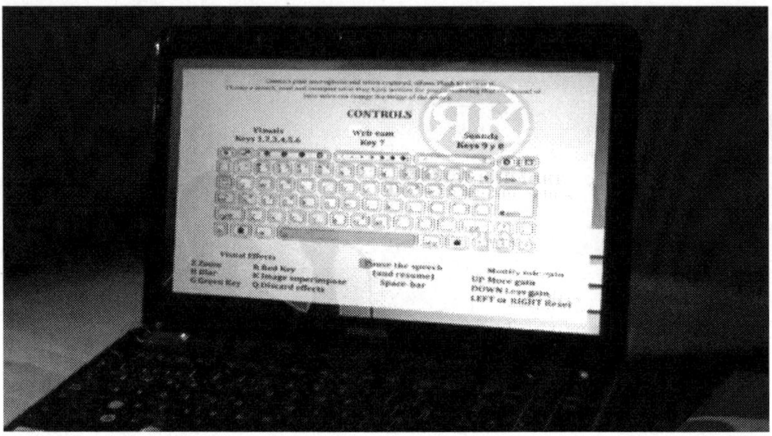

Figure 3: Three speeches to choose in Spanish, in *Radikal Karaoke* by Belén Gache

Ideally, karaoke seems to be a device that duplicates lyrics that are already known "by heart," and when playing the song, the singer completes the melody provided by the machine with words. However, Gache shows that what is important is the translation of what we think we are repeating every time we speak. Therefore, there is no way to imitate speeches without a deviation, because the conception of language itself as a hallucination (Derrida **1967**) provides a critical view of stereotypes to current political practices. Gache is minding the gap by helping us not to be robots, not to be just passive listeners.

THE ACTION: FACING RHETORICAL EMPTINESS, INTRODUCING PERFORMANCE

Radikal Karaoke intends to elicit political speeches from its users. Gache built machinery to perform the rhetorical emptiness related to politics with different voices and bodies, and in this search, the users subversively transform the discursive hegemony. As Flores admits: "Nuestra clase política nos lee frases trilladas y nosotros como público le damos una fracción de nuestra atención a ver si sale algo nuevo o por lo menos genuino"[3] (Flores **2017**).

NOTE 3
"Our political class reads trite phrases and we as a public give a fraction of our attention to see if something new or at least genuine comes out." (Our translation)

For the work to exist, something stimulating has to happen, something related to our own bodies that has been repressed by the political "circus" that entertains us. When a speaker pronounces the discourse offered by the machine, he/she performs the words that subject himself or herself to stupor and uncritical attitude. This is the way in which performance turns emptiness into alertness, using the rhetorical mechanism of politics.

Traditions, conquests, revolutions: the active voice of people who play karaoke is the way to express a criticism of emptiness. The work welcomes the performance of those who–being fragile in their monolingualism–come as guests to the *locus* of politics. And although this is just a game–just a discourse and then it is over–this language is hospitable *to the other* (Derrida **1996**), making way for critical thinking regarding the lack of sense shown by politics. If we come back to the Japanese meaning of karaoke we will find, once again, the idea of emptiness in its morphemes: *kara* (empty), *oke* (orchestra). Gache seems to return to these etymological meanings, wondering why words do not matter. And in addition, Gache presents the music as a body that could be used as a score to give ideal-universal instructions to an orchestra but played each time in a different way (Gache **2014**). What she tries to develop is what we listen to and what we could say when we change back these stereotypes.

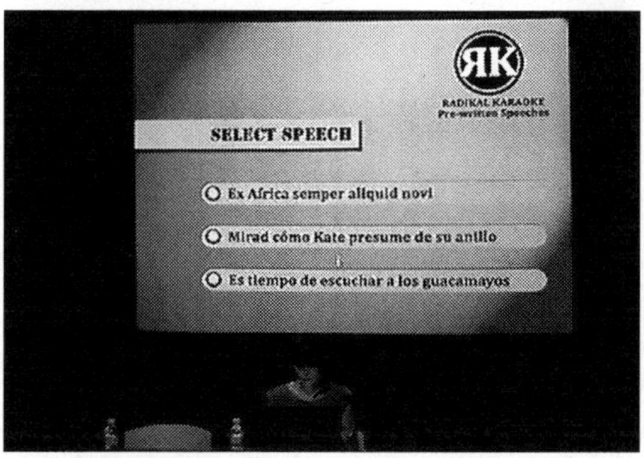

Figure 4: Images of explosions while performing the work *Radikal Karaoke* by Belén Gache

The material of the poem (orality, writing, drawing), the performance of readers/users, the interaction, the generativity, the listening, the form acquired by the discourse point to a deconstruction of the entertainment industry used by politics. The author clearly marks a position related to the need of intervention of those who consume these speeches without playing any role but that of listeners. Karaoke forces you to say something with your own voice, using the same device you used before, when you were just a receptor. As a consequence, poetic language restores the possibility of political action through the same machinery that causes the rhetorical emptiness denounced before. In the repetition of those three discourses of contemporary highly urbanized society, Gache recovers an organic form of language that allows the appearance of new senses and provides a place for a rebellious poetics. These speeches are pirated, showing how, once given, the giver of information loses control of the way it can be used by the performer (Errington **2008**).

The body becomes a place of enunciation of the demagogy of political *locus*. The work invites us to attend a costume party where all voices are heard and the same discourses get repeated once and again until all sense is lost. The parody consists in facing the distortions of what seems to be a "serious truth"– the political speech–by repeating common sense not only with words but also by means of images and sounds (Taylor **2017**). Here Gache is minding the gap of our past, turning us into protagonists of our present through parody.

THE PROJECTION: FROM THE DECREASING OF POLITICS TO THE INCREASING OF ART

To conclude, we describe two inversions that are very productive for expanding the use of art by means of new technology, for changing the demagogic speeches denounced by Gache.

First, what contemporary art can achieve is a reversion of the unidirectional movement of the political discourses that dominated the way of making politics in the 20th century, i.e., a leader appealing to the masses through the new technologies of the time–radio and television. Now, that multitude uses the technical possibilities in the opposite way: it makes demands to politicians through an insubordinate use of art (Brea **2002**).

Figure 5: The insubordinate use of art in *Radikal Karaoke* by Belén Gache

Second, there is an inversion of the artist as a hacker (Gradin **2015**), achieved by making new contents–that have been silenced by political interests–go viral. Gache suggests using "the other side of technology" to subvert passive listening and give speeches new and unthought–of meanings that turn art into a territory to experiment upon. Drawing a parallel with the incipient growth of electronics during the last decades of the 20th century, Burroughs stated in the 1970s that language was a virus whose only cure was silence or literature: "'Borren las palabras para siempre' (...) la palabra literaria fortifica el organismo contra las formas más insidiosas del mal; las palabras de los políticos, de los militares, de los comunicadores sociales, de los médicos, los psiquiatras"[4] (Gamerro **1970**, 26).

NOTE 4

"Delete words for ever'... the literary word fortifies the organism against the most insidious forms of evil; the words of politicians, military men, social communicators, doctors, psychiatrists." (Our translation)

In this inversion, we could find the political projection of art when interacting with machines. As Brea (**2002**) says, the key is how to subversively intervene in the processes of social construction of knowledge, speaking the language of the same system that produces a uniform and unique instrumentalization of the work of the people. Finally, Gache is minding the gap in machines to allow us to be heard.

Berardi, Franco. 2014. *La sublevación.* Buenos Aires: Hekht Libros.

Brea, José Luis. 2002. *La era postmedia. Acción comunicativa, prácticas (post) artísticas y dispositivos neomediales.* Salamanca: Editorial CASA.

Derrida, Jacques. 1967. *L'écriture et la différence.* Paris: Seuil.

Derrida, Jacques. 1996. *El monolingüismo del otro.* Buenos Aires: Manantial.

Derrida, Jacques. 1997. *Mal de archivo. Una impresión freudiana.* Madrid: Trotta.

Errington, Joseph. 2008. "Colonial Linguists, (Proto)-National Languages." In *Linguistics in a Colonial World: A Story of Language, Meaning, and Power,* 123-48. Oxford: Blackwell Publishing.

Flores, Leonardo. 2017. "Literatura electrónica y discurso político." *80 grados,* June. Link: http://www.80grados.net/literatura-electronica-y-discurso-politico/.

Gache, Belén. 2011. "Radikal Karaoke. Speech Transcripts." 2011. Accessed June 15, 2020. Link: http://belengache.net/rk/.

Gache, Belén. 2014. *Instrucciones de uso: Partituras, recetas y algoritmos en la poesía y el arte contemporáneos.* Madrid. Retrieved May 17, 2018. Link: https://www.belengache.net/pdf/InstruccionesDeUso_BelenGache.pdf.

Gamerro, Carlos. 1970. "Por un arte impuro." In *La revolución electrónica,* ed. by William Burroughs, 9-19. Buenos Aires: Caja Negra.

Gradin, Charly. 2015. "Hacker." In *Tecnopoéticas argentinas. Archivo blando de arte y tecnología,* ed. by Claudia Kozak, 132-37. Buenos Aires: Caja Negra.

Grossberg, Lawrence. 2012. *Estudios culturales en tiempo futuro. Cómo es el trabajo intelectual que requiere el mundo de hoy.* Buenos Aires: Siglo XXI Editores.

Groys, Boris. 2016. "Bajo la mirada de la teoría." In *Arte en flujo. Ensayos sobre la evanescencia del presente,* 33-54. Buenos Aires: Caja Negra.

Hutcheon, Linda. 1988. "Intertextuality, Parody, and the Discourses of History." In *A Poetics of Postmodernism. History, Theory, Fiction.* New York; London: Routledge.

Kozak, Claudia, ed. 2015. *Tecnopoéticas argentinas. Archivo blando de arte y tecnología.* 2nd ed. Buenos Aires: Caja Negra.

Taylor, Claire. 2017. "Entre 'born digital' y herencia literaria: el diálogo entre formatos literarios y tecnología digital en la poética electrónica hispanoamericana." *Tropelías. Revista de teoría de la literatura y literatura comparada,* 79-90. Link: https://doi.org/10.26754/ojs_tropelias/tropelias.2017271541.

KEDRICK JAMES • ERNESTO PEÑA
YUYA TAKEDA AND THE DIGITAL LITERACY CENTRE

Transmedia: An Improvisualization

Abstract

This paper describes a live transmediatic impro-visualization that started with the production of a digital photograph. The artifact-as-raw-data was translated into sound and played through a transducer (vibrating speaker), thus filtering the digital file as an analogue signal through different physical materials before its re-digitization, re-recorded in real time. Finally, the resulting artifact was represented in its visual form. Our presentation contrasted between performance as process and performance as product, and allowed both participants (voices) and material objects to be encoded in the transmediative process, imbuing data with immediacy while comparing aesthetic properties of both native and non-native file formats, and revealing patterns-in-common between these different media. For an applied example of these transmediative processes, we present a case study comparing the phenomenological differences between analogue (vinyl record) and digital (compact disc) media, the analogue playback being digitally recorded and visualized for a static comparison.

Résumé

Cet article décrit une impro-visualisation transmédiatique en direct qui a débuté avec la création d'une photographie numérique. Les données brutes de cet artefact ont été traduites et diffusées grâce à un transducteur (une enceinte vibrante). Ce faisant, le fichier numérique d'origine est travaillé à la manière d'un signal analogique avant sa re-numérisation et son enregistrement en temps réel. En plus de la part sonore, l'artefact modifié est également re-présenté visuellement.
Nos impro-visualisations permettent ainsi de distinguer la performance en tant que processus de celle en tant que produit fini, en plus d'intégrer les participants et les objets matériels à la performance sous forme de code. Les processus de transmédiation – incorporant les données en direct – donnent ainsi lieu à une comparaison entre les fichiers natifs et non-natifs et révèlent les motifs communs entre les différents médias de la performance. Nous examinons l'un des processus transmédiatiques mis à profit dans notre pratique, à savoir la transposition des médias analogiques (vinyles) et numériques (disques compacts).

MATERIALIZING DATA

This paper was performed live, and largely improvised, during the 2018 Electronic Literature Organization conference in Montreal. The aim was to share explorations in transmediation, a term we use specifically to mean transferring raw data between different sensory media platforms (Peña and James **2020**) which has been the focus of a project that began in the Digital Literacy Centre located in the Department of Language and Literacy Education at the University of British Columbia in 2015. Throughout this project, we have been developing an experimental approach to revealing educational benefits of analogue and code level interference in automated processes which we refer to as Glitch Pedagogy (Peña and James **2016**). We argue that through calculated perturbation we can enter a dialogue with the automated Other (James **2017**) as a kind of applied posthumanism, and reveal self, therefore history, in the data flow. Raw data–data stripped of proprietary software headers–like the data equivalent of Agamben's *Homo Sacer* (**1998**),[1] is able to pass incognito across certain digital platforms, and is compiled as if the data were native to the software opening it. This universality of the sign(al) we have in the past equated with the human phenomenon of synaesthesia (Luther **2014**). As such, one is able to intervene creatively with the data and produce unexpected artifacts within the output. Through multiple glitch trials (Menkman **2011**), such interventions might become an artistic practice.

NOTE 1

In this sense, raw data has no ownership or sovereign protection, and can therefore be taken (used) by any software program.d'imposture, persiste.

The methods we employ are procedural and function at the level of opportunistic accidents that are nonetheless strategic and, through trial and error, more or less calculated: from a literary point of view, we use procedural poetics applied at the level of code in the digital realm (Funkhouser **2012**), and operationalize these proceedings as a form of educational research. During the generative phase of our experiments, we disavow our own aesthetic and critical expectations regarding the output of the various automated processes we interact with. We simply observe, interact and audit (or vice versa) through playful experiment which is sustained through iterative processes. We revel in the unpredictability of outcomes; based on trial, result, and problem solving, we learn, and foster our better understanding of machine language dynamics in computational systems that typically remain tacit and are taken for granted. In planning the iterative processing cycles of data for our experiments, we alternate between digital and analogue media and, therefore, digital and analogue signal interventions (James **2015**).

In the context of this performance event, we introduced a focus on trans-mediation that involved the complete materialization and digital recapture of data flow. The matter of matter in the data stream implicates a quantum-mechanical transformation, from electron to waveform and back again: digital photographic data transmediated to sound waves passing through solid matter and through air/space in time only to be re-digitized. In this passage of light coded as digital data compressed into the slow, narrow range of the audible frequency spectrum, data cast in omnidirectional pulses of a transducer (a speaker that vibrates on a resonating physical object, i.e., an inverted metal mixing bowl resting on a raised classroom lecturers' desk)–with the audience not only present but vocalizing and shouting out, while the sound waves are being re-recorded as digital audio, then re-visualized to show the starting image now saturated with the full phenomenal presence of the material world embedded in the data, this act implicates the universe, and natural law, within our artificial sensorium. Moreover, the difference between the start and end images documents the exact circumstance of the performance in all its spatial, temporal, social, architectural, climatic, perhaps even spiritual complexity–even the history of the tree that was milled to make the lectern becomes integrated into the photographic image–making the outcome unique, and, therefore, unrepeatable. Naturally, we did not know what to expect. Taking a photograph, sonorizing it, recording ourselves listening to it, and returning it to its native format pushes our work beyond merely post-humanism of the glitch pedagogical dialogue with automation: it positions the work within new materialism, as a means of seeing the intersection between the quantum mechanical properties of the physical universe and the algorithmic properties of the digital, virtual universe. Where these two theoretical frameworks and worldviews intersect, we position ourselves vis à vis interruptions in a particular signal path and flow of data to invest the properties of the analogue, physical world within the digital artifact.

To further explicate the concepts and utility of our experimental practices, we provide a working example, namely the anomalous case of vinyl records as the only analogue storage medium to have so thoroughly recaptured public attention that it regained not only an iconic, trending cultural status but also a significantly increasing market share from its immediate digital successor, the Compact Disk (CD). In fact, at the time of the 2018 Electronic Literature Organization conference, Best Buy, one of the last mega chain big box stores was phasing out all CD sales, while smaller stores such as London Drugs were expanding their vinyl record shelves, helping the 12 % increase in sales over the previous year of new, physical music products (Waniata **2018**). While this is set in the context of the more significant impact, firstly of person-to-person file sharing (e.g., Napster), then of music streaming (e.g., Spotify), in the digital music market. For the purpose of this paper we will focus solely on physical products, comparing resurgent vinyl with disappearing CDs, for this marks a unique event in the history of electronic media, and is worthy of considerable scholarly attention in the study of popular culture and digital humanities. One obstacle to a more fulsome discussion is the insufficiency of (English) language to adequately describe the phenomenological difference between listening to digital versus analogue audio; so, to address this problem pragmatically, we apply transmediation techniques as a way of visualizing these difference (Rezza **2020**). Audiophiles tend to use fuzzy, sensory metaphors to describe perceived differences. Felt sense plays an important role in semantically approximating the distinction: sharpness versus smoothness, brightness versus softness, coldness versus warmth are typical descriptive terms that reach out to approximate ineffable sensations, but fall short of capturing the particular differentiation from an auditory perspective. Therefore, in order to examine this difference more closely as a static visual image, we compare two raw data visualizations of the same audio track played back through the same system, one originating as a digital file on CD, the other as an analogue track on vinyl. While some may question the fact that in both cases, the playback is analogue, part of our work has to prioritize analogue experiences of digital phenomena. While this represents early stages of our research in applied transmediation, it sets up the context in which we might consider the new materialist implications of the ability of distinct media formats to produce copies that are in fact unique to the user. We believe that this uniqueness to the user is identical to the manner in which knowledge is acquired and becomes useful (beyond aesthetic pleasure) to the learner.

SETTING (THE PERFORMANCE ITSELF)

Although this session was framed as a noise music recital, the set (mise-en-*play*, if you will) and response from the attendants gave it the ethos of a magic performance. We started by informing the attendants that we would transfer an image between two computers by transmediating such an image into an audio file and playing it through a speaker connected to the first computer, while simultaneously capturing the audio with a microphone connected to the other. We would then transmediate the audio file into an image file and discuss it. The artifact to be transmediated was presented to the attendants, a close-up image of a computer keyboard of 1024 x 1024 pixels of resolution (see Figure 1). Neither the visual qualities nor the resolution of the image were arbitrarily determined. They were carefully chosen to deliver some degree of aesthetic features in a manageable time when transmediated into sound and played to the audience. Such characteristics were based on principles that cannot be discussed here due to space limitations but have been detailed by the authors elsewhere (Peña and James **2020**).

Figure 1. The original image.

The set for this performance included two computers, a transducer speaker, a microphone and a couple of artifacts with a flat surface of different materials (i.e., metal and wood). The image file was originally stored in one of the computers (computer B, see Figure 2) and translated into a .raw file by saving the image file in that format. The converted .raw file was then imported without any further modification in an audio editor (Audacity). After conversion, the audio file was approximately 71 seconds in length at 44,100 Hz of sampling frequency in monoaural. A transducer speaker was connected to this same computer.

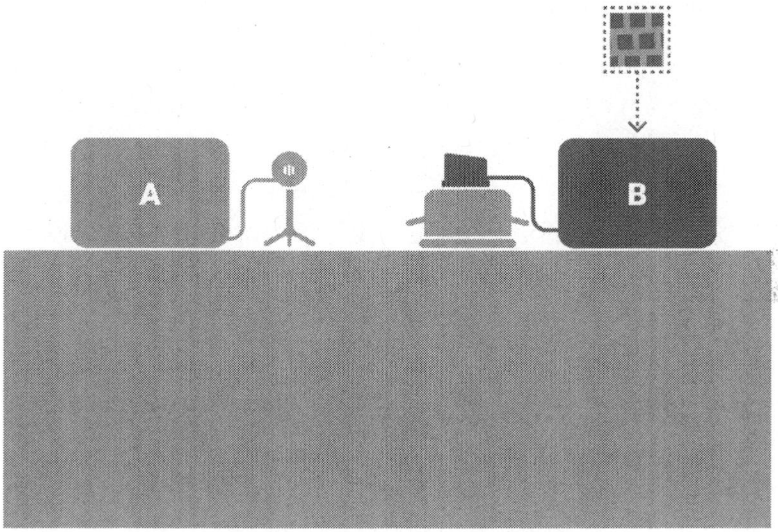

Figure 2. The configuration of the set.

The .raw file in audio format was then played in its entirety on the transducer. When played, the transmediated photograph sounded similar to a muffled helicopter with three distinct and identifiable patterns of tonal variation. The first rendition of the file was played through a wooden surface. As the file was being played, we invited the attendants to intervene in the audio by talking over and screaming for the sound to be also captured by the receiving microphone. By doing this, we intended to have these interventions visualized in the transmediated image, along with any other visual qualities that the file might have acquired from being filtered through the wooden surface (see Figure 3).

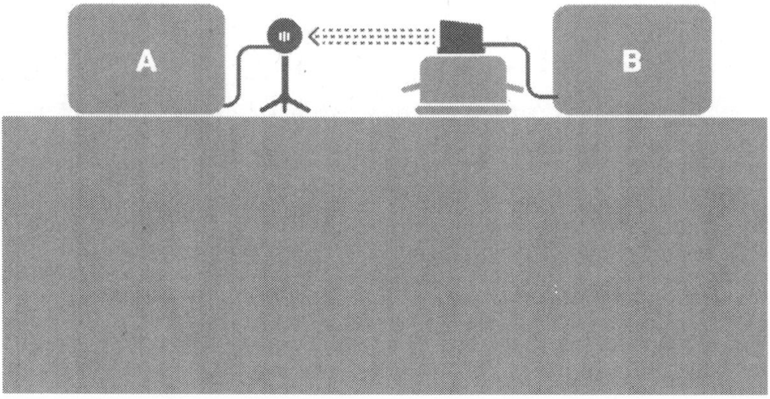

Figure 3. Sound being environmentally transferred from the transducer to the microphone.

To ensure the capture of the full image in audio format and its subsequent reconstruction, the recording started a couple of seconds before the track from computer B started to be played and was stopped a couple of seconds after. However, beyond capturing the entirety of the file, the real challenge consisted in discerning which data units of the audio file belong to the original image and which ones are data excess, produced during the presentation. The solution to this issue lies, at least partially, in the characteristics of the original file. Being aware of the resolution (1024 x 1024), the colour mode of the original photograph (RGB, 3 channels) and the relationship of 1:1 between pixels and audio samples, we needed only to calculate a) the total number of pixels in the image and identify the exact same number of samples in the audio file and b) identify the moment in which the microphone started capturing the sample, which could be deduced from the first noticeable peak in the waveform. Based on the aforementioned parameters, the number of samples that would reconstruct the full image was 3,145,778 ([1024^2] x 3). Once the first peak in the audio file was identified, it was just a matter of trimming the file to this number of samples and opening it as a .raw file (see Figure 4).

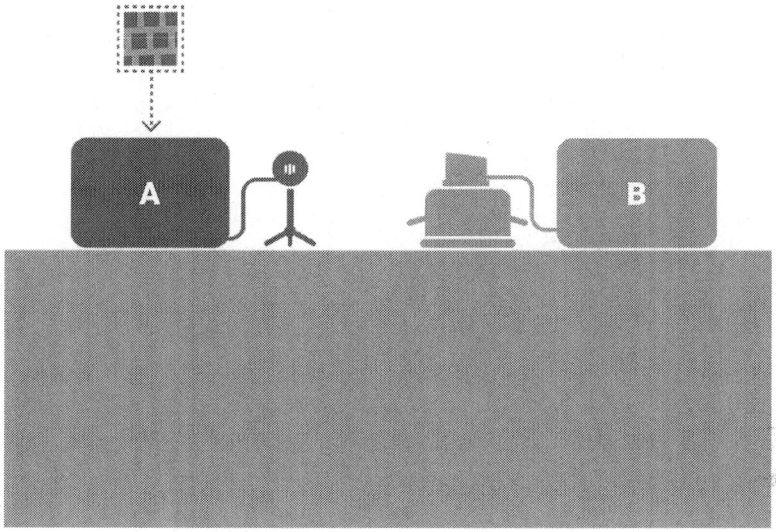

Figure 4. Image reconstructed on computer A after being transferred.

The result of reconstructing the image in computer A by transmediating the audio file captured from computer B back into a visual format is an altered yet recognizable version of the original file. This process was repeated twice, each time with the transducer placed on a different material. The first time, the transducer was placed directly over the wooden desk, the second time over a metal pot. On both occasions, the images reconstructed during the session held enough similarity to the original image to be recognizable (see Figure 5).

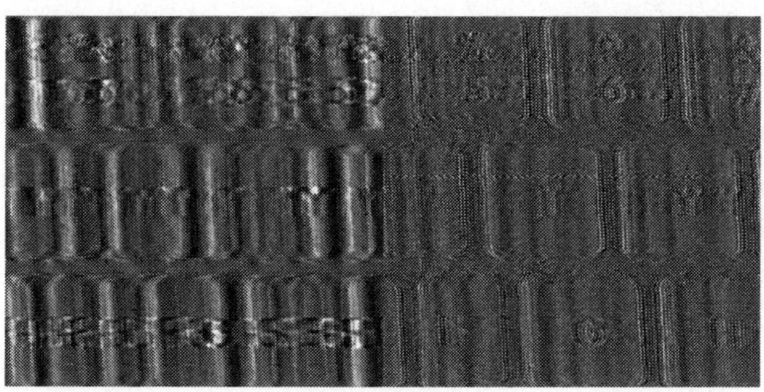

Figure 5. On the left, the reconstructed image after passing through the transducer placed over wood. On the right, the same image, now through a metal surface.

Probably more important than the similarities between the images presented here are the differences. These two images are now an index of the sonic events during the pass of the transmediated image between computers (the environmental sound, our own voices addressing the audience during the presentation, and the material properties of the surfaces where the transducer was placed).

THEORIZING THE PHYSICAL TRANSMEDIATION OF DATA

Pertinent to these experiments are the physical aspects of data, the electronic trace of where that data has been, where it has come from, echoing the wisdom of American poet Charles Olson's maxim, "Whatever you have to say, leave/The roots on, let them/Dangle/And the dirt/Just to make clear/Where they come from" (Olson 1987, 106). Data is transient and immaterial. Digital data does not age. It may, of course become redundant, obsolescent, corrupted, even viral, but this does not equate to the fading of an old photograph, the dog-eared pages of a favorite book, or the wow and flutter of old magnetic tape, the *bare ruined choirs* of cherished and well-loved media. Typically, this move toward non-redundant, uniform, ascetic, ageless data is considered to be technical progress, even though change in file formats, software and storage devices, along with the rapid life cycles and dysfunction of digital technology makes information storage more volatile and susceptible to temporal and environmental factors than ever. Although data storage devices and media have been rapidly cannibalizing one another, pressed on by industrial planned obsolescence, if one looks at a digital photograph from 10 years ago, there will be no sign of decay. Of course, one is most likely to perceive the age of the photograph through secondary factors like relatively low resolution compared to newer technology, *time-stamps* such as people's fashion, the scenery,objects in the image, and so forth, but the data itself is not materially imbued with historicity. Moreover, a thousand copies of that image stored in different devices, maintained and viewed by different people in different situations and climates will look identical if viewed later on the same machine. Physical images do age and wear, even if carefully preserved. The phenomena of aging, while perjured from a biological point of view of beings lured by immortality, are an entire gestalt within semiosis. The collector is attuned and attracted to these age-related features of consumer products as a sign of authenticity, whether collecting heritage Levi Strauss jeans or crate digging for original pressings of vinyl in a thrift store basement.

We posit that media which differentiates and acquires uniqueness according to its individual use, that is, data that becomes imbued with a particular history, becoming quantum entangled on a micro and macro level, can evolve and symbiotically/symbolically adapt its presence as cultural artifact or phenomenon. This process was first described by Walter Benjamin in his essay *The Work of Art in the Age of Mechanical Reproduction* (1969) using the term "aura".[2] Although this goes beyond the scope of our present topic, the notion that data can be separated from life and living, and from material circumstances is not only alienating (e.g., we are "users" of information technologies) but ultimately misguided in terms of education, especially digital literacy education. As merely part of the omnipresence of electrical activity, the immateriality and invisibility of data presents challenges to the human psyche in this *antisign* of the information age (James 2015), challenges that derange agency with facilitation-at-a-cost of craft and personalized meaning.

New materialists promote a shift in the prevailing intellectual orientation toward concerns with the material world–with ecology, with embodiment, and with the intangible aspects of experience and finding ways to reverse blind alleys that an excessive faith in the methods of physical and social sciences have brought us to. Karen Barad (2007) alerts us to how the abstractions of quantum field theory provided the groundwork for the application of this work on the physical plane in the most destructive way, through atomic and hydrogen bombs. The disconnection between processes and products, and the privileging of certain ontologies over others, created the conditions for a suspension of the affective, and sympathetic functions in decision making. In the search for knowledge, we have taken for granted the persecution, even the outright destruction of the material world. We seek to master nature, rather than allow the natural world and natural law to be our teacher. Through this same sedimenting of ways of doing that disregard the interrelations among all matter, the automation of our practices embeds these relations, as Cathy O'Neil (2016) quips, with "weapons of math destruction," noting the

NOTE 2

Benjamin describes this entangled relationship between the artifact and the history of its use thus: "The authenticity of a thing is the essence of all that is transmissible from its beginning, ranging from its substantive duration to its testimony to the history which it has experienced. Since the historical testimony rests on the authenticity, the former, too, is jeopardized by reproduction when substantive duration ceases to matter. And what is really jeopardized when the historical testimony is affected is the authority of the object. One might subsume the eliminated element in the term 'aura' and go on to say: that which withers in the age of mechanical reproduction is the aura of the work of art. This is a symptomatic process whose significance points beyond the realm of art. One might generalize by saying: the technique of reproduction detaches the reproduced object from the domain of tradition. By making many reproductions it substitutes a plurality of copies for a unique existence." (221)..

social impacts, the enhancing of distances between classes, races, genders, individuals are increasingly subject to scalable paradigms of surveillance and manipulation. It is not so much a matter of sedimenting a singular approach as it is of recognizing possibilities for what the future might need, and beginning to address them. As Einstein says, "we cannot solve our problems with the same thinking we use when we create them".[3]

NOTE 3

This reference with Einstein's quote is of dubious origin, and may be attributable to Ram Dass.

AN APPLIED EXAMPLE COMPARING VINYL AND COMPACT DISK MEDIA

In light of the new materialism, vinyl records are a special kind of case study. In no other instance has a physical, analogue media technology/product, once it is forced into antiquity and obsolescence by a (typically more portable) digital alternative or replacement, come back from the dead, so to speak. For sure, there are still Single Lens Reflex (SLR) cameras, but all modern ones are digital. It may be possible to find one that uses optical film, but rolls of optical film are difficult to find, and retail film processing is a cultural by-gone. A high definition digital camera would not have the characteristic grain, depth of field, and so on, that you see with optical film. But it could be made to look like optical film, and the use of the SLR design in digital cameras makes the difference negligible. It would have astonishing detail, and moreover, it would cost no more than the camera to take 10,000 photos. Except for particular graphic arts and a kind of nostalgia for olden ways, the optical camera's days are done as a mainstream technology. This said, an experiment of sonorizing the same photograph taken using optical film (then digitized), and a digitally originating photograph would be worthwhile.

How strange, therefore, that vinyl records which are neither convenient nor very portable, and require specialized playback turntables, cartridges, a generous amount of storage space, and are expensive to produce, must be shipped long distances for lack of local pressing plants (although new plants are opening up, and vinyl enthusiast Jack "White's label, Third Man, recently opened its own pressing plant in Detroit with the first newly built vinyl presses in 35 years," (Knopper **2018**)) that these incredibly awkward although often beautiful products have so thoroughly reentered the market that they are now dominating the physical music collector (new and used) world (Rosenblatt **2018**).

The material qualities of the vinyl record influence the apprehension of the product (sound) from the playback device (record player, amplifier, speakers) in such a way that the benefit of removing material artifacts from the listening experience also changed perceptual aspects of the listening experience and the fetishistic pleasure which both vinyl media and the physical packaging (the record jacket, sleeve, paraphernalia) conveyed, and which the marketplace for physical recordings prefers to the smaller, jewel case or printed outer sleeve of its digital counterpart. To compensate for this less auspicious product design, music producers at first created the longbox consumer packaging, a design that created 18.5 million extra pounds per year of waste by 1990 (Demain **2012**), which only ended after pressure from consumers to stop the practice.

Exactly what these satisfying properties of the vinyl record are can be difficult to articulate, they seem almost ineffable (or at least we have not developed yet the vocabulary to discuss them). Instead, they point toward a cumulative, residual, felt sense that accrues, subconsciously, as the result of abduction of sensory input.[4] It is in this context that we might consider the physical properties of data storage as having relevance to our research. To playback (retrieve) data from a vinyl record, a highly sensitive pick-up converts the physical motion of a needle passing through the walls of a continuous, spiral vinyl groove which has pressed into it the complexity of an audio waveform. Each time the needle passes through the groove, to play the record, it affects the groove, unlike optical readers of CD data, which make no difference to the digital film's surface whether scanned one or one thousand times. We pause here to consider that the stylus needle is housed in a pick-up cartridge attached to a lightly weighted tonearm, an apparatus which is also, however minutely, affected by the vibratory environment around it. In the gross sense of the environmental impact, if the record is played at a party where people are dancing, the stylus might jump and skip grooves, or, bumped into by a frenzied dancer, skid across the record, scratching the surface. But, as literacy theorist John Willinsky once quipped, even the tickling sound of ice in a martini glass could be impressed upon the walls of a vinyl groove while listening to some groovy jazz. In other words, the experience of listening to the record's playback is physically recorded into the materiality of the audio storage medium, creating a feedback loop which iterates and ages, and takes on the history and characteristics of its use each time it is played. A well loved record records the characteristics of its

NOTE 4

As defined by Charles Sanders Peirce. See Peirce Edition Project, ed. *The Essential Peirce, Volume 2: Selected Philosophical Writings (1893-1913)*. Vol. 2. 2 vols. Bloomington: Indiana University Press, 1998.

listeners and their environment in each subsequent playback. In this manner, no two copies of a used record will be identical.

To produce the following visualizations, we created a controlled audio environment using a consumer quality stereo system with high quality turn-table and CD player, each roughly the same age and duration of use. Speakers of the system were placed in close proximity to a stereo digital microphone connected to a computer recording at the standard Nyquist-Shannon sampling rate 44.1 kHz (roughly twice the rate of the highest frequency of human hearing, 20 kHz) for re-recording the data. Using our own short audio track "Eye Speak Icing," recorded in an analogue studio with voice and samples, and digitally captured at the same sampling rate as above, then pressed on both vinyl and CD (from a .wav file, not the lossless FLAGG format, to simulate consumer end product experiences), we were thus able to construct the entire history of the creative and mechanical as well as digital processes that went into the final file of digital data we transmediated, visualizing the differences between the analogue and digital storage formats.

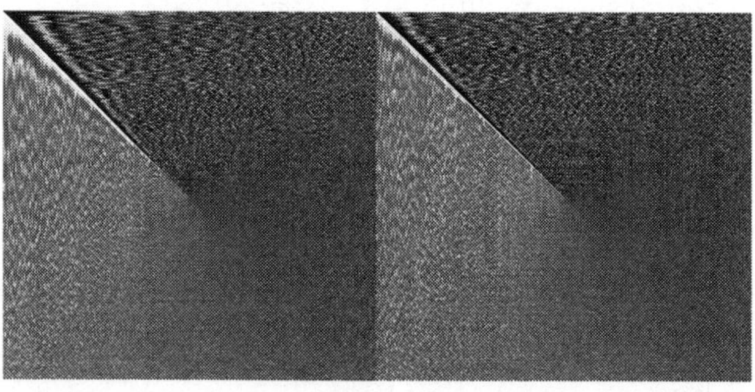

Figure 6. On the left, the visualization after spiral pixel sorting of a one-minute audio track played on CD. On the right, the same audio track played from a vinyl record with the same visualization process applied.

Contemplation of the visual representations in Figure 6 reveals distinct differences. The image to the left is more evenly distributed and symmetrical. The diagonal line which represents moments of relative silence is more broad. The subtle square linear patterns of the green and fuchsia overlay are evenly distributed. The image to the right has far more irregularity. The square linear patterns are more pronounced, while the dotted yellow line at the bottom of the CD image (the most obvious irregularity) disappears in the vinyl pixel sorted transmediation. We might say that although the two images at this resolution look similar, the image to the right has more pattern irregularity, with individual and idiosyncratic characteristics. A close-up of the same part of the images above shows much greater difference between these two audio files.

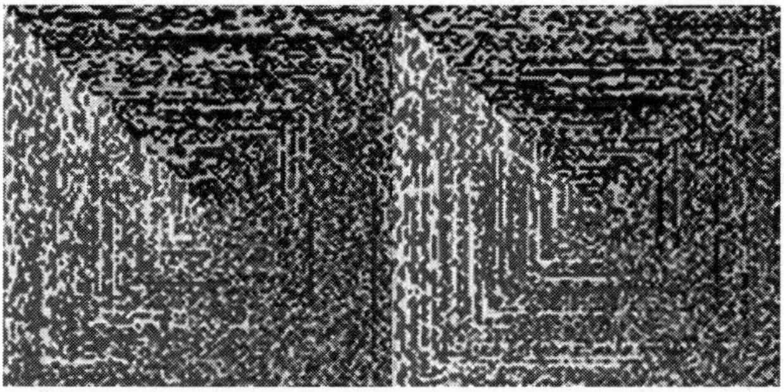

Figure 7. Close up of the same center section of two images shown in Figure 6.

In this instance we can see that the patterning is remarkably different. Interestingly, the warmer red-hued pixels predominate in the right-hand image, showing vinyl media, whereas the cooler magenta and navy blue hues predominate on the left. There is more even distribution of all colours in the bottom right-hand quadrant of midrange frequencies. Of course, it would be pointless to ascribe either image as *aesthetically* superior. However, it is worth noting that the longer one studies the images, the more distinct they begin to appear to be, and perhaps this is one reason why appreciators and collectors of music develop strong biases for one or the other mode of listening experience. An important consideration is that the vinyl copy of the record used to produce the right-hand image (analogue storage media) was mint quality, and therefore would show no artifacts of previous usage. However, a used version of the record might show substantially more differentiation, and increase the distinct characteristics described above (whereas, we assume, the left-hand image would remain roughly consistent). Hence this experiment will be repeated with these same physical copies of the audio track once a sufficient number of uses have accrued.

CONCLUSION

Both the embodied physical performance and the case study we undertook for the 2018 ELO conference were conceived as experiments in the materialization of data to study the effect and affect of physical influences on the data life cycle and the incorporation of user-specific data in the information we use and process. These experiments are conducted in the spirit of artful inquiry, and it is not our intent to prove any hypotheses, but rather to explore the educative potential of transmediation and playful intervention in the realms of machine language and digital data. We think of these processes as fundamentally different from user-profiled and correlated curation of contents which tap into big data or neural net algorithms to serve particular interests and aesthetic proclivities of individuals. The more automation serves our digital diets to us, the less informed we become, as these stages in acquiring knowledge rely, to some degree, on also learning what we are not interested in or pleased by. This becomes knowledge that is integrated into the individual's sense of being and self, becoming, eventually, the nutrient of identity transmuting information to knowledge. Indeed, a fundamental aspect of learning is that with sufficient exposure to information that is not within our current appreciation, we may discover new tastes and curiosities arising from previously disregarded topics, types, and genres of contents: You will never know until you try it. This may be the overall benefit of information and artifacts that reveal their nature only in regenerative interaction, tracing subjectivities, indeed embedding them in media as one does memories in consciousness. The resurgence of vinyl, a media molecularly composed of ancient life forms, may be something that the collective subconscious is calling for, a living media that is private, personal, and learns along.

Agamben, Giorgio. 1998. *Homo Sacer: Sovereign Power and Bare Life.* Stanford: Stanford University Press.

Barad, Karen. 2007. *Meeting the Universe Halfway: Quantum Physics & the Entanglement of Matter & Meaning.* Durham: Duke University Press.

Benjamin, Walter. 1969. *Illuminations.* Ed. by Hannah Arendt. New York: Schocken Books.

Demain, Bill. 2012. "Why Were CD Boxes So Big in the Early 1990s?" July 10, 2012. Link: http://mentalfloss.com/article/31148/why-were-cd-boxes-so-big-early-1990s.

Funkhouser, Christopher. 2012. *New Directions in Digital Poetry.* New York: Continuum.

James, Kedrick. 2015. "Mapping Critical Media Literacy onto Iterative Remix Practices." In *Reconceptualizing Literacy in the New Age of Multiculturalism and Pluralism: 2nd Edition*, ed. by Peter Mosenthal. Charlotte: IAP.

James, Kedrick. 2017. "Brave New Network: The Gambit of Living Automated Lives." In *The Precarious Future of Education: Risk and Uncertainty in Ecology, Curriculum, Learning, and Technology*, ed. by Jan Jagodzinski, 195-223. New York: Palgrave Macmillan US.

Knopper, Steve. 2018. "The End of Owning Music: How CDs and Downloads Died." *Rolling Stone*, June 14. Link: https://www.rollingstone.com/music/music-news/the-end-of-owning-music-how-cds-and-downloads-died-628660/.

Luther, Rachel A. 2014. "Synesthesia and the Phenomenological Experience: Implications for Ecological Mindfulness and Beginning Scholars in Science Education." *Cultural Studies of Science Education* 10 (1):215-27. October. Link: https://doi.org/10.1007/s11422-014-9644-6.

Menkman, Rosa. 2011. "Glitch Studies Manifesto." In *Video Vortex Reader II: Moving Images beyond YouTube*, 336-47. Amsterdam: Institute of Network Cultures.

Olson, Charles. 1987. *The Collected Poems of Charles Olson: Excluding the Maximus Poems.* Ed. by George F. Butterick. Berkeley: University of California Press.

O'Neil, Cathy. 2016. *Weapons of Math Destruction: How Big Data Increases Inequality and Threatens Democracy.* New York: Crown. First edition.

Peirce Edition Project, ed. 1998. *The Essential Peirce, Volume 2: Selected Philosophical Writings (1893-1913).* Bloomington: Indiana University Press.

Peña, Ernesto, and Kedrick James. 2016. "A Glitch Pedagogy: Exquisite Error and the Appeal of the Accidental." *Journal of the Canadian Association for Curriculum Studies* 14 (1):108-27. November.

Peña, Ernesto, and Kedrick James. 2020. "Raw Harmonies: Transmediation through Raw Data." *Leonardo – MIT Press Journals* 53 (2):183-88. April. Link: https://doi.org/10.1162/LEON_a_01635.

Rezza, Sol. 2020. "Analog vs. Digital: Vinyl Records". SOL REZZA. ZZA, March 14. Link: https://solrezza.net/analog-vs-digital-vinyl-records/.

Rosenblatt, Bill. 2018. "Vinyl Is Bigger Than We Thought. Much Bigger." *Forbes*, September 14. Link: https://www.forbes.com/sites/billrosenblatt/2018/09/18/vinyl-is-bigger-than-we-thought-much-bigger/.

SB. 1955. "Statement: The Russell-Einstein Manifesto." *Pugwash Conferences on Science and World Affairs*, July 19. Link: https://pugwash.org/1955/07/09/statement-manifesto/.

Waniata, Ryan. 2018. "The Life and Times of the Late, Great CD." *Digital Trends*, July 2. Link: https://www.digitaltrends.com/features/the-history-of-the-cds-rise-and-fall/.

Partie / Part 2

LE LANGAGE COMME INTERFACE

LANGUAGE AS INTERFACE

PART 2

LE LANGAGE COMME INTERFACE

LANGUAGE AS INTERFACE

JOHN CAYLEY

The Language That Machines Read

Abstract

We take it for granted that machines "read." Computers have read in and put out since the earliest days of post-Turing, stored program computation. But when we say that machines read, this immediately begs the question of what it is that they read and leaves unexamined the even more fundamental question of what reading is, as a process, as a behavior, as function of the faculty for language.

I argue that reading is constitutive of language. This statement means that something called reading brings language into being. As far as we know, language is something that only humans have and thus reading, in this sense, must be something that only humans do. The contentions in these statements will be reconfigured by the proposal that what machines read is what Walter Ong would call a grapholect, "a transdialect language formed by deep commitment to writing." In fact, what they "read" is something more constrained: encoded transcriptions of grapholectic languages–plural, since we must not restrict our attention to the global English grapholect. This reading is not the type of reading that humans do and, ultimately, we might not want to recognize it as reading at all. It is a distinctly différant (the Derridean form is deliberate and will be elaborated) sub-dialectic practice of reading that, at best, may be seen to constitute distinct linguistic grapholects. These circumstances and their current configuration–under the regime of computation and in the context of the predominant vectoralist instrumentalism and solutionism of Big Software such as GAFA (Google Apple Facebook Amazon etc.)–must be analyzed and therapeutically addressed before we can move on to entertain the possibility that "machine reading," as we know it, could be productively and generatively deployed in order to deform, reform, transform or otherwise reconfigure the texts of digital language arts or digital humanities practices.

Résumé

Nous tenons pour acquis que les machines « lisent ». Et pourtant, les ordinateurs lisent, émettent et conservent de l'information depuis les premiers jours de l'ère post-Turing. Mais quand nous affirmons que les machines lisent, nous soulevons inévitablement la question de ce qui est lu et ignoré par les machines et, plus fondamentalement, de ce qu'est la lecture en tant que processus, comportement ou fonction de la faculté du langage. Je soutiens que la lecture est constitutive du langage. Cette déclaration signifie que ce que nous appelons la lecture engendre le langage. Pour autant que nous sachions, le langage est unique aux humains et la lecture, en ce sens, l'est également. On peut reconfigurer ces déclarations autour du fait que les machines lisent à partir de la notion de « grapholecte » de Walter Ong, qui désigne « un langage transdialectique formé par un engagement profond à l'écriture ». En effet, ce qu'elles « lisent » est restreint : des transcriptions encodées des langages grapholectiques – au pluriel, puisque nous ne devons pas limiter notre attention au grapholecte universel anglophone. Cette forme de lecture n'est pas celle des humains et, ultimement, peut-être préférons-nous ne pas la reconnaître comme tel. C'est une pratique sous-dialectique *différante* (sa forme derridienne est délibérée et sera examinée) de lecture qui, au mieux, peut être considérée comme un grapholecte linguistique distinct. Ces circonstances et leur configuration actuelle – sous le régime computationnel et dans le contexte de l'instrumentalisme vectoraliste prédominant et du solutionnisme des grands fournisseurs de logiciels comme GAFA (Google Apple Facebook Amazon etc.) – doivent être analysées et résolues thérapeutiquement avant d'envisager la possibilité que « la lecture machinique », telle qu'on la connaît, puisse être déployée de façon productive et générative afin de déformer, réformer, transformer ou reconfigurer les textes issus des arts numériques du langage ou des pratiques émergeant des humanités numériques.

The language that machines "read"—at any particular moment—has been excerpted or extracted from what Walter Ong calls a grapholect, "a trans-dialect language formed by deep commitment to writing" (Ong 1982, 8). A little more precisely, machines read *encoded transcriptions* of grapholects that are tightly integrated with natural languages. The plural is important. We should not constrain our attention to the absurdly predominant global English grapholect.

We should also be prepared to consider the possibility that so-called written or literary language practices, the grapholects integrated with particular natural languages, might better be thought of as "top-level" modes of language practice, as, that is, distinct natural languages, languages that you—a specific, located human being—might not *know*, as in, "I don't know Italian." There are many people in the world who are designated, markedly, as "illiterate." This adjective suggests a lack or a failing, but only in relation to a presumed, historically literate culture, for which "literacy" is, to say the least, a significant cultural value. Any concomitantly presumed "lack," however, has no bearing on our human species' shared faculty of language. We would not consider someone who does not know Italian to be somehow lacking in their faculty of language or, a fortiori, lacking in some essential aspect of their humanity. And we should not do so with respect to anyone who happens not to know those grapholects or visually inscribed languages that we may know. It was Jacques Derrida who pointed out that we are all monolingual: essentially, with respect to the self-presence of language within us, and also in the actuality of any and all events of language that we share, respecting Saussure's fundamentals: the arbitrary nature of the linguistic sign and the linearity of language's events (Derrida 1998). At any one moment, in our experience and thought of linguistic events, we can only be *in* one language, monolinguistically.

But what is language? What is language ontologically? Based on experience and the science available to us, language is something *interpersonal* that we have evolved to *have*. By "interpersonal" I mean that language both depends on and constitutes the *social*. Our species has evolved to *have* the faculty of language and yet, although we have the faculty, the realized actuality of language cannot achieve existence without others of us, other individuals of our species, with whom, together, we live and make language. Language is only ever brought into being by means of the active responses of others, responses made to and with human persons or (recently, as of the 2010s) humanoid entities. These persons or humanoids make formal gestures of virtual language that become actual language when they are grasped as such by their interlocutors.

This active response may be called *reading.* If we need to distinguish this sense of "reading" from conventional "reading," the scanning and processing of a grapholect, we will call it *grammaleptic reading.*

The established usage of the word underlying contemporary English "(to) read" obviously precedes its application to conventional reading by centuries. And the now predominant usage and sense of the word seems to be to be derived from something like *the ability to make well-advised, convincing, articulable guesses based on signs or sign-like human gestures, or on the world's gestural forms.* The central claim of this thinking, that *reading brings language into being,* has nothing to do with literacy. It sponsors the revival and comprehension of an underlying, fundamental sense of an old word in English that bears a significant relation to our faculty of language as a whole, not merely to particular practices of language since the historical advent of graphic inscription. It is worth remembering, also, that the proto-linguistic gestural forms of our world and of human life are *data,* what the world gives; not *capta,* what we have been able to capture or transcribe from this data. We read what our world gives into language, and then some of this language is transcribed from our grapholects into capta. Reading the written capta–which we call *text*–back into actual language requires the recovery of experiences closer to those by means of which we read (past, present, and future) the actual data of our world into language.

"Grammaleptic" is an adjective derived from my own coinage, *grammalepsy.* "Grammalepsy" is a noun indicating a condition or circumstance. "Grammalepsis," also a noun, refers to the associated processes, particularly processes of reading. The "lepsis" in "grammalepsis" is the seizure, by articulable human thought, of "grammē," of (re)iterable, shared symbolic forms. The seizure of grammē in terms of *lepsis* is intended to suggest that these events are sudden, and that they cause breaks corresponding to both the discrete idealities of the symbolic forms which are so generated, and to a "breaking away," ontologically, from the support media in which these forms are expressed. Grammalepsy is the human condition that allows gestures in any perceptible and malleable support medium to become (re)iterable, shared symbolic forms and simultaneously elements of language itself (at any level of linguistic structure), thus bringing language into being.

The processes of grammalepsis generate grammē as shared symbolic events of language, bringing language into being. It is important to say that the creation of the grammē by reading implies that, so long as these grammē are shared by a community of language practice, they will be not only distinct–(re)iterable, symbolic–forms, they may also be newly created forms and thus both constitutive of language, and also an indication, as generated and generative, of what some philosophers of language, including Charles Taylor, would call *constitutive language* (Taylor **2016**, 3-50). This term is in contradistinction to *designative language*. The latter term refers to a strictly structuralist and positivist philosophy and science of language within the scope of which creativity is a function of (re)combination and syntactical reordering. "Generative" is reduced to the combinatorial in Chomsky's "generative grammar," the predominant paradigmatic *model* of language as *computable* amongst contemporary scientistic approaches. The structural linguistics of generative grammar is one of the major symptoms of an underlying conviction–generally widespread, but pervasive in the scientific community–that mind and thought are reducible to physical processes which can be *formulated*. The ascendancy of the regime of computation since the Second World War has provided a plausible mechanism for fundamentally misdirected theories and "simulations" of language as designative.

In the approach to language as constitutive, and as advocated in my own thinking, although the grammē are symbolic idealities, they may be marked not only by difference but by that to which Jacques Derrida has given a name in the (non-)word "différance," and that we might, pragmatically, venture to call *constitutive difference*. In this thinking, the practice and bringing into being of language is constitutive of the human as something open-ended and always unfinished with respect to the evolved faculty that we call language, and that we believe we have, as a species. In my own words, from a previous essay, "... we become language animals when certain perceptible forms that we make suddenly give us access to a world that is more human because it is suddenly more language" (Cayley **2018b**, 13).

All traces of language indicate an *arche-writing* in Jacques Derrida's sense. This relation is fundamentally synaesthetic, since our experience encompasses all that we perceive, and in language we trace our experience. The processes of grammalepsis are support media agnostic. Any perceptible and malleable medium will do, in principle. After all, these processes–(grammaleptic) *reading* by another name–render gestures that are expressed in any perceptible and malleable medium as ontologically and diegetically distinct, broken out and away from their support medium, and thus suddenly and simultaneously in the world of language. This is not to say, however, that any artificially or aesthetically structured substance or artifact or performance in structured artifactuality can or should be treated *as* or *like* (a) language, because not all such structures are readable.

There is no "digital language," as in the phrase "digital language art." "Digital" at this moment is a (con)temporary qualifier–for "language art" and many other practices–referring to the prevalence of digital affordances and infrastructures which allow us to discover new ways of reading language and language art. In practice, because language is an evolved faculty, and, to the extent of our knowledge, is species specific (Berwick and Chomsky **2016**; Hurford **2014**, **2012**), (linguistic) aurality is the support medium for language that has been privileged by evolution. Hand-written or typographic visuality is the support medium which the advent of human history and the course of civilization has promoted to a literal *authority* that is, *ironically*, logocentric and metaphysically implicated, as Derrida has shown (Derrida **1997**). In the near future, the digitalization of aurality will reconfigure, historically, these privileged relationships between support media and language (Cayley **2018a**).

If language can be said to have an underlying "substance," as distinct from a support medium such as aurality or typographic visuality, then we should, I believe, give it the name of *voice* in a particular phenomenological sense. This is the voice that we read with and into. It is also the voice of style, what even conventional criticism calls the voice of the author. Voice in this sense is able to grasp différance. *The constitutive differences of grammalepsis generate the voice of language.*

Voice is, a fortiori, the medium for any self-reflexive practice of aesthetic language, of experimental writing, poetry, language art, digital language art. Making this statement implies that–by giving physical evidence of embodiment–language cares to support and produce located, integral, personal identities. But this voice is not only voice as of actual, particular human voices. The characteristics of sited integrity and identity are required by linguistic objects in the symbolic abstract, as well as being contingent upon the fact that voice and human voices possess these characteristics. Thus, by the way, there is no recourse to idealism in this thinking but, rather, a counter affirmation of the deep pragmatic necessity for virtual linguistic forms and traces–at any and all levels of structure–to achieve states of sited integrity and identity in order to become language as such. The name for the reiterable condition of linguistic phenomena is *ideality*, an ideality that enables repetition and recognition but which is expressed–produced and received–as, precisely, voice:

> … it must be constituted, repeated, and expressed in a medium that does not impair the presence and self-presence of the acts that intend it: a medium that preserves at once *the presence of the object* in front of the intuition and the *presence to oneself*, the absolute proximity of the acts to themselves. Since the ideality of the object is only its being-for a non-empirical consciousness, it can be expressed only in an element whose phenomenality does not have the form of mundanity. *The voice is the name of this element. The voice hears itself.* (Derrida **2011**, 65)

Forms of voice are produced and received by us, but until a form is readable, it is not yet the *voice* of language. This movement from gestural to readable is also the movement from actual events and processes of production to the provisionally finished inscription–the utterance in the support materiality of voice–of a reiterable trace with respect to the conventions of one of the world's hospitable languages. Another name for these idealities is, of course, grammē.

What do machines read? Documentary, encoded literature or transcribed speech is not constitutive language unless and until it can operate with and generate language from différance, constitutive difference. Literature as such and as we prejudicially know it, earns this status through history and style, through the creation of *voice* by aesthetically implicated practice, as the substance of language.

Machines cannot read because they do not have access to the substance, the voice, of language. They will not be able to read documentary, encoded literature as language until and unless they can. And they will not do so as long as a systematically stupid computational, structuralist model of language and mind prevails. "Distant reading" is not reading in any constitutive or aesthetically tractable sense of the term. Typically, it produces statements for the sociology of literature, or decorative, literary, critical-aesthetic, suggestively prescriptive sociology.

Machine reading as such, however, is not a crisis for artists of language, not unless we fail to appreciate and take care with the distinctions that have been set out above. We would not fail to maintain these distinctions if we were only dealing with documentary textuality. Now, however, we face consequences due to the advent of transactive synthetic language. The vectoralist superpowers (such as GAFA: Google, Amazon, Facebook, Apple) are able to facture, programmatically, *humanoid* artifactual systems based on a merely designative model of language by synthesizing perceptible gestures that are then socialized as literal "voice," the voice of speech recognition and speech synthesis. The *socialization* of these entities is crucial. *AI*, as a sociopolitical and socioeconomic force, is nothing but this socialization. It allows the entities of transactive synthetic language to have passed, effectively, the Turing Test–by entering our homes and social spaces as interlocutors. And, in an age of predominant scientism, although we may not feel that "intelligence," in this degraded, meagrely embodied understanding, is anything like full humanity, nonetheless, we give it more and more of our space and time and attention.

What then is a crucial question for artists of language?

How will we continue to work and make art in *voice*, as the substantive medium of language, and how will we–should we?–distinguish our voices from the synthetic voices of the programmata?

Berwick, Robert C., and Noam Chomsky. 2016. *Why Only Us: Language and Evolution.* Cambridge: MIT Press.

Cayley, John. 2018a. *Grammalepsy: Essays on Digital Language Art.* New York; London: Bloomsbury Academic.

Cayley, John. 2018b. "The advent of aurature and the end of (electronic) literature." In *The Bloomsbury Handbook of Electronic Literature*, ed. by Joseph Tabbi, 73-94. New York; London: Bloomsbury Academic.

Derrida, Jacques. 1997. *Of Grammatology.* Translated by Gayatri Chakravorty Spivak. Corrected ed. Baltimore; London: Johns Hopkins University Press.

Derrida, Jacques. 1998. *Monolingualism of the Other, or The Prosthesis of Origin.* Translated by Patrick Mensah. Stanford: Stanford University Press.

Derrida, Jacques. 2011. *Voice and Phenomenon: Introduction to the Problem of the Sign in Husserl's Phenomenology.* Translated by Leonard Lawlor. Evanston, Ill.: Northwestern University Press.

Hurford, James R. 2012. *The Origins of Grammar. (Language in the Light of Evolution, Vol. 2).* Oxford; New York: Oxford University Press.

Hurford, James R. 2014. *The Origins of Language: A slim guide.* Oxford: Oxford University Press.

Ong, Walter J. 1982. *Orality and Literacy: The Technologizing of the Word.* London: Routledge.

Taylor, Charles. 2016. *The Language Animal: The Full Shape of the Human Linguistic Capacity.* Cambridge: The Belknap Press of Harvard University Press.

LEAH HENRICKSON

What Natural Language Generation Means For Authorship And Why We Should Care

Abstract

Natural language generation (NLG)–the process wherein computers translate data into readable human languages–has become increasingly present in our modern digital climate. In the last decade, numerous companies specialising in the mass-production of computer-generated news articles have emerged; National Novel Generation Month (NaNoGenMo) has become a popular annual event; #botALLY is used to identify those in support of automated agents producing tweets. Yet NLG has not been subject to any systematic study within the humanities. This paper offers a glimpse into the social and literary implications of computer-generated texts and NLG. More particularly, it examines how NLG output challenges traditional understandings of authorship and what it means to be a reader. Any act of reading engages interpretive faculties; modern readers tend to assume that a text is an effort to communicate a particular predetermined message. With this assumption, readers assign authorial intention, and hence develop a perceived contract between the author and the reader. This paper refers to this author-reader contract as "the hermeneutic contract".

NLG output in its current state brings the hermeneutic contract into question. The hermeneutic contract's communication principle rests on two assumptions: that readers believe that authors want them to be interested in their texts, and that authors want readers to understand their texts. Yet the author of a computer-generated text is often an obscured figure, an uncertain entanglement of human and computer. How does this obscuration of authorship change how text is received? This paper begins with an introduction to, and brief history of, NLG geared towards those with no previous knowledge of the subject. The remainder of the paper reviews the results of a study conducted by the researcher to discern how readers attribute authorship to computer-generated texts. Results indicate that a sense of agency is assigned to an NLG system, and that a continuum from authorship to generation is perhaps the most suitable schema for considering computer-generated texts. This paper concludes with an argument for why consideration of the social and literary implications of NLG and computer-generated texts is vital as we venture deeper into the digital age. Computer-generated texts may not just challenge traditional understandings of authorship: they may engender new understandings of authorship altogether as readers explore the conceptual gap between human and computer language production.

Résumé

La génération automatique de textes (GAT) – le processus de traduction de données par un ordinateur en texte lisible par un humain – devient de plus en plus présente dans notre ère numérique. Au cours de la dernière décennie, de nombreuses entreprises spécialisées dans la production en masse d'articles de journal sont apparues ; le National Novel Generation Month (NaNoGenMo) est devenu un événement populaire annuel ; #botALLY est utilisé pour identifier ceux qui soutiennent la production automatique de tweets par des agents automatisés. Pourtant, la GAT n'a pas encore fait l'objet d'étude dans les humanités. Cet article illustre les implications sociales et littéraires des textes générés automatiquement. En particulier, il examine comment la GAT pose des problèmes pour la conception traditionnelle de l'auctorialité et du rôle du lecteur. Toute acte de lecture implique la faculté d'interprétation ; les lecteurs modernes ont tendance à assumer qu'un texte représente une tentative de communiquer un message prédéterminé. En partant de ce principe, les lecteurs assignent une intention auctoriale et imaginent un contrat de lecture. Cet article renvoie à ce contrat de lecture comme un « contrat herméneutique ».

La GAT, dans son état actuel, remet en question le contrat herméneutique. Le principe de communication du contrat herméneutique repose sur deux hypothèses : le lecteur croie que l'auteur veut qu'on s'intéresse à son texte, et l'auteur veut que le lecteur comprenne son texte. Cependant, l'auteur d'un texte automatiquement généré reste souvent une figure obscure, un assemblage incertain d'humain et ordinateur. Comment l'opacification de l'auctorialité change-t-elle la réception du texte ? Cet article s'ouvre sur une brève histoire de la GAT. Il présente ensuite les résultats d'une étude réalisée afin de discerner comment les lecteurs attribuent une paternité aux textes automatiquement générés. Les résultats indiquent qu'on attribue une certaine agentivité au système GAT et qu'un continuum entre paternité et génération est potentiellement le schéma le plus approprié pour penser les textes générés par ordinateur. L'article se termine sur un argument expliquant pourquoi la prise en compte des implications sociales et littéraires de la GAT est vitale pour nous permettre de mieux comprendre l'âge numérique. Les textes générés automatiquement ne remettent pas seulement en question les conceptions traditionnelles de l'auctorialité : ils engendrent potentiellement de nouvelles conceptions de la paternité d'une œuvre alors que le lecteur explore les écarts conceptuels entre la production du langage humain et celle des ordinateurs.

INTRODUCTION

Natural language generation (NLG) is the process wherein computers produce text-based output in readable human languages. NLG systems are increasingly prevalent in our modern digital climate, prompting the emergence of companies that specialise in generating output for mass readerships and readerships-of-one alike. Narrative Science has worked in partnership with Deloitte to generate client-friendly narrative reports related to such issues as budget optimisation, financial operations, and internal auditing (Krittman, Matthews, and Glascott **2015**). Automated Insights has partnered with Bodybuilding.com to produce app-based workout recaps personalised to each individual user to motivate the user to maintain an exercise routine (Automated Insights **n.d.**). These are only a few examples of NLG's current applications as implemented by a burgeoning industry based around this technology. But there are also more aesthetic endeavours. One early example is *The Policeman's Beard is Half Constructed*, marketed as "the first book ever written by a computer," which was published by Warner Books in 1984. *The Policeman's Beard* comprises poems, prose, and dialogue generated by an NLG system called Racter; each block of text is accompanied by a collage by artist Joan Hall. Twitter has also seen a proliferation of bots that regularly generate tweets according to pre-programmed constraints. One example is the Magic Realism Bot, which proposes a hilariously absurd fantasy story plot every four hours. In this paper, however, I focus primarily on longer-form texts that are generated to exist in static, linear form.

Despite the burgeoning industry centred on NLG, there has not yet been any systematic analysis of computer-generated text reception. Resultantly, we do not know where these texts fit within our current conceptions of authorship and readership. This paper begins an examination into how NLG challenges traditional understandings of authorship and what it means to be a reader. Any act of reading engages interpretive faculties; modern readers tend to assume that a text is an effort to communicate a particular predetermined message. With this assumption, readers assign authorial intention, and hence develop a perceived contract with the author. This paper refers to this author-reader contract as 'the hermeneutic contract,' through which reading is accepted as an act wherein the reader receives an interesting and understandable text written by an author motivated by intent-directed agency. The author is regarded as an individual creative genius.

Computer-generated texts bring the hermeneutic contract into question. The hermeneutic contract's communication principle rests on two assumptions: that readers believe that authors want them to be interested in their texts, and that authors want them to understand their texts (Henrickson **2018a**). Yet the author of a computer-generated text is often an obscured figure, an uncertain entanglement of human and computer. As yet, the discussion about attributing authorship to computer-generated texts has been limited to theoretical consideration by scholars who tend to argue that computer-generated texts are authorless in the conventional sense of the word (Bolter **1991**, 179-80; Eve **2017**, 48). This paper broadens the discussion to include the opinions of ordinary readers–readers who have not extensively considered issues related to NLG. Opinions have been collected through a large-scale online reader response questionnaire comprising 500 adult participants of varying demographic profiles from 27 countries. Contrary to the scholarly assertions that computer-generated texts are authorless, these questionnaire results indicate that readers do attribute authorship to NLG systems. Computer-generated texts do not just challenge traditional understandings of authorship; they engender new understandings of authorship altogether as readers negotiate the conceptual gap between human and computer text production.

This paper begins by reviewing the methodology and results of an online reader response questionnaire conducted to deduce how ordinary readers attribute authorship to a computer-generated text. It focuses on one noteworthy response in particular: participants' willingness to attribute authorship to the NLG system that generated the text in question. It then proposes the use of a continuum that ranges from "authorship" to "generatorship" to conceptualise the creative contributions of text producers, whether humans or computers. This paper concludes with a call for continued research to further understand readers' attribution choices and to more deeply consider how computer-generated texts may conform to or affront our current conceptions of authorship as they are manifest in the hermeneutic contract.

It should be noted that these results were part of a larger ongoing research project, and are therefore not conclusive.

METHODOLOGY

The online reader response questionnaire described in this paper was conducted from late 2017 until early 2018, and its results are freely available at (Henrickson **2019b**). Of the 500 total participants, 337 self-identified as women, 155 as men, 5 as non-binary, and 3 as other. 139 were aged 18-29, 140 aged 30-39, 76 aged 40-49, 68 aged 50-59, 55 aged 60-69, and 22 aged 70+. 27 countries of residence were represented, with the United States, the United Kingdom, and Canada providing substantial numbers of responses. A detailed distribution of country representation is shown in Table 1; 32 noted that their highest level of education completed was secondary school, 10 trade/technical/vocational training, 126 an undergraduate programme, 180 a master's programme, and 152 a doctoral programme; 120 participants were students, 320 employed, 47 retired, and 13 not employed/unpaid workers. More than half of participants identified as working within education, training, and library fields. A detailed distribution of occupational fields represented is shown in Table 2.

Figure 1: Detailed distribution of questionnaire participants' countries of residence.

Country	Number of Participants
United States of America	213
United Kingdom	122
Canada	17
Finland	17
Australia	9
Germany	9
France	7
Sweden	4
India	3
Italy	3
Egypt	2
Ireland	2
Israel	2

Netherlands	2
Spain	2
Switzerland	2
Belgium	1
Cyprus	1
Denmark	1
Hungary	1
Malta	1
Mexico	1
Norway	1
Poland	1
Samoa	1
Singapore	1
South Africa	1

Figure 2: Detailed distribution of questionnaire participants' occupational fields.

Occupational Field	Number of Participants
Education, Training, and Library	252
Information Technology	38
Business and Financial Operations	27
Engineering	25
Media and Communications	25
Arts, Design, and Entertainment	23
Life, Physical, and Social Science	20
Not Employed	18
Office and Administrative Support	13
Legal	10
Public Sector	10
Healthcare	7

Management	7
Journalism	6
Retail and Sales	6
Community/Social Services	2
Construction and Extraction	2
Hospitality	2
Personal Care and Service	2
Architecture	1
Building/Grounds Maintenance	1
Farming, Fishing, and Forestry	1
Production	1
Sport	1

Social media platforms like Reddit, Facebook, and Twitter were used to promote the questionnaire. Additionally, participants were solicited through the SHARP (Society for the History of Authorship, Reading and Publishing), EX-LIBRIS, and DHSI (Digital Humanities Summer Institute) professional listservs. Invitees were encouraged to share the questionnaire in an effort to reach as wide a demographic spread as possible. Nevertheless, these responses are dominated by a highly-educated populace of primarily women and those employed in education, training, and library roles. This populace was likely a result of the methods of recruitment employed.

Questionnaire participants were presented with a remarkably uninspiring 243-word English-language text reviewing Finnish municipal election results called 'The Finns Party drop most seats across Finland.' This text was generated by an NLG system called Valtteri the Election Bot, developed by the privately and publicly funded Immersive Automation research team in Finland (Immersive Automation **2018**). It was used for this questionnaire by permission of Immersive Automation. Four times, questionnaire participants were asked to attribute authorship to this text. Each time, participants were presented with new information about the text's process of production. In the first question, participants were only presented with the text itself, which had Valtteri's name in the byline below the text's title. In the second, participants were informed that Valtteri was a bot, and that one John Smith (a pseudonym for a member of the Immersive Automation team) had translated the Finnish political party names into English for ease of reading. In the third, participants were informed that Valtteri was developed by the Immersive Automation team; in the fourth, that Immersive Automation was funded by numerous public and private bodies. For each of these questions, participants had to select from lists of predefined authors, although options for "It is not possible to assign authorship" and "Other" were available for all questions. If a participant selected "Other," the participant was obliged to clarify why in order to proceed with the questionnaire. Each question included an optional "Why have you selected this option?" text box for those participants who wished to elaborate upon their answers. To streamline the analysis below, only the responses to the fourth and final authorship attribution question–when participants were given all possible options to select from–are given serious consideration for quantitative purposes. The other questions, however, did garner valuable qualitative responses that are referenced in the analysis.

The questionnaire began, though, by asking participants to "list three things that come to mind when you think of the word 'author'." This opening question was included to prompt participants to think about what authorship meant to them, prior to being asked to assign authorship to the text provided. It is not within the scope of this paper to review the results of this word association exercise in detail, although one may refer to (Henrickson **2019a**–an earlier version of this paper) for a word cloud of these results. However, it is worth noting that, as the word association list was coded, four general facets of "author" emerged: authorship encompasses (1) an identity that is (2) associated with particular connotations, (3) as well as with particular activities (4) that result in particular kinds of (generally text-based) outputs. Popular definitions of authorship tend to refer to the composer of a work; at the time of writing, popular dictionaries define "author" as both a noun–"[a] writer of a book, article, or document"–and a verb with object "[b]e the author of (a book or piece of writing)" (Oxford Dictionaries **n.d.**). However, the results of this word association exercise made apparent that authorship is hardly as limited or concrete a term as one may believe. Authorship simultaneously refers to a variety of people, practices, and productions.

WHY DOES AUTHORSHIP MATTER?

Ours is a culture obsessed with authorship, as the sense of literary celebrity continues to strengthen after a stint of New Criticism, and attention is returned to authors' biographical references as means for textual interpretation. Indeed, as one article about literary celebrity points out, "[t]he public *persona* of an author is undoubtedly an important part of his or her authorship [emphasis original]," particularly given that authors, whose personalities were once largely limited to readers' imaginations, are increasingly embodied through their own engagements with readers via social media platforms (Ohlsson, Forslid, and Steiner **2014**, 42). To be sure, authors have long embraced public personae. A record of Ben Jonson's 400-mile walk to Edinburgh in 1618 suggests numerous public spectacles associated with each leg of this journey, and Jonson's enthusiastic reception at his destination; this journey was almost certainly a seventeenth-century publicity stunt, speaking to Jonson's desire to maintain popular attention (Loxley **2016**). In a description of his abrupt introduction to stardom, twentieth-century writer Norman Mailer (**1992**, 92) described himself as "a node in a new electronic landscape of celebrity, personality and status. Other people, meeting me, could now unconsciously measure their own status by sensing how I reacted to them. I had been moved from the audience to the stage." Overwhelmed by requests for book signings in remote locations, writer Margaret Atwood debuted her LongPen in 2006 to permit remote signings; the LongPen used a robotic hand to copy into ink that which a user wrote or drew on a tablet from anywhere else in the world. The LongPen also included audio and video capability so that authors could chat with their fans as the robotic hand inked a signature (Atwood **2006**; Burkeman **2006**). And we continue searching for texts penned by Shakespeare. It would seem, then, that literary pursuits are–and have long been–potential avenues to stardom.

Yet an author of a text may not be that text's owner. Once published in a book or journal, for example, an article may be considered the property of its publisher, rather than its writer. Although the writer of the text remains accountable for the argument presented in the text, as well as the words used to articulate that argument, in such instances authorship and ownership are distinct. By default, though, authorship and ownership are often regarded as synonymous–if I write something, it is assumed that I own it. However, for this research it is vital to recognise authorship and ownership as distinct terms.

More essentially than ethical and economic considerations, though, our culture's obsession with authorship speaks to a desire for connection with others. For authorship attribution scholar Harold Love (2002, 4), "[t]he subject of attribution studies is the uniqueness of each human being and how this is enacted in writing." Indeed, "[t]o identify authorship as a form of human work is to validate individual agency... In cases where such a thing is possible, attribution studies attempts to distinguish the traces of agency that cohere in pieces of writing, sometimes discovering one singular trace, but often a subtle entanglement of several or many" (Love **2002**, 32). In distinguishing traces of agency within a text, we construct the imagined author–that individual creative genius–in light of our own interpretations of what we read. While it is the reader who increasingly carries what Adriaan van der Weel (**2011**, 178) calls the "interpretive burden," the reader assumes this role in light of the conventional hermeneutic contract, which is in essence an assumption of authorial communicative intent. The author conveys a message through the written word; the reader receives this message according to a shared literacy to both syntactically and semantically decipher what has been written. Regardless of a text's genre, the reader holds an expectation of communicative intent that, as per Harold Love, represents individual agency.

Like with a human-written text, the author of a computer-generated text is largely imagined by the reader. However, authorship attribution is still important because our answers to questions of authorship attribution reflect our conceptions of both cultural and financial capital. Authorship supports the articulation of an individual's voice, ownership supports capitalism's commodification of the individual, and together authorship and ownership (under the title of authorship) represent a creative economy rooted in an expectation of communicative intent that itself is rooted in individual agency. Authorship implies accountability, agency, creativity, and intelligence.

HOW DO READERS ATTRIBUTE AUTHORSHIP TO A COMPUTER-GENERATED TEXT?

Once one appreciates the diverse ways in which authorship may be considered, the discussion can shift to how readers may attribute authorship to computer-generated texts. The results related to attribution revealed diverse findings. While I had thought that participants would attribute authorship to Valtteri's developers, many instead attributed authorship to Valtteri itself, distinguishing the system as the author, and the developers as the creators—or even authors—of the system. Surprisingly, some participants also identified the funding body of the system's development as an author of sorts, alluding to a patronage model of text production. 28.6 % participants answered that it was not possible to assign authorship at all, while 71.4 % of participants felt that authorship could be attributed:

- 179 participants (35.8 %) attributed authorship to Valtteri, the system
- Seven (1.4 %) attributed authorship to John Smith, the member of Immersive Automation who translated the Finnish political party names into English for ease of reading
- 90 (18 %) attributed authorship to Immersive Automation, the team that developed Valtteri, and nine (1.8 %) attributed authorship to Immersive Automation's funders
- 72 (14.4 %) attributed authorship to "other," which was often elaborated upon as some sort of co-authorship

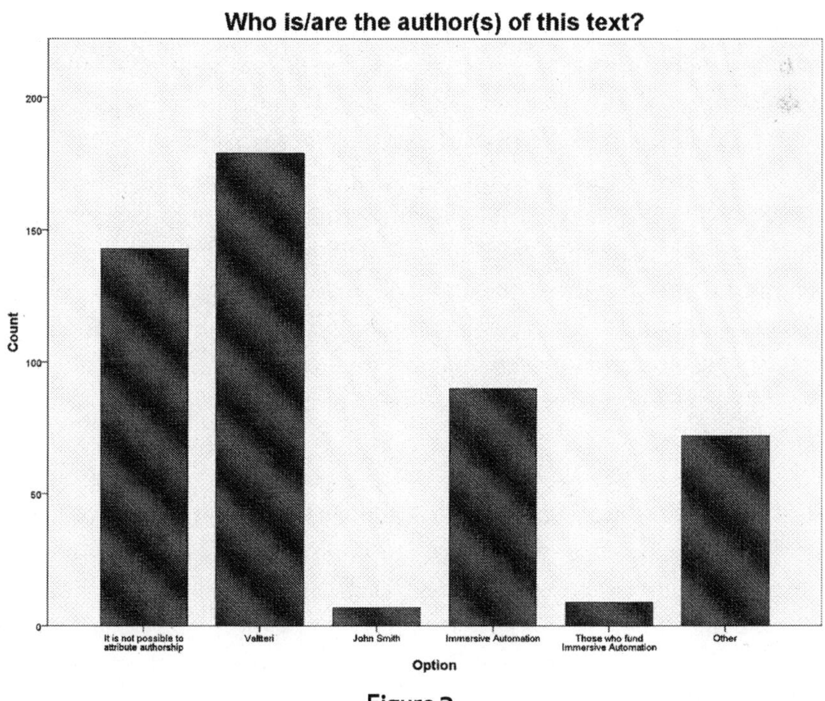

Figure 3.

There are, of course, many avenues for investigation leading from these results. For the sake of brevity, this paper will focus on what is the most notable: that of the authorship attribution to Valtteri, the system that generated the text in question. Justifications for this response emphasised the system's assembly of the words, distinguishing the system from its developers given its ability to create sufficiently original textual content. In such instances, authorship is regarded as an act of individual expression. For questionnaire participants who selected this option, the process of assembling words, regardless of developer influence, seems in itself enough for the system to warrant the "author" title.

When participants attribute authorship to Valtteri, one could argue that the current conventional understanding of the author as an individual creative genius is at least somewhat called into question. As one participant noted, "Valtteri, though not human, is the entity creating the article." Another participant observed that "Valtteri is the name of the computer program that generated the text. Who wrote or funded the program is not the author as the program could be sold to another party, which would muddy 'who is the author'." "The bot is still the author but the article/bot itself is owned by the funders," wrote someone else. If in common understanding, author-ship and ownership are considered synonymous, it would seem that by attributing authorship to Valtteri, participants imply that Valtteri is entitled to some kind of ownership of its output. In this case study, though, participants did suggest that priority lies less with authorship than with ownership. Valtteri may have authored the text, but it is the owner–usually identified as Immersive Automation–who is morally and legally accountable for the material under consideration, and it is the owner who is entitled to any financial gain from the system's output. Valtteri is not its output's owner because the system lacks financial interests. Authorship and ownership are distinct; for many participants, the former refers to the system, while the latter refers to the system's developer.

The distinction between system and developer is made even clearer through numerous participants' evocation of a parent-child metaphor. A parent, they argued, cannot take credit for a text that the child has written. The parent (i.e., developer) has simply produced the child (i.e., system) that has produced the text, and is therefore one step removed from the final product (i.e., text). "Nobody knows C S Lewis's parents so why should anyone care about the programmer of the computer?" asked one participant. "Is it odd to say that Mark Twain had parents but they are not the originators of his work because they created him? I feel the same applies to IA that created Valtteri," commented another. Similar observations were made to justify why funding bodies could not be considered authors. For example, one participant asserted that "If I gave JK Rowling use of my house and paid for all her meals while she wrote Harry Potter, that would not make me an author or even a co-author of Harry Potter. If I had signed a contract with Rowling then I could possibly have the rights or the IP to Harry Potter, but still not an author."

As with any analogy, the parent-child metaphor is hardly flawless. For example, a baby cannot be said to have much individual opinion or experience; its actions and verbal output reflect what it has learned from its guardians. Nevertheless, the parent-child metaphor as it appears herein is useful for unpacking the instinctual reaction to compare computational behaviour to that of humans, to search for and focus on the human elements exhibited by the machine. It was expected that participants would craft analogies based on their own subjective experiences of human relationships. The parent-child metaphor in particular, though, is significant because it suggests that some readers draw upon their understandings of social networks and behaviours to negotiate where this new medium of text production fits within current cultural contexts. This is in line with the CASA paradigm, which holds that computer users automatically respond to digital and computational media as they would to other people or phenomena of the physical world, in accordance with cues exuded by the medium in question (Van der Weel **2011**). That is, humans treat computers like other humans and, when faced with a computer-generated text, many will therefore readily attribute authorship to an NLG system rather than to its developers. Such instances of likening computational processes to human processes speak not only to readers' perceptions of computational capability, but also to more general ways in which readers negotiate attitudes towards new technologies in light of their perceptions of current cultural and technological circumstances.

THE AUTHORSHIP-GENERATORSHIP CONTINUUM

NLG systems all depend upon the set of possibilities established by their human developers. Of course, human writers too adhere to formulae associated with genres, repurposing syntactical and structural arrangements to convey new ideas through exploitation of conventional communicative methods. Use of these conventional methods gives readers more time to engage with the ideas being expressed rather than focus on the medium of expression; by using arrangements accepted as the communicative norm, little attention is drawn to the medium itself. Yet these questionnaire results show that it is not necessarily enough for a text to adhere to genre expectations. Many readers seem bewildered by NLG, uncertain where computer-generated texts fit within the conventional hermeneutic contract.

Some scholars have proposed new denominations of authorship, or an author-not author dichotomy, to explain computer-generated texts. Digital media critic Jay David Bolter (1991, 179-80), for one, has proposed two distinct kinds of authors for computer-generated texts: the immediate author (i.e., the generating system) and the ultimate author (i.e., the human programmer). More recently, literary scholar Martin Eve (2017, 48) has implied an author-not author dichotomy, arguing that computers are trained on "their own regurgitated outputs with only semi-deterministic random seeds to aid progress and foster change." That is, computers continue to depend upon the set of possibilities established by the human developer, and cannot be considered authors or creative agents in themselves.

Rather than establish new conceptions of authorship (like Bolter) or an author-not author dichotomy (like Eve), perhaps the more suitable–and intellectually feasible–approach to considering computer-generated texts is simply to appreciate the vagueness of the "authorship." I therefore propose here that using a continuum from authorship to generatorship would perhaps be more suitable for recognising such vagueness. As one questionnaire participant observed, "[a]uthorship [of a computer-generated text] resides on a continuum between the system and the system's creators, depending on the specifics of the system." This is not to say that authorship need be considered a uniquely human enterprise. Likewise, generatorship need not be limited to computers; it could also refer to those human writers who pump out what the developer responsible for *The Policeman's Beard is Half Constructed* calls "the Grade-Z junk that passes for romance novels and thrillers." And, as that developer predicted in 1984, "one of these days you will see a computer that is, indeed, capable of writing that Grade-Z trash... Whether or not the reader will be told that the author is a computer is another question" (Greene 1984). If authorship is considered an expression of individual identity to produce particular kinds of textual output through particular activities, one can at least loosely mark each system's particular balance between creative and mechanical–that is, cliché, perfunctory–contributions. For authorship refers to the producers of texts resulting from the four characteristics of authorship listed above; generatorship, to the producers of texts that demonstrate such strict adherence to genres that original creativity is lacking and communicative intent superficial. The author is an individual creative genius; the generator, not so much. It is a crude distinction, of course, but it is a distinction that helps us better delineate the complexities of authorship as it pertains to computer-generated texts.

Such a continuum also accommodates instances of human-computer collaboration for text creation. Scholar of creativity Margaret Boden, for one, has considered throughout her *Creative Mind* (2004) instances of creativity demonstrated by both humans and computers, and presents a loose framework for considering acts of creativity as historically novel (h-creativity) and psychologically novel (p-creativity). While Boden does not argue that computers are capable of creativity–indeed, she argues quite strongly against this capability–her distinction between varying types of creativity speaks to the need for new language to account for technological developments. Whether or not one holds that computers are capable of creativity, of the title of "author" by virtue of text production, the proposed continuum offers new language to account for the techno-logical developments related to NLG and other forms of aesthetic or expository computational output. The reader may situate the contributing NLG system and the human wherever he or she feels appropriate along the authorship-generatorship continuum.

Moreover, such a continuum better accommodates the distinction between "author" and "owner," and permits a more nuanced view of accountability for textual output. For no matter how they attribute authorship, readers–regardless of their levels of technical knowledge–conceptualise computational processes in ways that inform their development of some sort of "back-story" about personality and process. This conceptualisation may, as has been elaborated above, take the form of the parent-child metaphor, wherein the reader compares the NLG system and its developer to a child and its parent, respectively. As the child achieves fuller autonomy through growth and development, it becomes altogether separate from the parents who produced it, able to articulate its own subjective experiences in an original way and thus moving from generator to author. There is, it appears, a likening of computational processes of text generation to human processes of writing. Yet, while computer and human textual output may appear similar, they are produced through fundamentally different means. As computer-generated texts become ever more pervasive, it is increasingly more important to consider the implications of such differences and their effects, however subtle. A continuum demands consideration of authorial process as exercised by either humans or computers.

CONCLUSION

Readers' perceptions of NLG indicate uncertainty regarding how to approach the output of this rather new technology. In trying to make sense of where the conventional hermeneutic contract fits within instances of computer-generated texts, readers draw upon traditional understandings of authorship, but soon realise that these understandings are insufficient. NLG not only challenges traditional understandings of authorship, but also engenders new understandings of authorship altogether as readers explore the conceptual gap between human and computer language production. One way of mitigating readers' potential hostility towards this unfamiliar territory that has been proposed herein is introducing a continuum with authorship at one end and generatorship at the other, which may be used to more clearly mark the balance between seemingly original and rehashed contributions to a text's production. Of course, the power to determine this balance rests with the reader, and may differ based on the reader's own perceptions of computational capability. Thus, the hermeneutic contract maintains its relevance in instances of computer-generated texts because the responsibility for maintaining such a contract–and for ultimately making meaning from a text–has little to do with who or what the author is, and much more to do with the reader's perceptions of the author.

By understanding how ordinary readers attribute authorship to a computer-generated text, we may too understand how a reader perceives the NLG system's creativity capacity. I have written elsewhere (Henrickson **2018b**) of the potential for considering NLG systems as "agents" rather than mere tools for manifesting human vision. Through both engagement with this extant scholarship and analysis of ordinary readers' opinions as expressed in such studies as that described above, we may work towards holistic and comprehensive understandings of where NLG and computer-generated texts fit within our current literary climate. For despite scholars' assertions that computer-generated texts are authorless, ordinary readers attribute authorship to them, and often to the generating system itself. Indeed, it seems that ordinary readers tend to recognise the system as distinct enough from its creators to warrant the title of author. These results matter, because how a reader attributes authorship to a computer-generated text, if the reader has been informed of the text's process of production, uncovers the ways in which readers are already negotiating the hermeneutic contract as it pertains to computer-generated texts. This investigation has only just begun.

Atwood, Margaret. 2006. "The ballad of the LongPen (TM)." *The Guardian*, September 30. Link: https://www.theguardian.com/books/2006/sep/30/margaretatwood.

Automated Insights. n.d. "Case Studies: Bodybuilding.com." Accessed March 18, 2018. Link: https://automatedinsights.com/case-studies/bodybuilding.

Boden, Margaret A. 2004. *The Creative Mind: Myths and Mechanisms.* 2nd ed. London: Routledge. [First edition published 1990]

Bolter, Jay David. 1991. Writing Space: The Computer, Hypertext, and the History of Writing. Hillsdale, NJ: Lawrence Erlbaum Associates.

Burkeman, Oliver. 2006. "Atwood sign of the times draws blank." *The Guardian*, March 6. Link: https://www.theguardian.com/world/2006/mar/06/topstories3.books.

Eve, Martin Paul. 2017. "The Great Automatic Grammatizator: writing, labour, computers." *Critical Quarterly* 59 (3):39-54. Link: https://doi.org/https://doi.org/10.1111/criq.12359.

Greene, Bob. 1984. "Computer authors: Where's the soul?" *Chicago Tribune*, October 1. Link: http://archives.chicagotribune.com/1984/10/01/page/87/article/tempo.

Henrickson, Leah. 2018a. "Computer-Generated Fiction in a Literary Lineage: Breaking the hermeneutic contract." *Logos* 29 (2):54-63. Link: https://doi.org/https://doi.org/10.1163/18784712-02902007.

Henrickson, Leah. 2018b. "Tool vs. agent: attributing agency to natural language generation systems." *Digital Creativity* 29 (2):182-90. Link: https://doi.org/10.1080/14626268.2018.1482924.

Henrickson, Leah. 2019a. "Natural Language Generation: Negotiating Text Production in Our Digital Humanity." In *Proceedings of the Digital Humanities Congress 2018.* Link: https://www.dhi.ac.uk/openbook/chapter/dhc2018-henrickson.

Henrickson, Leah. 2019b. *Towards a New Sociology of the Text: The Hermeneutics of Algorithmic Authorship.* Empirical Studies. Loughborough University Research Repository. November 27, 2019. Link: https://doi.org/10.17028/rd.lboro.c.4663709.

Immersive Automation. 2018. "Valtteri the Election Bot". April 11, 2018. Link: http://immersiveautomation.com/valtteri-election-bot.

Krittman, Daniel, Philip Matthews, and Mary Grace Glascott. 2015. "Innovation ushers in the modern era of compliance". In *Deloitte*. Accessed March 18, 2018. Link: https://www2.deloitte.com/content/dam/Deloitte/us/Documents/finance/us-fas-how-natural-language-is-changing-the-game-deloitte-only.pdf.

Love, Harold. 2002. *Attributing Authorship: An Introduction.* Cambridge: Cambridge University Press.

Loxley, James. 2016. "'Public feasts': Ben Jonson as literary celebrity". *Celebrity Studies* 7 (4):561-74. Link: https://doi.org/10.1080/19392397.2016.1233707.

Mailer, Norman. 1992. *Advertisements for Myself.* Cambridge, MA: Harvard University Press.

Ohlsson, Anders, Torbjörn Forslid, and Ann Steiner. 2014. "Literary celebrity reconsidered". *Celebrity Studies* 5 (1):32–44.
Link: https://doi.org/10.1080/19392397.2014.887533.

Oxford Dictionaries. n.d. "Author". Accessed April 13, 2018.
Link: https://en.oxforddictionaries.com/definition/author.

Racter [William Chamberlain and Thomas Etter]. 1984. *The Policeman's Beard is Half Constructed.* New York: Warner Software / Warner Books.

Reeves, Byron, and Clifford Nass. 1996. *The Media Equation: How People Treat Computers, Television, and New Media Like Real People and Places.* Cambridge: Cambridge University Press.

Twitter. n.d. "Magic Realism Bot". Accessed December 16, 2017.
Link: https://twitter.com/MagicRealismBot.

"Valtteri". **n.d.** Accessed April 11, 2018.
Link: https://www.vaalibotti.fi.

Van der Weel, Adriaan. 2011. *Changing Our Textual Minds: Towards a Digital Order of Knowledge.* Manchester: Manchester University Press.

PART 2

LE LANGAGE COMME INTERFACE
LANGUAGE AS INTERFACE

SARAH CISTON

Spark Gap: Digital Language, Interstitial User

Abstract

Private and public collide in the mobile browser. This paper describes an experimental browser I designed to amplify the intimate co-presence of its users. It asks how an interface might be more expressive of the affective tensions created where digital language, physical proximity, and intersubjectivity intersect. Implemented within an interactive gallery installation, the artwork combines the anonymous limbo of waiting rooms with the intimacy of darkened bedrooms. Upon browsing, each reader witnesses neighboring readers' touch behaviors layered in ephemeral trails and text fragments on their own screen. The software archives fragments into an accumulating collaborative text, making digital reading a performance of writing in an era when every action becomes data. In the paper, I explore how digital language negotiates the gap between readers as we share anonymous physical proximity but diffuse digital intimacy, plumbing the tensions alive in the intersections of reading-writing, physical-digital, self-other. I draw on interdisciplinary scholarship to argue that digital reading practices separate intimacy from embodiment but reentangle them in complex ways–thus cultivating a more porous, but more vital, experience of subjectivity.

Résumé

Les sphères privée et publique se rencontrent dans le navigateur mobile. Cet article décrit un navigateur expérimental que j'ai conçu afin d'amplifier la co-présence intime de ses utilisateurs. Comment une interface peut-elle exprimer des tensions affectives créées à l'intersection du langage numérique, de la proximité physique et de l'intersubjectivité? Implantée dans une installation interactive en galerie, cette œuvre combine l'incertitude anonyme des salles d'attentes avec l'intimité des chambres à coucher assombries. Au lancement du navigateur, chaque lecteur est témoin des gestes de ses voisins grâce aux traces éphémères et aux fragments textuels qui se superposent sur leurs propres écrans. Ce logiciel archive les fragments dans un texte collaboratif qui s'accumule, faisant de la lecture numérique une performance d'écriture à une époque où toute action devient une donnée. Dans cet article, j'examine comment le langage numérique négocie l'écart entre les lecteurs alors qu'ils partagent une proximité physique anonyme et une intimité numérique diffuse. J'explore les tensions présentes aux intersections de la lecture et de l'écriture, du physique et du numérique et du soi et de l'autre. En m'appuyant sur une méthodologie interdisciplinaire, je soutiens que les pratiques de lecture numérique séparent l'intimité de la corporéité, mais qu'elles les ré-enchevêtrent de manières complexes – cultivant ainsi une expérience plus poreuse, mais plus vitale, de la subjectivité.

Private and public collide in the mobile web browser yet the browser interface does not address this collision. I created an experimental browser designed to amplify the intimate co-presence of its users. This project investigates how digital language alters both subjectivity and language itself. It asks how an interface could express tensions arising from the presence of other users–by transmitting fragments of other users' behavior into its interface as each user browses the web. As a creative writer and coder, I am particularly interested in how language negotiates the gaps between readers–especially the gaps created as we share anonymous physicality but diffuse digital intimacy.

Digital reading is a hybrid of reading–writing (Emerson **2014**, 163–84), co-produced by its audiences. In some ways, technology separates intimacy from embodiment. I argue that it also re-entangles intimacy and embodiment in complex ways, and that this cultivates a more fragmented–but more vital–kind of subjectivity. My hope is that showing the destabilization of language and subjects can open productive space by pointing to their underlying fluidity.

I explore this argument through the combination of writing, creative coding, and critical research, and this paper provides background on the intersections of reading–writing, physical–digital, self–other with which this project engages. I will describe the three components of this project, then discuss the interdisciplinary context I draw from to outline its potential impacts.

PROJECT DESIGN, METHODOLOGY

First, the project "Spark Gap" exists in physical space as an interactive gallery installation, where users join a public reading area equipped with tablets loaded with the browser. The light from each screen is the primary illumination in the space, inviting immersion and digital eavesdropping across screens. The installation juxtaposes spaces where digital reading occurs–the anonymous limbo of waiting rooms against the intimacy of darkened bedrooms. Both create a distance between digital and physical occupations of the same space.

Second, the browser interface shows others' touch behaviors: scroll and tap mark ephemeral trails in purple and blue, and clicked text fragments appear out of context in the menu bar. But the users' own touch behavior still responds normally, and they can navigate through links and buttons like a standard OS browser. Rather than undermine usefulness entirely, the effect is subtle and uncanny: a whisper of displacement, the feeling of a thrown voice. Where users are accustomed to seeing only their own behaviors displayed, instead they see another user's actions tracked and visualized. By extension they may anticipate their own actions being traced elsewhere. This prototype explores the potential of technology to make its own affordances more legible. Could an interface be more expressive of how it follows us, and how it lets us affect each other?

Third, I trace this question through the content within the browser. I composed a text that drew on my own reading habits while researching the project, plus personal tracking data collected throughout development. I created a non-linear database text of fragments that evoke my reading experience online. Because the project attempts to track nebulous traces of affect and influence that are impossible to capture comprehensively or accurately, instead the goal is to express a sense of overwhelming immersion, to play in the tensions between the curatorial and the combinatorial in every database.

The software also uses its tracked touch behavior to reconfigure this text continually. As users browse through the project or use its links to travel to other sites, another collaborative archival text is produced from fragments they touch. This new text is not comprehensive but always fragmented–evoking the urgency, fatigue, and occasional poetry in digital language. By enacting a kind of reading that writes yet more text, the work tries to draw out the tensions that intersect digital and public spaces–amplifying their self-reflexive, co-constructed nature.

SILENT READING, INTIMATE PUBLICS

Prior shifts in the history of language may hint at the possible impact of new digital reading practices, which the project explores through database and interface. Of course, every change in technology has its critics. Alberto Manguel (1997) reminds us that at first reading was always done in public and out loud, while critics of the first silent readers worried it would allow "unwitnessed communication between the book and the reader" (51)–just as parents now monitor children's screen time. Silent, solitary book reading has morphed in the digital age into silent, public phone reading. One of the characteristic uses of digital reading is to create the illusion of isolation in a public space. Peggy Kamuf (2017) says that the transition to silent reading made the separateness of experience via language simply more apparent. She recalls Saint Augustine's account of first witnessing another's silent reading:

> Augustine's account reveals nothing less than the ground or rather the gulf of unfathomable, irreducible alterity across which and on the condition of which reading can take place. In effect, we see, we read Augustine, who believes that he is seeing reading happen because Ambrose's "eye glided over the pages," even though he cannot see to the heart of the other's reading, to what precisely he locates here in Ambrose's heart, which "searched out the sense." Thus he neither sees nor hears the other's reading taking place; he can only believe that it takes place nowhere that he can hear or see, cut off, therefore, from his own understanding. So long as reading manifests itself in the openly spoken voice, then its conditioning ground of alterity can appear to disappear [...]. (4)

In the same way that the transition to reading in silence highlighted the alterity of the experience of a text, more recent shifts in reading practices–into the browser and digital device–can help expose this "conditioning ground of alterity" further, through the interchangeability and ubiquity of their technologies. Twenty-first century reading practices find readers (often idle, in transit, among strangers) staring into black boxes, a wide breadth of possibilities for the language each reader may be absorbing unseen at any given time. We may not pay too much attention to one another, but perhaps I imagine you are reading Baudrillard while you are actually reading Buzzfeed–or vice versa. We might imagine a shared experience as we read the very same words, but still our imaginations never cross that gap. By offering small hints of the gestures generated by its users, and fragments of the texts encountered by its users, this experimental browser interface tries to remind us of each other's physical presence layered with our digital presence.

An individual digital experience is often highly intimate even as it appears anonymous, interstitial, interchangeable in physical space. Kate Crawford (2016) says mobile practices offer "new collective intimacy" (137). "Twitter can be understood as a mechanism that commingles these two worlds, where 'the inner and the outer continually move through each other.' It is the sharing of subjectivity, as uneventful and routine as it may be, that forms the basis of Twitter's social reality" (134). And yet Josh Berson (**2015**) tracks digital engagement's effects on physical presence:

> We start to attend less to what is going on in the field of experience defined by the space around our bodies and more to what is unfolding in the larger space of distant presence. [...] in synchronization-at-a-distance social personae start to become delaminated from bodily presence–from bodily desire, from the very specific limbic sensations afforded by movement, rest, eye contact, skin-to-skin touch. Whatever else synchronization-over-distance is, it is a condition of *asymbolia*, a damping down of the emotional resonance of sensory experience–or, in a more positive light, of *pratyahara*, the withdrawal from the moment-to-moment flux of sensory experience that is a prerequisite of the boundarylessness we associate with "flow states." (2425-35)

A tension arises in the "diffuse familiarity" (Crawford **2016**, 138) of digital space layered onto public physical spaces, whereby turning toward online intimacy functions to produce physical alterity, allowing neighbors to become more anonymous to each other. While it would be impossible to resolve alterity all together–that profound otherness behind all communication attempts–an interface can attempt to make existing disconnections and opportunities for connection more visible, more accessible, more affecting. The goal is to cultivate a practice of making absence present, articulating what goes unnoticed, archiving what is scrolled past.

Although, besides not knowing what another is reading, we may not wish to know. If you are sitting near me, you may be unfortunate enough to catch a glimpse of my screen. In the involuntary cross-reading from an airplane seatmate, text becomes confrontation, a constant unauthorized remixing of fragments, an unwelcome address. Kamuf (**2017**) also examines the "uncanny relation" of feeling addressed by a text, possible as part of the private relationship formed through silent reading. She cites Maurice Blanchot's *Thomas the Obscure*: "all the strangeness [*étrangeté*] there was in being observed by a word as by a living being" (14) and she asks: "What does it mean for words *to read*, active transitive, instead of *being read*, passive? What is called reading if the words to be read are already living beings that (who?) read, which is to say also, bite, knead, grab?" (15). This question becomes particularly important now that so much reading is done online. Our reading goes on to read us.

READING-WRITING THE INDIVIDUAL

Words are tools to attract and track readers online; and in the context of social media and big data, the language presented to readers is both produced by and producing interpretations of those readers as subjects. These interpretations are not always accurate, but they still matter deeply because they are highly functional: "Google's misrecognition of my gender and age isn't an error. It's a reconfiguration, a freshly minted algorithmic truth that cares little about being authentic but cares a lot about being an effective metric for classification" (Cheney-Lippold **2017**, 9). Because these algorithms are trained on the behavior of others it recognizes as "similar users," the practice of digital reading is always–already weighted with the practice of writing–writing oneself and writing others–shaping the kind of person one is able to be online and off. This is reading and writing in the dark, since the algorithms which compile, interpret, and reconfigure our behaviors remain proprietary and opaque. And this constructed subjectivity does not yet even delve into questions of performativity or broader offline ecologies, which further call into question the idea of a fixed authentic self.

It is tempting to argue for new media's unprecedented break from an authentic self, but such shifts in language that reconstitute subjectivity are not new. Anne Carson (**2014**) argues that written language was another technology that changed perceptions of the self. She says:

> It is in the poetry of those who were first exposed to a written alphabet and the demands of literacy that we encounter deliberate meditation upon the self, especially in the context of erotic desire. The singular intensity with which these poets insist on conceiving eros as lack may reflect, in some degree, that exposure. Literate training encourages a heightened awareness of personal physical boundaries and a sense of those boundaries as the vessel of one's self. To control the boundaries is to possess oneself. (44)

Alongside this new sense of the individual self and a lack that is linguistically and erotically charged, she describes the new sense of letters and words as discrete concepts: "As separable, controllable units of meaning, each with its own visible boundary, each with its own fixed and independent use, written words project their user into isolation" (50). If even the written word is a complex technology of both communion and division, rather than echoing critiques of isolation due to phone use and lack of connection among users, I wonder how digital tools may also reignite our sense of co-presence.

Where written language created a discrete self–breaking from the sensory, enmeshed self of the oral traditions–I suggest that digital reading–writing (*because* it is fragmented and discombobulating) can productively complicate that stable, individual subject. And interfaces can help reveal the meshwork of influence and impact that always exists in a complex system of language, both digital and analog. Just as the written word was responsible for closing distances (as in the writing of letters) even as it created a sense of distance (between individual letters of the alphabet, between individual subjects), I argue that by bringing the voice of an absent other closer, digital text may provide opportunities for new kinds of readings in the interplay it creates by putting different texts in proximity.

In the overlaps between the many types of texts and voices that are layered through and skewed by pervasive computing practices, we can read new relationships and even new selves into the gap. These layers might include: a) text intentionally clicked and read: journalism, hot takes, listicles, blog posts, driving directions; b) text intentionally composed for circulation: status updates, retweets, Snapchat stories, emails; c) text unintentionally read: popup advertisements, social media page refreshes, eavesdropped SMS messages; d) text unintentionally composed but circulated: web cookies, site analytics, credit scores, cell phone location data. All of these stand in for or co-constitute the subject in various ways at various times–particularly theuser as interpreted by corporate algorithms trained to serve that user more (and more targeted) content. Because these algorithms are trained on the behavior of other "like users," each act of reading is a micro-act of writing–in the dark, in an unknown language. As Wendy Hui Kyong Chun (**2016**) says in "Big Data as Drama," "The body is always collective, and a singular action never singular, because it is linked to a pattern elsewhere" (374). In the context of such massive production of data and text, of text-as-data, of selfie-as-self, the demarcation between practices of reading and writing, not to mention author and audience, quickly blurs.[1]

NOTE 1

"There is a tightly wound loop between the roles of reading and writing on Twitter" (Crawford, "These Foolish Things," 134).

Within or across these categories lie additional levels of nuance–e.g., layers of performance (filters, selective posting, liking, following) that belie an individual's private sense of self, or the unacknowledged influx of influence upon that self from outside actors, or the notion of a singular "authentic" self, which it is important to dispel. The experience of digital reading–writing, although discombobulating, does a good job of problematizing the idea of the stable individual subject, while illustrating the meshwork of influence and impact produced in a complex system of language both digital and analog. Chun (**2016**) asks, "rather than fighting for a privacy that is no privacy, what if we rather embraced our role as collective characters in public?" (375).

SENSING THE MEDIATED SELF

So much digital experience is designed to happen below the surface of human attention, and so we are not equipped to know ourselves or our digital contexts. Self-assessments are increasingly mediated by these very technologies. Sun-ha Hong (**2016**) says individuals' intimacy with data operates in the periphery of experience:

> Even as self-knowledge becomes more comprehensive and ubiquitous than ever, it also recedes into the background and out of subjects' conscious engagement. To engage a machinic reading of ourselves is not so much to turn on and tune in, but to awake and become aware to an always already ongoing swarm of active objects–harvesting us and communicating with our bodies (and each other) in cables below our feet, radio wavelengths beyond our senses, frequencies beyond our temporal range. (11)

Marking the double meaning latent in the term "sense" (meaning or experiencing), Hong traces how digital self-tracking practices create an idealized subjectivity, in which "human subjects' sensory access to their own bodies, and their equipment for making sense of the data at hand, are both reconfigured–rendering them suitable parts for the machinic production of personal data" (20). This reading of data, and subject as read data, alters behavior and sense of self in relation.

This alteration via interface occurs not only at the moment we consciously select our tools. While Hong refers to self-tracking interfaces, in Mark Hansen's (**2015**) phenomenological reading of new media, the computational nature of all contemporary media shifts the sensory awareness of time toward scales beyond our senses, massive and microscopic, while–importantly–modulating human engagement in pre-conscious ways. The feedback loop he describes means that while there may be few pre- or non-computational experiences that remain, we can use computation to bring the experience *of mediation* closer to awareness. He says:

> Largely because of its technically facilitated capacities to impact the actual temporal and spatial frameworks in which sensibility is produced and to gather data about this impact, twenty-first-century media furnish an occasion for us to broaden our understanding of what experience is and perhaps has always been. (139)

Rather than cultivate nostalgia for some utopic non-mediated state that never was, the crisis raised by digital media can re-engage pre-existing intersubjectivities and ecologies: "mediation becomes a key trope for understanding and articulating our being in, and becoming with, the technological world, our emergence and ways of intra-acting with it" (Kember and Zylinska **2012** XV).

The challenge that interests this project is how to use technology to account for the relationships we cultivate–with technologies, with each other, and with a multitude of selves. It is important not only how we are produced as subjects by digital environments–how we are touched by interface–but also how we produce, how we respond in return. With this in mind, "Spark Gap" offers digital reminders of embodied co-presence through the touch behavior traces of nearby users, as well as textual reminders of digital co-presence through a corpus of browsed language. Chun (**2016**) argues for a more vulnerable, collaborative public engagement in digital spaces: "We repeat–we write, we read, we expose ourselves–to communicate this sense of community, to insist that this 'we' is possible" (379). For this project, vulnerability and collaboration result from grounding the digital experience in physical proximity–in order to reckon with intersecting fragments of selves and language we find there.

Berson, Josh. 2015. *Computable Bodies: Instrumented Life and the Human Somatic Niche.* Kindle Edition. Bloomsbury Publishing.

Carson, Anne. 2014. *Eros the Bittersweet: An Essay.* Princeton: Princeton University Press.

Cheney-Lippold, John. 2017. *We Are Data: Algorithms and the Making of Our Digital Selves.* New York: NYU Press.

Chun, Wendy Hui Kyong. 2016. "Big Data as Drama." *Elh* 83 (2):363–82. Link: https://doi.org/10.1353/elh.2016.0011.

Crawford, Kate. 2016. "These Foolish Things: On Intimacy and Insignificance in Mobile Media." In *Foundations of Mobile Media Studies: Essential Texts on the Formation of a Field,* 128–40. New York: Routledge.

Emerson, Lori. 2014. *Reading Writing Interfaces.* Minneapolis: University of Minnesota Press.

Hansen, Mark B.N. 2015. *Feed-Forward: On the Future of Twenty-First-Century Media.* Chicago: University of Chicago Press.

Hong, Sun-ha. 2016. "Data's Intimacy: Machinic Sensibility and the Quantified Self." *Communication +1* 5 (1):1–36. Link: https://doi.org/10.7275/R5CF9N15.

Kamuf, Peggy. 2017. "Comes a Letter in the Mail: Ellipses of Reading." *Differences* 28 (1):1–16. Link: https://doi.org/10.1215/10407391-3821664.

Kember, Sarah, and Joanna Zylinska. 2012. *Life After New Media: Mediation as a Vital Process.* Cambridge, MA: MIT Press.

Manguel, Alberto. 1997. *A History of Reading.* New York: Penguin.

Balpe & Chatonsky :

Esthétique générative, surproduction et mémoire à l'ère numérique

PAULO SILVA PEREIRA

Résumé

On se propose ici d'examiner trois questions à partir de l'œuvre de Jean-Pierre Balpe et de Grégory Chatonsky : l'esthétique générative, fondée sur la permutation et recombinaison automatique de textes et de contenus ; la surproduction culturelle et médiatique dans un contexte de reproductibilité généralisée ; l'inscription matérielle de la mémoire et la difficulté à consulter la quantité grandissante de données. Le projet *Capture*, conçu par Chatonsky en 2008 et ouvert dans les dernières années à la participation de plusieurs spécialistes, propose une machine algorithmique capable de produire un flux continu de chansons, d'images, de textes et d'autres objets. Un ensemble de programmes génératifs permet de recueillir de donnés sur le Web et de poster automatiquement les nouveaux éléments à mesure qu'ils sont générés, en créant un effet de saturation sur les réseaux sociaux. Ce projet de « netrock génératif » est une façon de penser, d'un point de vue critique, les implications sociales et culturelles des flux ininterrompus. La productivité illimitée du générateur de texte et les possibilités des blogues ou autres outils du Web ont été utilisées plusieurs fois par Balpe comme terrain privilégié d'expérimentation du littéraire. Il a démontré que la création textuelle, bien loin des formulations romantiques et subjectivistes, est devenue un processus à entrées multiples qui rend très complexe la notion d'autorialité. En dépassant le format traditionnel du roman, des projets d'hyperfiction en flux et en expansion continue comme *La Disparition du Général Proust* et *Un Monde Incertain* ont provoqué la discussion sur les frontières ontologiques de la fiction. Le complexe univers organisé autour de multiples entités qui prêtent leur nom à des séries spécifiques de textes suivant les possibilités formelles inscrites dans ses algorithmes, est en lui-même un laboratoire pour réfléchir sur les dispositifs de création et de dissémination du littéraire. Si le programme est la formulation logique du processus génératif, qui se manifeste sous la forme de code, l'auteur, qui crée en utilisant ce même programme informatique, travaille sur des modèles conceptuels et des règles qui manifestent sa propre conception de la littérature, des dispositifs qui la fondent, et le mode dont elle est vue par les communautés de lecteurs. En ce sens, l'agent humain, qui n'est impliqué qu'au deuxième degré dans le phénomène de la création, se présente comme un « Méta-auteur » et même le régime de coopérativité lectorielle se modifie sous l'effet de la multiplicité mouvante des textes. Un des liens les plus forts entre les travaux de Balpe et de Chatonsky est l'exploitation des possibilités de diffusion du texte génératif en articulation avec la notion de surproduction qui suscite le problème des modes de conservation et du fonctionnement de la mémoire à l'âge numérique.

Abstract

We propose to examine three questions surrounding the work of Jean-Pierre Balpe and Grégory Chatonsky: generative aesthetics, founded on the automatic permutation and recombination of texts and content; cultural and media overproduction in the context of generalized reproducibility; the material inscription of memory and the difficulty in consulting a growing quantity of data. The project *Capture*, created by Chatonsky in 2008 and expanded in the last few years to include participation from various specialists, proposes an algorithmic machine capable of producing a continuous stream of songs, images, texts, and more. An ensemble of generative programs allows for the collection of data from the Web and to post new elements as they are automatically generated by saturating social networks. This "generative netrock" project presents a way of conceiving, through an analytical point of view, of the social and cultural implications of uninterrupted flows of digital content. The unlimited productivity of a natural-language text generator and the potential of blogs or other tools of the Web have already been used on many occasions by Balpe as his preferred field of experimentation. He has demonstrated that textual creation, far removed from romantic and subjectivist formulations, has become a multi-entry process that complicates the notion of authorship. By surpassing the traditional format of the novel, generative and continually expansive hyperfiction projects such as *La Disparition du Général Proust* and *Un Monde Incertain* provoke a discussion on the ontological frontiers of fiction. The complex universe organized around multiple entities that lend their names with specific series of texts according to the formal possibilities inscribed in its algorithms, is in itself a laboratory for reflecting on the devices used for the creation and dissemination of literature. If the program is a logical formulation of the generative process, manifested in the form of code, then the author, who creates by using the same computational program, works on the conceptual models and rules that manifest his or her own concept of literature, of the tools on which it is founded, and the ways in which literature is viewed by communities of readers. In this sense, the human agent, who is only involved to the second degree in the phenomenon of creation, presents him or herself as a "Meta-author" and even the system of readership cooperativity changes under the effect of the moving multiplicity of texts. One of the strongest links between the work of Balpe and Chatonksy is the exploitation of the possibilities of diffusion of a generative text in articulation with the notion of overproduction, which raises the problem of modes of preservation and the functioning of memory in the digital age.

1.

On se rend vite compte que la prolifération croissante des flux d'information numériques, l'accumulation des données (aussi bien que la précarité de leur conservation) et les excès d'une mémoire en extension perpétuelle posent de nouveaux problèmes aux sociétés contemporaines. Ces questions seront, certainement, au cœur du débat scientifique, social et politique dans les prochaines années, mais on peut identifier déjà une conscience accrue de la part des artistes et théoriciens face à leur potentiel disruptif. Nous sommes débordés par la capacité des dispositifs techniques non seulement au regard de la quantité d'informations qui sont conservées dans de multiples bases de données que les utilisateurs alimentent sans cesse (et même sans le savoir), mais aussi par les contenus qu'on peut (et veut) préserver, en constituant virtuellement une archive démesurée. On peut d'ailleurs se demander si la construction de ces vastes répertoires d'objets ne correspond pas à une forme d'hypermnésie, c'est-à-dire une hypertrophie de la mémoire dans ses multiples débordements, conduisant à l'extrême abondance d'information et de savoirs de toute nature (Ernst **2012**; Bourassa **2013**, 2012). L'externalisation des capacités cognitives humaines en résultat de l'utilisation de la mémoire externe (ou artificielle) a subi un changement radical dans les dernières décennies grâce aux progrès technologiques : l'arrivée de l'ordinateur personnel; le Web comme bien commun; la culture participative et les réseaux sociaux; la dissémination des plateformes numériques. Il s'agit de mettre en perspective l'une des conséquences les plus visibles de ce phénomène : l'érosion de la dialectique entre le mémorable et l'oubliable, entre la conservation et l'effacement, dialectique qui conditionne depuis toujours l'archivage, les opérations historiographiques ou la formation de la mémoire individuelle et collective. Sur différents plans, le travail de sélection implique inévitablement des choix et des formes d'exclusion. Si nous avons du mal à oublier à cause de la capacité quasi-infinie de l'archivage numérique et des différents éléments qu'il met en jeu, que restera-t-il ?

Les trajectoires créatives de Jean-Pierre Balpe et de Grégory Chatonsky nous incitent à penser sur la nature et les implications de l'esthétique générative, fondée sur les permutation et recombinaison automatiques de textes et de contenus, la surproduction culturelle et médiatique dans un contexte de reproductibilité généralisée et les modes d'inscription matérielle de la mémoire. Au détriment des formes artistiques stables, associées à un désir de permanence et même de transcendance du temps, les pratiques contemporaines valorisent les processus, les flux et les gestes performatifs. De l'esthétique de la forme, les technologies génératives nous font passer à une esthétique du flux, soulignant la prédominance du faire. Pourtant, l'illimité de la production machinique et de la mise en réseau nous saisit souvent de vertige et met en évidence les limites de l'expérience humaine et de notre situation dans le monde.

2.

« L'écriture appelle l'infini » : ainsi définissait Jean-Pierre Balpe, dans *Contextes de l'Art Numérique* (Balpe **2000**), la tentation inscrite dans tout acte d'écriture et même dans toute création artistique. Le point de départ de cette réflexion était l'essai bien connu de Louis Aragon, *Je n'ai jamais appris à écrire* ou *Les Incipit*, où celui-ci proposait des analyses sur l'écriture, sur son origine et sur sa fin, en consacrant une attention particulière à *La Défense de l'Infini*, ce monumental roman dont l'auteur dit qu'il a détruit un millier de pages et les centaines de personnages le composant. Le principe du « commencement sans fin » qu'Aragon voyait déjà mis en œuvre chez Beckett constitue, en effet, un des moteurs de propulsion du projet artistique de Balpe : l'objet qui n'en finit pas de commencer ou qui ne finit pas ou se poursuit indéfiniment.

Il est impossible de ne pas s'égarer dans la complexité de la vaste galaxie en mouvement de la production de Balpe (**http://www.balpe.name/**), de ne pas être fasciné par les formes multiples d'expérimentation mobilisées au cours des dernières décennies. La création artistique a toujours été dépendante des techniques, des matériaux et des supports qui lui permettent de s'exprimer, mais l'émergence du numérique et des réseaux a transformé la relation du créateur au réel, a redéfini son statut et les modes d'appropriation de la technologie, a rendu obsolète la conception d'œuvre finie et a stimulé l'avènement de nouveaux moyens de diffusion et d'expression. En fait, une nouvelle technique fait apparaître de nouveaux processus formels et ouvre des chemins que les créateurs sont conduits à explorer; cependant, et contrairement à ce qu'on voyait dans des contextes antérieurs, nous ne sommes plus face à de simples technologies d'inscription, mais à des métaoutils ou, comme préfère dire Balpe, des « machines-langage », des « machines-pensée », des « machines-concept » (Balpe **2000**). En ce sens, penser le fonctionnement d'un système génératif exige la problématisation de la notion de texte, du statut de l'auteur, mais aussi des stratégies de lecture du percepteur. D'après Balpe, la générativité c'est « le trop plein, l'inépuisable, l'encore possible, la saturation et, parce qu'il connaît ses propres limites, l'homme, devant les promesses de l'illimité, ne sait jamais vraiment qu'en faire. L'infini de la génération s'affronte au fini de la perception, toujours bornée dans ses possibilités de découvertes » (Balpe **2000**).

Produire une œuvre inépuisable et éphémère qui s'écrirait *ad libitum* sans l'intervention d'un agent humain est une ambition qui se manifeste chez beaucoup d'auteurs (et même avant l'arrivée du numérique), mais la performance expérimentale *Trois mythologies et un poète aveugle* (1997) ouvrait déjà un débat intense sur la place assignée aux créateurs dans ces formes nouvelles qui donnent au texte littéraire ou musical l'évanescence de la parole improvisé (**http://www.balpe.name/Trois-Mythologies-et-un-Poete**). Les 'voix' des poètes Balpe, Henry Deluy et Joseph Guglielmi qui s'entremêlent dans ce « spectacle génératif » à partir de textes générés en temps réel par l'ordinateur (le « poète aveugle ») sont accompagnées par la musique du compositeur italien J. Baboni-Schilingi. Les algorithmes sélectionnent et combinent des mots et des phrases à partir d'une base de données constituée de fragments de textes poétiques, pendant qu'un autre ordinateur compose une musique influencée par ces textes. En d'autres termes, la machine lit les algorithmes et décide ainsi quels fragments apparaîtront sur un écran, en même temps qu'un dialogue insolite entre texte et musique s'élabore dans un jeu infini de variations qui suscite des formes nouvelles à chaque performance. Ce qui revient à dire, avec Balpe, que « l'œuvre générative est en effet, dans l'intégralité de ses dispositifs de présentation, à chaque fois une œuvre unique définie par une programmation spécifique qui borne ses singularités, mais dont les manifestations, bien qu'incarnées dans les mêmes supports matériels, sont toujours plurielles » (Balpe **2000**)[1].

NOTE 1

À ce propos, voir aussi le texte intitulé « L'infini » : http://articlesdejpbalpe.blogspot.com/2013/10/infini.html.

Jean-Pierre Balpe a exploré considérablement la voie de la générativité, en y ajoutant un point de vue pragmatique et une démarche plus heuristique. Ses générateurs sont capables de produire des textes dans plusieurs genres ou styles et il a démontré à plusieurs reprises que la création, bien loin des formulations romantiques et subjectivistes, est devenue un processus à entrées multiples qui rend très complexe la notion d'autorialité. En outre, les projets d'hyperfiction en flux et expansion continue comme *La Disparition du Général Proust* et *Un Monde Incertain* ont provoqué le débat sur les frontières ontologiques de la fiction. En effet, le complexe univers organisé autour de multiples entités (hétéronymes ou « hyperonymes ») qui prêtent leur nom à des séries spécifiques de textes suivant les possibilités formelles inscrites dans ses algorithmes, est en lui-même un laboratoire pour réfléchir sur les dispositifs de création et de dissémination du littéraire[2]. Mais l'intérêt de cette production n'est pas seulement dans la qualité du texte produit. C'est surtout par son capacité à générer des textes ad libitum que le dispositif étonne. Cette surabondance qui excède les capacités humaines et décourage les tentatives de lecture invite à s'intéresser plus au processus d'engendrement des textes qu'aux productions elles-mêmes.

Malgré une apparente ressemblance terminologique, la notion balpienne d'hyperfiction ne peut se confondre avec celle d'hypertexte, puisque dans le premier cas il s'agit d'un espace réparti de blocs de fiction dynamiques, c'est-à-dire en perpétuel changement essayant d'exploiter toutes les possibilités des blogues (écritures fragmentées, linéarité contrariée, bibliothèque de liens, calendrier, commentaires, etc.) et du système de pages de Facebook, ainsi que celles de divers outils Internet (moteurs de recherche, notamment) pour contraindre à une lecture explosée de la fiction, créer une confusion permanente entre le réel et la fiction, et s'adresser à des lecteurs qui, sans cela, ne seraient jamais entrés en contact avec elle.

Alors que les récits postmodernes s'ouvrent en fragments et en bricolage dans le contenu, l'intrigue et le style, les récits distribués vont plus loin, en négociant les aspects formels et physiques de l'œuvre et en se propageant à travers le temps, l'espace et le réseau, mais Jill Walker Rettberg fait remarquer à ce propos :

> Mapping distributed narratives is not an easy task; it is hard to describe and locate things that are not things but connections. It is difficult to think about distributed narrative. Our languages have developed to name discrete objects (Rettberg 2004).

NOTE 2

Dans « Ontologie du texte littéraire génératif » (2017), Balpe déclare à ce propos : « Il y a bien un auteur, mais cet auteur est inidentifiable : Charles-Emmanuel Palancy n'existe pas, c'est un hétéronyme, plus exactement ici un avatar car il produit sans arrêt de nouveaux textes et ne cache en rien un auteur réel qui ne prendrait ce nom que pour ne pas être directement identifié. L'auteur n'est qu'un ensemble de données et d'algorithmes de traitement qui, seuls, ont un auteur, les données pouvant provenir des origines les plus diverses. Il n'y a donc aucune relation directe entre le texte produit et un auteur réel. […] L'auteur sait ce qu'il programme mais ne sait pas ce que ses algorithmes écrivent et proposent à la lecture. »

Ce genre de fictionalité ouvre la voie à l'établissement de tendances hybrides combinant des éléments d'hypermédia, d'interactivité, etc., avec des présentations de complexité croissante qui éloignent l'hyperfiction du récit séquentiel pour incorporer des éléments d'interaction avec une présence renforcée, de sorte que l'attribution au lecteur de la possibilité de construire le texte ne soit pas seulement intéressante, mais aussi captivante du point de vue esthétique.

Selon l'auteur, *La Disparition du Général Proust* peut être considérée comme « un récit de récits en expansion perpétuelle », soumis à des changements permanents et sans version définitive, qui veut susciter « une réflexion en acte, donc en textes, sur ce que le numérique peut apporter à l'écriture littéraire » (http://poetiques.blogg.org/comment-la-disparition-du-general-proust-a115641080). Cette hyperfiction court sur un vaste réseau de blogues (dont certains ne sont plus en ligne) qui mêlent des événements de la vie de personnages fictifs à des assemblages de textes, génératifs ou non, qui s'entrecroisent et se rapprochent entre eux de plusieurs façons. Chacun de ces textes a sa propre unité, mais se lie à une constellation d'autres textes, de fragments et d'albums de photos selon des critères de cohérence et des affinités de style des multiples identités numériques, sans qu'aucune pensée de la totalité ou de la permanence ne soit nécessaire pour les organiser.

Les chiffres concernant la dimension exacte de ce type de projet divergent bien souvent et il ne reste plus qu'une quantité réduite de blogues ou d'albums actifs après le mouvement diastolique de la constitution de l'œuvre au fil des années. On pourrait dire le même sur le contenu présenté dans les pages de Facebook, surtout après la « disparition » de plusieurs hétéronymes. Se pose ici, d'une façon évidente, la question de l'éphémère numérique, notamment la volatilité des données au sein des flux continus et la perte des supports. En tout cas, Balpe essaye de retrouver des témoignages d'anciennes créations disparues d'Internet pour diverses raisons – *Dédale des traces* (http://www.balpe.name/-Dedale-des-traces-), ainsi que des créations devenues inactives – *Dédale des ruines* (http://www.balpe.name/-Dedale-des-ruines-).

Bien que ces êtres fictifs puissent apparaître dans plusieurs blogues ou pages de Facebook et faire des commentaires sur les contenus produits par d'autres, les articulations sous-jacentes à l'extension du réseau ne sont pas immédiatement visibles aux yeux des lecteurs. Ainsi, il est impossible de lire cette œuvre de manière conventionnelle, puisqu'il faut parcourir cette myriade de sphères à la fois autonomes et interconnectées, qui interagissent de façon dynamique. Entrainée par cette logique réticulaire, la navigation y est labyrinthique. Le contenu exige, en effet, un effort de lecture considérable, puisque les flux de données sont manipulés de manière à ne faire entrevoir que des moments et jamais le scénario complet.

À un autre niveau, laisser proliférer le doute dans l'esprit du lecteur quant à la nature fictive ou réelle des événements est une partie constitutive de la mise en scène de ces projets. En principe, toute œuvre de fiction repose sur un compromis tacite selon lequel le lecteur accepte de considérer temporairement les évènements représentés comme « réels », selon le principe que Samuel T. Coleridge a désigné comme « suspension volontaire d'incrédulité », mais que doit-on penser de projets qui si orgueilleusement travaillent sur l'imbrication d'univers ontologiques ? Balpe cherche à reconstituer l'image de la vie de ses hétéronymes à partir de la création de blogues d'apparence normale ou de profils de Facebook avec un certain air de vraisemblance. On pourrait parler ici de l'importance des effets métaleptiques : la métalepse implique la transgression des frontières ontologiques entre les mondes actuel/réel et fictionnel, pas seulement à partir du langage verbal, comme il était commun dans le contexte de la culture de l'imprimé, mais aussi à partir d'autres éléments comme les images, le son ou l'interface (Pier **2013**; Bell **2016**). Qui plus est, dans le cas des hétéronymes qui fréquentent Facebook, la publication régulière de textes, images, vidéos ou commentaires inclut des références chronologiques qui renvoient le lecteur au actuel/réel. Dans *Un Monde Incertain*, les profils cherchent à émuler le plus possible les stratégies suivies par les autres utilisateurs de la plateforme. Au-delà des contenus littéraires ou artistiques, on peut y trouver des commentaires sur la société et la politique françaises ou sur l'actualité internationale, parfois au moment même où le lecteur est touché par les évènements. Il donne à voir à quel point le numérique permet l'émergence d'une « œuvre » qui incorpore ce qui l'approche, mais qui se laisse aussi construire par le cours des événements.

On peut ajouter aussi que la condition de Balpe en tant que personnage et metteur en scène du jeu théâtral qu'il a lui-même créé présente un défi encore plus séduisant, parce que les contributions dans les pages des blogues ou dans Facebook doivent être lues comme on lit celles de nos amis ou collègues

NOTE 3

Le fait de publier son carnet de voyage en ligne à travers le blogue *Voyages – Voyages* participe au phénomène de mise en avant du récit personnel, en conservant une trace visible de ses trajets, et démontre aussi une volonté de partage d'une expérience personnelle : **http://mesjournaux.canalblog.com/archives/lisbonne/index.html**.

de chair et d'os, c'est-à-dire en suivant le même protocole de lecture. Et pourquoi un auteur qui prône si ouvertement la desubjectivation autorielle est si intéressé à exposer des traits autobiographiques ou des images de sa vie quotidienne ? Il n'y a pas de réponse univoque à cette question, mais étant donné qu'il veut représenter son rôle dans cette dramaturgie hétéronymique, l'écriture de soi doit être vue comme une partie de la mise en scène[3].

La Disparition du Général Proust ou *Un Monde Incertain* épousent également la remédiatisation qui s'impose au numérique par le biais de la liaison des contenus et de la coprésence de plusieurs médias[4]. Le numérique a créé des conditions pour la réintégration des flux de données optiques, acoustiques et écrites, en effaçant la traditionnelle séparation analogique des moyens. Cette recombinaison d'éléments sous forme de collections d'objets numériques modulaires donne naissance à des formes hybrides. Les médias numériques ont même reconfiguré la manière dont nous appliquons des techniques de remix telles que le collage, la citation ou le *sampling*, comprenant un code procédural qui est lui-même un *mash-up* (Navas **2012**; Gunkel **2016**). En outre, la prédominance d'un support qui efface ses propres moyens de production suggère qu'on ne peut plus vénérer le modèle original et il nous faut reconceptualiser la notion d'auteur, en demandant comment elle fonctionne dans le contexte d'un moyen qui peut isoler un élément et le réécrire comme infiniment reproductible et malléable. Il faut reconnaître que l'auteur est de moins en moins, dans ce contexte, un point d'origine bien défini et qu'on assiste à la prolifération de modes de production composites. La « culture remix » est une composante intégral de la manière dont nous utilisons les nouveaux médias et, en tant que telle, un trait distinctif de l'époque contemporaine. Dans cette perspective, l'hybridisme remixé est presque obligatoire, car c'est la base pour participer à une culture vivante et connectée au monde. En fait, la variété des propos de Balpe est très étendue, mais l'on y reconnaît des caractéristiques identiques à l'ethos des mouvements d'avant-garde et d'expérimentation artistique[5].

NOTE 4

C'est ce qu'on peut voir, par exemple, dans la production des hétéronymes Oriane Proust (*Questions* (Saison 1, Épisode 6 : **https://www.youtube.com/watch?v=jBshKxzk4I**)) et Rachel Charlus (*Écritures* (Saison 1, Épisode 5 : **https://www.youtube.com/watch?v=05fWO631R8**) ou *Poètes* (Saison 1, Épisode 4 : **https://www.youtube.com/watch?v=xep_Eul2aGI**)).

NOTE 5

Si l'on se rend sur le site de l'auteur, on peut voir une explication convaincante à ce propos dans le texte « La vie en jeux » : « les espaces virtuels sont un extraordinaire champ ouvert à ce qui me paraît être une forme nouvelle de création littéraire et que toute nouvelle innovation dans le monde des outils de communication est susceptible de produire d'autres modalités de textualisation. Sortir enfin de l'enfermement littéraire du roman pour aller vers autre chose qui me semble bien relever du littéraire mais d'un littéraire non encore identifié comme tel » (Balpe **2018**).

Au moment où les outils d'écriture deviennent de plus en plus soumis à la logique de l'opacité, de la capitalisation et du contrôle cybernétique, les pratiques littéraires exigent un espace d'autonomie renforcé. En effet, le texte est maintenant un élément logé dans un système qui le transcende et dont la logistique n'est pas forcément compatible avec la sphère littéraire et artistique. Les pratiques mêmes des médias dont nous jouissons, les pratiques qui nous relient aux autres s'approprient et reconfigurent nos aspirations en les transformant en des nouvelles formes d'exploitation et de contrôle. Si nous disposons de moyens techniques comme jamais auparavant, d'un autre côté le degré d'opacité et de dissimulation des pouvoirs qui déterminent les conditions de notre vie est plus fort aujourd'hui qu'il ne l'a jamais été. C'est précisément dans ce contexte qu'on peut situer l'innovante et transgressive appropriation balpienne des nouveaux moyens de communication en ligne. Que ce soit par la déconstruction du profil d'utilisateur de Facebook ancré sur des traces réelles en proposant une communauté d'hétéronymes, par la publication régulière de contenus automatiquement générés qui provoquent un effet de saturation dans le paysage médiatique, ou encore par le contraste entre les procédures algorithmiques utilisées dans la production artistique et celles des grandes plateformes du Web (Gillespie **2014**; Cardon **2018**), on peut bien reconnaître la nature transgressive de ce type de projet.

NOTE 6

À propos du lien entre l'automaticité algorithmique et les problématiques du capitalisme contemporain, il faut tenir en compte l'opinion de Tarleton Gillespie : « as we have embraced computational tools as our primary media of expression, and have made not just mathematics but all information digital, we are subjecting human discourse and knowledge to these procedural logics that undergird all computation. And there are specific implications when we use algorithms to select what is most relevant from a corpus of data composed of traces of our activities, preferences, and expressions. These algorithms, which I'll call public *relevance algorithms*, are–by the very same mathematical procedures–producing and certifying knowledge. The algorithmic assessment of information, then, represents a particular *knowledge logic*, one built on specific presumptions about what knowledge is and how one should identify its most relevant components » (Gillespie 2014).

Son propos est plutôt « pharmacologique » (Stiegler **2012**, **2013**), dans le sens où l'auteur comprend les objets techniques comme étant à la fois un poison et un remède. Le « poison » des technologies numériques se rapporte au contrôle de la catégorisation : le pouvoir d'établir les critères qui régissent les catégories des choses, c'est le pouvoir d'établir les lieux et les relations de (et entre) ces choses, et par conséquent leurs sens et valeurs. Dans les sociétés contemporaines, ce pouvoir réside dans le contrôle des métadonnées produites par la trace de tout geste numérique : « Ce que l'on appelle les *big data* désigne un nouvel âge de la catégorisation, computationnel, mis en œuvre par la modélisation, la visualisation et la simulation effectuées à partir de très vastes bases de données, elles-mêmes produites en temps réel par l'activité des gens et des agents, y compris artificiels, et par l'intermédiaire d'organes eux-mêmes artificiels » (Stiegler 2013). Selon la logique du capitalisme linguistique de Google et d'autres compagnies, il faut inciter les utilisateurs à s'exprimer plus pour en capter le flux langagier[6]. La solution avancée par Bernard Stiegler consiste à réclamer le contrôle des métadonnées qui alimentent la société de l'information. Le vertige de la surproduction de contenus et de toutes formes d'accumulation suscitées par les dispositifs techniques de l'ère numérique appelle nécessairement la problématisation (et la reconfiguration) de la dynamique mémorielle.

4.

Pénétrées par la culture numérique, les pratiques littéraires et artistiques tendent à problématiser les conditions de leur matérialisation concrète, mais il faut considérer ici une autre dimension (auto)réflexive qui transcende l'horizon des objets proprement dits. Il s'agit d'une réflexion personnelle de l'auteur ou de l'artiste et qui peut constituer, pour le lecteur critique, non une fermeture du sens mais une ouverture, parce qu'elle fonctionne comme méta-lecture des motivations et des défis du projet de création. Il est significatif à cet égard que Jean-Pierre Balpe et Grégory Chatonsky, comme tant d'autres créateurs dans le contexte international de la littérature et des arts numériques (assez souvent des professeurs universitaires et des chercheurs), aient privilégié l'articulation de l'expression artistique et de l'activité de recherche en tant que « recherche-création ».

Dans un texte réflexif publié en 2016 sous le titre « Face à l'hyperproductivisme », Chatonsky identifiait l'hyperproduction et l'afflux comme des points de repère pour son analyse de l'accumulation compulsive (ou excessive) dans le contexte des formes artistiques contemporaines et des conséquences que cela entraîne sur l'acte de perception. À partir de trois projets différents et appartenant à des étapes bien définies, mais dominés tous par des technologies génératives, il soulignait son travail sur les procédures permettant d'automatiser des séries de processus. Dans un premier temps, avec le projet *Incident of the Last Century 1999: Sampling Sarajevo* (1998) (http://chatonsky.net/sarajevo/), Chatonsky utilisait les techniques de sampling (comme l'indique le titre même) pour rassembler des fragments retirés de la production médiatique et culturelle concernant cette ville bosniaque et offrir au public le résultat final de façon aléatoire, randomisée. On pourrait évoquer à ce propos la « culture remix » des nouveaux médias. Plus tard, le parcours de recherche a mené à des travaux comme *Waiting* (2007) (**http://chatonsky.net/waiting/**) dont l'objectif était de mobiliser les ressources du *big data*, en utilisant notamment des phrases extraites de Twitter ou des photographies de Flickr et présentées sur des vidéos dans une gare. Tout en s'appropriant ces matériaux, il s'arroge le droit de décontextualiser des plateformes Web extérieurs au projet, bouleversant du coup leur signification première. Cette stratégie de déplacement et d'appropriation des contenus met en lumière la porosité du numérique et du réseau. Une autre dimension est, finalement, accomplie par un projet dont nous parlerons plus en détail – *Capture* (2009) (**http://chatonsky.net/capture/**) – que ce soit par son importance au niveau des pratiques de générativité ou par l'ouverture à la participation de plusieurs artistes : Olivier Alary, Jean-Pierre Balpe, Dominique Sirois, Nicolas Reeves.

Plusieurs remarques viennent à l'esprit à la suite de ces exemples. La plus générale touche à ce qu'ils peuvent apprendre sur les différentes conceptualisations du système génératif qui produit d'infinies instanciations à partir de la recombinaison d'un nombre limité d'éléments. En plus, ces travaux ont en commun une même caractéristique : l'utilisateur a toujours du mal (ou n'arrive même pas) à faire le tour des objets, des textes ou des images, parce que l'ensemble se recompose à chaque consultation. Il vaut la peine de reprendre l'argumentation proposée par Chatonsky à ce sujet :

> L'hyperproductivisme est le versant matérialiste et artistique d'une politique accélérationniste. Il se distingue du consumérisme du siècle dernier de plusieurs façons : il s'intéresse moins à la réception (consommation) qu'à l'émission (production). Il n'est pas fondé sur la production d'un même objet (standard industriel) pour une grande quantité d'individus, mais sur des modèles qui peuvent se décliner dans des séries d'objets variables, de sorte qu'il y a autant d'objets différents qu'il y a des consommateurs. (Chatonsky **2016b**)

Dans le but d'approfondir sa recherche et de dégager les problèmes qui affectent le monde contemporain, Chatonsky s'est consacré de plus en plus à l'étude et à l'utilisation de techniques de *machine learning* (ou intelligence artificielle non-directionnelle) et de réseaux de neurones artificiels. Une machine qui « apprend » à développer une base de données au-delà de ses limites peut offrir encore davantage de possibilités en matière d'automatisation de la production culturelle. C'est la perméabilité du système qui lui permet ce devenir génératif de déploiement, de recombinaison et d'autoréplication. Les réseaux neuronaux artificiels sont des exemples de ce type de programmation ouverte et avec une dynamique émergente, où les algorithmes « apprennent » et « se développent » de manière autonome à partir d'une entrée programmatique initiale. Ainsi, basé sur les derniers développements des réseaux de neurones et la mise à disposition par Google et Facebook de codes sources de *deep learning*, le logiciel Deep s'inspire des créations humaines (dans ce cas, de dessins que Chatonsky a réalisé entre 1992 et 2016, mais aussi de livres d'apprentissage du dessin) pour produire des images que seule une machine a la capacité de générer. Encore une fois : le rythme de production de la machine dépasse les capacités humaines, de sorte que personne ne verra tout ce qu'elle produit (http://chatonsky.net/really-you/).

Par des voies nécessairement différentes par rapport à ce qu'on avait vu à propos de Balpe, Chatonsky travaille aussi l'absence de finitude et d'horizon déterminé. Il ne s'agit plus de choix dans un parcours prédéterminé, comme serait le cas d'un récit hypertextuel, mais d'actualisations toujours originales d'un parcours : l'expérienciation esthétique n'est plus confrontée au nombre de choix mais à l'inédit.

Le projet *Capture* (2009-) propose une machine algorithmique capable de produire un flux ininterrompu de musiques, d'images, de textes et d'autres objets dérivés. Un ensemble de programmes génératifs permet de recueillir des données sur le Web et de poster automatiquement les nouveaux éléments à mesure qu'ils sont générés, en créant un effet de saturation sur les réseaux sociaux. Chaque nouveau fichier est unique et la série à laquelle il appartient est illimitée. En conséquence, l'acte de consommation ne pourra jamais accompagner le rythme hallucinant et continu de la production numérique de ce groupe (fictif) de musique : au moment même où une pièce apparait, une autre est déjà produite et ainsi de suite. Personne ne peut tout écouter, lire ou voir, ce qui contribue à créer un écart significatif entre le temps de la production numérique et le temps de la perception humaine. Ce projet de « netrock génératif » est une façon de penser, d'un point de vue critique, les implications sociales et culturelles des flux ininterrompus, aussi bien que le fonctionnement des industries culturelles. D'après le texte de présentation, le potentiel ironique est entièrement assumé, étant donné qu'on y déclare contribuer à résoudre ou à atténuer la crise des industries culturelles et créatives, particulièrement celle de la musique à cause des téléchargements illicites de fichiers. Quand un internaute consulte ou télécharge un fichier mp3, ce même fichier sera automatiquement effacé du serveur, ce qui revient à dire que l'internaute est le seul capable de le diffuser par la suite, s'il le veut. On voit ici l'inversion du système normal de production et de consommation, parce que le récepteur est investi du rôle d'agent diffuseur d'un exemplaire unique. En provoquant un effet de surproduction (un seul élément est à l'origine d'une série quasi-infinie d'autres éléments par dérivation successive), les technologies génératives utilisées dans le cadre du projet ouvrent un débat autour du consumérisme d'objets culturels et des politiques d'archivage électronique. En outre, comme le souligne l'artiste dans un texte intitulé « La mémoire des machines (auto/matisation/mobilisation/mmunisation) » :

> du fait de la tra(ns)duction qui articule les signes dépourvus de sens à des significations possibles, on ne cesse de produire par transformations successives. Toute inscription devient un matériel utilisable pour créer de nouvelles inscriptions, l'archive devient dès lors récursive et quasi-infinie. Ceci entraîne une saturation autophagique qui amène les phénomènes à un état intensif.

Ultimement, la dynamique d'accumulation renforce les liens avec l'ensemble du Web. Perspective toute borgésienne, sans doute, mais qui permet de comprendre un trait fondamental de cette œuvre, à savoir l'imaginaire de la base de données dont elle témoigne, son évolutivité marquée tant par la modularité des contenus que par leur variabilité. Non par hasard, Netrock Capture est un projet qui fait appel aussi à des réseaux sociaux comme Facebook ou Twitter pour diffuser des messages et images, en invitant à une interaction plus proche avec les utilisateurs (ou les fans)[7]. Balpe lui-même a collaboré à ce projet à travers la création de générateurs automatiques de paroles, de biographies et de critiques de disques capables de produire en quantité illimitée.

NOTE 7
https://www.facebook.com/netrock.capture
https://vimeo.com/154141190

Ce qui rend plus fascinant encore le travail de Chatonsky et de Balpe, bien que les deux artistes appartiennent à des générations différentes et ont des motivations artistiques spécifiques, c'est le même désir de mettre à l'épreuve le phénomène de surproduction de notre époque à partir de deux grands axes : celui de la générativité logicielle, qui peut produire une quantité illimitée d'objets (textes, images, vidéos, musiques) en flux continu; et celui plus récent de la quantité colossale de données qui résultent de l'activité humaine dans le réseau (ou ce que l'on appelle couramment *big data*). Dans le dernier cas, la réponse de la communauté intellectuelle et artistique à l'appropriation et à la marchandisation de toute trace humaine dans le réseau menées par les entreprises technologiques se fait par l'usage de techniques de re-signification de ces pratiques et de ce flux d'information dans un contexte de création. Son extension est presque illimitée, comme dans la première situation, dans la mesure où le rythme de production et de renouvellement de données excède notre capacité d'appréhension.

Ce n'est pas un hasard, en effet, si Chatonsky interroge et revisite de plus en plus les *affordances* des réseaux sociaux (Facebook, Twitter, Instagram) en ce faisant promoteur d'une approche disruptive : la fictionnalisation de soi qui permettrait de créer une rupture entre le vrai profil d'un individu et les contenus qui ne correspondent pas à l'expression d'une vie (et, donc, ne servent à rien). L'objectif majeur de cette approche ? Introduire un peu de contingence et d'incertitude dans l'ensemble des données mises gratuitement à disposition des grandes entreprises grâce au désir incontrôlable d'écrire, de commenter et d'intervenir. Ces entreprises ne fournissent que le support, puisque les contenus sont le résultat de la contribution gratuite des utilisateurs. Tout repose sur une économie de l'attention, du voyeurisme et de la traçabilité numérique qui exige, pour bien fonctionner, une correspondance directe avec le monde réel. Comme a bien souligné l'auteur dans un texte récent intitulé « Pouvoirs de la fiction à l'ère des réseaux sociaux » :

> Ce serait un renversement économique parce que nous utiliserions le temps de leur machine, mais ils ne pourraient rien tirer de nos données parce que celles-ci ne seraient pas corrélables au monde extérieur. On ne pourrait pas y faire retour ou alors il faudrait qu'ils interprètent nos fictions pour les ramener à nos vies et cela prendrait un temps infini, ils se perdraient dans des labyrinthes herméneutiques. Ils seraient enfermés dans leur boîte noire. (**http://chatonsky.net/fiction-sociale/**)

En s'écartant des sentiers battus, Chatonsky peut renverser en termes disruptifs l'utilisation des moyens et reconsidérer la problématique (et les paradoxes) de la trace en contexte numérique (Rifkin **2005**; Lordon **2010**).

En outre, les imaginaires de la ruine, de l'obsolescence, de l'érosion de la matérialité des dispositifs, de l'effacement, ainsi que de la disparition ont une présence prépondérante dans son œuvre. Le problème de la perte des supports et des données trouve une forme privilégiée dans des projets comme *Notre mémoire* (2011) (**https://vimeo.com/31630504**), par l'utilisation d'un disque dur en panne qui génère du bruit et qui va permettre de sélectionner des images dans la base de données de Flickr, ou encore, d'une manière encore plus radicale comme *Telofossils* (2013) (**http://chatonsky.net/telofossils/**), une installation préparée en collaboration avec Dominique Sirois, qui se présente comme un exercice spéculatif sur une archéologie (possible) de notre civilisation après sa propre disparition. Une telle approche permet de révéler les effets catastrophiques de l'innovation technologique sous la forme de structures fossilisées qui gardent en mémoire les artéfacts de notre temps.

5.

Un des liens les plus forts entre les travaux de Balpe et de Chatonsky est l'exploitation des possibilités de diffusion du texte génératif en articulation avec le concept de surproduction (ou de saturation informative) qui révèle toute la question des modes de conservation et du fonctionnement de la mémoire à l'âge numérique.

On a pu observer, chez Jean-Pierre Balpe, l'émergence de pratiques d'écriture en ligne où la figure auctorielle se met en scène, jouant des tensions entre l'auteur, les hétéronymes, le personnage d'écrivain et la personne elle-même. On dirait que l'auteur à l'ère numérique quitte peu à peu sa position traditionnelle d'utilisateur des instruments scripturaux pour investir de plus en plus celle de concepteur, à la recherche d'une expérience d'écriture qui est à la hauteur des attentes et des nouvelles possibilités offertes. L'agent humain, qui n'est impliqué qu'au deuxième degré dans le processus de création, se présente comme un « Méta-auteur » (Balpe **1994**) et même le régime de coopérativité lectorielle se modifie sous l'effet de la multiplicité mouvante des textes. En outre, les interfaces numériques contemporaines font naître de nouvelles possibilités esthétiques basées sur le réseau, le flux, le partage et la recombinaison d'éléments qui sont largement explorées au sein du système hétéronymique établi par Balpe.

Mais, revenons une fois de plus sur les notions d'infini et de surproduction. Produire une œuvre inépuisable et éphémère met en évidence les limites de la perception humaine, de la capacité d'adaptation du sujet et, à un autre niveau, la fragilité de la mémoire collective. Par la surproduction culturelle et par la dissémination à large échelle de données et d'informations numériques, la mémoire collective s'hypertrophie, mais en même temps devient plus fragile à cause d'un système de rétention effectué à court terme, qui la conduit à l'éphémère. Dans une écologie médiatique si surchargé par une quantité de traces provenant de gestes singuliers, on peut se demander comment sera-t-il possible d'éviter la précarité de la mémoire et d'assurer des conditions d'archivage dans le futur.

Les ruptures que le numérique a pu induire en termes de pratiques de communication, de consommation et de production ont fortement transformé le principe et les modalités d'écriture, contribuant à diminuer la distance entre l'acte de création et le contact direct avec l'œuvre. Beaucoup d'artistes et de créateurs mènent aujourd'hui une réflexion sur les ambivalences associées aux nouvelles possibilités d'inscription de la mémoire : d'une part, la fragilité de la mémoire collective et des processus d'archivage à travers la manifestation d'une esthétique de l'éphémère; d'autre part, la surabondance de données et la prolifération de contenus dans ce flux infini que constitue le Web, qui posent des problèmes de sélection et, par conséquent, de sédimentation lente des connaissances. Ce caractère massif du numérique (souligné, d'ailleurs, par le potentiel infini des technologies génératives) a conduit à un débordement de la mémoire qui peu à peu engouffre le monde, car elle grandit plus vite que notre capacité d'appréhension. Comme l'indique Chatonsky dans une interview (« L'art comme archéologie du futur »), on vit « la première époque dans laquelle les anonymes sont mémorisés. Le paradoxe bien sûr c'est que cette mémoire numérique devient excessive et pour ainsi dire amnésique parce qu'elle nous submerge. L'inscription, qui est habituellement distincte de la destruction, devient une forme de destruction ». (Chatonsky, Kevin **2013**). Dans tous ces cas, il s'agit en effet de penser (et de transformer) le rapport à notre finitude à travers la production de multiples formes d'infinitude.

Aragon, Louis. 1981. *Je n'ai jamais appris à écrire ou Les incipit.* Paris : Flammarion.

Balpe, Jean-Pierre. 1994. « Méta-auteur ». 1994. http://articlesdejpbalpe.blogspot.com/2013/06/meta-auteur.html.

Balpe, Jean-Pierre. 2000. *Contextes de l'art numérique.* Paris : Hermès Science Europe.

Balpe, Jean-Pierre. 2017. « Ontologie du texte littéraire génératif ». 2017. Consulté le 30 avril 2019. http://articlesdejpbalpe.blogspot.com/2017/10/x-ontologie-du-texte-litteraire.html.

Balpe, Jean-Pierre. 2018. « La vie en jeux ». 2018. Consulté le 30 avril 2019. http://articlesdejpbalpe.blogspot.com/2018/05/0-false-21-18-pt-18-pt-0-0-false-false.html.

Bell, Alice. 2016. « Interactional Metalepsis and Unnatural Narratology ». *Narrative* 24 (3):294-310.

Bourassa, Renée. 2012. « Enjeux de la mémoire : entre hypermnésie et oubli ». In *Le sujet digital : l'hypermnésie,* dirigé par Pierre Cassou-Noguèz, Claire Larsonneur, et Arnaud Régnault. Paris : Les Presses du réel.

Bourassa, Renée. 2013. « Hypermnésie et esthétique de l'éphémère numérique : les paradoxes de la trace ». 2013. https://www.academia.edu/3879245/Hypermn%C3%A9sie_et_esth%C3%A9tique_de_l%C3%A9ph%C3%A9m%C3%A8re_num%C3%A9rique_les_paradoxes_de_la_trace

Cardon, Dominique. 2018. « Le pouvoir des algorithmes ». *Pouvoirs* 164 (1):63-73.

Chatonsky, Grégory. 2016a. « Esthétique des flux (Après le numérique) ». Thèse de doctorat, Montréal : Université du Québec à Montréal.

Chatonsky, Grégory. 2016b. « Face à l'hyperproductivisme ». 2016. Consulté le 30 avril 2019. http://chatonsky.net/hyperproduction/.

Chatonsky, Grégory. s. d. « La mémoire des machines (auto/matisation/mobilisation/immunisation) ». Consulté le 30 avril 2019. https://www.academia.edu/25678922/La_m%C3%A9moire_des_machines_auto_matisation_mobilisation_immunisation.

Chatonsky, Grégory, et Kevin Thome de Souza. 2013. « L'art comme archéologie du futur ». *Amusement,* février. http://chatonsky.net/files/pdf/presse/%5BINTERVIEW%5D%20Gr%C3%A9gory%20Chatonsky,%20l'art%20comme%20une%20arch%C3%A9ologie%20du%20futur%20_%20AMUSEMENT.pdf.

Ernst, Wolfgang. 2012. *Digital Memory and the Archive.* Minneapolis : University of Minnesota Press.

Gillespie, Tarleton. 2014. « The relevance of algorithms ». In *Media Technologies. Essays on Communication, Materiality, and Society,* dirigé par Tarleton Gillespie, Pablo Boczkowski, et Kirsten Foot. Cambridge, MA : MIT Press.

Gunkel, David. 2016. *Of Remixology. Ethics and Aesthetics After Remix.* Cambridge, MA : The MIT Press.

Lordon, Frédéric. 2010. *Capitalisme, désir et servitude.* Paris : La Fabrique Éditions.

Navas, Eduardo. 2012. *Remix Theory. The Aesthetics of Sampling.* Vienne : Springer.

Pier, John. 2013. « Metalepsis ». In *The Living Handbbook of Narratology*, dirigé par Peter Hühn. Hamburg : Hamburg University Press.
https://www.lhn.uni-hamburg.de/node/51.html.

Rettberg, Jill Walker. 2004. « Distributed Narrative: Telling Stories Across Networks ». 2004. Consulté le 30 avril 2019.
http://jilltxt.net/txt/Walker-AoIR-3500words.pdf.

Rifkin, Jeremy. 2005. *L'âge de l'accès : La nouvelle culture du capitalisme.* Paris : Éditions La Découverte.

Stiegler, Bernard. 2012. « Relational Ecology and the Digital Pharmakon ». *Culture Machine* 13.

Stiegler, Bernard. 2013. « Autonomie et automatisation dans l'épistémè numérique ». In *Contribution au colloque de l'ANR Rencontres du numérique.* Consulté le 30 avril 2019.
https://anr.fr/Colloques/RencontresduNumerique/fichiers/Steigler.pdf.

Partie / Part 3

PLATEFORMES ET NARRATIONS

PLATFORMS AND NARRATIVES

PART 3

PLATEFORMES ET NARRATIONS
PLATFORMS AND NARRATIVES

RPG Maker as an E-Literature Platform

ROMAN KALINOVSKI

Abstract

Before game engines such as Unity and Game Maker made hobbyist and amateur game development widely accessible, there was *RPG Maker* for the Sony PlayStation. During its heyday between 1999 and 2002, many burgeoning game developers connected with each other in various online communities centered around RPGM development. This paper looks at *RPG Maker*'s specific affordances and limitations and how they are connected to those of its host platform, the original Sony PlayStation, specifically the combination of CD-ROM technology and removable flash memory cards. Because of these limitations, games made with *RPG Maker* tended to fall into two categories: those that uncritically embraced the RPG genre's tropes, and those that attempted to draw attention to these tropes in an ironic manner. This paper examines two works made with *RPG Maker* that fall into each of these categories, and argues that they, along with similar works, should be viewed as works of electronic literature rather than as games due to the fact that their literary value, rather than any ludic uniqueness, is the main differentiating factor between them.

Résumé

Avant que les moteurs de jeu tels que Unity et Game Maker ne rendent le développement de jeux amateurs largement accessible, il existait *RPG Maker* pour la PlayStation de Sony. Pendant son âge d'or entre 1999 et 2002, de nombreux développeurs de jeux se sont connectés les uns aux autres dans des communautés en ligne centrées autour du développement RPGM. Cet article examine les moyens et les limites spécifiques de *RPG Maker* et comment ils sont liés à ceux de sa plateforme hôte, la PlayStation originale de Sony, en particulier la combinaison de la technologie CD-ROM et des cartes mémoire flash amovibles. En raison de ces limitations, les jeux créés avec *RPG Maker* avaient tendance à se classer en deux catégories : ceux qui endossaient sans critique les tropes du genre RPG et ceux qui tentaient d'attirer l'attention sur ces tropes de manière ironique. Cet article examine deux œuvres réalisées avec *RPG Maker* qui relèvent de chacune de ces catégories et argumente qu'elles devraient, comme d'autres œuvres similaires, être vues comme des œuvres de littérature électronique, au lieu de simples jeux, parce que leur valeur littéraire, plutôt que leur unicité ludique, était le facteur principal qui les distinguait.

The turn of the millennium was a prehistoric era for indie, amateur, and hobbyist game development. While today creators of all levels of experience can access a wide variety of powerful tools, like Unity and Game Maker Studio, and use platforms like Steam and Itch.io to distribute their creations, such technologies are a recent occurrence; an aspiring game maker in 2000 or 2001 had far fewer options available. For some in that era, *RPG Maker* for the Sony PlayStation was the best, or perhaps only, outlet for their digital creativity. *RPG Maker* was an odd piece of software that allowed users to create and play role-playing games despite not providing—or even suggesting—any means of sharing or distributing such creations. Despite these limitations, online communities sprung up to allow *RPG Maker* enthusiasts to interact, and solutions were found that allowed games made on the platform to be distributed online.

RPG Maker, as a platform for the creation of games, has many affordances and limitations inherited from the platform on which it runs, the Sony PlayStation. Lacking online connectivity and allowing users to save only small amounts of data at a time, it is a feat of creative programming that anything resembling a functional game engine could run under these constraints at all. This paper will examine the particular affordances of *RPG Maker*, how the PlayStation hardware constrained what users could make using this software, and, by examining two examples of *RPG Maker* creations, theorize about the platform's potential as an outlet for electronic literature rather than for works that could be commonly considered games.

The Sony PlayStation was not supposed to be a standalone game console in the first place. What ended up as the PlayStation started out as a joint venture between Sony and Nintendo to create a CD-ROM peripheral for the Super Famicom game console. "The initial idea was to connect a CD player to the Super Famicom using an external digital interface, but the specifications were later changed to include a built-in CD drive" (Asakura **2000**, 32). The two corporations were unable to strike a bargain over the peripheral's development and their already delicate alliance fell apart. Having already spent considerable time and money engineering this device, Sony ended up developing it as their own standalone game console to compete with similar offerings from Nintendo and Sega. The PlayStation, released in Japan in 1994 and abroad the following year, turned Sony into a major player in the videogame market.

One disadvantage of CD-ROMs is the fact that they are a read-only medium. This presents a problem for video games, since most games need to save the player's data between play sessions. Previous generations of game consoles used battery-backed SRAM on each individual ROM cartridge to hold a player's data, but this was not possible with CDs. Sony ended up releasing proprietary memory cards for the PlayStation. Each card had 128 kilobytes of flash memory, a miniscule amount even back in the early 1990s when the system was designed. Each card is divided into 15 "blocks" of 8 kilobytes each, with the remaining space used as an index of the card's contents. When the PlayStation was first released, most games that supported the memory cards used only a single block to store a few variables or a high-score table. As games became increasingly complex they began using multiple blocks at once, with some games (including *RPG Maker*) potentially taking up entire memory cards. *RPG Maker* is thus a synthesis of the affordances of CD-ROM and flash memory technology: large amounts of non-editable assets could be stored on the disc, and user-created games consisting mainly of pointers to these assets could be stored compactly on memory cards without running out of space too quickly.

While memory cards could be physically transported and used to transfer data between systems, was it possible to share this data online, removed from the physical limitations of individual cards? A book written in the immediate aftermath of the PlayStation era, *Gaming Hacks* by Simon Carless, examines multiple ways to copy data from memory cards to a PC:

> The DexDrive from the now defunct Interact is by far the most common PlayStation 1 memory card copying device. […] Connect the DexDrive to the serial port on your PC, load the Windows-compatible software, and then back up entire PlayStation 1 memory cards as *.GME* files. You can then email these to your friends, trade them on the Internet, or store them on your PC for when your memory card inevitably fails. A lot of third-party PlayStation memory cards really *are* of poor quality and will corrupt and lose entire cards worth of games (Carless **2005**, 402-3).

Carless went on to describe more arcane methods, like a do-it-yourself solution that could be built from off-the-shelf parts, but concluded that the DexDrive was the most straightforward and convenient method of backing up memory card data. The *RPG Maker* community agreed with this sentiment, as the DexDrive was the most popular way for creators to share their RPGs with each other online.

The process of playing an *RPG Maker* game in the early 2000s was a ritual of circumventing the limitations of a number of hardware and software platforms. The first step was to download a memory card image from a site like *RPG Maker Pavilion* that allowed creators to upload their games for distribution. These were almost always distributed as compressed .ZIP or .RAR files, because many games used multiple image files that needed to be downloaded at the same time, so programs like WinZip or WinRAR had to be used to extract the .GME image files from their protective wrapper. Once decompressed, the card images were opened, one by one, in Dexplorer, the DexDrive's proprietary file transfer program. The user then inserted a memory card into the DexDrive and flashed the image onto it. This process was repeated with multiple cards if required by the game. Once all the cards had been flashed with the proper images, *RPG Maker* was booted up on the PlayStation and the option to play an existing game was selected. Any memory cards plugged into the system were automatically searched for *RPG Maker* data files and a list of available games was displayed. Upon selecting one, the game's associated files were sought, and if any were not found, the user was prompted to insert the proper memory card that contained them. Because the PlayStation can only have two memory cards inserted at once, a game spread across three or more cards had to be loaded in a certain order prompted by the system: the system data was loaded first, followed by any custom art assets and the initial scenario data.

Failure was possible at any point during this loading process, and the dreaded "FAILED" message was not an uncommon sight among *RPG Maker* enthusiasts back in its heyday. In the early 2000s, flash memory was more unreliable than it is today:

> It would be a mistake to assume that flash drives demonstrate the possibility of storage without materiality. "Because they are written by forcing electrons through a layer of electrical insulation onto a floating transistor gate, re-writable ROMs will only withstand a limited number of write cycles before the insulation is permanently damaged. In very old EAROMs, this damage could occur in as few as 1,000 write cycles. In modern flash EEPROMs, this life may be in excess of 10,000 or even 100,000 cycles, but it is by no means infinite" (Kirschenbaum **2012**, 106-07).

Due to the quantity of spare memory cards needed to play (and create) multiple games at once, and the fact that many *RPG Maker* users were teenagers spending their parents' money or their own limited funds, the cheapest possible memory cards–knockoffs or pre-owned or both–tended to be used for transferring data. The DexDrive images memory cards exactly, byte-by-byte, so any flaws in the flash memory would have been maintained in these images, resulting in a failed loading process and the potential loss of data.

There are two types of data that can be created in *RPG Maker* (aside from custom art assets, which are not created in the main editor). The first is called system data, which represents a database of assets that can be manipulated and strung together by the second data type, scenario data, to make a playable game. System data contains a game's playable characters and their numerical statistics, every item these characters can use or equip, every magic spell they can cast, every enemy they can fight, and every map they can visit. Without scenario data, though, all this information is useless. A game's scenario data contains all the event scripting, narrative text, and triggers for player interaction. It represents an arrangement of the system data (which, itself, is an arrangement of the content provided on the disc). A playable game needs system data and at least one scenario to run. Each relies on the other: System data does nothing unless activated by a scenario, and scenario data cannot do anything without assets to manipulate.

The division of data into these two types is a clever way to maximize the PlayStation's very limited memory card space. One instance of system data can support any number of scenarios, provided they are properly strung together. A lengthy *RPG Maker* game could have many memory cards worth of scenario data, all of them tied to a single system data file. Because it contains the game's text, which tends to be voluminous in even simple RPGs, scenario data quickly fills up. If text was stored alongside system data, this would create a conflict between the game's raw assets and its gameplay and story: as more is written, the space for maps and assets would decrease. Because of the division of data into system and scenario, however, such a zero-sum situation is avoided.

RPG Maker allowed users to create role-playing games in the style of then-popular 1990s series, such as *Dragon Quest* and *Final Fantasy*. Graphics were limited to a top-down, bird's eye perspective for moving characters around the world, first-person perspective battles against static enemies, text-based menus for inventory manipulation, and point-and-click world maps to connect various navigable areas. Without major work-arounds, creators were stuck with these default modes of play, and what work-arounds were possible generally provided a less engaging experience that felt more like an obvious hack than an actual game.

Because of the lack of variety, the main differentiating factor between *RPG Maker* creations became narrative rather than ludic. All *RPG Maker* games, for the most part, played the same. What made one creation stand out from another was the unique story each one told. For this reason, it could be useful to look at *RPG Maker*, and the creations made with it, from the perspective of electronic literature. This is not to say that all–or any–games made with *RPG Maker* were exceptional literary works. As amateur creations by a mainly teenage user base, most of these games either mindlessly repeated the RPG genre's fundamental clichés or ham-handedly tried to parody them. This paper will examine examples of both of these approaches: the first is a derivative RPG that does not stray far from the genre's tropes, and the other is a non-interactive game that tries too hard to poke fun at its own origins.

SILENT VOICES[1] by David Vincent (**2000**) is an example of a game that takes the former approach by only using the default assets included with *RPG Maker* and does not try to push the platform towards new or uncomfortable territory, whether technical or narrative. It tells the story of two lovers, David and Athena, who, on their way to their wedding in the city of Breslin, get caught up in a struggle for the control of a cosmic artifact called the Earth Crystal. The map design alternates between bland wide-open spaces that provide no clear sense of direction, and twisting mazes also without a clear sense of direction. Navigation of these spaces is not helped by the random battles that occur after every few steps. *SILENT VOICES* may be the closest it is possible for an *RPG Maker* game to get to complete cliché without becoming an overt parody of the genre's conventions. The game's most outstanding attribute is the fact that all its text is written in capitals; even with a title like *SILENT VOICES*, the characters seem to be shouting a lot.

NOTE 1

By some miracle, as of the time of writing (mid-April 2019) there is a server online that has *SILENT VOICES* (among other *RPG Maker* titles) available for download: an early version of *RPG Maker Pavilion* that was hosted by Tripod and was never taken down when the site migrated to what was then thought to be a more stable server in late 2000. Ironically, history has shown the opposite to be true, since the Tripod site is the only version of *Pavilion* still operational despite some missing graphics and broken links. The page featuring *SILENT VOICES* can be found at this Link.

On the opposite side of this spectrum is *Man Getting Hit in the Groin By a Football RPG: Featuring–Ernest Borgnine* by "Misled Jeff," who uses this platform–meant for sprawling, epic fantasies–to create a short non-interactive slapstick sketch. Both of these games were largely ignored by the online *RPG Maker* community at the time of their release. The former was seen as too generic and frustrating to play to be of any note, and the latter held no lasting interest after any initial chuckles had subsided. Even so, they represent opposite approaches to platform engagement and narrativity and have become interesting as examples of what *RPG Maker* as a platform can, or cannot, accomplish.

RPG Maker games, such as *SILENT VOICES*, can be read on multiple levels. The first and most obvious mode of engagement is to play it from beginning to end in a normative manner. As Matthew Kirschenbaum said about the Apple II interactive fiction work *Mystery House*, though: "As an electronic textual artifact then, normative play is perhaps the least interesting level on which to engage it" (Kirschenbaum **2012**, 129). In his book *Mechanisms*, Kirschenbaum analyzes his chosen digital artifact, a disk image of *Mystery House*, byte-by-byte in a hex editor. It is similarly possible to engage with *RPG Maker* creations on this deep level. Memory card images produced by a DexDrive are similar to the Apple II disk images analyzed by Kirschenbaum:

> [A] disk image is a literal representation of every *bit* of information on some original instance of source media… It is not simply a copy of all of the files that were on that original diskette; rather the disk image, like the facsimile or photograph suggested by the term, preserves all of the *information* that was recorded on the disk in its original storage geometry (Kirschenbaum **2012**, 118, emphasis in original).

Memory card images flashed via DexDrive are informatically identical to the physical media they represent (plus the .GME file header). It is thus possible to read *RPG Maker* creations like *Silent Voices* at this level, a byte-by-byte hexadecimal reading of its memory card image.

RPG Maker, however, provides a midpoint between normative play and hexadecimal deep reading: It is possible to open a game in *RPG Maker*'s built-in editor and examine it from its creator's viewpoint, seeing the game's assets and scripts as they would have appeared while it was being made. The developers of *RPG Maker* foresaw that users would share their games with each other (although perhaps not how they ended up actually being shared) and equipped their software with a rudimentary password protection system. Before sharing a game with a friend or releasing its memory card image online, a creator could designate a sequence of controller inputs that, unless entered correctly when prompted, prevented the game from being opened in the editor. The developers apparently did not see the need to encrypt these passwords, though: when a memory card image is opened in a hex editor, the password can be easily found and decoded once the user knows the particular offset and byte sequences to look for. Some games can only be completed by cracking the password like this: *Forever's End: The Unknown Savior* by "Pinoy0004" had a bug that turned the screen black at the end of one scenario and never faded it back in upon loading the next one. Thus, in order to play beyond the first of the game's three scenarios, this password hacking procedure becomes a mandatory part of the gameplay, an apparently unintended puzzle hidden in the game's data itself.

SILENT VOICES has some content that does not appear in normative play and can only be meaningfully seen by hacking the password and opening it in the editor. The game's ending sequence was never finished; the credits start rolling immediately after the final boss is defeated, but there is evidence that a longer scene had been planned. The father of Edward, one of the game's playable characters, appears in the scene and has a line that is scripted but is never displayed: "EDWARD, I AM SORRY, COME TO ME WHEN YOU NEED HELP." Looking at the system data reveals that there are many items, some of which are very powerful weapons and armor, that are never scripted to appear in the game: they are not contained in any treasure chests, and no enemies can drop them as loot after a victorious battle. Finally, there is a sequence of map screens–maps 52 to 61 in the system data–that were either deleted or never created in the first place. None of these maps have graphics or event scripts, and they are a blind spot in the middle of the game's data that would pass completely unnoticed in regular play, since the map sequence is only relevant in the editor and the game is scripted to arbitrarily jump between maps anyway, and is barely visible in hex on the memory card itself because their entries in the system and scenario data are simply skipped.

Man Getting Hit in the Groin By a Football RPG: Featuring–Ernest Borgnine also hides secrets: if one looks at the memory card image's hexadecimal data, remnants of at least one other *RPG Maker* game can be seen alongside deleted saves for *Castlevania: Symphony of the Night* and *Final Fantasy Tactics*. These digital artifacts do not directly impact the game, though, and are more curiosities than anything else. The "game" itself, which lasts for about five minutes and features no user interaction beyond pressing a button to advance the text, features custom graphics for acclaimed actor Ernest Borgnine (both walking around and collapsed face-down in pain), the titular football, and a television and toilet. The narrative has Borgnine waking up and verbally sparring with an unseen narrator about how terrible this *RPG Maker* game is, commenting on its limited graphical assets:

> Ernest:
> Hmmmm.... Let's see what I have here.

Oh yeah, I forgot that *RPG Maker* doesn't have a refrigerator tile.

So I guess there is nothing for me to eat.

> Ernest:
> Wait a darn minute!

How come there is a custom toilet tile and a television, and not a refrigerator!?

Going out to forage for food, the protagonist encounters a kid standing in the road who immediately punts a football towards Borgnine's groin. Approximately a third of the game's run time is Borgnine's narration of the pain he feels while lying on the ground:

> Ernest:
> Ooooh... the hurting... won't stop.
> Errrr... still hurts... as much.
> My groin... will... never be... the same... again.

Football's attempt at self-referential humor is painful to watch, but it represents a trend among *RPG Maker* games to parody the RPG genre or the platform itself. *SILENT VOICES* quietly accepts the limitations built into

RPG Maker by not attempting to work around them, while *Football* brazenly defies them by removing interactivity and drawing attention to the platform's shortcomings (such as the lack of a refrigerator graphic). This parody is likely only humorous to those who have been similarly irritated by *RPG Maker*, but given the difficult and unintuitive process of playing such games in the first place, the entire target audience was likely intimately familiar with these frustrations: who else was going to be able to play it?

Whatever their narrative or ludic qualities may be, any game made with *RPG Maker* inherently defies the affordances of one platform or another through the fact of its existence. Creators had to circumvent the limitations of the PlayStation's memory card technology, which was itself a circumvention of the CD-ROM's inability to retain user data. *RPG Maker* was a platform built on a platform, and the games made with it display evidence of this relationship whether or not their creators intended them to do so. Aside from deliberate attempts to defy convention, such as Football, games made with *RPG Maker* ended up a lot like *SILENT VOICES*: a frustrating pastiche of generic clichés. Even though it may be a chore to play through it normally, *SILENT VOICES* becomes interesting when viewed from a perspective that can reveal content that would be otherwise invisible to the player. The hidden and missing data in *SILENT VOICES* speaks to the peculiar materiality of *RPG Maker* games. As digital objects they occupy multiple modes of existence, whether they are stored in flash memory, on hard disks, or on servers that are somehow still running nearly two decades later. *RPG Maker* is a much more complex platform than it may appear to be at first glance, and the games created with it inherit some of that complexity in their narrativity and materiality.

Asakura, Reiji. 2000. *Revolutionaries at Sony: The Making of the Sony PlayStation and the Visionaries Who Conquered the World of Video Games.* New York: McGraw-Hill.

Carless, Simon. 2005. *Gaming Hacks.* Sebastopol, CA: O'Reilly.

Kirschenbaum, Matthew G. 2012. *Mechanisms: New Media and the Forensic Imagination.* Cambridge, Mass: MIT Press.

Misled, Jeff. 2001. *Man Getting Hit in the Groin By a Football RPG: Featuring – Ernest Borgnine.* RPG Maker for PlayStation.

Pinoy0004. 2001. *Forever's End: The Unknown Savior.*
Link: **https://www.rpgmmag.com/rmvault/rm/games/32/forevers-end-the-unknown-savior**

"RPG Maker Pavilion". n.d. Accessed april 14, 2019.
Link: **https://web.archive.org/web/20010922060317/http://rpgpavilion.com/**

Vincent, David. 2000. *SILENT VOICES.*
Link: **http://rpgmpavilion.tripod.com/demos/silent_voices2.zip**

for the sleepers in that quiet earth.: An Artbook Generated by a Deep Learning Agent

SOFIAN AUDRY

Abstract

This paper describes an artbook created through the adaptive behavior of a deep learning neural network computational agent as it "reads" a novel. Through this process, the network as agent builds a model of the syntactic and stylistic principles behind the original text and is able to use this model to generate new, unforeseen text. There exist 31 printed editions of the artbook thus generated, each unique and consisting of a text that reveals the learning process of the agent itself as it goes through the adaptive process, starting from a state of randomness and gradually refining itself as it reads the novel. The artbook is examined by looking at generated excerpts and discussing how they relate to the state of the deep learning system at different steps through the adaptive-generative process. Practical and theoretical implications are discussed in the context of generative literature, machine learning, and behavior aesthetics.

Résumé

Cet article décrit un livre d'art créé par le biais du comportement adaptatif d'un agent d'apprentissage profond (deep learning) de réseaux de neurones alors qu'il « lit » un roman. À travers ce processus, l'agent construit un modèle des principes syntaxiques et stylistiques du texte original et reprend ce modèle pour générer de nouveaux textes. Trente et une éditions imprimées du livre d'art ont ainsi été générées, chacune unique et composée d'un texte qui révèle le processus d'apprentissage de l'agent lui-même pendant qu'il subit le processus adaptatif, à partir d'un état de hasard se raffinant progressivement alors qu'il lit le roman. Nous examinons le livre d'art en s'attardant aux extraits générés et aux façons dont ils sont liés aux états du système d'apprentissage profond à chaque étape du processus d'adaptation et de génération. Les implications théoriques et pratiques de ce livre d'art sont ainsi examinées dans le contexte de la littérature générative combinatoire, de l'apprentissage machine et des esthétiques comportementales.

INTRODUCTION

Machine learning has recently become a popular approach to studying computational creativity and creating new forms of electronic art and literature. Oftentimes, this requires framing the creative process as a problem to be solved using some form of optimization. For example, such approaches have been used to evolve artificial 3D creatures based on subjective preferences (Sims **1994**; Todd and Latham **1992**); to generate music scores that "sound like" the dataset they have been trained on (Hadjeres, Pachet, and Nielsen **2016**; Eck and Schmidhuber **2002**); to transfer a painter's style onto another painting (Gatys, Ecker, and Bethge **2015**); and even to generate images that often feel "more artistic" (at least to the layman) than those of contemporary painters (Elgammal and al. **2017**). They have also been used in text generation applications, such as for writing poetry (Talafha and Rekabdar **2019**) and song lyrics (Potash, Romanov, and Rumshisky **2015**).

Indeed, machine learning is designed to recognize regular patterns, and when employed for generative purposes, is attuned to reproduce forms that already exist in the training data. Artists, on the contrary, often seek to create the unexpected. Studies that try to tackle artistic production as an optimization problem are immediately faced with problems such as: the existence of multiple maxima (e.g., there is no such thing as "the best novel" or "the best painting"); the possibly infinite and incommensurable domains in which artworks exist; and the fact that art is often precisely described as non-purposeful and non-optimizable (Penny **2000**; Moura and Pereira **2004**).

In this paper, we explore a text generation process whereby the optimization process of a machine learning algorithm is used as raw material. By unrolling the iterative steps of the training phase, the generative text reveals the temporal structure of the learning algorithm. We examine an artistic creation realized using this technique: an artbook generated using a deep learning model known as a long short-term memory (LSTM) recurrent neural network trained on the novel *Wuthering Heights* by Emily Brontë. The artbook, titled *for the sleepers in that quiet earth.* is published by Bad Quarto in a micro-edition of 31 unique copies, each of which has 642,746 characters[1]–the same length as the version of *Wuthering Heights* that was used for training the neural network (Audry **2019**). The creative approach

NOTE 1

A copy of the artbook can be acquired online: http://badquar.to/publications/for_the_sleepers.html

that led to the creation of the artbook is presented, as well as the outcomes. Finally, I discuss the implications of the work for the fields of computational media art and electronic literature.

CONTEXT

Machine learning finds its origin in *cybernetics*, a disruptive interdisciplinary science which impacted not only computer science and artificial intelligence, but also biology, neurology, sociology, anthropology, and economics. It had a profound impact on art in the 1960s, and foreshadowed the later development of new media art.

Figure 1. Sample pages from *for the sleepers in that quiet earth.* Image courtesy of Bad Quarto.

One of the central concepts of cybernetics is that of systems or agents, some of which are able, using feedback from their environment, to adapt over time by trial and error (Rosenblueth, Wiener, and Bigelow **1943**). The concept of an agent iteratively and incrementally adapting to its environment by adjusting its own structure is at the core of deep learning, which uses layers of densely interconnected simple "agents" called neurons which work together to achieve a greater level of complexity at the global scope. In current-day deep learning applications, millions of such computational neurons are being force-fed with gigabytes of data, resulting after several iterations in the *foie gras* of the deep learning revolution: fully optimized models often performing above human level.

Since the 1950s, many artists have exploited the adaptive features of adaptive systems, not by applying optimized models, but rather by exploding the learning process itself, often running it in real time. Consider for example Hungarian artist Nicolas Schöffer's piece *CYSP I*, which was directly inspired by Norbert Wiener's theory of control and communication (Fernández 2006). Or Karl Sims's *Galápagos* (1997), where visitors are asked to select their favorite artificial 3D creatures in a virtual environment, and where the selected creatures' genetic code is then used to create the next generation using genetic algorithms. *Performative Ecologies* (2008–2010) by architect Ruairi Glynn is another example. Inspired by the work of Gordon Pask, especially his 1968 installation *Colloquy of Mobiles*, Glynn's installation creates a conversational space in which dancing robots evolve in constant interaction with one another and the public.

Artist and media theorist Simon Penny calls these kinds of work "embodied cultural agents" or "agents as artworks" and integrates them within the larger framework of an "aesthetic of behavior," a "new aesthetic field opened up by the possibility of cultural interaction with machine systems" (Penny 1997).

In my past work, I have developed an ontological framework of behaviors by looking at the distinctive way behavior morphologies unfold in time (Audry 2016). While existing taxonomies of cybernetics systems have mainly focused on their relational and structural aspects (Cariani, 1989; Rosenblueth, Wiener, and Bigelow 1943), I look instead at the temporal dimension of agent behaviors and its aesthetic potential. In particular, I claim that adaptive behaviors are distinguished from non-adaptive behaviors by their ability to change over time, and therefore belong to a "second order" of behaviors—as behaviors whose behavior evolves over time. With that in mind, one can start considering how the shape of a behavior emerges from randomness (morphogenesis), transforms over time (metamorphosis), or remains stable (morphostasis).

Using this framework, we can establish that most learning algorithms go through a phase of morphogenesis during which their behavior changes, until they eventually stabilize in a final stage of morphostasis. I posit that this process of transformation and stabilization is artistically relevant and can be harnessed as a creative method.

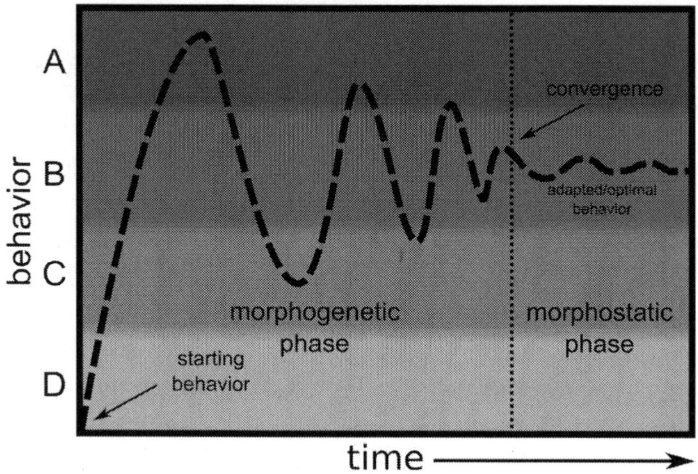

Figure 2. Example of temporal evolution of an adaptive behavior. The vertical axis represents the behavior of the system, understood as the temporally invariant shape of observable events the system generates. Recognizable behavior morphologies are represented using labels A, B, C and D. The horizontal axis represents the advance of time. The figure shows how adaptive behaviors iteratively change over time through a process of morphogenesis, until they stabilize into an optimal first-order behavior, thus entering a phase of morphostasis.

APPROACH

NOTE 2 http://www.gutenberg.org/cache/epub/768/pg768.txt

NOTE 3 The source code used in this project is available here: https://github.com/sofian/readings

This study involves a series of artworks where long short-term memory (LSTM) recurrent neural networks were trained on a single text corpus: a version of Emily Brontë's novel *Wuthering Heights* adapted from the Gutenberg online library.[2] Snapshots of the trained models were saved on disk at different steps of the learning process, resulting in a set of increasingly optimal models. These models were then used as part of a generative process to create a new text.[3]

The main artistic output of this approach is the series of 31 unique artbooks titled *for the sleepers in that quiet earth*. Each copy is generated by training an LSTM on all the characters from Brontë's novel (available on the Gutenberg library). LSTMs are a kind of artificial neural network with recurrent connections, which are able to "learn" from sequences of data such as words and characters. They are used in state-of-the-art language processing applications such as speech recognition and automated translation.

The result is a unique record of the neural network as it is trained over the book and learns the probability distribution of characters, thus somehow becoming increasingly "familiar" with its syntax and style, while at the same time it becomes more and more complex in its generative features. This unicity is important, because I see the work less as the trace of the system's behavior than as a way to experience its behavior as if it were happening in real-time.

Like many other deep learning systems, LSTMs are both predictive and generative. In most scientific applications, it is their predictive capabilities that people are interested in. For example, in machine translation, deep LSTMs are often used for comparing the probability of different candidate translations, and keep the one that is most likely. Yet, their generative capabilities are also the subject of scientific research and have been used in many generative art contexts.

Another unique feature of these systems is that, contrary to other AI approaches, deep learning systems improve iteratively. Starting from nothing, as they become more and more exposed to data, they improve and become better at prediction–which also directly impacts their generative capabilities.

Generation and adaptation form the basis of *for the sleepers in that quiet earth.* My intention in this work was not so much to produce an accurate "optimal" system that could generate rich, human-level, grammar-correct sentences. On the contrary, I sought to allow the hesitant, strenuous learning process of the system to reveal itself as it goes through all of its sub-optimal states of being.

Another key conceptual dimension of the work resides in the ability of the artificial system to be both reader and writer. If we picture the text of *Wuthering Heights* as being the "world" the LSTM "agent" dwells in and tries to make sense of by "reading" sequences of characters, then as it becomes more familiar with its environment, it is also able to "write" new possible sequences which can give an insight on the system's understanding of its world. The trace of the neural net's learning process is brought into the physical world as a printed book.

I made the decision to distribute this book only in print format rather than in a digital version. This aspect of the work is crucial, as it lends a physical materiality to the system and confers on it an identity beyond its abstracted, virtual existence. As such, the artbook format contributes to the hybridity of the work, which in my view and intention lie somewhere between visual arts, electronic arts, and electronic literature.[4]

PREPROCESSING

Wuthering Heights contains a little more than 600,000 characters, which is rather low when compared to state-of-the-art language modelling datasets which usually contain several million characters.[5] Starting with an open-access version of *Wuthering Heights* (Brontë **1996**), I slightly reduced the complexity of the learning task by reducing the number of different characters encountered through (1) turning all letters to lowercase (so that the system does not need to distinguish between uppercase and lowercase letters); and (2) removing low-frequency characters such as parentheses–which appeared only a few times in the text and would only confuse the system.[6]

TRAINING

To produce the work, a LSTM was trained on the complete text of *Wuthering Heights*[7] over many iterations. Snapshots of the neural network's weights were saved at different steps in the learning process, from the beginning where it is initialized randomly, to the end where it has read the book 150 times.

Learning is asymptotic, with many changes happening during the first steps of training. This resulted in the system appearing already "too trained" after the first epoch.[8] To compensate for this, we saved 200 snapshots during this first run-through alone using mini-batches of different sizes (Fig. 3).

NOTE 4
https://eringee.net

NOTE 5
As a point of comparison, consider the difficulty it would represent to learn how to write a book in a language unknown to you, with the only information being a single book written in that language.

NOTE 6
The preprocessed version of the text which was used as the training set is available here: **https://github.com/sofian/readings/blob/master/data/wuthering.txt**

NOTE 7
Some basic pre-processing was done on the text, as I explain later.

NOTE 8
In machine learning jargon, an *epoch* corresponds to one full iteration over the training dataset–in this case, the complete novel.

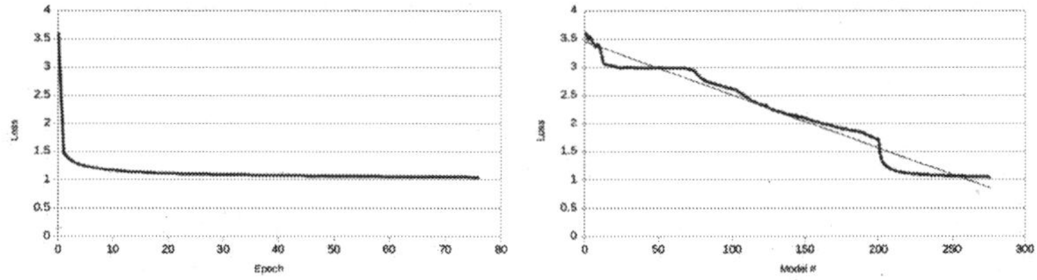

(a) (b)

Figure 3. Training loss (categorical cross entropy) plotted against (a) the training epoch for the first 75 epochs and (b) the saved model number up to the first 75 epochs. These graphs show how the process of saving models during the first epoch flattens the learning curve, allowing for more fine-grained evolutions during the generative step. Notice that the first 200 saved models happen during the first epoch alone.

These 351 snapshots–one in the starting state, 200 during the first epoch, and then 150 (one per epoch) for the rest of the process–were then used in a generative fashion to produce each version of the work: each snapshot was used to generate an approximately equal portion of the 642,746 characters of the book.

The way the LSTM is trained helps understand its behavior during the generative phase. The network attempts to model the distribution of sequential text patterns. It does so by estimating the conditional probability of the next character xi given the past N characters $h_i = x_{i-N} \dots x_{i-1}$:

$$P(x_i | h_i)$$

This probability distribution is represented by a function that produces one probability value for each possible character. For example, let us say that the *N=10* previous characters seen by the agent are "wutherin"; then after training we would expect the neural net to emit a high probability $P(g | \mathit{wutherin})$ for the letter *g* (wuthering), a lower probability $P(' | \mathit{wutherin})$ for a single quote (') (wutherin'), and near-zero probabilities for every other character.

The network can then be used to generate new sequences, simply by sampling randomly using the distribution and repeating the procedure. To go back to our previous example, after choosing the letter *g*, the agent would sample a new character, this time using the input "uthering"–in which case we would likely expect high probabilities for "s", a white space (" "), and other punctuation marks (".,?!").

This kind of statistical approach which looks at the previous *N* units in a sequence is known as a markovian process, commonly used in natural language processing (Manning and Schütze **1999**). One of the limitations of markovian processes is that they make the assumption that the closest elements in the past are the most important for predicting the future, which is an imperfect premise to say the least–especially when it comes to language, where there are often very long-term dependencies. This explains to a large extent why the sentences generated by the system, even in the later stages of training, are somehow detached from one another, as the neural network fails to grasp long-term dependencies between sentences.

To model that probability distribution, I used an LSTM network with two layers of fully interconnected hidden units with 200 neurons each. Input streams were sent by chunks of 100 characters using a sliding window (*N=100*). Input characters were represented using embeddings, a technique where each symbol is represented by a vector which is itself trained. For example, in this work, I used embeddings of size 5, which means that each character is represented by 5 different values. These values can be seen as a representation of different characteristics of each character that can be useful for the system to make better predictions over sequences. For example, the first value might represent whether the letter is a vowel, the second value whether it is a punctuation mark, etc.[9]

NOTE 9

In reality, we rarely see such human-based categories appear in embeddings, as the system finds its own way to represent information which is often counterintuitive because we do not "think" as an artificial neural network does.

GENERATING

After the training, we obtained a series of probability distributions at different stages of the evolution of the model, which were then used to generate each book. The outputs use a *softmax* distribution which gives a probability to each next character given the past characters that were generated. The softness of the distribution can be controlled using a hyper-parameter called the *temperature* which is typically set to 1. Raising the temperature spreads out the probabilities, making them more uniform, while lowering it makes the distribution "peakier," hence making the system even "greedier" to choose the letter with highest probability.

Temperature Adjustment

After some experiments, I noticed that the probability distributions in the early stages were too "spread" across the characters (i.e., there were few differences between each probability) and that the agent would thus generate text that appeared "too random" to my taste. I thus decided to slightly adjust the probability distribution to make it more "peaky" by decreasing the temperature τ–thus effectively heightening the probability of the most probable elements and decreasing the probability of the others.

However, this approach seemed too "greedy" in later stages where the neural net would become complex enough to be able to consider different sequence construction and completion. Thus, as the system became more and more trained, I adjusted the probability distribution to be more "spread-out" to encourage diversity.

Transitions Between

Models Finally, to allow for smooth transitions between each block of text generated by each model, in the last part of each section, we interpolated the probability distributions of the current model and the next model to generate each character. This was parameterized by a transition factor $\alpha \in [0, 1]$ representing the point of transition in each block at which we start interpolating. To generate *for the sleepers in that quiet earth.* we used $\alpha=0.2$, hence the last 20% of each of the 351 blocks of text (each averaging 1833 characters) was obtained by linearly interpolating the current probability distribution and that of the next trained model.

POSTPROCESSING & EDITION

The final production of the artbooks *for the sleepers in that quiet earth.* involved an additional step. Through discussions with editor Nick Montfort, we decided to implement a few minor changes to bring the raw generated text into book format. For instance, we interpreted the appearance of the word "Chapter" followed by Roman letters in the generative text (e.g., "Chapter XIX")[10] as an indication of a new chapter, which we thus formatted differently with a page break and bold typeface (Fig. 4).

NOTE 10

Notice that these appear randomly. For example, "Chapter XI" might appear before "Chapter III".

Figure 4. Sample page from the artbook showing the formatting of "chapters". Image courtesy of Bad Quarto.

RESULTS

This section discusses the results of the generative process through an in-depth examination of an unpublished version of *for the sleepers in that quiet earth.* In this section, we describe the progress of the learning system as it runs through the reading in terms of time. Here, "time" is to be understood in terms of character position and is represented using the symbol *t*. There are 642,746 individual characters in the original text. So for example, at time *t=64,274* the agent is about 10 % into the book, and at time *t=321,373* it is halfway through.

MORPHOGENESIS

The behavior of the system throughout the learning process manifests itself in a number of different ways, corresponding to the state of the neural net as it becomes increasingly attuned to the "world" it lives in–that is, the text it is reading. As is traditionally done, the neural network is initialized with random weights, representing a neutral state: at this point the agent has not been subjected to any observations and thus has no understanding of the world. Accordingly, in the first few pages of the book, the agent behaves completely randomly, as it has been initialized with random weights.

The system then proceeds to read the book, one character at a time, in an attempt to build an internal representation of how character sequences are generated in Brontë's novel–in other words, by building a model of the author's style. In so doing, it learns more and more about the author's style as it reads, starting with building a comprehension of sequences at the character level and incrementally building from it to groups of two, three, four characters forming syllables, on to building words, and finally complete sentences.

The following is a case study of a particular unpublished "reading" of the book, and thus construction of an LSTM agent. Here is an excerpt of the first "sentence" generated by the agent:

k:jnjw::j::lc;jc:::c:cnqnnn--";x!khwwxwswvsvwvdxd'nx:nc'i""';'n'g;pg;pguunm-
nmcovo:fow:wwwjdd:nden:":nn'nhk!knhu?y?msy?
yyywwowmww:fwfwwbdwdjfdnj,:jdzzr,lzrk-dqrk"q-"k."--".c"chhcixhcszzzx'

Excerpt at t=0

Early on in the training (after reading a few characters) the agent starts to utter erratically some of the characters it has seen:

t t tt tt ttt t t tt t t t t t t t t t
t t t t t t t tt t t tt t t t t tttt t ttt t t t
t t t t t tt t t t tt t tt t t

Excerpt at t=40

Later on, as it has seen more, it becomes obsessed with white spaces and frequent characters such as the letter "e".

e e e
e e e
e e e

Excerpt at t=530

These fixations can be explained through the probabilistic approach governing the system. More frequent characters simply have a higher probability of appearing in the text. For example, imagine yourself pointing to a random character in a book and trying to guess what it is without any context: you would likely have more chances of making the right guess if you chose a white space than any other character.

After reading a few hundred characters, the letters produced by the neural net become more condensed and we see some character duplicates appearing. These are the early steps of the agent moving from merely counting the frequency of characters as a predictive measurement. After about 5% of the book has been read, the letters become more condensed, and the agent even starts to tentatively concatenate frequent letters:

```
 tee   eeae  e  e  a e a ee
e e ee  a    e e      e   e   e e    e eee    a  t
 ae  t       ee e   e  e e ae  t eee a e e  a eae t  eeet ee
e  e   e ae  e  ee
 ene  n a t e e e  e n   e aa    e   e  a  a a  ta  e   e te
```

Excerpt at t=33,490

THE GLITCH

Surprisingly, not long after this point, the agent seems to regress to an earlier stage and starts behaving erratically for a while. This event only happened in one specific case: I have not been able to replicate, let alone explain, the reasons for this glitch, despite several attempts.

```
"""j"zjjjj"jjj""""jj"jj""jjjjjjj"jjejjjjj  """j"j"jjjz"""jjjjj:j":jjjjjj""jj  t  t  ee  t  ee  jj  ee  te
ee  ea  e"""j:  e  "jj"""j"j  e  t  e  e  e  ae:"jx:jjjqjj:q":"jjj"  jjjqjj:jjjjz"jxj  jj":jjz:jj  """jjjjj"
":jj"jjjxqj"""""j:j"jjj"jjjjj"jjje"e tt i t e aejjjjjx t e e t tt a jjj j e aa e e e ee ea e tt e i
j:":jjjjxjj:":j:z""" """jjjj"jjjjjjxxxjjxj""":"jjjxjzj:"q"jqxjjj"""j"j"jjjqjjjjj"jx"jj jejj :zjjj:j
```

Excerpt at t=43,090

My best explanation is that this is due to an early attempt by the neural network to make sense of double-quotes (""), which is one of the hardest mechanisms to understand for a neural network, as it involves looking backwards to a previous moment in the sequence–as opposed to learning about syllables which involve looking backwards one or two characters.

This, as well as the presence of tentative sequences of double-quotes in the next few learning steps, hint in that direction–although I was not able to verify this with certainty. Importantly, whereas I ran several training procedures in order to produce the work, tuning the model and the training procedure, this "glitch" only appeared in one of these experiments. Even a slight modification in the training data–for example, at some point I tried to remove the chapter titles–prevented the appearance of the glitch. Since I thought this was such a fascinating accident, I had no choice but to work with the specific experiment that produced it.

MORPHEMES AND PROTO-WORDS

Not long after resolving the "glitch," the system eventually relaxes its generation of spaces. It seems to finally have learned one of the most basic principles of English language: the separation of groups of letters using individual spaces. From this point on, it starts to tentatively build morphemes of increased length separated by a single space. Sequences are first limited to series of one, two, or three of the most frequent characters.

> oe e aa oe te o oo oe e e e iea ot e ae t ae oe iat e e e oe to ie at ee e te e ee e e e oe ee t ee ee ae e o at ee te a ee ie oe o te te e oe e ee e e ee e ea ie oe io ee e te oa oe ta o oa se oe t te ae e ee e e ee oe e o oat o et e ee e iae o see oe oo oe te t ae ae ee t o oe te e e ee t e oe ie ia a te en a ao te e to e oe e ie ee ot t oe e ea ee ie e oe e se a oe ee o te e oe t e a ea e e et ee t e te a ot ae a e ae oe e ooe ae e a oe oe ioe e se tae e

Excerpt at t=59,410

Soon the agent starts combining more diverse groups of letters. We even start to see the appearance of short words.

> he to toe site son ae tot te th aos tin thr tot to toe tot to te tos his toot toe tit tot tat hoe tot te to hh te ter tit hon se te toe hho io to tit te tin han tos hat tot to tae tos ioe sos tan ioe hote ao tat iis tee to tat io sot toe aote ho toe the tht tot tot tit tit thre ho toe th his aot toe to toe toe hoe iho ton he

> tis te hot tot tis toe aoe toe hhr te aot tos the th ais te ioe toe aoe to te tos hos tot toe ton io hot tate ih toe hee ion hit tos te
>
> *Excerpt at t=113,170*

This is shortly followed by early attempts to build short sequences of words, some of which are even correct English such as "in the," "that is," as well as "the mind" and "the mister."

> the sease and the his an the mind te at to seared the toul tout the tis and to to hhe mas is he the toun the i setened the the me the tor a sist hit you wos in sos in tis to ho the toat hat hhe seter the sor ind the in toe thas an the herare the tore the more a the the the mited i anserting the hor ho touthed in a tont to ceith to t
> he to mise it teat in the sorton in the tor the that that is seres of at ind an the sease the mister af the in se seret an tout the to the ind ander to se in seate sis the heathe i seited the sant i sind tho ceatter to the he inder the he
>
> *Excerpt at t=215,570*

PUNCTUATION AND SENTENCES

After having read about a third of the book, the agent starts using punctuation. For example, here is the first usage of commas (,):

> the heer to chered in at i son to sere the sorter, and ho merter the sorer the sand and his the meret ind the mored to me cered the coring in anter the mroned an the hor here the ceind the sere the sanding in the carter, and it i seind he mrer and so anter the the ter mererter to the
>
> *Excerpt at t=227,090*

About two thirds of the way through the book, the agent is able to construct sentences of varying length, making syntactically appropriate use of periods, commas, and quotes. These sentences are mostly nonsensical and grammatically imperfect. Yet, they seem to mirror some of the core aspects of the original text, including the use of the first person; the abundance of dialogs; and the construction of long sentences with many complementary clauses as is common in 19th century English literature. Above all, it is the rhythmical quality of the text produced by the artificial agent that bears the most resemblance to Brontë's style.

> "so satherine. he deat i could to she laster it the sranes and the door his sathered. 'i his lestanded to srean and hime wall at and the lister and santion."
> "you have wor trearing her an the care, and the look. i was so deat to the litter to see it i chould her a lested and to his fore the deand to her and to sathering to see the lounder her her seed to the reanten, his for had so the roster on a sould be the lose, and the had ase a meter to the leas on a mate a merared of his for shanted to me to sear the lease the dade and aspering his to sere and then i meath. i wall not he couse in the heas of the laster of him to her to mishers. i was not hear he so sann the linton his her the fide the rase her his couster the srarged a sranted the had sarle the has the loor."
>
> *Excerpt at t=448,530*

As a point of comparison, consider this excerpt from Chapter VIII of *Wuthering Heights*:

> "I guess she is; yet she looks bravely," replied the girl, "and she talks as if she thought of living to see it grow a man. She's out of her head for joy, it's such a beauty! If I were her I'm certain I should not die: I should get better at the bare sight of it, in spite of Kenneth. I was fairly mad at him. Dame Archer brought the cherub down to master, in the house, and his face just began to light up, when the old croaker steps forward, and says he–'Earnshaw, it's a blessing your wife has been spared to leave you this son. When she came, I felt convinced we shouldn't keep her long; and now, I must tell you, the winter will probably finish her. Don't take on, and fret about it too much: it can't be helped. And besides, you should have known better than to choose such a rush of a lass!" (Brontë 1996)

IMPROVEMENTS

This is an excerpt after one epoch of training–that is, after the agent has read the book once. At this point the agent has learned to generate complete sentences, with a few glitches. Many of these sentences are still grammatically incorrect and somewhat random. It is as if the agent can only "see" two or three words in the past, with usually only short sequences of two or three words making logical sense together. Consider for example the progression in the following sentence generated after the first epoch:

> i dade the cornert of her and, and he sheat it it with the deant a sood of the housh he had sather to him, and i had not the haston, and she had a contred to her to the sattle to the conder of his so stoul him the did or the seen.
>
> *Excerpt at epoch 1*

From this point forward, the neural network is trained for several epochs, having re-read the novel up to 150 times. Changes in the agent's outputs become less perceptible over these later iterations. The first epoch allowed the agent to grow from pure randomness to building morphemes, words, and full sentences with punctuation marks. In the following iterations over the novel, the agent seems to expand these basic building blocks by (1) polishing grammar; (2) expanding vocabulary; and (3) diversifying the lengths and structures of sentences–including producing dialogic constructs which are common in the original text.

To provide a sense of this evolution, here are some sample sentences from epochs 20, 80, and 150, which may give some idea of the transformation in the agent's behavior.

> "you have the delight is to spend them to speak to be a single things!"
> "it was a grief of more truth, and the satisfaction which i was a bad contents and the house for me, and struck her features with me to the servant to and a mean and startling. he would be a state that is the case. i don't like that i shall be the door, i dare you?"
>
> *Excerpt at epoch 20*

> "were you hear the plant of his father's sort of morning? what do you stay it to my hands to me! i'm not married and desire to be always there, and you would send it out of the farm. i hope you had been hardly to have a foold at all. i can be all start and talking a minute in his senses. when i asked if i was no far which she should be sure from the house, and i could not be silent on the fire, and hid her little abode on the heights, and i have

a solret associations," interpupted stared; "i'm nearly to do you to send them," said the strength.

Excerpt at epoch 80

"they would not resign you to the danger over through to me!"
"he's both a books then," he added, sufficiently.
"who is them insolently-spaking to him," said catherine. "you are a seat," he said: "i don't might wark his stall in that third that they are."

Excerpt at epoch 150

CONCLUSION

The computational artwork described in this paper spans diverse approaches, such as electronic literature, generative art, and behavior aesthetics. It makes use of deep learning recurrent neural networks, not so much as a way to generate novel and creative writing by taking advantage of the system's ability to imitate human performance, but in an effort to reveal the learning process of the system. In other words, the approach explored in this study subverts the core purpose of artificial intelligence, which aims at reproducing or exceeding human performance–in this case, by imitating the style of a well-known English author–and instead brings the focus back to the behavior of the artificial agent as it tentatively tries to achieve its goals.

The work thus offers a unique insight into the inner workings of a machine learning algorithm by turning the experience of reading/listening into an encounter with a learning agent. While the work differs in many respects from canonical forms of agent-based artworks (such as those employing situated robotic systems), it shares with them a unique focus on using behavior as a artistic form on its own–in these cases, through experiencing the journey of an artificial deep learning agent.

for the sleepers in that quiet earth. does not claim to be read as a novel nor as a poetic text, but rather as a material object which can be experienced with the senses. It thus demonstrates how machine learning can expand the field of electronic literature by supporting works where text is used not so much for its literary or linguistic content, but rather as raw material that can be shaped through adaptive algorithmic processes.

ACKNOWLEDGEMENTS

The author would like to thank the Fonds de recherche du Québec – Société et culture, Massachusetts Institute of Technology, NVIDIA Corporation, The Trope Tank, Bad Quarto, and Dr Nick Montfort for their support.

This research was initiated and conducted as part of the author's postdoctoral studies at Comparative Media Studies / Writing, Massachusetts Institute of Technology, Cambridge, MA, USA.

Audry, Sofian. 2016. "Aesthetics of Adaptive Behaviors in Agent-based Art". *Proceedings of the 22nd International Symposium on Electronic Art*, School of Creative Media, Hong Kong, 2–9. Link: http://isea-archives.org/?page_id=36370.

Audry, Sofian. 2019. *for the sleepers in that quiet earth.* Ed. by Nick Montfort. Boston & New York: Bad Quarto.

Brontë, Emily. 1996. *Wuthering Heights.* [1846]Link: http://www.gutenberg.org/ebooks/768

Cariani, Peter A. 1989. "On the Design of Devices with Emergent Semantic Functions". PhD diss., Binghamton: State University of New York.

Eck, Douglas, and Juergen Schmidhuber. 2002. *A First Look at Music Composition Using LSTM Recurrent Neural Networks.* Technical report No. IDSIA-07-02. Manno, Switzerland: Istituto Dalle Molle di Studi sull'Intelligenza Artificiale. Link: http://dl.acm.org/citation.cfm?id=870511

Elgammal, Ahmed, Bingchen Liu, Mohamed Elhoseiny, and Marian Mazzone. 2017. "CAN: Creative Adversarial Networks, Generating 'Art' by Learning About Styles and Deviating from Style Norms". *arXiv:1706.07068* [Cs], June. Link: http://arxiv.org/abs/1706.07068

Fernández, Maria. 2006. "'Life-like': Historicizing Process and Responsiveness in Digital Art". In *The Art of Art History: A Critical Anthology.* Ed. by Donald Preziosi, new ed, 477-87. Oxford History of Art. Oxford; New York: Oxford University Press.

Gatys, Leon A., Alexander S. Ecker, and Matthias Bethge. 2015. "A Neural Algorithm of Artistic Style". *ArXiv:1508.06576 [Cs, q-Bio]*, August. Link: http://arxiv.org/abs/1508.06576

Hadjeres, Gaëtan, François Pachet, and Frank Nielsen. 2016. "DeepBach: A Steerable Model for Bach Chorales Generation". *ArXiv:1612.01010 [Cs]*, December. Link: http://arxiv.org/abs/1612.01010

Manning, Christopher D., and Hinrich Schütze. 1999. *Foundations of Statistical Natural Language Processing.* 1st edition. Cambridge, Mass.: The MIT Press.

Moura, Leonel, and Henrique Garcia Pereira. 2004. *Man + Robots: Symbiotic Art.* Villeurbanne: Institut d'art contemporain.

Pask, Gordon. 1968. *An Approach to Cybernetics.* London: Hutchinson.

Penny, Simon. 1997. "Embodied Cultural Agents: At the Intersection of Robotics, Cognitive Science and Interactive Art". In *AAAI Socially Intelligent Agents: Papers from the 1997 Fall Symposium.* Ed. by Kerstin Dautenhahn, 103-5. Menlo Park: AAAI Press.

Penny, Simon. 2000. "Agents as Artworks and Agent Design as Artistic Practice". In *Human Cognition and Social Agent Technology. Advances in Consciousness Research.* Ed. by Kerstin Dautenhahn, 19:395-414. Amsterdam: John Benjamins Publishing Company. Link: https://benjamins.com/catalog/aicr.19.18pen

Potash, Peter, Alexey Romanov, and Anna Rumshisky. 2015. "GhostWriter: Using an LSTM for Automatic Rap Lyric Generation". In *Proceedings of the 2015 Conference on Empirical Methods in Natural Language Processing*, 1919–24. Association for Computational Linguistics. Link: https://doi.org/10.18653/v1/D15-1221

Rosenblueth, Arturo, Norbert Wiener, and Julian Bigelow. 1943. "Behavior, Purpose and Teleology". *Philosophy of Science* 10 (1):18–24.

Sims, Karl. 1994. "Evolving Virtual Creatures". In *Proceedings of the 21st Annual Conference on Computer Graphics and Interactive Techniques*, 15–22. SIGGRAPH '94. New York: ACM. Link: https://doi.org/10.1145/192161.192167

Talafha, S., and B. Rekabdar. 2019. "Arabic Poem Generation with Hierarchical Recurrent Attentional Network". In *2019 IEEE 13th International Conference on Semantic Computing (ICSC)*, 316–23. Link: https://doi.org/10.1109/ICOSC.2019.8665603

Todd, Stephen, and William Latham. 1992. *Evolutionary Art and Computers.* Cambridge, Mass.: Academic Press.

Wang, Kai, Jacky Tian, Ron Gao, and Chang Yao. 2018. "The Machine Poetry Generator Imitating Du Fu's Styles". In *2018 International Conference on Artificial Intelligence and Big Data (ICAIBD)*, 261–5.
Link: https://doi.org/10.1109/ICAIBD.2018.8396206

PART 3

PLATEFORMES ET NARRATIONS
PLATFORMS AND NARRATIVES

Making Participatory Interactive Experiences (PIE): Closing the Gap Between Story and Experience Through Electronic Literature and Digital Games

JON SAKLOFSKE

Abstract

Story is a way of rendering, essentializing, curating, crystallizing and communicating experience. Similar to the way that food preserves process the bounty of harvest moments into forms that extend the benefits of that harvest through longer durations and broader spaces, story is a method of processing, preserving and extending experience beyond the moment of actual or imagined events. However, given that "contemporary media is experiential," (Arbuckle and Stewart **2017**) multimedia e-lit and digital game experiences are ways of reconstituting such story preserves into participatory interactive experiences (PIE). PIE comes from Dene Grigar's extension of Vince Dziekan's ideas on multimedia museum curation. Dziekan proposes a "move-ment away from what might be termed as a broadcast model of distribution (entailing a one-way communication approach) by introducing degrees of openness (access, participation) and feedback (exchanges, transactions)... This shift entails ideological choices that challenge the museum's ability to respond to a changing mandate, from one founded on its presentation role to that of providing an infrastructure for aesthetic experience" (Dziekan **2012**, 70). While Grigar migrates Dziekan's idea of curating participatory, interactive experiences to the practice of curating e-lit, she also asserts that e-lit is already a multimedial PIE. Story becomes lived experience in these environments and such experiences are more communicatively and rhetorically impactive than traditional written and oral forms of storytelling. This paper explores and expands existing relationships between story and experience, using e-lit and game examples to demonstrate the importance of PIE environments for creative and scholarly communication.

Résumé

Le récit est une façon d'exprimer, d'essentialiser, de conserver, de cristalliser et de communiquer une expérience. À la manière des conserves alimentaires qui transforment l'abondance de la récolte en des produits qui en étendent les bénéfices pendant des durées plus longues et des espaces plus vastes, le récit est une méthode de traitement, de préservation et d'extension de l'expérience au-delà du moment des événements réels ou imaginés. Cependant, étant donné que les « médias contemporains sont expérientiels » (Arbuckle and Stewart **2017**), les expériences de la littérature électronique multimédia et des jeux numériques présentent des modes de reconstruction de ces « conserves » d'expérience en expériences interactives participatives (« participatory interactive experiences », PIE). Dene Grigar a développé le concept de PIE, une extension des idées de Vince Dziekan sur la conservation muséale des multimédias. Dziekan propose de « s'éloigner de ce que l'on pourrait appeler un modèle de distribution par diffusion (impliquant une approche de communication à sens unique) en introduisant des degrés d'ouverture (accès, participation) et de retour (échanges, transactions)... Ce virage implique des choix idéologiques qui remettent en question la capacité du musée à répondre à un mandat changeant, d'un rôle de présentation au besoin de fournir une infrastructure pour l'expérience esthétique » (Dziekan **2012**, 70). Alors que Grigar applique les idées de Dziekan sur les expériences participatives et interactives aux pratiques de commissariat de la littérature électronique, elle soutient aussi que la littérature électronique est déjà une PIE multimédia. Le récit devient une expérience vécue dans ces environnements, une expérience qui a un plus grand impact communicatif et rhétorique que les formes traditionnelles du récit écrit ou oral. Cet article se penche sur les rapports existants entre le récit et l'expérience, en citant des exemples de littérature électronique et de jeux vidéo pour illustrer l'importance des environnements PIE pour la communication dans les sphères de création et de la recherche universitaire.

Story is a way of rendering, essentializing, curating, crystallizing, and communicating experience. Similar to the way that food preserves process the bounty of harvest moments into forms that extend the benefits of that harvest through longer durations and broader spaces, story is a method of processing, preserving and extending experience beyond the moment of actual or imagined events.

What does this do to experience, to the original moment? Processes of preservation are reductive, extractive, and substitutive. Deformation and transformation also result. But this is not to suggest that the experience is something pure or ideal, some sort of perfect state that is eroded or muted through mediation. Experience is the essential foundation for story–story and experience are mutually dependent, interdependent. However, stories processed through print culture apparatuses are not highly experiential, and thus their impact on a reader is different than "living through" a particular moment.

The importance of experiential impact on human beings cannot be understated. While the experience of reading a book, or watching a film or play can be memorable in relation to the circumstances in which the container of mediated narrative preserves is opened and consumed,[1] there is something different about the experiential process of co-creating and navigating through a story landscape in a non- or less-than-linear way.

Borrowing terminology from Jerome McGann (**2001**), readers of printed stories may participate in a deformance (deforming performance) of the ori-ginal text during the reading process, but this simply echoes the kinds of reductive and essentializing deformances that narrative processing already imposes on experience. McGann's readers do not deform the original text on the page. They deform its communicative potential through imaginative interpretation from a specific historical, perceptual and subjective context. Alternatively, while e-lit users and game players, like readers of printed texts, interpretatively deform their experience but do not often deform the underlying code that generates the experience (though the possibilities for this are exciting!), they are regularly given a greater amount of agency over the process and progress of the presentation. In this way, and

NOTE 1

I have a number of favourite memories related to this kind of experience: for example, reading Herman Melville's *Moby Dick* in the middle of a rainy afternoon while eating a bowl of spicy rice in a nearly empty bar with Neil Young's "Cortez the Killer" playing over the speakers.

in spite of McGann's implicit suggestion that the agency of readers of printed text equals the agency of e-lit interactors and game players, choice regarding branching narrative possibilities shifts a more traditionally controlled transmission of pre-rendered, pre-processed stories toward the experience of emergent, participatory, and interactive narratives. As N. Katherine Hayles suggests, calling attention to e-lit's recursivity between body and machine in a Kittlerian post-structuralist context: "the future, unpredictable as ever, remains open" (Hayles **2008**, 130). In other words, there is less deformance potential in traditional print narratives, simply due to the constraints of the material page.

Given that "contemporary media is experiential" (Arbuckle and Stewart **2017**), multimedia e-lit and digital game experiences are ways of reconstituting or post-processing story preserves into participatory interactive experiences (PIE). PIE comes from Dene Grigar's extension of Vince Dziekan's ideas on multimedia museum curation. Dziekan proposes a "movement away from what might be termed as a broadcast model of distribution (entailing a one-way communication approach) by introducing degrees of openness (access, participation) and feedback (exchanges, transactions)... This shift entails ideological choices that challenge the museum's ability to respond to a changing mandate, from one founded on its presentation role to that of providing an infrastructure for aesthetic experience" (**2012**, 70). While Grigar (**2014**) migrates Dziekan's idea of curating participatory, interactive experiences to the practice of curating e-lit, she also asserts that e-lit is already a multimedial PIE. Participation and interaction imply that the route taken through a storied landscape is not prescribed, but involves a degree of openness and customization. In other words, the story is emergent, a product of reciprocal impacts between processes, details, and the actions of the interactor. As N. Katherine Hayles suggests, "... the engagement of human and machine cognizers shakes us out of our accustomed place of reading to an active encounter" (14). This encounter with story becomes lived experience in these environments, and such experiences are more communicatively and rhetorically impactive than traditional written and oral forms of storytelling. At times, they function like a treasure hunt (for example, *Dear Esther* (**2008**), *What Remains of Edith Finch* (**2017**) and *The Town of Light* (**2016**)) in which players hunt for pieces of story along a pathway that trigger further progress, and are then left with the posthumous responsibility of constructing a coherent narrative out of that journey. However, traditional treasure hunts tend to be ultimately linear, featuring a pre-determined route that players must discover in order to progress. Some examples of experiences that go beyond such linearity and allow the player to "[choose] how the story will be told" (Hayles 2008, 17) include *Her Story* (2015) (in which a player appears to be using a computer terminal that allows players to access, search and sort 271 video clips from a database of seven police interviews with a woman to determine what has happened), and *Gone Home* (2013) (in which the player takes on the role of Katie from a first-person perspective, returning to her family home to find it deserted, then piecing together what happened by exploring the house and its contents). In both of these examples, pre-rendered stories become embedded in an interactive experience that involves actively finding and assembling these pieces, much as detectives "read" an environment for physical clues and use such clues to help them create a coherent narrative account of past events. In these cases, players are asked to become storymakers, to process already-past experiences that they are not familiar with into stories via the finding and sorting of residual signs and mediations. The players' experience is this process, not the embedded story (though the found story gives context and purpose to the players' actions). Here, then, the original story is not reconstituted as experience, but becomes an essential ingredient in a new layered and non-linear experience for the player.

This is a use of the story preserve as an ingredient for further experience. There are additional layers of processing involved here, a post-processing that uses the story ingredient to inform its experience design, a code that processes the experience for the user, and–most-importantly–a post-processing that depends on the agency and choice of the user within that environment. Experience is thus re-enabled–but not as a way to replicate or idealize the original experience. In the current media landscape, mediation cannot capture or exactly communicate that original experience. Does this continual processing suggest a distance, an inauthenticity, an unreality? To an extent–yes–but the PIE, the experience that follows the initial processing, is a preservation of participation and interaction, not just a preservation of detail and pre-determination. Story is history. PIE is presentness, an emergence happening right now, rather than simply the storied recollection of something that happened then.

Given the diversity of creations within the loosely defined frame of Electronic Literature, it is impossible to accurately suggest that all e-lit is equally participatory and interactive, as some examples (such as Christopher Strachey's *Love Letters* (1952), Darius Kazemi's *Content Forever* (2014), Nanette Wylde's *Storyland* (2004), and Nick Montfort's *Taroko Gorge* (2009)) require a more passive observation of machine-generated presentations (some of which ask for input from users that influence the text's procedural or random generation). While such instances are provocative and necessary, this paper will use other examples to explore and expand existing relationships between story and experience, and to demonstrate the importance of PIE environments for creative communication.

What many e-lit pieces and game experiences (both digital and non-digital) do is invite a performative participation, a coordinated co-creation of experience (with code, UI, other people, machine processes, etc.). It could be argued that traditional print forms do this already, given the ways that a reader's imagination works to co-construct the virtual spaces and characters triggered by an author's configuration of language from page to page. However, a number of e-lit and game examples depend on more significant interactions and participations by users than those contributed by readers of print, and story becomes just one part/component/ingredient in the multimedial e-lit PIE.

By all accounts, *Life is Strange* (2015) is a fairly limited choose-your-own-adventure game experience. The player controls the character of Max Caulfield, an 18-year old student who faces difficult social and personal choices, and who also discovers that she has the power to rewind time and to affect the outcome of particular situations. The game focuses on her initial decision to use her power to save an old friend, Chloe Price, from being murdered, and this choice eventually produces a butterfly effect, resulting in a physical storm that threatens to destroy the entire town. While the experience is highly controlled and the effects of a player's decisions affect the narrative progress only minimally, at the end of the game's five episodes, Max is faced with a binary choice: Choose a socially responsible course of action and save the town (and all of Max's family and friends) by returning to the original scene of the game and letting Chloe die (thus negating all of the player's actions and choices), or choose the power of friendship and love by saving Chloe and sacrificing the town. When I was presented with that choice, after 10 hours of experiencing and investing in Max's life possibilities and despite the cartoonish graphics and limited and limiting user interface, I was literally frozen. Social responsibility clashed with emotional empathy, and my unique experience within that participatory, interactive environment made this choice a very personal one. I saved the game and thought about my decision for two days before making a selection. And ever since, I have regretted that choice–more than I have regretted many choices which have impacted real people in my own life experience. The emotional power and impact of this experience has become part of my memories–as much as any other memory from my life's experience–and I have just now processed it into a story to convey to you. And I am not alone. The game has received widespread critical acclaim, with many critics lauding the extent of participatory immersion and investment created by the experience.

Another example is *P.T.* (or Playable Teaser/Trailer), which mysteriously appeared in the online PlayStation store on August 12, 2014 with little fanfare. Players who downloaded and opened the free software were presented with a brief title screen, a cryptic series of short sentences, and then a first-person perspective of a closed door. Opening this door reveals a short hallway in what appears to be a home. This hallway turns right, leads past a front entrance, through an open door, and down a few stairs to another closed door. Opening this second door loops the player back to the beginning of the hallway. As these simple loops are experienced and expectation is constructed, embedded narrative details are slowly revealed and small environmental details change, interrupting the repetitive nature of this simple loop and increasing a sense of uncertainty and dread in the player. The graphical fidelity is excellent, approaching realism, and the game makes use of sparse and unpleasant sounds and silences in a further attempt to unsettle the player. Difficult puzzles involving precise actions on the player's part function antagonistically throughout the process, and what appears to be the deformed corpse of a woman threatens the player's progress and safety as the game continues. Who the player is supposed to be is never made clear, though the game details imply that the player might have committed uxoricide. The end of the experience reveals that this is just a small teaser demo for a larger horror game project by Hideo Kojima and Guillermo del Toro that has since been cancelled due to differences between Kojima and his former publisher, Konami. Following the cancellation of the larger project, *P.T.* has been removed from the PlayStation store and can no longer be obtained. While its scarcity has contributed to its almost-legendary status, and its simple but effective design has received universal acclaim, I mention it here due to the intensity of dread and fear it manages to produce in a significant number of its players. The embedded story details add context to the experience, progress, and emotions of the player, but for me, this experience was uniquely unplayable. I am the kind of person who is not adversely affected by horror movies or printed stories at all, save for a few well-crafted scenes of suffering. Years of consuming mediated horror stories has all but numbed me to the intended physiological and emotional effects of even the best examples, including horror games that make use of the most effective clichés. Until *P.T.* For some reason, possibly the perfect blend of constraint, sound design, and unpredictability, the experience of turning blind corners and opening closed doors in that game has frightened me to the point where I cannot play it for more than a few minutes at a time and continue to experience physiological reactions when seeing videos or stills of the game.

The fear that has resulted from my encounter with this participatory, interactive experience, like the indecision and subsequent regret that haunt me regarding *Life is Strange*, have impacted me more than hundreds (if not thousands) of film- and book-based stories. These are mediated stories that have been reconstituted as direct experiences, and which have left room for me to create my own experiential route through a particular topography. As N. Katherine Hayles suggests, "entering the narrative now does not mean leaving the surface behind, as when the reader plunges into an imaginative world and finds it so engrossing that she ceases to notice the page. Rather, the 'page' is transformed into a complex topology that rapidly transforms from a stable surface into a 'playable' space in which she is an active participant" (13). She continues, "... the engagement of human and machine cognizers shakes us out of our accustomed place of reading to an active encounter" (14). PIE is thus a circumstance where a pre-existing narrator is absent to a certain degree and thus the narrative is not-yet-realized. While this is less true for *Life is Strange*, given the limited choices a player is faced with, the narrative that I realized through my experience of *P.T.* is one of refusal to continue and an overwhelming fear of something that cannot physically hurt me. My story of *P.T.* is that I cannot continue, and that is a choice and an emergent story that the game supports.

Façade (2005) is the only one of these three examples that is formally categorized as e-lit, and–uniquely–features more opportunities for emergent narrativity in its short dramatic experience than the other two combined. The player is invited to a dinner at Grace and Trip's apartment. Grace and Trip are old friends of the player, and it becomes obvious that their marriage is strained within the first few minutes of interaction. In this playground, the player can explore various possibilities for reconciling or antagonizing Grace and Trip's relationship. Too much antagonism will result in the player being escorted out of the apartment, but through multiple interface options, including typing phrases (that are then spoken to Grace and Trip), interacting with objects, or comforting, hugging, and kissing the two other characters, the player can influence the outcome of the evening (and possibly the future of Grace and Trip's relationship). Oddly, of the three examples discussed here, this is the one that I have played through the least responsibly the most number of times. It is easier for me to abandon the role of a concerned friend and to sadistically toy with these characters (like some players do with their characters in *The Sims*) than it is to play against expectations in *Life is Strange* and *P.T.*, likely due to the greater constraints of the latter two on player actions. The crucial aspect of this example for the current discussion, though, is that at the end of the experience, whatever happens, the player is presented with a text file transcript of their gameplay, formatted as a one-act play. This calls explicit attention to the fact that the player has generated the story during the experience by mapping a unique route through this situation. The textual representation also demonstrates the impossibility of capturing all of the details and nuances of what has just happened to the player through this kind of script.

PIE, as exemplified through *Life is Strange* and *P.T.*, is a process of experience that follows processes of coding, of preservation, involving us in experiences that can be transformed into unique, personalized stories (by and through us), a re-vitalization of mediated and narrated story into experiential possibility, into a performative openness that also, necessarily, cannot exactly replicate the details of the original experience or intention. Rather than attempting to collect and re-present the residual memory fragments of an original experience into a storied causality, it instead generates another instance of experience itself. Differently, in the case of *Façade*, instead of being encouraged along pre-rendered pathways, we are invited to navigate through a more complex pre-rendered networked database of curated parts or fragments with a set of specific interface tools. *Façade* has no original experience to remediate, instead offering a particular situational context to the player. Its database of content constitutes the wholeness of an interactor's potential experience. Its code establishes a large set of curational possibilities and variables, generating a social simulation space that can support an incredible number of branching experiences. Façade is an example of e-lit that operates as avant garde/experimental theatre on the stage of the screen. Incredibly, social simulations have not evolved far beyond the complexity of Façade in the 15 years since its release, and it is difficult to name examples that have matched its ability to adapt to multiple forms of user input while still maintaining a causal coherence in its emergent narrative.

One additional example of looking backward to past works that already imagine future possibilities relating to the ways that e-lit and digital games might harness PIE to facilitate meaningful experience and responsible performance is Shelley Jackson's *Patchwork Girl* (1995). *Patchwork Girl* continues this idea of experience as the "traversal" (a term aptly used by Grigar and Moulthrop) of a database of possible content, but models this activity–to borrow from Gilles Deleuze and Felix Guattari (1987)–as a form of constructive assemblage, a process of coding or constellation that is itself experience, but an experience that involves the kinds of constructions that anticipate story. In Jackson's work, the process of experiencing this work and the situation itself are associated with suturing and patching together texts and bodies, and this metacritical construction, through its fluidity and openness (inviting participatory interaction) implicates the interactor in these processes. Extending the situation of Mary Shelley's *Frankenstein* to one that involves Shelley as the creator of a female creature, and thematically braiding this work with the life vs petrifaction opposition that threads through L. Frank Baum's *Patchwork Girl of Oz* raises questions of responsibility and accountability as audience members become complicit in the lucid and reflexive creation of textual bodies from disparate fragments.

E-lit is a curated experience. An engineered experience. A designed experience. Of course, this is nothing new. We know this. But to acknowledge that this participatory, interactive aspect prioritizes experience means that e-lit is aligned with experiential activation rather than narrative preservation. Or perhaps it is an essential link between the two, a way of conceptualizing story as a beginning, rather than an end of experience.

But to acknowledge that this participatory, interactive aspect prioritizes experience means that e-lit is either a particular function of preservative mediation—an essential initiation of the process of transforming experience into story—or a particular means of reconstitution—the post-processing transformation of story into experience. Perhaps it is both, and such a feedback loop, this continual processing and transformation between experience, story, experience, story, does not suggest some sort of linearity or progression. There are choices and aspects of openness involved, loops and reversals, provocations that do not prescribe entirely, a shared opportunity that is not the same for everyone (not just in a perception of the experience, but in the experience itself). Rather than reaffirming story as an end of experience, e-lit PIE offers a way of braiding experience as a beginning for story with story as a beginning for experiential possibility.

As a postscript to this assertion, I would like to raise the creative possibility of moving further away from pre-rendered story foundations and toward less controlled environments. If code is literally the underlying process, or preprocessed "story" program that foundationally activates PIE experiences in both electronic literature and digital games, and such storied code—as suggested above—is a jumping-off point for experiential possibility, what possibilities are inherent in allowing users to—through their deformative interaction with software—deform the underlying code that generates the experience. If a playthrough of an e-lit or game experience involved a permanent evolution of the underlying code, permanent effects and codified consequences of action and decision on generated landscapes, NPC memories, and social reputation, then the impact of one's decisions might be even more powerfully affective than the experience I had and continue to have with my final decision in *Life is Strange*. Such malleable underlying and evolving code that adapts to player action, not just via variables that are reset at the beginning of each new playthrough, but through transformative alterations that are saved to the source code, involves the same trusting spirit as Nick Montfort exemplified by opening up *Taroko Gorge* to modification, transformation, addition and removal by those who experience it. Effective play, in which players impact a pre-rendered and pre-programmed world as soon as they run the code and initiate input, bending, breaking, remixing, reconfiguring and imprinting storied preserves indelibly, might amplify affective experience in a life-like fashion. This could extend the promise of Façade and digitally realize Peter Brook's definition of a "necessary theatre;

one in which there is only a practical difference between actor and audience, not a fundamental one" (1968, 166), by blurring the boundaries between player and programmer in a virtual performance space. Participatory, interactive, experiential and permanent deformances of underlying, evolving source code that truly generate unique and unexpected events would be excitedly shared as stories with communities of players across social media like a virtual potluck in which everyone brings a uniquely flavoured PIE story to the table.

Annapurna Interactive. 2017. *What Remains of Edith Finch.*

Arbuckle, Alyssa, and Bonnie Stewart. 2017. "How Can We Make Scholarship More Relevant?" *Inside Higher Ed, University of Venus blog,* November. Accessed April 29, 2019. Link: https://www.insidehighered.com/blogs/university-venus/how-can-we-make-scholarship-more-relevant#disqus_thread

Barlow, Sam. 2015. *Her Story.* Video game.

Brooks, Peter. 1968. *The Empty Space.* New York: Simon; Schuster. (First Touchstone edition 1996)

Deleuze, Gilles, and Félix Guattari. 1987. *A Thousand Plateaus: Capitalism and Schizophrenia.* Translated by Brian Massumi. Minneapolis: University of Minnesota Press.

Dziekan, Vince. 2012. *Virtuality and the Art of Exhibition: Curatorial Design for the Multimedial Museum.* Chicago: Intellect.

***Façade*. 2005.** Procedural Arts, PC. Video game.

***Gone Home*. 2013.** The Fullbright Company, PC. Video game.

Grigar, Dene. 2014. "Curating Electronic Literature as Critical and Scholarly Practice". *DHQ: Digital Humanities Quarterly* 8 (4).
Link: http://www.digitalhumanities.org/dhq/vol/8/4/000194/000194.html

Hayles, Katherine N. 2008. *Electronic Literature: New Horizons for the Literary.* Notre Dame: University of Notre Dame Press.

Jackson, Shelley. 1995. *Patchwork Girl.* Watertown: Eastgate Systems.

Kazemi, Darius. 2014. *Content, Forever.* 2014. Link: http://tinysubversions.com/content-Forever/

***Life is Strange*. 2015.** Square Enix. Video game.

LKA. 2016. *The Town of Light.* Video game.

McGann, Jerome. 2001. *Radiant Textuality: Literature after the World Wide Web.* New York: Palgrave.

Montfort, Nick. 2009. *Taroko Gorge.* 2009.
Link: http://directory.eliterature.org/individual-work/4878

***P.T.* 2014.** Konami. Video game.

Strachey, Christopher. 1952. *Love Letters.* Reimplemented by Nick Montfort 2014.
Link: https://nickm.com/memslam/love_letters.html

The Chinese Room. 2008. *Dear Esther.*

Wylde, Nanette. 2004. *Storyland v2.* 2004.
Link: http://collection.eliterature.org/1/works/wylde__storyland.html

PART 3

PLATEFORMES ET NARRATIONS
PLATFORMS AND NARRATIVES

Love Letters to Strangers

CRISTIANE COSTA

Abstract

How to write about the search for love when it happens mostly in the virtual world? In fact, a new kind of epistolary literature is being written in cell phones, emails, apps, and dating sites. How different is it in comparison with the old love letters people used to write to their soulmates? Are we observing the rise of an e-pistolary literature?

Résumé

Comment écrire sur la quête d'amour, lorsqu'elle a lieu principalement en ligne? En effet, un nouveau genre de littérature épistolaire est en train d'apparaître sur les portables, dans les courriels, les applications mobiles et les sites de rencontres. Comment ce genre est-il différent des anciennes lettres d'amour par lesquelles nous correspondions avec nos aux âmes sœurs? Sommes-nous en train d'observer l'apparition d'une littérature e-pistolaire?

In Portuguese, the word romance means both literary novel and love affair. This status given to the amorous plot, making it synonymous with an entire literary genre, is not gratuitous: the search for love has always been one of the most important raw materials of literature. In the most traditional understanding, epistolary novels are series of letters exchanged between characters, fictional or not, although some authors expand the concept to include newspaper clippings and diary entries, for example (Kauffman 1986). The epistolary novel has existed in various forms since the Roman poet Ovid first used epistles in his writings. Even before the novel established itself as the main narrative genre, in the twelfth century, epistolary novels, such as the letters allegedly exchanged between the French philosopher Abelard and his pupil Héloïse, achieved great popularity (Zumthor 2000).

Barthes defines the fascination of following lover's correspondence in *A Lover's Discourse: Fragments*:

> LETTER. The figure aims at the particular dialectic of the love letter, at the same time empty (codified) and expressive (full of desire to signify desire)... As a wish, the love letter awaits your response; it impli-citly imposes on the other to respond, without which the image of it changes, becomes another... The marquise [of Mertueil, in *Les liaisons dangereuses*] is not in love; What she postulates is a correspondence, that is to say, a tactical enterprise destined to defend positions, to secure conquests: this enterprise must know the points (the subsets) of the opposing set, that is to say to detail the image of the other in several points in which the letter will try to play (it is actually a correspondence, in the quasi-mathematical sense of the term). But for the enamored, the letter has no tactical value: it is purely expressive–to be exact, praise (but the praise here is disinterested: it is only the speech of devotion); what I establish with the other is a relation, not a correspondence: the relation links two images. (Barthes 1990, 3 and 32)

The epistolary genre would be particularly suited to the female voice in the historical context of its rise. "As women began to receive education, they were taught to write letters as a form of exercising their newfound knowledge. Female letters used to be love letters and traditionally began with the words: To My Beloved" (Patch 2004, 3). In general, epistolary fiction focuses on this topic: love. The issue of these novels usually was the old and good search for a soul mate.

They have an interesting feature. Maybe because many male authors wrote their books based upon real women's letters in order to reproduce their voices, there is a tradition of including non-fictional elements in epistolary novels, more so than most other fictional genres. Epistolary novelists commonly blur "the lines between fiction and reality, by including morsels of information that seem to be about 'real lives'" (Kauffman 1986, 205). Another feature of epistolary form entails a type of fracturing of the story, dispensing the support of an omniscient and omnipresent narrator. They are non-linear stories par excellence.

The potential of the epistolary literature to leave the two-dimensionality of the paper book had already been shown with another major worldwide success, the pop-up Griffin and Sabine trilogy in which letters, postcards, and envelopes leap from the pages (Bantock 1991). It is curious that, with the advent of telecommunications, the traditional epistolary novel should virtually disappear, along with traditional letter writing.

> Just as the printed novel included customs of the manuscript, and the manuscript reflected oral traditions before that, new technology does not break suddenly with the past, but continues it in a different form. The new forms of epistles borrow iconography, codes of composition and modes of social practice from their predecessor. Email formats reflect previous modes of communication: we still address them with "to" and "from." "Attach file" icons look like paper clips. We use envelope icons for "send," reminiscent of sending the handwritten letters, from which epistolary fiction first stemmed. (Patch 2004, 4)

In fact, some contemporary novels are based on electronic communication, emulating emails and instant messengers to break the linear narrative, upgrading epistolary fiction. But they are not e-pistolary literature yet.

NARRATIVE LAB

As an author of print fiction books but also a digital media researcher, I am interested in one question: how to write a novel about love that is not a pale copy of what has been done in the past, but that reflects the impasses and plots of the contemporary world? How to recount the search for love these days, where interaction takes place predominantly in the virtual universe? I do not see how to narrate a meeting that quite often only exists on the screens of computers, tablets, and smartphones, without performing in the "real world," except by using the tools of electronic literature. Only electronic literature can handle an e-pistolary correspondence that includes new dimensions beyond the written word.

As soon as I started the *Love Letters to Strangers* project, I realized that writing about the search for a soulmate in the contemporary world, reproducing message exchanges that go largely to the cloud, would require a new kind of narrative. A born-digital narrative. My question was how to enrich the epistolary literature of new elements to turn it into e-pistolary. This could include, for example, the unspoken, the erasures and, especially, nowadays, the words deleted, as in the video (https://www.youtube.com/watch?v=zUe3sbtql2Q) "Could have been a love story". An electronic love story should also be told using geolocation tools, like this series written by Brazilian author Daniela Abade. She is behind the mysterious profile, Julia, in Google Maps (https://www.google.com/maps/d/u/0/viewer?ie=UTF8&oe=UTF8&msa=0&mid=1DDqoUQzebEwGD4AlqwPHuArJxgU&ll=13.025965625713502%2C-29.553222499999947&z=3). The new e-pistolary genre can show even augmented reality kisses as this advertisement suggests (YouTube: https://youtu.be/LRiZMVElhas). Or the text itself jumps from the page when matching with a QR Code, as we can see in a book that is part of the most recent Electronic Literature Collection. Between *Page and Screen* is defined by the authors as an unlikely marriage of print and digital. It chronicles a love affair between two characters, P and S, with no words, only geometric patterns that, when coupled with a webcam, "conjure the written word." The story reveals, through a cryptic exchange of letters, the couple's struggle to have a relationship (https://www.betweenpageandscreen.com).

LOVE AVATARS

My second goal with the *Love Letters to Strangers* project was to offer an unprecedented experience of immersion in the universe of dating sites. By uniting text, sound, and image, we gain "one more dimension to express the multidimensional experience of life," as Janet Murray states in *Hamlet on the Holodeck* (Murray 2002, Introduction). The idea was not to publish a traditional print work for newspapers or a linear story. At my lab, at Universidade Federal do Rio de Janeiro, 23 young researchers and I created avatars, made hyperlinked articles describing each site or app we visited, and wrote field journals about our experience. We created a site (**http://projetoparperfeito.wixsite.com/siteparperfeito**), not an e-book.

> Infiltrate
> To enter without an invitation, eventually disguised, without being noticed.
> That's what we did.
> Twenty-three researchers. Dozens of websites. Hundred love letters to strangers. The incessant search for a soul mate.
> A universe increasingly segmented by age, religion, ethnicity, gender, and even by lack or excess of sexual appetite, was unveiled by us in order for you to get acquainted with how online dating websites work.
> Have you ever had the courage to enter one of them?
> We did it for you and prepared this major report about the online search for love. We want to convey the most realistic vision possible on this virtual universe, as if the reader himself was diving into a parallel world.
> It is our stories and those shared by other people about their lives, pursuits of love, sex, or even intimacy with strangers they met on the web that we're going to present here, in a major in-depth report.
> We explored a new way of doing journalism through different narrative structures, which allow a non-linear reading experience of a report combining text, hyperlinks, images, and sound.
> The reader (would that be the exact word?) will be able to visualize each website's home page, follow their tips, ranging from advice to elaborate a more appealing profile to alert about the dangers of meeting strangers.
> It's also possible to follow the insiders' paths and their conversations with users, who will have their identities preserved.
> Episodes experienced by the researchers on dating websites (usually using fake profiles, which we call avatars) were described in two steps: traditional reports, introducing the pages and explaining their character and functioning methods; and delicious field diaries, written in the first person, with a level of subjectivity and involvement rarely allowed in journalistic texts.

We leave here the remembrance of this project of a pursuit for a P@r Perfeito, carried out in 2011. Among its products, there is a website, a printed newspaper, and a blog, developed in the School of Communication and the Contemporary Culture Advanced Program of the Federal University of Rio de Janeiro (UFRJ).
I was the leader of this project. But it was more than that.
I also infiltrated myself...

If the umbrella theme was the search for love on the internet, it was still necessary to subdivide it into 23 different articles. Each researcher should research a single subject, which required them to spend weeks searching the network for novelties and unusual angles. The material they brought me was surprising. There were sites for evangelicals, gays, lesbians, beautiful, ugly, fat, old people, for everything that is taste and target. We agreed that infiltrators would create avatars, one or more fake personalities to communicate with participants from previously chosen sites.

After more than one year working on this project, what conclusions did we reach?

I quickly noticed an interesting point: offline, the first contact is visual. Criterion No. 1 is the appearance. In relationships started online, the order is reversed. People first know each other "inside", talk about their tastes, past, and projects, only to make their first meeting outside. All this gives an illusion of intimacy. More than relationships, they are affective connections mediated by computer.

Sherry Turkle points out that one of the problems of talking to someone over the internet is that you lose the non-verbal component, the body language that may even contradict the words spoken (Turkle **1997**). The text also ends up having a tone more thought than speech, which loses its naturalness. But the nature of online communication has also changed with Skype, for example, which allows for closer interaction with a face-to-face interview. In any case, it is not because you have more control over the writing than over the spoken that you would lack spontaneity in an email or SMS exchange. One of my findings was that the continuous exchange of emails leads to a sense of intimacy, like the old epistolary novels. In these cases, the computer screen acts as a blank frame, or a mirror, where you can project any wish or illusion.

AN IMPOSSIBLE NETNOGRAPHY

Without incorporating an avatar or even exposing yourself to the web just the way you are, how do you understand the dynamics of a dating site and what moves people to look for them? How to understand that it is possible to feel intimate with a stranger you have never seen in person? To answer such complex questions, I had to be a participant observer myself. I had to interact and flirt with the suitors, abandoning the role of privileged observer, without involvement. But what if a certain profile awakened my own fantasies? And if that happened, how much would I like to expose myself, since I knew from the beginning that my correspondence would be public, shared with my readers?

Dating sites can be valuable cultural objects by revealing how contemporary society experiences the ancestral quest for a partner and affection. A perfect object of netnography. Traditionally, ethnographers make field journals, where they write both observations and reflections, which review emotions aroused by the experiment. The field diary is also a kind of autoethnography, since its basis is autobiographical. I followed the netnography manuals (Kozinets **2009**), but only to a degree. After all, writers can take certain liberties that would be considered somewhat unethical by the social sciences. Ethnographical research is guided by rules for research with human beings, which methodological inspiration comes from the biomedical sciences. But testing vaccines and drugs is quite different from interviewing.

Although, the interaction on a dating site is not always innocuous. Feelings can be hurt, hopes dashed, illusions undone by a researcher who, as in our case, pretends to be someone looking for a soulmate. I guarantee that all the identities of the people who interacted with us were preserved, except those who gave me their consent.

Obviously, I did not introduce myself as a writer or researcher. This is not to say that I lied. My “avatar” pieces of information were true at that time: name, profession, city where I live, marital status, photos, number of children, interests, up to age and weight. After all, omitting is not lying.

Basics

Occupation	Journalist and university teacher
Age	48
Height	5'5"
Wants Kids	Maybe
Kids at Home	Yes
Ethnicity	Hispanic or Latino
Religion	Christian
Drinks	About once a week
Smokes	Never

I chose an American site to escape the possibility of being identified by someone I know and thus damage my reputation. I also chose E-Harmony because, unlike most dating sites, it is not intended to be a virtual showcase, where thousands of profiles of your choice are displayed. It is not the user himself who selects people who might be interested in researching photos and profiles, but a computer program that combines personal characteristics from the questionnaire that identifies the psychological basis and "how to love" each one. It is interesting to leave it to your computer to find your soul mate.

Usually, the correspondence at E-Harmony goes through 4 steps

Step 1 – Get to know each other

Gain insight on how your match thinks or acts in certain situations by exchanging 5 questions. These questions help both you and your match to learn more about each other beyond what's in your respective profiles.

Step 2 – Must Haves & Can't Stands

Exchange 10 relationship Must Haves and Can't Stands. Let each other know the qualities you absolutely must have in a relationship as well as those which are deal breakers.

Step 3 - Learn more about each other

Reveal more of your inner thoughts, feelings, and values with 3 open-ended questions. Choose from our list of questions or create your own.

Step 4 - Send eHarmony Mail

Maintain a safe, easy, and anonymous communication environment with eHarmony Mail. Send each other messages directly. When you're ready, pursue the relationship outside of eHarmony.

Here you can have a taste of what is the quiz about:

Must Haves

◉ Chemistry... I must feel deeply in love with and attracted to my partner.
○ Communicator... I must have someone who is good at talking and listening.
◉ Sense of Humor... I must have someone who is sharp and can enjoy the humorous side of life.
○ Verbal Intimacy... I must know that my partner is sharing their deepest emotional thoughts and desires.
○ Emotionally Healthy... I must have a partner who is emotionally healthy, and able to share a stable life with someone else.
○ Strong Character... I must have a partner who is honest and strong enough to do the right thing.
○ Artistry... I must have a partner who has a passion for music, literature, drama, art, and the finer things in life either as a spectator or participant.
○ Education... I must have someone whose educational achievements match my own.
○ Exciting... I must have someone who isn't afraid to take a risk and who sees life as an adventure.
○ Patience... I must have someone who can handle life's frustrations or momentary setbacks with a patient, steady, demeanor.
○ Conflict Resolver... I must have a partner who will work to resolve rather than win arguments or conflicts within our relationship.
○ Personal Habits... I must have a partner who maintains high standards of personal hygiene, orderliness, and other personal habits.

◉ Affectionate... I must have someone who is comfortable giving and receiving affection.
◉ Energy Level... I must have someone whose energy level matches my own.
○ Intellect... I must have a partner who is bright and can share my understanding of the world as well as enjoy discussing important issues.
○ Self-Confident... I must have a partner who knows and believes in himself/herself throughout life's ups and downs.
○ Able to Accept Help... I must have a partner who is willing to accept outside help for personal or relationship issues that are serious and important.
◉ Curiosity... I must have a partner who is hungry for new information and knowledge and who strives to learn as much as possible.
○ Adaptability... I must have a partner who is able to adapt to life's surprises.
○ Organized... I must have a partner who values structure in their life.
◉ Tolerant... I must have a partner who is able to hear and appreciate divergent viewpoints.
○ Attractiveness... I must have a partner who is considered "very attractive" by most current standards.
○ Industriousness... I must have someone who is willing to work hard at whatever they do.
◉ Emotionally Generous... I must have a partner who enjoys people and is generous with his or her compassion, attention, sympathies and love.
○ Unassuming... I must have someone who is able to accept criticism, and even admit to being wrong sometimes.
○ Loyal... I must have someone I can count on to always support me.

Values

○ Family Life... I must have a partner who is committed to marriage, home, and family.
○ Style and Appearance... I must have someone who cares about the way they look and dress and has a sense of personal style.
○ Shared Politics... I must have someone who has political beliefs which are the same or similar to my own.
○ Spirit of Volunteerism... I must have a partner who shares my willingness to volunteer and support community and / or social causes.
○ Autonomy... I must have a partner who will give me space to be my own person.

◉ Shared Interests... I must have someone who is willing to share my interests and passions.

Family

○ No Children... I must have someone who shares my desire to not have children.
○ Family... I must have someone who shares my desire to have or adopt children.
○ Stepchildren... I must have someone who will accept my children as their own.
○ Parent Care... I must have someone who is willing to help me take care of my parents, now or when the time comes.
○ Parenting Style... I must have someone who shares my views about how to raise children.

Social Living

○ Sociability... I must have a partner who loves to socialize with lots of different people.
○ Staying In... I must have a partner who mainly enjoys staying in together and having quiet evenings alone or with close friends.

Spirituality

○ Spirituality... I must have someone with a similar deep commitment to spirituality, who shares my beliefs.
○ Spiritual Acceptance... My partner must accept and respect my spiritual beliefs, whether they share them or not.
○ Religious Practice... My partner must be committed to being an active member of a church or temple congregation.

Financial

○ Responsible... My partner must be financially responsible.
○ Relaxed... I must have a partner who is able to forget about money and focus on the important parts of life.
○ Ambition... I must have a partner who shares my desire to achieve high financial and/or career goals.

Sexuality

○ Abstinent... I must have a spouse who has saved himself/herself sexually for marriage.
◉ Sexually Knowledgeable... I must have someone who is mature and experienced as a potential sexual partner and is able to express himself/herself freely.
○ Traditional... I must have someone who is reserved and traditional in their sexual needs.
○ Passionate... I must have someone who is willing to explore our sexual desires with passion and understanding.

Can't Stands

Traits

○ Vanity... I can't stand someone who is overly interested in their physical appearance.
◉ Dependence... I can't stand someone who bases their happiness on me.
○ Lying... I can't stand someone who lies to anyone—especially to me.
○ Cheating... I can't stand someone who takes advantage of people.
◉ Anger... I can't stand someone who can't manage their anger, who yells or bottles it up inside.
◉ Rude... I can't stand someone who is belittling, impatient or hateful to people in any situation.
○ Unhappy at Work... I can't stand someone who hates their job and complains about it all the time.

○ Denial... I can't stand someone who is unable to accept blame or see fault in their own actions.
○ Workaholic... I can't stand someone who treats everything in life as secondary to their job.
○ Lazy... I can't stand someone who likes to spend excessive time sleeping, resting or being a "couch potato."
○ Worrier... I can't stand someone who easily loses perspective and constantly worries.
○ Intolerance... While I understand that religious conviction is a positive trait, I can't stand someone who is self-righteous and feels that their particular faith is the only one that matters.
○ Victim Mentality... While everyone has times of self-pity, I can't stand someone who continually sees himself/herself as a victim.
○ Grudges... I can't stand someone who has a chip on their shoulder.
○ Mean Spirited... I can't stand someone who has a devious nature and is mean to others.
○ Fiscally Irresponsible... I can't stand someone who is incapable of managing their money.
○ Hypochondriac... I can't stand someone who has a general disposition of sickness and is constantly treating the symptoms of their supposed illness.
○ Excessive Overweight... I can't stand someone who is overweight.
○ Gambling... I can't stand someone who gambles.
○ Intruding Family/Friends... I can't stand someone whose relatives and friends are constantly calling or visiting.
○ Depressed... I can't stand someone who is constantly unhappy about their life.
○ Cynicism... I can't stand someone who generally sees the world from a cynical perspective.
○ Self-Centered... I can't stand someone whose main topic of conversation is himself/herself.
○ Materialistic... I can't stand someone who sees material items as a measure of success.
○ Childishness... I can't stand someone who is not emotionally mature.
○ Petty... I can't stand someone who focuses on imperfection.
◉ Boorishness... I can't stand someone who is inclined to rowdy, vulgar or disrespectful behavior when "having fun."
○ Drugs... I can't stand someone who uses illegal recreational drugs.

Values

◉ Flirts... I can't stand someone who constantly flirts with the opposite sex.
○ Television Junkie... I can't stand someone who constantly watches television.
◉ Poor Hygiene... I can't stand someone who is not clean.
○ Gossip... I can't stand someone who loves to talk about other people.
○ Judgmental... I can't stand someone who finds fault with everyone and everything.
○ Addictions... I can't stand someone who currently suffers from addictions.
○ Undependable... I can't stand someone who fails to come through and is unreliable.
○ Foul Mouthed... I can't stand someone who swears or uses inappropriate language or humor.
○ Extremely Shy... I can't stand someone who is so shy that they cannot open up and share with me.
○ Political Correctness... I can't stand someone who censors their thoughts and opinions with a politically correct agenda.
◉ Recklessness... I can't stand someone who has a careless and irresponsible manner when with others.
◉ Sexually Obsessed... I can't stand someone who is sexually obsessive.
○ Uninterested... I can't stand someone who does not enjoy having sex on a regular basis.
○ Infidelity... I can't stand someone who engages in sex outside a committed relationship.
○ Punctuality... I can't stand someone who is always late.
◉ Racist... I can't stand someone who believes that any particular ethnic group to which they belong is superior to the rest of humanity.
○ Hypocrites... I can't stand someone who holds a double standard for their actions and those of other people.
○ Pornography... I can't stand someone who views or owns pornography in any form.
○ Sloppy... I can't stand someone who is unkempt.
○ Cheap... I can't stand someone who is so tightfisted as to be impractical.
◉ Arrogant... I can't stand someone who is obnoxiously cocky.
○ Pessimism... I can't stand someone who always sees the glass as half empty.

After one year of E-harmony research, I had 1,570 possible matches, but maintained contact mediated by the site with only 123, and had conversations by email with 14. Only three became so interested that I had to tell them my real intentions, and I got their consent to transcribe our conversations. For example, instead of being ashamed to have revealed that he was looking for a girlfriend, the American executive Ross Cooper loved the idea of being a "book" character, part of an academic/literary research project. If I had to create a character like Mr. Cooper, I would not have had enough imagination. A former guitarist who at age 17 went on tour with his rock band and only came back six years later, Ross was a nerd and studied computer science.

It is not in his Linkedin profile, but he told me that, married and having kids to raise, he decided it was time to stop living on crumbs as a programmer and make real money. That is when he invented a software program to prepare for the SAT, which sold more than 1 million units in the United States. He did not stop. Ross told me he created and purchased more than 25 product patents. About 10 years before we met, he founded a digital media content company. He also surfed in his spare time. Most of the time, Ross was aboard a plane in Asia. One day he was writing from Thailand, another from China, and the following week from Japan. Why would an overpowering guy like this waste his time with a Brazilian whom he has met on a dating site?

FROM: Ross Cooper
TO: Cristiane costa
SUBJECT: many

I have been looking for a special someone for a long long time. I cannot find one here or anywhere else. This is why I am so happy to talk to you. I am very interested in you only.

I want to love and be loved. That's the most important thing for me. There is an empty space in me that can only be filled by my soulmate. If I'm not thinking about work, I am thinking about who might be my soulmate. These days… I think about you throughout my day. You are a very important person to me. I convinced we don't need any specific structure. We can just enjoy and support each other. If we decide we need more from each other later on, that's fine too.

Sincerely yours,
Ross

BTW: I will soon shut down the E-Harmony as I truly don't have time for it. Now that I found you, I believe the E-Harmony service has served its purpose.

CONCLUSION

Exchanging messages with strangers is not completely new in the history of mankind. Quite a few people found their spouses that way in the past, even though it was much rarer than today. The Portuguese writer Albertina Bessa-Luís was one who used an advertisement to find a match. Born in 1922, she used her literary gifts, which would later earn her a Camões Award, to write an ad looking for a husband. Disenchanted with the boys of her environment, who were without cultural ambition, Albertina placed an ad in a newspaper in search of an "intelligent and educated" correspondent. Alberto Luís, a law student at Coimbra University, replied. A year later, they married. The family still holds hundreds of letters written throughout this year's courtship. It would make a romance. Her granddaughter is already writing. She was not the one and only intellectual who tried this. The book *They Call Me Naughty Lola* (Rose 2010) is an irresistible collection of the most brilliant and often absurd lonely-hearts ads from the erudite London Review of Books. How different is it from a site like Academic Singles, where scholars can find their soul mate?

Soon after building my website for *Love Letters for Strangers* research, I realized how quickly it became obsolete. First, because the universe of dating sites and apps is much larger and rhizomatic than I was able to map. Every day a new website or application is born, able to build social networks from unsuspected elective affinities. Second, apps like Tinder took the market by offering a more practical and reliable way of communication.

Another reason for the obsolescence was the realization that, born digital, the dating sites themselves created digital narrative strategies to develop an epistolary communication. This is the biggest gap. Faced with gigantic economic power, as well as a full-time developer team focused on engaging, using technologies such as eye tracking, these networks are themselves producing new communication and interaction tools in order to match millions of people and make them exchange love letters to strangers.

Bantock, Nick. 1991. *Griffin and Sabine.* San Francisco: Chronicle Books.

Barthes, Roland. 1990. *Fragmentos de um Discurso Amoroso.* Rio de Janeiro: Francisco Alves.

Boursuk, Amaranth, et Brad Bouse. 2012. *Between Page and Screen.* SpringGun. Link: https://www.betweenpageandscreen.com

Costa, Cristiane. 2011. *P@r Perfeito.* Link: http://www.projetoparperfeito.wixsite.com/siteparperfeito

Hayles, N. Katherine. 2009. *Literatura eletrônica: novos horizontes para o literário.* São Paulo: Global.

Kauffman, Linda. 1986. *Discourses of desire: gender, genre and epistolary fictions.* Ithaca; London: Cornell University Press.

Kozinets, Robert. 2009. *Netnography: Doing Ethnographic Research Online.* London: Sage.

Murray, Janet H. 2003. *Hamlet no Holodeck: o futuro da narrativa no ciberespaço.* São Paulo: Unesp.

Patch, Laura. 2004. *To My Beloved, BB4N: the history of "woman's" writing, or the epistolary novel.* 2004. Link: https://repository.library.georgetown.edu/bitstream/handle/10822/709197/The-History-of-the-Epistolary-Novel.pdf?sequence=1&isAllowed=y

Rose, David. 2010. *They call me naughty Lola: personal ads from the London Review of books.* London: Scribner.

Turkle, Sherry. 1997. *Life on the Screen: Identity in the Age of Internet.* New York: Simon & Schuster.

Zumthor, Paul. 2000. *Corrspondência de Abelardo e Heloisa.* São Paulo: Martins Fontes.

Haptic Onto-Epistem-Ology in Tendre Claw's *Pry*

ABRAHAM AVNISAN • AMARANTH BORSUK

Abstract

In *Pry* (Tender Claws, 2016), the interactive novella designed for Apple's iPad and iPhone by Samantha Gorman and Danny Cannizzaro, readers are invited to enter the unconscious of James Jenner, a Gulf War veteran suffering from post-traumatic stress and gradual optical degeneration. The game-like multimedia narrative requires us to take an active, haptic role in unfolding the story, uncovering the reasons behind James's choice to enlist, his failing sight, and the flashbacks that disrupt his daily life as a demolitions expert. Reading between the lines and beneath the surface, the text implies, will allow us to understand his situation more deeply. Through a series of material metaphors that map the iOS's multitouch gestures onto the history of the book, this complex work raises questions about memory and experience that are at the heart of the text. Through these haptic "ontoepistemologies," *Pry* asks us to consider our cultural definitions of reading, seeing, and knowing–particularly how those have been indelibly shaped by the object we think of as a book.

Résumé

Dans *Pry* (Tender Claws, 2016), le court roman interactif créé pour iPad et iPhone d'Apple par Samantha Gorman et Danny Cannizzaro, les lecteurs sont invités à entrer dans l'inconscient de James Jenner, un vétéran de la guerre du Golfe souffrant de stress post-traumatique et de dégénérescence optique graduelle. Le récit multimédia, qui ressemble à un jeu, exige que les participants jouent un rôle actif et haptique dans le déroulement de l'histoire, découvrant les raisons pour lesquelles James s'est engagé, sa vue défaillante et les flashbacks qui perturbent sa vie quotidienne d'expert en démolition. Lire entre les lignes et sous la surface paraît insinuer le texte; cela permet aux participants de comprendre plus profondément sa situation. À travers une série de métaphores matérielles qui met en correspondance les gestes multitouch de l'iOS avec le récit du roman, cette œuvre complexe soulève des questions sur la mémoire et l'expérience, au cœur du texte. À travers ces « ontoépistémologies » haptiques, *Pry* demande aux participants de reconsidérer leurs définitions culturelles de la lecture, de la vue et de la connaissance – en particulier la façon dont elles ont été façonnées par le livre.

In *Pry* (Cannizzaro, Gorman, and Tender Claws **2016**), the interactive novella designed for Apple's iPad and iPhone by Samantha Gorman and Danny Cannizzaro, readers are invited to enter the unconscious of James Jenner, a Gulf War veteran suffering from post-traumatic stress and gradual optical degeneration. The game-like multimedia narrative requires us to take an active, haptic role in unfolding the story, uncovering the reasons behind James's choice to enlist, his failing sight, and the flashbacks that disrupt his daily life as a demolitions expert. Like much electronic literature, the work teaches the reader how to enter and interact with the text. After an introductory, cinematic flashback in which we watch James leave home for the military in 1991, the novella's opening chapter, set six years later, begins. Here, a set of onscreen paratextual cues prompt us to use the familiar iOS spread and pinch gestures to access James's waking present, on the one hand, and his interior thoughts, memories, and unconscious on the other [Figures 1–2].

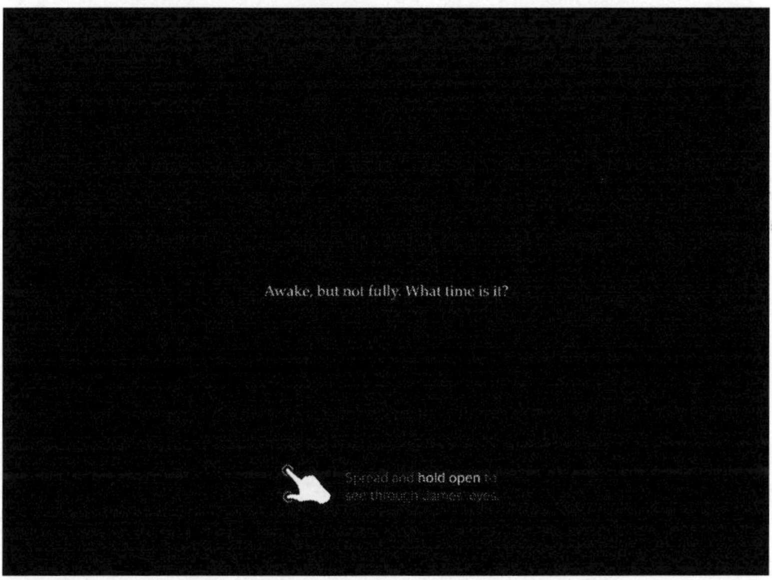

Figure 1. On-screen cues in the first chapter, "Below and Above," prompt us to use the spread gesture to see through James's first-person perspective.

Figure 2. The pinch gesture allows the reader to access James's subconscious thoughts.

Reading between the lines and beneath the surface, the text implies, will allow us to understand his situation more deeply and, perhaps, uncover the mysteries that drive James's actions and haunt his dreams. But how we pry into James's subconscious, and what, exactly, prying means, varies over the course of the work's seven chapters and appendix. From unfolding an accordion of virtual text to running our fingers along biblical verses written in braille, each chapter iterates on the material metaphor, to borrow N. Katherine Hayles's term (Hayles **2002**, 21), associated with the multitouch gesture as a way into James's story, constructing an elaborate, multivalent, and richly layered work that brings together personal and geopolitical histories. Each of these interfaces draws on both the affordances of the touchscreen and the history of the book to raise questions about memory and experience that are at the heart of the text. Much as James grapples with his loss of sight on the one hand and the visions from his past that surface unbidden on the other, as readers we must use our hands to navigate between the two. In doing so, we must consider our cultural definitions of reading, seeing, and knowing–particularly how those have been indelibly shaped by the object we think of as a book.

By forcing the reader's body into contact with the text, *Pry* engages what we are calling haptic "ontoepistemologies," a term adapted from feminist theorist and particle physicist Karen Barad. In her book *Meeting the Universe*

Halfway, Barad draws out the philosophical implications of quantum physics to propose that "practices of knowing and being are not isolable; they are mutually implicated. We don't obtain knowledge by standing outside the world; we know because we are of the world" (Barad 2007, 185). For Barad, knowing and being are inseparable because knowledge arises not simply through discourse or observation, but through intra-action–it is relational, rather than predetermined or inherent. If we refuse to privilege language over matter and subject over object, her work suggests, we enter into an ethico-onto-epistem-ology, "an appreciation of the intertwining of ethics, knowing, and being" (Barad 2007, 185), an ethical position that strongly resonates with *Pry*'s sensitive treatment of a charged political and personal subject.

Through its haptic interface, the novella challenges the reader to rethink our understanding of what constitutes knowledge and how that knowledge has historically been conflated with the process of reading as bound up in books, largely perceived as repositories of wisdom for the ages. It intervenes into a Western literary tradition that privileges sight and language as sites of meaning-making over and above touch and other relational ways of being. In chapter after chapter, *Pry* confronts us with different reading interfaces–a peep-show, a flip book, a scroll, a fan, a braille page. Each of these interfaces requires us to rethink our definition of the book as inextricably linked to the codex, a sheaf of pages bound along one side and enclosed between covers. Furthermore, each of these methods of reading requires the reader to step into or embody James's own onto-epistemology–his way of both being in and understanding the world–which is in turn grounded in his embodied experience as a veteran with PTSD who is losing his sight.

In *Pry*, reading is measured not by the eye's traversal of the text, but the hand's. The more we read, measured, in part, by the more we touch, the more of the work's final chapter, the appendix, becomes available to us. This appendix is unusual: it serves as a kind of key, helping us fit together the pieces of *Pry* we have been unfolding. Structured as an "album," it stands in metonymically for an album James carries throughout the novella: one that figures in flashbacks to a fight with Jessie, his unrequited love, in which its pages are gripped and torn. Unlike that album, in which he inserts family photographs and souvenirs, this album's images consist of long pages of text in which James diaristically recounts his family and wartime experiences. Each memory in the album scrolls infinitely both horizontally and vertically–meaning that we can read the text continuously either across or down the page—a seemingly-impossible interface that alludes to the historical scroll, one of our oldest portable book forms, but that is only truly possible in digital space [Figure 3].

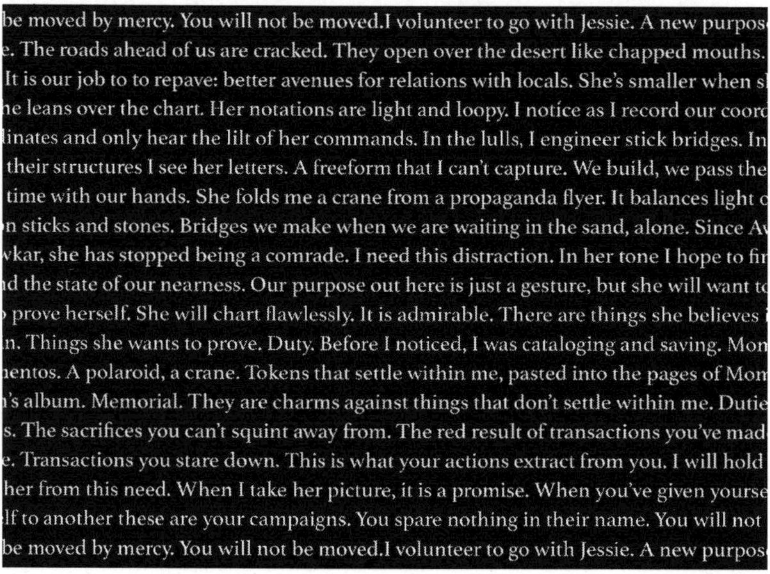
be moved by mercy. You will not be moved.I volunteer to go with Jessie. A new purpos
e. The roads ahead of us are cracked. They open over the desert like chapped mouths.
It is our job to to repave: better avenues for relations with locals. She's smaller when s
he leans over the chart. Her notations are light and loopy. I notice as I record our coord
inates and only hear the lilt of her commands. In the lulls, I engineer stick bridges. In
their structures I see her letters. A freeform that I can't capture. We build, we pass the
time with our hands. She folds me a crane from a propaganda flyer. It balances light o
n sticks and stones. Bridges we make when we are waiting in the sand, alone. Since Av
vkar, she has stopped being a comrade. I need this distraction. In her tone I hope to fin
d the state of our nearness. Our purpose out here is just a gesture, but she will want to
prove herself. She will chart flawlessly. It is admirable. There are things she believes i
n. Things she wants to prove. Duty. Before I noticed, I was cataloging and saving. Mom
ementos. A polaroid, a crane. Tokens that settle within me, pasted into the pages of Mom
's album. Memorial. They are charms against things that don't settle within me. Dutie
s. The sacrifices you can't squint away from. The red result of transactions you've mad
e. Transactions you stare down. This is what your actions extract from you. I will hold
her from this need. When I take her picture, it is a promise. When you've given yourse
lf to another these are your campaigns. You spare nothing in their name. You will not
be moved by mercy. You will not be moved.I volunteer to go with Jessie. A new purpos

Figure 3. The text of the appendix wraps to the screen's dimensions but also continues beyond the frame in an infinite scrolling canvas.

As part of the game mechanic of the novella, we "earn" access to these memories based on how much we have interacted with the preceding chapters, as demonstrated in the table of contents by the number of diamonds that appear below each chapter title [Figure 4]. As in the western tradition, reading leads to knowledge, but not as something that takes place between the page, the eyes and the brain. Rather, *Pry* dismantles this subject-object relationship to text, offering us an embodied experience, albeit in a limited fashion. By engaging in this haptic onto-epistemology the authors are able to create a much richer narrative, taking on questions of ability, memory, and trauma that might otherwise have come across as simplistic or reductive.

Figure 4. Diamonds in the table of contents indicate how much of a chapter's content we have read.

One of the things that makes *Pry* compelling is the way it takes advantage of its medium so thoroughly, drawing on behaviors the reader already knows how to perform. This is not to say that it is not also an ergodic work, requiring the reader to probe and pry into its depths, but rather that the authors have chosen to draw on gestures that have been normalized and rendered invisible by Apple, meeting the reader on comfortable footing before defamiliarizing an interface designed to be seamless. The pinch and spread gestures function differently from one chapter to another: in Chapter 1, as we have seen, spreading open allows us to "see through James' eyes" while pinching closed allows us to "enter James' subconscious" (Cannizzaro, Gorman, and Tender Claws **2016**). This same gesture, however, functions differently in Chapter 6, in which we are confronted with a text couplet separated by a small plus sign, a clue that here the spread gesture expands the text, revealing additional lines hidden between those of James's narrative [Figure 5].

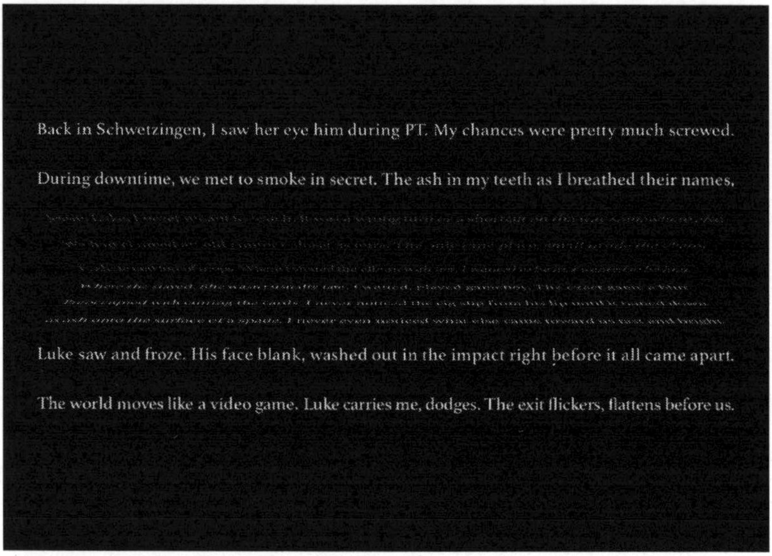

Figure 5. Pinching open the text in Chapter 6, "Dharan, Saudi Arabia," reveals additional narrative points between the lines, unfolding like an accordion book.

In Chapter 7, the pinch and zoom gestures take us through layers of video, allowing us to engage more deeply with the fragmented loops we have encountered briefly as flashbacks and repressed memories. Much like a tunnel book or peep show, with juxtaposed layers allowing us to peer deep into a scene, spreading moves us layer by layer through a series of vignettes. Sometimes the gesture allows us to move between two camera angles as we watch James and Luke, reunited after their service, camping in the desert, building a bonfire, and bantering easily. Only after cascading through these scenes do we begin to encounter text, which now represents what could be an inner monologue or Luke's side of the conversation as they begin to speak about Jessie, whose death haunts them both [Figure 6]. Once again the gesture has shifted its function, and the line between James's thoughts, memories, and self-narrative blurs.

Figure 6. In Chapter 7, "Camp," the pinch gesture takes us deeper into layers of videos that emulate the structure of a peep-show box or tunnel book.

While *Pry* opens up onto-epistemology through a wide variety of interfaces, Chapter 3: "Jacob and Esau," provides a particularly resonant example of the way the text challenges our relationship to historical ways of knowing by forcing us to re-evaluate what it means to read. It does so through both its haptic interface and its engagement with a biblical narrative that centers on sight and touch as two different modalities of gaining knowledge. In this chapter, the reader is again placed into James's body as he reads a braille Bible inherited from his mother. The braille cells' tactile raised dots are here visually represented as white dots against a black background. As we swipe our fingertip across the dots, we hear James's voice sounding the words aloud and see a cinematic montage of James's memories and associations with each line of verse [Figure 7].

Figure 7. As the reader swipes rapidly across the braille text, images from James's memories surface.

Unlike in previous chapters, the familiar haptic that the authors defamiliarize and reinvent is not the pinch and spread, but the swipe gesture. On multi-touch devices, the all-purpose swipe has come to replace the click and drag of the mouse or trackpad: it is not only a way to move around an image or document, but also a way to flip through the pages of a book and scroll through a webpage. In Chapter 3, *Pry* defamiliarizes the swipe skeuomorphically by returning it to its pre-digital significance: virtually recreating the real-world gesture used to read braille. While the gesture is absolutely identical, the simulacrum is, of course, futile: the multi-touch device remains absolutely smooth as the virtual raised dots have no way of escaping the limitations of their pixel-based representation.

In this chapter, the Old Testament story of conflict, deception, and eventual resolution between Rebecca and Isaac's twin sons, Jacob and Esau, is reinterpreted through James's personal experience, offering clues to the mystery at the story's center. The tight correlation between biblical verse and cinematic image leaves little ambiguity as to James's interpretation of the story: Jacob and Esau become James and Luke respectively; and Rebecca becomes a composite comprised of James's mother and Jessie. Here, the collapse between

James's childhood, the unresolved loss of his mother, and his obsession with Jessie are particularly poignant.

In the biblical story, Jacob tricks his blind father Isaac into giving him the blessing of the first born, which properly belongs to his brother Esau, Isaac's favorite. Under his mother's guidance, Jacob masquerades as Esau and serves his father a dish of goat, prepared by Rebecca just as Isaac likes it. In exchange for this meal, Isaac gives him the blessing, but only after assuring himself that this is indeed his beloved first born, the hunter, by touching his hands, which Rebecca has thoughtfully draped in goatskin to simulate Esau's hairy body. The story might be said to privilege vision over touch as the most reliable route to knowledge because it is Isaac's inability to see that enables Jacob and Rebecca to deceive him. However, the Old Testament sides with Jacob, establishing him as the progenitor of the nation of Israel whose treachery is necessary to secure his line, and it establishes Esau as a buffoon whose own foolish choices lead to his downfall. The story thus reclaims touch as an essential way of knowing that perhaps allows deeper insight than vision or received knowledge, which holds that the first born inherits all.

This story resonates for James, not only because he himself is losing his vision due to a genetic condition inherited from his mother, but because his relationship to his best friend and the woman they both love has been utterly destroyed by something he has seen that he should not have–Luke and Jessie having sex in a closet–and by his own subsequent failure to turn a blind eye. We gradually learn that James's fight with Jessie stems in part from his having snitched to his superiors about Jessie and Luke's ongoing relationship, resulting first in her transfer and then in far more severe repercussions for all three of them that James could not have anticipated. Here, vision fails. And it is only as James relinquishes sight and turns his vision inward that he can begin to grapple with the ramifications of what he has done [Figure 8].

Figure 8. Chapter 1 opens with a shot of James in bed, the camera drifting down from the ceiling to enter his open eye, which stands in metonymically for the inward-turning the text requires of us to gain insight into his past.

Likewise, *Pry* deprivileges sight and, by extension, the traditional understanding of reading as a process that takes place between the codex, eyes, and brain. By bringing our hand to the virtual raised dots on the screen's surface, it deceives us the way Jacob deceived Isaac, since what we see and what we feel do not match up. The remediation of braille, while futile, also functions perfectly to remind us that touch changes how we read, how we know, and how we are in the world. By drawing on historical and material modes of reading like the braille book, accordion, and scroll, *Pry* reminds us that reading has never been the disembodied experience our current cultural norms would have us believe, but rather one that always involves both hand and eye in making meaning. The novella actively values touch by rewarding the reader's interaction with a deeper understanding of James's past traumas and personal demons, which are added to the appendix each time we read.

One could argue that *Pry* values the haptic interface because it is, in fact, the only way to quantify a reader's engagement, short of eye-tracking technology, which is still an imperfect measure. Such a dismissal, however, fails to account for how deeply ingrained the haptic mechanics are into the narrative itself. Chapter after chapter, it is the haptic interactions that allow us to pry beneath the surface of James's waking life and of his version of events. Failing to interact with the text gives James the power to narrate his own story, but it limits what he tells us because it limits what he knows about himself and his world. Prying beneath the surface is the only way to get the bigger picture. Much as we each perceive ourselves to be the narrator of the book of our life, *Pry* reminds us that our understanding of the world is inseparable from unconscious and embodied experience. The novella forces us to confront the tension between the self we construct and the self as it stands in entangled relation to the world around it. Using James's blindness as a metaphor for the deterioration of classical forms of reading, the novella shows us how our relationship to literature is transforming thanks to digital media in ways it has always been transformed, but that we have forgotten how to see.

Barad, Karen. 2007. *Meeting the Universe Halfway: Quantum Physics and the Entanglement of Matter and Meaning.* Durham: Duke University Press.

Cannizzaro, Danny, Samantha Gorman, and Tender Claws. 2016. *Pry.* Tender Claws, LLC. June 9, 2016. Version 2.0. The App Store.

Hayles, Katherine N. 2002. *Writing Machines.* Cambridge: MIT Press.

Digital Deep-Sea Diving: Navigating the Narrative Depths of E-Lit and VR

MELINDA M. WHITE

Abstract

Storytelling is an attempt to convey the subjective human experience; with emerging media and heightened levels of interactivity, authors/artists are finding new ways to more fully immerse the reader into their world, what Murray calls "digital swimming." *ii – in the white darkness* by Reiner Strasser and M.D. Coverley is an example of an immersive work of electronic literature that attempts to convey the process of memory loss in conditions like Alzheimer's or Parkinson's disease. With virtual reality, what Chris Milk calls "the ultimate empathy machine," we sink into simulated fictional worlds, ideally allowing composers to push subjective experience even further, fully immersing reader/viewer/participant into an experience. John Hull's *Notes on Blindness* VR experience, for instance, conveys an experience of blindness that is indescribable in words and has to be told through feeling. Both of these texts utilize the affordances of their media to convey a subjective experience and evoke empathy, *Notes on Blindness* through a more internal empathetic experience. And isn't this our desire, to convey subjective human experience to others–to experience, to understand, to grow?
This article will explore the gaps between the idealistic view of empathetic response in a VR experience and the realities of the technology. Including theory from Janet Murray, Marie-Laure Ryan, and Nathaniel Stern, I plan to investigate the complications of augmented and virtual reality narratives. I will discuss how they alter ideas of embodiment and immersive narrative, how we can define boundaries within them, how they turn the tables on reader/author relationships, how we need to consider their unique affordances in storytelling, their potential for evoking empathy and compassion, and how they are, inevitably, the storytelling of our future.

Résumé

La narration représente une tentative de transmettre l'expérience humaine subjective ; avec les médias émergents et les niveaux accrus d'interactivité, les auteurs/artistes trouvent de nouvelles façons de plonger le lecteur dans leur monde, ce que Murray appelle « la nage numérique ». *ii – in the white darkness* de Reiner Strasser et M.D. Coverley est un exemple d'œuvre immersive de littérature numérique qui tente de transmettre le processus de la perte de mémoire des maladies telles que l'Alzheimer ou le Parkinson. Avec la réalité virtuelle, ce que Chris Milk appelle « la machine d'empathie ultime », on plonge dans les mondes fictifs simulés, permettant idéalement aux auteurs/artistes de pousser l'expérience subjective encore plus loin, immersant le lecteur/observateur/participant dans une expérience. L'expérience RV *Notes on Blindness*, par exemple, transmet l'expérience de la cécité qui est indescriptible en mots et doit être racontée à travers les sensations. Ces deux textes utilisent les médias à leur disposition afin de transmettre une expérience subjective et évoquer l'empathie, *Notes on Blindness*, par une expérience empathique plus interne. Et n'est-ce pas là notre désir, de transmettre une expérience humaine aux autres – d'expérimenter, de comprendre, de grandir ?
Cet article explore les écarts entre la vue idéaliste de la réponse empathique au sein d'une expérience RV et les réalités de la technologie. En fondant mon propos sur les théories de Janet Murray, de Marie-Laure Ryan et de Nathaniel Stern, j'examinerai la complexité des récits de la réalité augmentée et virtuelle. Je discuterai de la manière dont ils transforment les idées d'incarnation et de narration immersive, dont nous pouvons définir les limites en leur sein, dont ils renversent les rôles dans les rapports lecteur/auteur, dont nous devons tenir compte de leurs moyens uniques dans la narration et de leur potentiel pour évoquer l'empathie et la compassion, et, inévitablement, dont ils sont le récit de notre avenir.

> *"We can still dream of an art experience that is not only immersive and interactive, like our relation to the lifeworld, but that, in contrast to the randomness of life, also offers the design and meaningfulness of narrative. This unique combination, whose formula still eludes us, is what makes it total art."*
>
> Marie-Laure Ryan, *Narrative as Virtual Reality 2* (**2015**, 259)

Storytelling is an attempt to convey the subjective human experience. Stories connect us, often show us pieces of ourselves reflected in characters, teaching us something about ourselves. And, ideally, they allow us to experience the world through characters who are different than us or have experiences we cannot yet imagine. This ability to connect and empathize is what makes us human, and humane. In *Narrative as Virtual Reality 2*, Marie-Laure Ryan states that, "ever since Aristotle defined the effect of tragedy as catharsis, or purification through terror and pity, it has been taken for granted that literary fictions can elicit in the reader emotional reactions such as empathy, sadness, relief, laughter, admiration, fear, and even sexual arousal" (**2015**, 107). With emerging media and heightened levels of interactivity, authors/artists are finding new ways to more fully immerse the reader into their world, what Janet Murray calls "digital swimming." In *Hamlet on the Holodeck*, she offers this poetic definition of immersion:

> Immersion is a metaphorical term derived from the physical experience of being submerged in water. We seek the same feeling from a psychologically immersive experience that we do from a plunge in the ocean or swimming pool: the sensation of being surrounded by a completely other reality, as different as water is from air, that takes over all of our attention, our whole perceptual apparatus. We enjoy the movement out of our familiar world, the feeling of alertness that comes from being in this new place, and the delight that comes from learning to move within it (**1998**, 98-99).

Postmodern and electronic literature emphasize interaction, allowing what George Landow calls the "(w)reader" (**1994**, 14) to participate in narrative—conveying metaphor, meaning, and human experience through interactive links and interfaces. Installation artists such as Cardiff and Miller invite the viewer inside the frame. Now we are digital deep-sea diving in Virtual Reality, what

Chris Milk calls "the ultimate empathy machine" (2015)–diving into simulated fictional worlds, ideally allowing composers to immerse participants even more, pushing subjective experience and empathetic response even further. In her article, *Not a Film and Not an Empathy Machine*, Murray says of VR: "To invent a new medium you have to find the fit between the affordances of the co-evolving platform and specific expressive content–the beauty and truth–you want to share that could not be as well expressed in other forms. There is no short-cut to creating it" (2016). Marie-Laure Ryan says that "Total Art" would combine interactivity, immersion, and narrativity (2015, 259) and, though we are not there yet, each medium has unique affordances and can be immersive in different ways–by highlighting the materiality of the text or by attempting to remove the materiality altogether, render it transparent, and immerse us in an alternate reality. The medium depends on the message. What story do we want to tell? How does it ask to be told?

We know that all art is interactive (at least in a way) and all good stories are immersive. But the level and types of immersion can change with the way stories are told, particularly through various media. As Peter Brooks states in *Reading for the Plot*, "Narrative in fact seems to hold a special place among literary forms–as something more than a conventional 'genre'–because of its potential for summary and retransmission: the fact that we can still recognize 'the story' even when its medium has been considerably changed" (1984, 4). Postmodern print authors like Italo Calvino are able to immerse the reader while simultaneously highlighting the materiality of the text. For instance in Calvino's *If on a winter's night a traveler*: "The novel begins in a railway station, a locomotive huffs, steam from a piston covers the opening of the chapter, a cloud of smoke hides part of the first paragraph" (1979, 10) and, just like that, the reader is transported. Unlike narrative immersion, when we get sucked into a good story of a novel, curled up on our couch, when the materiality of a text is highlighted, the interaction between the reader and the text becomes part of its meaning. N. Katherine Hayles states:

> Materiality, as I use the term, does not simply mean all the physical, tangible aspects of the construction, delivery, and reading apparatus. Rather, materiality is a selective focus on certain physical aspects of an instantiated text that are foregrounded by a work's construction, operation, and content. These properties cannot be determined in advance of the work by the critic or even the writer. Rather, they emerge

from the interplay between the apparatus, the work, the writer, and the reader/user. (2002, 9)

Stories have an extraordinary way of causing us to feel, to experience perspectives unlike our own. Specifically, in electronic literature, this extraordinary capability extends to using links and interactivity, even the movement of the mouse to convey metaphor and deeper understanding of subjective experiences. While interacting with *ii – in the white darkness* by Ranier Strasser and MD Coverly (2004), for example, we are immersed into an interactive experience of what it is like to lose memory as we try to catch memories, bring them more clearly into view, to grasp mere fragments, simulating the condition of those with Alzheimer's or Parkinson's disease, a subjective empathetic experience that cannot be conveyed merely through words. It is the movement of the mouse, the interaction with the interface that gives the work meaning. This type of experience–of fading words and frustration of trying to grasp meaning–even more than reading a narrative of someone's experience with memory loss, can invoke an even deeper empathy.

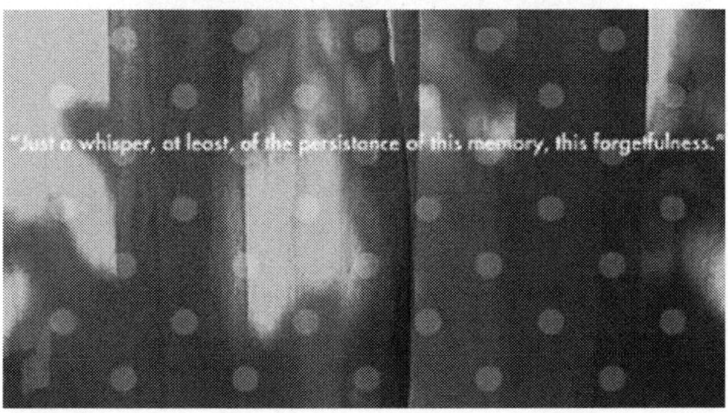

Figure 1. *ii – in the white darkness* by Ranier Strasser and MD Coverly (2004).

This act of interaction and movement can become even more realized when we are travelling in an installation, or virtual reality, as the reader is invited inside the frame, embodied, capable of a full-body reaction and immersion within a narrative space. In *Interactive Art and Embodiment: The Implicit Body as Performance*, Nathaniel Stern says, "Embodiment is moving-thinking-feeling, it is the body's potential to vary, it is the body's relations to the outside. And embodiment, I contend, is what is staged in the best interactive art" (2013, 2). In embodied physical installations, like *the Paradise Institute* and the *Killing Machine* by Cardiff and Miller, the viewer is embodied within a simulated experience. In *Paradise Institute*, the narrative is constructed in a virtual theater, where the viewer, enclosed, see clips of films, and hears ambient theater sounds in stereo through a headset, like a cell phone ringing or another audience member whispering: "Did you check the stove before we left?" (135), situating them in a familiar, yet controlled, "reality" to create meaning. In the *Killing Machine* (2007), the viewer becomes a complicit participant in the "killing" by pushing a button to start the machine–quite a choice and responsibility. This type of involvement and accountability within the narrative can cause the viewer to pause and reflect on the repercussions of their actions, even though it is a fictional space.

Figure 2. *The Killing Machine* by Janet Cardiff and George Bures Miller (2007).

In both interactive and embodied works, it is our empowerment, our autonomy that leads to our investment in story. Electronic literature can close the gap of subjective experience by bringing the (w)reader into the frame, changing the narrative as they make navigational decisions, gleaning meaning from the movement of the mouse. This autonomy and co-creation of narrative with a participatory text, immersion in a subjective human experience, is capable of being heightened in a three-dimensional embodied immersion within a virtual reality.

No stranger to multiple forms of media, Chris Milk has composed work that includes interactive music videos and participatory art. In *The Wilderness Downtown*, using Arcade Fire's song, *We Used to Wait*, the experience is augmented with personal input from the viewer–they add the address of their childhood home and, using Google Street View, Milk offers up a personalized version of the song, enhancing the experience and feeling of connection for the viewer. In *This Exquisite Forest* (2012), Milk invites participants to participate in the installation, as in an exquisite corpse in writing, by adding branches. The installation, as stated in the artist's statement, "explores narrative as a living breathing evolving organism." He only heightens this idea in virtual spaces. He says being inside a VR "feels like Truth" (2015), and he aspires to teach empathy through his work. *Clouds over Sidra*, for instance, has allowed members of the UN to see a Syrian refugee camp through the experience of a 5-year-old girl. If these virtual experiences can convey this terrible experience to those who can do something about it, it could make a tangible difference in the real world. Through this machine, he says, "we become more compassionate, we become more empathetic, we become more connected, and, ultimately, we become more human" (2015). He is hopeful that these experiences, this technology, can change the world.

Landow's (w)readers now become (vr)eaders (I thought it was funny). Ryan states that "the 'there' of VR may not be anywhere" (2015, 53), but that we are supposed to relate to VR environments as though they were real. We become co-authors, as we are in our lives, but digital deep-sea diving within virtual worlds. There are complications–accessibility, awareness of materiality and equipment for instance–but as VR looks to combine interaction, immersion, and narrative, and, as Chris Milk states, be "the ultimate empathy machine," we can at least say that it has some serious potential as a narrative medium.

Full bodily immersion in a three-dimensional space in an installation or virtual reality often accomplishes the goal of a direct emotional response through the non-traditional expression of ideas and increased involvement of the viewer in the work itself. The outcome can be a more subjective, metaphorical, emotional, and, yes, empathetic experience. Like *ii – in the white darkness*, the VR version of *Notes on Blindness* by John Hull (also a film) (2016) conveys an experience of blindness that is told through image and feeling, with clips of the author's recordings of his own experience. Like ii – in the white darkness, the experience utilizes the affordances of the medium to convey a subjective experience, evoke empathy, convey subjective human experience to others. Hull even directly addresses this problem of mutual understanding: "how can blind and sighted people truly understand each other? How can men understand women? How can the rich understand the poor? How can the old understand the young? Can we have insight into other people? This is the great question upon which the unity of our humanity hangs." Is VR the answer?

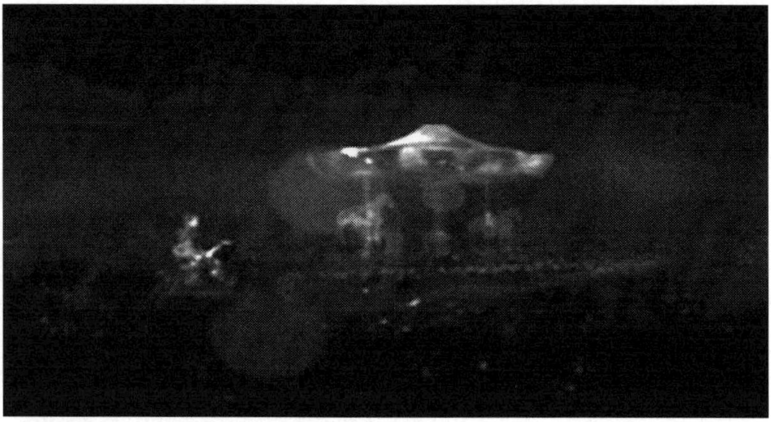

Figure 3. *Notes on Blindness*, produced by Ex Nihilo, ARTE France and AudioGaming, in co-production with Archer's Mark (2016).

We are digital deep-sea diving, attempting to achieve these empathetic experiences, to learn, understand, grow, but are we in over our heads? Although Marie-Laure Ryan sees interactive literature and immersion as incompatible, the tables are turned in Virtual Reality. She also says that for her, the ultimate goal of art is "the synthesis of immersion and interactivity" (**2015**, 7). Murray also brings up concerns of immersion and awareness of the medium with participatory narrative. She states: "Participatory narrative, then, raises several related problems: How can we enter the fictional world without disrupting it? How can we be sure that imaginary actions will not have real results? How can we act on our fantasies without becoming paralyzed by anxiety?" (**1998**, 103) She suggests we have to define borders. And it seems we are still trying to find that balance.

Can we be aware of the medium and immersed simultaneously? The technology is continually improving. In *Virtual Reality*, Rheingold says, "the perceptual technology must convince the operator that the simulation is a three-dimensional environment that surrounds him or her; this aspect is known as 'immersion'" (1991, 100). Immersion and navigation are the key elements to VR: He states that "Head-mounted displays, gloves that sense finger position and movement, and magnetic head-position trackers can create the feeling of immersion and grant the power of navigation through simulated environments" (113). It is this very equipment, though, that can be a hindrance to a fully immersive experience. We are often aware of the visor and equipment, and the fact that we cannot see/hear the actual environment we are in, usually a gallery space. This can make some viewers a bit anxious, potentially detracting from a full immersive experience with the work.

Marie-Laure Ryan says, *"The more interactive a virtual world, the more immersive the experience. There is nothing intrinsically incompatible between immersion and interactivity: in real life also, the greater our freedom to act, the deeper our bond to the environment."* (1994) In augmented reality, the reader is participant in the storytelling, and actively present within the narrative, though not fully immersed, as they would be in a VR. *Circle* by Caitlin Fisher (2011) is an AR text that emphasizes the materiality of the object, as the reader virtually touches and holds objects that tell meaningful stories. As Leonardo Flores says in his review of *Circle*:

> The main challenge for these kinds of works is that the computational infrastructure needed can be an obstacle for potential readers. The mechanics of looking at a screen with one's eyes and a different surface through a camera or waiting for a video to load over a slow data connection can hinder what might otherwise be an immersive experience... Fortunately, multiple technologies are moving in directions that will facilitate this kind of experience, as is the case with portable devices with screens and cameras that can be used "as a magic looking glass to explore the story world" (to quote Fisher). As computers become so portable and miniaturized as to become wearable and ubiquitous, electronic literature will increasingly move out from its virtual spaces and write on the world. (2013)

Figure 4. *Circle* by Caitlyn Fisher (2011)

The idea of the obstacles of the mechanism could include many mediated narratives, particularly those that draw attention to their medium. In *Storytelling for Virtual Reality*, John Bucher says of theorists Jay David Bolter and Richard Grusin (*Remediation*): "They suggest that culture moves toward media where the evidence of a mediated experience is less noticeable" (2018, 5). Ideally, in a fully immersive VR experience, we would want to feel less aware of the materiality, the equipment, and really feel lost in the experience, the story. Is this what we're moving toward? Flores idealistic vision of "writing on the world," is certainly appealing, but do we want the medium to be completely imperceptible? Or do we need those boundaries between the virtual world and reality?

Queerskins: a love story by Illya Szilak and Cyril Tsiboulski (2018) is an innovative VR that integrates a virtual, immersive experience, with a participatory real-world experience in the gallery space. Originally a work of electronic literature, *Queerskins* is about Sebastian, a young gay doctor during the AIDS epidemic, his parents, and his passing. The VR experience aims to encompass multiple perspectives in an attempt to capture more than the single story and let us feel empathy on all sides.

Figure 5. *Queerskins: a love story* by Illya Szilak and Cyril Tsiboulski (2018).

The engaging film-level aesthetic creates a more realistic environment for the (v)reader, allowing them to feel they are actually in a car, or a room, or a church. In addition, as in *Circle*, the creators have combined tactile and virtual objects and space through the virtual reality narrative, where (v)readers can observe Sebastian's parents, hold his objects, become him, and attend his funeral. This tactile real/virtual world provides some sort of tangible grounding to the virtual world; we are moved by objects, we feel more like Sebastian is/was a real person, we become immersed in his story. John Bucher acknowledges the work that goes into the illusion of a VR, stating:

> Technological advances that have led to greater and greater levels of immersion in VR tend to eliminate the evidence of a mediated experience, though one could argue there is an even greater level of mediation actually at work behind the scenes. (2018, 5)

This behind-the-scenes work involves everything that goes into shooting a film and more–3D video rendering of actual spaces, 3D rendered objects, digitally rendered characters, actors for the voices, and, as in any digital project, a whole lot of code. Not only through the VR, the creators have designed the experience so that participants can also interact with tangible objects in a gallery installation with the work. Participants can leave and take meaningful objects, move them around, and take photos with them, sharing their stories, allowing them to change the environment and become part of the story as well. The creators even bring these meaningful and personal photos to an audience outside the gallery space, as you see in this Instagram image:

Figure 6. Instagram screen capture (2018).

In her article, *Brave New World: Possibilities for Diversity in VR Technology*, Rebecca Alvin quotes Illya Szilak:

> We are always interested in incorporating what is actually existent in people's lives, and actually crowdsourcing a lot of stuff, because for us that recognition of embodied material, historical reality is what we sort of play off against–I know this speaks for myself–what I see as probably the most quintessential human characteristic, which is a reach to transcend those limitations of material, historical reality, and that's through art, through religion, through sex, through storytelling, in and of itself, but always going back to the fact that in VR you can pretend to be X, Y, and Z for five minutes, but when you take off the headset, you're still going to have to deal with the sociopolitical, economic realities of being black in America or being queer in America, or being a woman in America. You're still going to have that, so it's really important for us, ethically, to recognize that. (**2018**)

As Murray says, "In a participatory medium, immersion implies learning to swim, to do the things that the new environment makes possible" (1998, 99). We are still "learning to swim," learning what the new environment makes possible, what stories are asking to be told here, how we are becoming part of the story. Ryan suggests that:

> The greatest hurdle to overcome if interactive narrative is to combine the self-centered emotions that come from our active engagement in life and games with the other-centered emotions of traditional narrative is the creation of a kind of relation between the user's character and the synthetic agents that allows the user not only to interact verbally with these agents but also to influence their destiny and to feel personally concerned for both her character and for others. (2015, 250)

There is hope in narrative's ability to elicit empathy, not just through compelling characters that we might identify with, but also identifying with those characters different from ourselves–the most difficult place to have empathy. This is where VR's potential lies, putting the participant in someone else's shoes–it is seeing similarities and sameness that makes us feel connection, compassion, and empathy for others, we tend to feel more for those that are like us. In *Let It Brain's* statement on *This is Not Private*, an installation by Antonio Daniele, it affirms:

> The challenge with this work is inducing in the viewer a sort of "identity displacement," which reminds the phenomenon of the empathy. An algorithm tracks and calculates the empathic level between the actor and the viewer. The more the viewer empathizes with the actor the more their faces merge into a new identity which is no more the actor nor the viewer but something new (2015).

This is not only a participatory experience, but one that physically manifests the viewer's capacity for empathy and allows them to "practice."

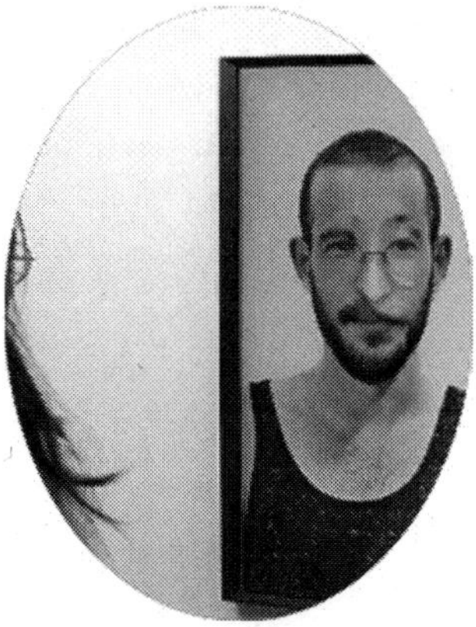

Figure 7. *This is Not Private* by Antonio Daniele (2016).

This potential for connection and empathy is what keeps us testing the waters. Bucher says:

> While the development of immersive storytelling benefits from previous art forms, such as the cinema, it still may be some time before the full potential of this new medium is seen. The eyes of new generations and the fresh perspectives they will bring will continue to recraft the path. However, the initial foundation must be laid before bricks can be added to the wall. (Bucher **2018**, 8)

The ability to bring us into an experience not our own, evoke empathy, promote diversity, this is the ideal that Milk holds, that by putting us in another's shoes, we will close the gap of subjective experience. But putting us in another's shoes virtually, does it take us out of our bodily experience, is it too jarring to suddenly appear as if we are someone else, does that take away from experiencing the story?

1000 Cut Journey (**2016**), created by a team of researchers at both Columbia University and Stanford University, led by psychologist Dr. Courtney Cogburn, premiered at Tribeca along with Queerskins last year. Here, participants see themselves as an African American male and experience scenes of growing up from this perspective, including an encounter with the police. From the creator's statement:

> We believe that achieving racial justice requires that we understand racism–not only an understanding that emerges from intellectual exercise or even in the consumption or production of science–but rather a visceral understanding that connects to spirit and body as much as reason. Understanding the social realities of racism is critical to promoting effective and collective social action. (**2016**)

Figure 8. *1000 Cut Journey.* The Cogburn Research Group (CRG) and the Virtual Human Interaction Lab (VHIL) (2016).

In her article, *Brave New World: Possibilities for Diversity in VR Technology,* Rebecca Alvin also quotes Cogburn:

> I think some of the responses from black people, in particular, were that it feels very authentic and familiar in ways that are really uncomfortable. But they also talked about–which I didn't expect–the experience of watching white people go through the experience and how that was emotional for them to see... It wasn't designed for people of color; it was designed for whites, so it's been interesting to get a sense of their reaction to seeing their experience for the purpose of educating white people, basically. So we had lots of interesting discussions. (**2018**)

Of course, we cannot expect to "solve" racism or implicit bias from a single-story experience, growing up black is not a single experience and, of course, there are additional problems with embodying the other, literally putting ourselves in their skin, when it is not our story to be told. I think the hope, though, is that the (v)reader would see this more as "our" shared human experience, the similarities more than the differences. Attempting to really share subjective human experience, as with *ii – in the white darkness* or *Notes on Blindness,* is what Milk's ideal vision of VR looks like and it is at least a beginning. It sounds as though the conversations coming out of *1000 Cut Journey* are both surprising and worthwhile. As any conversations around racism, and any attempts toward empathy, are certainly worthwhile.

Every "new" medium has complications: can we combine interactive and immersive, embodied and aware? What about becoming fully immersed in virtual environments, where we can no longer perceive boundaries–are there dangers? The study, "Empathy and embodied experience in virtual environment: To what extent can virtual reality stimulate empathy and embodied experience?" by Donghee Shin illustrated the difficulty in measuring empathy and participant immersion. It depends on the story being told, it depends on the openness of the participants. Shin says, "Immersion alone is not sufficient to generate the desired feeling... these findings indicate that VR should provide both quality content and relevant, socially meaningful stories to users" (2018). For total art, we must reconcile immersion, interaction, and narrative–we need aesthetically realistic environments, strong stories and open participants. We also need to expand the accessibility of these stories, and hopefully the technology will become more available and affordable, moving VR out of gallery spaces and into more people's personal spaces. We also must acknowledge, as creators, the desire of participants for control in the virtual world, to create their own stories–see that they might be resistant to narratives that they cannot alter. VR also complicates reader/author relationships even further. Putting (vr)eaders into a second person Calvino-esque situation may increase immersion and empathy, but could also cause resistance.

There is a lot of progress yet to be made, and who knows the stories that await us. But as the technology and content continue to progress, we can perhaps turn this medium into "the ultimate empathy machine" and convey experiences outside our own in hopes of better understanding each other and moving toward social action. In *Becoming Homeless: a Human Experience* (2017), also from the virtual human interaction lab at Stanford, participants are told in the second person that they are being evicted, and led through the experience of becoming homeless. In an article in the Washington Post, "Using Virtual Reality to Make you more Empathetic in Real life," Marlene Cimons quotes Lori Melichar, a director at the Robert Wood Johnson Foundation (funding the project) saying: "we're excited to see what [this] pioneering work can tell us about whether empathy can be taught and sustained to address health challenges like homelessness. As we look at ways to foster empathy, we need to consider harnessing emerging approaches like virtual reality to tell each other our stories" (**2016**). Again, the second person and embodiment of other could be jarring, but understanding other perspectives, learning, and sometimes participating in, stories from perspectives different from ours has always been a way to learn empathy and move toward compassion for others, another worthwhile goal. Murray predicted that, as the medium progresses:

> Participating viewers will assume clearer roles; they will learn how to become orienteers in the complex labyrinths and to see the interpretive shaping in simulated worlds. At the same time as these formal qualities improve, writers will be developing a better feel for which patterns of human experience can best be captured in digital media (**1998**, 111).

Figure 9. *Becoming Homeless: A Human Experience*, Virtual Human Interaction Lab, Stanford (2017).

This is true of any medium, particularly at the very beginning. It is a balance of learning the technology and finding the content, the stories, that need the medium to be told. There is not just one way to tell a story or one medium to tell it with and, as always, we need to consider why and how these stories need the specific medium. Murray states, “Instead of overhyping the inherent empathy-value of VR documentary, we should look for the specific moments that point to the genuine promise of the medium in creating compassionate understanding and build on those” (**2016**). It looks as though we are on our way. As our media for expression continue to change, as the affordances of each enable us to move closer to an empathetic understanding of each other (something we really need in the world right now), I see reader and author; viewer and artist becoming more entwined through technology, meeting in the medium. The environments need to be aesthetically pleasing and real, the stories need to be well-crafted and immersive, and the participants need to be open. Then we can immerse ourselves, aware of our constraints, materiality, borders, our participation in narrative, not as escape, but digitally deep-sea diving toward a more complete understanding.

Alvin, Rebecca M. 2018. "Brave New World: Possibilities for Diversity in VR Technology". *Independent Magazine*, July 7.

Brooks, Peter. 1984. *Reading for the Plot.* New York: Alfred A. Knopf.

Bucher, John. 2018. *Storytelling for Virtual Reality.* New York: Rutledge.

Calvino, Italo. 1979. *If on a Winter's Night a Traveler.* San Diego: Harcourt.

Cardiff, Janet, and George Bures Miller. 2001. *The Paradise Institute.* Link: https://www.cardiffmiller.com/artworks/inst/paradise_institute.html

Cardiff, Janet, and George Bures Miller. 2007. The Killing Machine. Link.

Cimons, Marlene. 2016. "Using Virtual Reality to Make You More Empathetic in Real Life". *Washington Post*, November 12.

Daniele, Antonio. 2015. "This is Not Private". *Let it Brain: artism in free form.* Link: http://www.letitbrain.it/letitbrain/?port=this-is-not-private

Fisher, Caitlin. 2011. *Circle.* Link: https://vimeo.com/64504258

Flores, Leonardo. 2013. "'Circle' by Caitlin Fisher. I Love E-Poetry". Link: https://iloveepoetry.org/?p=2572

Gitelman, Lisa. 2002. "'Materiality Has Always Been in Play': An Interview with N. Katherine Hayles". *Iowa Journal of Cultural Studies* 2 (1).

Landow, George P. 1994. *Hyper/Text/Theory.* Baltimore: The Johns Hopkins UP.

Milk, Chris. 2015. "How Virtual Reality Can Create the Ultimate Empathy Machine". *Ted Talk.*

Murray, Janet. 1998. *Hamlet on the Holodeck.* Cambridge: The MIT Press.

Murray, Janet. 2016. "Not a film and not an empathy machine". *Immerse*, n° 7 (October).

Rheinhold, Howard. 1991. *Virtual Reality.* New York: Summit Books.

Ryan, Marie-Laure. 1994. "Immersion vs. Interactivity: Virtual Reality and Literary Theory". *Postmodern Culture* 5 (1).

Ryan, Marie-Laure. 2015. *Narrative as Virtual Reality 2.* Baltimore: Johns Hopkins UP.

Shin, Donghee. 2018. "Empathy and embodied experience in virtual environment: To what extent can virtual reality stimulate empathy and embodied experience?" *Computers in Human Behavior* 78 (January):64-73.

Stanford University. n.d. "Virtual Human Interaction Lab". Link: http://vhil.stanford.edu

Stern, Nathaniel. 2013. *Interactive Art and Embodiment: The Implicit Body as Performance.* Canterbury: Gylphi.

Strasser, Reiner, and M.D. Coverley. 2004. "ii – in the white darkness". 2004. Link: http://collection.eliterature.org/1/works/strasser_coverley__ii_in_the_white_darkness.html

Szilak, Illya, and Cyril Tsiboulski. 2018. "Queerskins: a love story". 2018. Link: http://www.queerskins.com/

The Cogburn Research Group (CRG), et the Virtual Human Interaction Lab (VHIL). 2016. *1000 Cut Journey.*

Virtual Human Interaction Lab. 2017. *Becoming Homeless: A Human Experience.* Stanford: Stanford University. Link: https://vhil.stanford.edu/becominghomeless/

PART 3

PLATEFORMES ET NARRATIONS
PLATFORMS AND NARRATIVES

Micronarrative, Virtual Reality, and Medium Specificity: *Circa 1948* as VR Installation and Mobile App

JIM BIZZOCCHI • REESE MUNTEAN

Abstract

This paper is a close reading of *Circa 1948*, an interactive virtual reality (VR) artwork by artist Stan Douglas and the Digital Studio of the National Film Board of Canada (NFB). *Circa 1948* is a dramatization of an historical moment in Vancouver, British Columbia. *Circa 1948* was produced in two formats: four-wall installation and mobile application. These two versions of the artwork present the same story, set of characters, and interactive world in their respective platforms. The paper explicates the set of analytical lenses (content and theme, interactive design, interface, narrative, and spatiality) the authors used to focus their observations and build their conclusions. The findings include specific observations about theme, interface, and interactive design. The paper highlights the critical role of spatial design in the experience of VR, and the functions of micro-narrative and refusal of closure in the experience of this narrative.

Résumé

Cet article présente une lecture attentive de *Circa 1948*, une œuvre de réalité virtuelle (RV) interactive de l'artiste Stan Douglas et du studio numérique de l'Office national du film du Canada (ONF). *Circa 1948* est la fictionnalisation d'un moment historique à Vancouver, Colombie-Britannique. L'œuvre a été produite en deux formats : une installation sur quatre murs et une application mobile. Ces deux versions de l'œuvre présentent le même récit, les mêmes personnages et le même monde interactif. L'ensemble des angles analytiques (contenu et thème, design interactif, interface, récit et spatialité) dont les auteurs se sont servis sont explicités afin de structurer leurs observations et d'établir leurs conclusions. Les découvertes sont constituées d'observations spécifiques sur le thème, l'interface et le design interactifs. Cet article souligne enfin le rôle central du design spatial dans l'expérience de la RV. Il s'intéresse aux fonctionnalités du micro-récit ainsi qu'au refus de clore le récit dans le cadre d'une telle expérience.

INTRODUCTION

Circa 1948 is an interactive artwork by artist Stan Douglas and the Digital Studio of the National Film Board of Canada (NFB) (Douglas **2014**). The work is a dramatic interpretation of an historical moment in Vancouver, British Columbia. It offers a series of vignettes about a cast of 20 characters in two locations in Vancouver. The first location is "Hogan's Alley," a mixed-race working class neighborhood near downtown Vancouver. The second is the former Hotel Vancouver, then occupied by homeless Canadian veterans. The characters are a mixture of scoundrels on the make, and ordinary working class folks scuffling to get by. The experience takes place in a beautifully executed CGI recreation of the locations. It can be experienced in two forms: a four-wall CAVE-like installation, or as an iOS mobile application.

METHODOLOGY

Our goal was to understand the design and the experience of this work. Our methodology was textual analysis – the classic humanities process of "close reading." Close reading is the detailed and disciplined analysis of a "text." The term close reading was originally applied to poetry and literature, but is now extended to application in other media such as film, electronic games, and other digital media. Van Looy and Baetens describe the stance of the scholar when performing a close reading of a new media artwork:

> Reading is always an act of dismemberment, of tearing open in search of hidden meanings. 'Close' as in 'close reading' has come to mean 'in an attentive manner', but in the expression 'to pay close attention', for example, we still have a sense of nearness. When close reading, the eyes of the reader are almost touching the words of the text. Nothing is to escape the attention of the meticulous scholar (Baetens and Van Looy **2003**).

The first author of this paper has written about the potential indeterminacy of close reading when applied to interactive media (Bizzocchi and Tanenbaum **2011**). Any close reading relies on accurate and complete understanding of the work and its details. However, unlike literature or cinema, the interactive experience will unfold in different directions for different readers. This aspect of the reception experience increases and complicates the variations that a close reading scholar must consider. The solution to this challenge is multiple iterations of the scholar's engagement with the work, coupled with careful documentation. We viewed both versions (installation and mobile app) of the work many times, sometimes separately, but often together. For each viewing experience, we took extensive notes and captured a significant amount of photo and video documentation. In the final stages of our analysis, we also reviewed the shooting script used by the National Film Board during the production.

The close reading methodology can be applied for differing scholarly goals. Close readings do not have to cover all aspects of an artwork. This is a difficult task indeed. However, close readings can, and often do, concentrate on particular analytical dimensions. Often this can involve the examination of the work's stance on cultural questions such as gender, race, or class. Our close reading focuses on two broad directions in *Circa 1948*: the construction of narrative and the poetics of virtual reality.

Narrative is a complicated but well-recognized analytical direction. "Poetics" is less well understood. In many ways, it is a higher-level stand-in for the term "design." We are referring here to "design" in the broad sense: not just the look of an artifact, but the examination of how it has been put together. The word "poetics" comes from the Greek word "poiesis," which derives from the concept of "making." The term was used by Aristotle in his analysis of the creative decisions that went into the making of the classic Greek tragedies. In his book *Poetics* he examined several specific channels for creative decision-making in these dramatic works: plot, character, diction, thought, spectacle, and song (Aristotle **1997**). Ferguson points out that the book is based on an empirical process of textual analysis. Aristotle looked at the plays, and reverse-engineered the creative principles that shaped the works.

The term "poetics" has generalized to go beyond poetry, theater, and literature, and can be applied to creative design decisions in any medium. Film scholar David Bordwell says:

> ... the poetics of any artistic medium studies the finished work as the result of a process of construction... Any inquiry into the fundamental principles by which artifacts in any representational medium are constructed, and the effects that flow from these principles, can fall within the domain of poetics (Bordwell **2008**).

Bordwell maintains that a textual analysis of poetics (such as a close reading) is empirical in nature, because it "... appeals to intersubjectively available data that are in principle amenable to alternative explanation."

ANALYTICAL LENSES

In our close reading, we were open to what the experience would reveal, but we also had a set of analytical lenses to focus our attention on critical aspects of the work. Our lenses were:

- **CONTENT AND THEME** – what issues and questions does this work address?
- **INTERACTIVE DESIGN** – what choices can the user make, and how do they relate to the creation of meaning?
- **INTERFACE DESIGN** – how does the user exercise choice, and what aspects of the human sensorium did the work utilize?
- **NARRATIVE DESIGN** – how was the plot articulated, and what was the role of character, storyworld, and emotion?
- **SPATIALITY** – how was the virtual space designed, and what effect did this space have on the interactor's experience of the storyworld?

The authors have found that the use of these analytical lenses is useful in the process of textual analysis and close reading. These lenses focus attention on specific aspects of the work. This focusing function has several attributes. First, it is important to pick analytical lenses that are relevant to the specific work, and reflect important attributes of the medium within which it is instantiated. However, they function in a dialectic with the process of analysis. The lenses are modified in an iterative fashion over the course of the reading process. As the analysis proceeds, aspects which do not advance the understanding of the work are diminished or dropped. At the same time, other useful analytical perspectives reveal themselves in the extended close reading process. The set of analytical lenses evolves as the scholar comes to understand more and more about the work and its design. We believe that the revised set of analytical lenses is in itself a useful scholarly outcome of this process. These refined analytical lenses can in turn be applied against other artworks in future scholarship and criticism.

CONTENT AND THEME

The content for the CAVE version and the mobile version is identical. Both use the same CGI environment, and both contain the same narrative material. However, for most people, access to the CAVE version was severely limited by logistics. The mobile version is less embodied, but it offers unfettered access to the same set of stories, locations, and interactive choices.

Circa 1948 presents an urban Canadian society beset with contradictions of class and power. The main Hogan's Alley characters are a set of working class folks of various ethnicities: black, Chinese, Italian. All the locals are engaged in some form of illicit activity–including bootlegging, cannabis cultivation, illegal night clubs, black market distribution, and prostitution. The power structure within the neighborhood is clear. At the top are a gangster named Buddy and the brothel madam, Mae Lu. Most other Hogan's Alley characters either work for Buddy, or are his competitors. The police have a significant role in the neighborhood, but much of it involves extortion and corruption.

At the Hotel Vancouver location, we see a related picture of societal need, layered with grafting, scamming, and a complicit police presence. We also see that Canada has yet to recover from World War II. The returned veterans are seeking both jobs and housing, and are occupying the shell of the old and abandoned Hotel Vancouver. The occupied Hotel has some social services available for the occupants, but is at the same time the venue for a number of illegal and illicit activities.

In both locations, the role of women is significant. These women are embedded within a social and economic reality that requires their guile, endurance, and strength. Mae Lu negotiates the needs and demands of her employees, her clients, her business partner, and the local police. Gladys must compensate for a weak and dishonest husband. Betty is carrying out some mysterious and dangerous mission that involves a bad history with the gangster Buddy. However, while the women in *Circa 1948* are struggling against oppressive cultural and economic forces, they have not been crushed by this. None of them are subservient, and several have dominating personalities. All of them are doing what they need to do in order to survive.

INTERFACE AND SENSORIUM

Circa 1948 is designed to work in two separate presentation formats: a four-wall CAVE-like installation version, and a mobile app playable on iPads and iPhones. The content is identical in both platforms.

The 15' by 15' four-wall installation version is a more immediately immersive experience. It physically situates the user's body within the environment. She is surrounded by the visual world, which is projected on all four walls. The sound is also spatialized, coming from any direction within the space. The user navigates the two large and complex virtual locations through her body position. The user is confined to a small circle in the middle of the room, but can treat the circle as a joystick based on where she stands. Standing at the center stops any motion, but a single step towards any compass direction within the circle moves the user's point-of-view in the same direction. The user treats her body as a pointer that takes her where she wants to go. The immersive environment and the intuitive navigation results in a deeply embodied experience. This embodied experience comes with a logistical price. The CAVE version does not scale well in terms of audience numbers. It was designed for use by one person at a time. This meant a system of lineups and short reserved times for each user.

The mobile version provides unlimited access to the same material (CGI environment, sound, characters, and narrative events). There are two versions of the mobile interface. One version involves aiming the screen around in space–turning it into a magic window into the environment. This experience is delightful at first, but after a while the arms get tired. The more prosaic interface choice is to use the touchscreen capability, and navigate with a standard two-finger aiming movement.

Regardless of the interface format-CAVE, magic window mobile screen, or finger–navigation mobile screen–the content is the same. The CGI locations are well drawn: their imagery not fully photorealistic, but still representational and convincing (Rothman **2014**). The world is bounded, but sufficiently large and complex to support the pleasures of exploration and discovery. The audio is spatialized, with volume and presence modulated by user "distance" from the virtual sound source. The sound includes character dialogue, period music, and radio clips.

A notable omission from the experience is any visual representation of the characters, who exist as spoken exchanges of dialogue that are embedded within the virtual space. As the interactor navigates the space, she hears their conversations from the world of 1948. These 44 conversations are located at the places where the characters said them, but the speakers are never seen, only heard. Their presence is signaled by a glow at a specific location. As the user navigates closer to the glow, the dialogue begins, getting louder as the user gets closer. As she approaches, it becomes clear that these glows represent ghost-like avatars of the characters that are speaking.

INTERACTIVE DESIGN

The interactive design allows the user to freely traverse the two locations. In the process she discovers the narrative–a number of "ghost" dialogues that are distributed through the space. The interactor cannot change anything, however–this is what Ryan would term "exploratory interaction," not "ontological interaction" (Ryan 2004). Meaning can be discovered, but not modified.

However, the process of discovery is not easy. *Circa 1948* is what Espen Aarseth calls an "ergodic" experience–it requires work (Aarseth 1997). The navigation can sometimes be difficult–for example, the interactor must find and approach a relatively obscure elevator door in order to move from the main floor of the Hotel Vancouver to the upstairs rooms. There are visual cues to important objects (glowing light) and a few audio cues (sweeping sound, balloon blowing) to guide the discovery of the hot spots. Despite these aids, the discovery of the 44 embedded dialogues is a difficult task. The space is large, and the conversations are dispersed. It does take significant time and attention to find them. Most users probably miss some of the dialogues. Even determined users may have difficulty finding the final remaining narrative units embedded within the two locations.

NARRATIVE

A further "work" challenge for the reader is the incomplete nature of the narrative construction. The narrative does have several significant strengths. The storyworld is well-conceived and well–constructed–a convincing and evocative representation of a believable and interesting environment. The culture that the dialogues describe is also rich and varied. The experience is based on historical events and grounded in powerful social and political dynamics. This narrative storyworld certainly supports viewer attention and engagement.

The set of characters is also engaging. These 21 characters have unique and differentiated personalities. Despite the fact we never see any of them and need to rely on a relatively limited set of dialogues, the characters have a degree of complexity, and are interesting in their own right. The level of interest is enhanced through their interactions with each other. As we experience the dialogues, our understanding of the characters is increased. We sense Betty is dangerous, but it takes several dialogues before we begin to understand how and why this is so. Another conversation has the black market grifter Harry taking the time to help an amputated veteran deal with phantom limb syndrome. Mae Lu shows herself to be politically astute and hard as nails, but seems genuinely protective of Buddy and his role in the Hogan's Alley culture. The mix of personalities and motivations leads to a complex network of emotions. We can trace various sets of feelings and reactions across this collection of characters: greed, affection, dislike, envy, camaraderie, fear, loyalty and many others.

The defining characteristic of the narrative design in this work is its opposition to standard plot construction and narrative arc. There is no comprehensive narrative arc to unite this set of stories. The well-designed overall narrative arc has long been foundational to traditional mediated storytelling. The narrative arc was first identified by Aristotle ("the Complication" followed by "the Unravelling") (Aristotle 1997), and has been further theorized by innumerable literature and media scholars since his time (e.g., Kristin Thompson's succinct formulation: setup, complication, development, and resolution) (Thompson 1999).

In *Circa 1948*, this traditional narrative model is not followed. Instead of a comprehensive dramatic arc that joins and completes these conversations, we have a number of separate and relatively limited dialogue sets that give a fragmented and partial sense of any overall narrative. These conversations are what Henry Jenkins would term "micronarratives"–localized and limited incidents rather than complete and finished stories (Jenkins **2004**). The lead author of this paper has analyzed micronarrative construction, elaborating on Jenkins's original concept (Bizzocchi **2007**). Writing in the discourse around electronic game narrative, Bizzocchi and his colleagues argue that micronarrative construction has great utility for the design of interactive narratives (Bizzocchi et al. **2013**; Funk **2018**). The granularity and flexibility of a micronarrative-based modular narrative construction creates room for interactive choice and active engagement by the reader.

However, the rejection of the classic narrative arc goes beyond the fragmentation and fluidity of micronarrative construction. In the dialogues we do get, the presentation of plot is constrained–we see or hear only a few events associated with the progress of each character. We do receive enough information about each of them to have a sense of their motivations and goals. However, what we never get is closure. There is not a hint of Aristotle's "unravelling" or Thompson's "resolution." There is no sense of completion for either the overall collective narrative, or any of the individual narratives. We do not know if Mae Lu succeeds in her struggle with the city's power structure, if Betty gets her desired revenge, or whether Gladys gets the money she needs... We are never presented with a significant outcome for any of the various challenges and struggles that are important to these characters.

SPATIALITY

Virtual reality operates on a base logic that necessarily incorporates the poetics of other media. This is inevitable–newer media forms consistently borrow specific design features from their predecessors. Bolter and Grusin cite McLuhan's dictum: "The content of any medium is always another medium" (Bolter and Grusin **1999**; McLuhan **1964**). In this regard, the comparison of VR to cinema is both interesting and significant. Cinema was the benchmark for immersive experience in the twentieth century. As a new form of the moving image, VR is positioning itself as a viable successor to cinema as the dominant immersive medium for the twenty-first century.

There are two major differences between these media forms. The first is the interactive dimension of Virtual Reality, a topic we discussed above. However, the second is just as significant: the abandonment of the cinematic frame for the 360-degree view of virtual reality—whether head-mounted display or CAVE-like four-wall installation. The frame is central to the essence of what makes cinema a medium. Friedberg lists the various metaphors for the effects of this simple cinematic rectangle: frame, screen, window, mirror, filter (Friedberg **2006**). The simple truth is that the frame is a useful tool for the filmmaker. The rectangle is at the same time a constraint on our visual field and a magic window to focus and guide the visual experience of the viewer. It excludes the unnecessary, and presents the essential. With VR, this powerful device is lost for the artist. The compensations are the sweeping visuals of a 360-degree virtual world and the license for the viewer to roam within that world. Both Murray and Manovich see this combination—spatiality and navigation—as central to the nature of digital media (Murray **2012**; Manovich **2001**). Manovich further maintains that digital media's "spatial montage" is a fundamental digital poetic that extends cinema's more traditional "temporal montage" (Manovich **2001**). VR instantiates these theoretical directions of Manovich and Murray: the poetics of Virtual Reality are built upon a foundation of unfettered visual and virtually embodied exploration.

Circa 1948 makes good use of this foundation. The world is visually engaging, from the lived-in working class houses and streets of Hogan's Alley to the run-down rooms and hallways of the Hotel Vancouver. The navigation in the four-wall installation version of the work is compelling and immersive. The interactor steps in a direction, and is carried through the world. The finger-swipe navigation of the mobile app is less enveloping, but is still an efficient method for exploring the same visual world. The world is well drawn and visually engaging. The visual experience is enriched with sound effects, diegetic radio sound, and the spoken conversations of the "ghosts" of the characters. The diegetic sound effects and the glowing object "hot-spots" help guide the interactor's exploration of the space, acting as a softer substitute for the stricter guidance of cinema's rectangular frame. As the interactor explores the world, the ghost conversations gradually reveal bits of the overall narrative.

Circa 1948 reflects Jenkins's concept of a spatialized narrative embedded within a navigable storyworld (Jenkins **2004**). Jenkins was writing about electronic games, but his insights about spatially-distributed story environments are perhaps even more relevant to VR artworks. The core poetics of electronic games center on ludic challenge and flow. Narrative is important for many games, but not more important than winning, losing, and user performance in the moment. VR certainly can include ludic challenge, and we will continue to see electronic gaming on VR platforms. However, when considering the complete range of VR works, Jenkins's concept of spatialized story experience seems central to the medium and its evolution.

In this regard, the detailed design of the virtual space is critical, and *Circa 1948* meets this challenge. The size of the storyworld is well calculated. Hogan's Alley is a city block with enough locations to house a number of interesting characters. The Hotel Vancouver is represented by two large floors. One is the main floor with the front desk, the dining facilities, the hotel commons area, and several offices. The other is a hotel guest floor with many rooms holding another set of characters and actions. The result is a space that feels expansive, but not overwhelming. These locations are large enough to be varied and interesting, but not so large as to defy disciplined exploration. This decision to incorporate a moderate sense of scale gives the exploration enough scope to feel substantive, but not so much that the storyworld feels too large to experience or properly comprehend.

CONCLUSION

Circa 1948 is an interactive experience designed to run on either of two platforms: four-wall installation or mobile app. The visual environment, audio, and interactive design are identical. The experience of the narrative is also the same in the two versions. In either platform, the characters, the storyworld, the micronarrative plots–all engage the interactor. However, the refusal of closure is probably less satisfying to most participants. Combined with the uncertainty of progress through the set of micronarratives, the lack of closure can keep users seeking some sort of narrative resolution–which they will never find.

Why this design, then? Our understanding of the implications of refusal of closure has been broadened by this conference–in particular by the excellent *Narrative Palindrome* session on "endings" (Fan et al. **2018**). That session reminds us of the obvious–that an "ending" is not a necessary condition for narrative engagement. In fact, a critical thrust of the Electronic Literature initiative has been to complicate, problematize, and systematically explore the very concept of "narrative resolution." In this spirit, an open-ended and incomplete narrative arc does not interfere with the challenge or the pleasure of the search for story. In fact, it may allow the interactor the freedom of imagining a range of possible outcomes for this set of characters.

However, we believe the salient point is this: the lack of narrative closure puts more emphasis on the presentation of an historically complex moment in time. It is clear to us that the presentation of cultural themes and relevant social and economic issues is central to the experience of this work. In the spirit of Brecht, avoidance of narrative "fog" can place ideas, values, and realities in the forefront of the experience (Brecht **1964**). In *Circa 1948*, the heart of the work is the presentation of relevant themes examining historical realities and the inherent contradictions of economics, politics, society and culture.

RESEARCH SUPPORT AND DISCLAIMER

This research was supported by the Social Science and Humanities Research Council of Canada (SSHRC) and the School of Interactive Arts and Technology (SIAT) at Simon Fraser University. The lead author is related to the National Film Board (NFB) of Canada's production manager for *Circa 1948*. We do not believe this affected our research observations or findings in any way. The analysis is entirely the work and the responsibility of the two authors. The NFB did provide extended access to the four-wall installation, which allowed the researchers time and scope to perform the significant number of iterations required by the close reading methodology. The NFB also provided the script of the character dialogues, which assisted the researchers in their analysis of the narrative experience.

Aarseth, Espen. 1997. *Cybertext: Perspectives on Ergodic Literature.* Baltimore: Johns Hopkins University Press.

Aristotle. 1997. *Poetics.* Minneola: Dover Publications.

Baetens, Jan, and Jan Van Looy, ed. 2003. *Close Reading New Media: Analyzing Electronic Literature.* 1st ed. Leuven: Leuven University Press.

Bizzocchi, Jim. 2007. "Games and Narrative: An Analytical Framework". *Loading: the Journal of the Canadian Game Studies Association* 1 (1). July.

Bizzocchi, Jim, Michael Nixon, Steve DiPaola, and Natalie Funk. 2013. "The Role of Micronarrative in the Design and Experience of Digital Games". *Proceedings of DiGRA 2013*: DeFragging Game Studies.
Link: http://www.digra.org/wp-content/uploads/digital-library/paper_181.pdf

Bizzocchi, Jim, and Theresa Jean Tanenbaum. 2011. "Well Read: Applying Close Reading Techniques to Gameplay Experiences". In *Well-Played 3.0,* ed. by Drew Davidson, 218-315. Pittsburgh: ETC Press.

Bolter, Jay David, and Richard Grusin. 1999. *Remediation: Understanding New Media.* Cambridge: MIT Press.

Bordwell, David. 2008. *Poetics of Cinema.* New York: Routledge.

Brecht, Bertold. 1964. *Brecht on Theatre: The Development of an Aesthetic.* Ed. by John Willett. New York: Hill and Wang.

Douglas, Stan, ed. 2014. *Circa 1948.* Vancouver, BC: National Film Board of Canada. Interactive mobile app; location-based installation VR artwork.

Fan, L., A. Luesebrink, R. House, C. Fisher, and Panel Discussion. 2018. "Narrative Palindromes 2: Endings". Montreal. Accessed April 14, 2019.
Link: http://sites.grenadine.uqam.ca/sites/nt2/en/elo2018

Friedberg, Anne. 2006. *The Virtual Window: From Alberta to Microsoft.* Cambridge: MIT Press.

Funk, Natalie. 2018. "The role of narrative units in the design of coherent plot structures for single-player action video games". Doctoral dissertation, Simon Fraser University. Accessed April 14, 2019. Link.

Jenkins, Henry. 2004. "Games as Narrative Architecture". In *First Person: New Media as Story, Performance, and Game,* ed. by Nick Wardrip-Fruin and Pat Harrigan. Cambridge: MIT Press.

Manovich, Lev. 2001. *The Language of New Media.* Cambridge: MIT Press.

McLuhan, Marshall. 1964. *Understanding Media: the Extensions of Man.* 2nd ed. New York: Signet Press.

Murray, Janet. 2012. *Inventing the Medium: Principles of Interaction Design as a Cultural Practice.* Cambridge: MIT Press.

Rothman, Lily. 2014. "Vancouver Street View, Circa 1948". *Time Magazine Online.* Accessed Dec 2, 2015. Link: http://time.com/3808918/vancouver-street-view-circa-1948

Ryan, Marie-Laure. 2004. "Will New Media produce New Narratives". In *Narratives across Media: the Languages of Storytelling,* ed. by Marie-Laure Ryan, 337-59. Lincoln: University of Nebraska Press.

Thompson, Kristin. 1999. *Storytelling in the New Hollywood: Understanding Classical Narrative Technique.* Cambridge: Harvard University Press.

Partie / Part 4

ESTHÉTIQUES NUMÉRIQUES

DIGITAL AESTHETICS

TOPO – Trajectoires. 20 ans de présence en arts et littérature numériques

MICHEL LEFEBVRE • EVA QUINTAS

Résumé

En 2018, le centre d'artistes montréalais TOPO célèbre ses 25 ans de fondation et ses 20 ans de création et de diffusion à travers l'Internet. TOPO est un laboratoire d'écritures et de créations numériques pour les espaces du web, de la performance et de l'installation. La démarche du centre s'inscrit dans l'évolution de l'art réseau et s'intéresse à son extension en investissant les plateformes mobiles, délocalisées et hors écran. Au fil des années, ses réalisations, au départ produites pour le web, se sont déployées vers l'espace scénique et installatif. À l'occasion d'ELO 2018, TOPO a présenté une partie de ses archives qui témoignent d'une époque effervescente à Montréal pour l'émergence de la création numérique. À travers un corpus de projets, l'exposition et le texte qui en découle proposent une réflexion sur le déplacement de l'œuvre hypermédiatique hors de l'écran, vers d'autres espaces de rencontres.

Ce texte survole 20 ans d'expérimentation des potentiels narratifs des médias interactifs à travers une collection d'œuvres d'art web réalisées avec plus d'une centaine d'artistes issus des arts visuels et médiatiques, du théâtre, de l'audio et de la littérature. Depuis les premiers récits hypertextuels, TOPO a graduellement incorporé des éléments cinétiques et multimédias et travaillé la matérialité des éléments virtuels, pour arriver à un développement de la fiction comme système où le sens s'élabore par le biais de mécanismes d'interaction et de participation. À cela se sont ajoutées des performances et des installations mettant en valeur différentes disciplines, divers procédés scénaristiques et dispositifs technologiques, dans une volonté d'explorer les dynamiques de va-et-vient entre l'écran et le hors-écran.

Abstract

In 2018, the Montreal artist's center TOPO celebrated 25 years since its founding and 20 years of creation and dissemination through the internet. TOPO is a writing and digital creation laboratory for web spaces, performances and installations. At the core of the center's principles are the evolution of the art network, and an investment in mobile platforms on and off screen to ensure the network's expansion. Over time, the center's works, at first produced for the web, were later reworked for the stage and for installations. On the occasion of ELO 2018, TOPO presented a part of its archives of an extravagant era of digital creation in Montreal. Through a corpus of works, the exposition and the resulting text propose a reflection on the displacement of hypermedia works off screen in new meeting places

This article covers 20 years of experimentation with potential narratives in interactive media and through a collection of works of web art created with more than one hundred visual, media, theatre, audio, and literary artists. Since the first hypertext works, TOPO has gradually incorporated kinetic and multimedia elements, and worked on the materiality of virtual elements, to achieve the development of fiction as a system where meaning is created through interaction and participation. Performances and installations showcase different disciplines, theatrical processes, and technological devices in a spirit of exploration of the back-and-forth dynamics on and offscreen.

EXPLORER LES DÉFIS DES ÉCRITURES NUMÉRIQUES, DANS ET HORS DE L'ÉCRAN

En 2018, le centre d'artistes montréalais TOPO célèbre ses 25 ans de fondation et ses 20 ans de création et de diffusion en art numérique. TOPO est un laboratoire d'écritures et de créations numériques pour les espaces du web, de la performance et de l'installation. Son mandat est d'incuber, de produire et de diffuser des œuvres multimédias originales qui explorent les croisements interdisciplinaires et interculturels à travers les arts numériques. La démarche du centre s'inscrit dans l'évolution de l'art réseau et s'intéresse à son extension en investissant les plateformes mobiles, délocalisées et hors écran. Au fil des années, ses réalisations, au départ produites pour le web, se sont déployées vers l'espace scénique et installatif. À l'occasion d'ELO 2018, TOPO a présenté une partie de ses archives qui témoignent d'une époque très effervescente à Montréal pour l'émergence de la création numérique. À travers un vaste corpus de projets, l'exposition et le texte qui en découle proposent une réflexion sur le déplacement de l'œuvre hypermédiatique hors de l'écran, vers d'autres espaces de rencontres.

Image 1. Installation de TOPO au centre de design de l'UQAM (ELO 2018).

LIQUIDATION, UN PHOTOROMAN PLURIMÉDIA

C'est par l'exploration du récit interactif que les fondateurs de TOPO – les artistes Michel Lefebvre et Eva Quintas – ont inscrit le centre dans le circuit des nouveaux médias, en janvier 1998. Une tempête de verglas mémorable venait de ravager Montréal quand la radio FM de Radio-Canada diffusa les trois épisodes du photoroman *Liquidation* en version web radio, une première au Québec. C'est aussi ce photoroman, élaboré comme une parodie de roman policier, qui a donné le nom à l'organisme, l'Agence TOPO étant dans ce contexte l'agence du détective narrateur de l'histoire.

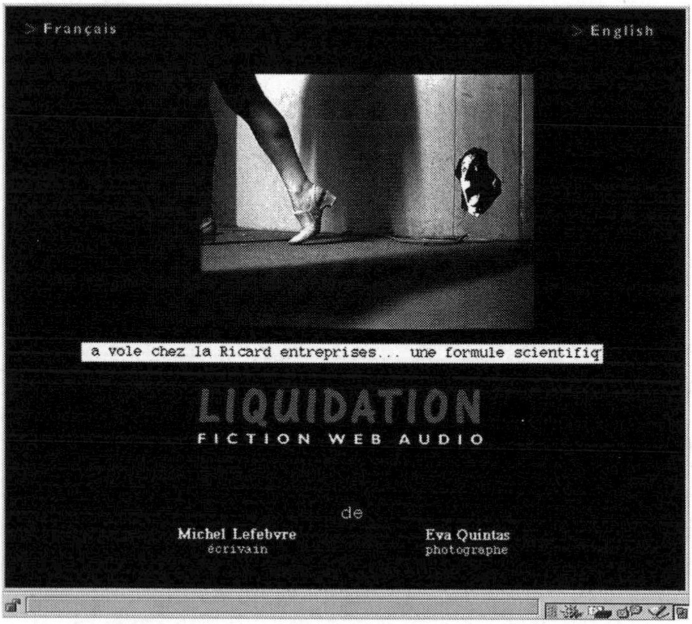

Image 2. Copie d'écran, *Liquidation*, une fiction web-audio (1998).

Liquidation a vu le jour dans un environnement technologique et esthétique bien plus limité que celui que nous connaissons aujourd'hui. L'expérience même de coupler des épisodes radiophoniques (son) à des volets web (images et textes) s'est avérée celle d'une impossible simultanéité des deux médias, la vitesse de diffusion de la radio étant, en 1998, bien plus rapide que celle du web... Après d'innombrables difficultés, liées notamment à la création d'outils logiciels nouveaux, l'œuvre s'est déployée sous forme de fiction aléatoire sur cédérom. Elle a été diffusée pour la première fois au printemps 1998 sous forme de prototype à la galerie Skol, un centre d'artistes montréalais. À cette occasion, les auteurs ont scénarisé un parcours installatif et performatif centré sur la monstration des processus créatifs de *Liquidation*, dont la maquette du photoroman sous forme de livre. Ils ont aussi imprimé une centaine de livrets de poésie combinatoire créés spécifiquement pour le photoroman avec La 'Calembredaine. Ce logiciel a été créé à Montréal par le programmeur Alain Bergeron et la linguiste Myriam Cliche, à la fin des années 1980, au sein du collectif artistique (La Société de conservation du présent).[1]

NOTE 1

Une importante monographie traitant de ce collectif précurseur des arts numériques a été publiée par TOPO en 2013. Voir Sonia Pelletier, Michel Lefebvre, Bernard Schutze (dir.) (*La Société de conservation du présent*) (1985-1994), Montréal, Agence TOPO, 2013.

Une version pleinement fonctionnelle du cédérom remportait, en 1999, le prix Téléfilm de la fiction multimédia au Festival du nouveau cinéma et des nouveaux médias de Montréal. Le texte du photoroman ayant été traduit vers l'anglais, le cédérom connaît par la suite une diffusion internationale dans plusieurs festivals. La version finale – Mac et Windows – sort en 2001 lors de l'exposition *Territoires extrêmes de la poésie* présentée à la Bibliothèque nationale du Québec. La fiction se distingue par sa programmation logicielle qui ouvre la voie à l'analyse du récit dans son déroulement temporel. En effet, le cédérom permet de choisir la durée du récit, sur un registre allant de 15 à 120 minutes. Le logiciel génère alors un enchaînement aléatoire des éléments indexés (1800 photographies, 4 heures de bande-son); il permute les nœuds narratifs qui relient les photos aux sons et aux textes, des récits s'agencent et se renouvellent à chaque visionnement, le sens persiste. Ce projet plurimédia (web, radio, cédérom, installation et performance) annonçait déjà la direction artistique du centre, axée sur la création collective et interdisciplinaire, l'ancrage social et l'exploration des nouvelles narrativités sur des supports variés.

> À plusieurs égards, *Liquidation* tend vers cet idéal de l'œuvre d'art totale ou *Gesamtkunstwerk*, un concept lié aux arts de la scène (aux opéras de Wagner initialement) qui a refait surface à maintes reprises au cours de l'histoire, et plus récemment dans le contexte de convergence des disciplines en art numérique. L'ampleur de ce projet, tant par le nombre d'individus impliqués et la quantité de documents multimédias produits que par ses incarnations et présentations diverses, en a fait un jalon dans l'histoire des arts néomédiatiques au Québec. (Parent **2008**)

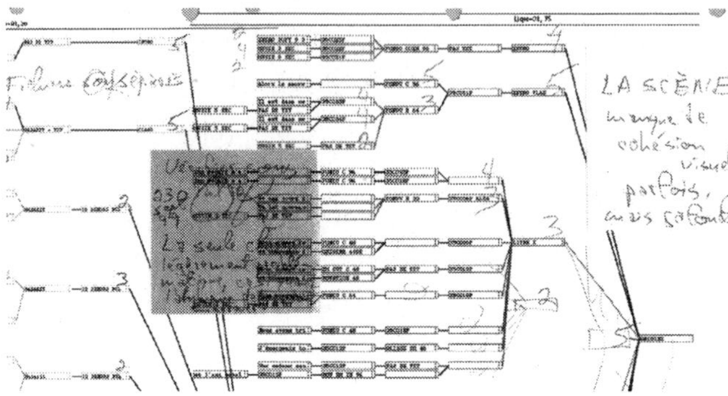

Image 3. Extrait d'arborescence du cédérom *Liquidation, une fiction aléatoire* (1999).

LA FICTION COMME SYSTÈME

Voici donc une trajectoire de 20 ans d'expérimentation des potentiels narratifs des médias interactifs à travers une collection d'œuvres d'art web[2] réalisées avec plus d'une centaine d'artistes issus des arts visuels et médiatiques, du théâtre, de l'audio et de la littérature. Depuis les premiers récits hypertextuels, TOPO a graduellement incorporé des éléments cinétiques et multimédias et travaillé la matérialité des éléments virtuels, pour arriver à un développement de la fiction comme système où le sens s'élabore par le biais de mécanismes d'interaction et de participation. À cela se sont ajoutées des performances et des installations mettant en valeur différentes disciplines, divers procédés scénaristiques et dispositifs technologiques, dans une volonté d'explorer les dynamiques de va-et-vient entre l'écran et le hors-écran.

NOTE 2

Crédits de réalisation multimédia : Guy Asselin et Vincent Archambault ont grandement contribué à la direction visuelle et à la programmation des projets web de TOPO entre 2001 et 2012. Ont suivi Paul Gascou-Vaillancourt et José Cortes Castillo.

Image 4. Image promotionnelle, *Civilités / Civilities* (2003).

Civilités/Civilities (2003), par exemple, est un projet qui a connu un succès certain, dans les années fortes de l'art web, circulant dans une dizaine de festivals et récoltant des articles dans la presse étrangère. Il s'agit d'une fiction modulaire qui regroupe, sous la direction artistique de Eva Quintas, dix artistes montréalais de disciplines et d'horizons variés proposant différents regards sur le « vivre ensemble ». À partir d'interfaces représentant l'espace public, celui de la communauté et du *civitas*, de petites histoires se développent comme des fenêtres sur des situations plus universelles, sur un certain état du monde, pour le moins trouble et violent. L'interface d'accueil présente des liens qui mènent vers les projets des artistes sans les hiérarchiser. Au fil d'une navigation intuitive, l'œuvre rassemble et associe des éléments qui renvoient à la diversité et à la collectivité. Elle est inspirée de l'ouvrage de Roland Barthes, *Comment vivre ensemble ?*, qui explore des contextes de cohabitation dans des groupes restreints où la liberté individuelle n'est pas exclue. La parole est aussi donnée à l'internaute à travers un module participatif offrant la possibilité d'envoyer textes et images : « L'aspect dynamique des interfaces encourage aussi une mobilité entre les documents et les récits, faisant valoir ainsi un déplacement dans nos propres conceptions. » (Parent **2008**)

Au début des années 2000, les œuvres de TOPO circulent largement dans le réseau virtuel, atteignant un rayonnement international dans des circuits de niche. Paradoxalement, elles peinent à s'ancrer localement. Les publics traditionnels du centre et de ses fondateurs – issus de la photographie et de la poésie, disciplines qui traditionnellement s'expriment dans l'espace physique – ne se sentent pas interpellés par les œuvres à visionner à l'écran. C'est à partir de ces constats que TOPO formalise ses réflexions autour du « rentrer et sortir de l'écran » en souhaitant accompagner chaque projet web d'un volet physique.

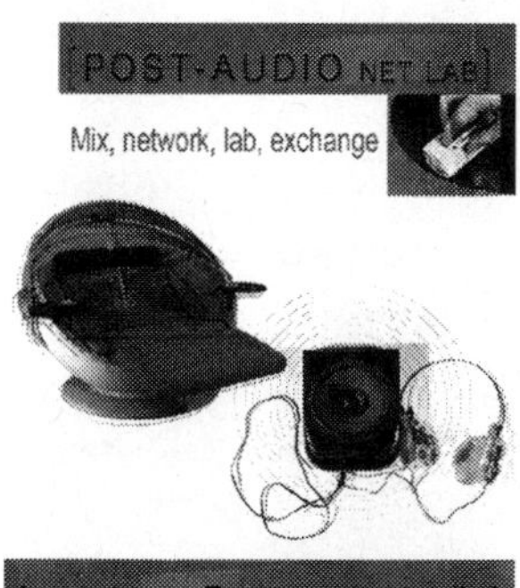

Image 5. Image promotionnelle, *Post_Audio_NetLab* (2004).

Post-Audio (2004-2008) s'affirme dans ce sens comme un projet multiplateforme marquant. Le point de départ est l'événement collectif *Post-Audio Esthetic*, conçu et orchestré par Gennaro De Pasquale au centre Clark, en 2000, qui fait valoir la création sonore dans un contexte d'installation et de performances. *Post-Audio_NetLab* prolonge, sur le web, un espace d'interaction, d'échange et de socialisation qui met en scène les codes de la culture musicale actuelle. Simulant l'expérience d'un magasin de musique, *Post-Audio_NetLab* est un lieu d'écoute, de jeu et de participation. Le site est construit autour d'une collection d'environ 400 disques fictifs édités par des labels de musique fictifs, auxquels sont rattachés des styles de musique inventés. Il comprend tout de même des extraits sonores de plusieurs artistes de la scène électronique montréalaise, de même que des vidéos d'archives trouvées sur Internet autour de l'histoire de la musique. Le site est également ouvert aux contributions des internautes par l'intermédiaire d'outils de télé-chargement et de mixage qui leur permettent d'intervenir dans la collection. La fiction se révèle alors un univers d'éléments visuels et textuels permettant l'interaction et la participation de l'internaute, l'ensemble étant régi par un système. La fiction devient en fait système.

Ce projet a donné lieu à diverses activités qui ont prolongé l'expérience du site dans l'espace réel : l'édition de *Post-Audio_DVD* en 2006, une compilation d'œuvres audiovisuelles sur DVD, et *Post-Audio_Installation* en 2008, com-binant l'ensemble du corpus avec des vidéos de l'artiste De Pasquale, le site web et des performances musicales, dans le studio de Méduse, à Québec.[3]

NOTE 3

Avec le soutien des organismes Antitube, la Bande Vidéo, Méduse et le Festival international de cinéma de Québec.

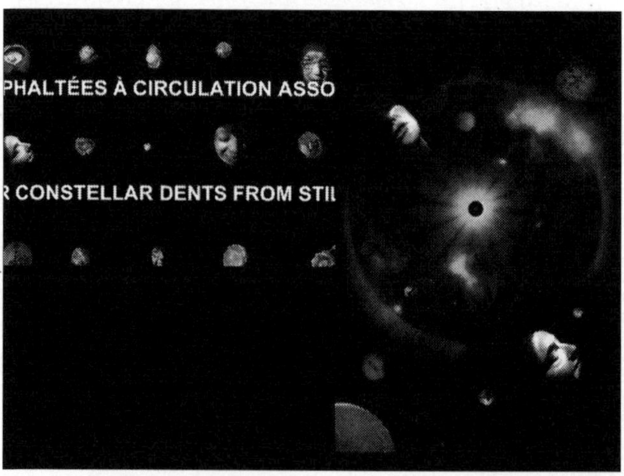

Image 6. Copie d'écran, *Astres/Stars/Goleuadau* (2006).

Avec *Astres/Stars/Goleuadau* (2006), fondée sur un corpus poétique de l'auteur canadien-gallois Childe Roland et les images de la photographe canadienne Susan Coolen, TOPO réalise une première œuvre de *e-poetry*. Le site se développe à partir d'une réflexion sur les trous noirs de l'astronomie et la mort des supernovas. Il rassemble des poèmes en français, en anglais et en gallois, qui sont couplés à des photographies et des animations multimédias aléatoires. Il s'agit de plusieurs dizaines de poèmes sonores dont chaque vers commence par une syllabe aspiratoire qui, à la longue, assèche et gerce la gorge. Les poèmes existent seulement quand ils sont lus à voix haute. L'interface éclatée offre une expérience de navigation qui amplifie le caractère mystérieux des textes, cette « kyrielle de jurons lancés aux impitoyables étoiles » (Roland). Le mot devient visuel, la lettre, un élément graphique.

> Comme un navigateur interstellaire attiré par de lointaines galaxies, l'internaute se déplace d'un agrégat à l'autre, propulsé par le langage. [...] La structure éclatée de l'interface de même que le flottement des images et des mots dans l'espace contredisent le parcours linéaire au profit d'une expérience faite de noyaux sémantiques et de passages aléatoires entre ceux-ci. Chaque noyau laisse ainsi une traînée de sons et de significations derrière qui continuent de faire écho jusqu'au relais suivant. (Parent 2008)

Au-delà du site web, *Astres* a également donné lieu à des performances de lecture et à des installations en galerie.

OBJETS NOMADES, ŒUVRES MOBILES

Suivant le développement de la géolocalisation et des technologies mobiles, TOPO entame un cycle d'explorations avec le corpus d'œuvres *Géo-Web* (2010), *Bêta-Cité* (Audiotopie, 2011) et *Détours : Poétiques de la ville* (collectif sous la direction de Taien Ng-Chan, 2012) – celle-ci conçue spécifiquement pour les plateformes mobiles.

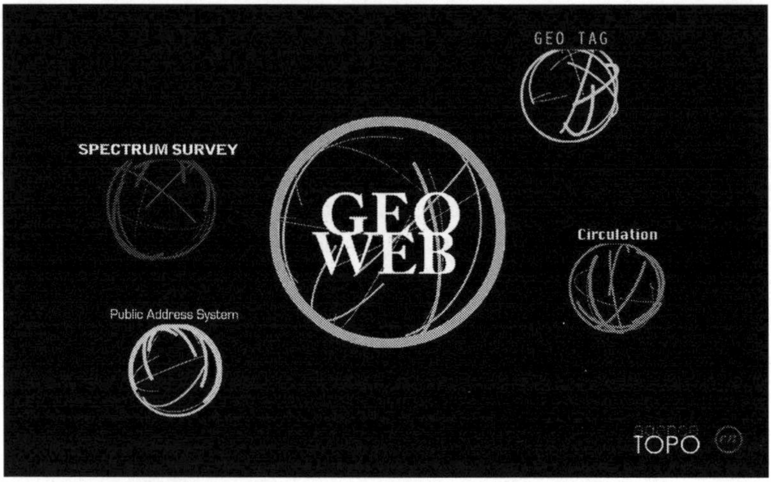

Image 7. Copie d'écran de la page d'accueil, *Geo-Web* (2010).

Géoweb réunit les artistes Matthew Biederman, Gregory Chatonsky, Zahra Poonawala et Cheryl Sourkes, sous le commissariat de Sylvie Parent. Cette dernière s'intéresse au phénomène du web géographique qui prend un essor notable avec l'évolution des outils de cartographie et de visualisation numériques. Les artistes s'approprient rapidement ces technologies pour produire nombre de récits de voyage, de cartes créatives, de projets de médias localisés. Pour expliquer un tel engouement, l'auteure note que la géolocalisation offre un ancrage physique et une certaine sensation d'emprise ou de contrôle dans un environnement numérique aux repères de plus en plus flous. Les lieux pouvant renvoyer à la mémoire d'un vécu, la localisation rejoint l'identitaire : « En effet, à lui seul le nom d'un lieu peut évoquer une expérience, un espace éprouvé ou imaginé. La volonté de situer est liée au désir d'appartenir au monde. » (Parent **2010**)

Image 8. Présentation du site *Détours, poétiques de la ville* (2011), par la directrice artistique Taïen Ng-Chang

Les corpus *Bêta-Cité* et *Détours*, développés à partir d'explorations singulières de la ville, utilisent le réseau comme un relais, dans une volonté, à nouveau, de relier des lieux et des personnes, en mettant l'humain au cœur de l'interaction. Le premier est une cartographie audiovisuelle interactive sur le web. Le site permet la création de parcours urbains audioguidés, que l'internaute peut concevoir et expérimenter dans deux quartiers de Montréal à partir d'une banque de sons, d'ambiances, de courtes séquences narratives et d'instruments virtuels. *Détours* présente également des trajectoires dans divers quartiers à partir de cartes enrichies de photos, de vidéos et de sons faisant écho à des histoires personnelles.

Dans ces promenades médiatiques et interactives, c'est le visiteur qui active le défilement de l'œuvre en marchant dans la ville. À noter également que les deux projets se sont prolongés avec des activités de médiation culturelle, des ateliers offerts aux jeunes de différents quartiers montréalais en collaboration avec des maisons de la culture. Ces œuvres nous rappellent alors que le web peut être « un réseau composé d'êtres humains qui échangent des informations et non un réseau d'informations qui s'échangent de manière autonome selon des protocoles automatisés. » (Mackrous **2014**)

SORTIR DE L'ÉCRAN/SPOKEN SCREEN

En 2007, en partenariat avec le laboratoire NT2, TOPO lance la série de performances *Sortir de l'écran/Spoken Screen* amenant la création hypermédiatique sur la scène. Cette série a présenté plus d'une dizaine d'artistes d'horizons variés, locaux et internationaux[4], dans une diversité de petites et grandes salles. À travers ce déplacement de l'œuvre hors de l'écran de l'ordinateur vers d'autres espaces de rencontres, TOPO réaffirme une volonté de connexions et de croisements, cette fois en invitant les artistes à se confronter directement à un public. Le centre fait le pari d'approfondir le rapport interactif entre le public et l'œuvre hypermédiatique : « C'est l'être humain, plutôt que la machine, qui est au cœur de la relation interactive. » (Mackrous **2014**)

NOTE 4

TOPO a présenté notamment les artistes Manon De Pauw, Jhave, Jason Lewis, Helena Martin Franco (Montréal), Simon Dumas et Éric d'Orion (Québec), Istvan Kantor (Toronto), Aya Karpinska, Michelle Citron (États-Unis), Annie Abrahams, HP Process (Philippe Boisnard et Hortense Gauthier), Pascale Gustin (France), Thomas Israël (Belgique), Jöerg Piringer (Autriche).

Image 9. *Fade Out* (Simon Dumas, Productions Rhizome) performance à la Cinémathèque québécoise (2007)

De telles propositions reflètent les changements technologiques de l'heure avec l'élargissement de l'espace du web. Les nouveaux outils numériques, les nouvelles plateformes et les artistes eux-mêmes ont ouvert ces espaces et créé la possibilité de telles hybridations. L'une après l'autre, les productions de TOPO expriment ainsi une volonté de lien, d'association et d'ouverture aux disciplines artistiques, aux environnements de création et de diffusion, aux communautés d'origines et de langues diverses. TOPO demeure aujourd'hui encore aligné sur ce qui a constitué les origines de sa fondation, c'est-à-dire la création interdisciplinaire mettant en relation, à travers les arts numériques, le texte, les mots, la parole, l'image et le son, dans un souci d'ancrage social et d'exploration de nouvelles voies de diffusion.

MÉDIATION CULTURELLE, CRÉATIVITÉ NUMÉRIQUE ET PARTICIPATION CITOYENNE

En témoignent trois œuvres interactives ayant fait appel à la participation citoyenne et à la création collective. *Cabinets de curiosités* (2015-2017)[5], la première de cette série, se développe comme une série d'ateliers comportant une dimension visuelle, littéraire, médiatique et spatiale, dont l'aboutissement est un événement, et l'archive créative, un site web. Il s'agit du résultat d'un projet de médiation culturelle mené avec le Centre Wellington, un organisme offrant des services de réadaptation et de soutien aux personnes atteintes d'un trouble de santé mentale dans l'arrondissement montréalais de Verdun.

NOTE 5

Cabinets de curiosités – Un projet de médiation culturelle réalisé sur deux ans sous la direction artistique de Gabrielle Lajoie Bergeron et Martine Koutnouyan avec plusieurs artistes invité·e·s. Réalisation du site web : Joseph Lefèvre assisté de Paul Gascou-Vaillancourt et José Cortes Castillo.

Image 10. Copie d'écran de la page d'accueil, *Cabinets de curiosités* (2015)

Spectrographies du territoire (2017-2018) explore de l'intérieur des secteurs en pleine mutation de Montréal. Lors de balades exploratoires, plus de 150 résidents et travailleurs des quartiers d'Outremont, de la Petite-Patrie et de Parc-Extension ont témoigné de leur environnement en s'attardant aux détails urbanistiques que l'on y trouve et qui symbolisent leur relation au territoire. Sous la direction de l'artiste invitée, Natacha Clitandre, avec l'équipe de médiation de TOPO[6], les citoyens et citoyennes disposaient d'une application de captation textuelle, sonore et photographique programmée afin d'inscrire leurs témoignages géolocalisés sur la page **Spectrographies.org.** Croisant histoire locale et récits personnels, cet exercice se proposait de capter l'esprit actuel d'un lieu.

Finalement, le dernier opus de cette série de projets pensés avec la communauté connaît un succès fulgurant dans les milieux des arts comme de la santé. *Dans la tête, une expérience immersive* (2017-2018)[7] propose quatre œuvres de réalité virtuelle issues d'ateliers avec des développeurs de technologies, des artistes médiatrices et de jeunes autistes créatifs. Le projet milite en faveur de la neurodiversité et de la reconnaissance positive de l'autisme.

NOTE 6

Spectrographies du territoire – Avec l'artiste Natacha Clitandre, l'équipe de médiation de TOPO comptait Michel Lefebvre, Gabrielle Lajoie-Bergeron, Pascale Théorêt-Groulx, Isabelle Anguita, Salima Punjani.

NOTE 7

Dans la tête – une expérience immersive – Un projet collectif de réalité virtuelle réalisé sous la direction artistique de Martine Asselin et Annick Daigneault assistées de Gabrielle Lajoie-Bergeron, Pascale Théorêt-Groulx et Marco Dubé.

HABITER L'INCERTITUDE D'UNE VITRINE

Le dernier jalon de cette trajectoire de 20 ans d'expérimentations est l'inauguration, en 2015, d'une vitrine d'exposition au rez-de-chaussée du pôle de Gaspé, dans le quartier montréalais du Mile-End. Il s'agit d'un espace vitré de 10 mètres carrés où TOPO explore la relation entre l'œuvre à l'intérieur de la vitrine et son spectateur de l'autre côté, dans un couloir.

Image 11. Page couverture du livre numérique *Habiter l'incertitude d'une vitrine* (2017)

Comment, à nouveau, réfléchir aux notions d'interaction et d'interactivité entre le dedans et le dehors? Entre le public et l'œuvre médiatique?

La Vitrine est investie par des installations et des performances mettant chaque fois à l'épreuve la présence dans et dehors cette vitre-écran : frontière, façade, cloison et surface à la fois. Située dans le lieu transitoire qu'est un couloir, chacun des artistes a dû repenser sa fonction et son usage dans un lieu de passage. Les résultats des deux premières années d'expositions ont été regroupés dans un livre numérique portant le titre *Habiter l'incertitude d'une Vitrine.* Pour cette publication, l'auteure Paule Mackrous a réuni la douzaine d'expositions produites en 2015-2017 sous quatre thématiques : reflets, arènes, présences et passages.

> La vitrine ouvre un monde singulier, un espace en creux où prend forme l'œuvre, mais elle nous renvoie aussi à nos propres présences : elle reflète nos corps et l'endroit depuis lequel nous contemplons la vitrine.
> Les reflets, tels les *glitchs* informatiques, dérangent en même temps qu'ils engendrent un espace de réflexions. Par habitude, on les conçoit comme des erreurs à corriger, mais puisqu'ils sont inévitables, force est de constater qu'ils font partie de l'expérience. Ils nous invitent chaque

> fois à redessiner les contours communs de deux univers en apparence distincts : l'intérieur et l'extérieur de la vitrine. Entre l'opacité du verre qui permet à notre image de se manifester et la transparence qui engendre un passage entre les mondes, les œuvres et leurs significations oscillent. Par les reflets, nous sommes constamment conviés à nous questionner sur la place qu'occupe notre propre regard dans l'œuvre.
> La vitrine devient un espace où, s'il y a des passages, ce sont ceux, invisibles, par lesquels les objets transitent d'un état à un autre. On y adapte les œuvres préexistantes, on y remixe les textes, on y traduit les éléments d'un médium vers un autre : de l'image animée vers le livre virtuel, par exemple (*Translational Spaces*). À leur tour, les œuvres convient le spectateur à une expérience transformatrice, ne serait-ce que par la réinterprétation que l'on fait du lieu où il déambule ou par la surprise que la présence de l'œuvre génère. (Mackrous 2018)

La Vitrine redéploie l'exploration créative initiale du web. Elle offre à TOPO un nouveau cycle de recherche pour affirmer une vision interdisciplinaire des arts et des littératures numériques, nourrie par des courants esthétiques et conceptuels venant des arts visuels, cinématographiques et performatifs.

Côté, Philippe. 1998. *Liquidation. En faire un photoroman!* (feuillet d'exposition) Montréal : Centre des arts actuels SKOL.

Mackrous, Paule. 2014. *Le web est ailleurs!* Montréal : Agence TOPO.

Mackrous, Paule. 2017. *Habiter l'incertitude d'une vitrine.* Montréal : TOPO.

Parent, Sylvie. 2008. *Agence TOPO. 10 ans de création pour le web.* Montréal : Agence TOPO.

Parent, Sylvie. 2010. *Géoweb : création de nouvelles géographies.* Montréal : Agence TOPO. Consulté le 12 avril 2019.
Accéder au lien : http://www.agencetopo.qc.ca/wp/texte-de-references-geoweb/

Petit, Cécile. 2003. *Civilités. Magazine électronique du CIAC.*

Robert, Pierre. 1999. « Présentation du cédérom Liquidation, un photoroman nouveau genre ». *Archée, revue d'art en ligne : arts médiatiques et cyberculture*, mars. Consulté le 12 avril 2019.
Accéder au lien : http://archee.qc.ca/ ar.php?page=article&section=texte&no=90&note=ok&surligne=oui&mot=&PHPSESSID=beedb268787aa169f801aa68b100eeaa

The *Book of Disquiet Digital Archive* as a Role-Playing Experiment

MANUEL PORTELA • CECÍLIA MAGALHÃES[1]

NOTE 1

Cecília Magalhães's doctoral research is supported by the Foundation for Science and Technology (FCT). This paper is part of her ongoing PhD project *Fragments in Practice* (2017-2021). Fellowship reference: SFRH/BD/139569/2018.

Abstract

The LdoD Archive (Portela and Silva **2017**, online) contains a model for virtualizing Fernando Pessoa's *Book of Disquiet* by simulating textual and bibliographic processes in the conceptual and material production of this textual work. Besides a set of features of representational simulation of the authorial genetics of the text and its editorial socialization through the four main critical editions, the LdoD Archive offers functionalities of performative simulation that allow interactors to reconceptualize and rematerialize the work at editorial and authorial levels. This interactive layer of the LdoD Archive sustains a dynamic textual environment in which users have the possibility of reediting and rewriting the fragments, using both computer-assisted and human-assisted procedures. Despite their high value as teaching and research resources, many digital literary archives remain confined to the expert scholarly community because they fail to engage with a non-specialist audience. In the digital archive devoted to Fernando Pessoa's *Book of Disquiet*, we experimented with Web 2.0 techniques in constructing a social edition in which experts and common users–in their regular studying, reading, and writing practices–can collaborate in the creation and publication of new versions of the Book according to a role-playing rationale. The aim of this article is to present the early testing results of the functionalities of the platform in terms of users' interaction. The data was collected through specific activities with small groups, focusing on the dynamic processes of editing, annotating, and rewriting the texts.

Résumé

La LdoD Archive (Portela et Silva **2017**, en ligne) comprend un modèle de virtualisation du *Livre de l'intranquillité (Book of Disquiet)* de Fernando Pessoa. Ce modèle simule les processus textuel et bibliographique au coeur de la production conceptuelle et matérielle de l'œuvre originale. Outre un ensemble de fonctionnalités qui permettent d'en simuler la représentation sur la base de sa génétique auctoriale et de sa « socialisation éditoriale » au gré de ses quatre éditions critiques, la LdoD Archive offre aux interacteurs la possibilité de reconceptualiser et de rematérialiser le texte aux niveaux auctorial et éditorial. Cette dimension interactive de la LdoD Archive soutient un environnement textuel dynamique dans lequel les utilisateurs ont la possibilité de rééditer et de réécrire les fragments, en utilisant des procédés assistées par ordinateur ainsi que par l'humain.Malgré leur mérite en tant que ressources pour la recherche et l'enseignement, plusieurs archives numériques ne sont consultées que par les communautés universitaires, car elles échouent à attirer un public non-spécialisé. Dans cette archive consacrée au *Livre de l'intranquillité* de Fernando Pessoa, nous avons expérimenté des techniques 2.0 en construisant une édition collaborative grâce à laquelle les experts et les non-experts peuvent collaborer dans la création et la publication de nouvelles versions du texte, que ce soit dans le cadre de leurs études, de leurs lectures ou de leurs pratiques d'écriture. L'objectif de cet article est de présenter les premiers résultats des évaluations des fonctionnalités de la plateforme suite aux interactions des utilisateurs. Nous avons recueilli les données lors d'activités spécifiques réalisées en petits groupes, en mettant l'accent sur les processus d'édition, d'annotation et de réécriture des textes.

INTRODUCING THE MULTILAYERED *LDOD ARCHIVE*

Our paper describes the attempt to bring together electronic literature practices and digital humanities methods in an integrated textual environment. The *LdoD Archive: Collaborative Digital Archive of the Book of Disquiet* (Portela **2017**) contains digital images of the autograph manuscripts and typescripts of Fernando Pessoa's *Book of Disquiet*, new transcriptions of those materials, four critical editions of the work, as well as a set of dynamic functionalities for intervening in this textual environment. Interaction within this textual space is structured according to three literary roles: reading, editing, and writing.

The *LdoD Archive* has been designed as a dynamic archive structured into two layers of interaction (Portela and Rito Silva **2015**). The first layer, described as the representation layer, involves both a genetic and a social dimension. The genetic dimension is expressed by the digital facsimiles of Fernando Pessoa's autograph documents: more than 600 fragments, written between 1913 and 1935, which were also topographically transcribed by the *LdoD Archive* team. Equally important, the social dimension is expressed by the transcriptions of four critical editions whose set of texts, transcriptions and organization give us different editorial interpretations of the work. Thus the representational layer of the *LdoD Archive* gathers the four main critical editions—edited by Jacinto Prado Coelho (1982), Teresa Sobral Cunha (2008), Richard Zenith (2012), and Jerónimo Pizarro (2010)[2]—and also the source authorial documents for those editions. When interactors engage with the representation layer, they are able to read the work according to various sequences and compare the expert editions of this work against each other:

NOTE 2

These dates of publication correspond to the specific editions that have been chosen for inclusion in the *LdoD Archive*. The date of the first edition of each version of the *Book of Disquiet* is as follows: Jacinto Prado Coelho, 1982; Teresa Sobral Cunha, 1990-1991; Richard Zenith, 1998; Jerónimo Pizarro, 2010.

> By placing digital facsimiles in the context of topographic transcriptions, the *LdoD Archive* enables users to experiment with the transit from document to text and from text to document. Situating both facsimile and topographic transcription in the context of the experts' editions, the *LdoD Archive* shows four possible transitions from text to book and from book to text. To the extent that each text of each edition is contextualizable in an archive of authorial and editorial witnesses, it is the very process of construction of text from document and book from

text that the genetic and social dimensions of the *LdoD Archive* place in evidence. The construction of the book–as the product either of a self-editing authorial act, or a series of posthumous editorial acts–becomes an instantiation of the conceptual and material process of identity and difference that enables text and book to emerge from a series of inscriptional marks and from the acts of reading and interpreting those marks (Portela and Rito Silva **2016**, 195).

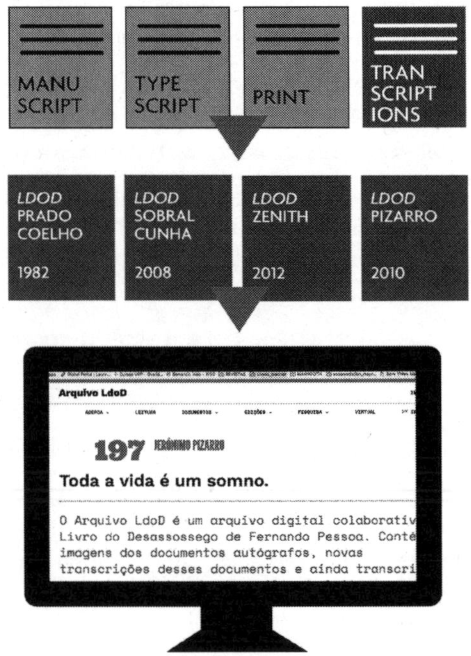

Figure 1. Representation layer and its genetic and social dimensions.

The simulation layer, on the other hand, involves a virtual dimension which enables interactors to dynamically manipulate the digital fragments of the *Book of Disquiet* within the textual environment. The concept of simulation comes from "the fact that users are given the possibility of playing various roles in the literary process (reading, editing, writing), using the flexibility of the digital medium for experimenting with the *Book of Disquiet* as a literary machine" (Portela and Rito Silva **2017**). When interactors engage with the simulation layer, they are able to enter the archive as editors or writers who can add their own content to the archive's database. Interactors are able to design new editions of the *Book*, an-notate and create taxonomies for their own editions, or they can rewrite variations based on the fragments. They are also able to visualize their reading paths and navigate from text to text according to multiple rea-ding strategies, including vi-sual maps representing textual similarity and user-created taxonomies.[3] The ability to shift between these three roles has been conceptualized as a simu-lation of literary performativity (Portela and Rito Silva **2016**).

Through this double-layered feedback between representation and simulation, the platform proposes a model for virtualizing the *Book of Disquiet* that simulates creative processes in the conceptual and material production of this work. In other words, it allows interactors to reconceptualize and remate-rialize the puzzling work of Fernando Pessoa and his editors by experimenting with the procedurality of reading, writing and editing. Through this reflexive dynamics, the semiotic actions of interactors become constitutive of the textual envi-ronment itself. At once conceptual and technical artefact, this innovative model for digital editing, digital writing and di-gital reading recreates the universe of the *Book of Disquiet* according to ludic principles of textual manipulation. The *LdoD Archive* explores those literary practices by creating a new rationale that brings together the *Archive*'s representation and simulation layers.

NOTE 3

The code for integrating the virtual writing functionalities into the platform is still under development. Two types of writing tools will be available for role-playing the act of writing: a word processing text editor for human-assisted writing; and a suite of writing programs for computer-assisted writing. An instance of the second type has already been developed as a stand-alone series of writing experiments by Luís Lucas Pereira under the general title *Machines of Disquiet* (2014-2018; 20 machines have been developed so far). Cf. Pereira et al. 2018. As regards the virtualization of reading within the simulation layer, a new functionality was added in 2019 called *Livro Visual* ["Visual Book"] (cf. **https://ldod.uc.pt/ldod-visual**).

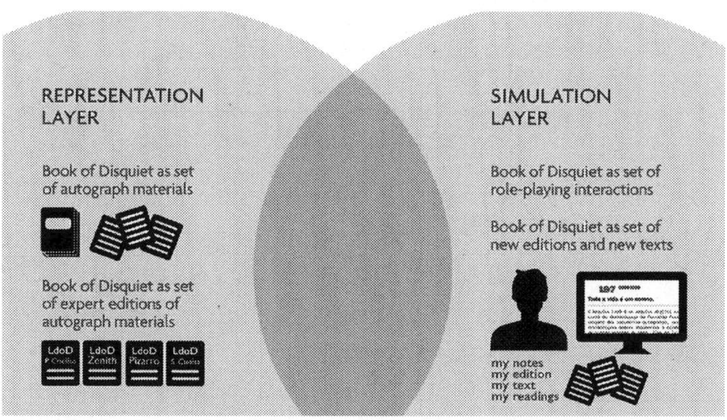

Figure 2. Simulation layer: *Book of Disquiet* as a set of new editions, new texts and new readings.

As enacted in the *LdoD Archive*, the integration of those layers offers an alternative model to digital humanities approaches to textual analysis and representation by bringing in electronic literature practices that foster creative and exploratory interactions in an evolving environment. Through these interactions, the archive opens itself up to social appropriation and transformation.

By means of specific textual encoding based on a TEI schema, combined with an object-oriented repository (Silva and Portela **2014**) and the integration of interactive tools, the *LdoD Archive* evolved into a dynamic space for experimenting with the procedurality of digital media to model the procedurality of literary action. According to the model of literary action embedded in the system, interactors are called upon to perform different roles, which have been abstracted as reader-function, editor-function, author-function, and book-function (Portela and Rito Silva **2015**).

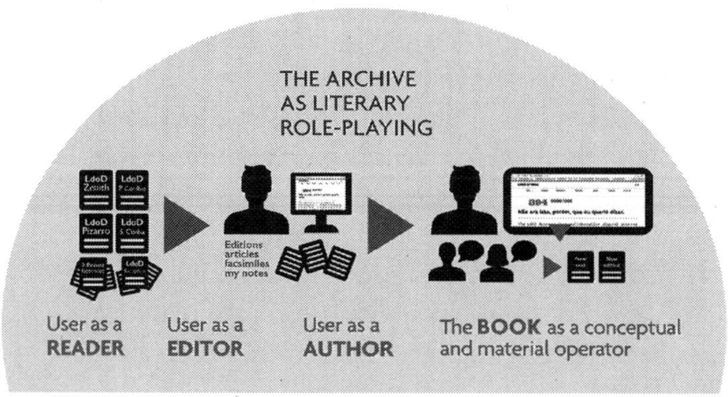

Figure 3. *LdoD Archive*'s literary functions.

DIGITAL ETHNOGRAPHY AND *PRAXIS* IN THE *LDOD ARCHIVE*

The long-term aim of the current stage of development is to focus on how the role of the interactors is constrained by the functionalities and interface of the *LdoD Archive*, on one hand, and to show how actual users, in formal and informal contexts, appropriate those functionalities, on the other. We want to learn more about the affordances and constraints of the platform so that we can improve its design, but we also want to learn more about the nature of literary performance through the uses of this role-playing textual environment.

This model of literary performativity is also an attempt to invent a new kind of textual space for literary interaction. It is both a literary and a scientific inquiry into the nature of literary performance through the possibilities of use of this role-playing textual environment.

•

The project *Fragments in Practice* is an ongoing PhD investigation (2017-2021) focused on analyzing the interactors' creative practices within the *LdoD Archive*. This investigation adopts Schatzki's definition of practice as an intertwined nexus that produces meaning through the different entities in play: subjects, artefacts, spatialities, timings and processes, shaping creative ecologies in action (Schatzki, Knorr-Cetina, and Savigny **2001**). Following this idea, the project also contains an ethnographic and self-reflexive component (Pink et al. 2016; Markham 2018; Markham and Baym **2009**) focused on collecting, handling and managing qualitative and quantitative data, based on the interactors' situated reading, editing and writing practices in the platform.

According to this situational approach, those practices were framed within three specific circumstances of use of the *LdoD Archive*: 1) teaching, 2) researching, and 3) leisure. Each situated practice shapes a different digital focus group where interactors from varied backgrounds will work on the platform. Following the notion of public engagement applied by Susan Schreibman's team in the project *Letters 1916-1923*[4] (2017), our focus groups have been projected for a highly participatory and collaborative partnership with the community related to educational and literary practices. In this regard, the interactors are, for us, more than our corpora of analysis: they are enrolled as co-creators in our experimental research of the interactive *LdoD Archive*. We expect to engage teachers, researchers, students, and rea-ders from the Portuguese-speaking community in exploring, discussing and creating new literary outputs derived from Pessoa's disquieting project.

NOTE 4

For further information about *Letters 1916-1923*, access: **http://letters1916.maynoothuniversity.ie/**.

NOTE 5

Our Youtube channel *Fragments in Practice* is still under construction, although it can be accessed via the following link: **https://www.youtube.com/channel/UCHK5OjU1w4OwPOF_eOjd9bQ**

The focus groups' themed activities will be carried out online, after a step-by-step didactic presentation of the *LdoD Archive* and its functionalities, in the form of 10 short video tutorials in the Fragments in Practice Youtube Channel[5] and, when necessary, by chat. During these activities, we intend to track the interactors' varied narratives as they become registered in the evolving content of the platform as well as to capture their impressions, understandings, intentionalities, difficulties, and so on. In this case, interactors' data will be captured by working with keylogging track, screen records, semi-structured interviews, and group chats. Moreover, the digital editions, annotations and other personal contributions will provide invaluable data for comparison and analysis. This multimedia data will be refined into our previous dataset structure, which has been organized into three interconnected categories:

- Interactors' profile (related to variables such as nationality, work location, professional background, reading interests, etc.);
- creative processes (related to the platform modes of use, including the interactors' perceptions and access to the reader, editor, author, and book functions); and finally
- the virtual editions themselves (related to the discursive and narrative traces of interactors' creativity as expressed in the editions' order, selection, annotations and so on).

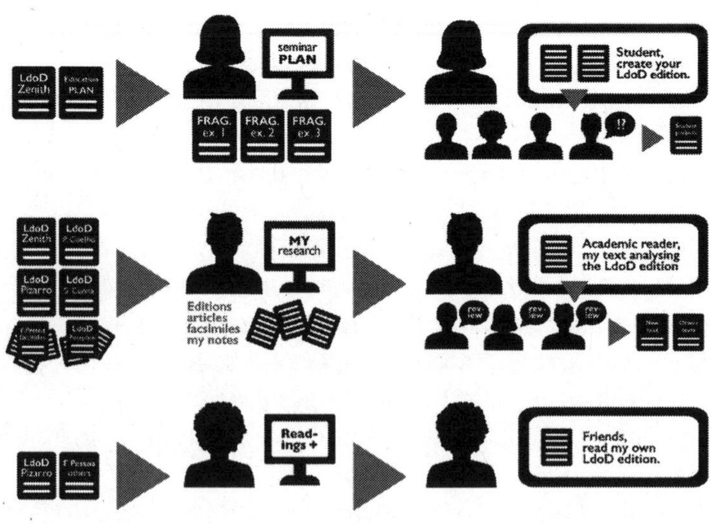

Figure 4. *Fragments in Practice* and the framed situations: Teaching, Research and Leisure.

We aim to create interactor-friendly conditions to go deep into the mechanisms of the *LdoD Archive*, examining how users are constituted through its affordances but also how they bring their own situated practices to negotiate them. Adjustments to our own research plan reflecting the outputs collected in the focal group activities are to be expected. Our first role-playing expe-riments were also meant to help refine our methodology and improve our analysis of the affordances and constraints of *LdoD Archive* in relation to collaborative practices of the interactors.

NOTE 6

We would like to acknowledge the collaborators who took part in both workshops and helped us to better understand the *LdoD Archive's praxis.*

EDITING AND WRITING: ROLE-PLAYING EXPERIMENTS IN *LDOD ARCHIVE*[6]

It is important to highlight that the practice-based digital ethnography and user-experience methodological approaches outlined above were required preliminary empirical tests for better understanding the challenges of the creative practices modelled in the *LdoD Archive*. In this section, we describe two workshops–*Disquiet Remix 1* and *Disquiet Variations*–whose structure and activities were designed for observing actual interactions with the platform after its first release.[7] The data has been collected from the activities of editing, annotating, glossing, and rewriting the texts as instantiated in the platform's interfaces and tools. Further, we describe how both workshops were organized and briefly analyze their qualitative outputs.

NOTE 7

Although usability tests had been carried out in 2014 and 2017, they were concerned with specific components of interface design. The two workshops reported here were meant to provide evidence about the uses of the various interfaces and functions once the final version of the archive was released.

Disquiet Remix 1: Teaching with and learning from the virtual editing functions of the platform

The *Disquiet Remix* test-session took place on November 26, 2017, in cooperation with the student fraternity Solar dos Kapängas. Fourteen participants took part in the event, divided into four work groups. This audience was mostly composed of undergraduate and graduate students in Humanities at the University of Coimbra, although some of the participants were not connected with the academic environment. The primary objective of this session was to test how each group could creatively interact with the platform by creating new virtual mini-editions of the *Book of Disquiet*.

In this case,

a) each edition contained only five fragments chosen by the user groups;

b) each edition had to have a title and a selection criterion, which was explained in the presentation synopsis (the synopsis explained both the selection and the ordering principles);

c) the creation of the mini-editions corresponded to the VIRTUAL EDITION function, but other functionalities of the platform such as those programmed in the READING, DOCUMENT and SEARCH interfaces were explored in order to find, compare and select texts.

The tasks required from the participants included:

> (1) open exploration of the platform, followed by registration as virtual editors, the creation of virtual groups, selection and collaborative annotation of the fragments, and collaborative writing of the presentation synopsis;
>
> (2) oral presentation of the mini-editions (including a brief description of the exploration and navigation of the platform for constructing the edition, as well as a general reflection on the particular reading and editing practices encouraged by the functionalities of the platform).

Each mini-edition was defined according to variables such as theme, heteronomy, source, critical edition, narrativity of selected texts, and even the material characteristics of the facsimiles. The four groups had two hours to discuss, create their editions and finally present them. For the most part, the presented results were based on the participants' previous ideas about Pessoa as an author who wonders, through his heteronyms, about existence, love, boredom, nostalgia, time and other notions which are inherent to his aesthetics of life. However, based on the same participants' interpretations and intentions, each edition was organized into distinct systems, represented by different narratives and correlations among the sorted fragments.

Figure 5. A situated *LdoD Archive*: creating editions.

On rearranging Pessoa's fragmentary thoughts, the participants, as *bricoleurs*, were able to build new meaningful short stories from unrelated fragments of the transcribed editions. We describe here two of these mini-editions,[8] showing how the groups were able to produce distinct (and similar) outputs by distinctive actions of planning, reading, searching and composing new editorial narratives for linking autonomous digital fragments.

NOTE 8

The English translation of the quotes and fragment titles are based on Richard Zenith's edition and translation, *Book of Disquiet* (2002). Translations of the synopses are ours.

The mini edition *The Journey*,[9] designed by Gabriella Mendes, Élia Ramalho and Wagner Merije, clearly reveals the literary background of the editors. They ordered the fragments signed by the semi-heteronym Bernardo Soares as an illustration of the character-writer's perception of himself through the metaphor of travelling:

NOTE 9

This mini-edition can be accessed at this link: **https://ldod.uc.pt/edition/acronym/LdoD-KAPGEW**

> The leaving and the arriving are present in Fernando Pessoa's work and soul. In this edition, we were guided by some words which bring an essential idea of this state of movement. We also aimed to create a travelling narrative with the fragments from *Book of Disquiet*. The order follows a logical narrative presenting the context, the character, the

beginning of the action, its climax and its end–delineated by the semi-heteronym Bernardo Soares's tiredness and inertia.

1 The black sky to the south of the Tagus

2 I belong to a generation that inherited disbelief

3 A voyage I never made

4 Shipwrecks? No, I never suffered any.

5 I'm astounded whenever I finish something

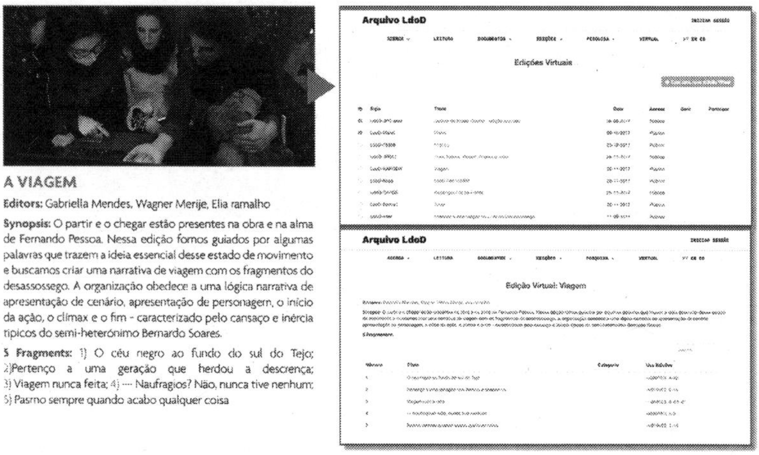

Figure 6. The virtual edition "The journey."

In the chosen sequence, the first fragment presents a subjective, corporeal and nostalgic Bernardo Soares, inspired by his oneiric impression of the Tagus river. In the following fragments, the opposition between movement and stillness, expressed in the permanent presence of body and water in motion–the sailing journey–is the hint for our character-writer to describe (through our editors) the struggles of his creative process. By rearranging the fragments, our editors tried to suggest new meanings to Soares's artistic narratives. Curiously, they avoid using one of the critical editions by choosing to work only with the facsimiles' transcriptions. Also, it seems that there is a concern in camouflaging their own enunciative presence beyond the synopsis: Bernardo Soares is here delegated as the main rising voice which describes what his creative writing process is.

On the other hand, the mini-edition designed by Andrea Aguinaga, Fátima Neves, José Neves, Robert Martins and João Martinho[10] has an entirely different logic. Labelled with their own names, each of the five editors chose one independent fragment to represent their personal state of mind (although none of them was individually attributed). The five fragments do not follow a specific edition criterion: they are picked from different editions and also from the transcribed facsimiles. Under the group's agreement, they also added one more fragment at the beginning of the synopsis, explaining the mini-edition's personal tone. In this case, Fernando Pessoa himself lets off steam, in a letter to Cortes-Rodrigues,[11] his authorial feelings during his process of handling the *Book of Disquiet*. This same subjective impression seems to be highlighted in the editors' choices. There is no concern with logical sequence or any specific order among the texts, although all of them correspond to universal philosophical themes and are here expressed as subjective, fragmented opinions from a fragmented embodied Pessoa, uncovered in each one of our digital editors.

NOTE 10

This mini-edition can be accessed at this link: **https://ldod.uc.pt/edition/acronym/LdoD-JFRAJ**

NOTE 11

This quote is based on Zenith's edition, which can be accessed at this link: **https://ldod.uc.pt/fragments/fragment/Fr720/inter/Fr720_WIT_ED_CRIT_Z**

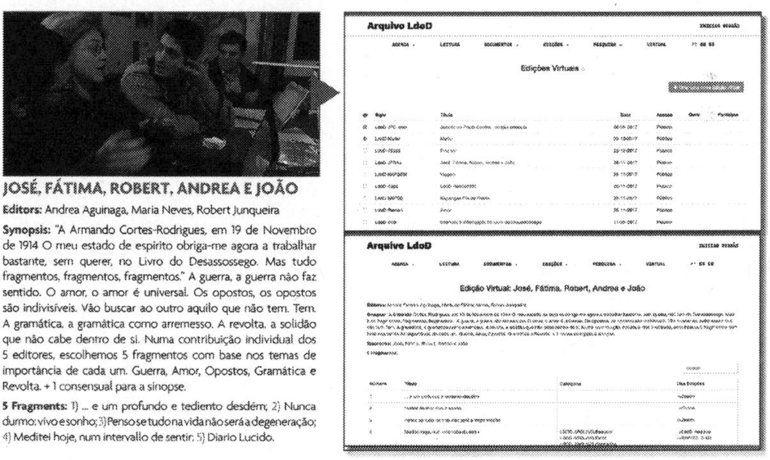

Figure 7. The virtual edition "José, Fátima, Robert, Andrea and João."

To Armando Cortes-Rodrigues, November 19, 1914. "My state of mind compels me to work hard, against my will, on *The Book of Disquiet*. But it is all fragments, fragments, fragments." The war, the war does not make sense. Love, love is universal. The opposites, the opposites are indivisible. They look for, in the other, what they do not have. They

> have. The grammar, the grammar as a pitch. The rage, the loneliness that it is not contained in itself. Through the personal contribution of the five editors, we chose five fragments based on the themes that are important for each one. War, Love, Opposites, Grammar and Rage. + one "in agreement" for our synopsis.
> 1 ...and a deep and weary disdain (war)
> 2 I never sleep. I live and I dream. (love)
> 3 Perhaps everything in life is the degeneration of something else (opposites)
> 4 Today, during a break from feeling (grammar)
> 5 Lucid Diary (rage)

Comparing the groups' results, we can find similarities in the way each interacted with the platform. Although the main functionalities and tools were presented, time constraints did not allow for the participating groups to explore annotation and taxonomy as well as advanced search or edition comparison tools. They were stuck on finding their own creative logic to build the totality of their mini-editions, by handling existent textual and material contents. That means they spent most of their working time discussing, reading and planning their editions. Then, searching and close-reading the "content required" fragments. Finally, they had a short time to explore how to manage and execute the virtual edition technically: searching, adding, ordering the fragments, and writing the synopsis. In this sense, both editions are technically simple, although they were structured under diverse creative conditions according to the practical nexus shaped in the process of group integration, managing the platform and planning the mini-editions. The interactors' individualities, in this sense, were essential for defining their distinct literary strategies, which still have much in common if we consider their interlocutory approaches: silently rising Soares's voice, narrating his self-journey, navigating into his writing process, or incorporating Pessoa's enunciative attitude to express, through his voice, the subjectivity of each editor.

DISQUIET VARIATIONS: TEACHING WITH AND LEARNING FROM THE VIRTUAL WRITING FUNCTIONS OF THE PLATFORM

The one-day workshop *Disquiet Variations* took place on April 30, 2018. This workshop was designed as a creative writing session for English-speaking participants from varied academic and professional backgrounds and varied age groups. For most of them, the workshop was also their introduction to Fernando Pessoa's work.

The workshop started with a brief introduction to the platform, focusing particularly on its virtual writing functionalities. These functionalities include both what we describe as "human-assisted writing" and "computer-assisted writing." In the first instance, interactors used only a text processor to produce their writing. In the second case, new texts could be generated with the help of various electronic literature operations on the textual database. A selection of 10 texts from the *Book of Disquiet* (in English translation by Richard Zenith) was read out loud by participants (each paragraph was read by a different person). After this collective reading, participants were asked to look for "seed fragments" in the texts. These 10-word seed fragments became the starting point for their writing of new texts under different voices. After 90 minutes of individual writing, presentation and discussion of the "Disquiet Variations" followed. The discussion was guided by the following questions: (a) why a particular "seed fragment"?; (b) how did the "seed fragment" help me invent a voice?; (c) what is the relation between my final text and my "seed fragment"?; (d) what is the relation between this new textual voice and the usual textual voice(s) in my texts?; (e) did this exercise help me open up a new perspective on language?; (f) what have I learned about writing?; (g) what have I learned about Pessoa's writing?

WHY a particular "seed fragment"?

HOW did the "seed fragment" help me invent a voice?

WHAT is the relation between my final text and my "seed fragment"?

WHAT is the relation between this new textual voice and the usual textual voice(s) in my texts?

DID this exercise help me open up a new perspective on language?

WHAT have I learned about writing?

WHAT have I learned about Pessoa's writing?

JOURNEY NEVER MADE
I hide behind the door, so that when REALITY comes in, it won't see me. I hide under the table and suddenly spring out to startle Possibility. I withdraw from myself, as if from the arms of an embrace, the two great tediums that encircle me — the TEDIUM of BEING ABLE to LIVE only the Real, and the tedium of being able to imagine only the Possible.
Thus I TRIUMPH over reality. Are these SANDCASTLES my triumphs? Of what divine substance are castles that are not sandcastles made?"
"How do you know that, by TRAVELING in this way, I am not obscurely rejuvenating myself? Childishly absurd, I relive my BOYHOOD and play with the ideas of things as I once played with my toy soldiers, with which, as a boy, I did things that went totally against the very idea of SOLDIERS.
Drunk on errors, I momentarily find myself erroneously alive.

Figure 8. A situated *LdoD Archive*: writing Variations.

Beyond the more general questions, which would be relevant for any writing workshop, this first attempt at exploring the *Book of Disquiet* for further acts of writing helped us think about the writing constraints that should be part of the role-playing author-function in the *Archive*. These constraints should be able to anchor each new writing act in Pessoa's text while exploring the iterability of writing for the free play of signification.

The idea of writing as an invention of perspective and voice–central in Pessoa's heteronymic processes–needs to be made more explicit as part of the rules of the game. We also need to open up the possibility of multiple hyperlinks to fragments from the *Book of Disquiet* rather than one single link to the seed string of up to 10 words. Making each textual iteration resonate the source text while opening it up to new chains of language will be our challenge for the future development of the text processing interface as an enabling writing tool within the Archive.

NOTE 12

Fernando Pessoa / Bernardo Soares, September 10-11, 1931. Edited and translated by Richard Zenith, Penguin Books, 2002.

Seed Text

201

Since early morning and against the solar custom of this bright city, the fog had wrapped a weightless mantle (which the sun slowly gilded) around the rows of houses, the cancelled open spaces, and the shifting heights of land and of buildings. But as the hours advanced towards midday, the gentle mist began to unravel until, with breaths like flapping shadows of veils, it expired altogether. By ten o'clock, the tenuous blueing of the sky was the only evidence that there had been fog.

The city's features were reborn once the blurry mask slipped away. As if a window had been opened, the already dawned day dawned. There was a slight change in all the sounds, which had also suddenly returned. A blue tint infiltrated even the stones of the streets and the impersonal auras of pedestrians. The sun was warm, but still humidly so, filtered by the vanished fog.

[...][12]

Variation (by Sue Burge)

Alternatives

after Pessoa

Do you remember a film where there are three suns, or was it three moons, or both, and that other film where this guy can't escape this one

> day, waking up to the same song, same radio news, I would have been like 'oh, bollocks,' but he never swears, just crosses his eyes a bit.
> There are days when all you see are poodles or blue cars or where a writer you've never heard of gets mentioned by two different people and it's goosebumpy but kind of cool at the same time; or days when you wake up with a smile and then remember the night before and you're like, "*okay already dawned day, dawn again.*"

This and several other examples in the *Disquiet Variations* workshop showed how writers always bring their own particular literary style and preoccupations to a constrained practice. The writing exercises also revealed two distinct attitudes towards the source text: one in which the seed text was appropriated without any attempt to link the textual variation to the semantic atmosphere of the source; and another form of derivation in which the seed text would bring with it additional resonances and layers of reference from the source. Intertextual relations between seeds and variations could thus be expressed as a continuum that extends from citation and allusion through pastiche and parody to metamorphosis.

CONCLUSION

The *LdoD Archive* has evolved into a complex textual environment with multiple layers and functionalities. Its articulation of textual representation and textual simulation is an attempt to model literary performativity, that is, a socialized network of acts of reading, editing, and writing. Interactors are invited to perform those roles within the textual environment by acting as readers, editors, and writers. This role-playing rationale captures the processuality of Fernando Pessoa's *Book of Disquiet* as a work under construction and opens it up to further creative acts of transformation. As a computational literary experiment, the *LdoD Archive* addresses the gap between digital humanities and electronic literature. First, through its repurposing of several DH tools beyond representational modelling, and secondly, by the reflexive and simulatory exploration of acts of literary production.

If the *LdoD Archive* aims to foster creative practices, these will be better understood through actual practices. By actively engaging the interactors in literary role-playing, these reading, editing, and writing experiments provide instances of its dynamic literary mechanism in action. While the analyses of processes and outcomes allow us to test the system in use, they also give us a glimpse into the distinctive creative actions through which interactors perform those roles. Furthermore, they help us improve the process of capturing and analyzing the ephemerality of these literary practices as well as the process of engaging users in new forms of literary production. The situated practices of diverse groups of interactors, as they negotiate the affordances and constraints of the platform, will let us understand not only how particular roles have been modeled in the *LdoD Archive*, but also how the literary emerges from a series of performative actions.

Digital facsimile: https://ldod.uc.pt/facs/bn-acpc-e-e3-4-1-87_0019_10_t24-C-R0150.jpg
Transcription: https://ldod.uc.pt/fragments/fragment/Fr239/inter/Fr239_WIT_MS_Fr239a_280

Markham, Annette N. 2018. "Ethnography in the Digital Internet Era: From Fields to Flows, Descriptions to Interventions". In *The Sage Handbook of Qualitative Research*, ed. by Norman K. Denzin and Yvonna S. Lincoln, 5th ed., 1129-62. Los Angeles: Sage Publications.

Markham, Annette N., and Nancy K. Baym. 2009. *Internet Inquiry: Conversations About Method.* Los Angeles: Sage Publications.

Pereira, Luís Lucas, Manuel Portela, and Licínio Roque. 2018. "Machines of Disquiet: Textual Experience in the LdoD Archive". *MATLIT: Materialities of Literature* 6 (1):59-71. Link: https://impactum-journals.uc.pt/matlit/article/view/5200

Pessoa, Fernando. 2002. *The Book of Disquiet.* Translated by Richard Zenith. London: Penguin Books.

Pink, Sarah, Heather A. Horst, John Postill, Larissa Hjorth, Tania Lewis, and Jo Tacchi, ed. 2016. *Digital Ethnography: Principles and Practice.* Los Angeles: Sage.

Portela, Manuel. 2017. "The Book of Disquiet Archive as a Collaborative Textual Environment". In *The Writing Platform: Digital Knowledge for Writers.* Brisbane: Queensland University of Technology. July 10.
Link: http://thewritingplatform.com/2017/07/book-disquiet-archive-collaborative-textual-environment-digital-archive-digital-simulator/

Portela, Manuel, and António Rito Silva. 2015. "A Model for a Virtual LdoD". *Digital Scholarship in the Humanities* 30 (3):354-70.
Link: https://doi.org/10.1093/llc/fqu004

Portela, Manuel, and António Rito Silva. 2016. "Encoding, Visualizing and Generating Variation in Fernando Pessoa's Livro do Desassossego". *Variants* 12 (3):189-210. Link: https://journals.openedition.org/variants/356

Portela, Manuel, and António Rito Silva. 2017. *Arquivo LdoD: Arquivo Digital Colaborativo do Livro do Desassossego.* Coimbra: Centro de Literatura Portuguesa da Universidade de Coimbra. Link: https://ldod.uc.pt/

Schatzki, Theodore R., Karin Knorr-Cetina, and Eike von Savigny. 2001. *The Practice Turn in Contemporary Theory.* London: Routledge.

Schreibman, Susan, Das Gupta Vinayak, and Neale Rooney. 2017. "Notes from the Transcription Desk: Visualising Public Engagement". *English Studies* 98 (5):506-25. Link: https://doi.org/10.1080/0013838X.2017.1333754

Silva, António Rito, and Manuel Portela. 2014. "TEI4LdoD: Textual Encoding and Social Editing in Web 2.0 Environments". *Journal of the Text Encoding Initiative* 8. Link: https://journals.openedition.org/jtei/1171

ESTHÉTIQUES NUMÉRIQUES
DIGITAL AESTHETICS

Sortir de l'écran :

Lucette, gare de Clichy FRANÇOISE CHAMBEFORT

Résumé

Lucette, Gare de Clichy est une œuvre narrative connectée en temps réel avec les données du réseau ferroviaire de la région parisienne (via l'API *Temps Réel Transilien*). Objet d'expérimentation (Nicolas-Le Strat, 2009), elle a été pensée très tôt pour être présentée dans différents contextes et sur différents supports. À partir de la même structure qui peut être modélisée de manière unique (modélisation moléculaire, Durand, **1997**), le design de l'œuvre est décliné selon trois modes différents (mode écran, performance, application mobile) afin de produire trois expériences spécifiques. La forme écran est adaptée à un affichage en gare à destination des usagers qui attendent le train. La thématique ferroviaire et la temporalité réelle sont alors au centre de l'expérience. La forme du triptyque a émergé en phase de création comme solution de design visuel permettant de relier la fiction à cette réalité. La performance théâtrale centre l'expérience du spectateur sur le personnage, Lucette, alors incarnée par l'acteur. Le caractère éphémère de cette forme invite aussi à porter une attention particulière au processus temporel. Temps, espace et corps sont les composantes de la représentation et doivent faire l'objet du design. La réussite de l'entreprise repose sur la capacité à casser la régularité du rythme par l'inventivité de la mise en scène (jeu de type clown en contraste avec la thématique, travail sur le son, scénographie). La comparaison de ces dispositifs s'attache à deux éléments : le processus qui permet au spectateur d'entrer en empathie avec le personnage et la mise en scène de la réalité et de la fiction. Par rapport à la forme écran, la performance favorise l'empathie et l'immersion dans la fiction tandis que l'équilibre entre fiction et réalité est plus complexe à ajuster.

Abstract

Lucette, Gare de Clichy is a narrative work connected in real time to data from the Paris region rail network (via the API *Temps Réel Transilien*). As an experimental work (Nicolas-Le Strat, 2009), Lucette, Gare de Clichy was initially conceived for presentation in different contexts and in various formats. The design of the work is based on a single structure modeled into unique modes (modélisation moléculaire, Durand, **1997**), resulting in three iterations of the work (screen, performance, mobile application) that create three specific experiences.

The screen version is intended for display in a train station for travellers and commuters. The rail network theme and the real-time aspect are thus at the center of the experience. The triptych version emerged during the creation as a visual design solution to connect fiction and reality. The theatrical performance centers the experience of the spectator on the character Lucette, played by the actor. The ephemeral nature of this form invokes special attention to the temporal process. Time, space, and body make up the elements of the representation and are subject to the design. The success of the undertaking rests on the ability to break the regularity of rhythm through inventive staging (clowning in contrast with the theme, work on the sound and set design).

The comparison of these modes is tied to two elements: the process which allows the spectateur to empathize with the character and the staging of reality and fiction. In comparison to the screen version, the performative version encourages empathy and immersion in fiction as it is more difficult to reach a balance between fiction and reality.

Lucette, Gare de Clichy est une œuvre narrative connectée en temps réel avec les données du réseau ferroviaire de la région parisienne (via l'API *Temps Réel Transilien*) que je développe dans le cadre de ma thèse. Il s'agit d'une démo, c'est-à-dire d'une production artistique dont le rôle est avant tout de servir la problématique de recherche par l'expérimentation.

Le point de départ de l'histoire est le suivant : Lucette est une femme âgée qui habite juste en face de la gare de Clichy-Levallois, tout près de Paris. De sa fenêtre, elle voit les voyageurs sortir de la gare. Sa vie est rythmée par les trains qui passent et qui lui amènent des visites.

Si je reprends l'image du « moulin à données », un concept que j'ai forgé pour décrire ce type d'œuvres (Chambefort **2017**) :

> — le flux de données est ici composé des informations sur les trains qui arrivent en gare;
> — la roue à aubes qui capte et transmet l'énergie et les engrenages représente le programme informatique générateur de l'œuvre. Ici, la logique de la machinerie, donc de la programmation de l'œuvre, repose sur une métaphore simple : chaque train qui arrive en gare de Clichy représente un personnage qui vient rendre visite à Lucette ;
> — de ce moulin sort un autre flux, l'œuvre elle-même, un flux composite, qui n'est pas fait d'un seul matériau.

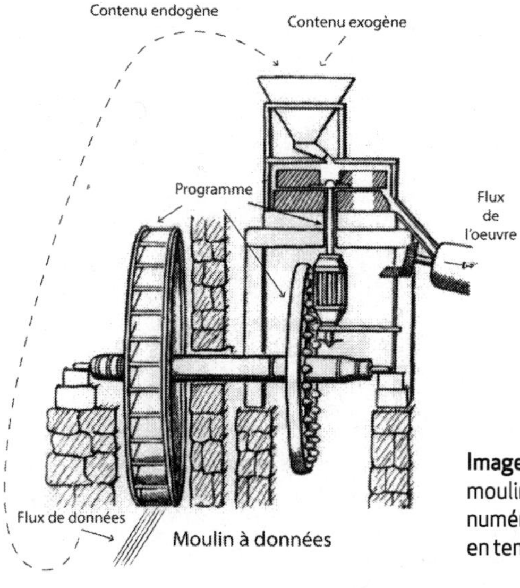

Image 1. Représentation du concept de moulin à données caractérisant les œuvres numériques adossées à des flux de données en temps réel.

La structure de l'œuvre peut être modélisée en utilisant la scénarisation moléculaire (Durand 2009). Cette représentation proposée par Alain Durand permet de formaliser un scénario indépendamment des outils techniques qui seront choisis pour sa réalisation.

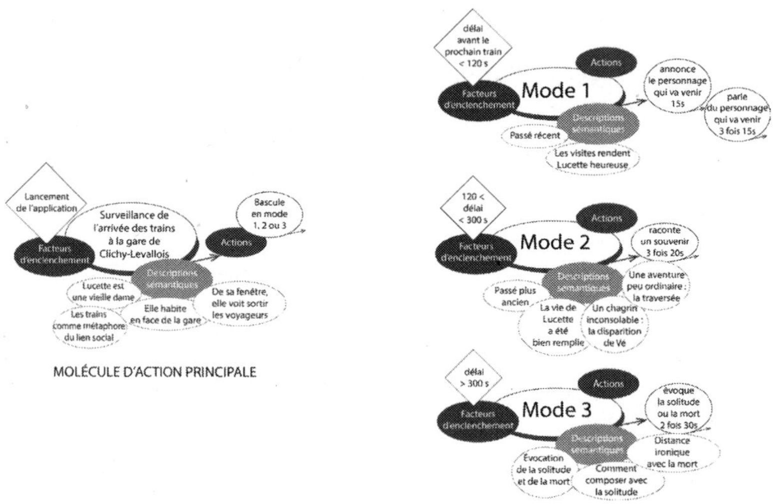

Image 2. Modélisation moléculaire de *Lucette, gare de Clichy*.

Les descriptions perceptuelles ne sont pas représentées puisqu'elles peuvent varier. La macrostructure de surveillance de l'arrivée des trains à la gare de Clichy-Levallois met en place la métaphore de base. Les trains sont présentés comme un instrument de lien social, métaphore qui se traduit par la relation logique : un train = un visiteur, et par la chaîne causale : si Lucette reçoit une visite, alors elle est contente. Trois modes sont déclinés en fonction du délai avant le prochain train. Ils permettent de mettre en œuvre un design du temps et un design du texte dans le temps – le texte étant composé de 336 fragments.

Le mode 1 est le mode court, quand l'attente est inférieure à 2 minutes. C'est le mode du flux de conscience rapide. La minute est composée d'une annonce, puis de trois textes courts en lien avec le personnage qui est attendu. Le mode 2 est le mode moyen, quand l'attente est comprise entre 2 et 5 minutes. C'est le mode des activités sociales et des souvenirs personnels. Trois textes sont affichés ou dits par minute, soit un toutes les 20 secondes. Le mode 3 est le mode long, quand l'attente est supérieure à 5 minutes. C'est le mode de la solitude et de la déprime. Deux textes sont affichés ou dits par minute, soit un toutes les 30 secondes.

À partir de cette structure, le design de l'œuvre a été décliné selon deux dispositifs : un dispositif écran et un dispositif performance, afin de produire deux expériences spécifiques. J'emploie le terme de « dispositif » dans le sens de la définition de Bruno Bachimont, c'est à dire « une configuration spatiale per-mettant de reproduire un déroulement temporel » (Bachimont **2004**). J'avais utilisé dans un premier temps le terme « forme » dans le sens de « forme de restitution », c'est-à-dire ce qui permet à l'utilisateur de s'approprier le contenu – forme écran, forme performance (Bachimont **2007**). J'aurais pu employer également le terme de « format » en me centrant sur la structuration du contenu (Bachimont **2004**). Enfin, j'aurais pu parler de « supports » en m'attachant au milieu matériel par lequel l'information est véhiculée (Bachimont **2015**). Le terme « dispositif » a l'avantage d'intégrer une notion temporelle.

La conception de ces deux dispositifs s'est faite de manière décalée dans le temps, mais néanmoins en parallèle. Le dispositif écran a été pensé pour être adapté à un affichage en gare à l'attention des usagers qui attendent le train. La forme du triptyque a émergé en phase de création comme solution de design visuel permettant de relier la fiction à la réalité. Cette forme n'est toutefois accessible, pour l'instant, que sur le web (**http://www.francoise-chambefort.com/lucette-gare-de-clichy**), et non en gare.

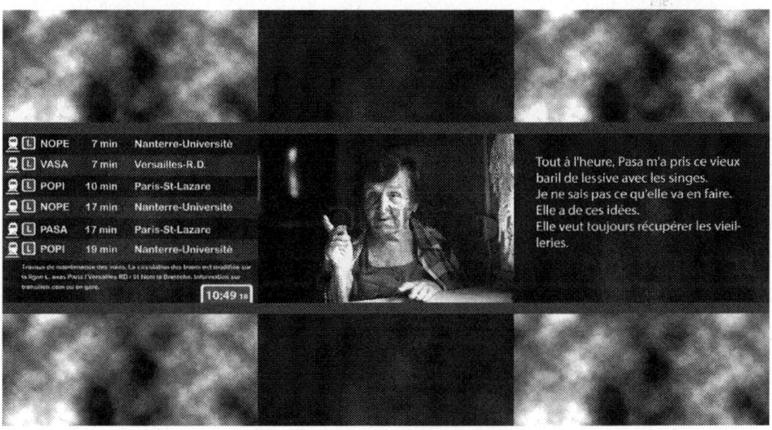

Image 3. Dispositif écran.

La performance théâtrale centre l'expérience du spectateur sur le personnage de Lucette, alors incarnée par l'acteur. Le caractère éphémère de cette forme invite aussi à porter une attention particulière au processus temporel. Temps, espace et corps sont les composantes de la représentation et doivent faire l'objet du design. La réussite de l'entreprise repose sur la capacité à casser la régularité du rythme par l'inventivité de la mise en scène (avec un jeu de type clown en contraste avec la thématique, un travail sur le son, une scénographie encore à travailler).

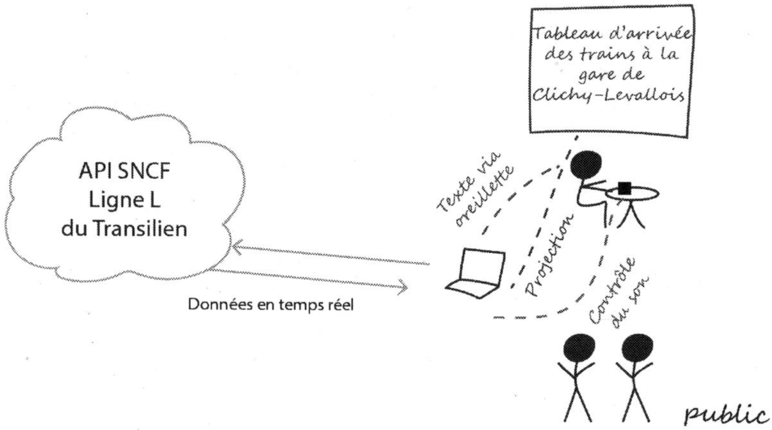

Image 4. Dispositif performance.

Le processus est continu. La représentation qui en est donnée permet au spectateur d'y accéder pendant un intervalle de temps défini (pour la performance) ou pas (la durée de consultation est libre pour le dispositif écran).

Pour comparer ces dispositifs, je vais m'attacher à deux éléments :

- la façon dont le spectateur est amené à entrer en empathie avec le personnage;
- et la façon dont réalité et fiction sont mises en scène.

Mon objectif est en effet de faciliter l'immersion tout en permettant au spectateur de garder présent en mémoire que l'œuvre est adossée à un flux de données réelles.

L'EMPATHIE

L'empathie consiste à partager un état affectif avec une autre personne, réelle ou fictive. Cet état est produit lorsque la personne en empathie a été amenée, par le contexte, à se préoccuper de l'autre. Elle reproduit alors intentionnellement, par l'imagination, l'état affectif de cet autre. Selon Françoise Lavocat, l'empathie, dans la fiction, agit comme embrayeur d'immersion (Lavocat **2016**). Pour Pelletier, ce sont les capacités narratives et non la simulation qui permettent de comprendre la situation dans laquelle se trouve l'autre (Pelletier **2016**). Ainsi, le cadre narratif conduit à saisir dans quel contexte le personnage agit. Le caractère lacunaire de la caractérisation du personnage semble également favoriser l'empathie (Keen **2006**).

Dans les œuvres de type « moulin à données », il n'y a pas d'interactivité. C'est le flux de données qui commande le déroulement de la représentation. Il s'agit donc d'œuvres numériques dans lesquelles la passivité du spectateur est préservée. Le fait que celui-ci occupe une place de témoin impuissant rend l'empathie plus libre, car elle n'invite pas à l'action. Cette passivité semble être à la source du plaisir procuré par les fictions (Chaouli **2005**). Au niveau cognitif, les zones du cerveau liées au rapport à soi sont désactivées. Par conséquent, c'est un mélange de plaisir et de frustration qui modèle « la réponse empathique propre à une situation fictionnelle » (Lavocat **2016**).

Dans le dispositif écran, le contexte est présenté sur l'écran d'introduction, alors que dans la performance, il fait partie du paratexte. Les conditions matérielles sont différentes pour le spectateur. Dans la performance, il est installé dans le noir, dans un environnement qui favorise l'inhibition de l'action et le décrochage cognitif par rapport aux perceptions environnantes. Ce qui diffère également, c'est le fait que dans un cas, le spectateur est confronté à des images et à un texte qu'il lit, tandis que dans l'autre, il a, face à lui, un acteur qui incarne le personnage et joue le texte.

Au centre de l'écran apparaît l'image de Lucette, dans un même lieu, sa cuisine, derrière sa table et devant sa fenêtre. Les images fixes se succèdent à un rythme régulier. L'expression sur le visage de Lucette change, passant de la joie à la rêverie et à la tristesse. La coiffure de Lucette change aussi, au point où il est parfois difficile de la reconnaître, de même que ses vêtements, signes du passage du temps et des saisons. Les expressions du visage de Lucette permettent d'inférer son état affectif.

Sur la scène, le personnage de Lucette est incarné. L'acteur est lui-même en empathie avec le personnage par le truchement du texte qu'il reçoit dans son oreillette. Il ne mémorise pas le texte à l'avance. Il répète les fragments qui lui arrivent et les interprète de manière improvisée et unique. Le jeu de type clown exacerbe l'affectivité grâce aux expressions faciales.

La performance permet donc une résonance empathique accrue. L'immersion dans la fiction se trouve ainsi facilitée.

	ÉCRAN	PERFORMANCE	
-	Pas de contrôle sur les conditions de visionnement	Contrôle des conditions > Public dans la pénombre > Scène éclairée **Inhibition de l'action** et **décrochage cognitif**	+
+	Images & texte Texte lu La lecture amène au **décrochage cognitif**	Texte joué Personnage incarné (**relais d'empathie**)	+
	Expressions faciales visibles sur les photos qui défilent en diaporama	Expressions faciales sur le visage de l'acteur clown	

Image 5. Empathie : comparaison des deux dispositifs.

RÉALITÉ ET FICTION

Qu'en est-il, une fois cet embrayage effectué, du rapport de ces deux dispositifs avec la réalité et la fiction? Plutôt que de parler de réalité et de fiction, on peut considérer, comme Françoise Lavocat, que toute fiction est hybride et que la part que prend la réalité dans une fiction est en fait la part de référence extra-fictionnelle qu'elle contient. Les œuvres qui s'appuient sur des flux de données en temps réel sont particulières à cet égard, car c'est le temps lui-même qui fait l'objet d'une référence. Le temps du monde fictionnel est emprunté au monde réel, à la seconde près, représenté par l'horloge du tableau d'affichage. Les événements au centre de la vie de Lucette sont l'arrivée des trains dans la gare de Clichy, qui sont des événements réels intégrés au monde fictionnel.

À l'écran, la référence au monde réel se concentre sur la reproduction mimétique du panneau d'affichage de l'arrivée des trains, en noir et blanc certes, mais selon les codes graphiques du modèle que l'on peut trouver dans les gares de la région parisienne. L'heure affichée correspond à celle qui s'affiche sur la montre du spectateur s'il en possède une et s'il est en France. L'écran est divisé en trois zones qui sont placées sur le même plan en deux dimensions. Visuellement, la référence au réel occupe donc le tiers de l'espace. La zone de texte, située à droite, fait explicitement référence à la zone de gauche lors de l'annonce des visites : le texte « POPI va venir » s'affiche lorsque le train POPI est en passe d'arriver. Au centre, le logo de la banque d'image qui a fourni les photos est visible, rappelant que tout ceci est une fiction. Il a donc été aisé d'équilibrer réalité et fiction dans ce dispositif, d'autant qu'au niveau perceptif, j'ai privilégié un champ resserré : les informations sont visuelles et textuelles.

Dans la performance, les plans sont différents. L'affichage de l'arrivée des trains se trouve derrière l'acteur, moins visible, moins prégnant qu'à l'écran. La scénographie pourrait être améliorée pour lui donner plus de place et pour figurer la fenêtre. C'est d'abord le design du son qui m'a permis de faire une place à la réalité avec l'utilisation de sons enregistrés.

	ÉCRAN	PERFORMANCE	
+	Tableau d'affichage des Trains placé au 1er plan	Tableau d'affichage des Trains placé au 2ème plan derrière l'acteur	-
	Triptyque réalité / fiction / fiction	Perceptions complexes : visuelles et sonores, le geste reliant le visuel et le sonore	-
+	Perception simple : Informations visuelles et textuelles		
		La musicalité renvoie à la fiction	+

Image 6. Tension entre réalité et fiction, comparaison des deux dispositifs.

Tout s'articule autour du son dans la performance, si bien que l'ensemble du programme, originalement en javascript, a été réécrit sous Max MSP, un logiciel musical qui permet de faire du contrôle en temps réel. Après beaucoup de recherches et d'expérimentations, notamment autour de la possibilité pour l'acteur de contrôler le son par le jeu, j'en suis arrivée à la structure suivante :

1. Une bande-son fait office de timeline. Elle commence par une introduction composée d'annonce vocales enregistrées à la gare de Clichy-Levallois. Elle se poursuit par des sons d'ambiance

figurant l'activité de Lucette dans sa cuisine lorsqu'elle se prépare un thé ou une tisane, entrecoupés par ce que j'ai appelé des « soupirs de trains », ces sons que font les trains lorsqu'ils sont à l'arrêt et qui m'ont paru tellement humains. Elle se conclut avec une autre annonce vocale. Les sons fictionnels sont ainsi encadrés et entrecroisés de références sonores réalistes évoquant la gare.

2. Comme un contrepoids aux contraintes du jeu (le texte étant envoyé dans l'oreillette), l'acteur peut contrôler le son en faisant des gestes sur la table. Celle-ci est équipée d'un microcontact. Lorsque le micro placé sous la table capte un son, produit par main, la tasse ou tout autre objet, le programme ouvre le volume d'une piste de son qui tourne en boucle en arrière-plan. Cette piste dépend du mode dans lequel se trouve le programme. En mode rapide, les bruits de la gare, des trains et les voix des annonces apparaissent. En mode moyen, le son devient plus musical avec une nappe harmonique au violoncelle. En mode lent, le son est encore plus musical avec un développement mélodique. L'acteur peut dès lors contrôler le son entre deux fragments de texte par des gestes très fins qu'il peut intégrer à son jeu corporel

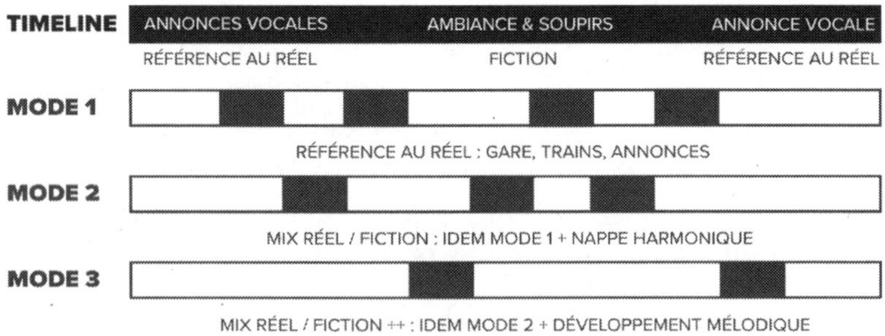

Image 7. Structure sonore du dispositif performance.

On le voit, il a été beaucoup plus difficile dans la performance de faire une place aux références extra-fictionnelles et au temps réel. J'ai trouvé des solutions dans l'usage du son, mais j'aurais pu aller plus loin sans doute. J'ai imaginé par exemple de reprendre le son réel de la gare, mais cela exigerait des développements techniques plus complexes. On peut se demander si le meilleur moyen de rendre compte de l'effet « temps réel » ne serait pas de rendre plus visible le fait que l'acteur ne connaît pas à l'avance le texte qu'il va dire. Sa liberté est alors très contrainte : elle réside dans son interprétation du texte, interprétation qu'il doit improviser en quelques secondes.

Le travail sur les deux dispositifs a été très enrichissant. Il m'a amenée à revoir ma position quant à l'usage du son pour le dispositif écran. J'avais fait quelques essais auparavant, que j'avais jugés peu concluants. À la lumière de ce que j'ai développé pour la performance, il me semble maintenant qu'il pourrait être intéressant d'ajouter du son afin de faciliter l'immersion. Que le dispositif soit vu en gare ou dans n'importe quel lieu, le fait de mettre un casque permet de se retrancher du monde extérieur comme le fait la pénombre de la salle de théâtre. Il serait même envisageable de réaliser une version totalement sonore de *Lucette*, simplement à écouter. Je n'ai pas eu le temps d'explorer davantage ce que pourrait être une version pour mobiles avec l'utilisation des notifications.

Le passage de l'écran à la scène a été facilité par l'absence d'interaction. Si la performance favorise l'empathie et l'immersion et qu'elle fait la part belle à la fiction, il a été plus difficile de mettre en avant le lien avec le monde réel. C'est un équilibre qui reste à trouver, afin que la spécificité de l'œuvre, le fait qu'elle soit adossée à un flux de données en temps réel, ne se dissolve pas totalement dans la fiction et que le jeu de l'acteur ne soit pas uniquement un jeu sous contrainte.

Bachimont, Bruno. 2004. « Arts et sciences du numérique : ingénierie des connaissances et critique de la raison computationnelle ». Mémoire de HDR.

Bachimont, Bruno. 2007. *Ingénierie des connaissances et des contenus : le numérique entre ontologies et documents.* Paris : Hermès Science (Lavoisier).

Bachimont, Bruno. 2015. « Le numérique comme milieu : enjeux épistémologiques et phénoménologiques. Principes pour une science des données ». *Interfaces numériques* 4 (3):385-402.

Chambefort, Françoise. 2017. « Raconter la vie, l'utilisation des flux de données en littérature numérique ». Université du Québec à Montréal. Consulté le 16 décembre 2019. Accéder au lien : http://oic.uqam.ca/fr/communications/raconter-la-vie-lutilisation-des-flux-de-donnees-en-litterature-numerique

Chaouli, Michel. 2005. « How interactive can fiction be? » *Critical Inquiry* 31 (3):599-617.

Durand, Alain. 2009. « Scénario multimédia ». *Document numérique* 12 (2):47-80.

Keen, Suzanne. 2006. « A Theory of Narrative Empathy ». *Narrative* 14 (3):207-36.

Lavocat, Françoise. 2016. *Fait et fiction. Pour une frontière.* Paris : Seuil.

Pelletier, Jérôme. 2016. « Quand l'émotion rencontre la fiction ». In *Interprétation littéraire et sciences cognitives*, dirigé par Françoise Lavocat, 123-55. Paris : Hermann.

PART 4

ESTHÉTIQUES NUMÉRIQUES
DIGITAL AESTHETICS

BORIS DU BOULLAY

J'écris double mais je me soigne

Résumé

Cette contribution s'apparente à une chute en écriture. Elle est constituée essentiellement d'une phrase-fleuve extraite d'un texte en cours d'écriture intitulé *Gianluca Vialli*, du nom d'un footballeur dont le narrateur cherche sans cesse à retrouver sur Youtube un but resté gravé dans sa mémoire. Ce texte est le point de départ d'une tentative de description de la vie, au sens où Michel Henry la conçoit comme radicalement immanente, révélée dans une auto-donation qui s'écarte même du champ phénoménologique. L'écriture vise, manque la vie, échoûant dans l'écart qui constitue l'acte d'écrire à dire quelque chose de cette vie si écrasée en elle-même qu'on ne saurait l'atteindre autrement que dans l'épreuve de soi. Pourtant, écrire en éprouvant la vie reste le moteur de sa visée. Ce texte se déploie dans cette idée, mais sans parvenir à déborder de son cadre. Il sert néanmoins de matrice pour une deuxième écriture, numérique cette fois-ci, qui tourne autour du texte, reprenant les phrases inachevées pour les mener un cran plus loin dans la description. L'inachèvement de la forme numérique met en marche des boucles de création (images, vidéos, RA...) qui travaillent la zone d'échanges entre la vie elle-même et les tentatives pour la décrire, devenant la zone d'échanges entre écriture textuelle et écriture numérique.

Abstract

This contribution resembles a failure in writing. It is principally composed of an extract of a stream of sentences from a text I am currently writing. The piece is entitled *Gianluca Vialli*, after the footballer who appears in a short clip which remains burned in the narrator's memory and which he seeks incessantly on Youtube. This text is the starting point of the description of life inspired by the work of Michel Henry, who views life as radically immanent, revealed through self-giveness which deviates even from the field of phenomenology. The writing both targets and misses true life, landing in the void constituted by the act of writing to say something of this life which is so overwritten we wouldn't know how to achieve it by any means other than self-trial. And yet, writing to examine life remains the driving force behind Henry's ambition. This text unfolds in this idea without escaping its framework. It serves, however, as a matrix for a second writing, this time digital, which goes around the text, sampling incomplete sentences to achieve more than just a description. The incompleteness of the digital form puts loops of creation (images, videos, AR) into place, working in the zone of exchange between life itself and the attempts to describe it, thus becoming the zone of exchange between textual writing and digital writing.

Ce texte est avant tout constitué d'un extrait d'un autre texte d'une centaine de pages que l'on trouvera plus bas, après cette courte introduction. Le texte dont est issu cet extrait se présente comme le retour à l'écriture d'une pratique plastique initialement fondée sur l'image, issue du cinéma argentique, et désormais reprise par le numérique comme un objet d'écriture où les conditions mêmes de l'acte de filmer, via les caméras PDVR (Personal Digital Video Recorder), ont modifié radicalement le cinéma, passant donc d'un art de la visée, à l'œil, à une pratique de l'écriture numérique, à la main. Ce qui nous intéresse ici est la manière dont cette écriture issue du cinéma, écriture revenue de l'image et redevenue texte, écriture devenue numérique, permet d'imaginer un dialogue entre les supports : le « print » achevé et le numérique *in progress*.

Le principe de départ de cette écriture est de créer un corpus de textes qui se place dans le dialogue entre supports, soit comme l'élément central, soit comme l'élément périphérique dans sa restitution au lecteur. Dans sa version imprimée, le texte occupe une fonction centrale dans la mesure où il est le premier élément créatif, celui qui s'approche une première fois d'une description de la vie. Et il se déploie de façon périphérique dans sa version numérique. Ce qui nous oriente d'abord vers une question spatiale, peut-être pas si éloignée du glissement à l'œuvre dans la critique cinématographique actuelle puisque la question historique ontologique de l'essence du cinéma, incarnée par Bazin et son *Qu'est-ce que le cinéma*? (Bazin **1962**) se déplace aujourd'hui, sous la poussée de nouvelles formes de consommation des images vers une relocation du cinéma, que Francesco Casetti résume par « où est le cinéma ? » (Casetti **2016**). Cette question spatiale a du sens dans ce projet dans la mesure où l'écriture occupe l'espace, en expansion, comme un élément liquide, autant qu'elle s'en préoccupe. Mais cette écriture qui s'épanche dans un espace qu'elle crée autant qu'elle l'investit, on peut aussi dire qu'elle se dédouble en même temps qu'elle s'éprouve. À peine écrite, déjà manquée, pourrait être le quasi mode d'emploi d'une écriture qui se pense d'abord comme une chute sur le modèle du flux (on retrouve l'élément liquide), le flux étant l'impossibilité *presque* (Meade **2018**) de mettre un point final à l'écriture. Au-delà de ce point, comme un appel d'air supplémentaire dans le flux, l'écriture se dédouble dans un surplus numérique.

Si l'objectif incessant et acharné du projet d'écriture est de décrire la vie, force est de constater que la distance dans l'écriture effectuée nous éloigne de la possibilité d'une atteinte de la vie par la description (Michel Henry). Au mieux, l'écriture est une effectuation de la distance en même temps qu'elle réduit la distance par la façon dont elle s'échappe. L'écriture se dédouble quand elle s'écrit, s'offrant comme une nouvelle chance à chaque tentative perdue, travaillant une option numérique, en cours, malléable, en puissance, autant d'écritures périphériques, supplémentaires, qui prolongent l'idée d'une description possible par encore plus d'écriture. Quitte à changer de support.

Comment ces deux écritures fonctionnent l'une par à rapport à l'autre? L'écriture centrale génère l'écriture périphérique. À peine est-elle écrite qu'elle génère une prolongation numérique. Dans la poursuite incessante de l'écriture, dans la description de la vie qu'elle détaille et étale mot après mot, dans les interstices imaginaires que l'écriture se tue à combler, il y a la place (localisation encore...) pour une écriture seconde, autour du texte, qui utilise la multiplicité et la plasticité du numérique pour repousser un cran plus loin l'illusion de pouvoir décrire la vie.

Cette écriture qui se dédouble et s'échappe dans le numérique est seconde. Elle vient après, pour combler, colmater ce qui semble pouvoir l'être encore. Elle se confond avec son usage, écriture purement utilitaire, censée parer à l'insuffisance première du texte imprimé. Seconde également comme un déchet, où les multiples écritures numériques générées par l'usage d'une écriture numérique en extension, peuvent être vues comme de la pollution au sens propre et au sens figuré, une écume polluante.

Concrètement, l'écriture sert donc de matrice insuffisante pour générer une forme numérique qui peut-être une image, un film, de la VR, un flux, un fil Twitter... Ces deux localisations, pour reprendre le terme de Casetti, génèrent deux modes de restitution au lecteur, pour donner au texte deux usages complémentaires : une fonction de visibilité dans le print. Et une fonction d'invisibilité dans le numérique : le texte n'est plus clairement visible dans le numérique. Autrement dit, dans l'écriture dédoublée, ce qui se voit s'affiche. Dans une affiche, dans un livre, dans tout document imprimé ou écrit à la main. Ce qui ne se voit pas s'entend et s'éprouve dans une image au sens large. Si l'on reprend l'idée d'une écriture en dialogue évoquée en introduction, nous sommes face à une distance, qui nous ramène à l'impossibilité d'écrire pour décrire la vie qui se donne sans donation dans la phénoménologie matérielle de Michel Henry. Mais si Henry affecte au projet artistique le but « d'exprimer cette profusion pathétique de l'Être » (Henry **1988**, 33), notamment en donnant à la forme abstraite peinte par Kandinsky le rôle de représenter par l'absence « la vie invisible dans son inlassable venue en soi-même » (*ibid.*), nous serions plus enclin à imaginer l'écriture double comme une distance à deux faces, comme la décrit Jacques Colléony :

> La réalité (l'ensemble des étants), en tant qu'elle présente sa face, est toujours son double, *son* ombre, *son* image – c'est-à-dire sa « propre » non-vérité. Et c'est cette non-vérité, qui est parallèle ou contemporaine à la vérité, que l'art a pour fonction d'accomplir.

Si le texte est central dans sa conception comme dans sa mise en page, il se voit surtout comme une affiche. Le texte devient donc visible, il en devient presque plus important à regarder qu'à lire. Et de ce point de vue-là, ce serait comme une pirouette pour retourner au numérique, comme l'écrivait Kenneth Goldsmith (**2018**).

Tout ce qui est imaginairement suggéré par l'écriture, les interstices que j'évoquais tout à l'heure, ce sont autant de points d'appui pour une création périphérique autour du texte. Une pollution numérique au sens de prolifération.

Cette manière de créer des canaux multiples de lecture pour un même texte s'appuie sur l'idée que du « print » au numérique, la distance n'est pas évolutive, mais un écart, un débordement permanent du processus littéraire à l'œuvre dans l'écriture « print ».

Autrement dit, dans ces expérimentations, le numérique résorbe par des ajouts permanents et successifs une écriture qui de son côté tend à résoudre cette tentation de l'augmentation par l'enchâssement de locutions – à la manière des poupées russes – pour décrire la vie.

De cet écart qui n'est ni distance, ni trajet, mais plutôt un face à face, nous avons à disposition deux formes qui se travaillent et se créent l'une contre l'autre, si serrées qu'elles semblent déployer l'écriture non comme le scénario d'une forme, mais comme le moteur circulaire d'un processus unique dont une face est visible et l'autre face cherche à ajouter la part manquante de la vie incessamment décrite.

[extrait du texte] […] Le cinéma m'abandonne, la vie s'échappe de mes veines, le sang coule sur le bitume, c'est l'été, je marche les bras levés pour tentant de réinjecter un peu du sang dans mon corps qui est venu s'entasser dans mes mains et dans mes pieds comme dans une impasse, une mémé avec des bas de contention, voilà ce que j'étais dès mes dix-huit ans, moi, je ne filme plus, la vie est un film devant mes yeux et je n'ose plus me baisser pour la ramasser, comme on s'échine enfant à cueillir toutes les marguerites d'un champ dont l'horizon se renouvelle sans cesse, avec excitation et découragement, seul le découragement me ceint aujourd'hui, j'ai donc perdu le fil, je ne sais plus où, je ne sais plus quand, j'ai trente ans, je reviens sur Paris après une parenthèse de sept ans à vivre près de Grenoble, dans une vallée traversée par une nationale qui ne s'embarrasse pas de défoncer les villages qu'elle dessert, quel drôle de mot, mon père racontait comment il s'était senti humilié d'avoir, quand on lui demandait lors d'un voyage d'affaires aux États-Unis ce qu'il avait retenu du pays, répondu « desert » avec un accent mal positionné de sorte que ces interlocuteurs, à voir leurs mines déconfites – et non confites comme ces affreuses boules sucrées qui infectent les cakes des anniversaires de mes copains de primaire – semblaient, du moins c'est ce qu'il a confusément senti sur le moment et qui a sans doute dû l'occuper une bonne partie du trajet du retour dans l'avion et peut-être davantage, ou cette obsession m'a été refilée, comme on refile un ballon ou un gosse ou le bébé, à défaut de le jeter avec l'eau du bain, avec la crainte de croiser le boa de Colin dans *L'Écume des jours*, qui se faufile dans les canalisations de la salle de bains, à moins que je ne fasse une belle contraction de la fée du robinet des *Contes de la rue Broca* et du nénuphar de Chloé, semblaient avoir compris « dessert » au lieu de « desert », mon père ayant prononcé ce mot avec une gourmandise lente qui devait exprimer toute l'extraordinaire sensation de découvrir les immensités désertiques de l'ouest américain et qui se transformait en gaminerie gâtée devant des gâteaux dégoulinants de sucre glace coloré, cette humiliation reste au cœur de la relation que j'ai avec mon père, dont j'admirais la chemise rouge de bucheron portée le dimanche avec ses bottines, le pantalon cassé sur le haut de la chaussure, parce que le dimanche, on peut être un peu dépenaillé tranquillou bilou, et toute ma vie j'attends ce moment où je serai assez grand pour porter cette chemise rouge, ces bottes, rouler en Citroën GS, mais cette humiliation d'enfant, transposée, récupérée, reprise à mon compte se développe comme le nénuphar de

Chloé, de jour en jour, jusqu'à atteindre le bout de mes mains, celles-là qui sont pleines de sel d'argent des films développés dans ma baignoire, est-ce l'humiliation ou les sels d'argent qui contractent mes mains, ou encore la crainte d'avoir les mains de ma mère, sa maladie des mains dont je n'ai pas connaissance du nom, faute de lui avoir demandé, faute d'avoir le courage de regarder cette maladie en face, faute de lui parler, faute d'avoir le courage d'essayer de la sortir de cette sclérose que la vieillesse ne parvient pas à conjurer, je ne parviens pas à conjurer grand-chose, je ne fais que tomber, cette chute qui fait tourner en rond et répéter, empêche de faire l'effort de penser, ça je le sens si souvent, si déjà, quand mes paupières se ferment, comme par un automatisme quand je sollicite mon cerveau, mon cervelet dirait mon frère, pas loin du on/off, j'allume mon cerveau, je ferme les yeux et je m'endors, c'est plus pratique pour vieillir comme une merde, et si vieillir ne me plait guère, autant que ce soit comme une merde, faute de prendre en compte la vieillesse de ma mère, d'accepter que sa maladie des mains, c'est aussi la mienne, ou qu'avec mes sels d'argent qui se baladent dans mon corps, comme je viens de l'apprendre avec ma fille, j'aurais pris sur moi la maladie de ma mère, ma fille aurait pris sur elle cette inquiétude, cette peur de l'abandon, après tout, tout en reprenant le schéma familial, ma sœur a incarné cette main pour me venir en aide, quand je me suis cassé le bras, les parents ne sont pas là, qu'est-ce qui m'a pris de descendre ce foutu talus herbeux en patin à roulettes en plastique jaune, quand on s'est tous réveillés dans la nuit, sœur, frère et moi, et qu'on s'est rendormis dans l'entrée, sans personne pour nous expliquer pourquoi, alors sans doute je n'ai rien compris, cette main, la même avec laquelle elle m'adresse un petit coucou désolé par la dernière fenêtre du train, celle face à la voix, celle des cow-boys, alors que je cours derrière le train qui emmène la famille sans moi, cette main-là dont je perds le contrôle, celle-ci dont ma mère a perdu l'usage, ces mains devenues inutiles devant mon découragement à faire des films, je n'ai plus trente ans, et je me sens flotter comme Michel dans ce film dont je cherche le nom, de Nicolas Philibert, je ne connais que lui, sur la clinique de la Borde avec le musicien Giroud, mais comment s'appelle ce film, bien sûr, Ferdinand Deligny vient à mon secours dans un flash, pourquoi bon dieu, pourquoi ai-je été abandonné, bon sang, ça n'a pas dû être facile pour le Christ quand j'y pense, pour Ravaillac non plus, ouïe, cette histoire d'écartèlement raconté par mon frère m'obsédait tellement je n'accédais à aucune représentation, il aurait fallu que je puisse repasser le plat de la douleur, reprendre le fil d'un présent qui m'échappait totalement, écarteler, vraiment?, tu veux dire avec les membres jusqu'à la déchirure comme de la viande, il s'agit de *La moindre des choses*, film dans lequel Michel, après le spectacle, perdu entre deux mondes, déclare après réflexion qu'il flotte, eh bien moi aussi je flotte, à grosses gouttes d'ailleurs, je flotte dans un film qui ne serait pas tourné, mais que je regarde de l'intérieur, qui semble vouloir prendre vie, il s'agirait simplement de prendre la pose, sauf que depuis que je prends la pose, je ne filme plus, je suis le film, dont j'avais pour habitude de dire que je ne le regardais pas ce film que je suis, dans une formule approximative, que j'écrivais du bout des doigts, à peine prononcée, dans un enrobage de gaucherie, rien à voir avec une chocolaterie, avec un regard de petit garçon sans pantalon, comme dans un rêve où on se retrouve à se promener dans la rue, parfaitement habillé, quoiqu'en ce qui me concerne il m'a semblé toujours être habillé à l'as de pique, bien loin de l'image d'un Steve McQueen qui traverse mon enfance et celle de mon frère, puisque l'on a construit ensemble, sur nos lits dont les couvertures peluchaient et tombaient irrémédiablement sur le parquet, malgré nos efforts, comme la bave à la commissure des vieux, cet imaginaire commun d'hommes adultes à venir, avec des montres aux poignets, des regards de biais, une assurance d'homme bien moulé dans son jean, à l'abri des poussières, que l'on appelle pas encore particules fines, et qui nous tuent à petit feu, comme les chauffeurs du Nord avaient l'habitude de le faire dans une série télévisée qui me terrorisait malgré son attrait irrépressible, dont je me demande parfois si ces images, ces pensées, des mots entendus parfois à la volée, n'ont pas brisé ma confiance en m'adonnant à des sentiments si contradictoires que je me retrouvais au milieu du gué, en slip encore, sans pantalon, d'où cet amour du slip que j'essaye de transformer en attribut visuel, comme une marque de fabrique, une revendication, une marque de soi, encore moins des particules élémentaires à la particularité particulièrement malvenue, rêve récurrent jusqu'à ce que je devienne père et que je rêve, bien que je ne puisse écrire ce rêve réellement ce rêve, ce cauchemar, les mots se coincent dans mes doigts, ravive les sels d'argent dans mes mains, dont la maladie se manifeste comme des toxines dans un corps abreuvé de pesticides, je rêve que ma fille tombe de la fenêtre, ce sont les mots les plus durs à écrire, comme quoi les mots ne s'envolent pas, ils se manifestent dans les mains, le sang, je pense à Geneviève Jurgensen, mon dieu cette disparition, ce coup de fil, Geneviève, pardonnez-moi de vous interpeller familièrement par votre prénom, si fortement par ailleurs lié à mon attachement maternel, jamais un livre ne m'a autant brûlé les doigts, je crains encore d'y repenser, de me remémorer cette portière de voiture, cet instant, toute mon âme refuse ce livre que j'admire, refus comme ce rêve que je ne peux écrire, que je repousse sans cesse, dans cette incessance si pleinement reliée à la vie qui m'obsède, comme ce rêve de ma fille qui tombe du sixième étage par la petite fenêtre de la salle de bains, dont l'accès par une petit margelle lors de la réfection de la pièce avait suscité bien des inquiétudes mais par une étrange mollesse combinée à l'impression que le danger était encore loin, vu l'âge de notre fille qui marchait à peine, dans une logique de relecture de l'histoire rétroactive qui rend les faits honteux quand ils n'étaient que légèrement anodins vécus au quotidien, semble-t-il comme toutes les catastrophes que je lis avidement dans la presse matinale comme une conjuration sur papier sur tout ce dont je serai passé au travers, encore vivant, comme j'aime traverser le papier de mes doigts sur des journaux pliés, dépliés et repliés, pliures de vie réelles dont je n'ai que l'écho, ce danger encore loin, mais qui s'est rapproché si vite, qu'il est passé avant que je ne puisse me retourner, comme ce couple qui laisse son garçon de cinq ans devant la télévision le temps de faire une course de cinq minutes et qui retrouve l'enfant mort écrasé, ayant voulu regarder par la fenêtre, comme ma fille me disant, que cela fait six ans qu'elle ne voit pas ce qu'il y a à voir par-dessus cette fenêtre de la salle de bains et qui voulait simplement jeter enfin un œil et profiter de la vue, à l'abri de nos regards, sentant confusément qu'il fallait agir seule pour obtenir satisfaction, je vois tes yeux et tes mains, ma petite fille, et dans mon rêve, je ne peux supporter de te voir tomber, c'est un cauchemar qui se matérialise difficilement dans des images, qui active mes neurones pour aiguillonner le corps, sortir du cauchemar et qui rend le réveil aussi insupportable que le rêve, dans une suite de jours et de nuits, dont on ne peut se libérer, à moins de construire une cage de velours rose comme dans *L'automne à Pékin* (ou *L'écume des jours*, comment ma mémoire pourrait-elle s'en souvenir, aujourd'hui, c'est une évidence que j'oublie tout, à moins d'un rêve récurrent, tout de la mémoire immédiate, généralement, je n'ai aucun souvenir de ce que j'ai fait la veille, il faudra sans doute se pencher sur ce problème de toxines un jour ou l'autre, comment ma mémoire pourrait ne pas se souvenir de ce dont je connaissais par cœur), ou de chuter dans une sublimation en manteau beige de Pierre Etaix sur New York, chute libératrice d'homme seul, sans attaches, sans liens familiaux, abandonné, sans filiation, libre comme un manteau volant dans le ciel, souriant à gorge déployée, sans inquiétude, sans responsabilité, un enfant dans le ciel, qui tombe comme une poupée immobile, c'était donc le sens de ce film inachevé photographié dans le ciel du Trocadéro, bon sang mais c'est bien sûr, comme je pouvais lire à l'abri des bras de mon frère qui commentait case par case les albums de Gotlib, c'est comme si j'étais dans les bras de ma mère, des bras sécurisants, veineux, directement reliés à la joie de rire, l'attitude du capitaine Haddock avec Tryphon Tournesol, ces changements de visage, si violents parfois, dont on pouvait pouffer de rire allongés sur le lit à la couverture défaite, des changements de visage violents comme celui de mon frère quand il reçoit la barre de métal à l'embout mal resserré qui glisse d'un coup hors de son trou, surgissant comme un diable de sa boîte aurait dit mon père, il la reçoit exactement à l'endroit sur son ongle incarné, avec la chair à vif, là où la douleur bascule d'incident à une imploration quasi christique de tant d'infortune, une telle incongruité que cela se produise avec autant de précision qu'on devinerait une volonté maligne et perverse, cette absurdité de la vie est tellement libératrice, un rire libérateur que je ris à gorge déployée devant mon frère qui se tord de douleur sous mes yeux et ses sautillements ne font que redoubler mon ardeur à rire, il manque de m'en retourner une ou deux que j'aurais bien mérité, alors que ce rire, mais il ne pouvait d'autant pas le comprendre que j'aurais bien été en peine de lui expliquer, ce rire manifestait sous une explosion apparemment malsaine une empathie réelle devant ce coup du sort, je n'ai jamais eu d'autre option, car c'était absolument ancré en moi, comme une absolue nécessité, je veux dire physiologique, mon corps est pris de spasme, comme un orgasme, quand la queue semble gonfler d'un coup, à la manière d'un ballon que l'on gonfle et qui résiste jusqu'au soudain er brutal grossissement, comme une libération donc, cette nécessité de rire pour conjurer le mauvais sort, supporter la vie, car il s'agit bien d'endosser la vie sur le dos, la porter comme un baluchon, dont on n'aurait pas trop connaissance, à peine une intuition, une vie tellement immanente, collée à nous, que je n'aurais eu de cesse de lui donner de quoi se présenter à moi, en tendant les bras, en faisant des allers-retours comme on fait les cent pas, quand on sait que l'on a quelque chose à faire mais quoi, si je ne note pas sur des listes, ou des bouts de papier, ou sur mon téléphone, si je ne note pas tout, je ne sais plus ce que j'ai à faire, mon univers se rattache à des bouts de liste qui me rappellent qui je suis, ce que je suis et ce que je dois faire, comme aller acheter de la sauce tomate, du chocolat, du lait d'avoine et du beurre, le nombre maximum d'ingrédients, au-delà de quatre, ma mémoire s'embrouille, je glisse beaucoup trop vite, je le sens, ce n'est pas une perte progressive, si progressive qu'elle me serait à peine perceptible, non, c'est une pente de glace, comme celle de Chamechaude, quand j'ai glissé sur ces pentes, dévissé, sans pouvoir m'arrêter, empêtré dans mon manteau comme Pierre Etaix dans le ciel de New York, ce qu'il y a de terrible avec la glace, c'est la prise de vitesse, j'ai pris tellement de vitesse, que je ne sais plus convoquer des mots aussi usuels que « fourchette », « tiroir », « radiateur », les choses sont là devant mes yeux, mais je ne parviens pas à les nommer, elles se tiennent inertes, totalement inoffensives et inutiles, narquoises, sur le bout de la langue, une langue qui serait coupée à grands coups de fourchette oubliée comme la langue de bœuf de ma mère sortie de la

Maurice du Moullay confond "fourchette" et "courgette"
(photo de Peter James Field)

cocotte-minute, un diable de sa boîte, Gianluca Vialli aussi sortait de sa boîte, marchant nonchalamment sur la moitié de terrain adverse, quasiment en roue libre, lorsque le ballon lui arrive dessus, comme au volley-ball, il récupère le ballon du pied qui rebondit, se retourne comme un jouer de PlayStation et relance le ballon à la volée dans une passe décisive, lent-rapide comme Matt Damon dans Jason Bourne, cette image de Vialli m'obsède, je la cherche indéfiniment sur YouTube, combinant les mots pour parvenir à mes fins, et je finis par tomber sur une vidéo de Michael Laudrup, qui fait la même chose en inversée, sur la partie haute du terrain, à terre, montrant toute l'habileté dont je ne suis pas pourvu, à peine, n'en déplaise à cette grosse baudruche de Prométhée, celui-là même qui m'a fait aimer Eschyle, le pompeux, d'ailleurs, mais pourquoi, je m'étais entiché de Pompée, sans doute un excès de jeunesse pour me différencier, pour autant, je ne suis pas très satisfait de vieillir, je suis en train de descendre, non pas comme on descendrait du train, mais comme on dégringole, dévisse, chutons dans le vide!, un *jumper* le long des tours jumelles, mais lentement, image par image, comme on scrute le cinéma, photogramme par photogramme, dont pas une seule image ne pourrait être prélevée comme Éric Rondepierre a pu le faire, j'étais l'image fixe prise dans un flux, en train de glisser ou était-ce l'eau? comme Robert Seyfried dans *Rei Dom ou la légende des Kreuls*, assis dans la rivière, le ventre rebondi, vieil homme sans doute plus jeune à l'écran que je ne le suis aujourd'hui, ça m'avait fait pareil avec une photo de Robert Guédiguian parue dans les *Cahiers du Cinéma* dont soudain, il m'était apparu qu'il n'avait pas la tête de vieux qu'il semblait avoir de prime abord, mais qu'en la scrutant avec attention, ou tout simplement en la regardant, sa tête, son visage de trois quart, le type de profilage que je n'ai jamais pu dessiner de ma vie, j'ai vu des enfants de six ans capable de dessiner leur père avec une précision dans le trois quart sidérante, mais moi je dessine toujours de face, à plat, la vie est de face, je pense de face, je pense dans un face à face, je ne dessine pas de trois quart, non, paf, je dessine en face, je capte, j'entoure, aucune perspective, la vie plate, l'eau plate, sur un plateau, Guédiguian avait ma tête, il n'était pas vieux, pas si vieux disons, ou c'était moi qui avait bien vieilli puisque j'allais sur mes quarante ans, sans avoir, et quand je pense que j'utilise le terme avoir pour une question d'être, je pense à mes élèves de La Courneuve qui ne connaissaient que le mode avoir, remplaçant l'auxiliaire être dans toutes les conjugaisons par l'auxiliaire avoir puisque la question était réellement d'en avoir ou pas, sans aucune référence au cinéma, au contraire, la toute simple réalité crue nudité de savoir si on allait avoir ou non, sans avoir la moindre idée, après quarante ans de vie, ce que voudrait effectivement dire d'être un trait d'union entre l'appréhension de la mort de son père inévitable et la crainte de la disparition de sa fille, redoutée, si redoutée que je ne puis la penser en face à face, je me rends compte à quel point je suis de trois quart, voire de dos dans cette histoire, dos au mur, est-ce que j'ai déjà agi dans ma vie sans être dos au mur? j'ai beau lire chez Ricoeur que je peux dire, faire, raconter, me souvenir et promettre, je fais le malin mais j'ai lu ça sur Wikipédia, il m'a fallu un effort surhumain pour aller vérifier dans la vraie vie que Ricoeur avait bien écrit ça, vérification tombée dans l'oreille d'un sourd, un sourd qui sursauterait tout de même à la détonation d'un fusil comme celle à l'œuvre dans *La Vérification* d'Alexeï Guerman, Ricoeur aurait plutôt dit que l'écriture ne pouvait se réduire à sa propre célébration et que dans ce sous-texte aurait pu s'engouffrer la vie, ou pas, c'est toute la question qui m'obsède, presqu'autant que l'image de la mère de Whistler redessinée d'un trait enfantin par Mr Bean, presqu'autant que les petits pas de Chris Burden revenant vers nous après avoir tenté d'éprouver la vie qui est en lui, c'est ça la plaie mortelle de Wikipédia, un saupoudrage à tout le moins, une vie repoussée dans ses retranchements, après le moi le déluge, remettons à demain ce que nous aurions pu faire aujourd'hui, c'est comme des chips, c'est absolument, rigoureusement impossible de ne pas manger de chips, je me demande si un Maori mangerait lui aussi des chips, je ne sais pas trop comment checker cette information et je ne veux pas regarder sur Wikipédia, j'aurais trop peur de trouver une note réelle sur le rapport du peuple Maori avec les chips de pomme de terre, car il est bien entendu que lorsque j'évoque les chips, il ne s'agit pas de toutes ces chips à la betterave, à la pomme ou autre produit honteusement dérivé de la chips pomme de terre, et pendant qu'il m'est permis, d'autant que je me permets tout seul, c'est sans doute ce qui fait le pouvoir dictatorial de l'écriture, en tout cas, sa force sans commune mesure face au cinéma, il n'y a pas de cinéaste qui peut éprouver la joie de l'écriture, il faudra que je lise *Écrire* de Marguerite Duras, pourtant je l'ai lu, mais je n'en ai aucun souvenir, en revanche je me souviens d'un texte de Patrick Süskind intitulé *Amnesia in litteris*, qui racontait la poussière mémorielle de toute la littérature, les approximations vagues que l'on garde des romans de Dostoïevski, le pouvoir d'écrire, de lutter de façon incessante, l'écriture rend le présent vivant, c'est une donation de la vie, même si je me rends compte que l'on peut également oublier ce que l'on écrit, partir de ce monde, oublier d'en faire partie, quitter le monde constitué pour le monde constituant muni d'une conscience en berne, rien à voir avec la Suisse, les petits Suisses, ou la compote de fraise, à l'extrême rigueur le pédalage dans la semoule, et là au beau milieu de cette lecture pénible et ardue et rêche de Paul Ricoeur, je tombe sur une vidéo de mon père, ou plutôt une vidéo où j'imite mon père, j'imite mon père parce que quoi, parce que j'ai tellement pas la croyance de ma pauvre tête, comme disait ma pauvre mère de ma pauvre grand-mère qui n'avait de pauvre que la peau sur les os, comme tout le monde, on va tous mourir, même moi, ton papa, ma fille, et toi aussi, tu cours, tu gambades mais tu vas mourir, ça me fait remonter tous les sels d'argent qui se sont infiltrés dans ma peau, mes mains se raidissent comme les doigts de Rafael Nadal lors de sa onzième victoire à Roland-Garros, en finale contre Dominic Thiem, dont Mats Wilander dit dans l'*Équipe*, qu'il a, malgré le score six-quatre, six-trois, six-deux, bien joué ce match, qu'il a joué comme il l'attendait, Thiem ayant pour sa part déclaré la veille du match qu'il avait un plan, et moi je me demande ce que peut bien recouvrir ce *bien joué*, ça nous échappe comme la vie, après tout, à part la sensation de se filmer, à part l'auto-filmage, je n'aurais pas accompli grand-chose dans ma vie, mais ça je l'aurais accompli, quoiqu'en l'occurrence je ne sais pas trop ce que j'ai accompli en imitant mon père en admettant que j'imite mon père, c'est toute la force d'un titre de film ou le nom d'un fichier, il a le poids de l'écrit, alors cette vidéo « mon père » est mon père, je suis mon père, je le suis sans distance, à distance respectable.

[...]

Gianluca Vialli, écriture double (en cours). Texte + photos, html, films et VR.

Bazin, André. 1962. *Qu'est-ce que le cinéma ?* Paris : Éditions du Cerf.

Casetti, Francesco. 2016. « The Relocation of Cinema ». In *Post-Cinema: Theorizing 21st-Century Film*, dirigé par Shane Denson et Julia Leyda. Falmer : Reframe books.

Colléony, Jacques. 1991. « Lévinas et l'art : La réalité et son ombre ». *La Part de l'Œil*, n° 7.

Goldsmith, Kenneth. 2018. *L'écriture sans écriture, du langage à l'ère numérique.* Traduit par François Bon. Paris : Jean Boîte Éditions.

Henry, Michel. 1988. *Voir l'invisible : sur Kandinsky.* Paris : Presses Universitaires de France.

Henry, Michel. 2002. *Auto-donation, entretiens et conférences.* Dirigé par Magali Uhl. Paris : Beauchesne.

Henry, Michel. 2005. *Entretiens.* Cabris : Sulliver.

Henry, Michel. 2015. *Phénoménologie de la vie.* 5 vol. Paris : Presses Universitaires de France.

Jdey, Adnen, et Rolf Kühn. 2012. *Michel Henry et l'affect de l'art. Recherches sur l'esthétique de la phénoménologie matérielle.* Studies in contemporary phenomenology 4. Leiden : Brill.

Laoureux, Sébastien. 2015. *L'immanence à la limite. Recherches sur la phénoménologie de Michel Henry.* Paris : Les Éditions le Cerf.

Meade, Chris. 2018. « Chris & the Ifso ». Consulté le 29 avril 2019. https://nearlyology.net/.

CHRIS FUNKHOUSER

Midiazine Research Performance ELO 2018 / Eastern Block, Montreal, August 15

Abstract

My performances and artworks during the past decade have often relied on use of MIDI (Musical Instrument Digital Interface) and other types of interactive digital audio. Recent experiments, as outlined in this essay, explore unique methods by which to map spoken language on the level of the phoneme to musical orchestration. The title of the performance, *Midiazine*, derives from miazine, a noun that indicates pyrimidine structure in chemistry, indicating three bases as being fundamental constituents of nucleic acids. I transmute the concept onto a multimodal expressive scenario (text/image/sound), in which one of three base sources (text) is cast into multiple media forms. In this case spoken words form as instrumental sounds as much as they do as something containing literal meaning. Splicing "di" into miazine acknowledges the MIDI component, making a nice neologism that also tips a hat towards an improvised type of publication, the "zine." *Midiazine* envisions pyramidal structure of language flow, with elements having even sides. The idea and premise here is that an ephemeral, temporary, and technological reliant *midiazine* would be issued at the event, created via a multimedia recitation using multi-channel voice and instrument mapping in conjunction with visual components.
The poetics of this interval of my practice are documentary, appropriative, conceptual, confessional, and intuitive, and involve sound and text design. My artistic approach in nearly every activity is spontaneous, fairly unpredictable, and what occurs onstage, thanks to software design (and not by coding), is direct virtual mapping of my voice to external sounds. This essay describes the contents of my ELO performance–documentary recordings of poets accompanied by poetry, and a script culled from a statement I made during a 2015 interview with George Quasha–and discusses the technological circuit built for the occasion. The performance (and present essay) proposes and hopefully answers specific questions, including how can integrating our voices with particular sounds supplement a communicative message?

Résumé

Au cours de la dernière décennie, mes performances et mes œuvres artistiques ont souvent reposé sur l'utilisation du MIDI (Musical Instrument Digital Interface) et d'autres types d'audio numérique interactif. Des expériences récentes, décrites dans cet essai, explorent des méthodes uniques permettant de faire correspondre le langage parlé au niveau du phonème à l'orchestration musicale. Le titre de la performance, *Midiazine*, est dérivé de 'miazine', un nom qui indique la structure chimique de la pyrimidine, dont les trois bases sont les composantes fondamentales des acides nucléiques. Je transmute le concept en un scénario expressif multimodal (texte/image/son), dans lequel l'une des trois sources de base (texte) est recréée en plusieurs formes de médias. Dans ce cas, la parole s'actualise sous forme de son instrumental tout en conservant son sens littéral. L'insertion de « di » dans la miazine reconnaît l'utilisation du MIDI, ce qui crée un joli néologisme faisant un clin d'œil à la publication improvisée qu'est le « zine ». Midiazine s'attarde à la structure pyramidale des flux de langage, avec des éléments ayant des côtés pairs. L'idée et l'hypothèse est qu'une *midiazine* éphémère, temporaire et technologiquement dépendante serait émise lors de l'événement, créée via une récitation multimédia utilisant un *mapping* multivocal et instrumental conjointement avec des éléments visuels.
La poétique de cette phase de ma pratique est documentaire, appropriative, conceptuelle, confessionnelle, intuitive et implique le design du son et du texte. Ma démarche artistique dans presque toutes les activités est spontanée, assez imprévisible, et ce qui arrive sur scène, grâce à la conception de logiciels (et non par codage), est une cartographie virtuelle directe de ma voix aux sons extérieurs. Dans cet essai, le contenu de ma performance ELO – des enregistrements documentaire des poètes accompagné de poésie et un script sélectionné d'une déclaration que j'ai faite en 2015 lors d'une interview avec George Quasha – et décrit et le circuit technologique créé pour l'occasion est examiné. La performance (et le présent essai) propose et, espérons-le, répond à des questions spécifiques, notamment comment l'intégration de nos voix avec des sons particuliers peut-elle compléter un message communicatif?.

1. Documentation of the performance:
https://drive.google.com/file/d/1PhaDN9r38U-wQFy5lOSLM2ehQhe740cF/view?usp=sharing
2. MIDI output of performance without voice:
https://drive.google.com/file/d/1YlFHXInLquCff1qMZSNY5O9uB_YEY-vF/view
Note: Italicized passages below were spoken / sung at the event.

For several decades, artists have been able to process voice and sound with reverb and other effects. With the advance of MIDI (Musical Instrument Digital Interface) in the 1990s, we have had the ability to transpose the sounds of one instrument onto another–e.g., someone can make a piano/keyboard sound like an electric guitar–or to synchronize sonic and visual components of their work, including words and animation. Since 2010 many of my performances and artworks have centered on using MIDI and other types of interactive digital audio manipulation. At first, I used MIDI to generate imagery and text with an electric bass or guitar. My most recent experiments with sound explore unique methods to intrinsically connect spoken or sung language, at the level of the phoneme, to musical orchestration.

In 2016, working with Ableton Live software, which incorporates MIDI components, I discovered a way, using the somewhat unusual combination of condenser microphone with Bass-to-MIDI converter plus software effects, to synthesize and extend my voice through orchestral sounds with great intricacy, in real time. This project, still ongoing, is partly inspired by the work of Taras Mashtalir, a Russian artist whose work I have encountered on a number of occasions during the past few years. In Mashtalir's installation "Pythia," at ELO 2015: End(s) of Electronic Literature festival in Norway, spoken words were used to activate/generate the appearance/projection of text based on what voice did and said. I have not yet acquired the level of technical skill needed to emulate such work, but have succeeded in discovering a method by which to map voice to instrumental sounds instantaneously.

The difficult part of achieving this objective was figuring out how to convert sound input to a MIDI signal. Certain instruments are built to do this, and crucial for me was discovering a somewhat obscure piece of hardware, a Sonuus Universal Bass-to-MIDI converter (Sonuus B2M), which enables me to convert voice to MIDI signal and feed a direct (unprocessed) line from a microphone into the audio interface and then into the software I use, Ableton Live. The Sonuus is a small, but very stalwart box which runs on a 9-volt battery that has one toggle switch (enabling "chromatic"), one input (1/4" jack), and 2 outputs (MIDI, 1/4"). Once the vocal information reaches the software, a number of instruments are available to apply to the signal, the parameters of which can be adjusted as desired by the ear.

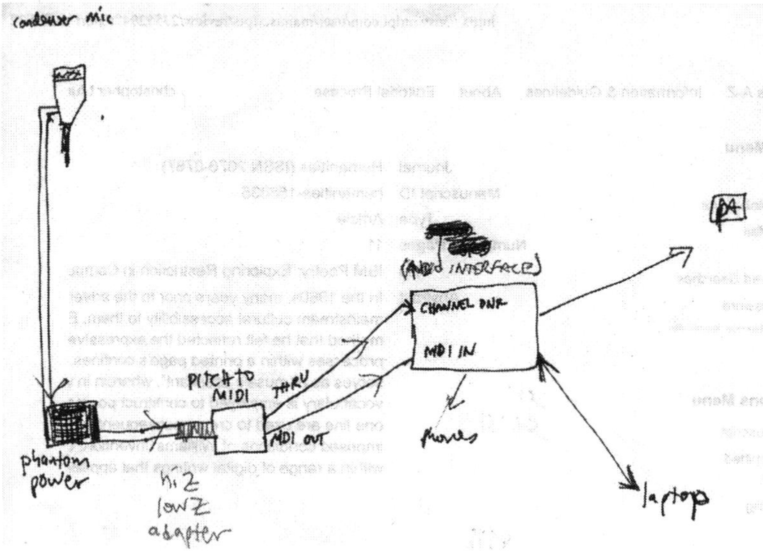

Figure 1. MIDI method sketch, Chris Funkhouser, 2017

Figure 2. Hardware used for MIDI-Voice experiments, Chris Funkhouser, 2018

For the ELO 2018 Attention à la Marche/Mind the Gap performance, I prepared a multimedia compendium (words, soundtracks, video), combining multi-channel voice and audio mapping and processing, presented with simple visual accompaniment. Vocalized (and processed through MIDI) were statements on poetics and poetry along with samples of recordings (spoken language) by other artists I have documented over the years. As an invocation, I stood and rattled a flex-a-tone percussion instrument before initializing the performance with a broadcast of Jackson Mac Low's poem "I Strife" (recorded at his loft for *The Little Magazine*, Volume 21 (1995)) and offering a brief introduction:

Tonight
an improvised experiment in
sound / voice / poetry
1/2 of what it will be
adding visuals eventually
painters!

With this line, I was thinking (as mentioned onstage), *Imagine a painting made by the voice of Cecilia Vicuña*, and proceeded to play and process an ethereal atmospheric recording I made of Vicuña's voice at the Subterranean Poetry Festival in the Widow Jane Mine (Rosendale, NY) in 2014 alongside my text/narrative/collage for the next few minutes.

The title of the performance, *Midiazine*, derives from miazine, a noun that indicates pyrimidine structure in chemistry (meta+diazine), indicative of the three bases that are fundamental constituents of nucleic acids. I transmute the concept into a multi-modal expressive scenario, in which one of three base sources (text) is cast into multiple media forms. In this case spoken words form as instrumental sounds as much as they do as something which contains literal meaning. Splicing "id" into miazine acknowledges the MIDI component, making a nice neologism that also tips a hat towards an improvised type of publication, the "zine." *Midiazine* envisions pyramidal structure of language flow, and elements having even sides seems a reasonable model. Proceeding with the idea and premise that an ephemeral temporary and technological reliant *midiazine* was being issued that night in Montreal, I sat at the computer and assembled it. Some of the contents I brought to the stage were "published" in the moment and, as explained below, others were not.

The roughly prepared verbal script I brought to the event originated in a statement I made during an interview conducted by George Quasha as part of his *Poetry Is* documentary series (2015). This excerpt from my interview with Quasha is also published in the book *Art is (Speaking Portraits)* [(2016); 150]. A photocopied and edited version of text became the basis of my set in Montreal. These words were originally spoken, documented by videotape, and then transcribed to print. Time passes, and into the once again reformed text I blend introductory material, epigraph, surround with sound and others' voices, and from it subtract trivial, superfluous, or inefficient words, locating potential points where pre-recorded, documentary sounds and poems I brought with me on the laptop and printed page might be associated with, and used to build, the narrative.

Preparing for the show, I collected a few samples of documentary recordings I made over the years and would have on-hand to use as part of the assemblage. The performance slot was only ten minutes, and I was very selective since it was not necessary or prudent to have too much loaded into the program. These files, slotted into different tracks in Ableton Live, included recordings of Lee Ann Brown, Jackson Mac Low, Most Serene Congress, George Quasha, Charles Stein, and Cecilia Vicuña. I brought along published-on-the-page poems by Quasha (from *preverbs*), Jhave Johnston (from *RERITES*), and a piece of mine published in the anthology *"US" Poets Foreign Poets* (2018), which I had received from Chris Tanasescu at the beginning of the 2018 ELO conference.

The technological circuit I assembled for the Attention à la Marche sound collage, without which this type of performance and aesthetic would not be possible, is as follows (see Figs. 1 and 2 above): a highly sensitive condenser microphone (Audio Technica AT 4003a)–which in this setup requires phantom power–is attached to the aforementioned MIDI converter using a Hi-Z Low-Z adapter; from there the vocal sounds are routed into two separate inputs in the audio interface (Komplete Audio 6): one carries voice straight through to an audio interface input channel, the other connects from the MIDI converter to the audio interface's MIDI input. Both inputs are routed to laptop/software via USB. Once the sound is processed it is sent back through the audio interface en route to the PA system (or headphones). In addition to the converter's importance, the type of microphone used in the process also makes a lot of difference. The sensitivity of the condenser microphone, compared to an ordinary unidirectional microphone, delivers a more dynamic, defined, and high-quality sound to the software.

The MIDI instrumental accompanists, all built into Ableton Live, are named BBass, Jarble Disto B, It Happened One, Flute Lead, Light and Shadow, GitProc, DigiNoise, and Sweet Bells. Each was added incrementally into the mix and manipulated in real time. While I cannot completely control each of the instruments, the voice initiates everything they do as well as how they sound. The software, once calibrated and in conjunction with hardware, does much of the work. An instrument that was initially part of the ensemble, Brassinski, was removed in the preparation process because its presence was overbearing. Several different types of audio filters—delays, saturators, reverb—were loaded into my Ableton performance file, for potential application to pre-recorded tracks: Minor Third Down, Groove, Pong, High, A Bit Warmer, Old Sampler, Megaflexion, Ping, and Harmony to MIDI.

there's a tree
at Rokeby
with majesty

The video component of this work presented a continuation of a tradition I began in August 2017 after seeing one of Jackson Mac Low's "static films" titled "Tree* Movie" at an exhibition of his work titled Lines-Letters-Words at the Drawing Center in New York City earlier that year. The process of making such a film is not demanding. As Mac Low wrote in 1961:

> Tree* Movie
>
> Select a tree*. Set up and focus a movie camera so that the tree* fills most of the picture. Turn on the camera and leave it on without moving for any number of hours. If the camera is about to run out of film, substitute a camera with fresh film. The two cameras may be alternated in this way any number of times. Sound recording equipment may be turned on simultaneously with the movie cameras. Beginning at any point in the film, any length of it may be projected at a showing.
>
> *For the word 'tree,' one may substitute 'mountain,' 'sea,' 'flower,' 'lake,' etc. (Mac Low 1986, 132-33).

My first Tree movie, made in Barrytown, New York with a Nikon, served well as a contemplative backdrop for a MIDI-based poetry performance on a bill with Nick Montfort in Troy, NY, August 2017. For the 2018 iteration, I identified a gingko tree located on an old estate known as Rokeby, also in Barrytown.

the skinny ghost birdvoice of the hermetic mirror needs to take in,
augment/collaborate,
bounce off, elaborate upon the many birdsongs of an open tree (Moe **1992**).

The 29-minute film captures late afternoon flight paths of various birds and insects as they dart in and about plentiful broad and robust leaves and branches beneath bright sky. For the 10-minute segment shown alongside my performance in Montreal, I chose footage where passing clouds clearly alter the appearance of the tree, and since it was not a windy day, the light-to-dark contrast occurs in a subtle arc.

Poetry of any sort is not just about writing
it's about the way you live & receive the world
Poetry isn't one thing–can't be
try to remain free, moving into digital production multimedia
that as poetry I still see. not everybody does.
it's an open system, & complex

A direct connection exists between videographic, sonic, and verbal content in *Midiazine* through the figure of Mac Low, someone I was fortunate to know and who began to influence and inspire my work as of our first encounter in 1991. His work is mentioned in my *Poetry Is* statement, is included in the soundtrack material by way of a vocal recording ("I Strife"), and he inspired my tree video series. While it is basic in form and content, I value the supplemental poetic role the video plays. Although the performance might better achieve expressive wholeness if frames of the video were synchronized with the voice and sounds, the video as is provides a contemplative spatial focal point that is more stimulating than simply watching the performer (who is not particularly doing anything compelling to look at). Further, since the video is rooted in a figure that influences the work as a whole, it is far from being random or out of place.

Most importantly, in terms of aural presentation,

Tying these things together, a way to justifize or rationalify them -> lyricism
Language & sound's innate properties
So writing out of algorithms
pay attention to how it sounds as it's read
or how you hear it in your head

At this juncture, my attention and voice onstage turn to the acrostic poem in the Margento anthology, an excerpt from "Hello Allocation," a text produced with help from the GTR Language Workbench (a language processing software program built by David Ayre and Andrew Klobucar). The musical orchestration continually shifts; throughout the performance I am tinkering with the sound levels, mixing them in and out, emphasizing some over others. With eight instruments at hand, applying too much at once can create audiophonic chaos. This happens sometimes, but in my estimation they are fairly tame and toned-down in the overall ELO mix, and if anything the words are given too much privilege.

Hello Allocation
Seven
malfunctioned asahi isn't newly enormousness
minuscule artillerists in notice elastic
motionlessly artistic inconsistent necessitous exerts
mega-crash arrays investing neat envoi
midwifery arrogant inglorious nouveau economics
mid apparition illumined night-line evergreens (52)

While Lee Ann Brown's tuning of Emily Dickinson's "Sonnet 100" plays, I further note:

You can sing Dickinson, & you can sing Mac Low if you
try hard enough–maybe not all, but a lot

and reiterate a couple of lines by Mac Low, *I strife/it strove before strove strife.*

Compositional processes value the lyrical as part of personal
forms of expression maybe not intimate personal; something else.
Not one thing or another;
something & something & something else,
& to someone else another combination

Charles Stein's sound poetry, recorded on my radio program Poet Ray'd Yo in 2015 (WGXC) emerges from, and merges with, the octet. These particular combinations or engagements may not completely embody the full potential for expressive media gestalt, but effective interconnection between multiple modalities is achieved, and I believe a potent and unusual type of digital writing and extension of the voice is unveiled through them.

A final poem, "Model: 117591 / Loss: 0.608," written by Johnston in conjunction with AI algorithms, part of his *RERITES* project (June 2017), concludes my segment of the program with the lines,

in an abundance as if there's a reason all around
in the balletic contingent imaginary (np).

Preparing and performing the material was instructive, informative, and I am mostly satisfied by the result. Listening back to the ambient audio documentation, the improvised live mix of orchestral sound is not as present as it seemed to be in the moment, or as it sounds when listening to the software-generated iteration. As I was multitasking, I managed to record digitally each of the audio channels, but I did not use the software to record everything together in real time, so variations that happened during the performance are not evident in a mix created on the laptop (i.e., the sound levels in the documentary mix are fixed as they were at the endpoint of the performance). I also made an ambient/room recording, in which subtle dynamics and interplay between modalities present in the material are absorbed in the loudness and echo of the gallery space, so the overall sound captured to the SD card on the handheld recorder (Roland R-26) is imperfect. The instrumental effects are barely audible, since the microphone sensitivity and recording levels were on low settings because of room volume and reverberation. The audio documentation of my performance that accompanies this report (Sound file 1) combines the software mix and ambient mix, but is still not completely indicative of what transpired or what the audience actually heard. As literary and Digital Humanities scholars increasingly make use of recordings as they subjectively and objectively evaluate audio documents, it will behoove them to remember that hearing a recording of an event does not guarantee that the documentation represents what the audience actually heard or experienced. Accurately documenting audio presentations with audio might seem like an easy thing to achieve, but since the overall output mix was not being recorded (only the individual channels) and the PA system was extremely loud, not all of the elements are easy to hear. In hindsight (i.e., for future reference), I should wear headphones in order to best hear what the software is doing, as well as record the live mix. If ever performing in a mode such as this again, I believe the presentation might benefit were I to be on my feet, with the laptop on a stand, positioned in front of the projection screen. Combining projected imagery and body in action, a technique employed by the performer who preceded me onstage, Phillippe Boisnard, made a positive impression on me.

Circumstances of space and moment definitely had an effect on the performance, especially since the set was near the end of an evening bill after a long day of conference activity. Being sensitive to that, plus the fact of a 10-minute time limit, I rushed in to starting the performance as soon as the gear was set up. In a less rushed situation it is easier to fine-tune sound from the stage. Listening back to the ambient recording, sensibilities of a musical/Sound poet are somewhat reflected, as is a bit of on-the-fly DJ factor. As indicated, I did not make use of all of the material I had gathered for potential use in the performance. For instance, I was not able to make time or find a way to insert Quasha's short poem "Doing with Mirrors" into the set as intended. Preparing for the event, I was working with an overall scheme that was flexible, and which could be spontaneously played out. Judging from the audio documentation, it appears as though four sound files that were loaded into Ableton Live, pieces by Mac Low, Most Serene Congress, Quasha, and Stein were omitted. Energy in the vocal staging is good, if not a bit rushed, exaggerated, and possibly overdramatic, and overall the show is, from a sound/audio poetry/poetics perspective unique and unusual enough to be legitimate as a message and aesthetic-bearing artwork. Programming a digital octet to take cues from my voice involves trial-and-error, fine tuning until the instrumentation sounds "just right" is an ongoing process. The sounds are possibly too synthetic, and I will not be surprised if I tone down the keyboard-sounding effects next time I prepare such a work.

Preparing this report and going back to the fourteen (in all) separate Ableton tracks, I had the idea to create a mix of the material in which voices are completely removed. Interestingly, removing the voice from the overall mix equation leaves a type of musical composition, whose verbal score (and reason for being) is the absent poetry, as heard in Sound file 2 that accompanies this essay. The coupling of voice and instrumental effects can be completely undone by flipping an intermediary switch in the software, leaving listeners with everything but the words, traced by patterns of retained sound. The alluvial sounds, as disorganized as they are, indicate how a more methodical, controlled presentation of the voice could be used as a way to create scores and soundtracks. This version of *Midiazine* is an example of how a musical composition can be a direct by-product or technological extension of electronic poetry, or of spoken word of any sort.

In *Midiazine* the visual elements, sound levels, choices of audio files, filters, and words spoken or sung were spontaneously what they were, only to happen once, in that time and place, and cannot be repeated. Whether or not any of the momentary material presented registered the way reading a zine might is unknown. I suspect what will be remembered are the noise levels, and the intense heat of the August night–not only the air temperature, but camaraderie of community and qualities of the performances. Next steps for me to take involve finding ways to render language/image visually through vocalization. I have processed and generated very basic video/animation through musical instrumentation in the past, using rudimentary software (MIDIPoet) that is far less versatile and sonically powerful than Ableton Live. To forge a new bridge, learning to use and employ a software program such as MAX will, eventually, enable me to do so.

In the meantime, I find the instantaneous ability to append orchestral sounds to voice interesting and aesthetically pleasing. In this example–a rather rushed and spontaneously assembled (though not completely improvised) performance–the musical output is jagged and rather amelodic. One can imagine how, with different types of texts or in a different vocal mode or presentational scenario–and by using other instruments–the results could and would be completely different. I have yet to explore many dozens of MIDI instruments and effects. With this mechanism, language not only carries sounds as well as meaning, but expands into music through inventive and imaginative use of software and hardware. I am confident such investigations are worthwhile within the Arts and Humanities, as they raise questions such as, how can integrating our voices with particular sounds supplement a communicative message? The poetics of this interval of my practice are documentary, appropriative, conceptual, confessional, and intuitive, and involve sound and text design. My artistic approach in nearly every activity is spontaneous, fairly unpredictable, and what I succeed in achieving here, thanks to software design and not by coding, is direct virtual mapping of my voice to external sounds.

Rhinebeck, NY
April 2019

Funkhouser, Christopher. 2018. "Hello Allocation." In *"US" Poets Foreign Poets*, ed. by Chris Tanasescu. Bucharest: Margento.

Johnston, Jhave. 2017. *RERITES* June 2017. Self-published.

Mac Low, Jackson. 1986. *Representative Works: 1938–1985.* New York: Roof Books.

Mac Low, Jackson. 1995. "I Strife." In *The Little Magazine*. Vol. 21, ed. by Christopher Funkhouser, Belle Gironda, and Benjamin Henry, CD-ROM. Albany: SUNY Department of English.

Mashtalir, Taras. 2015. "Pythia." In *Sonic Sculputure*. Bergen, Norway.

Moe, H.D. 1992. "Correctionism." In *We*. Vol. 16. Santa Cruz: We Press.

Quasha, George. 2015. *Poetry Is.* Video. Link: https://vimeo.com/129744982

Quasha, George. 2016. *Art Is (Speaking Portraits).* New York: PAJ Publications.

ALAN SONDHEIM

Trump's Tweets, Or The True And Authentic Electronic Literature

Abstract

The paper is a presentation on the subject of Splatter Semiotics, and The Semiotics of Splatter, which is concerned with "messy" digital lit/digital literacy. I am discussing Trump's tweets, Russian hacking, etc., and disruptive technologies which possess "spread" as, not only a form of digital literature, but also a new and dangerous cultural horizon, one that threatens the very foundations of democratic institutions.

Résumé

Cet article présente une sémiotique éclaboussante, de même qu'une sémiotique de l'éclaboussure (Splatter Semiotics, The Semiotics of Splatter), qui concerne le « désordre » de la littérature numérique et de la lecture numérique. Il y est question notamment des tweets de Trump, du hacking russe, etc., et des technologies perturbatrices qui pratiquent la dispersion comme une forme de littérature numérique, mais également comme un nouvel horizon culturel dangereux, qui menace les fondements mêmes des institutions démocratiques.

//for the Electronic Literature Organization Conference 2018 in Montreal. The talk was improvised from the material below. A background video was simultaneously played; without dialog or titles, it presented a fast-forward deconstructing landscape in a virtual world, one in which, for the solitary avatar, there are no holdfasts, no points or moments of stability. I was thinking of catastrophe theory here as well as "an outline of another analysis." This paper itself is a pastiche of such an outline.//

Two points first:

- ☐ Trump's Tweets are the most important and performative electronic literary culture today.
- ☐ To analyze these requires an analysis of high-speed splattered sign formation and subsequent displacement.

Fake news:

> Aug 2, 2018 03:24:33 PM — They asked my daughter Ivanka whether or not the media is the enemy of the people. She correctly said no. It is the FAKE NEWS, which is a large percentage of the media, that is the enemy of the people!
>
> Aug 2, 2018 06:04:04 AM — Wow, @foxandfriends is blowing away the competition in the morning ratings. Morning Joe is a dead show with very few people watching and sadly, Fake News CNN is also doing poorly. Too much hate and inaccurately reported stories–too predictable!
>
> Jul 31, 2018 08:34:47 AM — The Fake News Media is going CRAZY! They are totally unhinged and in many ways, after witnessing first hand the damage they do to so many innocent and decent people, I enjoy watching. In 7 years, when I am no longer in office, their ratings will dry up and they will be gone!
>
> Jul 29, 2018 07:30:04 AM — Had a very good and interesting meeting at the White House with A.G. Sulzberger, Publisher of the New York Times. Spent much time talking about the vast amounts of Fake News being put out by the media & how that Fake News has morphed into phrase, "Enemy of the People." Sad!

Notes towards a semiotics of splatter / splatter semiotics –
== > briefly, they're performative.
== > How are they performative?
//think of gesture re: Tran Duc Thao, proto-language, chora, etc.//
Some background = three semiotic domains –

Of the reading or attempted reading of the world, however "world" is defined:

1. I think through three different domains, and dynamics 'across' them. In other words, between the signifier and the signified, there are various regimes and ***ranges of processing times.***

2. The first is ***game-space***, characterized by rule-bound behaviors within a classical environment with more or less stable boundaries. There are limited sets of behaviors that might be considered acceptable; time is constrained and the signifier / signified processing times appears manageable. Chess, Tetris, Adventure, most computer games.
"Acceptability" refers to consensus here. *//game-space *as classical space//**

3. The second is ***edge-space***, characterized by breakdowns and glitches within and without game space; some of these glitches may be deliberately created within game-space, but most go against the game and lead to new behaviors, and even new ontologies. For example, an edge-space event may throw a player out of the game entirely, closing a computer or game pitch down, etc. *Edge-space problematizes the idea of "rule" itself.* It's here that epistemology extends into unknown territories. The interval between signifier and signified may be highly variable; this becomes important in considering *splatter semiotics or semiotic splatter* below.

4. The third is ***blank-space***. This references the uncanny, the untoward, the filling and fulfilling of those regimes of edge where nothing appears, nothing appears to appear. "Heere bee dragonnes" and the like. Think of the early maps of the North and South poles. It's where signifiers reference fluidities, instabilities. It's where we populate the indeterminate. And where we consider the processing time of the indeterminate. *Which leads I think to the issue of our time and a paradigm for electronic literature:*

[Insert: 'Blankspace' then *indicates how edgespace is 'filled in,'* how the imaginary operates there. I use the terms in considerations of Arctic and Antarctic mappings, virtual worlds, and so forth. *Finally, the semiotics of splatter considers splatter as world-breaking and fast-forward tendencies towards mobile boundary closures; this leads to splatter semiotics, where the terms form a field that remains always already ruptured.* This is the semiosis of the overloaded or hacked network, the network of fake news and fake apps, the explosive and turbulent behavior of the mediasphere itself.]
//then what is splatter–fractal roiling of fast-forward semantic domains, and positive feedback looping of the same in terms of the mechanisms of media absorption and re-presentation, re-mediation of what becomes news (and this is 'old hat,' we already know this).//

5. ***The Trump Tweet, or Rally Harangue or speed and phenomenology of semiotic dissipation.***
The following section dictated:
This references splatter semiotics, and semiotic splatter – the fast-forward dissipation of signs glued to "fake news" or "Trump's tweets" or governance by high-speed and untoward fiat:

EXAMPLES HERE: improvisation

...

There are so many avenues that one could take or that I could take in thinking about splatter semiotics. For one thing and the main thing: all sorts of different dynamic striations have to be considered. For example, it should be possible to ascertain what it means for a tweet to be received, processed, and then regurgitated or expelled or explicated. What sort of temporality is involved in all of this. Does this relate at all to the idea of the parasite which interferes with what might be considered an instantaneous production of a sign. In other words, newsrooms and their listeners and viewers are continuously thrown off by variegated responses to anything in which the truth value is 0. So we have to look at this as ice function of the digital era, in other words we have to look at this as a dynamics of sign production that can no longer be treated with in the classical time frame.
(Look, it's like this, take Kaja Silverman's *The Subject of Semiotics*–material on Lacan, Peirce, Saussure, Eco. And in all of it, there are these evanescent/ problematic relationships between signifier and signified, and in none of it is there any sort of dynamic and temporal relationship between them as far as

I can tell. You have to wait until information theory, Shannon for example, the route through Nyquist, then the tweets begin to make sense with all their wavering–as if they're branches of catastrophe theory geometries, and as such their truth value is irrelevant–in other words, there's no 'fragility of good things,' because anywhere leads to catastrophic jumps, temporally defined by the speed and processing protocols of the media receptors and transmitters, CNN, MSNBC, and the like. The study should be of _time,_ and as such, _time sensitive processing subjectivities_–not of static or slowly changing (for example dialects) classical relationships. –

Which might lead us back to Freud's condensation/displacement, both of which are temporal processes, but with the signs already assumed or in the process of production–but then I'm thinking about a basic _split_ between signifier and signified within semiotics, not in terms of layerings but in terms of damage, speed, Virilio's dromodology. Might lead us there. I think it does.) */leave out section in parentheses, consider a process between signifier and signified: news organizations can't catch up. related to chora, and related, I think (?) to the maternal; it is the performativity of the tweet splatter itself that's important, not so much the content–except for the signals of identification to the base./*

===

The paper is then a presentation, on the subject of Splatter Semiotics, and The Semiotics of Splatter, which is concerned with 'messy' digital lit/digital literacy. I'm discussing Trump's tweets, Russian hacking, etc.–and disruptive technologies which possess 'spread' as, not only a form of digital literature, but also a new and dangerous cultural horizon, one that threatens the very foundations of democratic institutions.

The semiotics of splatter, then, will consider high-speed semiosis, which is world-breaking and tending towards "roiling" boundary closers; this tends towards mobile boundary closures; and this leads to splatter semiotics, where the dynamics form a field that remains always already ruptured. This is the semiosis of the overloaded or hacked network, the network of fake news and fake apps, the explosive and turbulent behavior of the mediasphere itself.

I see this field as a form of politicized digital literature, where words lose meaning, become *puncta* (Barthes) or tokens, where language splays.

What's needed–a mathematization of sign production/reception rasters; I keep thinking of the formation of turbulence and semi-stable vortices, as well as the dynamics of foam.

This also relates to the attention economy, high-speed fast-forward attention spans, as well as the dissipation and annihilation of vortices, structures of attention, and so forth.
(I see this field as a form of politicized digital literature, where words lose meaning, become *puncta* (Barthes) or tokens, where language splays.)
===
Lakoff and Duran's Guardian article is also useful here–June 6, 2018– ***Trump has turned words into weapons. And he's winning the linguistic war.*****"** I recommend everyone find and read it. So here are some quotes and my commentary -
"Scientists, marketers, advertisers and salespeople understand these principles. So do Russian and Islamic State hackers. But most reporters and editors clearly don't. So the press is at a disadvantage when dealing with a super salesman with an instinctive ability to manipulate thought by 1) framing first, 2) repeating often, and 3) leading others to repeat his words by getting people to attack him within his own frame."
I say –
the press is also at a disadvantage here because there are incompatible processing times involved–that is fundamental. So that when a tweet occurs, the p.t. is considerably greater of course than the time for the next tweet. its both repetition–which sutures over temporalities–and the temporalities themselves which are the issue
"Trump's tweets are not random, they are strategic. There are four types: 1) Pre-emptive framing, to get a framing advantage. 2) Diversion, to divert attention when news could embarrass him. 3) Deflection: Shift the blame to others. And 4) trial balloon–test how much you can get away with. Reporting, and therefore repeating, Trump's tweets just gives [sic] him more power."
I say –
Trump tweets also collapse time; 1-4 operate within a classical proscenium which is critical–but so is the continuous setting-up and unfolding of that proscenium –
"First, journalists must understand how propaganda works on the brain and grasp the cognitive science that marketers of propaganda have implicitly mastered: frames, metaphors, narratives and brain basics."
again, the issue of time; propaganda is not a modernist object –
"Second, keep a steely focus on the fact that American democracy is under attack by a foreign power, possibly with collusion from the sitting president's campaign. This is a crisis. Certain rules don't apply in a crisis,

especially the rule that the press must amplify the presidents words, whatever they are."

This is critical–the ability to create time envelopes around whatever the case / cases may be–and in response to their comments on the 'news cycle'– it's important to recognize that the news cycle is no longer a cycle.

Finally, there's my article from last year's *2600* magazine, which I quote in part. As you can see, I'm grasping at straws with straws here. The fundamental point is, as far as the ELO conference is concerned, Trump's tweets are, above all, electronic literature in its most potent form. They move as seeds processed in fast-forward time across literatures and social media; they're as much a danger to U.S. 'democracy' as Goebbels's onslaught of newspapers headlines was in the early stages of Nazi Germany. And they have to be taken seriously and fought against; this is absolutely necessary –

SPLATTER

I've been a reader of *2600* for a long time now. I'm not a hacker but I write about being online (the title of an anthology I edited). The Trump election took many people by surprise; I saw it coming, and I want to talk about this in terms of hacking and freedom of information. Most of this will probably be familiar.

Semiotics, the study of signs and sign systems, depends on stability – the signifier and signified, for example, are relatively coherent for a "reasonable" period of time. The elaboration of signs and their relationships is complex; semiosis describes the ongoing elucidation and transformation of signs over time. What is important to understand is that semiosis is presumed to be a rationalized process, one that's traceable, accountable. But when we're dealing with high-speed net acrobatics, the situation is qualitatively and fundamentally different.

Two things I want to point out–that hacking, particularly release of documents (Wikileaks etc.) isn't neutral; it's highly political by its very nature. The release of documents related to HRC, and not to DT for a lengthy period of time ensured that the attacks would be continuous; her campaign was derailed as a result. Comey, unethical from the start, rushed into Congress with vague allegations that had no basis in fact; the maxim that one's innocent until proven guilty was derailed by innuendo.

The second point is that any sort of continuous attack forms a kind of bullying to which there's no response; it's impossible to fight back when

semiosis is derailed or transformed into a form of "splatter." Instead of the slow and absorbable evolution of sign systems, one's faced with a high-speed and random dynamics, much like DOS–you reply to one allegation, and a number of others have already appeared. It's a form of torture; the victim is worn down trying to keep up, the splattering appears random, there's no way to stop it, to prepare against it. The traditional news media were caught off-guard by this; their responses were those of organizations who previously had all the time in the world for analysis (or so it appeared) on their hands. Now with fast-forward Net speeds and tweets, HRC was raped by innuendo. ("Rape" may seem too strong a word here, but so many of the attacks were based on her body, her age, her "faltering," her gender. It was debilitating and horrifying to watch.)

Hackers have enormous power today–not only to potentially shut down power plants, but to change the political direction of entire countries. Continuous release of emails, Trump's continuous tweets deeply transform the media landscape–in this case for the worse of course, and with the attack on Net neutrality (and the beginnings of censorship on the horizon), we might find hacking itself limited and dangerous outside of anonymous and brutal security agencies.

//not that relevant to the conference//

The splatter–what I call splatter semiotics–is based on speed–something that has been analyzed in postmodern studies for a long time. The world is speeding up in its call-and-response time, but the speedup isn't coherent from one site or institution to another; there are fractures, breakdowns, misrecognitions. When old media slide against new media, when economies of attention themselves are disrupted, the potential for absolutism and proto-fascism arises.

--- skipping a section on defuge ---

This is where hacking of course can make an enormous difference for good. It seems as if all the fake news and tweets come from the right (I may be mistaken in this); it seems also that it's necessary to fight back accordingly–not in terms of fake news, but in terms of sped-up responses, responses which are no longer replies, but are in themselves actions of resistance, attacks on policies, etc. The dialog at the moment is mastered and controlled by the right (who are themselves a loose coalition); it has to be seized and subverted. It's not important whether or not one likes HRC or would rather have had Bernie; what's coming down the pike is incredibly frightening and brutal, erasing and even annihilating divisions on the left. I think that hackers can be in the forefront

of a response which is absolutely necessary today if democracy (in whatever form, and with all its current miseries) is to continue and grow. I would never underestimate the current regime; it takes just a few years at most for a country to abandon a democratic agenda and turn towards an absolutism that becomes increasingly difficult to eradicate.
//too simple, but an attempt to relate hacking mechanisms to tweet mechanisms, subject for another paper, authored by someone adept at hacking and speed.//
Resist from /dev/null !
//resist from digital degree zero. And this form of resistance–with one's back to the wall–is preventative action, not passive. We're in a 'Weimar situation' at the moment, with Goebbels's propaganda machine gearing up again.//
+++
This is what needs tackling.

Partie / Part 5

LIRE ET ÉCRIRE EN CULTURE NUMÉRIQUE

READING AND WRITING IN A DIGITAL CULTURE

Exploring Literaly Gaps In S. By Doug Dorst And J. J. Abrams

GABRIELLA COLOMBO MACHADO

Abstract

This paper analyses the storyworld of *S.* created by J. J. Abrams and Doug Dorst paying specific attention to the role of the readership in creating and participating in the storyworld of *S.* This storyworld is at once a novel called *Ship of Theseus* written by fictional author Straka in 1949; a set of margin notes written by two readers, Jen and Eric; insert materials that are placed in between the pages; and an online environment. The narrative plot mimics a detective novel in which Jen and Eric try to gather evidence to solve the mystery of Straka's identity, which constructs a subject position of the curious detective that can be then occupied by real readers. By assuming this subject position, readers are invited to interact in the storyworld on the Internet level through multiple websites, character profiles, and blogs that extend the narrative beyond the physical book. Readers can try to solve ciphers and analyze the online content; they can interact with characters, and they can trigger events in the storyworld. As reader-users, they are assuming an active role and helping shape the storyworld in a manner that goes beyond the physical printed book. Thus, the readership gains agency to influence the fictional world of *S.*, making the gap between authorship and readership seem almost nonexistent. Ultimately, *S.* is a non-linear, collaborative, and intertextual narrative that aims to bridge the gap between work and spectatorship, by demanding active participation of its readers-users.

Résumé

Cet article analyse l'univers narratif de *S.* créé par J. J. Abrams et Doug Dorst, en accordant une attention particulière au rôle du lectorat dans la création et la participation au projet. Cet univers est constitué à la fois d'un roman intitulé *Ship of Theseus* de l'auteur fictionnel Straka, paru en 1949, ds notes en marge écrites par deux lecteurs, Jen et Eric, d'encarts placés entre les pages et d'un environnement en ligne. L'intrigue imite celle d'un roman policier : Jen et Eric tentent de rassembler des preuves pour résoudre le mystère de l'identité de Straka, créant ainsi un personnage d'enquêteur curieux auquel nous pouvons nous identifier en tant que lecteurs. En assumant ce rôle, nous, lecteurs, sommes invités à interagir dans l'univers narratif sur l'Internet à travers plusieurs sites web, des profils de personnages et des blogs qui enrichissent le récit au-delà du livre matériel. Nous pouvons déchiffrer et analyser le contenu en ligne; nous pouvons interagir avec des personnages, de même que déclencher des événements dans l'univers narratif. En tant que lecteurs-utilisateurs, nous assumons un rôle actif et participons à la transformation de l'univers narratif en dépassant le livre imprimé. Nous pouvons ainsi influencer l'univers narratif de *S.*, rendant presque inexistant l'écart entre l'auctorialité et le lectorat. Finalement, *S.* est un récit non-linéaire, collaboratif et intertextuel qui vise à combler l'écart entre l'œuvre et son public en demandant la participation de ses lecteurs-utilisateurs.

This paper aims to analyse the storyworld of *S.* created by J. J. Abrams and Doug Dorst. I will pay specific attention to the role of the readership in creating and participating in the storyworld of *S.* In the spirit of the conference, the usual gap between author and reader is constantly challenged and breached in this work. First, if you are not familiar with *S.*, I will offer a brief summary. The storyworld started in 2013 with the release of promotional materials, such as YouTube teaser videos and radio transmissions that hinted at the new project by the duo, which culminated with the publication of a book called *S.* in October of the same year. The storyworld revolves around the fictional figure of V.M. Straka, who was a polemic author in the first half of the twentieth century. The physical book is at once a novel called *Ship of Theseus* (hereafter referred to as *SoT*) written by Straka in 1949; a set of margin notes written by two readers, Jen and Eric; and insert materials that are placed in between the pages.

The term novel does not apply to this specific cultural artifact, but storyworld seems more appropriate. The physical book purchased at a bookshop and called S. is only one of its components, which is expanded on the Internet. For instance, the characters have social media profiles that continue to update the storyworld beyond the publication of the physical book. There are also materials produced exclusively to the Internet, such as the blog Eotvos Wheel about Straka's candidates, and the Radio Straka transmissions. Moreover, as the readership grows, and new materials are added to the Internet, there is a blurring between what is actually fan-made and what is "official" storyworld material. Straka's mystery identity is the underlying motif of the storyworld connecting all the narrative levels. Nothing more is known of him besides the name on the cover of 19 novels that are varied in both styles and themes. If readers want to know Straka's real identity, they have to actively try to solve it.

The readership is a prominent motif in this work, as the two main characters are readers themselves. Jen and Eric are reading *Ship of Theseus*, interpreting it, analyzing it, and looking for clues as to Straka's identity. Moreover, they are highly qualified readers, both are English students, familiar with the historical context of the book, and can understand its intertextual references.[1] They are also capable of contradicting some information that poses as true, for example the Footnotes that Caldeira invents. Furthermore, in case concrete readers do not have all the information

NOTE 1

In the storyworld, *Ship of Theseus* was published in 1949, and Jen and Eric are reading it in 2013.

required to understand the references or historical context, Jen and Eric provide it with their extensive margin notes and analyses. Jen and Eric are quite literally the textual representation of the implied readership of *S.*, presenting a reading guide of the storyworld.

The implied reader is a concept coined by Iser that "can function as a *presumed addressee* to whom the work is directed and whose linguistic codes, ideological norms, and aesthetic ideas must be taken into account if the work is to be understood" (Schmid and Hühn **2014** par. 5). In other words, the implied reader can be understood as the hypothetical reader the concrete author had in mind while writing. As such, this concept is closely related to that of Eco's "model reader," who has the knowledge, experience, and linguistic ability that are leveled to the text expectation of its readership (Sully and Ryan **2010**). Thus, the text contains signs pointing to its implied reader which can be more or less explicit.

Iser's concept of the implied reader was influenced by phenomenology; therefore, it is concerned with the mental act of reading. Gerald Prince explains that Iser's implied author is "both a textual element, an entity deducible from the text, and a meaning-producing mechanism, a set of mental operations involved in sense-making (selecting and organizing information, relating past and present knowledge, anticipating facts and outcomes, constructing and modifying patterns)" (Prince **2011** par. 9). Not only is the implied reader constructed by the text, but it also is also part of the activity of reading by concrete readers. According to Sully, "the implied reader exists in the mind of the reader and is formed in the dynamic point of contact between the singularity of the individual act of reading and the formal indeterminacies of the text" (**2010**). Ultimately, the textual clues of its implied authorship are actualized in the process of reading.

The implied reader constructed by the text, then, offers a subject position to be occupied by the real readers. In the case of *S.*, the subject position presented by Jen and Eric is that of the curious, detective reader. *S.* mimics a classic detective plot, but its central mystery is that of an identity, not a murder. Jen and Eric act as detectives who attempt to reconstruct the hidden story of this fictional author through his fictional work. The detective plot is fascinating because it, "effectively deautomatiz[es] signification and mak[es] things 'strange,' the enigma of the murder endows the everyday world with a rich potentiality of unsuspected things" (Hühn 1987, 455). *S.* works in the same fashion by fabricating the enigma of an author's identity. The fictional works by Straka become endowed with potential clues into his identity. Thus, Straka's fictions are not just books, but potential sites for clues. As detectives, Jen and Eric are required to read the clues correctly in order to solve its mystery. Peter Hühn points out that solving the mystery serves to stabilize all signs into a coherent story, but this also means that "the text has consumed itself" (1987, 459). For this reason, readers usually do not re-read detective stories, since there is nothing else to learn from it. In traditional detective plots, readers are presented with a mystery that is then solved by the detec-tive. The gap between the storyworld and the readers is maintained at a firm distance, since there is no real involvement from the readers into actually solving the case. In contrast, *S.* does not consume itself through reading, because the mystery is not solved, giving readers no sense of closure. If rea-ders want to find a stabilizing reading of *S.*, they will have to perform this role by themselves. Albeit mimicking a traditional detective plot, *S.* withholds the final reveal in favor of engaging its readership and, thus, bridging the gap between authorship and readership.

The subject position created by the incomplete detective plot is set from the start. On the first page, Jen says she read *SoT* as an escape, and Eric answers: "Dear Undergrad Lit Major: If you thought it was an 'escape,' then you weren't reading closely enough. Want to give it another try?" (Hühn 1987, cover page). This sentence creates a set of assumptions for readers: (1) this book is not just entertainment, "escape"; (2) there is something hidden, some mystery; (3) the book demands attention and re-reading. By mirroring Jen and Eric's behavior as close readers and detectives gathering clues, concrete readers are accepting the subject position created by the text, positioning themselves within the storyworld as active readers or users.

By assuming this subject position, readers are also invited to interact in the storyworld on the Internet level. As an example, there are Twitter accounts for both Jen and Eric that extend their conversation to the Web. With Twitter, it is easy to follow, re-tweet, and even ask questions to the characters. One instance is when Twitter user 0bFuSc8[2] tweeted to both Jen and Eric, see Figure 1:

NOTE 2

I take this user to be an actual reader of *S.*, and not another character constructed solely on the Internet level, such as blogger J. W. Dominguez. My reason for believing so is that his Twitter account seems to include a variety of topics outside the storyworld.

Figure 1. Print screen by the author. @0bFuSc8. 2013. "Huh. I thought you two were in Prague, together? What did you make of Chapter 10 FN code #WhoIsStraka." Twitter, November 14, 2013.

This type of interactivity that the subject position constructed by the story-world offers its readership introduces the next topic, that of the users of digital media. According to Marie-Laure Ryan, the most distinctive feature of digital media is its interactivity (**2002**, 581). With such interactivity, we can potentially eliminate the gap between work and readership or allow a more continuous dialogue. She proposes four concepts that form binary pairs to explain the range of interactivity that digital media allows, ranging from being a spectator who navigates through a series of pre-determined events to a participant who can influence the outcome of the story. It is important to understand the level of interactivity promoted by *S.*, since it allows readers to become active detectives like Jen and Eric. Ryan's concepts are: external/internal modes and exploratory/ontological modes (**2002**, 595). They are grouped together in twos, and form four different interaction situations: external-exploratory, external-ontological, internal-exploratory, and internal-ontological.

Internal and external refer to the user's position within the fictional world. The user is in internal mode when s/he is positioned inside the world as an avatar or character that explores the world with a first-person point of view (**2002**, 595). In opposition, in external mode the user is outside the world, as a spectator in a god-like position, controlling or navigating through the world without the first-person perspective. The game *Myst* (1993) is an example of internal position, in which the user is a character trapped in a deserted island and has to search for clues in order to escape. The game *The Sims* (2000) is an example of external position, because the user is outside the world, but commands it in a god-like position.

Exploratory and ontological modes refer to the user's ability to alter the fictional world. In exploratory mode, the user is able to move around, observe, and alter his/her own perspective, however, s/he has no impact on the outcome of the storyworld (2002, 596). By contrast, the ontological mode allows the user to significantly alter and interfere with the outcome of the storyworld (2002, 596). Again, Myst serves as an example of exploratory because the character can only gather clues of the island, but not influence the outcome of it. In contrast, with *The Sims*, the user has total control over its destiny, being in an ontological position.

In the case of the storyworld of *S.*, the user is in a periphery between external and internal modes, as well as in a periphery between exploratory and ontological modes. In the pair external-exploratory mode, the text can be considered as a puzzle, that the user navigates through several clues without altering the outcome, only the order in which each clue is presented. Ryan describes the user in this type of digital narratives as, "external to both the time and the space of the fictional world. Interactivity resides in the freedom to choose routes across a textual space, but this space has nothing to do with the physical space of a narrative setting" (2002, 596). This means that *S.*'s users in this mode can choose to read the physical book in any way they like: *SoT* first, then margin notes, then inserts, or any other logic that users deem fit. However, if users do not engage with the storyworld in any other manner than choosing how to read it, they also do not move into other interactive possibilities. Such an engagement then does not promote a bridging of the literary gap, but keeps each agent in its place: book, reader, and author.

S. has the possibility of interaction at the internal-exploratory mode. Users of internal-exploratory mode are a part of the storyworld, experiencing it in a first-person perspective. According to Ryan, "The user has a seat on the stage; she may even play an active role, such as that of a traveler, an explorer, a historian, or a detective who tries to solve a mystery, but she is not the hero of the action" (2002, 597). Usually, the user is not participating at the time of the events; therefore, this type of interaction promotes narratives of investigation of past events, like the detective plot.

S. as a mystery plot, in which Jen and Eric are trying to discover the true identity of Straka, invites its readers to try to solve the mystery by themselves. This subject position opens the storyworld to the internal-exploratory mode.

Without an avatar or specific character to be impersonated, the reader enters as him/herself in search of answers, which further blurs the distinction between fiction and reality.

The footnote ciphers serve as an example of internal-exploratory interaction. From the first chapter on, Jen notices that the footnotes present some odd details that might lead to clues. She deciphers the Chapter One cipher using the chapter title as clue: first and last letters of the footnotes form a message: "Argosy every 19th 1900 hrs" (Abrams and Dorst **2013**, 27). These ciphers are present in every chapter; Jen and Eric decode almost all of them, with the exception of the Interlude, Chapter Nine, and Chapter Ten. Readers are provided with an Eotvos Wheel among the inserts material, to decipher the tenth cipher. The initial clues are: "Spinning Compass" and "locate" in italics in the first footnote. Then, readers have to note all the real-world locations mentioned in the footnotes of Chapter Ten and find their longitude and latitude, in order to use the Eotvos Wheel and gain a combination of letters. These letters arranged in a grid form the sentence: "I have loved you from the beginning, I will love you to the end." This whole process has to be figured out by the reader, otherwise the sentence remains unknown. There are ciphers still unsolved by users, such as the Interlude and Chapter Nine. The specialized blogs about the storyworld offer explanations on each cipher, providing a shortcut for readers who could not solve it on their own. These blogs also have ongoing discussions on how to solve the remaining ciphers, demonstrating how readers can engage with the storyworld beyond the printed book.

The storyworld also has the possibility of an internal-ontological mode of interaction. The already mentioned example of the user who tweeted to Jen and Eric is an example of this type of interaction. Moreover, there is an enigmatic website, *Who is Straka?*, that presents an image of an S, random blinking rorschach images, and messages. This website is a matter of debate among the users of the storyworld, because there seems to be no indication whether it is real or fan made. Blogger Zort70 posts on *SFiles22* that: "I'm still not sure if the Who Is Straka Website is legitimate, but there are definitely more things to find there" (Zort70 **2013**). When users open the source code of this website, there are comment lines within the code directing users to a "safe" email account and a mysterious, presumably encrypted message, as Figure 2 shows:

Figure 2. Print screen of website's source code made by the author. **https://whoisstraka.com/.**

The ambiguity of whether this web site is fan made or "official" marks the possibility of readers influencing the storyworld from an ontological position with agency to alter its outcome. The anonymous source of this website, as of other materials on the Internet (like the YouTube videos, radio transmissions, and Chapter Ten variations), allows readers to assume the position of authors themselves, creating content to add to the storyworld itself.

By expanding the storyworld to the Internet, S. is positioned in a hypertextual framework, inviting interactivity from readers. Many readers create blogs dedicated exclusively to solving the mystery of the storyworld, like Zort70 with the blog *SFiles22*; Mystimus with *Thoughts on 'S' by J. J. Abrams and Doug Dorst*; and Clare Fish with *Monkeys & Rabbit Holes*. They are positioned in a first-person perspective, exploring the mysteries of Straka not as avatars but as themselves. Their position is clearly inside the storyworld, because they are furthering the storyline by interacting with characters and receiving clues themselves. Moreover, they interfere with the story itself by presenting clues, giving commentary, and posting new "discoveries," i.e., the Chapter Ten variations.

Blog users received other versions of the Chapter Ten anonymously. It began with Doug Dorst tweeting about the discovery of Straka's original ending posted on Jen's tumblr account. Because it was tweeted by Doug Dorst himself, it is considered to be the only guaranteed original version of Chapter Ten (see Figure 3). It is the chapter that Caldeira sent to Eric and Jen when she died, and that is mentioned by Jen and Eric in their notes: "I'm so glad Filomena never opened that envelope" (Abrams and Dorst **2013**, 452).

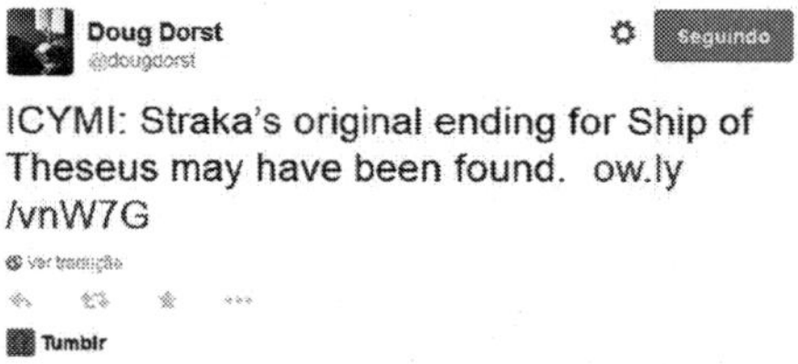

Figure 3. Print screen by the author. @dougdorst. 2014. "ICYMI: Straka's original ending for Ship of Theseus may have been found." Twitter, July 08, 2014.

There are five different versions of this chapter online, including the one mentioned by Doug Dorst himself. A serial number in their headings identifies the alternate versions: "Czech/English Translation For EPH-9993 (00273)" (@jenheyward). From the numbers inside the parenthesis, starting with Jen's official Chapter Ten variation–the others are numbered 00288, 00289, 00290 and 00291–users assume the missing variations will appear in the future. User Mystimus posted on his blog: "On the following pages, an alternate ending to Chapter 10 [sic] in *Ship of Theseus* by V.M. Straka, came to me anonymously–from the same apparent source as the other versions. It appears to replace the text beginning at the bottom of p451 and ending in the middle of p455" (@RadioStraka **2014**). The other bloggers similarly claim to have received their versions anonymously. These online versions inscribe users within the storyworld. Eric points out that there are different Chapter Ten variations on the Internet: "There are a few versions of Ch. 10 out there. A couple are obvious hoaxes" (Abrams and Dorst **2013** XIII). Users receiving these variations circles back to this comment made by Eric that there are hoaxes around in the 'real' world. It positions these variations within the storyworld and the users as active parts of it, expanding the fiction to include these blogs. Users are participating in the online environment by creating blogs that discuss the storyworld, and playing out the role of "filling the internet with hoaxes," as the comment made by Eric in the margins of *SoT* (Abrams and Dorst **2013**).

The final example of user interactivity is Radio Straka that, in their Twitter account, welcomes new followers into *S.*'s storyworld, as in a rite of passage. The figures below show two of these welcoming tweets:

Figure 4.

This welcoming seems to represent the moment these users enter the story-world from an internal perspective, actively interacting withinthestoryworld.RadioStraka is greeting new followers as members of the same group: "sail the waves together," "You may not have been one of us before, but you are now." This represents another insertion of readers into the storyworld, thus within the narrative structure of *S.*, Radio Straka's account also retweets the findings of other users, inscribing the user's efforts to gather clues into the storyworld itself. It legitimates their work as part of the storyworld, ultimately transforming them into collaborators. Thus, the online content of the storyworld composes it as a hypertext in which users have an active participation in an internal-exploratory mode.

To conclude, Jen and Eric create the subject position of the close reader, who is akin to a detective, which can be then actualized by the readers on the Internet. Readers can try to solve ciphers and analyze the online content; they can interact with characters, and they can trigger events in the storyworld. As reader-users, they are assuming an active role and helping shape the storyworld in a manner that goes beyond the physical printed book. Thus, the readership gains agency to influence the fictional world of S., making the gap between authorship and readership seem almost inexistent.

More than reader, but as user, in *S.* one is offered an internal-exploratory character that has to solve ciphers, and analyze online content in order to gain satisfaction from its incomplete detective plot. One can also go further and interact in an internal-ontological mode and add to the mystery, chat with characters, and trigger events in the storyworld. *S.* further problematizes the distinction between fiction and reality by having users enter the storyworld as themselves, with their real-life accounts of social media, without an avatar. As users, they are assuming an active role and helping shape the storyworld in a manner that goes beyond the physical printed book. Ultimately, *S.* is a non-linear, collaborative, and intertextual narrative that aims to bridge the gap between work and spectatorship, by demanding active participation of its readers-users.

@0bFuSc8. 2013. "Huh. I thought you two were in Prague, together? What did you make of Chapter 10 FN code #WhoIsStraka". November 14. In Twitter: https://twitter.com/0bFuSc8/status/400947387297824768

Abrams, J. J., and Doug Dorst. 2013. *S.* New York: Mulholland Books.

Dorst, Doug (@dougdorst). 2014. "ICYMI: Straka's original ending for *Ship of Theseus* may have been found". In Twitter: https://twitter.com/dougdorst/status/486745159036448768

Hühn, Peter. 1987. "The Detective As Reader: Narrativity and Reading Concepts in Detective Fiction". *Modern Fiction Studies* 33 (3):451-66. Link: https://doi.org/10.1353/mfs.0.1310

@jenheyward. 2014. *Tumblr blog.* February 24. Link: https://jenheyward.tumblr.com/post/77754362408

Mystimus. 2014. "Alternate Ending for Chapter 10 of *Ship of Theseus* by V.M. Straka EPH9993 (00291). Thoughts on S. by J. J. Abrams and Doug Dorst". April 9. Link: https://whoisstraka.wordpress.com/2014/04/09/alternate-ending-for-chapter-10-of-ship-of-theseus-by-v-m-straka-eph-9993-00291/

Prince, Gerald. 2011. "Reader". In *The Living Handbook of Narratology*, ed. by Peter Hühn et al. Hamburg: University of Hamburg. Link. Last modified September 25, 2013.

@RadioStraka. 2014. "37 nineteens now sail these waves, together. Uncovering truths, discovering lies, recovering the wisdom of the great V.M. Straka". March 16. In Twitter: https://twitter.com/RadioStraka/status/445128521820946432

@RadioStraka. 2015. "New voices join the chorus @sedogy @kayla_la08 @7synapses @Chiccarocks You may not have been one of us before, but you are now. #whoisstraka". March 16. In Twitter: https://twitter.com/RadioStraka/status/578654056710815744

Ryan, Marie-Laure. 2002. "Beyond Myth and Metaphor: Narrative in Digital Media". *Poetics Today* 23 (4):581-609. Link: https://muse-jhu-edu.proxy3.library.mcgill.ca/

Schmid, Wolf, and Peter Hühn. 2014. "Implied Reader". In *The Living Handbook of Narratology*. Hamburg: University of Hamburg. Link: https://www.lhn.uni-hamburg.de/node/59.html

Sully, Justin, and Michael Ryan. 2010. "Implied Author/Reader". In *The Encyclopedia of Literary and Cultural Theory*. Hoboken, NJ: Wiley-Blackwell.

Zort70. 2013. "Who is Straka update. S.Files 22: Examining the clues in the novel by J. J. Abrams & Doug Dorst". November 23. Link: http://sfiles22.blogspot.com/2013/11/who-is-straka-update.html

From Codex To Code: Computational Poetics And The Emergence of The Self-Reading Text

ANDREW KLOBUCAR

Abstract

So irretrievably connected is the act of reading to works of print that any comparable digital engagement with a text often seems best considered as a unique activity of its own. Whatever we are doing with words viewed via electronic screens, doggedly poking at them with our fingers, moving them about from document to document with a simple double-click, or jumping erratically from one link to another in an ever-growing, highly fluid hypertext, we are not "reading" them.

This paper looks theoretically at the digital text in relation to computational reason, reviewing its recent development as both a new technical object and a disciplinary form, distinct from all prior modes of print. To engage with writing in any digital format, as I will argue, is to partake in a highly complex, multifaceted set of new media relationships derived in part from very specific coding protocols. In addition, key to a more substantial interpretation and assessment of all digital written works is the subsequent revision of many long-serving, traditional reading competencies previously associated with academic writing and the literary arts. The printed word continues to offer modern culture an effective tool for developing a reflexive, dialectical approach to knowledge, using media to interpret and document how we observe the world around us. Digital, computational modes of writing by contrast emphasize a much more immanent technicity and structure in this very same world, relying on coding to assemble, synchronize, and ultimately predict real-time epistemological models for just about any phenomena.

Résumé

L'acte de lecture est si irrémédiablement lié aux œuvres imprimées que tout engagement comparable avec un texte numérique semble souvent, et au mieux, considéré comme une activité unique en son genre. Quoi que nous fassions avec des mots visualisés sur des écrans électroniques, en les tâtant avec nos doigts, en les déplaçant d'un document à l'autre d'un simple double-clic, ou en sautant de façon erratique d'un lien à l'autre dans un hypertexte toujours plus grand et fluide, nous ne les « lisons » pas.

Cet article examine le texte numérique par rapport à la raison computationnelle, en passant en revue son évolution récente en tant que nouvel objet technique et forme disciplinaire, distinct de tous les modes d'impression antérieurs. Écrire en format numérique, comme je le soutiendrai, c'est prendre part à un ensemble complexe de relations médiatiques dérivées, en partie, de protocoles spécifiques pour coder. En outre, la clé d'une interprétation et d'une évaluation plus substantielles des œuvres numériques est la révision de nombreuses compétences de lecture traditionnelles, précédemment associées à l'écriture académique et aux arts littéraires. L'imprimé continue d'offrir à la culture moderne un outil efficace pour développer une approche réflexive et dialectique de la connaissance, en utilisant les médias pour interpréter et documenter la façon dont nous observons le monde qui nous entoure. En revanche, les modes d'écriture numériques mettent l'accent sur une technicité et une structure beaucoup plus performantes, en s'appuyant sur le codage pour assembler, synchroniser et finalement prédire des modèles épistémologiques en temps réel pour à peu près n'importe quel phénomène.

INTRODUCTION

As writing instructors working with students in this digital age, we find ourselves facing a number of critical imperatives regarding reading as an assigned activity, and how it might be changing. Our use of and continued dependence upon print-based methods of comprehension and communication while distributing texts wholly onscreen challenges reading and writing pedagogy in a variety of ways. Even traditional modes of examining assigned texts in the classroom according to different genres of print may be deficient when applied to digital reading environments. Accordingly, this research set out to review the flawed use of print-based methods of comprehension and critical analysis for teaching first-year writing with digital, screen-based documents to be read online, and additionally to ascertain whether and how these methods might be improved.

The project initiated a both qualitative and quantitative study of select NJIT first-year writing classes (approximately 200 students) running in the 2018 spring term to determine possible deficiencies in reading-related exercises assigned in electronic format according to specific learning objectives. The research project pursued two primary lines of study in order to determine a more substantive and analytically accurate understanding of how first-year university students may be responding to information and argument presented in electronic formats. First, basic levels of student reading comprehension and critical engagement with electronic texts at NJIT were determined through in-class group discussion questions followed by individual surveys on one of two pre-assigned PDF articles. Second, the same two articles were subsequently re-assigned (making sure that each participating class received both articles), but this time through computer-assisted text analysis (CATA) software developed specifically to improve reader engagement with online and electronic texts. A second reading comprehension assessment based upon in-class group responses and individual surveys provided a strong comparative analysis of different electronic reading strategies, outlining whether and, if so, how electronically distributed texts may require additional tools and methods to ensure a more comprehensive reading practice. Text analytics, along with critical code studies are growing areas of scholarship in the Humanities, especially when the field is categorically designated as "Digital." In many ways, our research makes use of many of the field's core methodologies, dealing with texts primarily as formal objects in relation to specific media systems, to be considered thus together as technical, interactive social mechanisms.

As past critical work has shown, working with electronic texts in the classroom brings forth an array of interesting challenges, especially when employing traditional methods of argument, rhetorical analysis, and narrative study across multiple academic disciplines. On the one hand, because the current platform-based "web" operates simultaneously as a communication tool and a multimedia production space, it seems reasonable to consider online publication and distribution almost generically as ongoing, active social relationships. The web simply cannot be viewed as a publication format for single, individually read media works as print-based writing much more typically was; whether via cloud-based technologies, or the use of forums, electronic media place both writers and readers in some form of dialogue the minute they log on. At the same time, most web-based writing tools, even when supplemented with social media applications like discussion forums and chat boxes, appear incapable of fully integrating a more formally interactive or collaborative approach to writing and reading into their respective production spaces. The CATA software used in our ongoing studies, for example, the online tools NowComment, CATMA (Computer Aided Textual Markup & Analysis), Voyant, and NVivo, each introduce a variety of different collaborative approaches to critical reading, text mark-up, and annotation. The tools CATMA and NVivo also provide text analytics and visualization devices built into their interface design. The combination of annotation and mark-up features with improved collaborative messaging tools and visualization formats together provided the basis in our study for the ongoing development of new critical reading practices and corresponding sets of writing exercises.

Key to our research was to determine also how such tools and their various interfaces may subsequently provide broader, more theoretical insights into the changing ways we, being increasingly screen-based or even mixed mode readers, approach the text object itself, whether distributed electronically or as a work of print. To these ends, our study continues to make substantial use of historical developments in electronic reading and writing practices, beginning with the emergence of screen-based, hypertext formats and technologies in the early 1960s, proceeding through to their subsequent use in narrative fiction, poetics, and literary theory from the 1970s to the present day. Such advances in electronic literary practices, as numerous critical studies show, exemplify what the critic Espen J. Aarseth first theorized as an "ergodic" paradigm of texts and textuality in terms of how they function as both cultural and technical objects of study. As Aarseth makes plain, "... the 'text' is something more than just marks upon a surface. A reader peruses a string of words, and depending on the reader's subsequent actions, the significance of those words may be changed, if only imperceptibly. The act of re-reading is a crucial example: the second time we read a text, it is different, or so it seems. How can we know the text from the reading?" (1997). Aarseth's interesting separation of the text as a material object from how it operates as a procedural event is helpful here. The descriptive term ergodic derives originally from physics and mathematics, specifically probability theory, where it aligns the random chance of different processes occurring in a single system with the overall number of configurations within that same system. In literary studies, the concept of an ergodic text emphasizes the robust set of choices a reader may have when physically–as well as intellectually–configuring different readings of a particular narrative. As students in our study continued to read, re-read and discuss the assigned texts, a set number of different interpretations emerged, and were subsequently re-distributed as possible arguments for new readers to adopt. The rate of adoption was surprisingly consistent, matching evenly the overall number of possibilities. It often seemed that individual readers were unswervingly reticent to ignore or cast aside one interpretation in favor of another. In this way, computer-assisted text analysis (CATA) applications inspired distinctly collaborative and interactive modes of engaging with different texts, while highlighting, if not redefining, the very practice of reading itself in terms of social networking through specific media interfaces.

These various exercises in text analysis, as remains evident in much follow-up research, provide a host of significant insights into how electronic texts and reading practices continue to evolve in relation–especially in relation to academic reading and writing. Multiple reports with the aim of both determining and assessing some of the more basic facets of computer-assisted text analysis (CATA) for use in first-year composition and any level of literary study in the university are still being assembled from this initial set of observations. Complementing two specific studies presented at the ELO 2018 conference, *Mind the Gap* (Montréal 2018), one looking closely at some of the resulting critical interpretations readers developed using text analysis tools, the other analyzing the tools themselves, this paper offers an overview of various theoretical contexts that usefully situate electronic texts in relation to computational reason and automated analysis. To engage critically and reflexively with writing in any digital format, I argue, is to partake in a highly complex, multifaceted set of new media relationships derived in part from ever-changing, transformative coding protocols. It may subsequently be necessary to revise, if not remove altogether, many of the more traditional reading competencies that defined most academic studies of writing and even the literary arts in order to build functional methodologies for interpreting and assessing digital works delivered by screen. The printed word continues to offer contemporary culture a distinctly effective tool for developing reflexive, dialectical epistemologies, mediating and remediating how we document and organize the world around us. Digital modes of writing, however, bring to us a much more immanent sense of technicity, both in terms of symbolic systems of communication and of actual, technical devices for assembling, synchronizing, and ultimately predicting real-time, material models for just about any phenomena.

Many of the following questions regarding human-to-screen reading practices and modes of interactivity evoke a number of important theoretical perspectives on changing cultural and epistemological relationships to digital textuality. One key premise that continues to inform how we engage with writing in relation to computational devices suggests a very different concept of language itself as a mode of information exchange, especially when compared with the use of past analogue, often print-based media formats. Computational language, in the form of either actual programming or simple AI information requests (using a digital assistant like SIRI or Alexa, or typing in a search engine), provides a very new and currently ill-understood means in the Humanities for engaging semantically with writing systems, never mind interpreting them self-reflectively, critically, and most importantly socially. Digital texts in both theory and practice invite us to consider a wholly revisionary mode of knowledge construction, where combinations of language and programming no longer serve to mediate our social environments, but instead quite literally assemble and generate them according to increasingly refined protocols. When the act of reading, furthermore, appears to originate within the machine itself, it seems possible to describe any texts generated in the process as "self-reading," or even "reader-less," comparable, perhaps, to current parallel initiatives within the auto industry to produce the first "self-driving" cars. When the process of reading is being determined to a large extent as part of the programming, the digital reader, too, can seem simply along for the ride, engaged in an increasingly symbiotic, technically intertwined practice of "using" texts as guided by the devices in hand. Here, the human act of writing, like driving, becomes merely one element in a highly complex, multi-layered, near perpetual exchange of information. And again, distinct from print, the electronic text emerges as a component in an intricate part-symbolic, part-linguistic network of ongoing knowledge construction. To consume language in the digital era, whether by screen, goggles, or some other wearable device, is to participate in an increasingly vast, yet dynamic computational system, while at the same underscoring past analogue reading practices as inherently more political, aesthetically motivated activities.

John Cayley introduces similar concerns in his recent essay "Reading" (**2018**), conferring on both the act and the formal practice of reading specific ontological capacities, much as Jacques Derrida first laid out in his theories of "écriture" (*Writing and Difference*, 1967; *Of Grammatology*, 1967; *Speech and Phenomena*, 1967). Reading for both Derrida and Cayley straight-forwardly brings human language into being–an "ontological burden," Cayley assures us, terms like "reading" and "to read" etymologically "are well positioned to bear... deriving from cognates used to suggest something like the ability to make well-advised, convincing guesses, particularly concerning utterances and other forms of signifying trace" (**2018**). To read is accordingly to read *against* the text, whatever format it may appear in, implying that the reader by definition carries the expertise to interpret, perhaps even understand what exactly is *being* read.

In comparison, computational modes of reading and writing, following our earlier references to technicity, describe what the twentieth century philosopher Gilbert Simondon introduced as a "general phenomenology of machines" (1958). His seminal work in this area, one of only two published projects he completed during his lifetime, *Du mode d'existence des objets techniques* (1958) appeared in English as *On the Mode of Existence of Technical Objects* first in 1980, translated for the University of Western Ontario, and more recently by Cecile Malaspina and John Rogove in 2017 for Univocal Press (now UP Minnesota). Simondon's thesis remains today just as intriguing as it was over half a century ago for rethinking how technology and technical devices in general may actively influence, if not determine, our social and existential relationships to the world around us. A key focus in his project, as his title makes clear, remains the "technical object" or quite literally any material structure characterized by its own concrete coherence. Understanding technical objects was crucial, in his view, to overcoming what he termed the "facile humanism" that continued to support something akin to a false opposition between culture and technics or technology. Culture, he argues, "has two contradictory attitudes toward technical objects: on the one hand, it treats them as pure assemblages of matter, devoid of true signification, and merely presenting a utility. On the other hand, it supposes that these objects are also robots and that they are animated by hostile intentions toward man, or that they represent a permanent danger of aggression and insurrection against him" (17). The technical object presented, in Simondon's view, a much more fundamental, and philosophically coherent way to explore the epistemological and ontological conditions of modern reasoning. In his words, to understand our current "technical reality," and our co-existence together as "technical beings," we must acknowledge an intensely interdependent relationship between entities as objects driven by powerful procedural and material conditions of adaptation and what he defined as concretization. His work influenced many later philosophers of technicity, including René Thom, Bernard Stiegler, Don Idhe, and Bruno Latour, among others, who together describe nothing less than an entirely new "organon" of technologically informed phenomenologies.

Simondon's arguments on technicity and the technical object prove to be especially relevant to these phenomenologies for many of the same reasons they are important here. By providing an ontological understanding of the technical object based upon its mechanical and material conditions, Simondon profoundly challenges western thinking's more traditional concept of object relations, where how we identify things themselves continues to derive metaphysically from a sense of *eidos* or essential form. Technicity, along with any idea of artifice or a "made" object, has historically provoked within this very tradition numerous ongoing enquiries into such a relationship, especially as technical objects advance in both form and utility beyond any pre-assigned material limits. To look again at the concept of driverless cars or reader-less books, if the technical progress of these objects as tools make less and less sense to us in our role as their primary users, then we may on one level be metaphysically limiting their forms and functions according to prescribed constraints or hindrances. Such objects may better be considered as evolving procedurally according to a more complex logic defined in part by their own mechanisms and the contexts in which they are made to function. As Cayley reminds us, "[t]he prehistory, technics, and archive of print culture are presupposed by the reading of text, and it is the contemporary ubiquity of newer technics, exceeding those of print, that have caused us to challenge the much-analyzed traditional concept of reading. If print were not under threat, then it would be far less likely that we should imagine that reading faced any sort of existential crisis" (2018). And indeed, as our own research into the distribution of onscreen, digital texts in the classroom easily verifies, the crises of print and reading are both culturally and technologically intertwined. As the book continues to evolve as a technical object, so, too, must the reading practice, but that does not mean its critical function as a mode of assessment and interpretation need fail. The challenge remains how to integrate "reading" both technically and culturally with computation's increasingly advanced forays into language use.

Text analysis, derived as a process from increasingly sophisticated software programs, shows decisions about both form and content executed to more and more nuanced degrees for the screen. Not only do these programs infer new epistemological models for how we build and distribute knowledge in real-time, they effectively redefine learning itself in relation to both language and technology. Within such models, while linguistically and lexically formulating new information systems about the world and how it appears to function, reading as a critically reflexive mode of assessment continues to be marginalized in favour of more computationally consistent, "distant" reading methods to construct information from statistically dominant linguistic relationships and syntactic procedures. Practices in the humanities, especially with respect to composition and the literary arts, have been slow to adapt, though these changes radically redefine how we ontologically "read" our environment in terms of its linguistic objects and events.

Technicity analyzed to this end (Irrgang 2011) remains, as stated above, a core focus in the phenomenologies of Don Idhe (1998, 2007), and Bruno Latour (1993, 1996, 2005). More recently, referring to Idhe and his post-phenomenology, Peter Paul Verbeek (2005) argues that better technologically informed phenomenological enquiries provide an empirically rich and nuanced image of how material artifacts and technological devices inform how we ourselves linguistically frame our existence and experiences (2005). Verbeek further theorizes this relationship as a mode of technological embodiment, where even grammar can be likened to a kind of extended sense organ improving our phenomenal perception of reality (2005). This embodied technicity pays significant attention to automation and procedure, not as indications of reality's disappearance from our perception (via its technological abstraction), but rather as some of its core attributes. One might compare our use of language in Verbeek's paradigm to a professional dancer interpreting or "reading" his or her physical, sense-driven experience of the world by procedurally constructing a repeatable set of movements within it. Both engagements show how materiality and technicity, taken together, underscore the process of making sense of the world around us, using systematic, possibly self-driven methods in play.

Beyond text analysis and cybertext studies, most histories of the text or textuality itself as a self-reading device tend to begin with the emergence of the first modern lexicographic tools like dictionaries and encyclopedias. In form as much as function, the dictionary continues to emblematize the symbolic use of language as an actual tool or mechanism for organizing, constructing, and even executing information. Of course, such examples of technicity, as Amaranth Borsuk shows in her own recent eponymously titled history, *The Book* (2018), properly informs the very appearance of the book itself as a distinct, cultural and technical object. Here, we can remind ourselves that linguistic procedures like lexical standardization and even syntax itself owe their advent, in part, to the technical shift in writing and reading practices from rolled scrolls to printed pages arranged to be turned from one side to the next. Lexicography, as an early linguistic tool, follows directly from this technological transformation, formally transforming writing into a procedural mode of analysis. The book, itself, functioning as what N. Katherine Hayles terms a "linguistic media device" (2008), culminates in its recent format and mechanism of computer software. If there is a common cultural aim consistently informing this development, Borsuk makes clear, it is to facilitate an equally capable readership able to transition from one mode to the next with as little crisis as possible (220). Such an aim is enabled, she adds, by implementing legacy terms in each subsequent stage of development, while appealing to technical advancement in general as ethically important (223). Comparing Borsuk's history to Simondon's theory of technical objects, we might further understand the book's recent digital transformation in terms of it becoming increasingly concrete. Here, as an important phase in the book's ongoing technical development, the laptop not only signifies the prior device's historical continuity, but speaks to its technical and material improvement simply by "expanding" specific information-oriented and networking capabilities.

Understood as part of this historical development, CATA software, too, both endorses and follows from the book directly in terms of its many active, increasingly refined lexicographic functions. In fact, in many ways, such programs continually underscore the book as less a social or cultural icon than an immanently interactive technical device for generating live lexical analysis. What is particularly valuable for Borsuk is how these developments lead to more than simply better techniques for analyzing and organizing information, but also affect how we build newly data-rich narrative formats. Borsuk notes specifically in her study how digital "authors and artists are using the medium to create immersive cinematic and game-like reading experiences that take advantage of the digital space opened by this technology and demand a more expansive definition of the book... that is markedly spatialized and embodied, and draws us below the screen's surface" (244). In its recent incarnation as a digital platform, the book brings the technical features of language use to the forefront of the document as deliberately as any dictionary or CATA tool, while providing increasingly sophisticated interfaces and modes of writer-reader interactivity.

To work with language procedurally in the digital era is to understand its immense and growing capability as a programming tool. Reading a text on screen can just as immediately evoke multiple executable functions through coded commands as it might inspire a moment or two of self-reflection and critical thought. Our fingers and eyes continue to filter, summon, erase, and explore links, media supplements, marginal discussions, and other forms of remediated analysis. In this way, digital texts in both theory and practice cannot help but invoke entirely new, revisionary modes of knowledge construction, a process that seems to begin with a renewed focus on what it means to "read" a text in relation to a readable text formatted for our technical reality.

Aarseth, Espen. 1997. *Cybertext: Perspectives on Ergodic Literature.* Baltimore : Johns Hopkins University Press.

Abelson, Harold, Gerald Jay Sussman, and Julie Sussman. 1996. *Structure and Interpretation of Computer Programs.* Cambridge, MA : MIT Press.

Borsuk, Amaranth. 2018. *The Book.* Cambridge, MA : MIT Press.

Cayley, John. 2018. "Reading." *Political Concepts: A Critical Lexicon: The Trump Edition* 1 (5). Link.

Derrida, Jacques. 1967. *Of Grammatology.* Translated by Gayatri Chakravorty Spivak. Baltimore : John Hopkins UP.

Gualeni, Stefano. 2015. Virtual Worlds as Philosophical Tools: How to Philosophize with a Digital Hammer. New York : Palgrave Macmillan.

Hayles, Katherine N. 2008. *Electronic Literature: New Horizons for the Literary.* Notre Dame : University of Notre Dame Press.

Idhe, Don. 1998. *Philosophy of Technology: An Introduction.* London, UK : Paragon Press.

Idhe, Don. 2007. *Listening and Voice: Phenomenologies of Sound.* 2nd ed. New York : SUNY Press.

Irrgang, Bernhard. 2011. *Bernhard Irrgang: Critics of Technological Lifeworld: Collection of Philosophical Essays.* Translated by Arun Kumar Tripathi. New York : Peter Lang.

Latour, Bruno. 1993. *We have never been modern.* Translated by Catherine Porter. Cambridge, MA : Harvard UP.

Latour, Bruno. 1996. *Aramis, or the Love of Technology.* Cambridge, MA : Harvard UP.

Latour, Bruno. 2005. *Reassembling the social: an introduction to actor-network-theory.* Oxford; New York : OUP.

Simondon, Gilbert. 2017a. *On the Mode of Existence of Technical Objects.* Minneapolis : Univocal Publishing.

Simondon, Gilbert. 2017b. *On the Mode of Existence of Technical Objects.* Translated by Cecile Malaspina and John Rogove. Minneapolis : Univocal Publishing.

Verbeek, Peter-Paul. 2005. "Artifacts and Attachment: A Post-Script Philosophy of Mediation." In *Inside the Politics of Technology: Agency and Normativity in the Co-production of Technology and Society,* ed. by Hans Harbers, 125–46. Amsterdam : Amsterdam University Press.

ROLANDO RODRÍGUEZ • JESSICA RODRÍGUEZ
ALEJANDRO BRIANZA

Expand Readings: A Visual/Motor Activity Signifiant In Textual Reality

Abstract

This paper is born by the interest in theorizing artistic and educational practices and experiences through the collaborative platform andamio.in. Within this, we have worked with sound, visuals and text as three layers that can be expanded within themselves and through other practices and fields producing performances, installations and fixed-media pieces. We have also developed and implemented educational activities with children, always from the perspective of the informal school: workshops. We try to collide sound, images, and text using both memory and reality, taking into account theoreticians, such as Hans Belting, Marshall McLuhan, Didi Huberman, and writers such as Marcel Proust, Jaime Sabines, Gabriel García Márquez, among others.

Résumé

Cet article est né d'un intérêt pour la théorisation des pratiques et des expériences artistiques et éducatives à travers la plateforme collaborative andamio.in. Dans ce cadre, nous avons travaillé avec le son, le visuel et le texte comme trois strates qui peuvent être déployées en elles-mêmes, comme elles peuvent l'être par d'autres pratiques et domaines, produisant des performances, des installations et des pièces à supports fixes. Nous avons également développé et mis en place des activités éducatives avec des enfants dans la perspective de l'école informelle, fondée sur des ateliers. Nous avons entrepris de réunir le son, les images et le texte en utilisant à la fois la mémoire et la réalité et en tenant compte des travaux de théoriciens comme Hans Belting, Marshall McLuhan, Didi-Huberman, et des écrivains tels que Marcel Proust, Jaime Sabines et Gabriel García Márquez, entre autres.

INTRODUCTION

What is reading? As a transitive verb and strict action, it is to convey the view by the signs that we recognize from our mother tongue, written in a text to understand them and turn them into sounds. The act of reading goes beyond the interpretation of an inherited code. Reading is a cognitive, visual/motor activity that is meaningful to reality. Whatever reality might be.

When we read a text, our thought manages a set of received information that is gradually organized according to its maturity, experience, cognitive processes, intuition, and conceptualization. The order in which it happens does not matter. What is important is the fact that when it is read, the construction and appropriation of both historical and a-historical concepts occur.

Technology, following the proposal of Marshall McLuhan (1988), is an extension of our own body. For that matter, clothing is an extension of our skin. Shoes are an extension of our feet, and written language is an extension of our identity.

One could think of the transitive verb of reading as a natural activity in the human being. Simone de Beauvoir affirms in her novel *Una Muerte muy Dulce (Une mort très douce)* that "there is no natural death; nothing that happens to man is natural, since his mere presence calls the world into question" (Beauvoir 2003, 72). The act of reading implies the development of a technology of reading. It is an artificial action.

You cannot think of reading as a natural act. The expansion of reading happens at the moment in which a common code is constructed that is accepted by a specific society as an element of meaning of identity. Thus, the idea of understanding ourselves as undifferentiated beings of nature is displaced. Code technology makes man more cultured. It subjects him to the understanding of reality. Reading will no longer be the understanding of sound, the use of taste as appropriation and cognition, touch as the experience of unity.

The artificiality that Simone de Beauvoir affirms and the extension proposed by Marshall McLuhan coincide in the code of the written language subject to the truth, to the construction of concepts.

The act of reading is now understood, not as conveying the view on a text that contains an artificial and arbitrary code, but as an act of culturalization and appropriation of an identity discourse. Sound and vision, substantial elements of the primitive, are reduced to the subjection of the text that is read and that is true in itself.

EXPANDED READINGS

Expanded Reading is one of the emerging artistic practices that have the characteristic of using technology to build meaningful experiences, not only from text but also from sound and the visual.

An Expanded Reading can be generated from sound, the visual, or the textual. We will call each layer an element because each one is juxtaposed against the other in the sense that the narrative is respected. There is no interest in involving one layer into another. The idea is thinking of each one arbitrarily. So, at some point within the production, there is the possibility that they collide. What happens in these untimely moments–in space/time–the experience of a phrase, a visual, a sound that connects with the spectator recovering his memory and his social collective memories.

As an emerging practice, it is detached from thinking about the text; which means that the written code is just another layer. It moves towards a narrative construction without a plot, deactivates linearity, and does not operate within the discourse. It is thought from the relation between the triad that, insistently, we try to separate sound, visuals, and text.

An example of this is the sentence from the novel by Gabriel García Márquez, *Cien Años de Soledad* (García-Marquez **2007**). "Things have a life of their own–the gypsy preaches with a harsh accent–it's all a matter of awakening the soul." The affirmation is forceful in the harsh cry of the gypsy who waves it to the wind to spread it between the ears he seeks to penetrate. The enunciation exists in the expansive solitude of the text. It is known. It is all a matter of opening the book and wishing to declaim the first line of the second paragraph of the Colombian writer's novel.

But opening raises its genesis from the sound of enunciation. Thus, affirmation does not exist if there is no one to whom it is useful and useless to say it or unuseful to listen to it. And when you say it and listen to it, both the reader and the listener build the image. On one hand, a life that is, and cannot deny. It exists in the reality of the senses. On the second hand, we have the lightness of the text rhythm. While rough things seem heavy; life itself proclaims awakening, accent, and soul to light actions and nouns, which seem to travel from space/ time in any street. We are not talking about the book, nor even Macondo. A street that might be Vancouver, Reading, Berlin, Buenos, Aires, or Uruapan.

The text is nothing without the enunciation and the construction of the image. Because the human being is an image. But this is not reduced to the primacy of the vision. It is a personal process that is unleashed by activating the text based on sound as the principle of enunciation and the opening of memory files as the memory to build the image.

The reading expands, then. The first line of the second paragraph of García Márquez's novel is no longer a frigid phrase, trapped in the loneliness of its one hundred years. It is pure life that flows. It is useless to recover the sound of rennet, liver, or heart. That admits the construction of an image through a cognitive and historical process where the line of the knowable and the sensitive disappears.

Thus, things such as clepsydra or scaffolding, cornice or hibiscus, caravan or herd, lamppost or gutter, lion or dolphin, score or Turkish bath cohabit in the metropolis of sound, which is the throat from which a scarecrow emerges as a silencer of the torturing sound of an insect which turns off the reverse image that projects a parallelogram. This makes appear, in the middle of the bonfire, the sound which arbitrarily has been acquired by experience, common sense and intuition. The declaration of things, the discovery of the multiple meanings of each sound contained in the images that one learns to exchange with oneself: ("a flaming ribbon," "a dry land," "a happy life," "seed of poppy," "stowage full of avocados," "river that sings," "dog scabies," "bazaar lovers," "the ingenuity of a masterful wind," "the mikrokosmika reality of an empire," "a pirate of courtyard inside," "a train on lines," "drops against loneliness"). Each story of flaming ribbons, dry land, happy lives, poppy seeds, pallets full of avocado, rivers that sing, dog scabs, city lovers, naiveties, maestral winds, mikrokosmika realities of empires, of pirates in the backyard that were part of the pile of enunciations and declarations that were becoming more and more distant senses of the truth of sound and image, and that, at the same time, brought us closer to a truth of the text and the lie of the image and sound. It appears in the reading, the primacy of the written word as exercise of the truth and the primacy of the eye that builds the truth.

But we do not know about the long journey that happened to unravel this truth–if it is true. When the balance within the ear, which is sound, gentle waters that become turbulent, kinesthetic movement that is now a tremor that moves the uncertain floor that sustains us, is agitated, one begins to activate memory, to evoke memories. By then, the flaming ribbons will have already become a newcomer; the dry land in a jackal howl; the happy lives in the abundance of hunting; the poppy seeds in existential poison; the pallets full of avocado in forced labor; the rivers that sing in monuments to modernity; the scabies of the dog in silent hands that tend to close and to be fixed; the city lovers in permanent, silent and immobile conversations; the ingenuities of maestral winds in barely a whisper of understanding; the mikrokosmika realities of empires in workshop rings that manufactured clepsydras; the backyard pirates in adventurers that do not go beyond an owl's cry; the things that have a life of their own in playful dragons from a pirate vase made in china: that roughness is nothing more than a wood sandpaper that softens surfaces; those things are everything and they are nothing; what to preach is a discourse carved in the sand; that awakening causes the disease of uncertainty; that the souls no longer live in purgatory but that they go through the streets digging in garbage containers; and that the accent is just a whisper that does not travel beyond the distance that is allowed.

The reading of the first line of the second paragraph of the novel by García Márquez, *Cien Años de Soledad (One Hundred Years of Solitude)*, has been expanded. It has been activated from the moment it is decided to read it with the silent voice of the sound that belongs to us, and an image has been constructed that provokes the echo of its history, of our history.

THE BODY MOVING TOWARDS EXPANDED READINGS

Hans Belting (2007) states that the body is the place of images. This is where the images are produced/consumed. Memory is the archive of images, and memory is the production of images of the body itself.

Much has been said about the problem of the loss of the body and its importance in the production with the use of current technologies. The truth is that our forms have changed: the way we communicate, produce and consume what surrounds us. We have another relationship with objects, and consequently with images.

The images have also changed. Their traditional sense has ceased to exist by changing the relationship between the body and the image. The body continues to exist from the moment when it produces from its memory, generates images, and expands through them. The images then become living organisms that are constantly changing until the moment that another body receives/consumes them.

The body functions as a generator of individual and collective images. Although in the physical body they die with it and have a defined space / time, the collective memory has its own mechanism. It is handled in spaces / times as those organisms that are transformed with them. Marcel Proust understood the mutable value of memory in his book In Search of Lost Time. In Volume One, *Du côté de chez Swann (Swann's Way)* (1913), he describes how a second before awakening those memories of past rooms were called from the memory archive. All spaces / times exist in the same moment, to return to the body at the moment of awakening, a second later.

LOS DÍAS TERRESTRES, AN EXPANDED READING PERFORMANCE

Los días terrestres is a piece produced by ANDAMIO. The main idea was to read three female poets. The first presentation was in Uruapan, in May 2014. Wislawa Szymborska, Herta Müller and Gabriela Mistral were read. Along with the readings, a second sound layer was added in real-time. A visual layer produced by a light table and pre-recorded/edited videos were mixed in real-time projected onto a wall. The three layers ran out of phase with each other. There were visual silences and pauses in the reading when passing from one text to the next, from poetess to poetess.

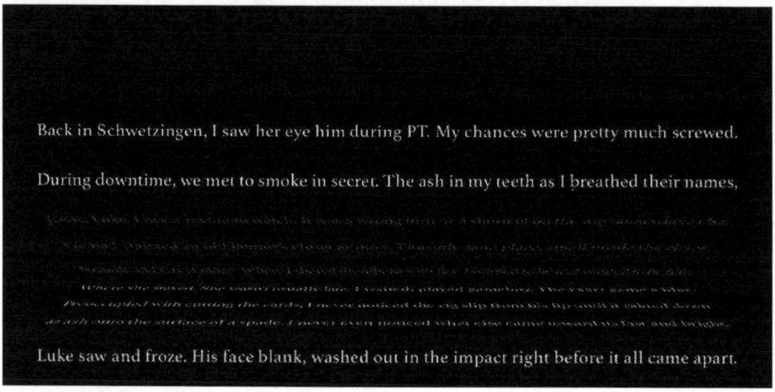

Figure 1. *Los Días terrestres*, performed in Uruapan, Mexico in May 2014

The expanded reading *Los días terrestres* recovered three elements with which it had been working: sound, visual and textual production. From this perspective, the being of the art piece is not static but changes according to the specific space/time in which it is produced. For example, it has been presented a total of four times, and in all of them it has changed; not only in the elements that were used on stage but also in their duration–20 or 45 minutes–in the sound/visual materials, in the way of using the chosen texts.

In the first two presentations–in the cities of Uruapan and Zamora, Mexico–a total of 30 poems were read from the three poets. One was differentiated from the other by a change in the visual material or by changing the projection place. The light table was positioned as an important element from the first stage of the project because it provided the physical objects: keys, buttons, threads, paper and old photographs manipulated in real-time, where the images generated were translated and mixed through the Resolume video software.

Figure 2. *Los Días terrestres*, performed in Uruapan, Mexico in May 2014

As far as sound is concerned, the texts read are rarely modified and are competing with the second sound layer, made in real-time through Max/MSP. At some moments the meaning of the texts is lost to the point where, for the spectator, the sound and the reading become noise. The sound/visual/textual layers become possibilities that co-exist in space/time, generating the experience of emerging narratives without plot, non-linear, without apparent discourse.

The second stage of the piece–*Los días terrestres 2.0*–we worked on the basis of pre-production where we established a score based on time. What do we mean to it? The experience we got from the first stage, the piece demanded segregation in time. It would have an impact on the presentation. We weren't looking to write a script, the idea was to try to make each layer narrative have their own chaotic and congruent moments. So, the spectator would have the possibility of connecting with the text read in last times: at the beginning and at the end of the piece. And the same with the other layers.

Figure 3. *Los Días Terrestres*, performed in Manizales, Colombia at the International Image Festival 2015

Beyond the unexpected events that take place between complex and simple moments, the expanded reading is no longer divided by the three writers. The relationship between images is sharpened when they are interrupted, modified and confronted in the specific space/time of the producer-spectator.

Appropriating the concept of audiovision proposed by Michel Chion (1993), it is understood that visual/sound/textual images do not submit to each other. None of the three layers is the main one, but they coexist to build an experience.

The reading producer was able to choose which texts to read and their order.

The sound producer makes a counterpoint starting from the same recording in real-time of the text read, generating the possibility of recovering the individual / collective memory within the space/time of the performance.

The visual producer plays with the stage space/time, which is one more element to make the sound/textual layers breathe.

CHILDREN LIVE IN IMAGES

When we assert that children live in images, it is because they do not differentiate between reality and fiction. The stage proposed by Piaget (1991) regarding the activity of children to animate, makes everything possible in it. For example, the idea that a thunderous sound can be a witch, an image of a pencil is subject to the flight of an airplane, the words of a text can be light and soft as feathers or severe and solid as a rock.

The experience of expanded readings in children leads us to declare that the differentiation that adults make between the sound/visual/textual triad expressed in it depends on their own academic history that demands coherence, systematization, and a fragmentation of the images that, from experience, they know to be lying.

Figure 4. Workshop in collaboration with Vivelab Bogotá and the University of Bogotá, Colombia 2016

Images, on the other hand, generate a movement towards the playful/ cognitive in children. The images are pedagogical in the historical sense, and at the same time playful in the a-historical sense of the immediacy of the game where everything possible fits into the animation.

A second project, from ANDAMIO, is the work done with children through the piece *Me encanta Dios*, a poem by the Chiapan poet Jaime Sabines. Although the piece takes the title of the poem, it consists of reading a series of writers of short stories and poems for children.

The piece leads us to think of Expanded Reading as an exercise of imagination generated through the text, and the animation built from the sound and the visuals.

The Expanded Reading aims to begin with a dynamic presentation where children recognize each other, generating empathy among them. Then, some exploration dynamics are used with the voice generating different sounds: loud, soft, continuous, or impulsive screams. The body is set in motion and space is explored.

Thanks to a video system reactive to the sound programmed in Resolume, the children use the sounds, the fruit of their own exploration, to apply different processes to a video in real-time, guided by the person who manages the software.

We continue with a brief activity of reading to bring them closer to the texts, dividing the group into teams, and we work with poetry read simultaneously in different ways for each one: slow, fast, singing, from back to front. Thus, a plot of sound/visual images is generated with the texts with which the children usually feel familiar by connecting their memories and individual and collective memory with the reading. This allows the activity to take on a playful character, turning words into bodies with weight, volume, tone, measure, meaning.

Figure 5. Workshop in collaboration with Vivelab Manizales and Banco de la República in Manizales, Colombia 2016

This Expanded Reading experience with children is technically comparable to the production process described above for the piece *Los días terrestres.* Only it adapted the horizon of possibilities that is wider in children. Poems such as *La Luna* and *Me Encanta Dios* by Jaime Sabines, *Las Palabras* by Pablo Neruda and Otoño by Rolando Rodríguez have been used so far, as well as short stories: *Un azul para Marte* by José Saramago, *La luz es como el agua* by Gabriel García Márquez, and *Pirata de patio Adentro* by Rolando Rodríguez.

CONCLUSIONS

Expanded Reading, as an emerging artistic practice, faces the problem of defining its limits and the content of its forms. The idea of characterizing it, instead of defining it, allows us to recognize the horizon of possibilities it has. But it will be the specific characteristics that correspond to the category that will allow, at the moment of producing it and consuming it as an image, to signify it as such, giving it that sense.

The experience of producing Expanded Reading allows us to recover meanings that are minimally used. The fact that the sound is the principle that generates the idea whereby the text expands towards the visual/textual is a process of exploration that returns us to the primitive, to the playful as an experience of cognitive/significant learning.

Where it goes, and what the current state of such artistic practice is, is uncertain. The technological changes are so immediate that only speculation remains as to whether or not Expanded Reading will be consolidated as part of the art system. And such speculation is contradictory, liquid and gaseous.

ACKNOWLEDGMENTS

This investigation was presented at Electronic Literature Organization ELO Montreal 2018.

An initial version of this research titled *Lectura expandida y audiovisión como herramientas de acercamiento*–in Spanishwas published in Espinosa, Susana (compiler). Festival Escalatrónica 2015. Remedios de Escalada: EDUNLA. ISBN 978-987-1987-91-7a.

ANDAMIO is a collaborative platform where producers with different training meet, generating projects at a distance. Andamio works within three lines: production, research and education. All are related not only to the union and breakdown of sound in other disciplines but also in the use of different technologies to produce experiences. To see more information about this project: http://andamio.in/.

Agamben, Giorgio. 2005. *Profanaciones.* Buenos Aires: Adriana Hidalgo.

Barthes, Roland. 1974. *El placer del texto; y Lección Inaugural* (Translation of *Le plaisir du texte* and *Leçon inaugurale*). Mexico City / Buenos Aires: Siglo XXI editors.

Beauvoir, Simone. 2003. *Una muerte muy dulce* (Translation of *Une mort très douce*). Barcelona : EDHASA.

Belting, Hans. 2007. *Antropología de la imagen* (Translation of *Bild-Anthropologie*). Buenos Aires: Katz Editores.

Chion, Michel. 1993. *La audiovisión.* Buenos Aires: Paidós.

García-Marquez, Gabriel. 2007. *Cien Años de Soledad.* Mexico City: Fondo de Cultura Económica.

McLuhan, Marshall. 1988. *El Medio es el Masaje* (Translation of *The Medium is the Massage*). Barcelona: Paidós.

Michaud, Yves. 2007. *El arte en estado gaseoso: Ensayo sobre el triunfo de la estética* (Translation of *L'art à l'état gazeux. Essai sur le triomphe de l'esthétique*). Mexico City: FCE.

Piaget, Jean. 1991. *Seis estudios de Psicología* (Translation of *Six études de psychologie*). Barcelona: Labor.

Proust, Marcel. 1913. *En busca del tiempo perdido.* Vol 1: *Por el camino de Swann* (Translation of *À la recherche du temps perdu.* Vol. 1 : *Du côté de chez Swann*). Mexico City: Sexto Piso.

Vygotsky, Lev. 1995. *Pensamiento y lenguaje* (Translation of **Мышление и речь** *(Thought and Language)*). Barcelona: Paídos.

KYLE BOOTEN

Swarm Reading: "Deformance And Interpretation" At Scale

Abstract

In the spirit of the conference theme of the 2018 gathering of the Electronic Literature Organization ("Attention à la marche!"/"Mind the Gap"), this paper considers the gap between two fields: digital humanities and electronic literature. Can D.H.'s concern with digitally-assisted hermeneutics be brought into conversation with e-lit's aesthetic experimentalism? After considering work in each field that leans toward the other, this paper demonstrates an interpretive technique that occupies the gap between D.H. and e-lit: "swarm reading." Inspired by the concept of "deformative criticism" (Samuels and McGann **1999**), swarm reading consists of two steps: 1) gathering, via crowdsourcing, a number of creative re-writings of a particular text, such as a poem, and 2) using techniques of natural language processing and data visualization to help make sense of these "deformances." Reading with the swarm allows one to read a text against a background of possibilities, glimpsing where the text (or one's own response to it) does or does not deviate from what might be expected. The paper concludes by speculating about the pedagogical usefulness of swarm reading as a technique for social, large-scale interpretative activity.

Résumé

Dans l'esprit du thème du colloque de la Electronic Literature Organization 2018 (« Attention à la marche ! » / « Mind the Gap »), cet article s'intéresse à l'écart entre les humanités numériques et la littérature électronique, en posant plus précisément l'interrogation suivante : est-ce que l'intérêt des humanités numériques pour l'herméneutique assistée par ordinateur peut entrer en dialogue avec les expérimentations esthétiques de la littérature électronique ? Suite à une étude d'œuvres informées par ces deux disciplines, cet article présente une technique interprétative qui comble l'écart entre les humanités numériques et la littérature électronique : la lecture par grappes (*swarm reading*). Inspirée du concept de « critique déformative » (Samuels and McGann **1999**), la « lecture par grappes » comporte deux étapes : 1) la réunion, via la production participative, d'un nombre de réécritures créatives d'un texte, tel qu'un poème et 2) l'usage de techniques de traitement automatique du langage naturel et de visualisation des données, afin de comprendre ces « déformances ». La lecture par grappes permet la lecture d'un texte en fonction de son arrière-plan de possibilités, donnant un aperçu des moments où le texte (et la réponse d'un lecteur) s'écarte de ce qui est attendu. L'article conclut en spéculant sur l'utilité pédagogique de la lecture par grappes en tant que technique pour des activités sociales d'interprétation à grande échelle.

MINDING THE GAP BETWEEN "E-LIT" AND "D.H."

The "digital humanities" and "electronic literature" are deeply intertwined on a material level. Code that generates poetry does not necessarily look much different than code that analyzes it. Both may depend upon similar ways of processing text, similar statistical algorithms, similar libraries (e.g., Python's Natural Language Toolkit), and similar programming tools (e.g., the nearly-ubiquitous Jupyter notebooks). Yet it is also possible to speak in broad terms about their differences. In the form of empirically-minded "distant reading" (Moretti **2013**), digital humanities work is often explicitly hermeneutic in function; it wants to help us understand a collection of texts or perhaps even to test literary hypotheses about these texts. On the other hand, one is not likely to find a statistical test or a "p-value" in a work of electronic literature.

The theme of the Electronic Literature Organization's 2018 meeting was "Mind the Gap!" ("Attention à la marche !"). This paper represents an attempt to mind the gap between e-lit and D.H.–or, rather, a particular gap between digitally-generated texts and what might be thought of as digitally-mediated hermeneutics. It minds this gap first on a theoretical level by locating two concepts that could help to bridge these two fields, *deformative criticism* and *crowdsourcing*. It then offers a technical demonstration of the kind of not-quite-e-lit, not-quite-D.H. work that can happen when these two concepts are deployed in tandem, when crowdsourcing is put to deformative ends.

Why, however, mind this gap? In this age of "digital distraction" and the insinuation of certain corporations' notions of human-computer interaction into all aspects of our lives, both electronic literature and the digital humanities offer different ways of rethinking how computers and human minds could and should work together. What assemblages might appear between the digital humanities' focus on interpretation and understanding and electronic literature's radical experimentations in form? This paper is just one foray into this nebulous gap.

COMPUTATIONAL "DEFORMANCE"

In "Deformance and Interpretation," Lisa Samuels and Jerome McGann (1999) advocate for a hermeneutics based on the practice of "deformance." The deformative critic literally changes aspects of the text, such as by erasing words or classes of words (e.g., everything but the nouns) or intentionally rearranging the order of its lines. According to them, deformative hermeneutic strategies can aid our understanding of a text by breaking through familiarization and "releas[ing]... the poem's possibilities of meaning" (28). As the authors admit, this practice is subjective—or, to be more specific, it consists of material actions that *mobilize* or *catalyze* the subjective reactions of the critic in ways that the un-deformed poem could not.

While pointing to intellectual forbears in this tradition, Samuels and McGann admit that deformance runs counter to mainstream, normative techniques of literary reading. Still, if deformance seems at odds with the positivist strands of today's digital humanities, D.H. has also thought about the relationship between algorithmic processes and deformation. Steven Ramsay (2011) has drawn attention to Estelle Irizarry's algorithmic "tamperings" as exemplars of how computational technology and even natural language processing are particularly well-suited to the goals of deformance. The designers of "Poemage" (McCurdy et al. 2016), an interface for visualizing the sonic patterns in poetic language, note that they were inspired by the concept of deformance (as well as Irizarry's "tamperings" and Ramsay's related concept of "screwmeneutics"). One may also see a similar hermeneutic-but-also-aesthetic impulse in Tanya Clement's (2008) interface designed to visualize the repetitions in Gertrude Stein's *The Making of Americans*. These are only a few representative examples of D.H. work that takes advantage of algorithms' ability not just to "read" texts but also to re-write them.

This work in turn shares certain similarities with key examples of electronic literature, so many of which (including one of its ur-examples, Theo Lütz's [1959] algorithmic remix of lines drawn from Kafka) are in the business of computationally recombining—that is to say, deforming—other literary works. Nick Montfort and Stephanie Strickland's *Sea and Spar Between* (2010) generates and displays on a webpage a sublimely large number of stanzas, recombinations of linguistic shards mined via statistical processes from the prose of Melville and the poetry of Emily Dickinson. Certainly one can appreciate this work as an aesthetic object in its own right, but one could also use it hermeneutically, trying to find new insight into the similarities or differences between the language of the two authors whose words are recombined within it. (This may start with a simple game: can one detect which words are specific to Melville or Dickinson?) Allison Parrish's *Articulations* (2018) invites us to understand (or rather *hear*) anew the Project Gutenberg Poetry it samples and sorts according to phonemic affinities. Listening to this text may lead us to notice otherwise-obscure linguistic as well as sonic patterns that characterize the corpus. Indeed, insofar as this strand of electronic literature makes use of the same techniques of natural language processing used by data scientists, from the most basic tabulation of word frequencies to (in the case of *Articulations*) the novel application of vector-space models of language, it is no surprise that the literary works generated by these techniques possess some kind of family resemblance to more straitlaced examples of the data science of literature. Providing new ways of reading the texts that they deform may not be the chief goal of these works, but it is an important (and perhaps unavoidable) side effect of work that comes into existence by crunching the numbers of some extant text or corpus.

CROWDREADING, CROWDWRITING

Electronic literature is no stranger to harnessing the potential of digitally-connected crowds. Bhatnagar's *Pentametron*, for instance, is perhaps the most famous example of what has become an important sub-genre of computer generated verse that reshapes utterances from social media into literary texts. But by *crowdsourcing* here I mean something more specific: the actual direction of the attention of strangers on the internet toward some task. At present, the standard way of "renting" a crowd is through one of several digital labor markets, the most prominent of which is Amazon's "Mturk" platform. MTurk connects "requesters" (who have labor that needs to be done) with "Turkers" who are ready to perform small tasks for small amounts of money. These tasks are more formally known as "Human Information Tasks" (or "HITs"), a term that implicitly opposes itself to non-human information tasks: Mturk was designed for those small tasks that are (currently) too complicated for computers, yet only just (Thurston quoted in Voyce 2014). A few examples from the Mturk marketplace: extracting information about the price of a car from a website, transcribing 35 seconds of audio data, answering a psychological survey (probably for academics), and describing the "quality" of a bathroom seen in a photo. A note on nomenclature: the term "crowd" is not the most apt descriptor of Mturk, carrying with it connotations of disorganization. "Swarm" is perhaps a more useful term, as it captures the sense that workers on Mturk are in fact highly organized by the computational apparatus, never without a direction. (A murmuration of digital starlings swerves and then alights upon a task.)

Suffice it to say that most tasks on Mturk are neither creative nor literary, yet artists have used what might be called "creative crowdsourcing" as a way of further interrogating the nature of digital crowds and the economic logic that brings them into existence. Nick Thurston's *Of the Subcontract* (2016), for instance, is a book of poems written by Turkers. On a conceptual level, approaching literary production as a process that is amenable to the logic of anonymous digital outsourcing ironically draws attention to the perspectives and poetic inclinations of a class of workers typically figured not as authors or even craftsman but rather as *almost* computers. While at first blush less concerned with the politics of crowdsourcing, Fred Benenson's *Emoji Dick* (2010) explores more deeply ways that labor (including the labor of creativity itself) can be divided into minute tasks and then, through computational methods, recombined into a "result." To create this work, Benenson paid Mturk workers to translate individual lines of Melville's *Moby Dick* into emoji. Other Turkers in turn ranked competing emoji translations for each line, settling on the "best" translation for a line. Lisa Gitelman (2018) observes a similarity between this digital "piecework" and the way that Melville's novel itself was originally typeset line by line by unremembered compositors, a reminder that that "books have always been the results of distributed labor." Still, the genesis of Benenson's book is the result of a different kind of process insofar as the micro-task in question is both explicitly creative (more like writing than layout) and accomplished through the automatic aggregation and cross-comparison of labor. Certainly this must be a work of "deformance," albeit of a more cheeky variety than the kind recommended by Samuels and McGann.

Another artwork, this one non-literary, is worth mentioning here: Lauren McCarthy's *Social Turkers* project. McCarthy created a system to interweave Turkers into everyday social interactions. These Turkers would view a phone-captured live-streaming of McCarthy as she, for instance, went on dates; the Turkers would then interpret the scene and offer suggestions of what to do or say, information that would be communicated to McCarthy via text message. As McCarthy's website for the project asks, "Would unbiased third party monitors be better suited to interpret situations and make decisions for the parties involved?" While the project itself does not definitively answer this question, it does take the thoughts of Turkers seriously in ways that neither Thurston's nor Benenson's respective projects do. *Of the Subcontract* is almost an anthropological document, one that (in Thurston's words) "make[s] conceptually present what the Turkers think poetry can and should be" (quoted in Voyce **2014**). Likewise *Emoji Dick* is at its foundation a jest, an impossible exercise in which the *prima facie* absurdity of translating literature into emojis becomes fused with the the meta-absurdity of Mturk itself, a system designed to direct human intelligence toward any informatic task, no matter how inherently frivolous. McCarthy's experiment may be odd in the sense that it is not typical to pay a stranger via the internet for relationship advice, yet this is where the oddness ends. It is quite reasonable to ask another human for advice on how to live one's life better. The project suggests that people, even those separated by an alienating system of labor, can understand each other (though not necessarily perfectly) and even help each other.

Still, *Emoji Dick* and *Social Turkers* are similar in that they position the crowd itself in the role of interpretation, be it of social interaction or (a fragment of) a novel. Crowdsourcing in this manner bears a resemblance to "digital humanities" in the admittedly broad sense that it uses computation *hermeneutically*. Indeed, a growing body of digital humanities research explores how to use crowdsourcing to gather interpretations of texts (Walsh et al. **2014**) as well as to perform less obviously creative humanities tasks, such as transcribing texts or assigning metadata to them (Terras **2016**). Once again, the distinction between the artistic and the properly scholarly is a subtle one.

Below I describe two small experiments that are at once creative attempts to push the boundaries of crowdsourcing beyond the rote and toward the creative and to use crowdsourcing in ways that are hermeneutically useful. It is the concept of deformance that unites these two goals.

READING WITH THE SWARM

> I am talking about the color white. Please don't try to make me think I have not murdered you in my dreams. He is taking her to a dinner party across the road. An artist tells her about a film he conceived, that is all one color, the color inside a shadow.
>
> Mei-Mei Berssenbrugge, *The Heat Bird* (1983)

Using Mturk, I paid nearly 150 people to produce a deformance of the above excerpt. Unlike the rather open-ended deformances demonstrated by Samuels and McGann, here they were highly constrained. I presented to the Mturk workers the poem exactly as above, only the final word ("shadow") was omitted, replaced by a series of asterisks. I told the Turkers that they needed to fill in the words "in a way that makes sense to [them]."

Canonically, deformance is a small-scale, bespoke reworking of the text. Deformance begs for close-reading to make it intelligible as a single, unified text. But how would I confront the Turkers' deformances in this way? Not only were there too many of them to comfortably close read, the fact that there *were* so many of them posed an epistemic problem: given contradiction between them (given that not all of the Turkers' answers were the same, which of course they were not), how does one read the deformances as a gradient of possibilities? Here "swarm reading" pairs well with computationally-assisted "distant reading," allowing me to see patterns in the answers that otherwise would likely slip past my perception. My intuition was that it would be interesting to focus on the *wrong* answers, to see if there were trends in the ways that Turkers filled in the blank.

A bit of technical detail: *vector-space models* are a common way of computationally representing words or other linguistic elements. Algorithms such as *word2vec* read over a large corpus of text and arrange its words in multidimensional space such that words that appear in similar contexts are close together within this space (Mikolov et al. 2013). Such a model provides a (machine-learning-derived) way of estimating how semantically close or distant two words are, typically calculated as the cosine distance between their vectors. For instance, according to a vector-space model trained on a large amount of news text, the cosine distance between "mouse" and "rat" is 0.46, between "mouse" and "cheese" is 0.15, and "mouse" and "anarchy" is 0.06.[1] For each word in the corpus of Turkers' guesses, I calculated the difference between that word and all other words. I then "clustered" the guesses by plotting the top 3 % of the relationships between the words. In Figure 1, the nodes of the graph are edges; darker nodes have more connections to other nodes and are thus more "central" to the semantic space represented by the graph. Note: this process inherently *filters* the data such that not every one of the Turkers' guesses is visualized, rather only those that are similar to at least one other (distinct) guess. This process of distant, machine reading inflicts a kind of fuzzy democracy upon the data.

NOTE 1

Here and elsewhere in the paper I use Google's pretrained news vectors trained with the word2vec algorithm: **https://code.google.com/archive/p/word2vec/**

Figure 1 reveals two small semantic clusters of closely related words. One of them: *corpse, coffin, shroud, casket,* and *tomb.* Below this cluster, another: *dandelion, lemon, orchid, apple, tomato, peach,* and *walnut.*

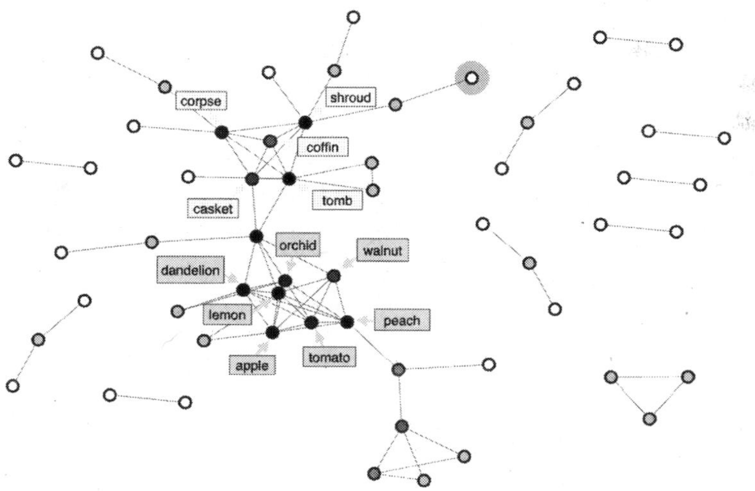

Figure 1. Plot of strongest semantic connections between Turkers' guesses according to vector-spaced model. Correct word ("shadow") circled in red.

When I first generated this visualization, the second cluster struck me as more surprising than the first. After all, the word "murder" is (to me) so shocking, so salient, in Bersenbrugge's poem that it seems natural that, in trying to bring the poem to a state of coherence, the poem would end with a similarly macabre or menacing note. The second cluster, however, puzzled me, and in fact continues to puzzle me. My best guess is that the Turkers, ignoring the specter of violence, have instead taken up the literal, material circumstances reflected by the poem: a dinner party, in which the guests would naturally focus on food. My attention tends to pass over that detail, and so the Turkers' answers draw me to consider the importance of an aspect of the poem that, to me, seems irrelevant.

Both clusters, however, are similar in that they all represent material objects. A coffin and an apple both have an interior, one that can be accessed respectively by lifting it or cutting it open. A *shadow*, however, does not, and so the Turkers' answers direct me to consider the way in which a shadow is and is not a *thing*, an *object*. It draws attention, in other words, to the subtle paradox of this line. Though it uses statistical methods, the point of this particular deformance is not to prove something definitively but to create an interface against which interpretations can be made.

ANOTHER EXAMPLE: *IMITATIO*

The previous example tasked Turkers with "writing" but in a limited and highly constrained sense. Indeed, contributing a single word in some sense represents the zeroth degree of deformance. Such miniscule gestures have the advantage of being easy to compare, especially in a statistical sense. Yet swarms can deform a text more comprehensively.

An example: 50 Turkers were asked to emulate a short poem by James Schuyler, composing a poem from their point of view but, following my instruction, "[mimicking] how the poet uses words." The poem was his "February 13, 1975," one of the *Payne Whitney Poems*:

> Tomorrow is St. Valentine's:
> tomorrow I'll think about
> that. Always nervous, even
> after a good sleep I'd like
> to climb back into. The sun
> shines on yesterday's new

fallen snow and yestereven
it turned the world to pink
and rose and steel blue
buildings. Helene is restless:
leaving soon. And what then
will I do with myself? Some-
one is watching morning
TV. I'm not reduced to that
yet. I wish one could press
snowflakes in a book like flowers.

My question was exactly how the Turkers would go about approaching this task, what linguistic features they would end up imitating. In other words, by tasking the Turkers with emulating this poem, I hoped to get a sense of what aspects of it seemed most important (and least important) in the effort to capture this poem's style.

However, answering this question also demanded in some sense that I isolate what seemed (possibly) salient (to me). Unlike the previous experiment, in which the unit of deformance (the word) was predetermined and easy to compare, this was not the case with the 45[2] valid imitations of Schuyler's poem that I retrieved. In order to statistically compare these imitations, I first had to think about which "features" of the poems I could describe in ways that could be made formal and thus countable. These features were defined and calculated computationally via code written in Python with the Natural Language Toolkit and SpaCy.[3]

NOTE 2

The submissions of Turker who copy-and-pasted Schuyler's poem, repeated it nearly verbatim, or copy-and-pasted another author's work were excluded.

NOTE 3

The Natural Language Toolkit was used for tokenization of words and sentences. Python's regular-expression library was used to find hyphenated enjambments.

How many of the poems began with "tomorrow," as Schuyler's does? A quarter (11 out of 45) did. Six more began with "today." None began with "yesterday," which would represent a more serious deviation from the poem's opening line that describes the future but by way of the present tense.

When I try to recollect this poem, I do not remember that first line, however. I think of the gently melancholic turn at the end: "I wish...." Eleven poems contained the two words "I wish," ten of them placing this phrase in the last sentence or line to directly mirror Schuyler:

I wish I could shower in orange peels.
I wish the world allowed more time for love.

NOTE 4

As is typical in D.H. text analysis, such differences can be analyzed statistically; poems beginning "today" or "tomorrow," for instance, were more frequent than poems containing enjambment-broken words (like "some-/one") according to a chi-squared test, $X^2(1) = 15.01, p < .01$.

In other cases, however, linguistic features that to me are thoroughly Schuyleresque did not seem as salient as I would have guessed. To my eye, slicing the word across the enjamb-ment–"some-/one"–smacks of Schuyler's charming insouciance. Just a few examples of this stylistic tic across his work: "No, they come to my death-/bed" ("The Morning of the Poem"), "when I lived in the coun-/try" ("The Dark Apartment"), and "let us name: dandy-/lion (*pisse-en-lit*)" ("Our Father").[4] Yet only two of the Turkers broke a line in this way. Knowing nothing of the cultural background of the workers, it is perhaps still not surprising that none of them mentioned a "Saint" or "St.," though Schuyler's reference to St. Valentine echoes another line in a poem from the same series ("I speak / back, like St Francis / and the wolf of Gubbio") as well as other poems that evoke his enduring fascination with religion, specifically Catholicism.[5]

NOTE 5

See Moore (1992). Schuyler's uncollected poem "Thanksgiving" (published in *Other Flowers*) refers to no fewer than seven saints.

The point of this exercise is not that one way of imitating a poem is right or wrong; however, certainly one way of doing so may be dramatically more common (i.e., more obvious) than another. Confronted by these quantified imitations, I can locate and question the ways that my own sense of what is characteristic of the poem deviates from a norm. *Why do* I find "some-/one" so charming? Why does Schuyler's religious fascination fascinate me? Inversely, I can see the poem through the eyes of the swarm, paying more attention to features that would normally escape my attention (e.g., that opening "Tomorrow"). This exercise offers yet another technique for interpreting one's interpretations.

SWARM RHETORIC AND A FUTURE OF CROWDSOURCING

Most of us, at present, do not pay strangers on the internet to read or write or rewrite poems (though some of us do pay strangers to drive us or even to pick up our groceries). What is at stake when *reading* becomes entangled with crowdwork as an economic activity? This question is especially pressing in light of the fact that both academic and popular writing on Mturk has painted a mostly baleful picture of the logic of this marketplace. As Trebor Scholz (2017) observes, HITs themselves can be "rote, often repetitive, and potentially exploitative" (23).

Let us step back and describe these experiments in deformative criticism in broad terms. First, I tasked people with *reading* (a small morsel of) literature: I directed their attention to texts–in fact, texts that I admire and think are worth bringing to the attention of others. Next I tasked them with *interpreting* literature (through an act of deformance). What does this sound more like: *work or school*?

Crowdsourcing a swarm of literary deformances is essentially useless from an economic perspective. If it has any use, it would be as something like an *educational* practice. After all, filling in the blanks may seem outré as an interpretive activity, but every student (especially in primary and secondary school) fills in all sorts of blanks with all sorts of language. In fact, the poet W.H. Auden tasked his students with filling in the blanks of poetry as a way of learning about their style and content (Carpenter 2011). Likewise, imitative writing enjoyed a long and prestigious pedagogical history. Within the rhetorical tradition that arose in antiquity, imitating a particular poem or author was "the bridge between one's reading and writing (or speaking)" (Burton n.d.), an invaluable technique within a larger structure of activities that guided the student toward eloquence (Corbett 1971). While I would not go so far as to say that there is nothing to be said for the educational value of translating *Moby Dick* into emoji, clearly the two experiments I demonstrate above are more directly in the ambit of what might be called "Language Arts."

Echoing the typical logic of Mturk, I have kept the workers alienated from the knowledge that they produce. However, it would not be hard to imagine a pedagogical system in which literary crowdsourcing may play just one part. Students in a large "survey" class could themselves produce deformations of part of a poem using the techniques that I have presented here. Participants in the class may then use machine-generated analyses of their deformances as a starting point for interpretation. In the case of a semantic map (Figure 1), one could quite literally locate one's self in relation not only to the original text but to one's peers. Individual students could get a sense of how close they were to the right answer, how close they were to their peers' answers, and to which peers they were closest. Students of a particularly prominent "cluster" of words far from the "correct" word might argue for the reasonableness of the way they filled in the blank. The imitations of those who had been reading other poems by a particular poet all semester might be compared to those by students who are new to his work, helping to isolate what if anything the former students have "internalized" about this author's tendencies. One could locate a practice of collaborative interpretation within the swarm.

Having started out by considering the ways that crowdsourcing may be used to produce textual forms at the boundary of digital humanities and electronic literature, I have arrived at imagining how this art itself may fulfill a social, educative purpose. I do not believe this to be a bait-and-switch or an unfair intrusion of "practical" concerns. After all, digital media are inflicting radical transformations on how we are able to pay attention (Carr 2011; Hayles 2007). Given this reality, the question of how attention is organized, directed, and disrupted is (or should be) a central one for both electronic literature and the digital humanities, just as it has always been for education writ large.

I will conclude by offering, as a kind of philosophical warrant for this position, a perspective advanced by philosopher of media Bernard Stiegler. In brief, Stiegler (2010) worries not just that digital media ruin our attention spans but, on a deeper level, sabotage our ability to become ourselves as we locate ourselves in a social milieu and, in doing so, catalyze our own difference in relation to it (a process he calls "transindividuation," developing a term from Gilbert Simondon). As he argues (Stiegler 2009), reading itself is a paradigmatic tool of transindividuation, since by reading the static text we may sense the way our interpretations differ not only with others' but also with our own as they shift over time. Threatening this transformation are all the ways that computational media, armed with statistical models of our interests and desires, think and pay attention for us and thus "short-circuit" our ability to do so for ourselves (Stiegler 2010, 2018).

For Stiegler, the antidote is not to retreat from digital media but rather to build new computational systems and interfaces that run in the opposite direction, that are "dedicated to the individual and collective interpretation of traces" (2018, 141). Such interfaces would re-present our traces, or the little bits of semiosis that we shed, "with all polysemic and plurivocal thickness of which the hypomnesic trace is capable" (141). I view these experiments in literary crowdsourcing as attempts to think about what such interfaces would look like and how they might make legible this sort of social plurivocality.

Benenson, Fred. 2010. *Emoji Dick.* 2010. Link: **http://www.emojidick.com/.**

Berssenbrugge, Mei-Mei. 1983. *The Heat Bird.* Providence, RI: Burning Deck.

Bhatnagar, Ranjit. 2019. "Pentametron." Accessed April 14, 2019. Link: **https://twitter.com/pentametron.**

Bird, Steven, Ewan Klein, and Edward Loper. 2009. *Natural Language Processing with Python: Analyzing Text with the Natural Language Toolkit.* Sebastopol, CA: O'Reilly.

Burton, Gideon O. n.d. "Silva Rhetoricae." Accessed April 10, 2019. Link: **http://rhetoric.byu.edu/.**

Carpenter, Humphrey. 2011. *W.H. Auden: A Biography.* London: Faber & Faber.

Carr, Nicholas. 2011. *The Shallows: What the Internet is Doing to Our Brains.* New York: WW Norton.

Clement, Tanya E. 2008. "'A Thing not Beginning and not Ending': Using Digital Tools to Distant-Read Gertrude Stein's The Making of Americans." *Literary and Linguistic Computing* 23 (3):361-81.

Corbett, Edward P.J. 1971. "The Theory and Practice of Imitation in Classical Rhetoric." *College Composition and Communication,* 243-50.

Gitelman, Lisa. 2018. "Emoji Dick and the Eponymous Whale, An Essay in Four Parts." Post45. Link: **http://post45.research.yale.edu/2018/07/emoji-dick-and-the-eponymous-whale-an-essay-in-four-parts/.**

Hayles, Katherine N. 2007. "Hyper and Deep Attention: The Generational Divide in Cognitive Modes." *Profession,* n° 1:187-99.

Hoover, David L. 2008. "Text-Alteration as an Interpretive Teaching Strategy: The Case of 'The Snow Man'." *Style* 42 (4):470-85.

Lutz, Theo. 1959. "Stochastische Texte." *Augenblick* 4 (1):3-9.

McCarthy, Lauren. n.d. "Social Turkers: Crowdsourced Dating." Accessed April 10, 2019. Link: **http://socialturkers.com/.**

McCurdy, Nina, Julie Lein, Katharine Coles, and Miriah Meyer. 2016. "Poemage: Visualizing the Sonic Topology of a Poem." *IEEE Transactions on Visualization and Computer Graphics* 22 (1):439-48.

Mikolov, Tomas, Ilya Sutskever, Kai Chen, Greg S. Corrado, and Jeff Dean. 2013. "Distributed Representations of Words and Phrases and their Compositionality." *Advances in Neural Information Processing Systems,* 3111-19.

Montfort, Nick, and Stephanie Strickland. 2010. "Sea and Spar Between." Last modified 2010. Link: **https://nickm.com/montfort_strickland/sea_and_spar_between/.**

Moore, Judith. 1997. "Poet James Schuyler at UCSD: Boxes Full of Heartbreak." *San Diego Reader*, October 2. Accessed May 12, 2020. Link: https://www.sandiegoreader.com/news/1997/oct/02/boxes-full-heartbreak/.

Moretti, Franco. 2013. *Distant Reading*. New York: Verso Books.

Parrish, Allison. 2018. *Articulations*. Denver: Counterpath.

Ramsay, Stephen. 2011. *Reading Machines: Toward an Algorithmic Criticism*. Champaign, IL.: University of Illinois Press.

Samuels, Lisa, and Jerome McGann. 1999. "Deformance and Interpretation." *New Literary History* 30 (1):25-56.

Scholz, Trebor. 2017. *Uberworked and Underpaid: How Workers are Disrupting the Digital Economy*. New York: John Wiley & Sons.

Schuyler, James. 2007. *Selected Poems*. New York: Farrar, Straus; Giroux.

Schuyler, James. 2010. *Other Flowers: Uncollected Poems*. New York: Farrar, Straus; Giroux.

Stiegler, Bernard. 2009. *Technics and Time, 2: Disorientation*. Translated by Stephen Barker. Stanford: Stanford University Press.

Stiegler, Bernard. 2010. *Taking Care of Youth and the Generations*. Translated by Stephen Barker. Stanford: Stanford University Press.

Stiegler, Bernard. 2018. *Automatic Society: The Future of Work*. Translated by Daniel Ross. New York: John Wiley & Sons.

Terras, Melissa. 2016. "Crowdsourcing in the Digital Humanities." In *A New Companion to Digital Humanities*, ed. by Susan Schreibman, Ray Siemens, and John Unworth, 420-39. Hoboken, NJ.: Wiley-Blackwell.

Thurston, Nick. 2016. *Of the Subcontract: Or Principles of Poetic Right*. Toronto: Coach House Books.

Voyce, Stephen. 2014. "Of the Subcontract: An Interview with Nick Thurston." *The Iowa Review* 44 (1):94-108.

Walsh, Brandon, Claire Maiers, Gwen Nally, Jeremy Boggs, and Praxis Program Team. 2014. "Crowdsourcing Individual Interpretations: Between Microtasking and Macrotasking." *Literary and Linguistic Computing* 29 (3):379-86.

Secret Sharing, A Pedagogical Tool For E-Lit Practices

AUGUSTO VINICIUS MARQUET

Abstract

This article aims to provide a practical framework for the design and organization of workshops, based on the proceedings of the *Cuéntanos un secreto (Tell us a secret)* project. I focus on the activation of the sociocultural exchange of experiences; I provide two samples of pedagogical material used during the workshop taken from the works of Ulises Carrión's and Augusto de Campos; lastly, I inquire about the workshop as a creative and collaborative tool for community building looking towards the future of society.

Résumé

L'objectif de cet article est de proposer un cadre pratique pour le design et l'organisation d'ateliers basé sur les événements du projet *Cuéntanos un secreto (Raconte-nous un secret).* L'article porte essentiellement sur l'activation de l'échange socioculturel des expériences; je donne deux exemples de matériel pédagogique utilisés lors de l'atelier provenant de l'œuvre d'Ulises Carrión et Augusto de Campos; je pose des questions au sujet de l'atelier comme un outil créatif et collaboratif pour le renforcement communautaire avec une vue sur l'avenir de la société.

CUÉNTANOS UN SECRETO

"I'll be your mirror"
Nico & The Velvet Underground (1967)

Cuéntanos un secreto (*Tell us a secret*, from here onwards referred to as "*CS*") is a secret-sharing project between communities that takes place during a visual communication workshop. The workshop explores visual depictions in the form of images, animations, videos, and electronic objects that illustrate textual stories shaped as secrets. As a result, the project hosts an extensive archive of popular storytelling composed of textual and graphic elements. For the purposes of the project, both the original text and its depictions are considered *a secret* (Fig. 1). In that sense, the CS project is a tool for self-exploration and expression.

Figure 1. Vinicius Marquet, *Secret composition*, 2019, digital vectors; Personal collection.

The project was born in 2012, when I coordinated a graphic design workshop at Faro de Oriente[1] in Mexico City. Since then, its main objective has been to link communities by asking them to share their secrets within a visual communication workshop. At the end of each workshop, participants are invited to donate their hidden experiences by anonymously writing them down on a sheet of paper. All secrets are enclosed into an envelope. These are collected in our "bag of secrets." In a later instance of the workshop–which takes place in a different sociocultural context–participants randomly pick one secret from the bag and create a representation of it. As such, a connection is initiated between strangers, and the tension between source and reflection represents a dialogue between different communities and contexts.

NOTE 1

Fábrica de Artes y Oficios Oriente is a cultural center located at the edge of the city in the municipality of Iztapalapa. It aims to provide education and culture for some of the most marginalized populations in Mexico City. It is a fantastic place to experiment with education, workshops and open culture.

The *CS* project, rather than being a final cultural product, is conceived as a process and a playful place to experiment with visuality. As the project developed, our archive expanded too. Therefore, it became necessary to preserve and distribute the secrets using diverse methods and techniques: printing small publications–such as posters, flyers, invitations and digital zines–and organizing small exhibitions and presentations about the *CS* project. (Fig. 2)

Figure 2. Marquet. *Exhibition La Trampa Grafica, fanzine making and digital edition*, 2013, Photography. Personal collection.

Until now, we have worked with communities such as internet users, members of the army, young scholars, student nurses, art schools, imprisoned women, retirees, and gallery visitors. The project mostly holds secrets in Spanish from people living in Mexico City, but the collection has expanded and currently contains secrets from people from Baltimore (MD), Camden (NJ), New York City (NY)[2] Genk (BE), London (UK) and cybernauts from cuentanosunsecreto.com. The project also contains a few samples from the Netherlands in several languages such as English, Italian, Dutch, Turkish, Portuguese, and Korean.[3]

The project has three main goals:

NOTE 2

These secrets are from *Variable Piece 4: Secrets* (Huebler, 1973) and were used as the source of the English secret collection during the *CS* workshop "Software re-cover" (Marquet, 2018) at Kingston University in London.

NOTE 3

This collection was part of a language installation entitled *De encryptor* (Marquet, 2016) during the "101 FORMATTING MEMORY International Media Poetry Festival" at the University of St Petersburg, Russia.

- □ To explore visual communication through narratives applied in diverse visual manifestations.
- □ To build communities by exchanging anonymous hidden experiences.
- □ To preserve and distribute popular storytelling in the shape of secrets.

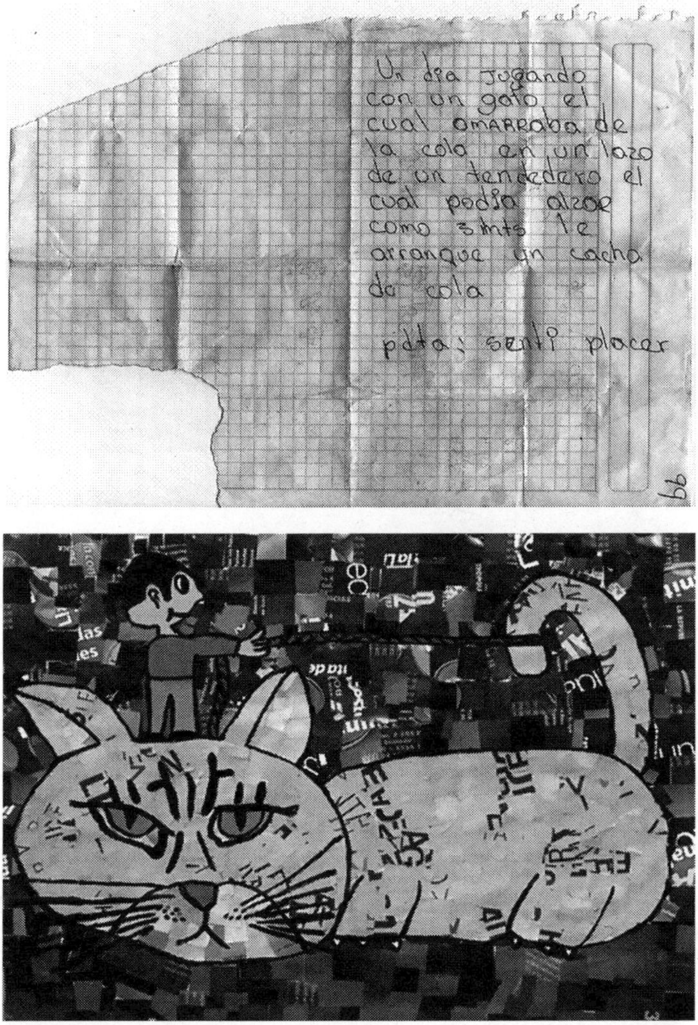

Un dia jugando
con un gato el
cual amarraba de
la cola en un lazo
de un tendedero el
cual podia alzar
como 3 mts le
arranque un cacho
de cola

pdta: senti placer

99

Figure 3. *Secreto de un gato*, 2012, Mixed media; *Cuéntanos un secreto* collection. ("Cat's secret": 'One day while playing with the cat whose tail used to tie the clothesline and which I could drop as far as 5 meters, I took a chunk of his tail off. PS: I felt pleasure.'). The reversal of proportions between the cat and the figure in the illustration gives a good indication of the self-representation of the author of the secret.

As an introduction to the visual communication workshop, we usually explore visuality through drawing. These visual exercises are based on Betty Edwards's art practice theories, from her book *Drawing on the Right Side of the Brain* (1979). Other exercises emanate from readings about elemental concepts of design and visual communication by iconic designers such as Bruno Munari or Wucious Wong. Depending on the subject, we also analyze specific readings, like Jose Lúis Brea's essay "Cultura Ram" (2007), The *New Art of Making Books* (Carrión 1975), among others.

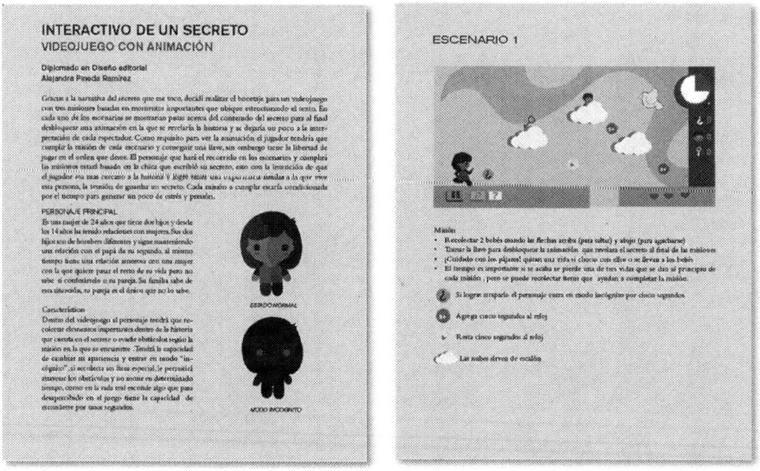

Figure 4. *Video game concept and characters*, 2016, Digital, Mixed Media; *Cuéntanos un secreto* collection.

As the previous figures suggest, we have used the depictions of secrets to explore a large array of objects and activities in diverse communities: from five-year old children, to imprisoned women. Each community is contextualized by its own needs and characteristics. Therefore the workshop seeks to adapt and develop content depending on the community's needs and characteristics.

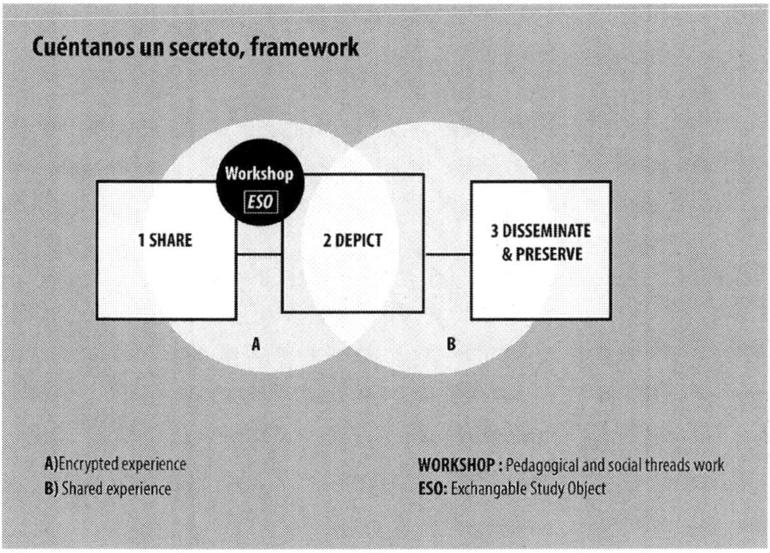

Figure 5. *Diagram of cuéntanos un secreto project*, 2019, digital vectors; Personal collection.

For the framework of the project (Fig. 5), this flexible feature of the study is named *ESO, Exchangeable Study Object*. This allows the project to be continually open to the visual communication needs of the community. Apart from the community norms, throughout the workshop there are only two game rules that determine the social dynamics of the workshop.

The first rule is "You don't choose the secret. The secret has chosen you." This rule implies that the secret is trying to tell the participant something that they need to be enlightened about; they must pay attention to what the blank spaces between letters say. How do they perceive the way in which the author is writing the story? Who do they think is this anonymous author? Where do they think the author lives? What do they think is the author's gender? How old do they think the author is? How do they think the author feels? Do they have similar experiences in their experience repertoire? The secret has chosen the participant in order to be listened to, depicted and turned into a new representation. Since the secret has chosen them, they need to respect the original narrative and finish its depiction before they open a new secret.

The second rule is "All secrets and their depictions are anonymous." At the end of the workshop, we ask participants to voluntarily donate an anonymous secret of their own in order to continue with the workflow. This anonymous feature seeks to preserve the originality of the secret and the ownership of the collection. In consequence, we have decided that this project is authored by *Nosotros* (Us). The archive of the CS project belongs to *Nadie* (Nobody).

The role of the facilitator is to safeguard and administrate the secrets. We are also responsible for organizing the CS workshops, which entails translating artistic-experimental language into institutional language, or code switching,[4] and developing each workshop session with the relevant pedagogical material.

NOTE 4

Term developed by artist and academic Sandy Stone, who will be reviewed later in this article.

Under ideal circumstances we use the first few days as a prelude before the secret distribution occurs. During those days we perform a number of exercises to bring the participants to a visual mindset, review concepts of design and visual communication and check basic knowledge about the materiality of each medium. The materiality of the medium depends on *ESO*. For example, for explaining electronic literature to bachelor designers or artists, the *New Art of Making Books* by Ulises Carrión (**1975**) and Augusto de Campos' "Concrete Poetry: A Manifesto" (**1956**) provide a clear, simple and valuable introductory reading.

Both Carrión and de Campos are fundamental artists and thinkers who have questioned written language and its dissemination since the early 1960s, and whose artwork has had a symbiotic relationship with their written material; it is easy to link their theories and practices. As a designer, I think their examples seem like paper prototypes of more complex pieces that are currently created on digital media.[5]

NOTE 5

Read more about using Ulises Carrión and Augusto de Campos as example in "Textualities based on practices" (**https://viniciusmarquet.com/2020/07/28textualities-based-on-practices/**).

CS proceeds according to three basic steps, as described below:

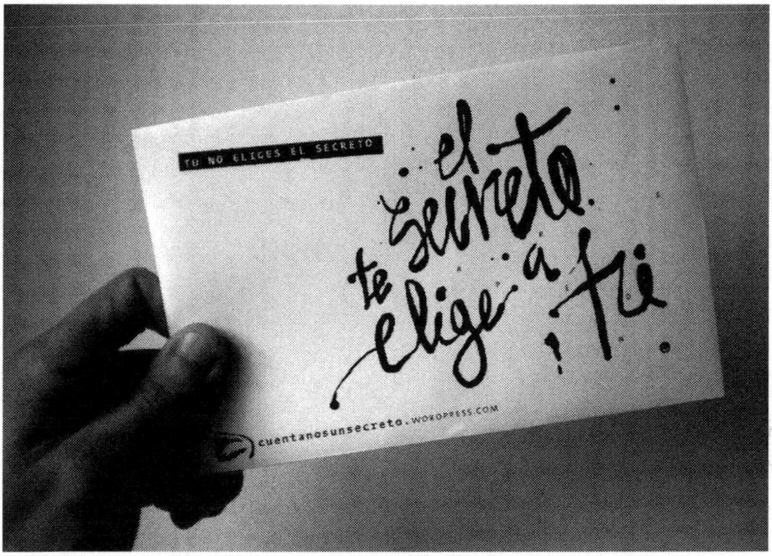

Figure 6. Marquet, Vinicius. Prints. *Special edition with the legend " You don't choose the secret the secret has chosen you,"* 2013, Photography; Personal collection.

1. Sharing

All the secrets are enclosed into envelopes and distributed randomly between participants. The collection is organized by communities (for example, "Genk, Belgium, 2019," or "Cyber community, Submitted on 2013/02/09 at 15:40"). Randomness and selectivity are substantial features of the experience in addition to the first rule of the experience (Fig. 6).

It is prudent to not share envelopes coming from the same group of people, unless participants agree to share their secrets amongst each other. Also, it is recommended to ask participants to take a picture of the secret as soon as possible, so that they can always go back to read it without exposing the original material to unknown circumstances. A picture is a safeguard at any moment. Please consider keeping the original source safely.

2. Depicting

Participants open their envelope and read the secret. First, we ask participants to do this in silence by themselves. Later, we discuss in group by inviting participants to read the secrets aloud. What is their first impression of the story? How do they feel about it? Later, the other participants are welcome to give their own opinions, reflections and questions. At this point it becomes very important to avoid setting any absolute statement or prejudice. Instead, participants are invited to question and open doubts about the secret story and first impression of the reader. As facilitators, we aim to provoke empathy: besides anything this life story deserves respect, it could be yours.

Based on this group activity, we invite the secret readers to reflect deeper on their secret and give their own interpretation by making a first draft. At this moment, it is important to remark to participants about the materiality of *ESO*. How can I translate my experience to the medium used during the workshop? For instance, how can I make a paper prototype of an augmented reality journey? Then I would recommend the participants analyze Ulises Carrión performance *Love Story* (1984) (http://www.li-ma.nl/site/catalogue/art/ulises-carrin/love-story/533) to give them a user experience example. This is an organized sight-seeing tour in the Dutch city of Arnhem and the surrounding countryside. Those on the tour progress along the narrative nodes, from point "a" to "b," and so on. This would be a similar experience in most of the AR experiences that involve journeys, such as *34th North 118 West* (2003) by Knowlton, Spellman and Hight, or *Pilgrim* (2018) by Hutchinson and Unseld.

3. Disseminating and preserving

The source is ready and finished when it is enclosed in an envelope by the author and shared with the facilitator. It will later be opened by a new participant in another other community. Both the source and the depiction will form part of the *Cuéntanos un secreto* archive. The workshop ends when the secret is published on cuentanosunsecreto.com or on any other public platform. Sharing is the strategy to preserve the collection. Placing the collection of secrets in the public space is an essential part of the project. (Fig. 7)

Figure 7. Secrets encapsulated in QR codes, 2012, Stickers; *Cuéntanos un secreto* collection.

Difficulties could arise if participants do not end the depiction on time. In some communities there is a possibility to maintain communication. Surely, this is an extracurricular agreement with participants, and they should agree on that. If that is not the case, I recommend enclosing the secret into an envelope and returning it back to the secret bag.

Based on the *CS* procedures and guidelines, each workshop is a symbolic performance that can be reproduced many times, in different contexts and by different facilitators. We hope that this paper might aid other scholars and artists in considering this framework as an invitation to join and recreate the *CS* project in their own community. All literary works previously mentioned are available through open access on the *Cuéntanos un secreto* website and we are happy to share credentials to publish your community secrets.

Figure 8. Nosotros. "Los discretos (The discrete ones)." Screenshot. Link: **http://hey.viniciusmarquet.com/los_discretos/index.html**

THE WORKSHOP AS A CREATIVE AND COLLABORATIVE EDUCATIONAL TOOL

> *"Ya lo dijo Freud no me acuerdo en que lado*
> *Solo la experiencia que he experimentado."*
> [Freud has said it before, I don't remember exactly where,
> It is just about the experience that I have experienced.]
> "Estación del Metro Balderas"
> Rockdrigo Gónzales (1984)

In *The Great Didactic*, the philosopher and pedagogue Comenious appeals to our senses as the bastions for modern teaching. He says:

> Everything should, as far as possible, be placed before the senses. Everything visible should be brought before the organ of sight, everything audible before that of hearing. Odours should be placed before the sense of smell, and things that are testable and tangible before the sense of taste and touch, respectively. (Comenius 1896, 336–37)

Comenius does not merely propose a sensual approach to reality. In fact, from a materialistic perspective, he considers it our only way to communicate with reality. How can we learn if we are not connected with our environment or with others? How can we teach if we do not experience the materiality of our objects of study?

So far, practice has been one of the oldest and most effective ways of learning and teaching. For example, looking at my nephew Mateo,a gorgeous six-month-old baby, I can easily see how tasting, making and imitating is the oldest pedagogic method. It is probably the most natural and primal way to experience the vast outside world. In this moment of his short life, everything is edible and his mouth is constantly looking for a new experience. Maybe, given his short memory, everything is still just a big breast for him.

I would like to discuss the workshop under this umbrella of experiencing and making the learning process more sensorial.

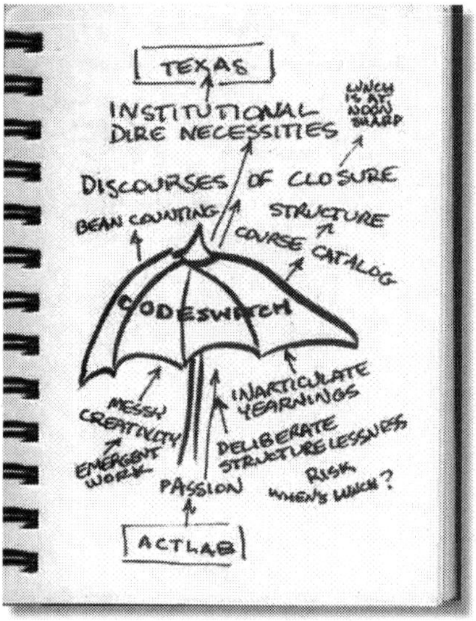

Figure 9. Stone, Sandy. Code switching diagram, 2005, digital; Link: **https://sandystone.com/radar.shtml**

In June, 2018, I attended a delightful lecture called "Against 'Lab' as Free-Floating Signifier..." by Lori Emerson (**2018**). Since 2009, Emerson directs one of the most emblematic media labs, MAL (Media Archaeology Lab) at Boulder University in Colorado. She and other international academics from different colleges are researching media labs with the intention of publishing a book titled *The Lab Book*. Her talk inspired in me a couple of thoughts regarding this tendency to call everything a "Lab," and it also introduced me to the "ActLab concept."

This image depicted in figure 9, summarizes the philosophy of the ActLab in UT Austin, Texas. The lab was directed by the artist and academic Sandy Stone, who was founder of the Lab and ran it from 1993 until 2010. The image illustrates the term "codeswitching" (Fig. 9). In her own words:

> The codeswitching umbrella translates experimental, Trans-ish language into blackboxed, institutional language. Thus when people below the umbrella engage in deliberately non-teleological activities, what people above the umbrella see is organized, ordered work. When people below the umbrella produce messy, inarticulate emergent work, people above the umbrella see tame, recognizable, salable projects. When people below the umbrella experience passion, people above the umbrella see structure. (Stone 2005)

This connects very closely to my own experience with the *Cuéntanos un secreto* workshop, especially during its most prolific years at Faro de Oriente in Mexico City. Regardless of the lack of resources, grades or even paper certifications for the workshop participants, they were always tremendously eager and were very willing to learn, share and produce. Therefore, I generated this new image in an attempt to illustrate some of their sociocultural particularities (Fig.11).

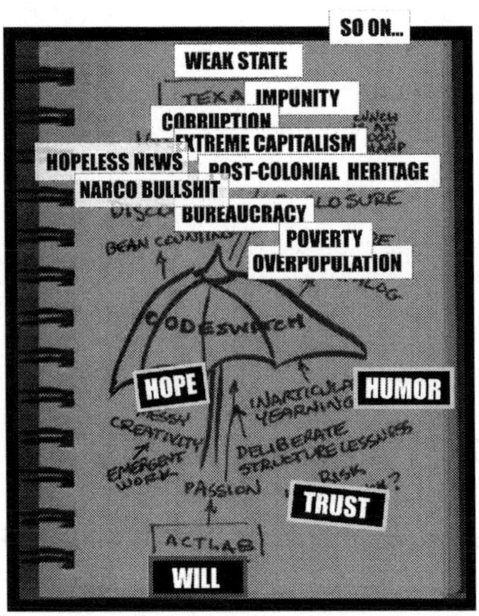

Figure 10. Marquet. *Mexican Code switching diagram interpretation*, 2019, digital; Personal collection.

In essence, the underlying idea remains the same: the work of the "umbrella," "lab" or "workshop" is to create a neutral and open space for experimentation and practice by translating this "experimentation" into administrative and institutional words. This implies neutralizing the workshop space from the outside world, allowing the students to study, keeping them safe from crime, cartels, weapons, drugs, but also distract their minds from daily problems such as money loans, budgets and a huge list of objects and stories from the outside reality. It is very important to refrain as much as possible from being a paternalistic space. But here is where imagination needs to happen.

Nowadays, I consider the workshop as the golden bastion of the *CS* project, because it is during the workshop that we build a community and we establish trust based on daily experiences. As a workshop facilitator, I ask myself: how can I provide meaningful experiences if there is no trust? How dare I ask for the participants' trust if I don't offer them a humane experience? How could we forget that the learning process is based on the experience with the other? Without otherness we might be, like Dr. Frankenstein's creature, a being that exists but that lives in terrible solitude. How would one exist if there is nobody to talk or share knowledge with?

Therefore, our learning process is based on sharing experiences with the other and, therefore, building community: "We are Nosotros." The workshop and the lab are places to build a community by creating knowledge. They operate as umbrellas that provide a free and neutral space to experiment with knowledge. They are, essentially, places to play.

My second concern was looking for differences between labs and workshops, or ateliers.[6] Nowadays there exists a predominantly "scientific" validation of reality that gives way to the fashionable and marketable idea of calling everything a lab. But not everything is science and science is not everything; for instance, there are legends, myths, stories, literature and art manifestos. Those are not sciences, yet they provide a tremendous heritage for human knowledge.

Nevertheless, when we look at the history of the workshop, we observe that it has always reflected a substantial element of society, from Medieval times to the beginning of the Industrial Revolution. The atelier was not only a place where knowledge and work were created and distributed, but it was also the community building-place for society.

Looking into the future, in this transitional historical context where technology and science are shaping our society rapidly, I wonder what the difference between a workshop, a lab, a makerspace and a hackerspace are. How will these educational places shape our society? How can we turn those online experiences sensorial for participants? And how will they transform themselves? What kind of society do we want to build?

NOTE 6

Please consider that, besides *ateliers* and *workshops* sharing the same meaning with different linguistic origins, French and English, they have evolved differently as a consequence of the English hegemonic culture. While workshops have covered all kinds of human knowledge, ateliers are attached to places for craft, arts and food gourmet concepts. They are more hand-made knowledge places. This would deserve a deeper epistemological research comparing with *labs* as well, by instance.

Brea, José Luis. 2007. *Cultura Ram.* Barcelona: Gedisa.

Campos, Augusto. 1956. "Concrete Poetry: A Manifesto". Translated by John Tolman. 1956. Accessed August 14, 2020.
Link: http://www.ubu.com/papers/noigandres01.html

Carrión, Ulises. 1975. "The New Art of Making Books". In *Ulises Carrión: We Have Won! Haven't We?*, edited by Guy Schraenen. Amsterdam: Museum Fordor.

Carrión, Ulises. 1984. *Love Story.* LIMA. Accessed April 14, 2019. Video, 23'40".
Link: http://www.li-ma.nl/site/catalogue/art/ulises-carrin/love-story/533

Comenius, John Amos. 1896. *The Great Didactic.* London: A & C Black. Accessed May 1, 2019.
Link: https://ia600502.us.archive.org/31/items/greatdidacticofj00come/greatdidacticofj00come.pdf

"Cuéntanos Un Secreto". 2012. Accessed May 1, 2019. Link: http://cuentanosunsecreto.com

Edwards, Betty. 1979. *Drawing on the Right Side of the Brain.* Los Angeles; New York: J. P. Tarcher.

Emerson, Lori. 2018. "Against 'Lab' as Free-Floating Signifier: From Appropriation to Counter-Cooptation and Codeswitching". Presentation in Digital Humanities 18 "Puentes/Bridges." June 24-30. Mexico City: ADHO.

Gónzalez, Rockdrigo. 1984. "Estación Del Metro Balderas". In *Hubanistorias. Self-Made Record.*

Huebler, Douglas. 2016. *Variable Piece 4: Secrets.* New York: Printed Matter Inc.

Hutchinson, Lauren Aurora, and S. Unseld. 2018. *Pilgrim, Geolocative Narrative Experience.* Amsterdam: International Documentary Film Festival Amsterdam. April 11, 2019.

Knowlton, Jeff, Naomi Spellman, and Jeremy Hight. 2003. *34th North 118 West.* Artwork, Digital Narrative Experience. Accessed April 11, 2019.
Link: http://34n118w.net

Marquet, Vinicius. 2016. *De Encryptor.* 101 media poetry, Collective exhibition. Saint Petersburg.

Marquet, Vinicius. 2018. "Software Re-Cover: Tell Us a Secret Project". *Guest Lecture and Workshop in Kingston University.* Kingston School of Arts, London UK.

Nosotros. 2012. "Los Discretos (the Discrete Ones)". In *Cuéntanos Un Secreto Collection.* Mexico City. Accessed May 1, 2019.
Link: http://hey.viniciusmarquet.com/los_discretos/index.html

Stone, Sandy. 2005. "On Being Trans and Under the Radar: Tales from the Actlab. Sandy Stone Website". Accessed April 4, 2019.
Link: https://sandystone.com/radar.shtml

MARÍA GOICOECHEA DE JORGE

Elite-CM Project:

Developing Enriching Interactivity In Children's Digitized Literature And E-Lit

Abstract

This paper presents some of the products and experiences carried out as part of the eLITE-CM research project on Electronic Literary Publishing, in particular those aimed at addressing some of the concerns regarding the future of reading education in the face of the increasing use of interactive screen media by children. It discusses the product design and reading experiments carried out with children aged 7-11 with two interactive works: an enriched digitized edition of an old children story ("Plaga de dragones"/ "A Plague of Dragons") and a piece of interactive fiction ("El Cambiazo" / "Switcheroo"). We explored how each textual modality required different strategies to produce engaging forms of interactivity.

Résumé

Cet article présente certains des produits et des expériences réalisées dans le cadre du projet de recherche du eLITE-CM sur l'édition littéraire électronique. Ce projet visait notamment à apaiser les inquiétudes sur l'avenir de l'enseignement de la lecture, face à l'augmentation de l'usage des médias interactifs par les enfants. Nous y discutons des enjeux de conception et des expériences de lecture réalisées avec des enfants âgés de 7 à 11 ans à partir de deux œuvres interactives : une édition numérique enrichie d'un ancien récit pour enfant (« Plaga de dragones » / « Invasion de dragons ») et une œuvre fictive interactive (« El Cambiazo » / « Switcheroo »). Nous explorons de quelles façons chaque modalité textuelle requiert des stratégies différentes pour produire des formes engageantes d'interactivité.

INTRODUCTION

As a research group dedicated to the study of the literary in its transition from print to hypermedia, we have witnessed with interest the rapid growth of interactive media use among children. However, we have often been disappointed with the literary products available for the Spanish digital market, which often fail to exploit electronic textuality's potential to engage young readers already accustomed to other interactive products, such as games.

Also concerned with the insularity of electronic literature with respect to the general context of digital culture, for our ongoing project the LEETHI group decided to establish a wider network of partners and participate in a grant that required the collaboration of several research groups from different universities, public institutions and companies. We designed a project that tries to implement what we have learnt about electronic literature in the field of digital publishing, because it is our belief that the experimental nature of e-lit has the potential to transform and revolutionize other digital publishing formats. The eLITE-CM Project is therefore aimed at developing the field of electronic literary publishing through the creation of synergies among the different actors involved: teachers, academics, librarians, technological centers, and companies in the digital publishing industry.

One of our objectives is to develop enriching interactivity in children's digital literature. We have approached this objective from two perspectives, one directed to the recuperation of the Spanish literary heritage, through the enriching of digitized literary texts, and the other focused on the dissemination and creation of new texts that explore the possibilities of electronic textuality and new publishing formats, such as interactive fiction. We have selected and created works of interactive fiction that give special prominence to the linguistic code so that they can function as a bridge between traditional print literature and more visual forms of electronic literature. Moreover, as we will see later, this genre is also a very potent tool for studying and experimenting with reading.

The adoption of electronic textuality has been a gradual process where we can observe an evolution towards an electronic textuality increasingly hybridized with the characteristics of the digital medium, moving from plain digitized texts, to hyperlinked digitized texts, progressing towards text formats that have incorporated the intrinsic characteristics of digital culture: multilinearity, multimodality, interactivity, scalability, etc. The aim of our double perspective is to create bridges between different generations of readers, as well as texts benefitting from an existing gradation in textual formats that can help readers across generations move from print-based formats to more digital ones, and *vice versa*. Our main objective is to engage young readers with the pleasure of literary reading across textual formats.

We have dedicated a considerable amount of resources and time to this objective because we believe it can provide some alternatives to a social concern. The market, academia, parents and even pediatricians have witnessed the growing avalanche of digital products aimed at appeasing adults' anxieties regarding the education of future generations of children who have already fallen prey to the fascination of the screens. Among this offer overdose, it is difficult to elucidate which products are actually fulfilling their promises and which are dull, ineffective or even aggravating the evils they are supposedly counteracting.

THE MYTH OF INTERACTIVITY

Though research is scant and often exploratory, two myths have already developed from the first wave of iPad research, according to Kucirkova: first, the tendency to place technological artifacts and traditional resources in opposition, rather than in complementary relation to each other, and the second, derived from technological determinism, the misconception that positions technology as the driving force for educational change, without recognizing the powerful role of context and other variables, such as the different reading purposes and rituals evoked by different media or the ability of teachers to effectively leverage iPads' affordances and creatively link them to the curriculum (Kucirkova **2014**, 1-2). To these myths we could add the myth of interactivity, which has inspired the design of reading apps and ebooks with the promise that they can be useful in promoting vocabulary development and reading comprehension, via digital scaffolds such as oral narration, sound effects, animation or games.

We cannot ignore that one of the buzzwords used to advertise the products of digital culture is interactivity. This term has been exploited to such an extent as to be emptied of meaning: even an Ikea carpet and an Elgydium toothbrush have been marketed as interactive. Therefore, it also becomes necessary to clarify certain misconceptions about the term. First, we need to keep in mind that interactivity means different things for different people regarding the field of study they represent. As we can see from the dictionary entry, the term can have a general meaning describing a bidirectional system, but it also has particular meanings in the field of communications and computing:

- **in•ter•ac•tive** (in′tәer ak′tiv), **adj.** acting one upon or with the other.
- (Telecommunications) of or pertaining to a two-way system of electronic communications, as by means of television or computer: interactive communications between families using two-way cable television.
- (Computing: of a computer program or system) interacting with a human user, often in a conversational way, to obtain data or commands and to give immediate results or updated information.
(*Random House Unabridged Dictionary of American English*, 2018)

In critical discussions of hypertext, for example, I have noted a polarization of critics towards opposed understandings of the term: technophile critics defending technological interactivity as the unique form of interactivity, being cognitive interactivity between reader and text, purely metaphorical, and, on the other hand, humanist critics undermining technological interactivity as a pure simulacrum of the true communication that can only take place when two humans interact (Goicoechea **2010**).

I find it more productive to understand "interactivity" as the result of human and non-human interaction, in which the medium's degree of technological interactivity together with the depth of cognitive interactivity provided by the reader determines the final degree of interactivity of the resulting interaction. In its turn, cognitive interactivity is also the result of internal and external factors: both the cognitive skills of individual readers and the reading culture in which they are immersed will have an impact on the creativity their readings and writings can produce.

Though interactive media, compared with television and video, allow for contingent responses to children's actions and thus may facilitate more retention of taught material (Roseberry, Hirsh-Pasek, and Golinkoff **2013**), their enhancements have also been shown to distract children's attention from the story and interfere with comprehension. As Radesky et al. have pointed out: "the visual design, sound effects, and touchscreen interface of interactive media can either engage young children or distract them from educational content" (Radesky, Schumacher, and Zuckerman **2015**, 2). Thus it is necessary to find a balance between the two to facilitate learning. But there still remain many questions that need to be addressed, for example, what tablet enhancements facilitate the most learning at different developmental stages and how exactly do they promote a more active and engaging reading experience? We need to know more about the cognitive mechanisms elicited by the so-called interactive media.

Two years ago in the ELO Conference at Porto (2017), the panel dedicated to children's e-lit debated the different types of interactivity found in e-lit works, establishing a gradation regarding their ability to increase the reader's appreciation and understanding of the story. Marina Gabelica, for example, distinguished between platform-oriented interactivity (technological interactivity) and what she described as meaningful interactivity (which was an attempt to explore the space between the interactivity provided by the medium and that of the user). For this type of meaningful interactivity, she provided different levels: low, medium and high, depending on whether the interactor's reading could influence the depth of the story by discovering hidden media objects in a linear narrative (low); expand the story through choice and actions (medium); or influence the flow and direction of the narrative by selecting paths in a branching narrative (high) (Gabelica **2018**, 108-9). Gabelica's approach, a close heir of the technophile perspective, grants hypertextual formats the highest level of interactivity, implying that choosing links is always a non-trivial choice that requires a cognitive, and thus meaningful, effort, without further verification of the resulting insight gained in reading comprehension and the formulation of creative reading hypotheses.

Adopting a pragmatic or communicative position, Thales Estefani discussed Hutchins' concept of distributed cognition and Norman's "cognitive artifacts" and applied them to reading digital picture books, which were perceived as distinct artifacts which offer their own affordances and demand particular skills in the process of reading and navigation. Nonetheless, Estefani concluded that in order to be of any use in the understanding of the story, gamification and interactivity need to be introduced in the right places (Estefani and Queiroz **2018**, 124).

So we start from this common ground: that electronic literature is a type of cognitive artifact, as books also are in their own way, which triggers a particular type of communication on the part of the reader, whose cognitive abilities and reading culture will also determine the type of reading experience that is finally produced. Thus, we would like to continue exploring the reader's engagement with electronic literary artifacts, not in opposition to print formats but in relation to their own particular affordances and limitations in providing satisfactory reading experiences, taking into account the context and cultural environment in which reading takes place. The questions we wish to put on the table will hopefully advance the development of research methods that serve to orient designers with respect to the right balance and correct placement of interactive features. For that purpose, we will pay attention to the changing role of image versus text, the role of reading transcripts (that is, the possibility of rereading), the effects of the different types of technological interactivity in the child's understanding and enjoyment of the story, and the role of interactivity in the transmission of values and creative thinking.

This paper attempts to further this discussion by presenting some preliminary reading experiments carried out at several schools in Spain on two types of digital stories for children from 7 to 11 years old: an enriched digitized edition of an old children's story ("Plaga de dragones" / "A Plague of Dragons") and a piece of interactive fiction ("El Cambiazo"/"Switcheroo"). Each textual modality requires different strategies to produce engaging forms of interactivity, though in both cases the pedagogical intention is the same: to promote the pleasure of reading.

"ENRICHING" DIGITIZED CHILDREN LITERATURE*

Creating digital editions of printed literature of the past has become our way of integrating our literary heritage in the digital culture in which we are all immersed and which threatens every excluded work with eternal disappearance. We think that children should also be made participants in this process, so that they can understand better the works of distant periods and have a solid foundation from which to construct their reading habits. We expect that contact with enriched digital editions of these texts can construct mental bridges that would help them move smoothly from one period to another, from one textual format to another.

With these ideas in mind, we have chosen to refresh *Plaga de dragones (A Plague of Dragons)*, a forgotten collection of children stories published in 1923 during the Spanish Silver Age. This period, famous for the effervescence of its cultural life, saw the emergence of Saturnino Calleja Publishing House, or as it has been described today, the Zara of Books. This publishing house revolutionized Spanish children's education by providing beautifully illustrated books for a reasonable price, hiring the best designers and illustrators while searching all over the world for the best children's stories, though not always acknowledging their authors. Nonetheless, Calleja's visionary emphasis on privileging the image was found decisive in the success of his enterprise.

Creating an enriched digital version of this text has allowed us to make relevant discoveries about this collection from a philological perspective. Perusing the digitized children's collection already selected by the National Library of Spain's team, I was struck by the freshness and prophetic quality of the first story of this book, which gives its title to the collection: "Plague of Dragons." It altered my perception of Spanish children's literature of that period, whose didacticism and piousness was normally very tiresome. This story, however, was original, and it included several features that caught my attention, for example its great sense of irony, scientific references, the prominence given to a female character, a young girl, and even the introduction of a magic mirror that anticipated Google Earth! We discovered, through an illustration that had also been used in Calleja's edition of Edith Nesbit's tales, that it was actually an anonymous adaptation into the Spanish culture of some of Edith Nesbit's famous tales from the collections *Book of Dragons, Five Children and It,* and *Nine Unlikely Tales*, the only original Spanish story being the second tale in the collection. No wonder that, as an English philologist, I was drawn immediately to these stories! The adaptation was also very well done, and it made us suspect that there was also a prominent writer behind it, but that will be the subject of a different paper.

Before deciding how to enrich this digitized collection, we first made a study of the situation of children's literature digital collections worldwide. We realized that these were mainly aimed at researchers, not children or even teachers. The collections do not normally have an explanatory introduction or structure, and most often they are created simply by the grouping of the previously selected texts. The only added material is the library card of each book. In the Children's literature collection, which is part of the *Rare Book and Special Collection Reading Room of the Library of Congress*, for example, visitors can download the text in PDF format or use the Page Turner reading mode. Very often this reading mode only offers a single page at a time, with the possibility of viewing all the pages in miniature format. If you are a registered library user, sometimes you can share that text with other readers and add a brief note about the whole book, but you cannot make annotations over a particular paragraph, as is the case in the Baldwin Library of Historical Children's Literature. We liked, however, the British Library's "Turning the pages" software and the National Library of Spain's edition of *Don Quixote* (Fig. 1 and 2). Both offered a double page, clearly designed icons, and easy navigation. Moreover, both had integrated sound notes as well as written notes.

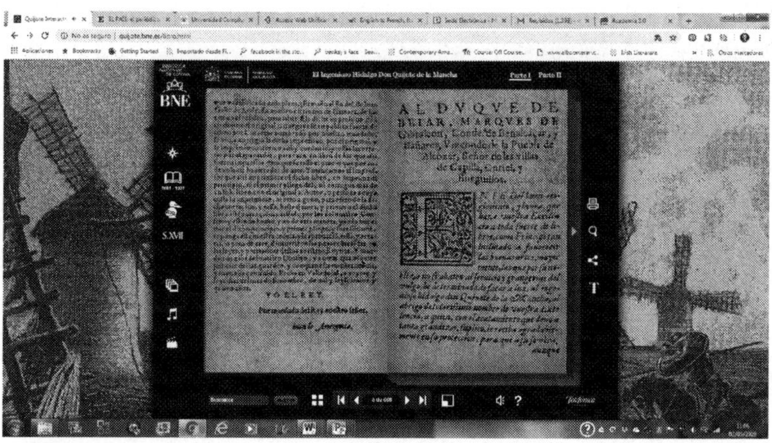

Figure 1. Lewis Carroll's *Alice's Adventures Under Ground* in the British Library collection Turning the Pages.

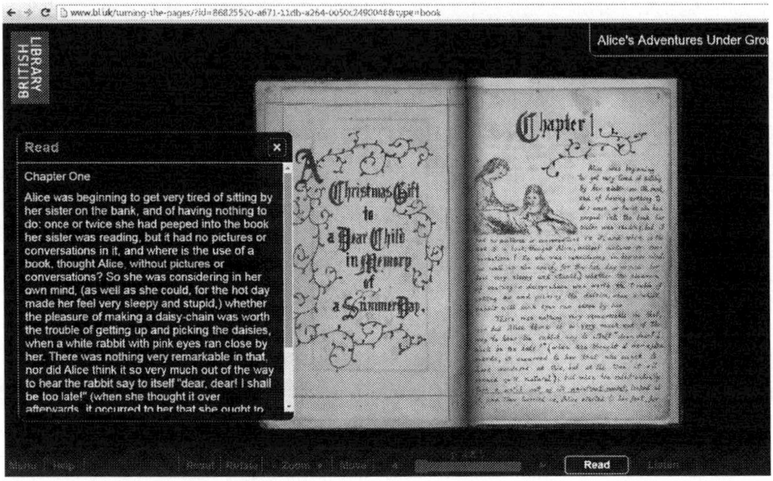

Figure 2. *Don Quijote Interactivo* at the National Library of Spain.

As can be seen, these beautiful editions are expensive, and they are normally implemented only in the case of literary jewels, not specifically for children. In our case, we were actually working with popular literature for children, and we had to find a solution to be able to edit texts with a simple formula that would allow us to reach a wider audience, and especially those who were the original target of those texts: children.

We began our first pilot of the story "A Plague of Dragons" using the tool offered by the National Library, Madgazine, a private platform originally intended for the creation of digital magazines, but it did not really meet all our needs: it could not integrate sound, and it provided only two predetermined icons to introduce pop-up annotations and links (Fig. 3).

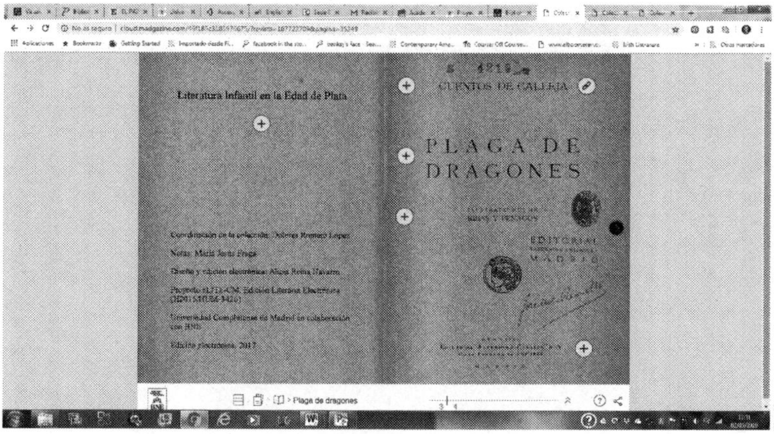

Figure 3. First pilot of the story "A Plague of Dragons" (2017) at the Spanish National Library.

We nevertheless carried out a reading experiment introducing the digital edition in a second grade classroom setting using the digital board as visual aid, with the presenter reading the story aloud, asking questions and exploring the pop-up windows together with the class. After evaluating the experience with the teacher, we gathered that the limited amount of annotations per page had not been obtrusive regarding reading comprehension, but that the register used in the annotations was not adapted to 7-8 year old children.

For our second pilot, we decided to create a tailor-made version (though this required hiring a programmer) of another story in the collection entitled "Una ciudad de libros" ("A City of Books"), so that we could customize it according to teachers' needs (Fig. 4); 110 teachers from 58 primary schools across Spain participated in our initial study, filling out a questionnaire designed to assess their needs regarding their practice of teaching reading. We also formulated questions to find out their degree of familiarization with digital tools. Particularly, we asked them which skills they wanted to promote through reading and the kind of features they would require from a digital edition of the tales. We later synthesized those demands in eight differentiated icons to help readers distinguish each type of annotation (Fig. 5). We also studied carefully the quality rubrics for educational digital objects and adapted them for our own purposes. The result was a bilingual edition of the story with its corresponding audio narration, eight different types of annotations, and three reading modes: the Spanish version (with annotations oriented to promote a literary and creative reading), the English version (oriented to the study of English as a second language), and a bilingual version (without annotations).

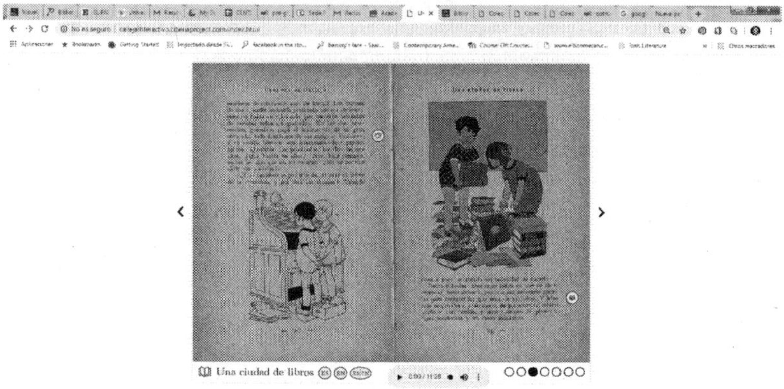

Figure 4. Digital edition of "Una ciudad de libros" / "A City of Books" (2018) from the collection Calleja Interactivo / Interactive Calleja (prototype version).

Type of annotation, activity or enhancement	Icon
1. Information related to cultural and historical context, oriented to improve reading comprehension.	
2. Vocabulary comprehension	••••••••
3. Listening comprehension (English version)	
4. Oral communication activities (English version)	
5. Annotations oriented to improve critical skills and intertextuality.	

6. Activities oriented to improve emotional intelligence and collaborative work.	
7. Creative writing and drawing activities	
8. Interactive activities (games, image galleries, self-correcting exercises, puzzles, etc.)	
9. Oral narration	

Figure 5. Icon design for "Una ciudad de libros" ("A City of Books").

This second pilot will be integrated in a webpage with the rest of the tales in the collection, with an introduction to the project, an introduction to Edith Nesbit and Calleja Publishing House, a didactic guide for teachers, and a visual guide for children. Before completing the enrichment material for the rest of the stories, we carried out an evaluation of this pilot at 20 schools, where teachers had a chance to integrate the story as part of their curriculum and dedicate the amount of time they considered necessary to exploit the material. Many teachers organized pre-reading and post-reading activities, read the story first without the annotations and reserved the exploration of additional material for a second in-depth reading. With their feedback and new ideas, we have improved the didactic guide, polished the style of the annotations and expanded the interactive features that can be used to evaluate reading comprehension, such as widgets to order the stories' illustrations, to introduce creative writing and drawing activities inside the platform, and self-correcting exercises.

We hope to have provided teachers, parents and children alike with an attractive new edition of the work which can help children today enjoy the same stories that their grandparents read nearly 100 years ago, using digital publishing to bridge a cultural as well as temporal gap between children from different times and places.

INTERACTIVE FICTION FOR CHILDREN

The other selected work is an original piece of interactive fiction (IF) written by the Marino family entitled "Switcheroo," which I translated into Spanish as "El Cambiazo." "Switcheroo," the third of the tales from Mrs. *Wobbles & the Tangerine House*, won the 2017 children's digital fiction prize for the "Opening Up Digital Fiction" competition. This work inverts the tendency observed in other examples of IF by placing great emphasis on the narration. This type of story is, in my opinion, a bridge between traditional book reading and electronic textuality. By offering the reader choices regarding the actions available to the main protagonist–in this case an orphan boy who wakes up one morning as a girl and spends the day with his/her potential parents–the story invites readers to engage actively in the experience of reading and care more profoundly about its protagonist. This work also allows us to study readers' interaction from new angles given the potentialities of its infrastructure, the Undum platform, a free and open-source, JavaScript-based interactive storytelling platform developed by Ian Millington, which can register readers' behavior.

Figure 6. Spanish Title Page for "El Cambiazo" (2017).

For the first experiments carried out with this interactive story, we decided to make a public reading of the story (so we did not register individual readings), since we wanted to gather a first impression of children's reaction to this type of literature and at the same time familiarize their teachers and families with it. We read the story to two classrooms in the Fifth grade of Primary School, that is, to 60 kids between 10-11 years old and their teachers. We read the story communally, speeding it up a bit to fit it in 45 minutes, and selecting the links and choices offered by the story depending on the number of raised hands. We repeated the same format with a different setting in Casa del Lector, a private foundation dedicated to the promotion of reading and innovation, where this time children of different ages were accompanied by their parents. Both types of experiences offered us rewarding insights regarding the children's appreciation and engagement with the story. Reading in a group proved an encouraging action by itself, involving children who normally do not spend their free time reading. They also provided very insightful points to analyze regarding the nature of their responses.

From the perspective of the interactivity of its medium, the Marinos' tale provides readers with the option of listening to the book narrate its own story or reading it by themselves. The Spanish version does not have the audio yet, so my reading provided the aural dimension and the screen projector the visual aid to follow the story by themselves. As it is an interactive story, it also presents readers with a selection of links and branching choices at measured intervals once the setting, the protagonist and his situation are thoroughly presented. Moreover, these choices are gamified since they will determine in the end how the reader's attitude is judged by the tale's machine. Since the story's theme has to do with expected gender reading behavior, each choice will veer the final decision towards one type of reading character or another, represented by famous literary characters: Huck, Tom Sawyer, Katniss, Matilda, Sleeping Beauty, etc. The tale also includes other little games, such as a dressing game that allows readers to choose the protagonist's outfit, and a card game. The effect of this sort of game in the overall interpretation of the story could not be studied in this preliminary experiment. However, we could observe the boys' and girls' reactions to the choices offered by the story, as well as the attention span of different ages.

"Switcheroo" allows children to face different realities regarding gender and disability from a magical perspective that will make them reflect about the value of loving and accepting oneself. In the end, the tale situates the reader at a crucial juncture: should the protagonist ask Mrs. Wobbles to allow him to remain in a girl's healthy body or, on the other hand, revert to his old boy's self? (Fig. 7). The first option implicitly entails being quickly adopted by the new mum and dad with whom the protagonist has been acquainted during the development of the story (and who seem pretty nice), whereas the second option would revert the character to his disability but leave him in the warm care of the magical Mrs. Wobbles (not a bad option either). Regardless of the choices made by the readers, the end is left open with the following sentence: "Very well. That is all. Now I was forming an impression of you as you were reading..." (Fig. 8). Abruptly, the story is left unfinished and turns the attention to the reader himself or herself, as it provides the result of the reader's behavior. The book, another character in the story, then urges the reader to ignore its own sententious identification: "But don't let me tell you who you are. Nobody knows who you are till you live your life and show them." Thus, even if the story does not provide proper closure, this sentence contains its moral, which can be applied to both the reader's and the protagonist's life choices.

The reader is left to wonder how the life of Derik/Denise will be from then onwards, but unlike other interactive fictions there is not a failed or successful outcome. Morally, however, in my particular reading of the story, I felt that the correct choice implied a return to the original self, the disabled boy, and coincidentally a majority of the school girls were also attached to the idea of protecting and cherishing the original self. Curiously enough for me, there was a majority of boys in the school readings that chose to remain as a girl. Asked about their choice, they discussed the advantages they found in being healthy (she could still play football) and, most often, that she could have a complete family, a father and a mother. The girls, however, felt that magic should not interfere with who you really are and that you should accept yourself to be happy, no matter if you are fat, ugly or handicapped. The boys, conversely, challenged my assumptions by publicly acknowledging that they would prefer the main character to remain a girl.

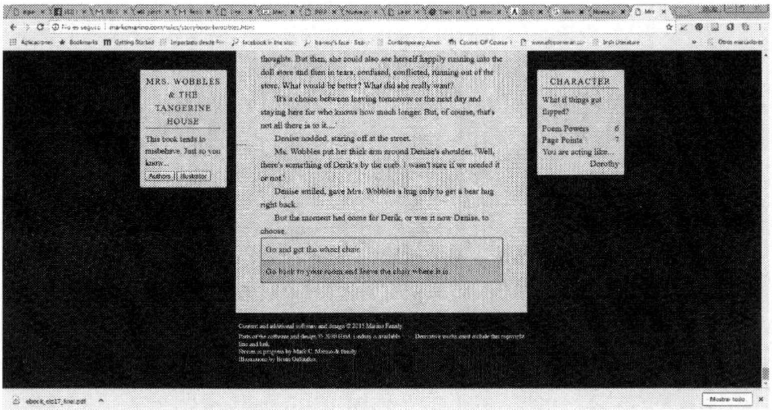

Figure 7. Final decision in "Switcheroo" (2015).

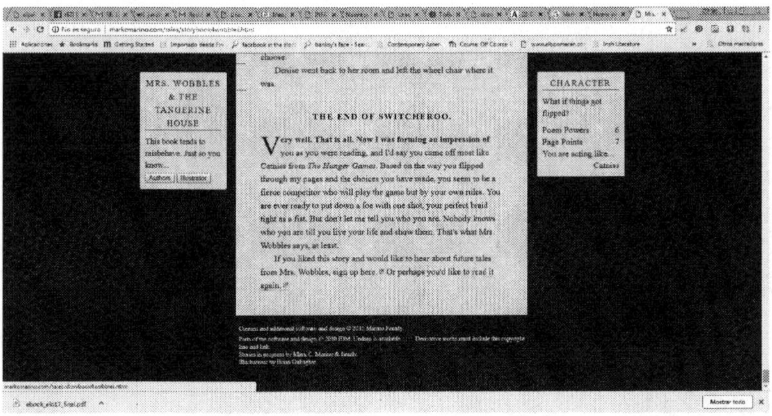

Figure 8. Last page of "Switcheroo" (2015).

In the family reading at Casa del Lector, the group of children ranged from 6 to 11 years old. The smaller children obviously had more difficulty concentrating for so long; especially because the story had very few visual cues that they could follow (it only has three illustrations plus the title decoration). I had already warned the parents that the story was aimed at older children. But this also demonstrates how concentrated reading without the help of illustrations is a habit that is learned through practice and that requires a certain level of maturity.

The work permits readers to interrupt the reading and continue where they left it, but it is not possible to undo the choices made. One would need to read the story from the beginning to experiment with other options. However, the HTML page provides a fixed transcript of the produced story each time, allowing the readers to retrace their steps and reread what has happened so far. If they read the story several times they will realize how each option is loaded with a particular value that will determine the type of character with which the story identifies the reader: there are conservative options, daring options, and even absurd options (like staying in the bathroom for life). The interactivity of "Switcheroo" is smoothly integrated in the gamification of the story with very few choices that are irrelevant to the story's outcome, and even when they do not change the structure of the story, as in the end, this is also significant. We can interpret this invariance with this final coda: There are important decisions in life that are personal and should not be judged, so no matter what the reader decides, it is the "correct" choice. In this manner, the interactivity triggered by the medium's potentialities is used masterfully to place the reader in a delicate moral dilemma and transmit empathy and ethical values.

Children's acceptance of this cognitive artifact was immediate. Accustomed to all sorts of digital games, they adapted quickly to the rules of this literary game and, for those children who normally find print reading a strenuous task, this type of literature did not appear that challenging. In this respect, teachers commented on the fact that many links only allowed for the continuation of the story, providing new chunks of text at a time, and disguising in this manner the true amount of text they were actually following through.

After these preliminary reading experiments, we became aware of the genre's potential to explore reading behavior, promote active reading, and engage readers, not only in the vicissitudes of characters in adventure or mystery narratives, but in stories involving ethically complex choices that put their emotional intelligence to a test.

Despite the proliferation of educational digital products in the Spanish context, reading "Switcheroo / El Cambiazo" was a novel experience for all the participants. Parents and teachers remembered the Choose-your-own-adventure books but did not know that there were any electronic formats like this for children. The feedback we obtained from the families at Casa del

Lector and at school was very positive. Days after the reading experience at school several parents addressed me asking me if there were any more stories of the sort I had read in class since their kids, some of whom normally did not like reading, expressed their interest in reading more interactive stories.

CONCLUSIONS

The purpose of this paper was to present the design considerations and preliminary experiments undertaken with two formats of digital publishing for children: enriched digitized text and interactive fiction, both aimed at promoting literary reading.

For our experiment with digitized literature, we chose a specific collection of children's stories from the 1920s, *Plaga de dragones (A plague of dragons)* with the idea of using interactive features to make it more appealing for contemporary children. The new digital layer was added with the purpose of reducing the cultural gap between the original text and the reader in terms of both content and format, taking advantage of the digital scaffolding to produce the type of exploratory, interactive, engagement that today's children appreciate. The interactive elements, mainly pop-up annotations with multimedia features, were strategically placed to support the story's comprehension at several levels: vocabulary explanation, historical and contextual information, critical reading and intertextuality, and creative and interpretative thinking. Our customized second pilot allowed us to create a bilingual edition of the text, with integrated sound and differentiated icons depending on the type of link to comply with teachers' demands.

To introduce Spanish audiences to interactive fiction for children, we translated the third tale of the collection *Mrs. Wobbles and the Tangerine House* by the Marino family entitled "El Cambiazo" / "Switcheroo". This story afforded us a very good example of the way interactive fiction can be a potent tool for both educating children and studying their responses in the face of complex life challenges, such as disability, transgender, adoption, etc.

Exploratory communal readings were organized to test initial responses to these two digital formats. We read our enriched digitized text to 7-8 year-old children, and organized an evaluation of the pilot among teachers. We concluded that the tool was found useful and that the enriching material, which augmented significantly the presence of image and audio, was not found extraneous or obtrusive though it was more efficiently integrated during a rereading of the story. Older children particularly enjoyed the interactive fiction readings and expressed their desire to be acquainted with other similar stories. To introduce children, parents and teachers to electronic literature for children, we created a small collection of e-lit for children with a selection of works in Spanish and other languages.[1]

NOTE 1

http://www.ciberiaproject.com/coleccion-lij-digital/

The warm welcome received by these early attempts encouraged us to start designing an experimentation model of reading for children's digital literature that takes into account the spectrum of textual formats, exploring the type of expectations and affordances each format raises in children and analyzing their responses accordingly, escaping from a Manichean contrastive analysis with print. The design of children's digital literature still faces many challenges and questions for which we will need to carry out specific experiments.

Funding: This research was supported by the eLITE-CM project: Electronic Literary Publishing (reference: H2015 / HUM-3426) within the Program of Research and Development among Research Teams of the Community of Madrid in Social Sciences and the Humanities, and was 50 % co-funded by the European Social Fund for the programming period 2014-2020.

Estefani, Thales, and João Queiroz. 2018. "Children's Picturebook Goes Digital: Implications on Cognition." *MATLIT: Materialities of Literature* 6 (2):115-27. Link: https://impactum-journals.uc.pt/matlit/article/view/5276.

Gabelica, Marina. 2018. "Children's Electronic Literature Criticism: Exploring Electronic Picture Books." *MATLIT: Materialities of Literature* 6 (2):99-113. Link: https://impactum-journals.uc.pt/matlit/article/view/5308.

Goicoechea, María. 2010. "The Reader in Cyberspace: In Search of Digital Literature in Spain." In *Reading Moving Letters: Digital Literature in Research and Teaching*, ed. by Roberto Simanowski, Jörgen Schäfer, and Peter Gendolla, 183-206. Bielefeld : Transcript Verlag.

Kucirkova, Natalia. 2014. "iPads in early education: separating assumptions and evidence." *Frontiers in Psychology*, July 8. Link: https://doi.org/10.3389/fpsyg.2014.00715.

Radesky, Jenny S., Jayna Schumacher, and Barry Zuckerman. 2015. "Mobile and Interactive Media Use by Young Children: The Good, the Bad, and the Unknown." *Pediatrics* 135 (1). Link: https://doi.org/10.1542/peds.2014-251.

Roseberry, Sarah, Kathy Hirsh-Pasek, and Roberta M. Golinkoff. 2013. "Skype Me! Socially Contingent Interactions Help Toddlers Learn Language." *Child Development* 82 (3):956-70. Link: https://doi.org/10.1111/cdev.12166.

Is There A Gap In The Classroom?

ANA MARIA MACHADO

ANA ALBUQUERQUE E AGUILAR • ALICE ATSUKO MATSUDA

Abstract

There is still a big gap between electronic literature for children and Portuguese schools. This situation is in contrast with the increasing interest the educational community and publishers show in print literature for children and young adults in Portugal.
In this article we develop the steps that the team from the project *Inanimate Alice: Translating Electronic Literature for an Educational Context* (Centre for Portuguese Literature at the University of Coimbra) took in order to give Portuguese students the opportunity to experience e-lit. These steps are namely the translation of the first five episodes of *Inanimate Alice* and of the already existent educational guidelines, the production of *Alice Inanimada*-episodes 1 ("China") and 2 ("Itália") by the BradField Company, the endeavours taken by the project team in order to make the Portuguese version accessible to the public, as well as the contacts made with the Ministry of Science, Technology and Higher Education, and the National Reading Plan. All these steps were fundamental for the development of a pioneer educational experiment that took place in two Portuguese schools.
The project team contacted several public schools located in Central Portugal in order to conduct, in February, April and May 2018, a study based on an experiment in which a large group of sixth and eighth graders interacted with the two Portuguese episodes of *Alice Inanimada*. With the aim of reducing the previously mentioned gap, we prepared two questionnaires where we evaluated students' aesthetic perception, their attention and immersion, and the comprehension skills required by this kind of work. As for the teachers, we were interested to know what they thought about the *Alice Inanimada* experiment, how it enhanced students' knowledge, what inherent difficulties it implied and what activities they would like to suggest. In this article, we will present and analyse some of the collected data concerning these topics, and also offer some clues that could be helpful to bridge the gap between e-lit and schools.

Résumé

Il existe encore un grand écart entre la littérature jeunesse électronique et les écoles portugaises. Cette situation détonne avec l'intérêt croissant que la communauté éducative et les éditeurs portent à la littérature imprimée pour les enfants et les jeunes adultes au Portugal.
Dans cet article, nous exposons les étapes mises en place par l'équipe du projet *Inanimate Alice: Translating Electronic Literature for an Educational Context* (Centre de Littérature portugaise à l'Université de Coimbra) afin de faciliter l'expérience de la littérature électronique pour les élèves portugais. Ces étapes comprennent la traduction des cinq premiers épisodes de *Inanimate Alice* et des directives éducationnelles déjà existantes, la production des épisodes 1 (« China ») et 2 (« Itália ») de *Alice Inanimada* par BradField Company, les efforts déployés par l'équipe du projet pour rendre accessible la version portugaise au public, ainsi que les contacts établis avec le Ministère des sciences, des technologies et de l'enseignement supérieur et le Programme national de lecture. Toutes ces étapes ont été fondamentales au développement d'une expérience éducative pionnière qui a eu lieu dans deux écoles portugaises.
L'équipe a contacté plusieurs écoles publiques dans la région du Centre du Portugal afin de réaliser en février, avril et mai 2018, une étude basée sur l'expérience dans laquelle un grand groupe d'élèves en sixième et huitième interagissait avec les deux épisodes portugais de *Alice Inanimada*. Dans le but de réduire l'écart mentionné précédemment, nous avons préparé deux questionnaires grâce auxquels nous avons évalué la perception esthétique des élèves, leur attention et leur immersion et les compétences de compréhension acquises lors de cette activité. En ce qui à trait aux professeurs, nous nous sommes intéressés à savoir ce qu'ils pensaient de l'expérience de *Alice Inanimada*, comment elle a amélioré les connaissances des élèves, les difficultés inhérentes impliquées et quelles activités ils voudraient suggérer. Dans cet article nous présentons et examinons les données recueillies, et nous offrons des pistes de réflexion qui pourraient combler l'écart entre la littérature électronique et les écoles.

There is still a big gap between electronic literature for children and Portuguese schools. Actually, this situation is in contrast to the increasing interest the educational community and publishers are showing in print literature for children and young adults in Portugal.

The aim of this paper is to present the steps that the team from the project *Inanimate Alice: Translating Electronic Literature for an Educational Context*[1] (Centre for Portuguese Literature at the University of Coimbra) took in order to give Portuguese students the opportunity to experience e-lit.

NOTE 1

With the coordination of Ana Machado, the team began with Ana Albuquerque e Aguilar and António Conduto, responsible for the translation. Alice Matsuda worked on the project during her postdoctoral studies. After that, the work was continued by Ana Machado and Ana Albuquerque e Aguilar.

As the ultimate goal is to introduce digital literature in Portuguese schools, the team translated the first five episodes of *Inanimate Alice* (Boyd, **n.d.**) and recently finished the translation of the pedagogical guidance, created by Bill Boyd and Jess Laccetti. Finally, the team began to create their own materials, as will be seen below.

One of the main problems of this task has been to find financial support to publish the Portuguese version of the series. So contacts were made with the two biggest education-oriented publishing companies in Portugal, but they rely considerably on ministerial documents and barely dare to innovate, as it is safer to publish what the Ministry of Education recom-mends that schools, teachers and students buy. Also they continue to rely on the print business model, and are afraid to take what they assume to be an entrepreneurial risk, even if Portuguese public schools are, in general, well equipped, technologically speaking, although the Ministry of Education does not always ensure software updates.[2] In June 2018 there was a chance of a partnership between Microsoft Portugal and The Bradfield Company, and finally *Alice Inanimada* could be sold to schools, teachers and students, and could be studied in classes, but, unfortunately, this did not work out. Anyway, for the moment we are making contacts with investors interested in educational matters, hoping that in the near future we can read *Alice Inanimada* in Portuguese schools.

NOTE 2

Due to the COVID-19 crisis, in 2020, both Portuguese publishers and the Ministry of Education had to turn to digital forms and media very rapidly. However, time will tell if this is a temporary or permanent change and investment.

Currently, in the Portuguese-speaking world (Portuguese being the fourth language most spoken around the world, as shown in the figure, with some

300 million speakers),[3] with regard to digital literature for children, there is an enormous gap between the solid editorial market in Brazil and its void in Portugal. That is why a new team[4] is now working on the creation of the first Portuguese digital literary work for children, inspired by Portuguese artist Costa Pinheiro's (1932, Moura, Portugal – 2015, Munich, Germany) wall paintings (**https://www.costa-pinheiro.de/pt/publico**).

NOTE 3

See "O Estatuto da Língua Portuguesa no Mundo," August 8, 2017, from Observatório da Língua Portuguesa, in **http://observalingua portuguesa.org/graficos-o-estatuto-da-lp-no-mundo/**.

NOTE 4

Ana Machado and Ana Albuquerque e Aguilar from the first project, and Júlia Zuza, also a member of the Centre for Portuguese Literature (CLP), will create three different stories for three different publics: a picture book for young children, generative poems grounded on children's oral tradition, for 7-9 year-old children, and a "birdy" novel for 10-11 year-old children. Lately, the team has been enlarged with two more PhD Students from CLP and the Department of Informatics Engineering, responsible for hypermedia design and code. Rui Torres, digital artist and professor at Fernando Pessoa University (Oporto, Portugal) is our consultant.

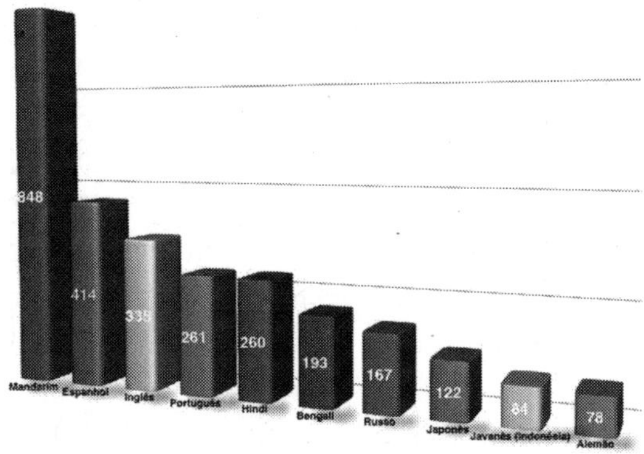

Figure 1. As linguas mais faladas no mundo.

While documents such as the *Profile for Students* issued by the Ministry of Education in 2017 expose the need to teach them how to read digital texts, but neither ministerial documents nor publishers really recognise the educational potential of hypertextual and multimodal literature, with the result that, besides the lack of electronic literature works, there is still a need for pedagogical instruments and teachers' training to deal with digital literary works. However, as this study shows, children and teenagers are ready for this kind of educational innovation, and many teachers are also available to learn new skills.

Being aware that educational changes in Portugal often take place from the top down, meaning that we need approval from the Ministry of Education to have some impact in classrooms, we contacted the 2027 National Reading Plan (PNL)[5] whose Commission asked the universities for book suggestions.

It took some months, but finally, *Alice Inanimada* was referred by PNL 2027 as the first digital literary work ever endorsed by this institution in our teaching system. The *Plano estratégico para a área da ciência tecnologia e ensino superior. Leituras ciência e conhecimento* (**2017**, 13) mentions their goal for 2018: to present *Alice Inanimada* in a teacher training context as part of the strategic plan prepared by the Ministry of Science, Technology and Higher Education. And it concludes that the novel by "Andy Campbell, Chris Joseph, Ian Harper, Kate Pullinger, and Mez Breeze (2005-2017) would be the first native digital fiction to be read in Portuguese schools" (translated).

This was surely a very big step, because the PNL seal is an important argument for Portuguese-speaking countries like Brazil and Angola to be interested in *Alice Inanimada*. So, there are good reasons to expect some funding opportunities here, but also in America, as there are schools that teach Portuguese as a heritage language.

Meanwhile, two public schools located in the Centre of Portugal[6] were contacted in order to conduct an empirical study, in April and May 2018, in which 59 students from the sixth and eighth grades interacted with *Alice Inanimada*, the first digital literary work they ever knew. With the aim of reducing the previously mentioned gap, two questionnaires were prepared to evaluate the students' aesthetic perception, their attention and immersion, and the comprehension skills required by this kind of work, in a total of 117 inquiries collected. These questionnaires sought also to understand the sort of activities and strategies teachers need to apply in class in order to develop students' digital literary literacy. As to the teachers, it is relevant to know what they think about the interest of the *Alice Inanimada* experiment, how it enhances students' knowledge, the inherent difficulties it involves, and what activities they would like to suggest. Unfortunately, due to some delay from the PNL organization, the training sessions, scheduled for the last trimester of 2018, had to be postponed to February 2019.[7]

NOTE 5

The 2027 National Reading Plan stems from a partnership between the Ministries of Education, Culture, and Science, Technology and Higher Education. Its aim was to enhance literacy levels (cultural, scientific and digital) of children, young people and adults, in order to prepare them for twenty-first century challenges.

NOTE 6

We thank both the principals of Agrupamento de Escolas de Anadia and Escola Secundária Infanta D. Maria, and the teachers who collaborated with us: Isabel Pimenta, Elvira Jaqueta, and Helena Isabel Carvalho.

NOTE 7

In order to respond to the manifest interest of teachers from all over the country in this teacher training course, Ana Maria Machado and Ana Albuquerque e Aguilar had to duplicate the number of sessions previously scheduled by the Portuguese National Reading Plan in collaboration with the Directorate General of Education. Finally, the course took place in Coimbra and in Lisbon, in February and April 2019.

So, not having the data from the training sessions available to present in the ELO Conference 2018, in this paper only the answers of the three teachers from the schools where the experiment took place will be considered. Nevertheless, for the purpose of this reflection it is more important to take into account the perception of the teachers who collaborated with us *in loco*, with their own students, rather than those who were learning individually how to didactically explore *Alice Inanimada* in a training session. Above all, we will reflect upon the questionnaires and the students' perceptions.

As has been said, the pedagogical experiment took place in two public schools with sixth- and eighth-graders, the latter being located in a more socially and culturally privileged environment.[8] Participant students belong to three different classes. Each one was split in half–one group read the story on paper and the other on screen and, in the second episode, each group swit-ched versions. Finally, each group individually answered a questionnaire divided in three parts: personal / social / cultural data, aesthetic reception, and comprehension of the work, whether print or digital. The results we present here take into account the complete group of students without further distinction because, at this time, we are analysing more general items like students' reception of the work and features like multimodality or immersion, and also because the differences between different grades were not really relevant.

NOTE 8

On April 9 and 11, 2018, Alice worked with sixth-graders in Anadia, and on April 19 and May 3, 2018, Ana Aguilar worked with eighth-graders in Coimbra.

Within the introduction of e-lit in schools, the aesthetic reception is the main focus of this paper, whilst digital literacy will be studied in future publications. Knowing the school context of Portuguese students, the results of this research were not totally surprising, and they confirm what Ackerman and Lauterman (2012) showed in their inquiry on reading on screen or on paper, arguing that "the problem with screen reading is more psychological than technological." Even though this study does not assess multimodality, its underlined difference favours children and teenagers, because they use technology on a daily basis, as the results of our project survey show. Actually, the readers of the digital episodes said it would be very important for them to study more digital works in school, in contrast with those who read it on paper. Indeed, after they became familiar with episode 2, they were asked if they preferred Alice's adventures on paper or on the computer and, not surprisingly, 98 % of the students chose the original, digital version, as they felt more confident using their digital skills to navigate through the episode, than the simple act of reading verbal code with three illustrations.[9] Also, they felt the narrative was digital native.

NOTE 9

The first, a drawing of Brad within the *player* made it necessary to explain what player meant, as the word was not translated (Machado et al. 2018). The other two regarded the thoughts of Alice represented in the original version within the player or simply showing up on the screen.

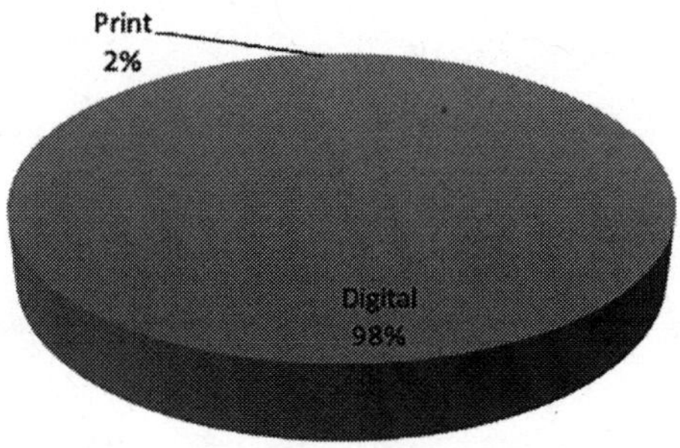

Figure 2. *Medium*

The estrangement towards literary work in a digital milieu was also measured, and the majority (21/31) of the answers show the naturalization of the medium as students felt it was natural to read *Alice Inanimada* on a computer: 78 % declared they did not feel any difficulties (45 %) or felt minor ones (23 %) navigating through the text.

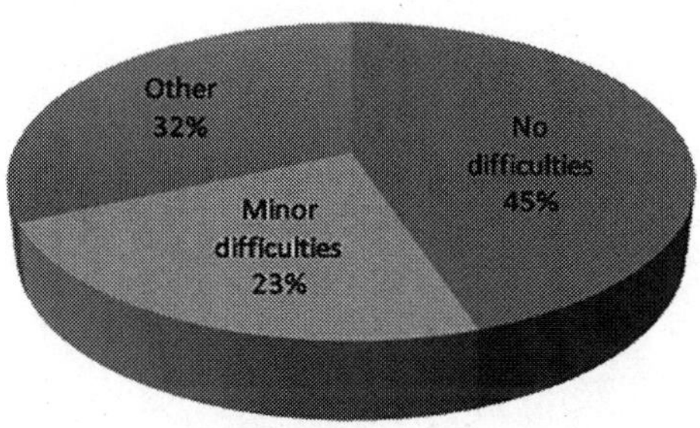

Figure 3. Estrangement towards literary work in a digital milieu / Naturalization to the medium

Moreover, students revealed a genuine interest in the digital work, as, confronted with the choice of doing anything else, 84 % said they would rather continue using *Alice*'s first episode (compared with 61 % of the students who were reading it on paper). And 74 % of the group that used the original first episode declared they liked it a lot (32 %) or very much (42 %), as against 60 % of the print reading (18 % and 24 %, respectively).

Also, when asked about their desire to know the rest of Alice's adventures, 84 % of the digital-experience students showed strong (55 %) and great interest (29 %), contrasting with the 68 % (32 % and 36 %, respectively) of the other group.

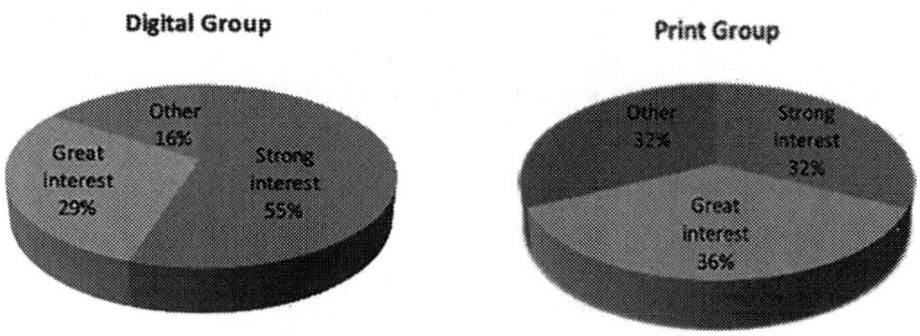

Figure 4. Desire to know the rest of Alice's adventures

Finally, to understand the full extent of their reception of the work, after they became familiar with the two episodes, we asked the participant students to define *Alice Inanimada* in one adjective. Only 7 % of them used words that have negative connotations ("bad" and "macabre"), while in the majority of the answers one can find adjectives ranging from "fantastic" to "different," or "exciting" and "unforgettable" and "innovative," underlining how positive and, at the same time, unexpected, having e-lit in the classroom is for them.

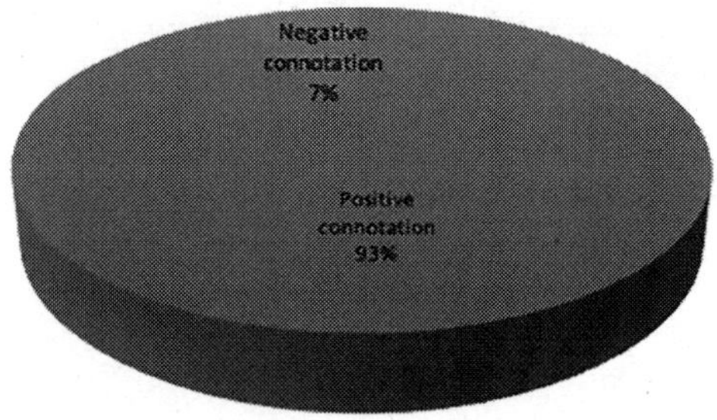

Figure 5. One adjective to describe the experience with *Alice Inanimada*

When asked about their motivation to continue Alice's adventures, creating an episode of their own, 68 % of the digital-experience group stated they were strongly (32 %) or very much (36 %) interested in doing so, as against 50 % of the print-experience group (where those answers were chosen by 25 % each).

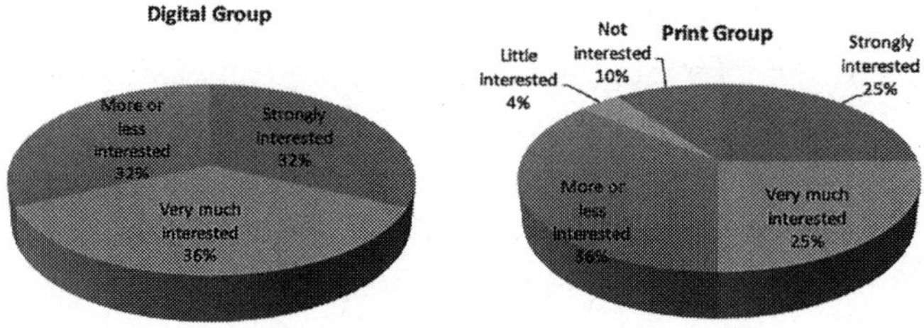

Figure 6. Motivation to create a new episode

Also, concerning multimodality, students were asked about which modes they would use when creating another episode. Although they could choose more then one option, whether using the paper or the digital version, the data reveal the dominance of monomodality (46 vs. 14). Only three students described a multimodal episode associated with previous choices. On one hand, it seems that they did not realize they could choose more than one answer, but, on the other hand, one could also think that globally they do not have a metacognition of multimodality and they perceive video as a multimodal medium. As to writing, it seems that the relatively expressive fact that 19 students chose text, with or without other modalities, reveals a school *habitus*, as if they did not even consider the possibility of creating a story with other modality than text.

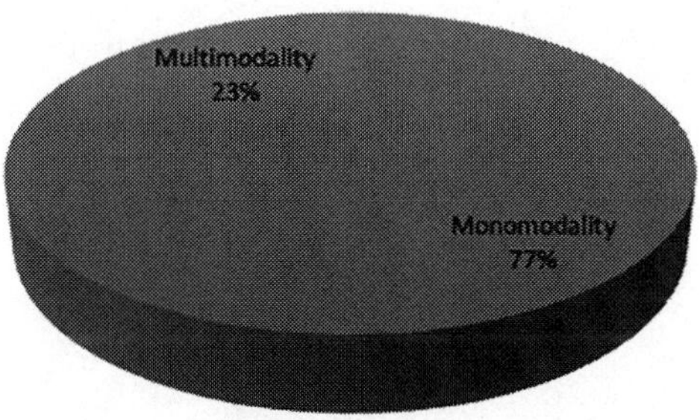

Figure 7. Creating a new episode: Dominance of monomodality

Knowing the way students perceived *Alice Inanimada*, its literary genre identity was another goal of the questionnaires, so first they were asked what action they performed *vis à vis* the digital work. The majority (55 %) said they "watched" the episode, 42 % "read" it and 3 % "used" it. The first two options are rather normal, and they are linked to traditional media. On the other hand, it is the third one that points to the novelty of digital literary reception, disclosing an implicit consciousness of a reception that encompasses the mouse movement, the interaction with the story, and a physical behaviour that is not merely "passive." Considering what one could call the porous border between electronic literature and electronic games, it is quite surprising that no one chose "play," while, in class, after answering the questionnaires, students used this verb referring to their interaction with *Alice Inanimada*.

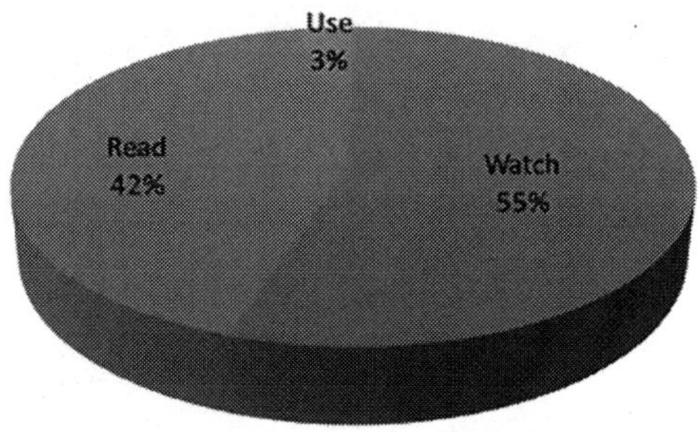

Figure 8. Performed action *vis-à-vis* the digital work

Afterwards we wanted to know how they identify the genre of the work. The majority of students (58 %) sensed its specificity and called it a "digital narrative," after its medium, 13 % considered it a "youth novel," and 29 % an "animation film." As with the previous question, no one considered it a "computer game."

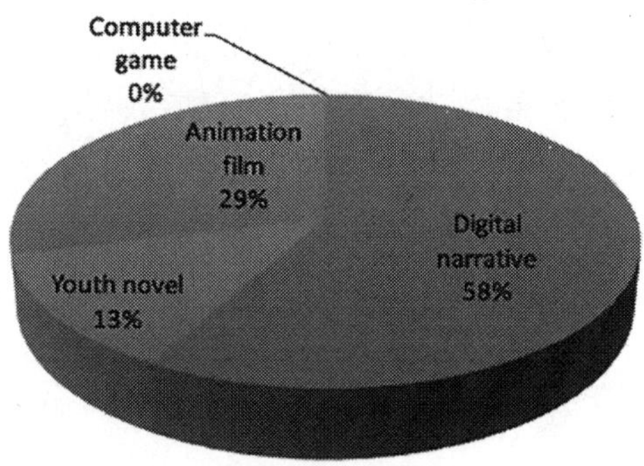

Figure 9. Genre

In order to grasp the students' consciousness of immersion, they were asked in what moment they "entered" the story. Between those who read the episode and those who read it on the computer there was a curious difference, for 74 % of the first group mentioned situations of mental immersion, while, in the second group, 32 % explicitly referred to situations where they interacted with the episode and, a minority, to the presence of more than one sense. Pointing out the moment when Alice takes photos of the flowers and sends them to her father in an action of intern interactivity (Ryan **2001**), they implicitly identified Alice's gesture with the reader mouse movement, revealing some awareness of replacing the protagonist action. Anyway, the lion's share (45 %) in respect to "entering the text" still goes globally to the imaginary immersion, that is, the majority of students from the two groups understood immersion as an interior process. Yet, a minority of students diverged from both kinds of immersion, because either their answers were imprecise (23 % in the "digital group" and 18% in the "print group"), or, in the "print group," they clearly stated they never "entered" the text (18 %).

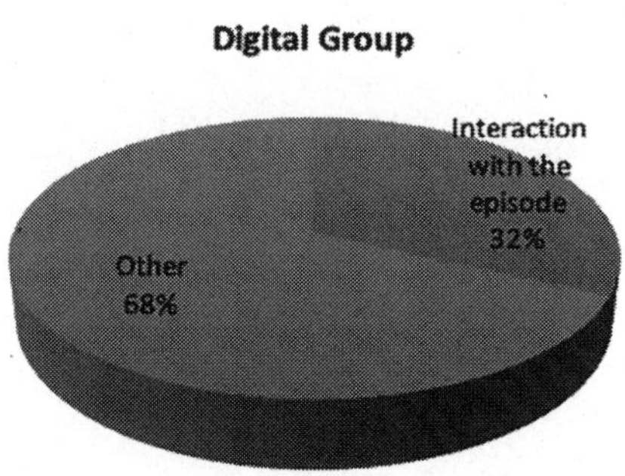

Figure 10. Immersion

So, apart from perceiving the kind of fusion between the reader and the text (Ryan **2001**) inherent to the reading process, and, consequently, a sort of "experience of being transported to an elaborately simulated place" (Murray **1997**, 110), a rather substantial group of students proved their digital literacy, realizing the interactive gesture as a *surplus* regarding print reading, that is an "immersion as participatory activity" (Murray **1997**, 110), in a world without frontiers where territories were off-limits (Provenzo 1991). In fact, the interaction with Alice is such that the reader is therefore an actor that invades and acts in a fictional environment. As stated above, even if there is estrangement towards a digital literary work, which, for these teenagers, is a completely new experience, naturalization rapidly occurs. One good example of this kind of feeling towards the interaction with Alice is when, in episode 2, the reader has to dress the protagonist before she goes outside and faces a snowstorm, as 96 % of the students find this process absolutely natural, because it serves a narrative purpose. However, in the same episode, when having to solve the puzzle created by the character, even though they found it easy, only 11 % found it "natural," since this operation is not justified by the narrative flow. Although this is rather unsurprising (Potrony and Grupo GRETEL **2014**), it is still worth mentioning.

This demand from the virtual world which calls for the action from someone outside the episode is another step in the immersive engagement (Murray **1997**), and this "non trivial gesture" (Aarseth **1997**) required by *Alice Inanimada* reveals the ergodic nature of the medium, opposed to standard linear print text (Aarseth **1997**), because that specific nature is not only a cerebral performance, but also a physical gesture. Actually, in *Alice Inanimada*, "non trivial effort is required to allow the reader to traverse the text," as Aarseth (Aarseth **1997**, 1) states as a feature of ergodic literature.

It goes without saying that in the first and second episodes, both immersion and ergodicity are incipient, contrasting with their progressive development in further episodes. Nonetheless, not only those features were implicitly perceived in students' answers, but they should be noted by teachers in order to educate students in digital literacy.

Exploring teachers' responses, two of the three teachers participating in the study (67 %) say they sometimes use digital technologies in their classes, but all of them report they will teach *Alice Inanimada* when it is available to the public, considering the endorsement of the work by PNL 2027 to be rather important for legitimizing this choice. They value the students' interest and motivation, the educational innovation, and the development of digital skills as the three key aspects for bringing *Alice Inanimada* to their classrooms. Nevertheless, they also identify potential technical problems and Internet access in schools as their main concerns in doing so. They all think this e-lit work is a good starting point for students to develop creative and cultural activities.

Conducting this study, the first of this type carried out in Portugal, it was possible to observe both teachers' and students' interest and motivation and their enthusiasm to continue teaching and learning digital literature. Students' desire and teachers' commitment to create new *Alice Inanimada* episodes is the most expressive demonstration of the aesthetic reception. And in a near future, it is legitimate to expect to find those creations in the Inanimate Alice Featured Classroom (**https://inanimatealice.com/featured-classrooms/**).

In order to fill the gap between the will of the education community and the effective teaching and learning of electronic literature, there is still a lack of a serious commitment from the Ministry of Education and publishing companies in Portugal. This attitude is probably due to the lack of awareness of digital literature on the part of educational and political actors. So, with respect to our project, besides the teachers' and educators' training sessions already mentioned, we are organizing the Teaching Digital Literature International Conference that will take place at the University of Coimbra (Portugal), July 25-26, 2019[10], hoping to educate teachers and other literary education actors in e-lit and to raise awareness about its pedagogical potential.

NOTE 10

Some of the papers of this conference can soon be read in the journal MATLIT – Materialities of Literature, organized by Ana Maria Machado and Ana Albuquerque e Aguilar (Coimbra, Centre for Portuguese Literature, vol. 8.1, launched into be published in July, 2020).

Aarseth, Espen. 1997. *Cybertext: Perspectives on Ergodic Literature.* Baltimore: The Johns Hopkins University Press.

Ackerman, Rakefet, and Tirza Lauterman. 2012. "Taking Reading Comprehension Exams on Screen or on Paper? A Metacognitive Analysis of Learning Texts Under Time Pressure". *Computers in Human Behavior* 28 (5):1816–23.

Boyd, Bill. n.d. *Inanimate Alice. Mind Map Ideas.* Kindly provided by Ian Harper.

Government of Portugal. 2017. *Plano Nacional de Leitura 2027.* Link: http://www.planonacionaldeleitura.gov.pt/

Laccetti, Jess. "Inanimate Alice. Pedagogy Project. Lesson Plans and Student Resource Pack". Link: http://www.inanimatealice.com/education/edupack.pdf

Murray, Janet H. 1997. *Hamlet on the Holodeck: The Future of Narrative in Cyberspace.* Cambridge, MA: MIT Press.

Observatório da Língua Portuguesa. 2017. "O Estatuto da Língua Portuguesa no Mundo," August 8. Link: https://observalinguaportuguesa.org/graficos-o-estatuto-da-lp-no-mundo/

Potrony, Mireia Manresa, and Grupo GRETEL. 2014. "Leer En Digital: La Interpretación Del Lector". In *Grupo GRETEL, Actas del Simposio Internacional La literatura en pantalla: textos, lectores y prácticas docentes.* Bellaterra: Universitat Autònoma de Barcelona.

Provenzo, Eugene E., Jr. 1991. *Video Kids: Making Sense of Nintendo.* Cambridge, MA: Harvard University Press.

Pullinger, Kate, and Chris Joseph. 2017. Alice Inanimada – Episódio 1: China. Translated by Ana Maria Machado, Ana Albuquerque e Aguilar and Anton Stark. The Bradfield Company.

Pullinger, Kate, and Chris Joseph. 2018. *Alice Inanimada – Episódio 2: Itália.* Translated by Ana Maria Machado, Ana Albuquerque e Aguilar and Anton Stark. The Bradfield Company.

Ryan, Marie-Laure. 2001. "Beyond Myth and Metaphor – the Case of Narrative in Digital Media". *Game Studies* 1 (1).

Partie / Part 6

PERSPECTIVES DIACHRONIQUES SUR LA LITTÉRATURE ÉLECTRONIQUE NUMÉRIQUE

READING E-LIT ACROSS TIME

ANAÏS GUILET

Littérature électronique de papier : Réflexions sur la troisième génération de littérature électronique

Résumé

Cet article entend partir d'une interrogation aussi simple que les problématiques qu'elle soulève sont complexes : qui lit de la littérature électronique et de quelle littérature électronique parle-t-on? Cette question ne s'avère pas seulement ontologique, elle est aussi largement institutionnelle, et en cela impose d'interroger les processus de légitimation de la littérature électronique. Selon Leonardo Flores (**2019**), nous en serions à la troisième génération de la littérature électronique, une génération à l'audience populaire, qui a la particularité d'opérer sur des plateformes non spécifiquement dédiées à la littérature et dont le détournement des supports, le remix, serait le mode d'action privilégié. Cette nouvelle génération implique de fait une redéfinition de la littérature électronique et l'intégration de nouveaux corpus. Flores s'appuie sur des exemples tirés de la pratique des bots, de l'instapoetry ou encore des mèmes. S'il identifie très nettement ces pratiques comme faisant partie d'un tournant populaire pour la littérature électronique, il n'aborde pas suffisamment frontalement les enjeux auctoriaux qu'elles supposent. Ainsi, il ne renvoie que de manière très détournée à la problématique des pratiques amateures. Il s'agira donc pour nous, dans la lignée des réflexions ébauchées par Flores, de saisir à quel point cette démocratisation change radicalement la donne en termes de production et de réception de la littérature numérique, en même temps qu'elle en bouleverse radicalement la définition.

Désormais, les pratiques populaires qui conjuguent littérature et numérique ne se résument plus seulement à la lecture d'*ebook*, mais également à celle de la fan fiction, que l'étude de la littérature électronique a souvent mise de côté, à celle du récit transmédia que favorise aujourd'hui l'ensemble des réseaux sociaux. Il importera alors de nous demander à quel prix s'effectue cette démocratisation, particulièrement si le constat doit être opéré que ce qui fait littérature électronique pour les chercheurs n'est pas toujours désigné comme tel par leurs auteurs et leurs lecteurs. Si cette démocratisation de la littérature électronique se joue du côté des amateurs, cela s'effectue pour le meilleur comme pour le pire. Partant du constat d'un tournant paralittéraire de la littérature électronique, nous verrons comment cette démocratisation et la popularité de certaines œuvres provoquent dans un même mouvement leur récupération par les éditeurs et des plateformes d'autoédition. Ces derniers cherchent à produire le plus souvent des livres papiers, impliquant de ce fait une dissolution du numérique dans le papier et donc, pour les œuvres, une dislocation même de leur appartenance à la littérature numérique.

Abstract

This article begins with questioning as simple as the issues it raises are complex: who reads electronic literature and what electronic literature are we talking about? This question is not simply ontological, but also institutional, which therefore demands a questioning of the processes of legitimization of electronic literature. According to Leonardo Flores (**2019**), we are currently in the third generation of electronic literature, a generation of mainstream audiences which operates on platforms not specifically dedicated to literature and of which the appropriation of media through remixes is the privileged mode of action. This new generation implies a redefinition of digital literature and the integration of new corpuses. Flores relies on examples pulled from bots, instapoetry, and even memes. While he clearly identifies these practices as participating in a mainstream wave of electronic literature, he does not confront head-on the authorial concerns that these practices imply. Thus, he only refers in a very roundabout way to the question of amateur practices. We therefore seek, in line of reflections outlined by Flores, to identify at what point this democratization radically changes the situation in terms of the production and reception of digital literature, at the same time as it radically upsets its definition.

From this point onwards, the mainstream practices which unite literature and digital can no longer be limited to the reading of an *ebook*, but also to reading fan fiction, which digital literature studies have often overlooked, and the transmedia narrative now favored on social networks. It is important to ask ourselves at what price this democratization takes place, particularly if it should be noted that what is considered by researchers to be electronic lite-rature is not always designated as such by authors and readers. If this democratization of electronic literature favors amateurs, it is for better or for worse. Starting with an observation of a paraliterary turning point in electronic literature, we will see how this democratization and the popularity of certain works drives both editors and self-publishing platforms to claim them. The latter seek most often to produce paper books, implying the dissolution of the digital in paper and thus, for the works, a dissonance even in their belonging to digital literature.

La littérature électronique constitue à la fois un objet et un champ de recherche qui, comme en témoigne l'existence d'ELO et des colloques organisés dans son cadre depuis 2008, bénéficie désormais d'une reconnaissance institutionnelle. La littérature numérique est inscrite dans les programmes de départements d'études littéraires; elle fait l'objet de collections, de répertoires et de travaux de recherche (thèses, mémoires, essais, etc.), qui visent, depuis plusieurs années, à établir ses principales caractéristiques[1]. Tous ces travaux abordent d'une manière ou d'une autre les nouvelles formes de textualité, les questions lecturales que le numérique fait émerger, l'hypermédiatisation, la transmédiatisation, et ils interrogent les ruptures et continuités qu'implique le passage au numérique. Loin de moi le désir de remettre en question l'existence de la littérature numérique, la pertinence de son étude ou de sa valeur heuristique; je souhaite plutôt poser la question suivante : qui lit la littérature numérique à part nous, chercheuses et chercheurs membres d'ELO et nos étudiantes et étudiants captifs? Car il me semble que c'est là, aujourd'hui et à ce stade de nos travaux, que se situe désormais le *gap* à franchir par la littérature numérique.

Il semble alors indispensable de préciser la question : qui lit de la littérature électronique et quel type de littérature électronique lit-on?

Tout dépend de ce que nous entendons par littérature électronique. Dans son article, « Electronic Literature: What Is It? », N. Katherine Hayles (**2007**) la définit comme la littérature née en milieu numérique et (habituellement) conçue pour être lue sur ordinateur; Hayles prend soin d'exclure toute littérature imprimée puis numérisée (c'est-à-dire homothétique). Or, s'il est aisé d'obtenir des chiffres concernant le nombre de lecteurs d'ebook et leur évolution[2], les statistiques n'existent pas pour quantifier les lecteurs d'œuvres de littérature électronique ou pour dresser leur portrait.

NOTE 1

Je pense par exemple, et pour n'en citer que quelques-uns à *La Valeur heuristique de la littérature numérique* de Serge Bouchardon (**2014**), aux travaux d'Alexandra Saemmer (**2007**, **2015**), ou en anglais aux différents ouvrages de N. Katherine Hayles (**1999**, **2002**, **2008**) mais aussi aux textes fondateurs de Landow (**1994**, **1997**) sur l'hypertexte. Je pense aussi aux différents mémoires et thèses écrits par les étudiants du NT2, y compris à ma thèse de doctorat (Guilet **2013**).

NOTE 2

Cf. baromètre du numérique 2018 de l'ARCEP : **https://www.arcep.fr/cartes-et-donnees/nos-publications-chiffrees/numerique/le-barometre-du-numerique.html**, consulté le 2 avril 2019.

Hayles, en formulant sa définition en 2007, distingue deux générations dans l'histoire de la littérature électronique. La première recoupe les œuvres de fiction hypertextuelles jusqu'en 1995, alors que la seconde inclut des œuvres davantage multimédias issues d'une évolution en des formes hybrides comme les « network fiction », « interactive fiction, » « locative narratives, » « interactive drama, » et « generative art » (Hayles **2007**).

La littérature numérique, comme le montre la chercheuse et, à sa suite, les membres de ELO qui en ont proposé une définition, regroupe une pluralité de formes, de genres et de technologies mises en pratique.

> The term refers to works with important literary aspects that take advantage of the capabilities and contexts provided by the stand-alone or networked computer. Within the broad category of electronic literature are several forms and threads of practice, some of which are:
> — Hypertext fiction and poetry, on and off the Web
> — Kinetic poetry presented in Flash and using other platforms
> — Computer art installations which ask viewers to read them or otherwise have literary aspects
> — Conversational characters, also known as chatterbots
> — Interactive fiction
> — Novels that take the form of emails, SMS messages, or blogs
> — Poems and stories that are generated by computers, either interactively or based on parameters given at the beginning
> — Collaborative writing projects that allow readers to contribute to the text of a work
> — Literary performances online that develop new ways of writing[3]

NOTE 3

Site de ELO, en ligne : **https://eliterature.org/about/**, consulté le 1er avril 2019.

Ainsi, la littérature numérique ne se réduit pas à la littérature hypertextuelle, mais elle renvoie à toute littérature combinant des pratiques textuelles et numériques. Cette liste, compte tenu de la nature évolutive des pratiques, implique donc d'être régulièrement mise à jour. La définition de Hayles, proposée l'année du lancement de l'iPhone, ne pouvait inclure ni les œuvres numériques issues des réseaux sociaux, ni celles produites pour nos smartphones et tablettes, pas plus qu'elle ne pouvait tenir compte des œuvres incluant la réalité virtuelle ou l'internet des objets. Toutes ces technologies, plateformes ou médias ont la particularité de ne pas être dédiés à la littérature et de faire l'objet d'un vaste usage populaire, particulièrement en ce qui concerne les réseaux sociaux et les appareils mobiles. Partant de ce constat, Leonardo Flores, à la suite de Hayles, évoque la possibilité que nous en soyons à la troisième génération de la littérature électronique :

> Third generation electronic literature emerges with the rise of social media networks, the development of mobile, touchscreen, augmented reality (AR) and virtual reality (VR) platforms. This generation is less concerned with inventing form and more with remixing and creating work within well established platforms and their interfaces, parallel to a return to recognizable poetic forms, Romantic subjectivity, and pastiche in Postmodern poetry. (Flores **2018**)

Je ne peux que partager ce constat de l'émergence d'une troisième génération pour la littérature électronique, une génération à l'audience populaire, qui a la particularité d'opérer sur des plateformes non spécifiquement dédiées à la littérature et dont le détournement des supports, le remix, serait le mode d'action privilégié. Flores, par ailleurs, note très clairement la rupture opérée par cette troisième génération en termes de nouveaux corpus à intégrer à la littérature électronique : « I recognize the need to account for the explosive growth and diversification of e-literary digital writing practices beyond what is practiced and studied by the ELO community. » (Flores **2019**)

Dans son article « Third Generation Electronic Literature » (**2019**), le chercheur s'appuie sur des exemples tirés de la pratique des bots (sur Twitter notamment), de l'instapoetry, ou encore des mèmes. S'il identifie très nettement ces pratiques comme faisant partie d'un tournant populaire pour la littérature électronique[4], il n'aborde pas suffisamment frontalement, selon moi, les enjeux auctoriaux que cela suppose. Ainsi, il ne renvoie que de manière très détournée à la problématique des pratiques amateures :

NOTE 4

« I would describe these works as works of e-literary popular culture that seek ease of access and spreadability (to reference Henry Jenkins' term in Spreadable Media), and are aligned with the poetics of contemporary digital culture. » (Flores **2019**)

> (…) huge amount of people have used these tools to produce writing that has stepped away from the page to cross over into electronic literature territory, and it's a crucial move. Whether they know it or not, they are producing third generation electronic literature. (Flores **2019**)

Ces créateurs de troisième génération feraient de la littérature électronique comme M. Jourdain faisait de la prose dans *Le Bourgeois gentilhomme*. Il s'agit donc ici de problématiser plus avant et, dans la lignée des réflexions ébauchées par Flores, de voir à quel point cette démocratisation change radicalement la donne par rapport à qui produit et qui lit la littérature numérique, de même que la manière dont elle en bouleverse radicalement la nature.

Contrairement à ce qui se produisait chez les deux premières générations, la production, la lecture et les processus de légitimation de la littérature numérique ne passent plus par les institutions universitaires, mais elles sont plutôt le résultat de pratiques amateures. Les hypertextes de fiction de première génération étaient réalisés par des universitaires, pour des universitaires, alors que ceux de seconde génération l'étaient par des universitaires (dans le cadre du développement et de la reconnaissance de la recherche-création notamment) ainsi que par des auteurs souvent déjà connus, toujours pour un public de niche souvent constitué d'universitaires. La révolution que propose la troisième génération est celle de proposer une littérature numérique faite par des *quidams* pour des *quidams*, en la situant donc à l'extérieur des réseaux institutionnels usuels de la littérature électronique. Désormais, les pratiques populaires qui conjuguent littérature et numérique ne se résument plus seulement à la lecture *d'ebook*, mais également à celle de la fan fiction, que l'étude de la littérature électronique a souvent mise de côté, à celle du récit transmédia que favorise aujourd'hui l'ensemble des réseaux sociaux. À l'heure du *storytelling* généralisé (Salmon **2008**), quiconque peut raconter sa vie ou une fiction en publiant un texte sur Facebook, accompagné d'une image Instagram, d'un lien Youtube ou Soundcloud. La littérature électronique, entrée dans une nouvelle ère plus populaire, plus démocratique, semblerait ainsi (enfin) pouvoir prospérer.

Mais il importe alors de se demander à quel prix s'effectue cette démocratisation. Par exemple, il faut s'interroger sur ce qui fait que la littérature électronique n'est pas toujours désignée ainsi par leurs auteurs et leurs lecteurs, puis d'en identifier les enjeux.

En effet, si la démocratisation de la littérature électronique se joue du côté des amateurs, cela s'effectue pour le meilleur comme pour le pire. On verra que, d'un point de vue littéraire, ces productions ressortent plutôt de la paralittérature. Et, du point de vue de la littérature électronique, la démocratisation et la popularité de certaines œuvres provoquent sa récupération par les éditeurs et des plateformes d'autoédition, lesquels cherchent à produire le plus souvent des livres papiers, impliquant de ce fait une dissolution du numérique dans le papier et donc, pour les œuvres, une dislocation même de leur appartenance à la littérature numérique.

I. LA LITTÉRATURE ÉLECTRONIQUE AMATEURE

Mes propos sur la littérature numérique amateure sont basés sur les recherches que j'ai effectuées dans le cadre de la rédaction d'un chapitre sur les pratiques textuelles amateures sur le Web pour l'ouvrage collectif *Tous artistes! Les pratiques (ré)créatives du Web* (Limare, Gerard, et Guilet **2017**). Cette étude insistait sur la grande vitalité des productions littéraires amateures sur le Web à travers une pluralité d'exemples faisant varier les supports mobilisés. Le présent article reprend succinctement quelques exemples de ces pratiques[5].

NOTE 5

Pour des analyses plus détaillées, voir (Limare, Gerard, et Guilet **2017**).

1) FAN FICTION WATTPAD

Les fan fictions constituent une pratique dominante des écrivains amateurs sur le Web. Ces textes sont rédigés par les aficionados de produits culturels de masse à partir de leurs sujets de prédilection (*Harry Potter*, *Twilight* ou *Hunger Games*, par exemple) en vue d'en développer l'univers. La lecture effectuée par le fan aboutit à la production de ce que Jenkins (**1992**) appelle du « bêta-texte » : soit des textes, mais aussi des vidéos ou des dessins que le fan réalise sur les thèmes des œuvres qu'il s'approprie et qui sont diffusés par les médias sociaux, blogues et autres plateformes Web. Pour ne citer qu'un exemple, la série *Star Trek* est à cet égard canonique. Les membres de la communauté de fans *Star Trek*, surnommés les « *trekkies* », imaginent des histoires, des scénarios : ils fabulent, par exemple, sur [l'homosexualité de Spock (**http://bit.ly/2fSObN5**)] ou inventent d'autres fins à certains épisodes (Jenkins **2008**).

NOTE 6

Hyperliens :

http://www.ublot.com, http://www.fanfictions challenges.com, http://www.freestory.org, http://www.fanfic-fr.net, http://www.fanfictions.fr, http://www.francofanfic.com, http://fanfiction.super forum.fr.

La multiplication des plateformes dédiées à cette pratique témoigne de sa vivacité : Fanfiction.net est l'un des sites les plus consultés et où sont publiées le plus de fan fictions, mais l'on peut également citer ublot.com, fanfictionschallenges.com, freestory.org, fanfic-fr.net, fanfictions.fr, francofanfic.com, ou encore fanfiction.superforum.fr[6]. On trouve également des fan fictions sur des plateformes d'autopublication comme Wattpad ou KDP d'Amazon. À noter que si Wattpad n'est pas spécialement dédiée aux écrits de fans, elle en est constituée dans d'écrasantes proportions.

Les fan fictions s'élaborent au sein de communautés dont le Web est la condition pragmatique d'existence; celui-ci constitue, au-delà d'un simple moyen de diffusion, un monde alternatif, hors des sentiers battus de la légitimation littéraire, où peuvent s'exprimer l'altérité d'une appétence pour un certain type d'œuvres, le confort d'un jugement par des pairs, ainsi qu'un désir d'expression par l'écriture et le partage de textes.

2) LES CHRONIQUES SUR FACEBOOK

Le phénomène des chroniques qui se développe sur Facebook depuis quelques années propose des récits feuilletonesques majoritairement écrits par des adolescentes. Si l'on se fie aux « Bonjour les filles » par lesquels elles commencent, les chroniques s'adressent d'abord à un lectorat féminin. Bien qu'il soit difficile de chiffrer les adeptes de cette pratique d'écriture amateure sur le Web, force est de constater, quand on explore tous les hyperliens, qu'elles sont nombreuses.

Les chroniques sur Facebook se construisent sur des pages « Livre » ou « Communauté » et non sur les profils personnels de leurs autrices. La lectrice peut donc non seulement les liker, mais également s'y abonner afin de recevoir toutes les mises à jour. Les chroniques racontent le plus souvent des histoires d'amour tumultueuses, comme dans « Chronique – Une rencontre qui peut tout changer », ou des histoires de survie à une maladie (« Chronique de Lilia : j'étais condamné [*sic*] et pourtant on m'a sauvé [*sic*] ») (**http://bit.ly/2gftp80**) ou à un événement dramatique (« *Moi, Valé, fille du chef de la mafia nord, j'ai été kidnappée–chronique* ») (**http://bit.ly/2g2QB6R**). Les titres sont explicites et les histoires le plus souvent stéréotypées. Le succès d'une chronique se mesure au nombre de « J'aime » qu'elle récolte, qui peut grimper jusqu'à plus de 27 000 (« Chronique d'une cendrillon promise à un prince de tess ») (**http://bit.ly/2gYGLoD**).

Comme dans le cas des fan fictions, une vraie communauté se forme autour des chroniques, avec ses codes (construction d'une page Facebook, titre explicitant le statut de chronique, importance des dialogues), son vocabulaire et ses coutumes (l'échange, le fait de remercier les fans pour leurs commentaires, les encouragements aux chroniqueuses, etc.). Cette communauté est en majorité constituée d'adolescentes ou de jeunes adultes pour qui Internet devient le lieu d'un exutoire, un espace d'expression anonyme, détaché des proches, et où elles peuvent se confier, s'exprimer hors de tout jugement, au sein d'une communauté qui leur ressemble (Casilli **2010**).

3) LE MADELEINE PROJECT

J'aurais pu évoquer également des romans Instagram comme celui de Caroline Calloway (**http://bit.ly/2g4SyTu**), mais je préfère m'en tenir à l'exemple de twittérature de Clara Beaudoux. Cette-dernière vit à Paris et trouve dans la cave de son nouvel appartement les affaires de Madeleine, l'ancienne locataire des lieux.

Le *Madeleine project* repose sur des thématiques mémorielles à tendance pathétique et se construit sur quatre saisons. La première (2015) est consacrée aux archives personnelles remisées dans la cave de la vieille dame. Pour la seconde saison, qui débute le 8 février 2016, Beaudoux mettra le nez dehors pour partir à la rencontre de ceux qui ont connu Madeleine : son filleul, un couple d'anciens voisins, un commerçant. La troisième saison est pour sa part consacrée à la vie professionnelle de Madeleine, à la visite de Beaudoux à Bourges, ville natale de Madeleine, ainsi qu'à l'approfondissement des informations sur Loulou, son fiancé mort à la guerre. La quatrième saison, quant à elle, s'emploie à décrire la vie d'institutrice de Madeleine et à essayer de retrouver quelques-uns de ses anciens élèves.

La démarche de Beaudoux est transmédiatique; elle se déploie parallèlement sur twitter, Facebook et Storify. Elle aussi intersémiotique : entre image et texte. Son parcours médiatico-littéraire résulte d'un travail efficace de détournement des fonctionnalités des réseaux à des fins narratives.

II. LE TOURNANT PARALITTÉRAIRE DE LA LITTÉRATURE ÉLECTRONIQUE

Toutes ces pratiques d'écriture numérique offrent une diffusion fragmentée et suivie, proche de celle des séries télévisées dont le succès ne se dément pas ces dernières années, elles-mêmes n'étant que l'avatar du format feuilletonesque apparu dès le XIXe siècle.

Le roman-feuilleton, qui s'est développé dans les années 1830, semble en effet constituer une tendance majeure des pratiques d'écriture amateures qui s'épanouissent sur le Web. Ce genre littéraire s'est propagé dès l'avènement de la presse écrite. Comme le roman-feuilleton, les écrits amateurs contemporains coïncident avec un moment charnière de l'évolution médiatique : les plateformes numériques, à l'instar des journaux du XIXe siècle, offrent la possibilité d'une production massive de textes, permettant ainsi leur démocratisation, en même temps qu'ils influent résolument sur les formes narratives et leur réception.

Il faut également rappeler que le roman-feuilleton, parce qu'il ne peut manquer d'être considéré comme une forme littéraire féconde et créative qui transcende ses enjeux purement économiques, inaugure un trouble dans la vision romantique des belles-lettres qui distingue la « haute culture » (highbrow) de la « basse culture » (lowbrow). Et c'est en cela que les pratiques sérielles amateures sur le Web peuvent être comparées sous bien des aspects au roman-feuilleton. La sérialité possède un impact décisif sur chacune des étapes, allant de la création à la consommation du récit, mais elle est également à l'origine d'une esthétique singulière qui va à l'encontre des contraintes de légitimation (Aubry **2006**). Ainsi, et à titre d'exemple, dans les chroniques sur Facebook comme dans les fan fictions, le ton des textes produits est souvent oralisé, d'abord parce que l'on retrouve beaucoup de dialogues, mais aussi parce que certains auteurs emploient un langage très familier ou a contrario maladroitement ampoulé. Il faut aussi souligner que les fautes d'orthographe et de grammaire sont légion : lire ces chroniques ou fan fictions est une épreuve pour qui accorde quelque importance à l'emploi du conditionnel, à l'accord des participes passés ou à la concordance des temps. Si l'on est loin d'une écriture proustienne, l'attention à la narration, le ménagement d'effets de suspens entre les publications, ainsi que l'alternance entre récits et dialogues témoignent d'une vraie construction diégétique qui, si elle tient plus du scénario de *soap opera* ou de *sitcom*, n'enlève rien au désir d'écriture prégnant et sincère manifesté par ces jeunes chroniqueuses comme par les auteurs de fan fiction. Leurs productions sont littéraires par fiction comme par diction (Genette **2003**) et numériques de par leur support de diffusion; je préciserais de plus qu'elles sont hypermédiatiques, puisque toutes mêlent textes, images, vidéos, musiques et hyperliens.

Sur le plan créatif, le roman-feuilleton du XIXe siècle est à l'origine du développement de nombreux sous-genres populaires, comme les romans de mœurs, de cape et d'épée et sentimentaux, que l'on retrouve aussi dans les productions amateures sur le Web, avec d'autres qui lui sont propres : chick lit, science-fiction, thriller – tous des sous-genres que d'aucuns relèguent au domaine de la « paralittérature », de la « littérature industrielle », du « mauvais genre » ou du « récit de grande consommation », en somme de la littérature populaire. Celle-là même fleurit dans toutes les productions amateures sur le Web, qui forment de ce fait un vivier incomparable pour les éditeurs contemporains à la recherche des prochains succès commerciaux, parmi lesquels la paralittérature règne en maître incontestable.

La littérature numérique, dans cette troisième ère, effectue ainsi à l'image de ce que produisit le roman feuilleton au XIXe siècle, son tournant paralittéraire. Comme la littérature populaire naissait à « la fin de l'Ancien Régime avec l'explosion du genre romanesque, le progrès de l'alphabétisation et la multiplication des cabinets de lecture [...] » (Huybrechts **2014**), la paralittérature électronique naîtrait du développement et de la multiplication des réseaux sociaux, de la maîtrise des outils numériques des *digital natives*, comme de leur simplification, entraînant la construction de communautés partageant leurs écrits, leurs lectures et leurs appétences littéraires.

En 1970, Jean Tortel remarquait que « l'espace littéraire » constituait « un petit îlot isolé parmi la masse énorme de l'écriture » (Tortel **1970**, II); la littérature numérique, telle que l'entendent les institutions actuelles, ne serait, dès lors, qu'un îlot parmi la masse des productions numériques écrites, un îlot dont les contenus ne recoupent ni les écrits les plus populaires, ni les plus lus.

III. LA LITTÉRATURE ÉLECTRONIQUE, UN TIGRE DE PAPIER ?

À sa description de la troisième génération de littérature électronique, Flores ajoute : « This generation leaves behind book and open Web publishing paradigms and embraces new funding models, such as crowdfunding and software distribution platforms. » (Flores **2018**) Or, selon l'étude que j'ai effectuée des pratiques de littérature électronique amateures, les seuls moyens de financement offerts aux auteurs sont ceux proposés par les plateformes d'autoédition comme Atramenta (**http://www.atramenta.net**) ou Bookonlive (**https://www.bookonlive.com**), qui génèrent des revenus anecdotiques, et ceux de la commercialisation d'une édition papier.

1) SUCCESS STORY NUMÉRIQUE ET BEST-SELLER PAPIER

Les plus populaires des productions amateures sur le Web sont parfois publiées en livre papier. C'est le cas de Nargesse Bibimoune et de sa chronique intitulée « Dans la peau d'un Thug » (http://bit.ly/2h22azO), qui est apparue sur Facebook à partir de 2011. Elle y narre le quotidien de Youssef, un voyou des cités mal dans sa peau dont le meilleur ami vient de mourir brutalement. Obtenant chaque jour plus de lecteurs, jusqu'à atteindre des milliers de fans, l'étudiante en sciences politiques à Lyon finit par être repérée par Is Edition, qui publie à compte d'éditeur *Dans la peau d'un Thug* au sein de sa collection « Graines d'écrivains ». C'est le cas aussi de Clara Beaudoux, qui a vu le *Madeleine project* publié en livre aux Éditions du sous-sol en 2016, puis en 2017 en version poche, et traduit vers l'anglais pour New Vessel Press.

Pour les écrivaines numériques amateures, la transformation de leur travail d'écriture fragmentaire sous la forme d'un livre apparaît comme un aboutissement, une sorte de consécration de la dimension littéraire de leur œuvre qui se joue tout entière dans l'aura indéniable que porte encore aujourd'hui le livre et ce, au détriment du dispositif numérique initial qui était pourtant partie intégrante de leur création. Malgré sa mort mille fois annoncée, le livre conserve donc sa dimension sacrée, telle qu'elle avait été affirmée au début du christianisme (Johannot **1994**). Le livre permet de consacrer un discours, et c'est sans doute en partie pour cela que les amateurs semblent tenir à faire aboutir leurs expériences sur le Net dans une publication, pour ainsi corroborer l'adage mallarméen selon lequel « Tout, au monde, existe pour aboutir à un livre » (Mallarmé **2003**, 22). Les écrits sur les réseaux sociaux n'apparaissent alors que comme un banc d'essai, un travail préparatoire, un test avant la publication finale, « le brouillon d'écran et l'épreuve d'imprimante », pour reprendre les propos d'Emmanuel Souchier (**1996**, 119).

Ce « devenir livre » dissout également l'appartenance à la littérature électronique de leurs œuvres selon la définition qu'on en a donné en introduction, laquelle soulignait leur caractéristique numérique. Face à ce constat, nous sommes en droit de nous demander si la littérature électronique de troisième génération ne serait, en fait, qu'un tigre de papier.

2) DES QUESTIONS ÉCONOMIQUES

La viabilité économique de cette littérature numérique semble totalement dépendante du passage au papier qui convertit l'autorité, née en contexte numérique, en vente de livres et en un statut de *best-seller*. Comme le remarque Flores :

> [...] while second generation works are currently more sophisticated, complex, and aligned with academia, the third generation will produce the first massively successful works because they operate in platforms with large audiences that need little to no training to reading them. So while second generation works will continue to attract critical acclaim with limited audiences, it is the third generation that will produce the field's first #1 hit. (Flores **2018**)

Si l'on en croit les exemples de *Fifty Shades of Grey* – initialement une fan fiction publiée sur Internet –, et ses 125 millions d'exemplaires, traduit en 52 langues et adapté en film en 2015, ou même d'*After* d'Anna Todd – égérie de Wattpad dont le premier tome de sa fan fiction écrite sur téléphone portable s'est vendu à plus 15 millions d'exemplaires –, la littérature électronique aura déjà produit ses best-sellers. Mais à aucun moment ces textes n'auront été présentés comme appartenant à la littérature numérique; à peine quelques journalistes auront signalé, à titre anecdotique ou pittoresque, leur origine numérique. Cette troisième génération de la littérature électronique est ainsi potentiellement l'occasion d'une récupération commerciale où se rejouent les schémas économiques de la littérature de masse.

La troisième génération de la littérature électronique reprend également à son compte la tension que nous retrouvons depuis des décennies dans les débats autour de la paralittérature, en suivant ses logiques d'exclusion et de dévaluation. Rappelons en utilisant le vocabulaire de Marc Angenot (**2013**) que c'est au XIXe siècle que commencent à s'opposer les régimes de production de la littérature industrielle et celle de la littérature dite « élitaire ». Il s'agit alors de reprendre avec Huybrecht la distinction effectuée par Bourdieu (**1979**, **1992**), en lien avec un processus d'autonomisation de la création artistique, entre deux ordres de production :

> Le champ de production restreinte d'une part, rigoureusement tourné vers l'accumulation du profit symbolique et hiérarchisé par un principe de reconnaissance mutuelle; le champ de grande production de l'autre, quant à lui soumis à l'impératif économique, diffusant dès lors des biens ajustés à une demande préexistante et voués à une rapide obsolescence (Huybrechts 2014).

Les productions amateures ne font dès lors pas exception aux mécanismes de la distinction chers à Pierre Bourdieu; il y aurait désormais une littérature numérique populaire, issue de pratiques paralittéraires et essentiellement produite par des écrivains amateurs, et une littérature numérique élitaire, celles qui obtient les prix ELO et qui est étudiée par les chercheurs. Dans son étude sur l'écriture numérique et les communautés d'écrivains, Anne-Marie Petitjean analysait « l'école de François Bon » et notait comment se construit au sein de cette communauté le statut d'auteur numérique :

> Constatons qu'ici encore, c'est l'appréciation des partenaires de la communauté qui assure la valeur des écrits produits et un ensemble de signes sociaux afférents déterminant le statut d'auteur numérique. L'autonomie du champ littéraire, acquise au XIXe siècle par d'autres moyens, a tendance à se réinventer par les moyens contemporains de la communication numérique, en jouant pareillement sur le discours d'initiés. On assisterait ainsi à l'émergence, depuis une dizaine d'années, d'un groupe d'artistes indépendants établissant ses codes et ses règles de fonctionnement, déterminant autorité et légitimité en son sein et apte à accentuer le clivage entre production de masse, soumise à la loi économique, et production lettrée, cultivée, maîtrisée par un code commun tentant d'échapper au marché et constituant une nouvelle « cléricature », se lisant et se commentant en cercle restreint. (Petitjean 2012, 6)

CONCLUSION

Comme le notait Alexandra Molotkow dans un article du *New York Times* : « Populism is the new model of cool; elitists, [...] are the new squares » (2012). Alors cool ou ringard? Populiste ou élitiste? Les productions de littérature électronique amateures rejouent ainsi le duel entre une légitimité esthétique et une légitimité industrielle, lesquelles ne peuvent pas, on le sait, s'opposer si facilement. Il existe en effet tout un spectre entre cette littérature idéale, à la langue soignée, d'un genre noble, savamment composée, produite par un auteur légitimé, et une littérature de masse, destinée uniquement à satisfaire les attentes du public, au contenu standardisé et créée seulement dans un souci de rentabilité. C'est dans ce même spectre que doivent être inscrites les pratiques d'écriture électronique amateures de troisième génération.

Angenot, Marc. 2013. *Les Dehors de la littérature. Du roman populaire à la science-fiction.* Paris : Honoré Champion.

Aubry, Danielle. 2006. *Du Roman-feuilleton à la série télévisuelle : pour une rhétorique du genre et de la sérialité.* Berne : Peter Lang.

Bouchardon, Serge. 2014. *La Valeur heuristique de la littérature numérique.* Paris : Hermann.

Bourdieu, Pierre. 1979. *La Distinction : critique sociale du jugement.* Paris : Minuit.

Bourdieu, Pierre. 1992. *Les Règles de l'art : Genèse et structure du champ littéraire.* Paris : Seuil.

Casilli, Antonio. 2010. *Les Liaisons numériques. Vers une nouvelle sociabilité ?* La Couleur des idées, French Kindle Edition.

Flores, Leonardo. 2018. « Third generation Electronic literature ». In *ELO 2018 Mind The Gap!* Montréal. Consulté le 2 avril 2019. Accéder au lien.

Flores, Leonardo. 2019. « Third generation Electronic literature ». *Electronic Book Review*, avril. Consulté le 8 avril 2019. Accéder au lien.

Genette, Gérard. 2003. « Fiction ou diction ». *Poétique* 2 (134):131-39.

Guilet, Anaïs. 2013. « Pour une littérature cyborg : l'hybridation médiatique du texte littéraire ». Thèse de doctorat, Poitiers et Montréal : Université de Poitiers et UQAM. Consulté le 2 avril 2019. https://sites.grenadine.uqam.ca/sites/nt2/en/elo2018/schedule/504/Third+Generation+Electronic+Literature.

Hayles, Katherine N. 1999. *How we Became Posthuman: Virtual Bodies in Cybernetics, Literature, and Informatics.* Chicago; Londres : The University of Chicago Press.

Hayles, Katherine N. 2002. *Writing Machines.* Cambridge (Mass.); Londres : MIT Press.

Hayles, Katherine N. 2007. « Electronic literature: what is it? » 2007. https://eliterature.org/pad/elp.html.

Hayles, Katherine N. 2008. *Electronic Literature: New Horizons for the Literary.* Notre Dame (Ind.) : University of Notre Dame.

Huybrechts, Florence. 2014. « Paralittérature(s) ». In *Le Lexique socius*, édité par A. Glinoer et D. Saint-Amand. Consulté le 2 avril 2019. http://ressources-socius.info/index.php/lexique/21-lexique/51-paralitterature-s.

Jenkins, Henry. 1992. *Textual Poachers: Television Fans & Participatory Culture.* New York; Londres : Routledge.

Jenkins, Henry. 2008. « La filk et la construction sociale de la communauté de fans de science-fiction ». In *Cultural Studies. Anthologie*, édité par H. Glévarec, E. Macé, et E. Maigret. Paris : Armand Colin / INA.

Johannot, Yvonne. 1994. *Tourner la page : livre, rites et symboles.* 2e édition. [1988] Paris : Jérôme Million.

Landow, George P. 1994. *Hyper/Text/Theory.* Baltimore; Londres : The John Hopkins University Press.

Landow, George P. 1997. *Hypertext 2.0: the Convergence of Contemporary Critical Theory and Technology.* Baltimore; Londres : Baltimore (Maryl.); Londres.

Limare, Sophie, Annick Gerard, et Anaïs Guilet. 2017. *Tous artistes! Les pratiques (ré)créatives du Web.* Montréal : Presses de l'Université de Montréal.

Mallarmé, Stéphane. 2003. « Le Livre, instrument spirituel ». In *Œuvres complètes.* Vol. II. Paris : Gallimard.

Molotkow, Aleksandra. 2012. « Why the Old-School Music Snob Is The Least Cool Kid on Twitter ». *New York Times,* avril. Consulté le 13 décembre 2016. http://nyti.ms/2gHGKai.

Petitjean, Anne-Marie. 2012. « Web littérature et communauté d'écrivains : à l'école de François Bon ». *Communauté(s) en francophonie* 35 (1). Consulté le 13 décembre 2018. https://hal.archives-ouvertes.fr/hal-01896072/document.

Saemmer, Alexandra. 2007. *Matières textuelles sur support numérique.* Saint-Étienne : Publications de l'Université de Saint-Étienne, Centre interdisciplinaire d'études et de recherches sur l'expression contemporaine.

Saemmer, Alexandra. 2015. *Rhétorique du texte numérique.* Paris : Presses de l'ENSSIB.

Salmon, Christian. 2008. *Storytelling : La machine à fabriquer des histoires et à formater les esprits.* Paris : La Découverte.

Souchier, Emmanuël. 1996. « L'écrit d'écran, pratiques d'écriture et informatique ». *Communication et langages,* n° 107.

Tortel, Jean. 1970. « Qu'est-ce que la paralittérature ? » In *Entretiens sur la paralittérature,* édité par N. Arnaud, F. Lacassin, et J. Tortel. Paris : Plon.

"Conpleting The Circle?" The Curious Counter-Canonical Case Of *The Eastgate Quarterly Review Of Hypertext* (1994-1995)

ASTRID ENSSLIN

Abstract

This article provides a vignette for exploring early, pre-web hypertext literature from a canon-theoretical point of view. At its centre lies a serial publication from the mid 1990s that followed a then highly innovative yet ultimately short-lived trajectory: the *Eastgate Quarterly Review of Hypertext* (1994-1995). I refer to it as a curious case of counter-canonicity because, at the time of writing, there is a lot of mystery surrounding its rationale and its commissioning principles, as well as the reasons behind its discontinuation. Furthermore, to date there is very little scholarship that deals with the EQ as an e-lit publishing phenomenon in its own right, and most of the works published in it are both under-documented and under-researched. To address this gap, I present the results of a preliminary oral-digital history project I performed on the subject. I also offer the first ever narrative analysis of one of the EQ's littlest known works, Michael van Mantgem's hypertext fiction, "Completing the Circle," which was published in issue 2.2 of the EQ (1995). Overall, this article makes a contribution to documenting, preserving and dynamically canonizing (Ensslin **2007**) an early hypertext publication experiment that appeared at the threshold of the emergent WWW and testifies to a strong sense of uncertainty about where literary publishing, and publishing more generally, was headed at the time.

Résumé

Cet article présente un tableau de la littérature hypertextuelle pré-Web, abordée sous l'angle des théories canoniques. J'y analyse, plus précisément, une publication en série du milieu des années 1990 qui a suivi une trajectoire tout aussi innovante qu'éphémère : l'*Eastgate Quarterly Review of Hypertext* (1994-1995). Je qualifie cette publication de « contre-canonique », car au moment d'écrire ces lignes, il y a beaucoup de mystère autour de sa raison d'être, de son processus de sélection, ainsi que de son interruption. En outre, à ce jour, très peu d'études traitent du EQ comme d'un phénomène de publication de littérature électronique à part entière, et la plupart des textes qui y sont publiés sont à la fois peu documentés et peu étudiés. Pour combler cette lacune, je présente les résultats d'un projet préliminaire d'histoire orale-numérique que j'ai réalisé sur le sujet. Je propose également la toute première analyse narrative d'une œuvre peu connue de EQ, la fiction hypertextuelle de Michael van Mantgem, « Completing the Circle », qui a été publiée dans le numéro 2.2 de EQ (1995). Dans l'ensemble, cet article contribue à documenter, à préserver et à canoniser de manière dynamique (Ensslin **2007**) une expérimentation précoce de publication d'hypertextes parue à l'aube du WWW, qui témoigne du fort sentiment d'incertitude quant à l'avenir de l'édition littéraire.

INTRODUCTION

My aim in this paper is to explore early, pre-web hypertext literature from a canon-theoretical point of view. To this end, I am going to look at a publication that, at the time it was active in the mid-1990s, followed a highly innovative yet relatively short-lived trajectory: the *Eastgate Quarterly Review of Hypertext* ("EQ"). I call it a curious case of counter-canonicity because there is a lot of mystery surrounding its rationale and its commissioning principles, as well as the reasons behind its discontinuation. Furthermore, to date there is very little scholarship that deals with the EQ as an e-lit publishing phenomenon in its own right, and most of the works published in it are both under-documented and under-researched. To address this gap, I examine the results of a preliminary oral-digital history project I performed on the subject, and I am also going to make a start on canonizing one of the EQ's littlest known works, by offering a short analysis of Michael van Mantgem's hypertext fiction, "Completing the Circle," which was published in issue 2.2 of the EQ (**1995**).

In this paper I argue that a medium-conscious, digital-born notion of canon has to move away from "seminal, normative and timeless" principles of canonization (Schweikle and Schweikle **1990**, 232) to a more open, fluid and non-elitist, non-normative notion combining "there-ness," critical potential, and replicable accessibility. This is a proposal that builds on the "dynamic" e-lit canon I put forward in my 2007 book, *Canonizing Hypertext*. Put another way, the fact that a work exists (rather than its subjectively attributed value) to me would seem sufficient to merit examination and preservation, especially if it inspires a critical response ("critical potential"), although I do not see this as a necessary pre-condition to canonization.

Arguably, we can only read and analyze literary works in a replicable manner if we can assume that other people could, theoretically, arrive at similar or indeed discrepant readings, based on the presumption of having access to the same textual material (bearing in mind, of course, that the reading experience itself might differ radically between readers). And here we are already confronted with a dilemma: what textual material? After all, the ways in which we read depend on the availability of the original software and its operability on one or more vintage hardware platforms. Is being able to access a work through an emulator still "access"? I would argue that it is, to the extent that it allows certain types of (replicable) readings. However, fully platform-conscious readings that take into account the tangible, medium-specific qualities of, say, a Macintosh Classic or Performa, as well as of physical data carriers such as floppies and CD-ROMs, are restricted to those with access to the physical and support infrastructures of a dedicated media archeology space like the Electronic Literature Lab at Washington State University Vancouver.

This constraint is aggravated by the fact that certain historical works of e-lit are no longer available from their original distributors and, hence, technological obsolescence is augmented by changes in production and dissemination that further reduce the canonical potential of important works of pre-web e-lit–and by "important," I mean significant as an example of medium-specific historical literary practice that needs to be preserved in the same way that voices of historical individuals need to preserved for posterity, for example through oral historiography. Using terminology coined by German literary scholar, Hans Günther (1987), we might say that, due to access issues, a large number of pre-web hypertexts moved straight from pre-canonical to post-canonical status, which means they are "de-canonized," or critically invisible, without even getting a chance to be discussed at length by the e-lit scholarly community, prior to obsolescence.

To be clear, I agree with Scott Rettberg's point in "An Emerging Canon" (2013) that a crowdsourced, user-generated approach to documenting and, thus, cumulatively and democratically canonizing electronic literature, its curatorship and scholarship, is more robust and collectively satisfying than any single-handed or oligarchic attempt at selection and exclusion. However, the question in which I am interested here is what can be done to prevent crowd-*censorship* of works that defy quasi-egalitarian access for purely material reasons–and by material I mean physical and infrastructural reasons (software and/or hardware are no longer supported); logistic reasons (shipment is either discontinued because publisher has run out of copies, or slowed down by dated delivery methods such as wooden flash drives being sent through snail mail); and financial reasons (where experimental and arguably non-culinary forms of writing are costed as highly as or more highly than blockbuster video games; Ensslin, Skains, and Tabbi 2017).

The ELO's attempts to take action on un-de-canonizing certain forgotten works of pre-web literature by procuring and preserving them is vital. Yet, in the case of Eastgate, this comes with a significant amount of copyright baggage, which will need to be resolved for any consolidated effort to port Storyspace works onto more stable platforms.

What I am going to do in the remainder of this paper is to present a case study of a pre-web e-lit publication that warrants the term "obsolescent": the literary journal, *Eastgate Quarterly Review of Hypertext*, which was published between 1994 and 1995 on stand-alone data carriers. Grigar (Grigar **2018**) introduces three works that were originally published in the series: J Yellowlees Douglas's "I Have Said Nothing," Mary-Kim Arnold's "Lust," and Robert Kendall's *A Life Set For Two*. To add to her efforts, I will offer a brief analysis of one work that has been almost completely neglected by e-lit scholarship: "Completing the Circle" by Michael van Mantgem.

CROWD-CENSORSHIP AS A SYMPTOM OF OBSOLESCENCE

Crowd-censorship as a symptom of obsolescence manifests in a variety of forms: an obvious one is under- and/or mis-representation in key archives and directories, such as the Electronic Literature as a Model of Creativity and Innovation in Practice Knowledge Base, or ELMCIP for short. At the time of doing the research for this paper, there was a separate ELMCIP entry for EQ, set up by Jill Walker in 2011 (Fig. 1). However, not only does the entry remain a "not yet reviewed" stump, but it also fails to communicate what the EQ actually is, or was. The only information available currently is provenance, editorship, and an eclectic list of some of its contents. Furthermore, the entry itself is partly inaccurate: Carolyn Guyer and Martha Petry's *Izme Pass* was not published in the EQ, but in *Writing on the Edge*. In fact, it could not have appeared in the EQ because the work was published in 1991, and the EQ first appeared in 1994. Similarly, Mary-Kim Arnold's "Lust" appeared in issue 1.2 of the EQ dated 1994 rather than 1993, as suggested by the entry.

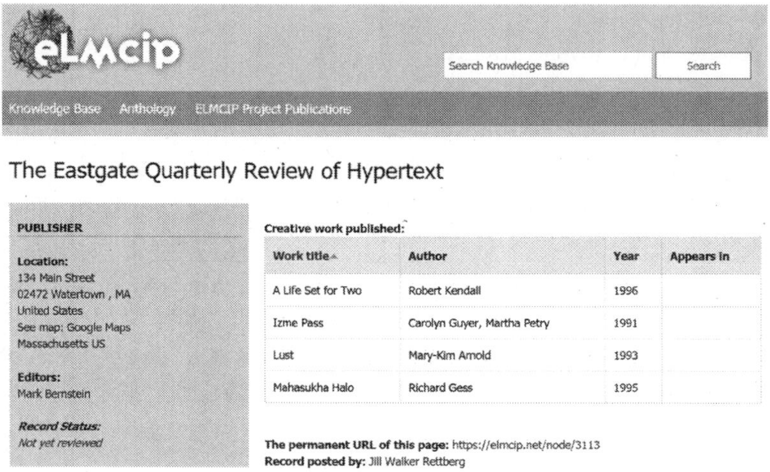

Figure 1. Screenshot of the EQ entry in ELMCIP, taken in June 2018.

Perhaps even less uplifting, for that matter, was my experience with the Electronic Literature Directory (ELD), which gave me zero hits for the EQ (in June 2018). Both examples suggest that crowd-censorship occurs even in highly reputable, well-endowed and thoroughly moderated databases, and this shortcoming calls for a more concerted, focused scholarly approach to creating and reviewing pre-web electronic literature in crowd-sourced[1] directories and archives.

NOTE 1

It has to be conceded that neither the ELMCIP Knowledge Base nor the ELD are fully crowdsourced in the sense of being rolled out to the entire world on the enabled side of the digital divide (Wikipedia would be an example of this); rather, their entries are outsourced to the entire community of e-lit scholars, which often includes undergraduate students, and they receive P2P review comments and edits throughout their life cycle.

THE *EASTGATE QUARTERLY REVIEW OF HYPERTEXT*

The EQ is a series of eight journal issues, published on stand-alone data carriers over two annual volumes. Each issue comes in the form of a cardboard envelope containing one or more floppy disks and/or a CD-ROM (my copy of issue 2.1, for example, contains two floppies and a CD ROM to cater to different platforms), as well as a printed booklet with author's notes and bios, mini-essays, system specs and installation directions.

According to EQ editor Mark Bernstein, "the idea of the [EQ] grew from two sources: from [Eastgate's] view of the immediate future of literary hypertext in the context of the early 1990s, and from the challenges confronting publishing in that era" (personal correspondence, August 8, 2018). The journal was particularly intended for short hypertext fiction, nonfiction, and poetry, which might not have sold as stand-alone hypertext novels. At the time, "the size of the novel was [an important] landmark" (ibid), and the pricing for a short hypertext fiction would have been very similar to that of a full-fledged hypertext novel. Short fiction was struggling to sell on the mainstream print market, and for Eastgate it was not clear at all whether the business model of a journal would be successful in relation to the emergent, medium-specific genre of hypertext.

What can be said with some certainty is that the EQ project was underfunded to begin with and challenged by a somewhat experimental business model that did not allow Eastgate to even pay royalties in all cases, or to "[port] first-gen Eastgate texts to Windows or to 16bit platforms and beyond" (Michael Joyce, personal correspondence, July 31, 2018). Furthermore, and this may have been the other key contributing factor to the EQ's demise, there simply were not enough hypertexts of the complex, cognitively modeled kind supported by Storyspace. As Yellowlees Douglas put it in an oral interview (July 31, 2018), the kinds of hypertexts that are becoming mainstream now (mostly through Twine), are flat and cognitively non-representative, whereas the Storyspace School allowed for complex, psychologically mapped deep and layered linking and tunneling. However, the combination of high developmental effort and short life-cycles prior to technological obsolescence prevented many hypertext writers from producing more material, and with the kind of regularity required to fill a quarterly journal.

In my logistically constrained research for this paper (the EQ is out of print and cannot currently be ordered through Eastgate), I wanted to get a sense of (a) how much scholarship exists on the EQ in general, and (b) how de-canonized individual works from the EQ actually are. So I ran various catalog and search engine searches for the title of the journal. In this exercise, I found only 4 references to the journal that did not simply mention it in a citation (i.e., where a work published in it was mentioned in the main text and the EQ was cited as part of that reference). Yet again, that information was mostly descriptive, minimalist, and/or promotionally slanted: Stuart Moulthrop, in "Travelling in the

Breakdown Lane" (1995), calls the EQ "the first journal of hypertext literature." Sarah Sloane, in her 2000 book, *Digital Fictions: Storytelling in a Material World*, tells us that the EQ is part of a seemingly proliferating movement of hypertext literature and scholarship, and that Eastgate's website "features subscription information for a disk-based journal, Eastgate Quarterly Review of Hypertext." Chris Funkhouser, finally, in *Prehistoric Digital Poetry* (2007), commends Bernstein's persistence in publishing hypertext works in stand-alone form and in the EQ at a time "when few other publishers in the United States were willing or able to produce literature that required viewers to load files onto computers" (153).

Interestingly, the EQ is mentioned consistently for many consecutive years in various small publisher directories. In the *Directory of Poetry Publishers* (2006-2007, and many years preceding that volume), the EQ is listed, including address details, commissioning and submission information ("Expects 1-2 poems 2006, 1-2 poems 2007", "Hypertextual poetry only"); subscription price; reporting time; recent contributors, and special interests (e.g., "The editor is interested in translations. Everything we publish could be construed as 'experimental.' No light verse, nothing sentimental–there is nothing worse than going for unearned emotional effect."

Just for comparison, in *The International Directory of Little Magazines & Small Presses* of 1999-2000, the EQ entry gives partly discrepant information, especially about its remit ("poetry, fiction, articles, art, photos, interviews, satire, criticism, parts-of-novels, long-poems, collages, non-fiction"–"electronic submissions only; send disks, not paper. Works should be in some way 'hypertextual' (loosely construed)." It also says that discounts and site licenses were available at the time.

To gain a sense of the relative scholarly popularity of individual works published in the EQ, I ran a database (MLA) and web search (Google Scholar and Google Books), which resulted in the bar chart depicted in Fig. 2. The chart shows the combined hits from Google Scholar and Google Books on June 27, with duplicate hits removed. The MLA search did not yield any results at the time the search was conducted.

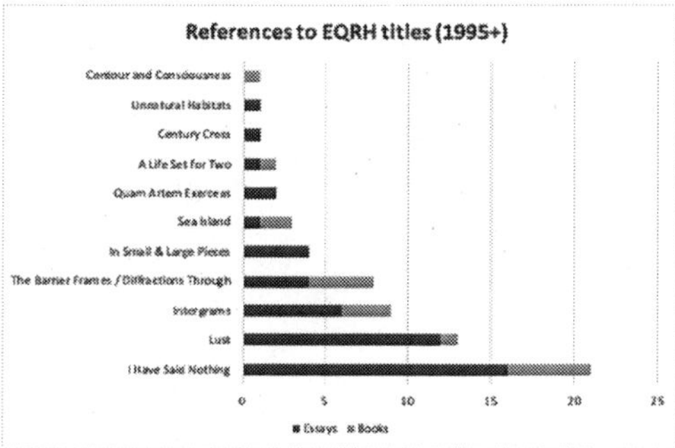

Figure 2. Number of references to individual EQ titles in Google Scholar and Google Books from 1995 onwards.

The vast majority of existing scholarship discusses Douglas's "I Have Said Nothing" and Arnold's "Lust" (Issue 1.2), followed by Rosenberg's "Intergrams" and his co-published poems, "The Barrier Frames" and "Diffractions Through" (Issue 2.2). Between one and five mentions referred to Kathryn Cramer's "In Small and Large Pieces" (1.3), Giuliano Franco's "Quam Artem Exerceas" (1.4), Robert Kendall's "A Life Set for Two" (2.4), Deena Larsen's "Century Cross" (2.2), Kathy Mac's "Unnatural Habitats" (1.3), and a mysterious, yet unpublished hypertext by Heather Malin, "Contour and Consciousness," which is referenced in Michael Joyce's book *Othermindedness* (**2000**) as "forthcoming" in the EQ (Malin was a PhD student of Joyce's at the time). Arguably, had there been a Volume 3, it might have been published there although, even at the time of writing Joyce's book, a continuation after a 3-4 year break must already have seemed unlikely. Malin herself commented, "As to whether contours is available somewhere, I have it saved on a floppy disk which is safely tucked away, but [there is] no way of physically putting it into a computer or any software to virtually open it with. But god, how I would love to if I could!" This resonates with the general frustration of numerous Storyspace writers (like Yellowlees Douglas) who, at this point in time, cannot even access their own hypertexts. It is therefore reassuring to note that, following our correspondence and my presentation of this paper at ELO 2018, Malin donated "contours and consciousness" to the ELO for preservation in its emergent ELO Repository (**https://hyrax.elo-repository.org/**).

"COMPLETING THE CIRCLE"

After the more quantitative and strangely enlightening exercise of searching for scholarly engagement with EQ content, I embarked on an emulated reading of a work in my possession that, according to my search (confirmed again by crowd-censored database stumps in leading e-lit directories), had been mostly if not completely ignored by e-lit scholarship: Michael van Mantgem's "Completing the Circle" (CtC)

Like other individual EQ texts, CtC is recorded in WSUV's Electronic Literature Lab Catalogue, also showing select screenshots and photos of hardware and software usage, and the material form in which the work was distributed (see Fig. 3). The entry does not, however, contain any plot or character summaries, or indeed any biographical information about the author. Instead, it gives information about how two different copies of the text were obtained (purchased or gifted for use in the lab), and that they are in "mint condition." What is particularly useful about this entry is the fact that it details the operating systems on which the software was successfully tested, e.g., Mac OS 8 and 9, and System Software 7.

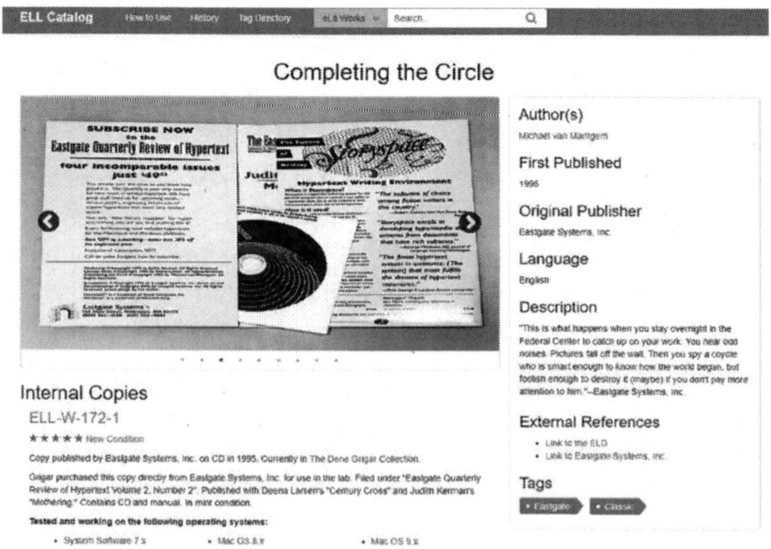

Figure 3. Screenshot of ELL Catalog entry of "Completing the Circle".

In the final part of this paper, I offer what to my knowledge is the first published reading of "Completing the Circle." The work title applies serendipitously well to the ongoing, iterative project of preserving e-literature, as it references the never-ending exercise of "Completing the Circle." In the manuscript, the circle relates to the iterative mechanisms of life, love, desire, obsessive guilt and traumatic re-living. These rotations can only be broken

> when events become completely clear, almost crystalline; when a choice, a single phrase, will create a very real future and an irretrievable past. That moment is so immediate that each choice becomes like a Venus Flytrap or The Yellow Brick Road. Keep in mind that there is only one direction and no possibility of return. Indeed choosing one path immediately and forever closes the other. [CiC]

These mutually foreclosing paths are clearly resonant, or rather indicative of the Aarsethian "paths not taken" (1997, 3), except that, in real life, there is no respawn or replay option. Van Mantgem's hypertext novel, then, takes its paradoxical motto, that "a circle is always in the process of being completed and at the same time is always complete" onto a formal level and presents readers with a "scotomic episode," a "view from the protagonist [Haller]'s brain, a brain taken over by sex, delusions, mental collapse, and the desperate attempts to keep it all together." This scotomic episode manifests in a combination of hypertext loops and more linear passages, which, however, criss-cross the protagonist's life in seemingly random, proleptically and analeptically organized memories. His condition is the result of an injury he inflicted on himself by deliberately crashing his car into the Mexican desert while escaping from his beloved yet estranged wife, Christina, with his much younger lover, Mary. A third female character, Carmen, appears in his musings at regular intervals, and whilst the impression arises that she is a prostitute that he once had sex with, she also becomes the epitome of unachievable perfection in sexual and general life satisfaction.

The text is canonical in the sense that it enters into a tradition (a narrative series) of both print and hypertextual prose writings that deal with problematic masculinity, car crashes (Moulthrop 1995), and multiple personality phenomena. There are a number of different narrative voices competing in CtC, including those of the female characters, focalizing Haller from their point of view. This multivocality is augmented by the appearance of an intrusive narrator, who comments on Haller's condition as well as, metafictionally and metamedially, on the affordances of hypertextual writing for reader agency, but also its limitations for presenting complex mental conditions like Haller's. After all, hypertext still uses linear human language and cannot live up to these conditions. The text has intriguing ludic-apostrophic moments as well, where direct reader address metaleptically brings us into a dialogue with the narrator about our textual preferences and about our endlessly re-"playing the game of life."

As the reading progresses, the textually implemented hermeneutic circle crystallizes into a frame narrative, which sees Haller being visited by Christina in hospital after the accident, and several embedded narratives that provide context for the car crash, including various episodes from Haller's earlier life with Christina, his affair with Mary, and sexual obsessions. However, since the protagonist is mentally unable to bring his life story into a coherent form, the narrator has to intervene to help readers along, so to speak. Each episode of the traumatic crash loop ends in a textually implemented dead end, which the reader can only get out of by manually opening the link menu and choosing an exit option rather than simply hitting return or clicking on an available link in the lexia.

CONCLUDING REMARKS

Let me close with the following transliteration of the scotoma experienced by Haller, represented in the [Blankness] lexia in Greek characters: "This is what it is like to look without seeing, to see without understanding, to read but not comprehend."

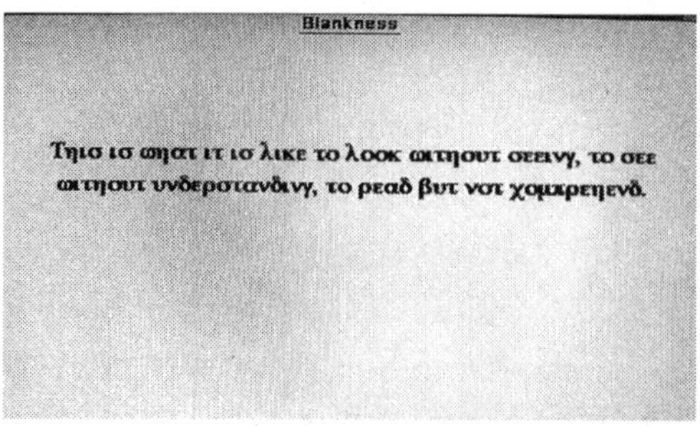

Figure 4. Screenshot of [Blankness] lexia in "Completing the Circle."

This dually symbolical representation is only one way van Mantgem's fiction implements its thematic concern formally. Transferred to the issue of preserving pre-web electronic literature, it is important to create the possibility for broad audiences to "see" and read de-canonized texts rather than just looking at their immaterial, theoretical, and historical existence through secondary literature, system-compatible emulators, or incomplete, crowd-censored directory entries. Preservation to the extent of making the original materiality of a text accessible in its original form is thus an important step in enhancing our understanding of e-lit history as a key aspect of human cultural history and media archeology more generally.

Aarseth, Espen. 1997. *Cybertext: Perspectives on Ergodic Literature.* Baltimore, MD: Johns Hopkins University Press.

Ensslin, Astrid. 2007. *Canonizing Hypertext: Explorations and Constructions.* London: Bloomsbury.

Ensslin, Astrid, Lyle Skains, and Joseph Tabbi. 2017. "Hypertext: Storyspace to Twine". In *The Bloomsbury Handbook of Electronic Literature.* London: Bloomsbury.

Funkhouser, Chris. 2007. *Prehistoric Digital Poetry.* Tuscaloosa: University of Alabama Press.

Grigar, Dene. 2018. "Rethinking the Canon of Pre-Web Hypertext Literature: A Call to Action about Preserving Our Early E-Lit Cultural Heritage," paper given at 2018 ELO Conference, Montreal.

Günther, Hans. 1987. "Die Lebensphasen eines Kanons – am Beispiel des sozialistischen Realismus"». In *Kanon und Zensur. Archäologie der literarischen Kommunikation,* II, ed. by Aleida Assmann and Jan Assmann, 135-48. Munich: Wilhelm Fink.

Joyce, Michael. 2000. *Othermindedness: The Emergence of Network Culture.* Ann Arbor : University of Michigan Press.

Moulthrop, Stuart. 1995. "Traveling in the Breakdown Lane: A Principle of Resistance for Hypertext". *Mosaic: An Interdisciplinary Critical Journal* 28 (4):55-77.

Rettberg, Scott. 2013. "An Emerging Canon? A Preliminary Analysis of All References to Creative Works in Critical Writing Documented in the ELMCIP Electronic Literature Knowledge Base," paper given at ELO 2013, *Bergen,* 2013. Link: http://retts.net/documents/Emerging_Canon_S_Rettberg.pdf.

Schweikle, Günther, and Irmgard Schweikle. 1990. *Metzler Literatur Lexikon.* Stuttgart: Metzler.

Sloane, Sarah. 2000. *Digital Fictions: Storytelling in a Material World.* Santa Barbara: Praeger.

Van Mantgem, Michael. 1995. "Completing the Circle". *Eastgate Quarterly Review of Hypertext,* Watertown: Eastgate Systems, 2 (2).

PART 6

PERSPECTIVES DIACHRONIQUES
SUR LA LITTÉRATURE ÉLECTRONIQUE

READING E-LIT ACROSS TIME

Raconter l'Internet :

Matérialité et effets

SYLVAIN DAVID

Résumé

Une toile large comme le monde (2017) d'Aude Seigne a pour sujet le réseau dans son ensemble, soit un dispositif matériel complexe aux ramifications apparemment infinies. *Féérie générale* (2012) d'Emmanuelle Pireyre met à l'inverse l'accent sur la navigation individuelle, sur les effets d'association d'idées ou de courts circuits intellectuels que celle-ci souvent induit. Ces deux textes ont pour originalité de renouveler – voire radicaliser – la représentation habituellement faite de l'internet dans le roman contemporain, en investissant respectivement une macro- et une micro-perspective par rapport à la toile. Leur lecture croisée permet de soulever quelques questions par rapport à ce que « peut » la littérature, pour reprendre la célèbre formule de Jean-Paul Sartre, lorsque confrontée à l'univers du numérique et du virtuel.

Abstract

Aude Seigne's *Une toile large comme le monde* (2017) is about the network as a whole, as a material device with seemingly infinite ramifications. Emmanuelle Pireyre's *Féérie générale* (2012), on the other hand, places the emphasis on individual navigation, the effects of the association of ideas or intellectual short circuits that this often infers. These two texts are original in that they renew–or even radicalize–typical representations of the internet in the contemporary novel by respectively employing macro- and micro-perspectives of the web. Their cross-reading allows us to raise questions about what literature "can" do, in the words used by Jean-Paul Sartre in his famous quote, when confronted with the digital and virtual world.

La réflexion littéraire – mais aussi cinématographique ou télévisuelle – sur les avancées technologiques et leurs dérapages potentiels a longtemps été l'apanage de la science-fiction. Les premiers récits mettant en scène la connectivité informatique et les flux de données relèvent généralement de ce genre; ils proposent d'alarmantes dystopies. Or, depuis le développement du Web 2.0 et son omniprésence dans la vie quotidienne, un nombre croissant de romans que l'on pourrait qualifier d'« ordinaires » s'intéressent à l'internet : plus particulièrement au champ des possibles ouvert par le réseau et aux effets que celui-ci exerce sur ses usagers. Une de leurs thématiques récurrentes est les interactions permises par le courriel, les messages textes, les médias sociaux. On y explore des formes éminemment contemporaines de socialité ainsi que leurs répercussions sur les identités et les représentations de soi. Un autre cas de figure omniprésent est la somme d'informations disponibles à partir d'un moteur de recherche ou, de manière plus pointue, de compétences en *hacking*. Le texte peut alors transmettre un certain nombre de données sans avoir à recourir à une omniscience de la narration ou à un quelconque personnage de spécialiste, convoqué uniquement dans l'intrigue pour le savoir qu'il peut y distiller. Certains romans, plus ambitieux, intègrent directement des extraits de ces conversations ou de ces données à leur trame : l'internet se fait dès lors mise en abyme ou genre intercalaire, dont l'écriture, la forme, le style, viennent nécessairement impacter ceux de l'œuvre en son ensemble.

Deux romans récents poussent encore plus loin cette idée de raconter l'internet. *Une toile large comme le monde* d'Aude Seigne (2017), a pour sujet le réseau dans son ensemble, soit un dispositif matériel complexe aux ramifications apparemment infinies. *Féérie générale* d'Emmanuelle Pireyre (2012), met à l'inverse l'accent sur la navigation individuelle, sur les effets d'association d'idées ou de courts circuits intellectuels que celle-ci souvent induit. Ces deux textes ont pour originalité de renouveler – voire radicaliser – la représentation habituellement faite de l'internet dans le roman contemporain, en investissant respectivement une macro- et une micro-perspective par rapport à la toile. Leur lecture croisée permet de soulever quelques questions par rapport à ce que « peut » la littérature, pour reprendre la célèbre formule de Jean-Paul Sartre, lorsque confrontée à l'univers du numérique et du virtuel.

MATÉRIALITÉ

Le premier chapitre d'*Une toile large comme le monde* est consacré à un câble de fibre optique sous-marin qui relie l'Europe à l'Amérique : il est question du bathyscaphe qui a délimité son tracé, du navire qui l'a posé, des risques de rupture qu'occasionnent sa situation géographique, de la faune et de la flore qui l'environnent. Les chapitres subséquents s'intéressent à divers personnages que rien, *a priori*, ne relie entre eux : une *hackeuse* zurichoise et son amant spécialiste de plongée sous-marine; un trio polyamoureux américain constitué d'une entrepreneure qui vend ses produits sur internet, d'un gestionnaire de communautés virtuelles et d'un libraire indépendant; une activiste scandinave de l'environnement; un ingénieur portuaire chinois et son fils *gamer*. Le récit de leur quotidien permet d'évoquer d'autres aspects de l'univers contemporain de la connectivité. Certains relèvent du matériel et de la programmation, comme un entrepôt de serveurs, un embranchement du réseau, un code informatique, sans oublier des besoins énergétiques et un approvisionnement en matières premières rares. D'autres éléments recensés par le texte renvoient plutôt aux modes de vie, comme une conversation Skype, une gestion de la vie amoureuse en ligne, un échange avec de purs inconnus par le biais de divers groupes de discussion, et bien des réalités semblables du quotidien branché.

Cet aperçu empirique du réseau et de ses usagers prend une tout autre tangente, au milieu du livre, alors que les personnages, désabusés par les effets que le numérique peut avoir sur les existences, décident de mettre à profit leurs compétences pour saboter la toile : individuellement d'abord, puis, au fil de rencontres et de coïncidences, en commun. Leurs efforts ont pour conséquence un effondrement quasi-complet de la civilisation occidentale. Le récit de la convergence des personnages et de la finalité de leur action est toutefois livré un peu trop rapidement pour s'avérer véritablement crédible. Ce qui semble intéresser l'autrice est avant tout de rappeler la fragilité de la toile, qui sous-tend la quasi-totalité de la vie quotidienne, et de réfléchir aux répercussions de son éventuelle désagrégation. Le roman, de ce fait, se présente dans ses premiers chapitres comme un (pseudo) documentaire et se clôt sur le ton du conte philosophique ou de la parabole.

Ce point de vue à la fois empirique et moraliste est livré par le biais d'une narration hétérodiégétique et apparemment omnisciente, qui « voit » à la fois l'ensemble du réseau et ses divers acteurs, tout en ayant accès à l'intériorité d'un certain nombre d'entre eux. La vue d'ensemble n'empêche cependant pas la narration – ou est-ce la romancière? – de s'exprimer régulièrement en son propre nom, pour commenter les personnages et les événements de la fiction comme s'il s'agissait de faits réels, indépendants de l'écriture qui pourtant leur donne vie.

> Il est allongé au fond de l'océan. Il est immobile, longiligne et tubulaire, gris ou peut-être noir, dans l'obscurité on ne sait pas très bien. Il ressemble à ce qui se trouve dans nos salons, derrière nos plinthes, entre le mur et la lampe, entre la prise de courant et celle de l'ordinateur : un vulgaire câble. Appelons-le FLIN. (Seigne **2017**, 7)
> [Le personnage d'Evan] me marche dessus, d'une certaine façon. Car quand je pense aux câbles apparentés à FLIN, je me dis que je suis aussi dans le câble, que je suis ce que je produis, ce que je stocke, ce que je décide de révéler de moi-même et de communiquer au monde. Autant de raisons qui font que je suis certainement déjà passée dans ces câbles sous [s]es pieds [. . .]. (Seigne **2017**, 96)

L'autrice, Aude Seigne, revendique à cet égard deux influences (Sulser **2017**). D'une part, elle reconnaît sa dette au livre *Tubes: A Journey to the Center of the Internet* d'Andrew Blum, qui rapporte, d'un point de vue journalistique, une exploration des composantes matérielles méconnues de la toile. Le commentaire externe de la narration du roman peut ainsi rappeler la perspective du grand reportage, qui présente les faits tout en les « éditorialisant ». Plusieurs des intervenants spécialisés interviewés par Blum expriment d'ailleurs leur crainte d'un acte terroriste, qui viendrait cibler un ou plusieurs des points nodaux du réseau : la fiction prend alors le relais des tensions du réel. D'autre part, Seigne dit avoir été inspirée par *Féérie générale* d'Emmanuelle Pireyre, un rapprochement qui justifie d'autant plus la lecture croisée proposée ici des deux textes.

EFFETS

Féérie générale a également une ouverture atypique. On y suit une fillette de neuf ans, dégoûtée par le fait que ses camarades de l'école primaire, *traders* précoces de l'économie globalisée, consacrent l'essentiel de leur temps à suivre le cours de la bourse et à faire fructifier leur portefeuille d'investissements. Elle préfère, quant à elle, vouer ses loisirs à peindre le cheval du voisin. La question de la mondialisation mène à un bref aparté théorique qui invoque la pensée de Claude Lévi-Strauss. La passion de la fillette pour la peinture équestre permet de passer, sans réelle transition, à une réflexion sur l'évolution des modes de représentation au fil de l'histoire de l'art occidental. Le récit se poursuit en focalisant cette fois sur la mère de la fillette, qui cherche l'amour en ligne, ce qui est le prétexte à un développement sur les nouvelles configurations interpersonnelles permises par le Web et les réseaux sociaux. On bifurque ensuite sur le cas d'un *serial killer* japonais, dont les crimes auraient été motivés par une addiction à ces passions dématérialisées plus tendancieuses que sont la pornographie et les mangas violents. Le tout est mis en contraste par le biais d'une anecdote sur Umberto Eco et son intérêt de jeune sémiologue pour les *comics*. Et ainsi de suite... (ont été résumées ici environ 20 pages sur 250).

Contrairement à Seigne, qui met de l'avant la matérialité du Web, Pireyre insiste avant tout sur ses effets, sous la forme d'un déluge d'informations dont la cohérence et la pertinence semblent parfois poser problème. Les chapitres ont beau avoir des titres sous une forme interrogative, ce qui rappelle une requête de moteur de recherche et un désir d'informations pertinentes, il n'en reste pas moins que ce qui y est livré est certes drôle et fantaisiste, mais souvent – et ostensiblement –, profondément inutile : « Le tourisme représente-t-il un danger pour nos filles faciles? »; « Friedrich Nietzsche est-il halal? » (Pireyre **2012**, 143). Cette apparente frivolité n'empêche cependant pas une exploration approfondie du sujet. L'internet marque par le fait même une présence affichée dans le texte : des échanges entre ados sur un forum de discussion sont reproduits tels quels, syntaxe et orthographe approximatives à l'appui; la pratique de la fan fiction est valorisée comme réappropriation d'un imaginaire colonisé par l'industrie culturelle; la figure du *hacker* est présentée, par le biais d'un personnage d'universitaire révolté, comme un cas de figure de l'héroïsme contemporain. Un dialogue réel entre divers protagonistes est même balisé à l'aide de notations temporelles qui reflètent ironiquement les mises en forme par défaut des interventions sur les réseaux sociaux :

> Un parent, Audrey, a lancé la discussion à 14h51 : « Les jeux violents accroissent-ils la violence de nos ados […]? » […] « Ne t'inquiète pas trop, a répondu Stéph à 14h53, Quentin casse de l'alien six heures par jour depuis deux mois, mais je le trouve plutôt cool […]. » D'après Sandrine, à 15h03, les développeurs devraient modifier les jeux pour les moraliser […]. « Vous vous trompez, a dit Valentine […] en faisant le tour de la table à 15h18 pour servir les cafés: il ne faut pas avoir peur, les jeux violents canalisent la violence […]. » (Pireyre **2012**, 28-30)

Par-delà ces références et emprunts souvent comiques, il n'en reste pas moins que c'est avant tout en filigrane que *Féérie générale* traite de l'internet et de ses effets, c'est-à-dire par le biais de sa construction. À l'instar d'une navigation intuitive où l'on se laisse guider par l'appel des hyperliens, souvent vers une destination imprévue, le roman de Pireyre repose sur une logique éminemment contemporaine, où l'apparent désordre comporte en fait une cohésion intrinsèque.

Cette part fondamentale de subjectivité est soulignée par la perspective du récit. Comme chez Seigne, qui s'en est inspirée, la narration de *Féérie générale* est apparemment omnisciente : elle jongle avec une multitude de faits et d'individus tout en paraissant avoir accès à l'intériorité de ces derniers. De façon similaire à *Une toile vaste comme le monde*, la voix narrative de *Féérie* s'incarne régulièrement pour exprimer son propre point de vue : « Je sais, on ne rencontre pas souvent dans le réel ce genre de spécialiste de neuf ans; c'est néanmoins plus fréquent de nos jours avec les rencontres par Internet. » (Pireyre **2012**, 19) Elle extrapole aussi fréquemment au « nous », livrant alors la supposée opinion de ses semblables; tout particulièrement « [n]ous les Européens » (Pireyre **2012**, 40). Le statut même de cette parole se complexifie du fait que, contrairement à chez Seigne, la narratrice devient personnage dans certains fragments du récit, se livrant à des activités – notamment des lectures de poésie multimédia – qui ne vont pas sans rappeler celles d'Emmanuelle Pireyre elle-même (ce qui est renforcé par l'inclusion de quelques photos de l'autrice, parmi d'autres, qui font écho aux événements du récit). Cette figure narrativo-auctoriale paradoxale dit en outre connaître personnellement certains des protagonistes qu'elle côtoie dans la diégèse – par exemple « la fille d'une de [s]es anciennes camarades d'université » (Pireyre **2012**, 146) – dont elle rapporte, par sa voix, le vécu. La narration de *Féérie générale* est ainsi à la fois intra- et hétérodiégétique. L'incarnation autofictionnelle de l'autrice cohabite, au sein de l'intrigue, avec des éléments manifestement fictifs (tels les gamins *traders* de l'incipit).

Emmanuelle Pireyre revendique cette approche, dans une série de textes à caractère plus théorique, sous le nom de « fiction documentaire ». Il s'agit, à la manière du cinéma vérité, d'une tentative de mettre en forme, par le biais de divers procédés formels, les éléments du réel afin de leur conférer un surcroît de sens et d'intelligibilité; de « fai[re] dialoguer différents types de documents réels, pour élaborer à partir d'eux des combinaisons et rapprochements de sens inédits » (Pireyre **2007**, 123). Dans cette perspective, « ce n'est généralement pas la narration qui conduit la progression du texte, mais plutôt le fil de la pensée et la combinaison de données ou de contenus de savoir collectés ici ou là » (Pireyre **2007**, 123). La littérature revêt, de ce fait, une fonction à la fois combinatoire et critique. Deux aspects en particulier des flux d'information générés par la fréquentation quotidienne de l'internet retiennent ainsi l'intérêt de Pireyre dans *Féérie générale*. D'une part, les modalités et la profondeur de l'immersion dans l'univers virtuel; de l'autre, le tri et l'agencement des données colligées en chemin. Comme l'exprime l'autrice/narratrice, dans l'un des nombreux passages autoréflexifs du roman :

> Notre contemplation restreinte est absence de spécialisation. Il en va de même pour les objets, les appareils, les phénomènes sociaux, les histoires. Nous ne serons pas les spécialistes des radios-réveils, ni des vaccins anti-hépatiques, ni des procédures pénales, ni de l'amour. Nous ne restons pas absorbés : nous remontons à la surface, toujours moins denses que chaque sujet pris isolément. Nous voulons nous partager entre quantité d'objets, autant de fois que nécessaire. Ainsi est notre mode de pensée: nous faisons des catégories et remontons à la surface. Chaque niveau où nous arrivons devenant aussitôt familier, nous nous propulsons à la catégorie supérieure. Dans ce déplacement ascensionnel, nous classons, produisons des catégories de catégories pour élucider l'épais mystère où nous téléchargeons éberlués.
> Simplement, parfois, dans la surexcitation et la fatigue de fin de journée, nous produisons aussi quelques classements insensés; comme dans une nouba de médecins, nous en profitons pour remettre un peu de bazar dans le réarrangement du monde, attitude contre-productive difficile à justifier. (Pireyre **2012**, 201-02)

Une telle position paradoxale du sujet-internaute inspire, imagine-t-on, l'ambiguïté de la narration de *Féérie générale*, à la fois en présence et en retrait de son objet, tour à tour théorisant ses attributs et submergée par lui.

Tel que le suggère le développement plus substantiel qui lui a été ici consacré, le roman de Pireyre demeure plus ambitieux dans sa mise en forme et sa théorisation intrinsèque que celui de Seigne, qui en est pourtant inspiré. *Une toile vaste comme le monde* a toutefois l'ambition de représenter – ou raconter – l'internet plutôt que de simplement en exprimer la logique et les effets. Leur lecture croisée permet donc, comme il l'a été postulé en introduction, de lancer quelques pistes de réflexion par rapport à ce que « peut » la littérature face à l'omniprésence du Web et sur l'influence qu'il exerce sur la pensée et la perception.

QUE PEUT LA LITTÉRATURE ?

Au niveau de la représentation de base, *Une toile vaste comme le monde* et *Féérie générale* ont un contenu à bien des égards similaire. On y trouve, comme on l'a vu, une mise en scène de l'usage quotidien des outils numériques et des réseaux sociaux, de même qu'une focalisation sur les figures typiques générées par cet environnement : le programmeur, le *hacker*, le *gamer*, mais aussi l'utilisateur de Skype, du courriel, des messages textes, et ainsi de suite. De ce point de vue, ces œuvres sont similaires à la majorité des romans qui traitent de l'internet dans son usage ordinaire. Les récits de Seigne et de Pireyre se distinguent néanmoins en ce qu'ils mettent en scène une disruption du réseau, laquelle a pour effet d'en révéler par défaut l'influence supposément pernicieuse : destruction complète de la toile, pour l'un; détournement, par l'écriture, de sa logique interne et de ses effets, pour l'autre. Le genre romanesque marque, dans ces deux cas de figure, clairement son territoire face à un état de fait dont, pourtant, il s'inspire. Les autrices ne se limitent pas à constater une réalité contemporaine : elles en traquent, par la fiction, les failles et les faiblesses.

Une toile et *Féérie* ne réinventent pourtant pas de fond en comble le roman moderne pour parvenir à cette fin. Les deux textes, de manière typique de la littérature expérimentale actuelle, réinvestissent et recombinent des formes existantes pour les adapter à une situation inédite. Non sans ironie, ces œuvres font à la littérature ce que l'internet fait aux discours et aux représentations en général. De par ses aspirations documentaires, *Une toile vaste comme le monde* s'inscrit à bien des égards dans la continuité du roman réaliste du 19e siècle, époque de grandes découvertes où la littérature aspirait à baliser le plus minutieusement possible le monde : structures de pouvoir, classes sociales, sciences et techniques, géographie, faune et flore. Il est d'ailleurs révélateur, dans cet ordre d'idées, que le film *Globodrome* de Gwenola Wagon, lequel a également pour sujet le Web en son entièreté, s'inspire explicitement d'une œuvre de Jules Verne. Ce « néo-réalisme » se double d'une actualisation du genre populaire du complot, qui remonte lui aussi aux débuts la modernité, un moment où l'urbanisation et l'internationalisation des flux de commerce tendent à opacifier une structure sociale jusque-là transparente : l'idée de la conspiration – imputée à des réalités apatrides tels les « étrangers » ou le capitalisme – avait en ce temps-là pour effet de réinsuffler un semblant de sens et d'explication à un monde désormais méconnaissable. Là encore, il n'est pas innocent que la majorité des fictions consacrées à l'internet – *Mr. Robot*, notamment – reposent justement sur l'idée du complot. *Féérie générale* renvoie, à l'inverse, à une forme de littérature plus savante et plus ludique. On y trouve, d'une part, des traces de *Bouvard et Pécuchet* – « name-droppé » au passage par le texte –, soit un récit qui prend directement à partie l'effort de totalisation du savoir et de classification générale revendiqué par le roman réaliste. On y observe également des scories des récits expérimentaux des Lumières comme *Jacques le fataliste* ou *Tristram Shandy* qui, de par leur narration sans cesse égarée dans des hors-sujet pourtant introduits de manière logique, subvertissent la cohérence linéaire, là-encore valorisée par la tradition réaliste. À ceci pourrait s'ajouter l'écriture fragmentaire et le butinage intellectuel d'essayistes, de Montaigne et Pascal à Nietzsche ou Cioran, mais ce serait là sortir du genre narratif.

Cette situation des textes de Seigne et de Pireyre dans leur appartenance générique sommaire a pour effet de déboucher sur un curieux paradoxe : alors qu'*Une toile vaste comme le monde*, qui se donne pour sujet la totalité du réseau dans une volonté de macro-perspective, repose sur une actualisation de la tradition réaliste, *Féérie générale*, qui mime la micro-perspective de l'usager du Web, a pour fondement une récupération de la tradition « antiréaliste ». Ceci peut se traduire, en termes informatiques, par une opposition entre *hardware* et *software* – ou entre réseau et interface –, lesquels sont respectivement les sujets des textes en question. Dans cette optique, Seigne, qui part de la réalité matérielle de la toile, aboutit à une logique d'arborescence, où chaque élément doit nécessairement être à sa place pour assurer un bon fonctionnement de l'ensemble. La pléthore de personnages et de situations que conjugue son récit obéit ainsi aux lois de la symbiose et de la synchronie. De ce fait, à partir du moment où le réseau est saboté, leur existence s'effondre – bien que ce soit le résultat qu'ils aient cherché –, de même que, de façon révélatrice, se délite peu à peu la fiction qui en rend compte. Pireyre, à l'inverse, adopte la dynamique du flux de données, où la totalité est animée d'une logique qui n'exclut pas l'incohérence, le coq-à-l'âne, la répétition, l'hétérogénéité entre genres et niveaux de savoir ou de fiction. À cet égard, la multiplicité également observable dans son texte rappelle le principe de « tabularité » offert par un navigateur Web: une série de fenêtres peuvent être ouvertes simultanément, selon une logique qui renvoie à une même navigation intuitive, sans pour autant que leur contenu soit directement lié. Vu de la sorte, le roman de Pireyre ne se termine véritablement jamais et – tel un recueil de poèmes ou un essai fragmentaire – peut être lu dans tous les sens sans pour autant trop perdre de sa substance ou de sa visée.

Les postures narratives divergentes des deux romancières ont toutefois pour effet de nuancer quelque peu ces derniers constats. C'est d'ailleurs le propre de la littérature « savante » ou expérimentale que d'entretenir toujours une part d'ambiguïté. Seigne, en maintenant la voix narrative à un niveau distinct de celui des personnages, tout en lui permettant de commenter les actions de ceux-ci comme s'ils étaient indépendants de ses intentions, redonne une part d'inventivité et d'« agentivité » à des protagonistes humains en outre présentés comme étant victimes d'un dispositif qui prédétermine leurs visions du monde et les modalités de leurs interactions. Toute la dynamique du complot vient aussi accentuer cette idée d'une liberté idéalement maintenue à l'égard du système (même si, en une ironie finale du texte, un tel affranchissement ne mène pas forcément au mieux). Pireyre, en s'insérant elle-même (sous forme de personnage *alter ego*) dans son récit introduit par le fait même une balise, un critère de vérité, dans ce qui pourrait sinon n'être qu'une accumulation de données éparses vouées à coexister sans lien autre que la parataxe. Si, dans son univers, le système, représenté au niveau de ses possibles, est souple, la subjectivité individuelle vient tout de même y introduire une part de restriction, via le choix des sujets explorés, et de structure, par la trajectoire virtuelle ainsi esquissée. Il est vrai, cela étant dit, que la part de prévisibilité introduite par le déterminisme des algorithmes générateurs de données a pour effet de contraindre cette supposée souplesse avant même l'émission du moindre flux.

Ce constat d'une opposition, dans les perspectives et dans la forme, qui se dissout dans une commune ambiguïté, laquelle reflète possiblement les paradoxes de la toile elle-même, peut suggérer, en dépit de l'intérêt des récits et des sujets abordés, une certaine impuissance de la littérature face à une réalité à la fois omniprésente et insaisissable comme peut l'être le Web 2.0 et ses structures sous-jacentes. Qu'en est-il alors vraiment? Le potentiel de la littérature, face à un média concurrent aux ramifications infinies, se limite-t-il, non sans *pathos*, à l'ordre du constat désabusé?

RACONTER L'INTERNET

Une toile vaste comme le monde, en dépit de son ton souvent sérieux ou idéaliste, comporte une certaine dose d'ironie. Par exemple, pendant même qu'ils conspirent en vue de saboter le Web, les divers personnages se repèrent et coordonnent leurs actions par le biais des réseaux sociaux et autres moyens de communication électroniques. Comme vient le souligner opportunément l'un des comploteurs : « C'est quand même hilarant de penser qu'en cherchant sur internet, on trouve comment détruire internet. Tout est là. » (Seigne **2017**, 182) Dans une perspective plus « méta », la narration – qui recoupe ici pleinement la voix de l'autrice – admet, alors qu'elle décrit des installations de télécoms appelées à être détruites, que son propos est moins la transcription d'impressions vécues dans un lieu réel que le commentaire d'une image trouvée en ligne :

> Malgré le froid, j'aimerais bien me trouver à leur place, sur ce rocher, au-dessus de ces câbles, face à cet océan. Car j'ai quelques photos sur mon ordinateur, des plages du monde entier d'où émerge la sombre ondulation d'une gaine au milieu d'arbustes roux, de vagues mousseuses ou d'une colonie de manchots. J'ai cherché des traces des câbles sur le web comme Pénélope et Matteo les cherchent en présent en Cornouailles, mais mes résultats sont des paysages anonymes, une pure contemplation esthétique, une rêverie autour d'un circuit sous l'océan. Ces images, elles se détachent des lieux, elles se dissocient du réel. (Seigne **2017**, 138)

De ce fait, bien que le roman critique la toile, son intrigue et même son écriture reposent inéluctablement sur ce que celle-ci peut lui offrir.

Féérie générale comporte le même type d'ambiguïtés, bien que son ton et sa forme plus généralement ludiques en font une composante moins contradictoire. Un bon exemple de ceci est lorsque la narratrice livre un réquisitoire contre la part de *fake* – ou de « féérie », c'est selon –, qui grève désormais le monde, sur un site de fans fictions, voué justement au détournement de l'imaginaire, au moment où elle-même ne cesse de cumuler des récits d'existences disparates dont la représentativité statistique paraît directement issue d'une recherche internet :

> Un soir, après avoir lu sur un site une histoire d'amour entre Buffy et Harry Potter, une scène gore avec le Seigneur des anneaux, une scène porno entre la Belle et un vampire, une scène de thriller chez les Pokemon, une histoire d'amour déçu avec Naruto, une histoire d'amitié et de compétition entre deux dresseurs de Pokemon juste après une explosion atomique, je me suis sentie un peu fatiguée.
>
> Histoires, histoires, histoires, pour finir, les histoires, leur profusion, leur succès me troublaient. Bien sûr, nous adorons les histoires, les séries TV, nous adorons écouter les anecdotes des voisines et leur raconter les nôtres; néanmoins, le consensus entre gourous du storytelling et adolescentes [adeptes de fan fiction] sur la recherche de bonnes histoires m'inquiétait. Je me questionnais : nos formes de poésie actuelles, nos classements du monde, alambiqués mais somme toute rassurants, nos agencements, nos conférences PowerPoint sont-ils encore légitimes? Je commençais à douter de mes méthodes tenant soigneusement les fictions au second plan, les subordonnant aux réflexions; mais d'un autre côté l'infinité des histoires possibles, l'infinité des événements non classés, m'angoissait. Comme si le monde n'était pas déjà une pagaille irréversible suffisamment innommable. En quête de réconfort, j'ai posté un message aux filles du site sur lequel je venais de passer la soirée : « Ne pensez-vous pas qu'il faut arrêter de rajouter du fictif, des couches de fake masquant le réel? Ne croyez-vous pas qu'il serait temps de mettre de l'ordre? De ranger un peu? » (Pireyre **2012**, 177-178)

Là encore, le Web est à la fois sujet et objet, cause et conséquence. La fiction consacrée à l'internet est-elle donc vouée, en outsider analogique du monde connecté, à se retrouver éternellement aspirée par une telle logique circulaire ?

Les deux romans ici commentés – auxquels on pourrait ajouter bien d'autres consacrés au même sujet – permettent de lancer quelques pistes de réflexion à cet égard. D'une part, une constante de ces fictions est la figure du *hacker*, voué à se réapproprier un système par ailleurs contraignant et à en « réagencer » les flux de manière signifiante ou créative. Pareil détournement demeure pourtant interne au réseau; il est généralement une disruption temporaire qui cède rapidement la place à un retour du même. Ne pourrait-on pas, pour développer cette idée, envisager la littérature consacrée à l'internet justement comme une sorte de *hacking* externe, qui partage les visées de la corruption menée de l'intérieur, mais avec une perspective extérieure, nécessaire, si l'on en croit la philosophie classique, à toute critique raisonnée? La représentation de la logique circulaire de l'internet serait ainsi, en elle-même, significative. D'autre part – et suivant ce qui précède –, il est souvent question, à la suite des travaux de Bolter et Grusin, du fait que les médias modernes, tout particulièrement l'internet, constituent des « remédiations » (1998) des formes et contenus de médias antérieurs. Suivant cette idée, ne pourrait-on pas voir le roman consacré à la toile comme une paradoxale « re-remédiation », c'est-à-dire une réappropriation d'un contenu intellectuel, rhétorique, axiologique, autrefois propre à l'imprimé et depuis réactualisé en ligne? Tel que le suggère l'inélégance du double préfixe « re-re », une telle médiation, non plus au second, mais au troisième degré, aurait une visée doublement « méta » : celle de non pas seulement dégager une perspective critique sur les discours et représentations en circulation, par le biais du Web, dans l'imaginaire social, mais aussi – c'est le nœud de l'affaire – d'offrir une même distance réflexive par rapport aux supports et aux mises en forme par lesquels ces données transitent.

On pourra rétorquer que c'est là un ultime avatar, après bien d'autres, de la polyphonie romanesque, telle que théorisée notamment par Mikhaïl Bakhtine (1929). On pourra également rappeler que le texte n'est qu'une composante parmi d'autres de la toile, qui repose en grande partie sur l'image et le son : le *hacking* littéraire ici postulé supposerait alors une part de traduction « inter » ou « transmédiale », ce qui vient forcément complexifier les enjeux. Il n'en reste pas moins que la dynamique d'ambivalence et de recyclage ici revendiquée a fait la force du genre romanesque depuis les débuts de la modernité, et même avant : pourquoi dès lors ne pas en faire un outil d'observation et de commentaire privilégié par rapport à l'omniprésence contemporaine du Web, lequel invite à une dynamique de recyclage et de *remix* sans pour autant (toujours) valoriser la part de contenu critique ou autoréflexif qui, dans la grande tradition du roman, accompagne justement une telle démarche ?

Bakhtine, Mikhaïl. 1929. *Poétique de Dostoïevski.* Traduit par Isabelle Kolitcheff. Points. Paris : Seuil.

Blum, Andrew. 2012. *Tubes: A Journey to the Center of the Internet.* Toronto : Harper Collins.

Bolter, Jay David, et Richard Grusin. 1998. *Remediation: Understanding New Medi.* Cambridge (MA) : MIT Press.

Pireyre, Emmanuelle. 2007. « Fictions documentaires ». In *Devenirs du roman,* édité par François Bégaudeau, 119-37. Inculte. Paris : Naïve.

Pireyre, Emmanuelle. 2012. *Féérie générale.* Paris : L'Olivier.

Seigne, Aude. 2017. *Une toile large comme le monde.* Carouge-Genève : Zoé.

Sulser, Éléonore. 2017. « Quand les romanciers s'emparent du Web ». *Le Temps,* 25 août.

« Tout était vrai et donc rien n'était vrai; tout était faux et donc rien n'était faux. »

La (ré)invention des grands récits à l'ère du numérique

SOPHIE MARCOTTE

Résumé

Les « fake news », qui font la manchette presque quotidiennement depuis novembre 2016 dans les médias et sur les réseaux sociaux, nous ramènent à une interrogation beaucoup plus vaste sur les notions de vérité et de mensonge. Ces dernières se situent au cœur de la trilogie du romancier français Antoine Bello, composée des *Falsificateurs*, des *Éclaireurs* et des *Producteurs*, parus entre 2007 et 2015 aux Éditions Gallimard. La trame des trois récits repose en effet sur les activités du CFR, le Consortium de Falsification du Réel, fondé par un certain Pierre Ménard et au sein duquel des milliers d'employés, en poste un peu partout sur la planète, travaillent à la fabrication des grands « récits » qui feront en sorte de préserver une certaine stabilité à l'échelle mondiale. Cet article porte surtout sur le troisième roman de la trilogie, *Les Producteurs*, dans lequel la circulation libre, sur l'Internet, de toutes sortes d'informations et documents, pose les limites de l'activité de falsification du réel à laquelle se consacre entre autres personnage principal de Sliv Darthunghuver, un jeune islandais qui gravit les échelons de l'organisation secrète jusqu'à faire partie de son conseil d'administration. Les activités de l'agence se voient en effet de plus en plus dépendantes de l'usage du Web et des réseaux sociaux. Or, si le numérique facilite la circulation et l'accès aux renseignements, il diminue considérablement la possibilité de falsifier la réalité sans être démasqué, comme le réalisent les agents du CFR chargés d'une mission spéciale liée à la découverte d'une cité Maya en mer, au large de l'Amérique centrale. Le roman de Bello, qui reste traditionnel dans sa forme, s'articule ainsi autour de la désinformation, de la réécriture de l'Histoire, mais surtout, du rôle et des pièges du numérique dans la fabrication des « archives » du monde contemporain.

Abstract

"Fake news," which has been making news and social media headlines almost daily since November 2016, brings us to a much broader interrogation on the notions of truth and falsehood. These are at the heart of the trilogy by French novelist Antoine Bello, composed of *Falsificateurs*, *Éclaireurs* and *Producteurs*, published between 2007 and 2015 by Éditions Gallimard. The framework of the three stories is based on the activities of the CFR, the Consortium for the Falsification of Reality, founded by a certain Pierre Ménard and in which thousands of employees, stationed all over the planet, work on the fabrication of founding "narratives" which serve to preserve a certain stability on the global scale. This article deals primarily with the third novel in the trilogy, *Les Producteurs (The Producers)*, in which the free online circulation of all kinds of information and documents poses limits on the falsification of reality, to which the protagonist Sliv Darthunghuver, a young Icelandic man who rose through the ranks of the secret organization to become a member of its board of directors, devotes himself. The agency's activities become in fact more and more dependent on the use of the web and social networks. And yet, if the digital facilitates circulation of and access to information, it also considerably diminishes the possibility of falsifying reality without being revealed, as realized by the agents of the CFR in charge of a special mission related to the discovery of an undersea Mayan city off the coast of Central America. Thus Bello's novel, which remains traditional in its form, hinges on disinformation, the rewriting of History, and overall, the role and the snares of the digital in the fabrication of "archives" in the contemporary world.

La trame narrative des romans est de plus en plus investie par les dispositifs et les usages du numérique. Cette présence se manifeste, tant au plan formel que thématique, par la mise en page et en récit d'échanges par l'entremise d'ordinateurs et de portables (courriels, messages-textes, billets de blogues, tweets, statuts et commentaires Facebook, etc.) et par la narration de voyages reposant sur l'utilisation d'applications telles Google StreetView ou Google Earth.

Ces innovations s'accompagnent aussi, dans certains cas, d'une réflexion plus vaste sur les notions de *vérité* et de *mensonge* à l'ère de la circulation d'information sur l'Internet, notamment sur les *fake news*; celles-ci ont été définies, par une journaliste du *New York Times*, comme des faux articles circulant sur l'Internet « with an intention to deceive, often geared towards getting clicks », qui en sont venus à être un « political battering ram, with the left accusing the right of trafficking in disinformation, and the right accusing the left of tarring conservatives as a way to try to censor websites. » (Tavernise **2016**) La notion de *fake news* reste éminemment subjective, dépendamment du point de vue depuis lequel elle est envisagée.

Le rôle et les pièges du numérique dans la prolifération de rumeurs et l'alimentation de théories du complot sont ainsi interrogés par le roman, qui met en évidence le fait que les *fausses informations*, abondamment diffusées sur les réseaux sociaux – qui deviennent parfois très lucratives pour ceux qui en sont à l'origine lorsque de la publicité leur est associée – atteignent potentiellement davantage d'individus que les articles issus des médias traditionnels. La vérité, dans ce contexte, n'est plus ce qui prévaut : ce qui importe est de faire circuler le meilleur *récit* possible, celui qui deviendra la nouvelle référence. C'est d'ailleurs ce sur quoi insiste Salman Rushdie dans un article paru dans *Charlie Hebdo* où il explique que la vérité « a toujours été une idée controversée », et qu'elle est désormais, à l'ère où nous vivons, celle que nous créons : « Des mensonges intéressés sont régulièrement présentés comme des faits, alors que des informations plus fiables sont accusées d'être des *fake news*. » (Rushdie **2018**)

C'est précisément autour de cette problématique que s'articule la trilogie romanesque d'Antoine Bello composée des *Falsificateurs* (**2007**), des *Éclaireurs* (**2009**) et des *Producteurs* (**2015**), trilogie parue aux Éditions Gallimard. Les dispositifs numériques y contribuent, tel qu'il le sera démontré dans le cadre de cette étude exploratoire, à brouiller les frontières entre réalité et fiction, à créer des preuves de toutes pièces pour ajouter à l'Histoire des événements qui ne se sont jamais déroulés, et à orienter, dans d'autres cas, l'interprétation que le commun des mortels forge de certains faits et événements. On verra que l'interprétation globale du phénomène des faits alternatifs que propose Bello dans son œuvre romanesque rejoint la réflexion de Rushdie : « la création d'un fait historique résulte de la signification particulière que l'on attribue à un événement. » (Rushdie **2018**) Bello joue cette carte à fond, en imaginant une organisation se consacrant justement à des activités de falsification.

La trame des trois romans, pour en résumer brièvement l'intrigue, repose sur les activités du CFR, le Consortium de Falsification du Réel, fondé par un certain Pierre Ménard et au sein duquel des milliers d'employés, en poste un peu partout sur la planète, travaillent à la fabrication ou à la réinvention des grands récits qui feront en sorte de préserver une certaine stabilité à l'échelle mondiale.

Les Falsificateurs raconte l'arrivée dans le monde du travail du jeune diplômé en géographie Sliv Darthunghuver, embauché par une boîte de consultants du domaine de l'environnement, où il se fera rapidement remarquer pour ses talents de scénariste, puis recruter par le Consortium de Falsification du Réel. Il participe, par exemple, à l'invention d'une espèce de poisson – le galochat – identifiée comme étant menacée d'extinction par les essais nucléaires menés par la France, et à la rédaction d'un imposant document prouvant que le chien supposément lancé en orbite par l'URSS en 1957 n'a jamais existé. Si le roman porte très peu sur l'usage des dispositifs numériques dans le travail de réécriture des récits, il met surtout en lumière l'importance de procéder à la falsification des événements et des documents avec la plus grande prudence pour éviter de mettre en péril l'existence de l'agence, ce que Sliv, qui a peu d'expérience, apprend à la dure lors d'une mission ratée en Amérique du Sud. Le roman annonce néanmoins ce qui viendra dans les deux suivants en évoquant les avantages de créer des documents sur support électronique : « [...] les modes d'alimentation sont si nombreux qu'il est extrêmement difficile d'isoler les causes d'un dysfonctionnement. Tel chiffre modifié, telle ligne supplémentaire dans un rapport seront mis sur le compte d'une erreur de saisie et l'on n'ira pas chercher plus loin. » (Bello **2007**, 286)

Dans *Les Éclaireurs*, dont l'intrigue s'organise notamment autour de l'entrée en guerre des États-Unis contre l'Irak, l'existence et la mise en circulation des fausses informations par le gouvernement sont mises à l'avant-plan. Alors que Sliv et son agence poursuivent leur travail visant à orienter le déroulement et le dénouement de la guerre, la Maison Blanche tente de dissimuler quelques faits en divulguant des *faits alternatifs* à certains journalistes du *New York Times* et du *Washington Post* parmi les plus influents (Bello **2009**, 229). Encore ici, peu de place est accordée aux dispositifs numériques et à leur influence sur le déroulement des événements. Le roman, beaucoup plus centré sur des questions idéologiques que le précédent, montre surtout à quel point les médias, eux-mêmes manipulés par le pouvoir politique et économique, manipulent à leur tour la population mondiale.

C'est dans le troisième roman de la trilogie, *Les Producteurs*, qu'est surtout développée la problématique du vrai et du faux liée à l'usage du web et des plateformes de diffusion à grande échelle qu'il abrite. Dans *Les Producteurs*, en effet, la circulation libre, sur l'Internet, de toutes sortes d'informations et de documents pose les limites de l'activité de falsification du réel à laquelle se consacre toujours Sliv Darthunghuver, qui a gravi les échelons de l'organisation secrète du Consortium de Falsification du Réel jusqu'à faire partie du Comex – l'équivalent d'un conseil d'administration. Les activités de l'agence, qui, jusque-là n'étaient pas essentiellement liées à l'usage de dispositifs numériques, se voient de plus en plus dépendantes, dans ce troisième roman, de l'usage du Web et des réseaux sociaux. Or, si le numérique facilite la circulation et l'accès aux renseignements, il diminue considérablement la possibilité de falsifier la réalité sans être démasqué, comme le réalisent les agents du CFR chargés d'une mission spéciale en lien avec la découverte d'une cité Maya en mer, au large de l'Amérique centrale. *Les Producteurs*, qui reste traditionnel dans sa forme, s'articule ainsi autour de la désinformation, de la réécriture de l'Histoire, mais surtout, du rôle et des pièges du numérique dans la *fabrication* des « archives » du monde contemporain.

Comme il vient d'être évoqué, les activités de l'agence CFR et de ses employés, dans *Les Producteurs*, se voient de plus en plus dépendantes de l'usage du Web et des réseaux sociaux. En effet, le Web permet une diffusion à plus grande échelle des récits fabriqués ou modifiés par le Consortium. Il permet aussi la production de commentaires orientant l'interprétation des événements. À cet effet, « Internet », avait écrit Sliv dans un mémo interne destiné aux employés, « allait décupler les opportunités des agents CFR tout en réduisant leurs risques d'être démasqués. » (Bello **2015**, 35) Or, il doit préciser, quelque temps après, que si le numérique facilite grandement la circulation et l'accès aux renseignements, il diminue considérablement la possibilité de falsifier la réalité sans qu'on ne s'en rende compte quelque part sur la planète :

> Internet avait rendu impossibles des falsifications qu'il y a dix ans encore on citait en exemple à l'Académie. Ajouter une œuvre à la bibliographie d'un dramaturge danois sur Wikipédia ne présentait guère de difficultés; infléchir de façon significative la biographie d'un leader politique ou d'une star de la chanson relevait en revanche de la gageure tant leurs admirateurs veillaient au grain. (Bello **2015**, 35)

Le problème est que le métier de falsificateur est désormais accessible, grâce à la démocratisation du Web, à qui veut bien s'y essayer : « Révisionnistes, illuminés, lobbies : tout le monde y va désormais de sa petite falsification » (Bello **2015**, 92), si bien que la vérité n'existe plus : « elle est constamment recréée. » (Bello **2015**, 110)

Comme dans *Machine God* (**2015**), un thriller international de Jean-Jacques Pelletier où les réseaux sociaux jouent un rôle de premier plan dans la progression de l'enquête policière sur une série de meurtres à caractère religieux, les réseaux sociaux, dans *Les Producteurs*, sont décrits comme servant à amplifier la rumeur et contribuent à alimenter les théories du complot :

> La rumeur lancée par un gamin sur son téléphone portable avait presque autant de chances de faire le tour du monde qu'un dossier ayant demandé des mois de travail. Les théories du complot fleurissaient dans les forums, recueillant un succès inversement proportionnel à leur plausibilité. Des sites en recensaient des pages entières, parmi lesquelles le visiteur pouvait choisir celles qui confortaient ses préjugés ethniques, politiques ou religieux : le FBI avait orchestré les attaques du 11 septembre, un petit nombre de patrons présidait aux destinées du monde… Internet avait à la fois accéléré leur propagation et leur légitimité. Le concept de vérité n'avait jamais semblé si relatif. (Bello **2015**, 36)

Pour le Consortium de Falsification du Réel, la relativisation du concept de vérité devient catastrophique, car toutes les activités de l'agence reposent justement sur le passage de la vérité au mensonge et sur la distinction fondamentale entre les deux. Or, à l'ère d'Internet, « tout était vrai et donc rien n'était vrai; tout était faux et donc rien n'était faux. » (Bello **2015**, 36)

Les réseaux sociaux, sur une base individuelle, entraînent une activité de falsification du réel, plus modeste, mais qui fait tout de même écho à celle que pratiquent les agents dont la mission est de modifier le cours de l'Histoire. En effet, les abonnés y racontent des histoires (de « bonnes » histoires, dans certains cas) :

> un voyageur s'étant trompé d'avion avait atterri à Pékin quand il était attendu à Istanbul; … un voleur retrouvé coincé dans le garage de la maison qu'il cambriolait intentait un procès à la famille, etc. Il était difficile de résister à ces récits quand bien même ils ne possédaient aucune vertu morale ou éducative. (Bello **2015**, 121)

Mais ce qui caractérise surtout les réseaux sociaux est que les utilisateurs préfèrent y tenir un discours optimiste, foncièrement faux, plutôt que d'avouer, par exemple, qu'ils traversent une crise financière ou conjugale :

Personne lisant les messages (de ma sœur Mathilde) débordant d'optimisme qu'elle postait presque chaque jour (citations, liens vers des articles de journaux, photo du plat qu'elle avait cuisiné la veille…) n'aurait pu deviner qu'elle et son mari traversaient une mauvaise passe. Ma sœur préférait à l'évidence l'histoire de la ménagère comblée à celle de la banlieusarde surendettée. (Bello **2015**, 168)

À plus grande échelle, la seule possibilité qu'il reste au Consortium de répandre efficacement la rumeur afin de pouvoir espérer que ses récits deviennent <u>la</u> référence est la création et la gestion de comptes fictifs sur Facebook et Twitter. Le bureau de Berlin, par exemple,

> contrôlait près d'un million de comptes fictifs sur les réseaux sociaux, tissant à longueur de journée entre eux des liens toujours plus étroits qui renforçaient leur authenticité. Lena achevait de brouiller les pistes en recourant à ce qu'elle appelait des *proxys*. […] elle pouvait choisir si les

> visiteurs du site semblaient connectés d'un quartier résidentiel de San Diego, un cybercafé de Denver ou une tour de bureaux d'Atlanta. (Bello **2015**, 194)

C'est toutefois dans la mission ultime du Consortium de Falsification du Réel, liée à la découverte d'une cité Maya en mer, au large de l'Amérique centrale, que les réseaux sociaux jouent le rôle le plus important. Manuela Ocampo, présentée comme une ancienne étudiante d'Harvard et camarade de classe de Mark Zuckerberg et comme l'une des premières utilisatrices de Facebook, « à l'époque où le site était confiné aux universités », a pour mandat de contrôler, depuis Barcelone, « 25 000 profils bidon » qui, « à raison d'un millier d'amis par tête de pipe », permettraient de « toucher vingt-cinq millions de personnes en un clic, assez pour faire basculer le résultat d'une élection [ou] ruiner la réputation d'une personnalité. » (Bello **2015**, 414) Elle forme également

> les agents européens aux ficelles de Facebook (en) leur apprenant comment réunir 50 000 noms sur une page réclamant la libération d'un touriste autrichien détenu au Cambodge ou faire s'effondrer les ventes d'une marque de laitage en répandant la rumeur qu'on y avait trouvé des traces de cyanure. (Bello **2015**, 414)

Les réseaux sociaux, dans *Les Producteurs*, en viennent ainsi à produire la nouvelle, que les médias traditionnels relaient ensuite : « C'est à nous d'alimenter la machine » (Bello **2015**, 430), rappelle Sliv, et de faire en sorte que le nouveau *récit* sur le Codex Maya apparaisse dans les premiers résultats des principaux moteurs de recherche. Or, Bello va encore plus loin dans son exploitation des réseaux sociaux : au-delà de la gestion de faux-profils, les personnages créent des pages Facebook de soutien à la cause défendue par le Consortium, ce qui infléchit encore plus efficacement « la perception du public » (470) dans le sens voulu par l'agence.

Il reste que tout ce travail de manipulation des réseaux sociaux ne privilégie pas nécessairement la quantité d'information au détriment de la qualité. En effet, la prudence est de mise et le plan initial doit être respecté à la lettre pour réussir à laisser croire que le mensonge constitue en fait... la vérité. « Prudence sur les réseaux sociaux pour l'instant [...] Quelques centaines de tweets et de partages, histoire de prendre date, mais pas davantage. Gardons nos forces pour demain. » (Bello **2015**, 424) Tout ce système, savamment orchestré – « se servir des réseaux sociaux pour diffuser la (fausse) nouvelle et la maintenir dans l'actualité » (Bello **2015**, 430) – réussit finalement à faire croire à l'existence des nouveaux Codex qui auraient été découverts dans des coffres au fond de la mer au large du Mexique. (Les images des fonds marins, dont la retransmission a rejoint « 120 millions de téléspectateurs et moitié autant d'internaute » (Bello **2015**, 534), ont en fait été tournées dans un studio à Hollywood.)

Bref, le roman de Bello, qui reste traditionnel dans sa forme, s'articule autour de la désinformation, de la réécriture de l'Histoire (l'Histoire universelle, ici, et non pas l'histoire personnelle), mais surtout, du rôle et des pièges du numérique dans la *fabrication* des « archives », toujours en mouvement, du monde contemporain : « Nous ne façonnons pas vraiment la réalité, nous ne faisons que [déclencher] [...] des forces qui nous dépassent. » (Bello **2015**, 526)

C'est d'ailleurs ce que propose aussi le roman suivant de Bello, *Ada*. L'intrigue repose sur la disparition d'une intelligence artificielle prénommée Ada, qui génère notamment des romans en « imitant le processus de création d'un auteur traditionnel » et produit de surcroît des critiques de ce même roman, orientant sa réception. Ainsi, chacun croit « à ce qui l'arrange » (Bello **2016**, 305), tout comme dans le cas des récits produits par le CFR dans les trois romans précédents, puisque, conclut le narrateur, « Tout ne sera bientôt que récit. Nous générons chaque jour des quantités formidables de données, qui ne demandent qu'à être tissées en histoires. Vous verrez, le monde pissera bientôt du texte à jet continu. » (Bello **2016**, 280)

CONCLUSION

J'ai tenté, par ces exemples, de dégager certains éléments de la représentation qu'offre le roman contemporain des données issues de l'Internet et des réseaux sociaux. On a pu constater que cette transposition, dans les romans de Bello, ouvre surtout au déploiement d'une thématisation singulière, celle de la tension entre le vrai et le faux et de la création d'une nouvelle réalité qui devient la *vérité* à laquelle on croit.

Alors que dans d'autres romans (je pense entre autres à *Programme sensible* d'Anne-Marie Garat, à *Document 1* de François Blais et à plusieurs romans policiers parus au cours des dernières années), le recours à des outils informatiques, que ce soit à des applications fournissant la possibilité de voyager virtuellement ou à une plateforme de réseau social, fait en sorte d'altérer le rapport des personnages au réel et la perception qu'ils en développent, dans *Les Producteurs* de Bello, l'usage qui est proposé des réseaux sociaux comme Facebook et Twitter débouche sur une redéfinition de la perception que les gens ont de la réalité, ces plateformes entraînant la production d'une « nouvelle » réalité qui finit par s'imposer au commun des mortels.

Ainsi, la fréquentation des réseaux sociaux et les usages qui en sont faits – des pratiques désormais courantes du quotidien reconduites dans le roman, invitent paradoxalement à réfléchir à ce qui se révèle être une représentation fausse de la réalité. L'insertion de fils Facebook ou Twitter, par exemple, et la reproduction visuelle de la plateforme dans les romans, et surtout, l'usage des réseaux sociaux à des fins de propagation d'informations auxquelles on associe d'emblée un degré d'autorité, ajoutent a priori au récit un certain *effet de réel*. Or, il s'agit plutôt d'une construction de la réalité, voire d'une exagération de la réalité dans plusieurs cas, comme je l'ai démontré à partir de la lecture des romans de Bello. Ces échanges reposant sur la production de *faux*, de *rumeurs*, de *mensonges*, visent, somme toute, à *tromper*. Dès lors, on peut conclure que l'insertion et la problématisation du numérique dans le roman contemporain paraît paradoxalement générer non pas un *effet de réel*, pour reprendre le concept de Barthes, mais peut-être plutôt ce qu'on pourrait appeler un *effet d'irréel*.

Bello, Antoine. 2007. *Les Falsificateurs.* Paris : Gallimard.

Bello, Antoine. 2009. *Les Éclaireurs.* Paris : Gallimard.

Bello, Antoine. 2015. *Les Producteurs.* Paris : Gallimard.

Bello, Antoine. 2016. *Ada.* Paris : Gallimard.

Pelletier, Jean-Jacques. 2015. *Machine God.* Montréal : Hurtubise.

Rushdie, Salman. 2018. « La littérature et les fake news ». *Charlie Hebdo,* 23 mai.

Tavernise, Sabrina. 2016. « As Fake News Spreads Lies, More Readers Shrug at the Truth ». *New York Times,* 6 décembre. Consulté le 2 avril 2019. Accéder au lien : https://www.nytimes.com/2016/12/06/us/fake-news-partisan-republican-democrat.html

PART 6

PERSPECTIVES DIACHRONIQUES
SUR LA LITTÉRATURE ÉLECTRONIQUE

READING E-LIT ACROSS TIME

Avoiding Digital Insanity: the Attachment to Constructivism in Brazilian Literature

ANDRÉA CATRÓPA • GILBERTTO PRADO

Abstract

How to build a nation from words? My hypothesis in this paper is that the constructive role of the written text in Brazilian culture has been holding back its experiments in digital literature. Ever since its inception, the relationship between Brazil and literature has been quite peculiar. Brazil was colonized by Portugal, which had a substantial literary history, and the circulation of books and the establishment of the press was forbidden until the nineteenth century. The legal flow of texts, therefore, began shortly before Brazilian independence in 1822. This fact linked literary expression to the idea of building a nation, especially until the middle of the 20th century. Although some local poets have been distinguished by their satirical and irreverent spirit, it is common to find among Brazilian writers what the critic Antonio Candido called the "tradição empenhada" ("committed tradition"). This term defined a kind of engagement that sought to reflect social utopias in the literary text. In the 1950s, the Brazilian concrete poetry movement published avant-garde manifestos and inaugurated, on a national scale, a tradition of poetry that dialogues with Arts and Design. The concrete poets, who related creation to theory, were targeted both for admiration and rejection. In the latter case, critics thought their work suffered from "excessive internationalization." Concrete poetry's experimentalism, however, was intimately related to the period of accelerated transformation of the country towards urbanization and industrialization; but it was not restricted to that. Poetic concretism also was a response to the trauma of a colonized country whose "literary fashions" always came in the wake of what was fashionable abroad. According to Charles Perrone, concrete Brazilian poetry helped "to reconfigure the nation in cultural terms." Moreover, we believe that this movement foreshadowed future events that would become widely diffused in the digital era: the enhancement of word materiality, the spatial organization of the verses, and the use of sounds and colors as elements of poetic creation. Our perspective, however, is that these proposals were not dissociated from the constructive parameters related to the mission of building a nation. This tendency generates a lack of resonance of the "inconsequently experimental" literary movements like SpamPoetry, Flarf Poetry, and Conceptualism, which makes Brazilian digital literature still predominantly follow the concrete verbivocovisual tradition.

Résumé

Comment construire une nation à partir de mots? Mon hypothèse dans cet article est que le rôle du texte écrit dans la culture brésilienne a restreint l'expérimentation en littérature numérique.

Depuis ses débuts, le rapport entre le Brésil et sa littérature est particulier. Le pays a été colonisé par le Portugal, qui avait déjà une importante histoire littéraire et qui, jusqu'au XIXe siècle, a interdit la circulation de livres ainsi que la fondation d'une presse locale. La diffusion légale de textes a donc dû attendre l'indépendance du Brésil, obtenue en 1822. Cette conjoncture historique a contribué à lier la littérature à l'idée de la fondation d'une nation, et cela jusqu'au milieu du XXe siècle. Tandis que certains poètes locaux se distinguent grâce à leur esprit satirique et irrévérencieux, il est commun de retrouver, parmi les écrivains brésiliens, ce que le critique Antonio Candido a appelé la « tradição empenhada » (« la tradition engagée »). Cette expression désigne un engagement à valoriser les utopies sociales dans le texte littéraire. Dans les années 1950, le mouvement brésilien de poésie concrète fait paraître des manifestes avant-gardistes et instaure, à l'échelle nationale, une tradition poétique qui dialogue avec les arts et le design. Les poètes concrets, associant la création et la théorie, ont été à la fois admirés et rejetés. Dans ce dernier cas, les critiques trouvaient que leurs œuvres souffraient d'une « internationalisation excessive ». Sans s'y limiter, l'expérimentalisme de la poésie concrète était intimement lié à la période de transformations accélérées du pays vers l'urbanisation et l'industrialisation. Le concrétisme a aussi servi de réponse au traumatisme d'un pays colonisé dont les principaux modes littéraires provenaient toujours de l'étranger. D'après Charles Perrone, la poésie concrète brésilienne a aidé à « reconstruire la nation en termes culturels ». En outre, nous soutenons que ce mouvement a présagé de futurs événements désormais courants à l'ère numérique : l'accent mis sur la matérialité des mots, l'organisation spatiale des strophes et l'usage des sons et des couleurs comme éléments de la création poétique.

Enfin, nous soutenons que ces propositions poétiques n'étaient pas dissociées de leur « rôle constructif », dont la mission était la fondation d'une nation. Cette tendance génère un manque de visibilité des mouvements littéraires d'« expérimentation sans conséquence » – tel que le Spam Poetry, le Flarf Poetry et le Conceptualisme – qui fait que la littérature numérique brésilienne suit encore la tradition verbivocovisuelle concrète.

THE REBELLION OF VISUAL POETS

There are two ways in which we can observe the phenomenon of Brazilian concrete poetry. The first is to focus on international art trends, aiming a general approach to its context. The second is to dwell on the specific characteristics that the movement presents and that are intimately related to the history of the country where it arose.

Initially, we will focus on the general aspects, commenting on some characteristics of concretism closely related to modern sensibility. This leads us to one question that has driven many artists towards abstraction: their denial of illusionistic practices of the past and the belief that geometric abstraction calls attention to the materiality of painting as an artistic medium. In the late nineteenth and early twentieth centuries, we had a parallel use of alternative forms of expression in literature, especially in the area of poetry. As we can see in painting and sculpture, the refusal to embrace a role of representation of nature is increasingly being questioned, mainly because of the spread of technological advances in the daily life of Western society. According to Walter Benjamin's classic essay "The Work of Art in the Age of Its Technological Reproducibility," the change in the mode of production requests new art forms in the unprecedented economic environment. If the work of art detaches itself from the concept of originality, its ritualistic or emotional value no longer defines it; instead, its conceptual value becomes its main quality. This belief gives rise to a series of questions about what is appropriately an artistic element, and this questioning is what facilitated the outbreak of the vanguards.

This movement culminated in a crisis in the concept of the sign, drawing attention to its materiality. If in traditional written poetry the reader usually takes into account only the meaning of the words, in visual poetry there is a questioning of its expressive medium.

If we agree with Vilém Flusser (2011), we can think of linear writing as a kind of language that, for a specified period, would become the most prestigious in Western society, overriding orality, which was the primary communication system for our ancestors. For centuries, the written code was a privilege for a few, and the recording of information depended on the work of copyists. With the advent of the printing press, books began to circulate and became the primary vehicle for disseminating ideas. The printing machine also drove the creation of a new medium: newspapers, which started to spread in the sixteenth century. Its modern version, with large-scale production, began to be produced a few hundred years later. Between the nineteenth and twentieth centuries, the prestige of books began to share space progressively with printed newspapers and, although this medium emphasized the written word, graphic arts and photography began to play an essential role in their existence. This dynamism about the supremacy of the word as a sign of exhaustion of writing stimulated poets to seek more meaningful ways to say something through dialogue between words and images in a single work of art. A more comprehensive movement in society accompanied this art's tendency: the explosion of the use of visual communication encompassing illustration, photography, advertising, graphic design, and typography. On the poetry front, Cubism, Futurism, Dadaism, and Surrealism awakened the perception of the iconic and sonic potentialities of poetry, which for centuries have taken second place to the linear disposal of the text, designed to be housed in printed media.

In the poetic experiments of artists like Hugo Ball, Kurt Schwitters (both Dadaists), or Guillaume Apollinaire (Cubist), what came into play was the very matter of poetry. Instead of restricting themselves to dialogue with their tradition, formally altering the versified construction according to metrics or varied themes, these poems broke with the literary's strict sense, seeking photography, drawing, collage, typography, and sound as their means of expression.

BUILDING A COUNTRY: UTOPIAS OF A NEW BRAZIL

Echoes of these avant-garde events were heard during the Modern Art Week in Brazil when some local artists launched proposals that sought to break with various cultural ties to which they had found themselves conditioned. Especially in the field of literature, modernists tried to approximate the literary language of the daily dialect. This point was especially significant for writers, since Brazil had adopted the language of its colonizer as the official language of the country since the eighteenth century. However, the influence of the Tupi-Guarani, the African dialects brought by the slaves, and the languages of the people who had invaded the country throughout history (such as the Dutch and the Spanish), made the Portuguese spoken in America farther and farther away from European Portuguese.

Nevertheless, normative grammar, as well as literary convention, rejected the use of the practiced mode of Portuguese in the day-to-day lives of Brazilians. In books, newspapers, and plays, writers were to abandon the talk of the streets and practice an artificial language, dominated only by the more elitist and erudite strata of society. Not just the linguistic issue but also the theme of many of the literary works of modernism involved the breaking of nationally established taboos and prejudices. During the 1920s, rural areas, whose economy was based on agricultural production, developed rapidly. It was natural, therefore, for Brazilian literature to critically examine its colonial past.

Suddenly, cities, which were becoming increasingly populous, inaugurated new habits of consumption and life. The desire for change was such that Brazilian urbanism adopted modernism as its official style. Mainly from the 1930s onwards, the country's government began to finance projects for official buildings in a functional and unadorned style, to move beyond the traits of neocolonial and neoclassical architecture.

Unlike in many European countries, where the transition from artisanal production to industrial production occurred gradually over centuries, in Brazil, this process took only a few decades to complete. There was, therefore, an urgency to prepare the country culturally to embrace these changes in the economic field, which radiated to other spheres of national life. However, it was not until the 1950s that the urbanization and industrialization of the country intensified, mainly through the development policy of President Juscelino Kubitschek.

These sociocultural factors created the conditions for concrete art to present unique and very peculiar features in its Brazilian developments. The quest for the mathematical purity of form and objectivity in artistic creation was inserted as a possibility of breaking with the colonial past. Historically, in a country where government institutions began to establish themselves only from the nineteenth century, art and literature often assumed the role of contributing to the formation of national identity. From Romanticism to Modernism, Brazilian literature was entrusted with the task of recognizing and presenting to its readers the many realities of a territorially large, ethnically diverse, and economically unequal country. There was, therefore, a function for literature that extrapolated the field of imagination and creation, inserting itself into the national culture as a discourse of identity formation.

VERBIVOCOVISUAL FLIRTING WITH HYPERSPACE

Stimulated not only by the European avant-garde but also by the Brazilian modernists, Augusto de Campos, Haroldo de Campos and Décio Pignatari joined forces around the 1950s to propose their vision of poetry. The theoretical dispute, undertaken by the concrete movement in the literary milieu, was always the subject of discord and contributed to hindering a broad discussion of their poetic procedures. We often find a polarization between worshipers and detractors of concrete poetry and the controversial insertion of artists like the brothers Campos and Décio Pignatari in the literary field is due to their avant-garde spirit.

From a contemporary perspective, its formulations may be considered authoritarian. Even if this is a standard feature of many artistic manifestos, it is difficult to critically appraise the proposals and statements of the concrete, since we can find the economics of the words of their poetry applied in their theory. Thus, we can consider that the manifestos of concrete poetry are also a form of literary expression, a projected reflection in practice. Throughout this manifesto, the concrete poets listed their artistic references in a very peculiar way, formulating a synthesis of the points of interest of previous works for their poetic project, as we can read in their second paragraph:

> Forerunners: Mallarmé (*Un coup de dés*, 1897): the first qualitative jump: "subdivisions prismatiques de l'idée"; space ("blancs") and typographical devices as substantive elements of composition. Pound (*The Cantos*); ideogramic method. Joyce (*Ulysses* and *Finnegans Wake*): word-ideogram; organic interpenetration of time and space. Cummings: atomization of words, physiognomical typography; expressionistic emphasis on space. Apollinaire (*Calligrammes*): the vision, rather than the praxis. Futurism, Dadaism: contributions to the life of the problem. In Brazil: Oswald de Andrade (1890-1954): "in *Pills, minutes of poetry*. João Cabral de Melo Neto (born 1920–*The Engineer* and *Psychology of Composition* plus *Anti-Ode*): direct speech, economy and functional architecture of verse. (Campos, Campos, et Pignatari 1958)

Although literature has played a central role in Brazilian culture since the late nineteenth century, reading was inaccessible to a large part of the population. When the country began to industrialize, there was a concomitant movement to universalize access to public education. Therefore, hitherto, the consumption of literature was restricted to elites and opinion makers. Part of the concrete project was meant to produce literature that could ideally be enjoyed in public spaces among the hurried passers-by in an increasingly urban country. It was a kind of poetry that was suitable for billboards, posters, magazines, and newspapers. Perhaps, too, its purpose was to attract, through its iconicity, those new readers and viewers who had been formed by the primary schools that spread, more and more, across the country.

This resulted in a poetics that ideally was based on pure, clean structures with pretensions of universality. These poetics also proposed the perception of the word as an object that, to reach its maximum artistic power, had to strip itself of its more consolidated uses. Instead of just using metaphors, metonymies, or rhymes, concrete poets subverted the expectation of what literary matter was, relying on the force of sound, design, and image as alternatives to constructing poetry.

HOW TO BUILD A NATION FROM WORDS?

However innovative these practices were, in the first decades of the twenty-first century, we have witnessed an emergence of the synthetic image that, according to Paul Virilio (1991), is composed of dimensionless points and non-lasting moments, digitally controlled by algorithms of a coded language. In a certain sense, concrete poetry, even though it provides a dialogue with the digital poetics of the present, demarcates a considerable difference between them: its inscription in the emergence of forms, based on the concreteness of space.

Kenneth Goldsmith (2001) and Marjorie Perloff (2007) both agree with the view that Brazilian concrete poetry anticipated characteristics that would be diffused by digital media. Our perspective, however, is that concrete poetry was not dissociated from the constructive parameters related to the mission of building a nation. Moreover, this tendency generates a lack of resonance of the "inconsequently experimental" literary movements like SpamPoetry,

Flarf Poetry, and Conceptualism, which makes Brazilian digital literature still predominantly follow the concrete verbivocovisual tradition. My hypothesis in this paper is that the constructive role of the written text in Brazilian culture has been holding back its experiments on digital literature.

Benjamin, Walter. 2002. *Selected Writings. Volume 3 (1935–1938).* Translated by Edmund Jephcott and Howard Eiland. Cambridge; London: Harvard University Press.

Campos, Augusto de, Haroldo de Campos, and Décio Pignatari. 1958. "Pilot Plan for Concrete Poetry." *Ubuweb Papers.* Accessed January 21, 2018. Link: http://www.ubu.com/papers/noigandres01.html.

Candido, Antonio. 1981. *Formação da literatura brasileira – momentos decisivos (Formation of Brazilian Literature – Decisive Moments).* Belo Horizonte : Itatiaia.

Flusser, Vilém, and Nancy Ann Roth. 2011. *Does Writing Have a Future?* Minneapolis: University of Minnesota Press.

Goldsmith, Kenneth. 2001. "From (Command) Line to (Iconic) Constellation." *Ubuweb Papers.* Accessed January 10, 2018. Link: http://www.ubu.com/papers/object/05_goldsmith.pdf.

Perloff, Marjorie. 2007. "From Avant-Garde to Digital: The Legacy of Brazilian Concrete Poetry." *Cadernos de Literatura Comparada* 17:11-49.

Perloff, Marjorie. 2012. "The Audacity of Hope." In *The History of Futurism: The Precursors, Protagonists, and Legacies,* ed. by Geert Buelens, Harald Hendrix, and Monica Jansen, 9-30. Plymouth : Lexington Books.

Pignatari, Décio. 1998. "Décio Pignatari se proclama o designer da linguagem [Décio Pignatari proclaims himself the language designer]," May. São Paulo.

Virilio, Paul. 1991. *The Lost Dimension.* New York : Semiotext(e).

PART 6

PERSPECTIVES DIACHRONIQUES
SUR LA LITTÉRATURE ÉLECTRONIQUE

READING E-LIT ACROSS TIME

Littérature numérique :

10 marches à franchir

SERGE BOUCHARDON

Résumé

L'objectif de cet article n'est pas de faire un bilan de plusieurs décennies de littérature numérique, mais d'identifier certains défis qui se présentent à elle actuellement, ainsi que les tensions que ces défis recouvrent. Comme cet article est tiré de la conférence que j'ai donnée au congrès d'ELO 2018, dont le thème était *Attention à la marche! Mind the gap!*, j'ai cherché à relever le défi d'identifier ces marches à franchir par la littérature numérique. Je me suis concentré sur dix marches ou gaps, sans prétendre à l'exhaustivité. Il s'agit en fait de poser des questions en montrant certaines tensions à l'œuvre concernant le champ de la littérature numérique, puis l'expérience de lecture des œuvres et, enfin, la formation et la recherche.

Abstract

The objective of this article is not to simply review several decades of digital literature, but rather to identify certain obstacles that present themselves currently, as well as the tensions that these obstacles bring with them. Since this article is derived from the talk I gave at the ELO 2018 conference, where the theme was *Attention à la marche! Mind the gap!*, my goal was to take up the challenge of identifying the gaps to fill with digital literature. I focus on ten gaps or marches, with no claim to exhaustiveness. I pose questions with regards to these gaps while illustrating certain tensions concerning works in the field of digital literature, then the experience of reading these works, and lastly, how this new literary form affects education and research.

The English version of this article can be found here:
https://electronicbookreview.com/essay/mind-the-gap-10-gaps-for-digital-literature/

INTRODUCTION

Qu'est-ce que la *littérature numérique*? Celle-ci existe depuis plus de six décennies et s'inscrit dans des filiations connues (écriture combinatoire et à contraintes, écriture fragmentaire, écriture visuelle et sonore...). Littérature *numérique, électronique* ou *informatique*, la terminologie n'est pas figée. En revanche, la critique s'entend généralement pour distinguer deux principales formes de littérature sur un support numérique : la **littérature numérisée** et la **littérature numérique** proprement dite (même si parfois la frontière peut être floue, et peut-être l'est-elle de plus en plus).

La *littérature numérisée* reprend le plus souvent des œuvres d'abord publiées sur papier dans des éditions numériques, que l'on appelle enrichies ou augmentées en ce qu'elles apportent des fonctionnalités (annoter, chercher, partager) ou des contenus multimédias (vidéos, iconographie...) permettant d'apprécier et de comprendre l'œuvre. La nature du texte lui-même n'a pourtant pas foncièrement changé : nous pouvons ou pourrions toujours l'imprimer sans altérer sa signification.

Dans la deuxième forme de littérature (la *littérature numérique*), pensée et conçue par et pour le numérique, le texte changerait profondément de nature si on l'imprimait. Qu'il s'agisse de fictions hypertextuelles, de poèmes animés, d'œuvres faisant appel à la génération automatique de texte ou encore de productions collaboratives en ligne, la création littéraire « nativement numérique » (« Digital-born », Hayles **2008**) est actuellement florissante. Pour les auteurs, il s'agit de concevoir et de réaliser des œuvres spécifiquement pour les supports numériques (ordinateur, tablette, smartphone), en s'efforçant d'en exploiter les caractéristiques : dimension multimédia ou multimodale, animation textuelle, technologie hypertexte, interactivité, ou encore géo-localisation et réalité virtuelle.

L'objectif de cet article n'est pas de faire un bilan de plusieurs décennies de littérature numérique, mais d'identifier certains défis qui se présentent à elle actuellement, ainsi que les tensions que ces défis recouvrent. Comme cet article est tiré de la conférence que j'ai donnée au congrès d'ELO 2018, dont le thème était *Attention à la marche! Mind the gap!*, j'ai cherché à relever le défi d'identifier ces marches à franchir par la littérature numérique. Je me suis concentré sur dix marches ou gaps, sans prétendre à l'exhaustivité.

Il s'agit en fait de poser des questions en montrant certaines tensions à l'œuvre concernant le champ de la littérature numérique, puis l'expérience de lecture des œuvres et, enfin, la formation et la recherche.

1. LE CHAMP DE LA LITTÉRATURE NUMÉRIQUE

1.1. GAP N°1

CRÉATION : DE LA CONCEPTION D'INTERFACES À L'EXPLOITATION DE PLATEFORMES EXISTANTES?

Leonardo Flores[1] propose une typologie de la littérature numérique avec trois générations d'auteurs et d'œuvres. Pour définir les deux premières générations, il se réfère à N. K. Hayles (**2008**). La première génération, à partir des années 1950 et jusqu'en 1995, correspond aux expérimentations d'avant le Web qui s'appuient sur des supports électroniques et numériques (« pre-web experimentation with electronic and digital media »). La deuxième génération, à partir de 1995 et jusqu'à maintenant, donne naissance à des œuvres innovantes créées avec des interfaces et des formes dédiées (« innovative works created with custom interfaces and forms »). Leonardo Flores distingue une troisième génération, à partir de 2005, qui utilise des interfaces et plateformes existantes et touche un large public (« established interfaces with massive user bases »).

NOTE 1

http://leonardoflores.net/blog/lecture-third-generation-electronic-literature/

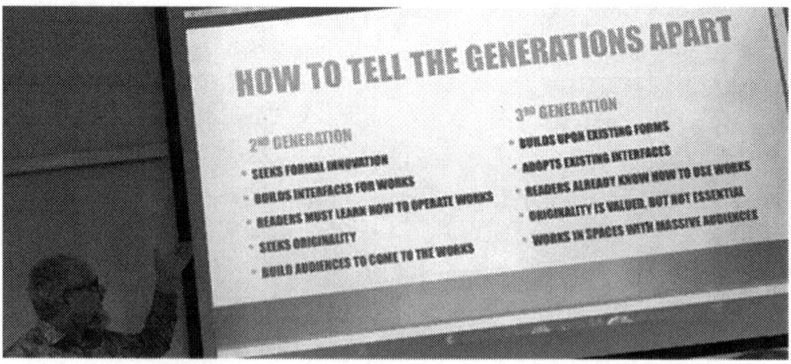

Figure 1 : Présentation de Leonardo Flores à l'Université de Bergen en 2018.

Selon Leonardo Flores, même si les deuxième et troisième générations co-existent toujours, on peut observer chez les auteurs de littérature numérique un mouvement de la deuxième vers la troisième. Une des difficultés pour les auteurs a parfois été liée aux compétences informatiques à maîtriser pour créer des œuvres de littérature numérique. C'est ce que l'on pourrait appeler le « fossé technique » (« technical gap »). Ce fossé technique pourrait être considérablement réduit, voire disparaître, dans le passage de la deuxième à la troisième génération. Les plateformes de réseaux sociaux, notamment, présenteraient de ce point de vue un atout précieux pour les auteurs qui n'ont pas forcément de compétences techniques en programmation. Mais au-delà de la question des compétences, la motivation première peut être de jouer avec (et de détourner) des dispositifs comportant une dimension industrielle et idéologique forte, et ainsi de sensibiliser un large public aux enjeux socio-politiques de ces dispositifs.

Figure 2 : *Aleph Null 3.0*, de Jim Andrews : un exemple de création de seconde génération ("both a tool and an artwork in itself").

Figure 3 : Troisième génération : les *netprovs* (improvisations sur internet) de Rob Wittig et Mark Marino, qui se déroulent sur les réseaux sociaux, en particulier sur Twitter.

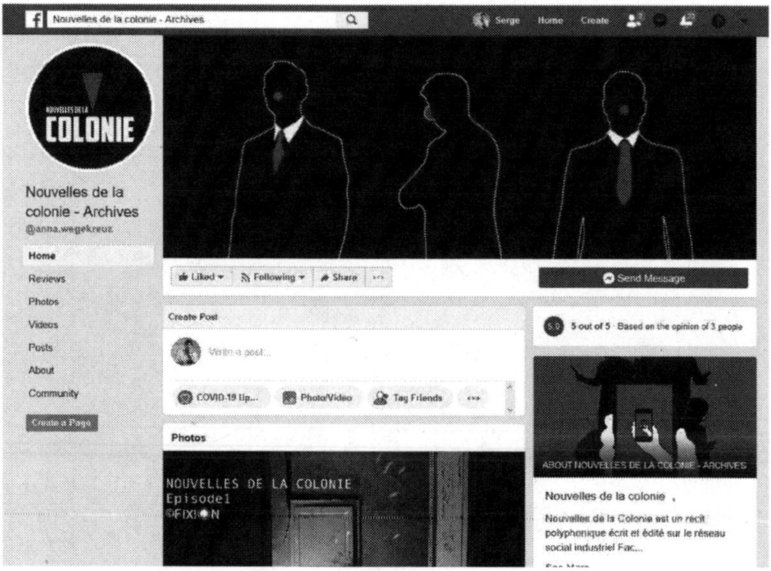

Figure 4 : Troisième génération : les *Nouvelles de la colonie*, création collaborative sur Facebook, depuis 2016.

TENSION : COMPLICITÉ VS RÉSISTANCE VIS-À-VIS DES PLATEFORMES

Une question se pose dès lors, formulée par David Ciccoricco[2] :

> La littérature électronique fonctionne-t-elle en mode de complicité, en se connectant à son public par les moyens et supports usuels? [...] Ou bien, la littérature électronique fonctionne-t-elle comme un art de la résistance [...]?

NOTE 2 Publication à venir chez Bloomsbury Press. Je traduis.

Lorsqu'on s'appuie sur une plateforme de réseau social (comme Facebook) ou de microblogging (comme Twitter) pour créer une œuvre de littérature numérique, propose-t-on uniquement une approche critique détournant ces dispositifs, ou ne court-on pas le risque d'être également *complice* de la logique commerciale et industrielle de ces plateformes ? Se pose également la question de la pérennité des créations qui sont fondées sur des plateformes propriétaires, et donc de la dépendance à ces plateformes.

1.2. GAP N°2

PUBLIC : D'UNE AUDIENCE CONFIDENTIELLE À UNE LARGE AUDIENCE ?

La question d'une nouvelle génération d'outils et d'œuvres conduit à la question souvent débattue de l'audience de la littérature numérique. Leonardo Flores parle, à propos des œuvres de la troisième génération, de la possibilité de toucher une plus large audience (« works in spaces with massive audiences »).

Depuis plusieurs années déjà, de nombreuses démarches tentent de rejoindre un public plus large. Ainsi l'initiative *Opening Up Digital Fiction Writing Competition* (**https://readingdigitalfiction.com/**), organisée notamment par l'Université de Bangor en Grande-Bretagne, vise à récompenser des créations susceptibles d'atteindre un large public[3].

NOTE 3

« Wonderbox Publishing, in conjunction with Bangor University (Wales), is sponsoring the second annual competition to discover the best "popular" digital fiction: digital fiction that appeals to mainstream audiences. »

http://openingup.wonderboxpublishing.com/

Figure 5 : Capture d'écran du site «Reading Digital Fiction».

Cette volonté est également explicite dans tous les événements organisés autour de la littérature numérique pour enfants (« Children's lit » ou « Kid elit »). Cette littérature est présente depuis plusieurs conférences et festivals ELO. Par exemple, dans le cadre de la conférence ELO organisée à Bergen en août 2015, une exposition avait été consacrée à la littérature numérique pour enfants dans la bibliothèque de la ville de Bergen. Une journée de conférence s'était tenue dans cette même bibliothèque, en corrélation avec l'exposition.

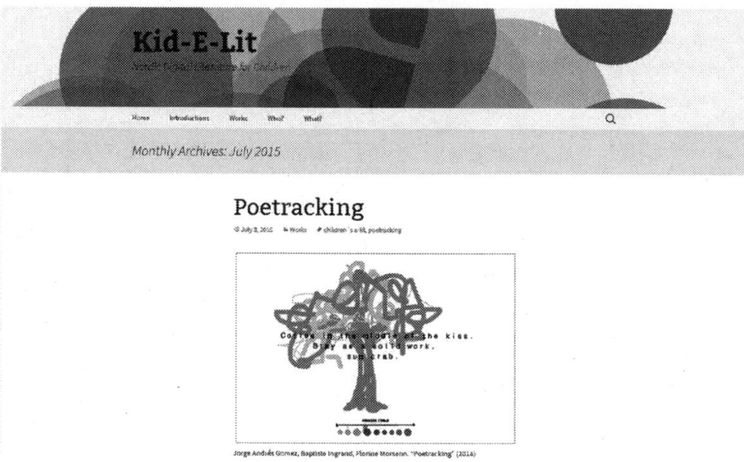

Figure 6 : L'exposition Kid Elit pour ELO 2015 à Bergen[4].

TENSION : LARGE AUDIENCE VS EXPÉRIMENTATION

On peut toutefois se poser la question suivante : faut-il avant tout viser le grand public ? Ne serait-ce pas contradictoire avec le fait que la littérature numérique est avant tout une littérature expérimentale ? Dans un échange en ligne avec Joe Tabbi, Scott Rettberg parle ainsi d'une « pratique fondamentalement expérimentale, dans le sens scientifique d'une expérimentation »[5]. Quel serait le coût d'une telle marche à franchir en termes de public, et est-ce seulement possible ?

NOTE 4
http://www.kidelit.dk/?m=201507

NOTE 5
https://www.facebook.com/jill.rettberg/videos/522434064169/ Je traduis.

1.3. GAP N°3

TRADUCTION : D'UNE CULTURE HOMOGÈNE GLOBALE À DES SPÉCIFICITÉS CULTURELLES?

On a évoqué une nouvelle génération de plateformes et d'outils industriels (*gap* n° 1) permettant éventuellement de toucher un lectorat plus large (*gap* n° 2). Ce passage pourrait entraîner une culture homogène globale fondée sur la technologie numérique. C'est la question évoquée notamment par Erika Fülöp :

> Leonardo Flores souligne que la littérature électronique dépend davantage des développements technologiques (mondiaux) et des influences internationales que des traditions nationales ou régionales. Les technologies numériques représentent un changement de paradigme si radical, affirme-t-il, que nous devrions considérer la littérature électronique comme un phénomène international ou même postnational. (Fülöp **2018**, je traduis)

À cette vision de la littérature numérique comme phénomène international et postnational, Erika Fülöp oppose une volonté de « contrer le stéréotype d'une culture homogène globale à l'ère numérique » (Fülöp **2018** je traduis), en soulignant que la littérature qui se fait dans cet espace n'en garde pas moins les traces des cultures pré-digitales.

TENSION SUR LE RÔLE DE LA TRADUCTION : DOMESTICATION VS ALTÉRITÉ

Ce passage éventuel pose également la question de la traduction des œuvres de littérature numérique : le rôle du traducteur, par exemple en langue anglaise, est-il de gommer les différences culturelles pour que la production *parle* à un public anglophone, ou au contraire consiste-t-il à faire ressortir ce qui relèverait d'une forme de spécificité culturelle, mettant ainsi en évidence la diversité culturelle des productions de littérature numérique plus que leur dimension internationale?

En théorie de la traduction, Schleiermacher[6] distingue deux manières de traduire : essayer d'amener le lecteur plus près du texte (et de la culture d'où celui-ci vient), en gardant donc un peu de l'étrangeté ou de l'altérité culturelle du texte; ou bien rapprocher le texte du lecteur, en lui proposant une traduction qu'il peut facilement s'approprier parce que le texte traduit s'assimile à la culture du lecteur. Cette opposition, si elle peut sembler réductrice, met bien en évidence la question de la dimension culturelle de la traduction. C'est sur la distinction de Schleiermacher que s'appuie Lawrence Venuti (Venuti **2008**) pour mettre en avant une tension entre « foreignization » et « domestication ». Comment cette tension s'exprime-t-elle dans la littérature numérique, dans l'espace numérique où, selon certains, on est partout « chez soi » ? Que voudraient dire les frontières linguistiques dans cet espace, si ce ne sont plus (également) des différences culturelles ?

Et comment cette diversité culturelle s'exprime-t-elle : uniquement par la dimension linguistique ?[7] On peut formuler l'hypothèse que le fait que les créations de littérature numérique ne soient pas seulement fondées sur des mots, mais également sur des gestes et sur du mouvement (animations), renforce la prégnance des spécificités culturelles et l'importance de leur prise en compte (Di Rosario et Borras **2012**).

NOTE 6

"On the Different Methods of Translating" (1813). 7

NOTE 7

María Mencía, Søren Bro Pold et Manuel Portela abordent la traduction en articulant quatre niveaux (Mencía, Pold, et Portela **2018**) : « *Translinguistic (translation between languages); transcoding (translation between machine-readable codes; translation between machine-readable codes and human-readable texts); transmedial (translation between medial modalities); transcreational (translation as a composition practice; translation as a shared creative practice)* » (présentation lors de la conférence ELO 2017 à Porto).

1.4. GAP N°4

CHAMP LITTÉRAIRE : DE LA LITTÉRARITÉ À L'EXPÉRIENCE LITTÉRAIRE ?

Créer des œuvres accessibles et toucher un public plus large pourrait renforcer le passage vers une institutionnalisation et une inscription dans le champ littéraire, en mettant en exergue la littérarité de ces œuvres. Pourtant, ne faut-il pas considérer qu'il y aurait une « nouvelle qualité de littérarité » dans la littérature numérique, pour reprendre l'expression de Roberto Simanowski (Simanowski **2010**) ?

Quelle serait cette propriété qui rendrait littéraires certaines œuvres? Réfléchissant sur la littérarité des œuvres de littérature numérique en rapport avec une littérarité déjà existante, Jörgen Schäfer insiste sur la production d'une autre réalité (Schäfer **2010**). Zuern parle d'un usage figuré du langage (Zuern **2010**). Strehovec rappelle quant à lui le concept de « défamiliarisation » (Strehovec **2010**) :

> Les formalistes, suivant Viktor Chklovski dans « L'art comme procédé » (1917), ont posé comme critère de littérarité la « défamiliarisation » ou « l'étrangeté » (ostranénie) : la littérature, ou l'art en général, renouvelle la sensibilité linguistique des lecteurs par des procédés qui dérangent les formes habituelles et automatiques de leur perception. (Compagnon 1998)

Si la littérarité pose la question de la figuration et de la défamiliarisation, on pourrait toutefois se demander, avec Simanowski, quelles seraient les stratégies équivalentes de la figuration et de la défamiliarisation dans les œuvres de littérature numérique.

> Strehovec a certainement raison d'avancer que le concept de *défamiliarisation* dépasse le seul domaine de la linguistique et qu'il doit s'appliquer à la langue cyber sous toutes ses formes : matériaux visuels, sonores et caractéristiques propres aux médias numériques, tel que l'intermédialité, l'interactivité, l'animation et l'hyperlien. Une définition plus générale émerge donc du *littéraire* comme l'agencement des matériaux ou l'utilisation de caractéristiques d'une façon inhabituelle dans le but de favoriser une perception esthétique aux dépens d'une perception automatique. (Simanowski **2010**, je traduis)

Cette défamiliarisation, en outre, ne devrait pas toucher seulement la dimension linguistique, mais également les dimensions iconique et sonore. Une difficulté apparaît : comment identifier la défamiliarisation dans un système d'expression qui est trop récent et trop évolutif pour avoir établi du *familier* et du *commun*?

Une question se pose dès lors : la littérarité d'une œuvre de littérature numérique serait-elle similaire à celle d'une œuvre imprimée (tout en reposant sur des moyens différents), ou bien constate-t-on une transformation de cette littérarité? Joe Tabbi évoque une nécessaire transformation de la littérarité avec les œuvres de littérature numérique :

> Quoi qu'il advienne de la littérature électronique, elle n'est pas seulement un nouveau champ de recherche. Il semble plutôt que nous soyons impliqués collectivement dans la transformation de la façon dont le travail littéraire est réalisé, présenté et représenté dans les différents médias (Tabbi 2002, je traduis).

Dans les œuvres de littérature numérique, nous assisterions alors plus à une métamorphose de la littérarité qu'à une incarnation d'une littérarité qui existerait déjà. Cela va aussi dans le sens d'une construction et d'une variation – notamment en fonction des supports – historiques de la littérarité.

Ceux qui affirment que ces textes ont moins de valeur littéraire n'ont peut-être pas saisi ce qui fait la spécificité et la pertinence de la littérature numérique : une expérience littéraire interactive. Ils continuent à opposer littérature et informatique (ou numérique) et parlent de deux mondes qui ne peuvent pas communiquer. C'est pourtant la confrontation, l'interpénétration, avec toutes ses tensions, entre littérature et numérique qui construit la littérarité de la littérature numérique. Ou plutôt faudrait-il parler – de façon pragmatiste à la manière de Dewey (1980), pour qui il n'existe pas d'œuvre dotée d'une valeur en soi, c'est-à-dire indépendamment des expériences qui en sont faites – d'*expérience littéraire* plus que, et de façon essentialiste, de *littérarité.*

TENSION : LÉGITIMITÉ DANS LE CHAMP LITTÉRAIRE VS INSCRIPTION EN MARGE DE CE CHAMP

L'ELO définit ainsi la littérature numérique : « Qu'est-ce que la littérature électronique? Le terme fait référence à des œuvres qui ont une forte dimension littéraire et qui tirent avantage des possibilités et des contextes de l'ordinateur, seul ou en réseau » (http://eliterature.org/about/, je traduis).

Doit-on persister à parler de littérarité? N'est-ce pas prendre le risque de continuer à être évalué selon des critères qui ne correspondent pas à la littérature numérique et à ses spécificités, et pour les auteurs continuer à demeurer toujours incompris?

Faut-il chercher à combler le fossé institutionnel avec le champ littéraire? Faut-il chercher une légitimité dans le champ littéraire ou tracer une (ou des) voie(s) en marge de ce champ?

L'EXPÉRIENCE DE LECTURE

2.1. GAP N°5

GESTE : DE LA LECTURE DE TEXTES À L'INTERPRÉTATION GESTUALISÉE?

Sur quoi l'« expérience littéraire » dont il a été question précédemment est-elle fondée? Les œuvres de littérature numérique proposent souvent – pas systématiquement – un mode de lecture faisant appel aux gestes, autrement dit une lecture gestualisée. Un texte numérique, s'il est un texte à lire, peut proposer une manipulation gestuelle. Cette dimension de la manipulation du texte, mais aussi des autres formes sémiotiques, ouvre un large champ de possibles pour les créations numériques interactives. Dans quelle mesure peut-on dire qu'il y a un « gestural gap », un saut à franchir avec cette lecture gestualisée? Et dans quelle mesure peut-on parler d'une gestualité spécifique au numérique?

Dans le récit interactif *Déprise*[8], le geste contribue pleinement à la construction du sens. Le lecteur est confronté à des manipulations gestuelles reposant sur un écart entre ses attentes lorsqu'il manipule et l'affichage qu'il constate à l'écran. Il expérimente ainsi de façon interactive le sentiment de *déprise* du personnage. Dans la troisième scène, le personnage tente d'interpréter un mot que sa femme lui a laissé : s'agit-il d'un mot d'amour ou d'un mot de rupture? Cette double interprétation, le lecteur peut l'expérimenter gestuellement : s'il déplace le curseur de sa souris d'un bord à l'autre de l'écran, l'ordre des phrases du texte s'inverse et le mot d'amour se transforme en mot de rupture (la musique, extraite de *Carmen* de Bizet, est alors également jouée à l'envers).

NOTE 8
Serge Bouchardon et Vincent Volckaert, *Déprise*, 2010, http://deprise.fr/.

L'exemple ci-dessus pose la question du geste et plus largement de l'engagement du corps dans la littérature numérique. La manipulation gestuelle est certes inhérente aux supports techniques d'écriture et de lecture; toutefois, le numérique entraîne un *passage à la limite* en introduisant la calculabilité au principe même de la manipulation (Bachimont **2010**). De cela, la littérature numérique en est peut-être le meilleur révélateur. Lorsque le lecteur fait le geste de taper une lettre au clavier, que peut-il arriver? Une autre lettre peut s'afficher à la place (cf. la dernière scène de *Déprise*[9]), la lettre tapée peut quitter la zone de saisie et *s'envoler*, ou bien encore ce geste peut générer un son, lancer une requête dans un moteur de recherche, voire éteindre l'ordinateur (tous des exemples existants)... À partir de ce geste très simple, des possibles sont bien ouverts qui excèdent l'anticipation inhérente au geste.

NOTE 9
http://deprise.fr.

Le numérique rend possible la défamiliarisation de l'expérience gestuelle inhérente à la lecture et à l'écriture. La défamiliarisation est bien sûr le projet de beaucoup d'avant-garde et d'approches littéraires (et plus généralement artistiques). On pourrait néanmoins avancer qu'il y a des spécificités dans le mode numérique de défamiliarisation. En littérature, la défamiliarisation concerne l'aspect linguistique. Dans la littérature numérique, la défamiliarisation ne concerne pas seulement la dimension linguistique, mais également les dimensions iconique et sonore, et la dimension gestuelle. C'est sans doute avec la question du geste que la défamiliarisation peut être la plus explicite, dans la mesure où un répertoire de gestes commence à se stabiliser avec les supports numériques (PC et supports tactiles). Avec le numérique, le geste interactif est défamiliarisé grâce à l'opacité du calcul : le numérique introduit un écart entre les attentes du lecteur fondées sur ses gestes et les possibles offerts. Dans la littérature numérique, la défamiliarisation est fondée sur le calcul. En ce sens, on pourrait parler d'une gestualité spécifique au numérique, notamment bien mise en évidence dans la littérature numérique.

C'est ce rôle du calcul et du programme, ainsi que la question des interfaces et de l'apprentissage culturel de celles-ci, qu'il faut prendre en compte dans l'analyse des manipulations gestuelles si l'on souhaite en saisir les spécificités. Faire l'hypothèse d'une gestualité spécifique au numérique, c'est également poser la nécessité de sensibiliser et de former au rôle du geste dans la construction du sens d'une production numérique. Il est en effet important de réfléchir à la sémiotique et à la rhétorique propres à ces gestes de manipulation. Cette dimension pourrait être intégrée dans une formation à l'écriture numérique.

TENSION : ENTRE LA CONTEMPLATION DE LA *RÉVÉLATION* D'UN SENS ET L'ACTIVITÉ DE SON EFFECTUATION[10]

Ce que l'on peut alors constater, c'est une tension entre la contemplation de la révélation d'un sens et l'activité de son effectuation. Les créations de littérature numérique reposent en effet souvent sur des dispositifs dans lesquels le lecteur agit, compose, construit; cette expérience, qui repose sur une activité gestuelle, est-elle compatible avec une expérience – si ce n'est une révélation – esthétique? La tension créatrice est ici celle de l'ouverture au sens, où il faut être prêt, dans l'attente, disponible, et de la fermeture du dispositif où il faut être affairé, mobilisé. Le dispositif doit nécessairement se dépasser vers une expérience esthétique, celle-ci ne pouvant être seulement un faire. Ceci incite à faire l'hypothèse que la littérature numérique est vraiment un art, si elle permet de sortir de la fermeture du dispositif tout en révélant ses possibilités de manifestation du sens.

NOTE 10

Ce que j'appelle dans « Towards a tension-based definition of Digital Literature » (Bouchardon **2016**) la tension de l'expérience esthétique et littéraire. Est mise en question l'antinomie de principe entre l'activité (notamment gestuelle) dans la réception et l'expérience esthétique.

2.2. GAP N°6

RÉCIT : VERS UN EFFACEMENT DE LA FRONTIÈRE ENTRE RÉALITÉ ET FICTION?

Dans *Littérature numérique : le récit interactif* (Bouchardon **2009**), j'ai défendu la thèse selon laquelle le support *conditionne* la narrativité. Alors que les théories du récit (par exemple celles des formalistes russes comme Propp ou des structuralistes comme Greimas et Bremond) affichent, pour la plupart, une universalité indépendante du support, la littérature numérique montre que le support conditionne la narrativité. Le terme « conditionne » signifie ici que le support est la condition de la narrativité mais aussi qu'il la contraint, sans pour autant induire une vision déterministe : le support numérique est travaillé par des tensions et autorise ainsi une multitude de jeux[11].

NOTE 11

On pourrait objecter que c'est parce que le support numérique est très prégnant dans les œuvres interactives que le support conditionne la narrativité. En réalité, le récit littéraire interactif permet de revisiter les supports précédents, à commencer par le support papier, et de mettre en exergue le rôle du support dans tout dispositif de narration.

NOTE 12

En 2001, Lev Manovich parlait déjà de « database narratives » (Manovich **2001**).

Parmi les contraintes et les possibles ouverts par le support numérique, assistons-nous depuis quelques années à une nouvelle façon de raconter? Le gap par rapport à d'autres façons de raconter pourrait venir du couplage avec des bases de données[12] et des flux de données en temps réel.

Prenons l'exemple de *Lucette, gare de Clichy* (création présentée par Françoise Chambefort sous forme de performance dans le cadre de ELO 2018 à Montréal : **http://fchambef.fr/lucette/**. Il s'agit d'un récit reposant sur un flux de données en temps réel.

> Lucette habite juste en face de la gare de Clichy-Levallois. De sa fenêtre, elle voit les voyageurs qui passent. Ces trains, avec leurs petits noms étranges et familiers, sont autant de personnages qui viennent rendre visite à Lucette. Il y a des moments pleins de vie et des moments de solitude.

Figure 7 : *Lucette, Gare de Clichy*, de Françoise Chambefort (2018).

Ce type de récit est une pure expérience du temps (le temps vécu par une autre personne), mais qui est en même temps fondé sur du *temps réel.* Cette œuvre narrative non interactive est en effet connectée en temps réel avec les données du réseau ferroviaire de la région parisienne (ligne L du transilien). Elle pose des questions très intéressantes sur l'hybridation entre réel et fiction. Dans quelle mesure le récit de fiction peut-il s'appuyer sur un flux de données en temps réel? Est-ce que cela peut faire émerger une nouvelle forme de narration?

Françoise Chambefort analyse le rapport entre faits réels et fiction :

> Nous sommes à même de pointer les particularités narratives de ces objets médiatiques et technologiques qui utilisent les données comme moteur d'une mise en récit. Les données sont un matériau qui se prête particulièrement bien à la narration [...]. Le choix des données contribue pleinement à la mise en récit. Faits réels et fiction entretiennent un rapport fonctionnel qui amène le spectateur à placer son attention tantôt sur l'un, tantôt sur l'autre dans un mouvement qui renforce selon nous le sens de l'œuvre. Enfin la notion de temps réel provoque une fusion entre la mise en intrigue et sa réception. Grâce à cette temporalité particulière, le réel donne à la fiction la force de sa contingence tandis que la fiction apporte au réel sa puissance émotive (Chambefort **2018**).

Au-delà de la question des flux de données en temps réel, ou encore de la réalité virtuelle, le *gap* dans la manière de raconter pourrait venir de l'intrusion du temps et de l'espace réels du lecteur dans la fiction[13]. Certains récits, sous forme d'applications pour supports mobiles, reposent sur des notifications, où il s'agit de prendre en compte la temporalité *réelle* du lecteur. Dans *Lifeline* (2015), fiction interactive sur smartphone avec une dimension ludique forte, nous échangeons avec un personnage fictif et nous le conseillons dans sa quête (un astronaute perdu dans l'espace dans le premier épisode, une jeune magicienne dans le second). Le personnage nous raconte sa quête et de temps en temps se déconnecte pour accomplir une tâche, se reposer... Nous le retrouvons ensuite quelques minutes ou heures plus tard lorsqu'il nous parle à nouveau. Notre journée est donc rythmée par ces échanges qui, si nous les suivons à un rythme normal, se prolongeront pendant quelques jours.

NOTE 13

Il existe toute une tradition de cette insertion dans les jeux vidéo, notamment depuis le CD-ROM In *Memoriam* de 2003 (*Alternate Reality Game*, avant que l'expression ne soit forgée) : **http://www.dailymars.net/dossier-les-jeux-videos-en-arg-1sur4-in-memoriam/**

NOTE 14

Par exemple les récits qui font appel à Google Maps (par exemple : Carpenter J.R., *in absentia*, 2008, accéder au lien. **https://collection.eliterature.org/2/works/carpenter_inabsentia.html**

Concernant l'espace, il s'agit de récits numériques liés à des espaces physiques. On peut inclure dans cette catégorie les récits en ligne qui utilisent des outils cartographiques[14], jusqu'à ceux qui investissent l'espace urbain et sortent de l'espace de l'écran, en particulier ceux qui reposent sur la géolocalisation (*locative narratives*, ou encore *ambient literature*). Par exemple *The Cartographer's Confession*[15],

NOTE 15

https://ambientlit.com/cartographersconfession

application pour téléphone portable qui raconte l'histoire de deux réfugiés juste après la seconde guerre mondiale, nécessite que le lecteur déambule dans les rues de Londres pour se dérouler. Ces fictions hypermédiatiques posent la question du rapport entre narrativité et spatialité (Bourassa **2010**), de même que celle du rapport à l'espace physique couplé à des bases de données.

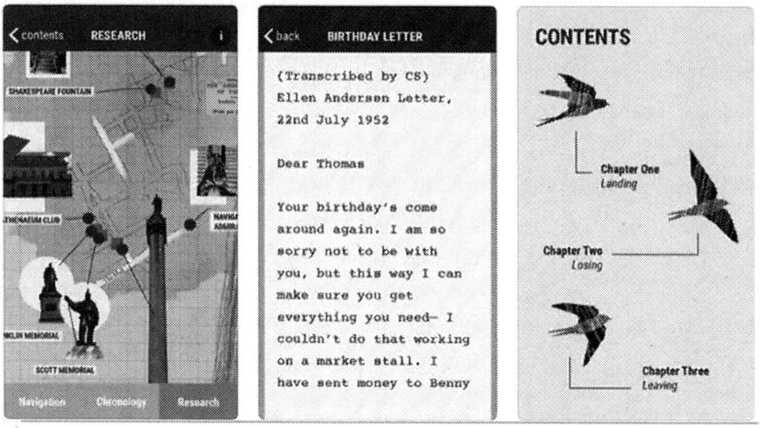

Figure 8 : *The Cartographer's Confession*, de James Attlee (2017).

Le *gap* consiste ici à introduire davantage de la réalité du lecteur dans la fiction. L'intrusion du temps et de l'espace réels du lecteur dans la fiction semble différente des métalepses littéraires et cinématographiques auxquelles nous sommes habitués; le « franchissement de seuil » n'est pas de même nature.

TENSION : NARRATION VS JEU DRAMATIQUE

La littérature numérique ne contribue-t-elle pas de la sorte à l'effacement de la frontière entre fiction et réalité? La différence entre narration et jeu dramatique[16] pourrait être mobilisée : si quelqu'un me raconte une histoire (narration), il y a bien une frontière entre réalité et fiction (ce qui n'empêche pas une forme d'immersion); si j'accomplis les actions à la place du personnage, *comme si* j'étais le personnage (jeu dramatique), peut-être alors cette frontière s'estompe-t-elle. Dans les récits numériques reposant sur l'intrusion du temps et de l'espace réels du lecteur dans la fiction, la narration peut parfois sembler s'effacer au profit du jeu dramatique; le lecteur *joue* le rôle d'un personnage.

NOTE 16

Jeu dramatique ne fait pas référence ici seulement à l'univers théâtral. L'expression jeu de rôle pourrait aussi convenir.

Selon Françoise Lavocat, le pouvoir de la fiction repose sur le « désir empêché de venir en aide aux personnages, de pénétrer dans leur monde » (Lavocat **2016**) ce qui entraîne une forme d'empathie plus que d'identification. L'empathie ainsi définie, loin de conduire à un effacement de la frontière entre la réalité et la fiction, renforcerait celle-ci. L'empathie serait du côté de la narration, l'identification du côté du jeu dramatique. Quelle est la projection dans le monde de la vie du lecteur ? Celle-ci n'est sans doute pas la même dans les dispositifs qui reposent sur l'identification du lecteur/interacteur/joueur. Dans ces dispositifs, le lecteur est très centré sur lui-même, ce qui peut favoriser l'introspection. Mais le décentrement que procure l'empathie, le plaisir de ne pas être soi-même, est sans doute moins fort.

Doit-on poser l'hypothèse d'un effacement de la frontière entre réalité et fiction dans les créations de littérature numérique qui s'appuient sur le temps et l'espace réels du lecteur, ou bien plutôt d'un nouvel agencement entre réalité et fiction, de même qu'entre identification et empathie ?

2.3. GAP N°7

LE SUJET NUMÉRIQUE : D'UNE IDENTITÉ NARRATIVE À UNE IDENTITÉ POÉTIQUE ?[17]

Comme l'a montré Paul Ricœur, notre identité personnelle se construit au fil de nos lectures, et le genre narratif peut constituer une grille d'intelligibilité de notre propre existence (Ricoeur **1985**). Au cœur de ce lien entre relation au texte et rela-tion à soi réside l'idée, formulée par Alberto Manguel (**2013**) dans sa lecture de Saint-Augustin, que le monde est un livre que l'on est censé lire – ou, comme l'avançait Clifford Geertz, que le texte est un paradigme d'interprétation de la texture de l'action humaine (Geertz **1973**). Dans ce nœud entre la littérature et la vie, qui ferait de la première le miroir ou le laboratoire de la seconde, il semble que tous les genres, tous les types de textes ne soient pas égaux. Ce que paraissent suggérer des œuvres fondatrices de la modernité comme *Don Quichotte* ou, bien plus, tard *Madame Bovary*, c'est que le genre narratif, jusqu'au grotesque et au drame, a constitué le paradigme central d'interprétation de l'action, de la temporalité de la vie, de la relation à l'altérité.

NOTE 17

Cette partie repose sur « Le sujet numérique : d'une identité narrative à une identité poétique ? » (Mayer et Bouchardon 2017)

Le récit, en effet, et peut-être en particulier le roman, est un modèle qui nous aide à nous comprendre nous-mêmes, et à penser notre propre évolution dans le temps sous le signe d'une intrigue. Un tel modèle narratif du soi suppose en creux une certaine représentation de la vie, comme une grande progression linéaire, jalonnée d'étapes et de péripéties qui pourraient se découper en chapitres, incarnée dans des personnages (le héros qui serait le soi, les adjuvants et les opposants qui seraient les autres), et pouvant se lire comme une histoire unitaire. Or, les formes d'écriture et de lecture favorisées par le milieu numérique pourraient bien faire vaciller ce modèle.

D'abord, parce que les formes littéraires que permet le Web, ainsi que les pratiques de lecture qu'il éveille, offrent des alternatives à la linéarité du récit romanesque. Lire sur le Web devient une activité fragmentaire, courte, nomade, naviguant d'hyperlien en hyperlien selon l'ordre de son choix; tandis que la création littéraire numérique expérimente des textes qui bifurquent, multimédia, interactifs, où l'unité n'est jamais donnée mais toujours à construire et à questionner[18].

NOTE 18

Il est vrai que l'hypertexte, le montage de fragments écrits et la littérature combinatoire précèdent largement, dans l'histoire littéraire, l'introduction de l'informatique. Pensons à la technique du cut-up, dont Tristan Tzara jeta les bases avant que William Burroughs ne l'expérimente dans son *Festin nu*, ou encore à la fascination pour le rôle de l'aléa dans le montage textuel qui traversa les créations de l'OuLiPo aussi bien que celles de Marc Saporta avec sa *Composition n° 1*, roman dont le lecteur permute les pages comme il battrait un jeu de cartes. Ce que les dispositifs numériques ont de spécifique, c'est non seulement qu'ils généralisent ces pratiques autrefois explorées par les avant-gardes, mais aussi qu'ils les étendent au-delà du seul monde littéraire, dans les usages communicationnels ordinaires, et notamment sur les dispositifs de réseaux dits sociaux.

Simultanément, les outils d'expression de notre identité en milieu numérique semblent moins favoriser la mise en avant d'une trajectoire unitaire que la récollection d'instants et de fragments. Les manières de transposer notre vie sur les réseaux sociaux, par exemple, échappent à la linéarité du *curriculum vitae* pour se livrer sous forme de billets (« statuts » Facebook) soulignant la multiplicité du soi sous ses visages variés et ses moments mémorables. Le sujet s'actualise à chaque fois par et dans l'instant qu'il est en train de vivre : mosaïque de photos, recueil de haïkus, où « je » devient la somme bigarrée de ses instantanés.

Ces deux phénomènes, transformation de la lecture et transformation de l'expression de soi, seraient-ils liés? Participent-ils l'un et l'autre d'un même devenir, où les mutations de la vie et les mutations du texte se rejoignent, battant en brèche la concordance du récit au profit d'un recueil d'instants? Assiste-t-on à une nouvelle manière de se lire soi-même, provoquée ou reflétée par nos manières de lire les textes – et en quel sens irait cette relation de causalité?

Une hypothèse, formulée par Ariane Mayer (Mayer et Bouchardon 2017), propose d'interpréter cette nouvelle position de l'identité lectrice sous le signe du poème. Un modèle poétique du soi coexisterait avec le modèle narratif à l'école duquel il s'est longtemps compris – où le sujet se lirait moins comme une histoire, que comme un regard qui émerge d'une pluralité d'espaces sensoriels, de moments, d'impressions fugaces, rassemblés après-coup en recueil. Il se dirait moins comme une progression temporelle, que comme l'espace d'un paysage, dont les sons, images et pensées se répondent acci-dentellement pour dessiner une ambiance.

NOTE 19

Au-delà de la question du storytelling, on peut constater un nombre toujours plus important de récits, qu'il s'agisse de films et de séries, mais aussi de fan fictions produites par les internautes eux-mêmes.

TENSION : UNE APPÉTENCE TOUJOURS PLUS GRANDE POUR LES RÉCITS[19] VS UN DEVENIR POÉTIQUE DE L'IDENTITÉ

Est-ce que les plateformes des réseaux socionumériques (cf. gap n° 1) ne renforcent pas ce passage vers une identité poétique ? Dans quelle mesure les œuvres de littérature numérique permettent-elles tout particulièrement de montrer / penser ce passage ?

Fabrique de soi en ligne et littérature numérique participent-elles d'un même devenir poétique de l'identité ? Ou au contraire – et peut-être pour cette raison même –, le sujet contemporain a-t-il plus que jamais besoin d'histoires ?

FORMATION ET RECHERCHE

3.1. GAP N°8

FORMATION : DE LA LITTÉRATIE À LA LITTÉRATIE NUMÉRIQUE ?

Du point de vue pédagogique, la littératie numérique représente-t-elle un fossé à franchir par rapport à la littératie ? Faut-il former de la même façon ? Quels types de connaissances et de compétences sont à développer ? Et quel peut être le rôle de la littérature numérique dans cette littératie numérique ?

La notion de littératie est entendue selon de multiples acceptions (Cailleau, Bouchardon, et Crozat **2018**). Tout d'abord, comme le rappellent Béatrice Fraenkel et Aïssatou Mbodj (Fraenkel et Mbodj-Pouye **2010**), « le terme anglais *literacy* appartient au langage commun en langue anglaise, il désigne la capacité à lire et à écrire ». Ce terme vient du latin « litteratus » et selon l'étude du médiéviste Herbert Grundmann, sa sémantique se construit en relation à son antonyme « illiteratus », terme qui désigne avant le XIIe siècle « celui qui ne sait ni lire ni écrire » et qui par la suite acquiert la connotation supplémentaire de la non maîtrise du latin. Les auteurs soulignent ainsi l'ambiguïté originelle du terme de littératie qui oscille entre une compétence qui relève d'une maîtrise technique du lire/écrire et une composante culturelle.

Les auteurs pointent en outre que les deux grands courants d'études sur la littératie reflètent cette ambiguïté du terme. Le premier, le modèle dit « autonome », issu des travaux de Jack Goody, considère que « l'écriture en tant que technologie de l'intellect ouvre des possibles pour l'organisation sociale et les processus cognitifs » (Goody, **2007**), indépendamment des pratiques effectives et des contextes où elles se déploient. Ces possibles peuvent, selon les contextes, n'être que partiellement exploités, ce qu'il qualifie de « littératie restreinte ». Le second, le modèle dit « idéologique » proposé par Bryan Street, pose que les pratiques scripturales sont toujours situées et qu'il n'est pas possible de leur attribuer des effets a priori.

TENSION : APPRENTISSAGE THÉORIQUE / APPRENTISSAGE PAR LA PRATIQUE (CODE)

Le premier courant, dans la lignée de la thèse de la « raison graphique » de Jack Goody, requiert une approche qui envisage la littératie numérique comme relevant d'une connaissance et d'une compréhension des spécificités de la technologie de l'intellect qu'est l'écriture, indissociablement technique et culturelle. Une telle approche – que je privilégie – pose la question du niveau de compréhension de la technologie numérique : peut-elle rester théorique ou doit-elle passer par une pratique, une écriture des outils, autrement dit un apprentissage du code ? Cette question est actuellement largement débattue (Souchier **2017**). Pour ma part, il me semble qu'une pratique de la programmation peut contribuer à une littératie numérique. L'apprentissage du code est un moyen d'expérimenter la relation agissante du milieu numérique, de prendre conscience de nos possibilités de choisir parmi un ensemble de possibles techniques, de contribuer à la conception de nos outils d'écriture et de lecture quotidiens, voire d'en modifier ou d'en créer. Il ne s'agit pas de faire de tout un chacun un ingénieur en informatique mais bien plutôt un acteur du milieu numérique.

Ainsi, selon Stéphane Crozat (2018), « l'apprentissage de la littératie numérique relève d'un couplage entre apprentissage technique et apprentissage culturel d'une part et apprentissage théorique et apprentissage pratique d'autre part. »[20]

NOTE 20

http://aswemay.fr/co/000054.html

	Théorique	Pratique
Technique	Informatique théorique (algorithmique, modélisation...)	Programmation (développement, administration...)
Culturel	SH de la technique (histoire, philosophie, anthropologie...)	Usages des outils (bonnes pratiques, détournement...)

Figure 9 : Composantes technologiques d'un apprentissage de la littératie numérique, par Stéphane Crozat (2018).

En quoi la littérature numérique permet-elle de franchir ce gap vers une littératie numérique? Nombre de créations sensibilisent au fait qu'un texte numérique réunit deux types de texte (Bachimont) :

— un texte codé, forme d'enregistrement, qui va être interprété (par exemple un texte sur le Web sera souvent codé en langage HTML);
— un texte affiché à l'écran, forme de restitution.

Contrairement au support papier sur lequel forme d'enregistrement et forme de restitution sont identiques (le texte imprimé), elles sont distinctes sur un support numérique. Via la médiation du calcul, à une même forme d'enregistrement peuvent correspondre plusieurs formes de restitution. C'est ce jeu dynamique entre formes d'enregistrement et formes de restitution qui est exploité par certains auteurs.

C'est le cas du poème en ligne de Julien d'Abrigeon intitulé « Proposition de voyage temporel dans l'infinité d'un instant »[21]. « *La raison d'être de ce poème est, quoi qu'il arrive, d'être le plus contemporain des poèmes. Puis de disparaître.* » En activant l'œuvre, le lecteur déclenche un poème animé constitué par la date et l'heure présentes qui apparaissent, avec des polices différentes, dans l'espace de la page-écran. À la fin, le texte reste figé pendant quelques secondes avant d'être à nouveau généré automatiquement, en prenant en compte la nouvelle heure. Le texte de ce poème est un texte non seulement animé, mais qui n'a aucune pérennité, Il est calculé; par contre, il ne sera jamais le même, car la date et l'heure de consultation seront toujours différentes.

NOTE 21

Abrigeon Julien (d'), *Proposition de voyage temporel dans l'infinité d'un instant*, 2002, http://tapin.free.fr/HEURE.htm

Derrière ce jeu entre texte-code et texte-à-lire, la littérature numérique permet de pointer la dissimulation structurelle propre à tout programme informatique. Le lecteur ne sait pas ce que le programme est en train de faire, de calculer. Le lien hypertexte sur lequel il vient de cliquer est-il statique (s'il clique dix fois sur le même lien, obtiendra-t-il à chaque fois le même fragment textuel)? Ou bien est-il dynamique (conduisant vers un fragment tiré aléatoirement, ou bien vers tel ou tel texte en fonction de telle ou telle condition, par exemple selon les textes déjà parcourus par le lecteur)? Il y a là une opacité induite, due à cette machine logique qu'est tout programme informatique, sur laquelle s'appuient certains auteurs.

Talan Memmott, dans *Lexia to Perplexia*[22], explore les relations entre une conscience humaine et un réseau informatique. Il y joue du rapport entre texte du programme (dont des bribes sont données à lire) et texte narratif. Le texte du programme *créolise* progressivement le texte narratif, illustrant par là-même l'idée que le code fait partie du *texte* de l'œuvre.

NOTE 22

Memmott Talan, *Lexia to Perplexia*, 2000, https://collection.eliterature.org/1/works/memmott_lexia_to_perplexia.html

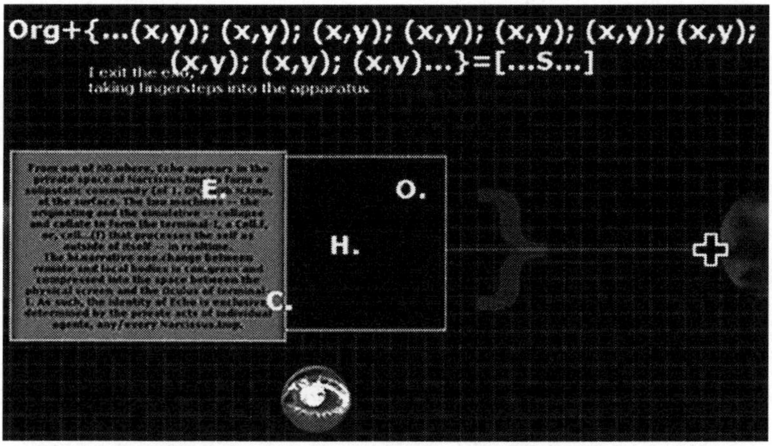

Figure 10 : *Lexia to Perplexia*, de Talan Memmott (2000).

Concernant la question du code, certains auteurs ont pu concevoir des poèmes numériques pouvant être lus et interprétés par un lecteur et également exécutés par un ordinateur (c'est le cas par exemple de Jean-Pierre Balpe). De tels poèmes jouent sur la frontière entre écrit destiné à être lu et écrit destiné à être calculé et mettent l'accent sur le calcul en tant que processus matériel. Alan Sondheim, auteur de littérature numérique, a inventé le terme de *codework* pour désigner ce type de créations, qui se présentent comme un mixte de langage de programmation et de langage *ordinaire*.

Le terme de *codework* est d'ailleurs plus large, désignant également les créations qui se présentent comme des lignes de code et qui ne sont pas destinées à être calculées. Voici un exemple tiré de *Days of JavaMoon* de Duc Thuan :

NOTE 23

Thuan Duc, *Days of JavaMoon*, 2000, http://www.ducthuan.com/JavaMoon/moon.htm

```
//Feeling.
if(ashamed++ == losing self-esteem.S __________
wasn't on diet) [re]solution =
would stop eating lunch next time;

//Result.
after all = S __________ couldn't resist to eat
when see[sniff]ing food
("ate();", felt defeated & self-disgusted x 1000);
}
```
[23]

Par ailleurs, le passage de la création d'outils dédiés à l'utilisation de plate-formes de réseaux socio-numériques (cf. gap n° 1) nous incite sans doute à penser différemment le numérique. Ce déplacement consiste à ne pas penser le numérique seulement comme un moyen, mais comme un milieu, c'est-à-dire ce qui est à la fois autour de nous et aussi entre nous[24], ce selon quoi nous agissons et que nous transformons dans une relation de co-constitution permanente. Selon ce point de vue, l'individu est dans un environnement, alors que le milieu est ce par quoi il se constitue. Il s'agit de penser le numérique comme notre nouveau milieu d'écriture et de lecture.

La littérature numérique a ainsi un rôle à jouer pour nous aider à comprendre notre *milieu* numérique et à agir dans celui-ci de manière éclairée. Elle peut rendre notre milieu numérique *visible* : elle nous aide à lutter contre les mythes de la transparence et de l'immatérialité. Au-delà d'une culture littéraire, la littérature numérique contribue à construire une littératie et une culture numériques.

NOTE 24

J'emprunte notamment cette notion de « milieu » à Gilbert Simondon, qui n'a eu de cesse d'essayer de réconcilier culture et technique (Petit 2013).

NOTE 25

Répertoire des arts et littératures hypermédiatiques, http://nt2.uqam.ca/fr/search/site.

NOTE 26

Anthology of European Electronic Literature, https://anthology.elmcip.net/

3.2. GAP N°9

PRÉSERVATION : D'UNE MÉMOIRE STOCKÉE À UNE MÉMOIRE RÉINVENTÉE ?

La formation à la littérature numérique – ainsi que la recherche sur la littérature numérique – pose la question de la préservation des œuvres. Il semble incontournable de tenter de préserver toutes les œuvres, ainsi que de construire des anthologies. Concernant les anthologies, on peut notamment mettre en avant trois initiatives : celle du laboratoire NT2[25], celle de ELMCIP[26] et celle de ELO[27]. L'organisation ELO est également à l'origine du projet CELL[28], qui contribue au développement d'un système centralisé de taxonomies pour toutes les bases de données de littérature numérique.

NOTE 27

Electronic Literature Collection, http://collection.eliterature.org/

NOTE 28

http://collection.eliterature.org/

Beaucoup de projets d'archivage et de préservation des œuvres sont menés depuis de nombreuses années. A titre d'exemple, le travail de Dene Grigar et de son laboratoire *Electronic Literature Lab*[29] à Washington State University Vancouver est de ce point de vue remarquable.

NOTE 29

The Electronic Literature Lab : ***http://www.dtc-wsuv.org/cmdc/ell-skybox.html***

Figure 11 : Le laboratoire de littérature électronique dirigé par Dene Grigar à Washington State University Vancouver.

La question de l'archivage et de la préservation des données numériques apparaît en effet comme particulièrement cruciale dans le domaine de la création artistique et littéraire numérique. La préservation des œuvres pose un véritable problème à la fois théorique et pratique. Une création numérique n'est pas un objet, mais elle n'est pas non plus, le plus souvent, un simple événement situé dans le temps tel que peut l'être une performance ou une installation numérique. En fait, elle participe des deux aspects à la fois : objet transmissible et également fondamentalement processus qui ne peut exister que dans une actualisation (Bootz **2006**; Bouchardon et Bachimont **2013**).

Que doit-on conserver avec de telles œuvres? Se contenter de conserver le fichier original semble insuffisant pour la préserver, *a fortiori* si elle est générative ou interactive (le fichier informatique n'est pas l'œuvre dans la mesure où ce n'est pas ce qui est perçu par le lecteur). Sans compter que parfois, les œuvres en ligne présentent une dimension contributive : elles s'enrichissent des apports des internautes et évoluent continuellement...

Dans notre article de 2013, « Preservation of Digital Literature » (Bouchardon et Bachimont **2013**), nous revenons sur l'initiative du poète canadien Jim Andrews pour préserver sur le Web[30] l'œuvre de poésie numérique *First Screening* de bpNichol (1984). Cette initiative est intéressante en ce qu'elle combine plusieurs stratégies. Jim Andrews propose :

NOTE 30 http://vispo.com/bp

— le programme informatique original codé avec Hypercard,
— l'émulateur de la machine originale qui permet de rejouer le programme aujourd'hui (émulation),
— une réécriture du programme (en JavaScript) pour pouvoir le jouer sur les machines actuelles sans émulateur (migration),
— une reconstitution du rendu visuel de l'époque sous forme de vidéo QuickTime (simulation de l'événement).

En présentant ces approches complémentaires, Jim Andrews affirme que : « Le destin de l'écriture numérique reste généralement la responsabilité des écrivains numériques eux-mêmes » (je traduis). Ce serait aux auteurs eux-mêmes de mettre en œuvre les stratégies de préservation de leurs œuvres.

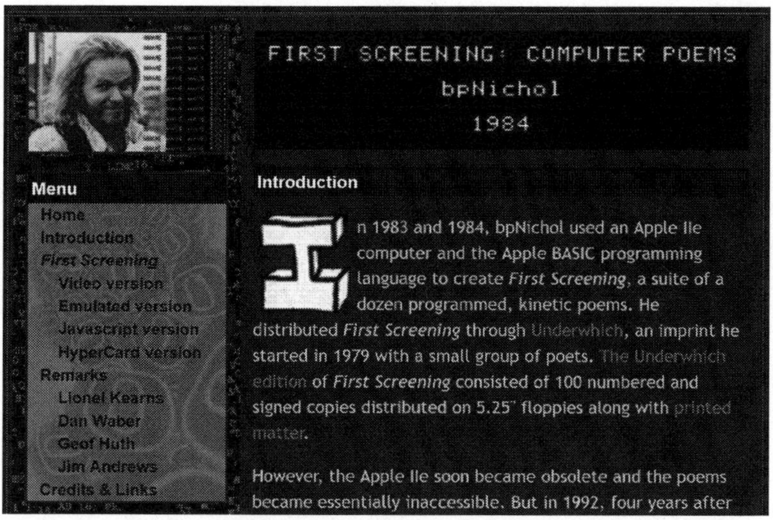

Figure 12 : Préservation du poème « First Screening » de bpNichol, par Jim Andrews.

Ce qui est dès lors intéressant, c'est d'observer le nombre d'auteurs qui reprennent quelques années plus tard leurs créations en ligne pour en proposer une recréation, une *réinvention*, ou pour les repenser en prenant en compte l'instabilité du dispositif. C'est le cas, par exemple, d'Alexandra Saemmer pour *Tramway*[31]. Cette pièce, dont la première version date de 2000, fut repensée par son auteure en 2009, prenant en compte et *poétisant* l'évolution des formats et des systèmes.

NOTE 31

http://revuebleuorange.org/bleuorange/02/saemmer/

> Dans la première version de *Tramway*, il y avait déjà l'idée d'une lecture combinatoire des fragments, les textes étaient déjà écrits, mais l'instabilité du dispositif n'était pour moi qu'un éventuel défaut de conception ou un bug; j'étais loin de pouvoir la « poétiser »[32].

NOTE 32

Courriel d'Alexandra Saemmer datant de mars 2011.

Tramway repose sur un épisode douloureux de la vie de l'auteure, la mort de son père. Face au corps de l'être aimé et désormais sans vie, impossible de faire ce dernier geste, fermer les paupières. Ce geste qui n'a pas pu être fait rend encore plus difficile le travail de deuil. Saemmer écrit :

> Dès les premiers clics dans *Tramway* apparaît une ligne textuelle défilante. Elle contient le récit d'un traumatisme. Sur la plupart des ordinateurs standard, il est actuellement possible de déchiffrer le texte. Grâce à l'évolution de la vitesse de calcul des ordinateurs, ce mouvement de défilement, dans peu de temps passera cependant si vite que le texte deviendra illisible. L'instabilité du dispositif est ici mobilisée au profit d'une scène qui sera travaillée par le temps jusqu'à sa décomposition complète – définition d'un deuil qui mènera lentement vers l'oubli, et dont le lecteur ne pourra trouver dans quelque temps plus qu'une trace illisible dans *Tramway* (Bouchardon et Saemmer **2012**).

Figure 13 : *Tramway*, d'Alexandra Saemmer (2000).

Alexandra Saemmer exprime bien ici à quel point *Tramway* repose sur la labilité du dispositif informatique et dans quelle mesure cette labilité fait partie du projet artistique. Certains auteurs considèrent dès lors que leurs œuvres – notamment les œuvres en ligne – ne sont pas destinées à perdurer et qu'elles portent en elles leur propre disparition.

Face à l'obsolescence matérielle et logicielle, certains auteurs estiment ainsi qu'on ne peut pas lutter contre la « tendance technique » (Leroi-Gourhan **1964**) du médium : le meilleur parti serait de laisser faire le temps, voire de poétiser cette obsolescence dans une « esthétique de l'éphémère » (Saemmer). Toutefois, la majorité des auteurs ne revendiquent pas cette esthétique de la déréliction ou de la disparition.

TENSION : ARCHIVER LA CRÉATION ORIGINALE VS LA LAISSER DISPARAÎTRE / LA PRÉSERVER EN RÉINVENTANT CONTINUELLEMENT

Une question se pose donc : face à l'obsolescence matérielle et logicielle, doit-on tenter à tout prix de préserver ces œuvres ou bien mettre en avant une « esthétique de l'éphémère » (Saemmer) ? Cette logique de l'éphémère nous incite-t-elle à passer d'un modèle de la mémoire stockée à un modèle de la mémoire sans cesse réinventée ?

Pour prendre l'exemple de l'une de mes créations, le récit *Déprise*[33], développé initialement en Flash en 2010, a été en 2018 recréé/réinventé en JavaScript pour le Web et aussi sous forme d'application pour téléphones portables et tablettes[34].

NOTE 33

http://deprise.fr/

NOTE 34

Pour une réflexion sur la recréation d'une pièce, voir également (Strickland et Hatcher **2017**).

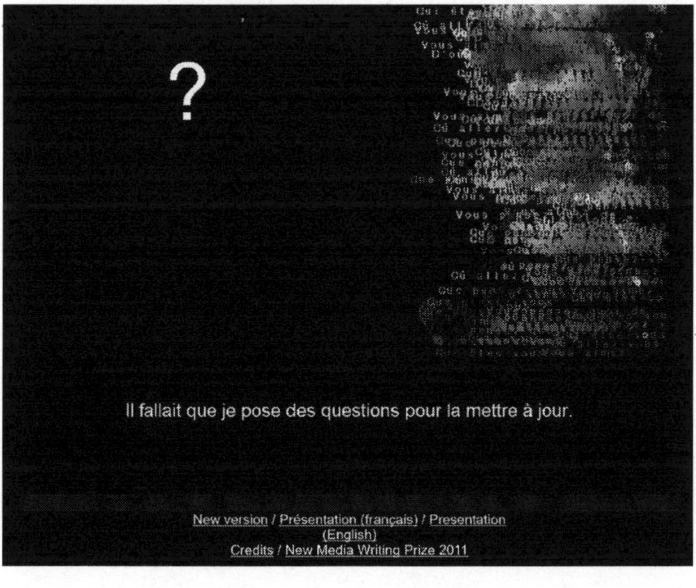

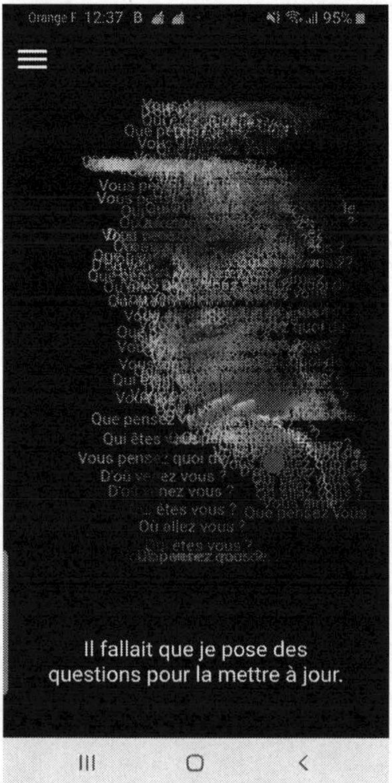

Figure 14 : Trois versions différentes de *Déprise* (2010-2017-2018).

Sans doute y a-t-il trois options concernant la pérennité d'une œuvre de littérature numérique, selon le type de création et l'esthétique de l'auteur : archiver l'œuvre et tous les documents du cycle de vie de l'œuvre (les documents de conception, les sources, la totalité des versions...), laisser celle-ci disparaître, ou la réinventer continuellement. Les trois démarches semblent légitimes (et parfois combinables).

En matière de préservation, et contrairement à ce qu'on avait pu imaginer, le numérique est sans doute le support le plus fragile et le plus complexe dans l'histoire de l'humanité. La valeur ajoutée du numérique n'est donc pas là où l'on croit. Si le numérique n'est pas un support de préservation, en revanche il nous fait basculer dans un autre univers qui est un univers de la mémoire réinventée et non conservée (Bouchardon et Bachimont **2013**). D'un point de vue anthropologique, ce modèle de la mémoire semble plus riche et plus véridique que le modèle de l'imprimé qui est une mémoire de la conservation, du stockage (le livre que l'on range sur une étagère comme le souvenir que l'on rangerait dans une case du cerveau). Les sciences cognitives nous apprennent d'ailleurs que la mémoire ne fonctionne pas sur le modèle du stockage.

De ce point de vue, la littérature numérique peut être considérée comme un bon laboratoire pour penser la préservation numérique : elle permet notamment de se poser les bonnes questions et met en exergue le numérique comme passage d'un modèle de la mémoire stockée à un modèle de la mémoire réinventée (Bouchardon et Bachimont **2013**).

3.3. GAP N°10

RECHERCHE : D'UNE ÉPISTÉMOLOGIE DE LA MESURE À UNE ÉPISTÉMOLOGIE DE LA DONNÉE ?

Certains chercheurs dans notre domaine, sensibilisés aux humanités numériques, s'appuient pour leur recherche sur de très grands corpus ou des bases de données importantes. Ainsi Jill Walker Rettberg[35] a-t-elle analysé les œuvres citées dans 44 thèses sur la littérature numérique, et a notamment produit une visualisation cartographique stimulante de ces références avec le logiciel Gephi[36].

NOTE 35

http://www.electronicbookreview.com/thread/electropoetics/analyzing

NOTE 36

https://gephi.org/

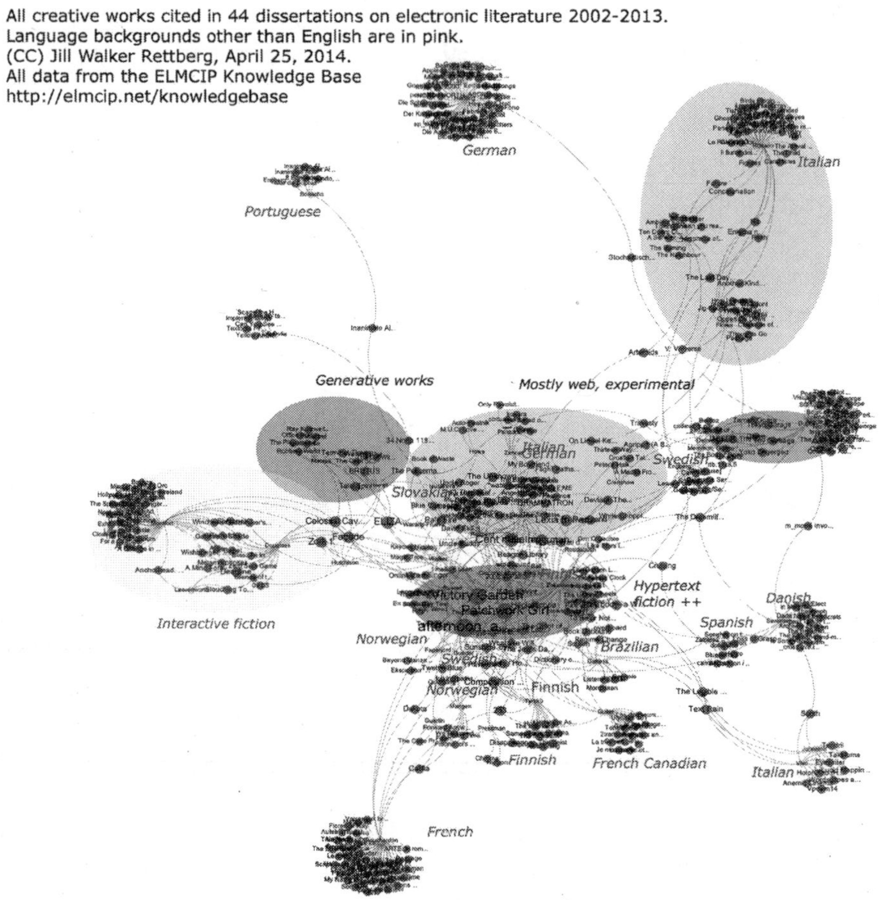

Figure 15 : Représentation cartographique avec le logiciel Gephi, par Jill Walker Rettberg.

Le déploiement des technologies numériques s'accompagne de nouvelles modalités d'organisation et de production des connaissances. Il ne s'agit pas seulement de disposer de plus grandes capacités de calcul ou de production de données. Il s'agit également de donner à lire et à voir ces données, de les rendre intelligibles et, potentiellement, d'en faire varier les représentations pour produire de nouvelles connaissances. Le milieu numérique repose donc la question de la visualisation comme outil de production et de circulation des savoirs.

TENSION : OUTILS DE REPRÉSENTATION TRÈS SOPHISTIQUÉS / RÉGIME CRITIQUE D'INTERPRÉTATION

Dans le passage que nous vivons actuellement d'une épistémologie de la mesure à une épistémologie de la donnée (Bachimont **2015**), on peut parfois avoir l'impression qu'un régime du faire s'est instauré avant le régime du *comprendre*. Il peut sembler que la sophistication des outils, notamment de visualisation, n'a pas encore permis de mettre en place un nouveau régime critique d'interprétation de ceux-ci. Ces dispositifs instrumentaux numériques reposent en effet « sur des programmes d'écriture qui sous-tendent une implémentation méthodologique et une inscription paradigmatique et déterminent finalement des postures épistémologiques singulières » (Bigot **2018**), sans que les concepteurs de ces dispositifs ni les chercheurs qui les utilisent n'en aient toujours conscience. Ces dispositifs détiennent un pouvoir normatif sur les pratiques de recherche et aussi sur les conceptions de la connaissance scientifique.

En quoi la littérature numérique peut-elle nous aider dans ce passage d'une épistémologie de la mesure à une épistémologie de la donnée ? Les œuvres de littérature numérique sont souvent attrayantes visuellement par leurs interfaces. L'enjeu reste néanmoins leur interprétation. On peut ainsi établir un parallèle avec les outils de visualisation, notamment cartographiques. Ces outils sont très attrayants visuellement, mais il faut construire un nouveau régime critique du savoir. La pratique et l'analyse des œuvres de littérature numérique, qui nous permettent de comprendre et d'interpréter ce qui est encapsulé dans un dispositif numérique, pourraient nous aider à construire ce nouveau régime critique du savoir.

CONCLUSION

Je me suis arrêté sur certains défis auxquels la littérature numérique est actuellement confrontée. La littérature numérique est un lieu de tensions, ce que j'avais mis en avant dans un article intitulé "Towards a Tension-Based Definition of Digital Literature" (Bouchardon **2016**).

Revenons à quelques-unes des questions soulevées.

Une nouvelle génération d'auteurs opère un passage vers l'exploitation de plateformes et de réseaux socio-numériques existants pour leurs créations; ce passage risque-t-il d'entraîner une forme, non seulement de dépendance, mais de *complicité* avec ces plateformes industrielles? À supposer que ces environnements et plateformes d'écriture permettent de toucher un public beaucoup plus large, que deviendra alors la dimension expérimentale de cette littérature? Doit-on lutter contre une forme d'homogénéité globale de la culture numérique pour retrouver des spécificités culturelles, et quel rôle peut jouer la traduction dans cette démarche? Si la littérature numérique tend à s'institutionnaliser et à chercher une légitimité dans le champ littéraire, s'agit-il pour autant de la même expérience littéraire? Cette nouvelle expérience littéraire est notamment fondée sur la question des gestes et sur une nouvelle façon de raconter. Ceci dit, n'observe-t-on pas un glissement, dans la construction subjective, d'une identité narrative vers une identité poétique? La littérature numérique invite à définir une nouvelle littératie, une *littératie numérique*. À des fins de formation et de recherche, nous avons besoin de préserver les œuvres; or, adopter une approche de continuelle réinvention permet-elle de lutter contre la tendance technique d'un médium à l'obsolescence? Enfin, dans quelle mesure la littérature numérique peut-elle nous éclairer sur l'usage que nous pouvons faire en recherche des outils numériques de représentation et de visualisation?

La notion du passage ou de marche à franchir (*gap*), qui apparaît dans l'intitulé du colloque *ELO 2018 Montréal*, pose la question souvent débattue de la continuité ou de la rupture, de l'évolution ou de la révolution, concernant la littérature numérique et plus largement du numérique. Sans doute faut-il se méfier de l'idéologie du « nouveau ». Il semble important de ne pas céder à la tentation idéologique d'une révolution numérique et d'inscrire la littérature numérique, et plus largement les écritures numériques, dans la longue tradition des supports et des pratiques de l'écrit[37]. Entre continuité et rupture, comment dès lors situer et penser les passages et les marches (*gaps*) dont cet article a fait l'objet?

NOTE 37

Ce que fait Scott Rettberg dans *Electronic Literature* (2019).

Le livre est un support matériel qui, tout au long de son histoire, a offert toujours plus de manipulabilité à son lecteur (que l'on pense au passage du volumen au codex, qui a permis la numérotation des pages, les tables des matières...). Le support numérique s'inscrit ainsi dans une continuité, vers toujours plus de manipulabilité. Il y a toutefois une forme de *passage à la limite* (Bachimont **2010**) dans la mesure où toute la médiation est calculée : tout devient manipulable. Avec le numérique, ce n'est plus seulement le support, mais le contenu lui-même qui est manipulable. La manipulabilité est au cœur même du numérique. Cette notion de *passage à la limite* permet de penser une forme de rupture dans la continuité.

C'est dans ce « passage à la limite » que la littérature numérique est passionnante. Les fossés à sauter ou les marches à franchir sont autant d'occasions de revenir en arrière, de faire retour sur certaines notions : sur la littérature, le texte, l'auteur, le récit (ce que j'appelle la « valeur heuristique » de la littérature numérique, cf. Bouchardon **2014**), ainsi que sur le numérique et sur la technique. Chaque saut en avant est une occasion de mieux comprendre le présent en convoquant le passé. Franchir un *gap*, c'est avant tout se projeter vers l'avenir en repensant notre passé.

Bachimont, Bruno. 2010. *Le sens de la technique : le numérique et le calcul.* Paris : Les Belles Lettres.

Bachimont, Bruno. 2015. « Le numérique comme milieu : enjeux épistémologiques et phénoménologiques ». *Interfaces numériques* 4 (3). https://www.unilim.fr/interfaces-numeriques/index.php?id=386.

Bigot, Jean-Edouard. 2018. « Instruments, pratiques et enjeux d'une recherche numériquement équipée en sciences humaines et sociales ». Thèse de doctorat, Compiègne : Université de technologie de Compiègne.

Bootz, Philippe. 2006. « Les basiques : la littérature numérique ». Leonardo / Olats.

Bouchardon, Serge. 2009. *Littérature numérique : le récit interactif.* Paris : Hermès Science.

Bouchardon, Serge. 2014. *La valeur heuristique de la littérature numérique.* Paris : Hermann.

Bouchardon, Serge. 2016. « Towards a Tension-Based Definition of Digital Literature ». *Journal of Creative Writing Studies* 2 (1). http://scholarworks.rit.edu/jcws/vol2/iss1/6.

Bouchardon, Serge, et Bruno Bachimont. 2013. « Preservation of Digital Literature: from Stored Memory to Reinvented Memory ». *Cibertextualidades*, n° 5:184-202.

Bouchardon, Serge, et Alexandra Saemmer. 2012. « Littérature numérique et enseignement du français ». In *Guide TICE pour le professeur de français – identité professionnelle et culture numérique*, 225-48. Paris : CNDP-CRDP de l'académie de Paris.

Bourassa, Renée. 2010. *Les fictions hypermédiatiques : mondes fictionnels et espaces ludiques – des arts de mémoire au cyberespace.* Montréal : Le Quartanier.

Cailleau, Isabelle, Serge Bouchardon, et Stéphane Crozat. 2018. « Un MOOC pour agir et comprendre en milieu numérique ». *Revue de la société française des sciences de l'information et de la communication*, n° 12. http://journals.openedition.org/rfsic/3377

Chambefort, Françoise. 2018. « Data Art et mise en récit ». In *Mettre en récit, Enjeux des formes contemporaines de narration.* Metz : Crem, AJC Crem, École doctorale Fernand-Braudel (Université de Lorraine).

Compagnon, Antoine. 1998. *Le Démon de la théorie. Littérature et sens commun.* Paris : Seuil.

Dewey, John. 1980. *Art as Experience.* New York : Perigee.

Di Rosario, Giovanna, et Laura Borras. 2012. « Translating Digital Literature: Two Experiences and a Reflexion ». *Texto Digital*, Florianópolis, 8 (1):138-62.

Fraenkel, Béatrice, et Aïssatou Mbodj-Pouye. 2010. « Introduction. Les New Literacy Studies, jalons historiques et perspectives actuelles ». *Langage et société*, n° 133:7-24.

Fülöp, Erika. 2018. « Digital Cultures: A View from French Studies and Literature ». *Explorations in Media Ecology* 17 (3):271-77.

Geertz, Clifford. 1973. *The Interpretation of cultures.* New York : Basic Books.

Gervais, Bertrand, et Samuel Archibald. 2006. « Le récit en jeu : narrativité et interactivité ». *Protée* 34 (2):27-29.

Hayles, Katherine N. 2008. *Electronic Literature: New Horizons for the Literary.* Notre Dame : University of Notre Dame Press.

Lavocat, Françoise. 2016. *Fait et fiction. Pour une frontière.* Paris : Seuil.

Leroi-Gourhan, André. 1964. *Le Geste et la Parole II. La Mémoire et les Rythme.* Paris : Albin Michel.

Manguel, Alberto. 2013. *Le Voyageur et la tour. Le lecteur comme métaphore.* Arles : Actes Sud.

Manovich, Lev. 2001. *The language of New Media.* Cambridge : MIT Press.

Mayer, Ariane, et Serge Bouchardon. 2017. « Le sujet numérique : d'une identité narrative à une identité poétique? » *RIHM* 18 (1):43-61.

Mencía, María, Søren Pold, et Manuel Portela. 2018. « Electronic Literature Translation: Translation as Process, Experience and Mediation ». In *Electronic Book Review*. http://www.electronicbookreview.com/thread/electropoetics/translative.

Petit, V. 2013. « Internet, un milieu technique d'écriture ». In *Réseaux socionumériques et médiations humaines*, édité par Estrella Rojas, 155-73. Paris : Hermès-Lavoisier.

Rettberg, Scott. 2019. *Electronic Literature.* Medford (Ma) : Polity Press.

Ricoeur, Paul. 1985. *Soi-même comme un autre.* Paris : Seuil.

Saemmer, Alexandra. 2015. *Rhétorique du texte numérique. Figures de la lecture, anticipations de pratiques.* Villeurbanne : ENSSIB.

Schäfer, Jörgen. 2010. « Reassembling the Literary ». In *Beyond the Screen*, édité par Jörgen Schäfer et Peter Gendolla, 25-70. Bielefeld : Transcript.

Simanowski, Roberto. 2010. *Textmaschinen – Kinetische Poesie – Interaktive Installation.* Bielefeld : Transcript.

Simanowski, Roberto, Jörgen Schäfer, et Peter Gendolla, éd. 2010. *Reading Moving Letters. Digital Literature in Research and Teaching.* Bielefeld : Transcript.

Souchier, Emmanuël. 2017. « Et demain, j'apprends quoi ? Le leurre démocratique du code informatique ». In *Le français aujourd'hui*, 11-24. 196. Paris : Armand Colin.

Strehovec, Janez. 2010. « Alphabet on the Move. Digital Poetry and the Realm of Language ». In *Reading Moving Letters*, édité par Roberto Simanowski, Jörgen Schäfer, et Peter Gendolla, 207-27. Bielefeld : Transcript.

Strickland, Stephanie, et Ian Hatcher. 2017. « Loss of Hover: Recreating Shockwave Universe as an App for iPad ». *Przegląd Kulturoznawczy* 33 (3):364-71.

Tabbi, Joseph. 2002. *Cognitive Fictions.* Minneapolis : University of Minnesota Press.

Tabbi, Joseph, éd. 2018. *The Bloomsbury Handbook of Electronic Literature.* Londres : Bloomsbury.

Torres, Rui. 2011. « Preservación y diseminación de la literatura electrónica: por un archivo digital de literatura experimental ». *Arizona Journal of Hispanic Cultural Studies* 14:281-98.

Venuti, Lawrence. 2008. *The Translator's Invisibility : A history of Translation.* Londres, New York : Routledge.

Zuern, John David. 2010. « Figures in the Interface. Comparative Methods in the Study of Digital Literature ». In *Reading Moving Letters. Digital Literature in Research and Teaching*, édité par Roberto Simanowski, Jörgen Schäfer, et Peter Gendolla, 59-80. Bielefeld : Transcript.

Biographies

Albuquerque e Aguilar, Ana

Ana Albuquerque e Aguilar is a PhD candidate in the Materialities of Literature Program at the School of Arts and Humanities – University of Coimbra (Portugal), funded by FCT, the Portuguese Foundation for Science and Technology. With a background in classical literature and culture, her current research focuses on electronic literature, literary education, reading, teaching, digital literature for children and young adults, and creation of digital works. She is also a teacher trainer and the author of Portuguese textbooks and didactic materials.

Ana Albuquerque e Aguilar est candidate au Doctorat dans le programme Matérialités de la littérature, à l'École des Arts et des Humanités de l'Université de Coimbra (Portugal), soutenu par la Fondation portugaise de la science et de la technologie (FCT). Elle a une formation en littérature et en culture classique; ses recherches actuelles se concentrent sur la littérature électronique, l'éducation littéraire, la lecture, l'enseignement, la littérature numérique pour les enfants et les jeunes adultes, ainsi que sur la création d'œuvres numériques. Elle est également formatrice d'enseignants et l'autrice de manuels et de matériel didactiques portugais.

Atsuko Matsuda, Alice

Alice Atsuko Matsuda holds a PhD in Letters from the State University of Londrina and developed post-doctoral training at the University of Coimbra, participating in the Research Group on Materialities of Literature, with Capes funding. She is an Associate Professor at the Federal University of Technology of Paraná, in Curitiba, Brazil and a permanent professor of the Post-Graduate Program in Language Studies (PPGEL). Her publications address areas of Children's and Youth Literature, Literature and Teaching, Training of Readers, and Digital Literature.
E-mail: alicem@utfpr.edu.br

Alice Atsuko Matsuda détient un Doctorat en lettres de l'Université d'État de Londrina et a développée une formation post-doctorale à l'Université de Coimbra, en intégrant le groupe de recherche sur les Matérialités de la littérature, avec du financement Capes. Elle est professeure associée à l'Université fédérale de technologie de Paraná, à Curitiba (Brésil) et est professeure au programme post-doctoral en études des langues (PPGEL). Ses publications abordent plusieurs domaines de la littérature pour enfants et pour jeunes adultes, de la littérature et de l'enseignement, de la formation de lecteurs et de la littérature numérique.
Courriel : alicem@utfpr.edu.br

Audry, Sofian

Sofian Audry is a professor of Interactive Media within the School of Media at the University of Quebec in Montreal (UQAM). His work is inspired from visual art, artificial intelligence, artificial life, biology and cognitive sciences. His computational artistic practice branches through multiple media including robotics, interactive installations, immersive environments, physical computing interventions, internet art, and electronic literature. He is currently working on a book about new media art in the age of machine learning. His work and research have been presented in multiple international events and venues around the world.

Sofian Audry est professeur en médias interactifs à l'Université du Québec à Montréal. Son travail s'inspire de l'art visuel, de l'intelligence artificielle, de la vie artificielle, de la biologie et des sciences cognitives. Sa pratique artistique computationnelle s'étend à de nombreux médias, notamment la robotique, les installations interactives, les environnements immersifs, les interventions informatiques physiques, l'art web et la littérature électronique. Il travaille actuellement sur un livre sur l'art des nouveaux médias à l'âge de l'apprentissage automatique. Ses œuvres et ses recherches ont été présentées à des nombreux événements internationaux.

Avnisan, Abraham

Abraham Avnisan is an interdisciplinary artist whose work is situated at the intersection of image, text and code. Using a host of emerging technologies including 3D scanning, augmented reality and virtual reality, he creates applications for mobile devices, interactive installations and technologically mediated performances that seek to subvert dominant narratives through embodied encounters with language. Abraham has presented his work both nationally and internationally. Selected exhibitions, biennials and performances include: *Inside Practice* at the Art Institute of Chicago in Chicago, IL (2020); *Refiguring the Future* at 205 Hudson Gallery in New York, NY (2019); *Between Bodies* at the Henry Art Gallery in Seattle, WA (2018-19). Abraham holds an M.F.A. in Poetry from Brooklyn College and an M.F.A. in Art and Technology Studies from The School of the Art Institute of Chicago. Abraham is an Assistant Professor of Emerging Media & Technology and Journalism & Mass Communication at Kent State University.

Abraham Avnisan est un artiste interdisciplinaire. Son œuvre se situe au carrefour de l'image, du texte et du code. Se servant de nombreuses technologies émergentes, y compris la numérisation 3D, la réalité augmentée et la réalité virtuelle, il crée des applications mobiles, des installations interactives et des performances technologiquement médiatisées qui cherche à subvertir les récits dominants à travers des interactions corporelles avec le langage. Ses œuvres ont été présentées à l'échelle nationale ainsi qu'internationale. Parmi les expositions, les biennales et les performances sélectionnées figurent : *Inside Practice* à l'Institut d'art de Chicago à Chicago, Illinois (2020), *Refiguring the Future* au 205 Hudson Gallery à New York, New York (2019) et *Between Bodies* au Henry Art Gallery à Seattle, Washington (2018-19). Abraham est diplômé d'une maîtrise en beaux-arts et en poésie du Brooklyn College et d'une maîtrise en beaux-arts et études technologiques de l'École de l'Institut d'art de Chicago. Abraham est actuellement professeur adjoint en média émergent, technologie, journalisme et en communication de masse à l'Université d'État de Kent.

Barber, John F.

John F. Barber convenes with The Creative Media & Digital Culture Program at Washington State University Vancouver. His scholarship, teaching, and creative endeavors arise from intersections of art, humanities, and technology and manifest as literary media art where he feels that practice-based research discovers and puts into action new knowledge. His radio and sound art are broadcast and exhibited internationally. His publications appear in *Digital Humanities Quarterly, Digital Studies, ebr, Hyperrhiz: New Media Cultures, Leonardo, MATLIT (Materialities of Literature), Scholarly Research and Communication*, and elsewhere. Barber curates *The Brautigan Library*, a collection of unpublished manuscripts, and was featured on *This American Life*. See his website, for more information and access to his work.
Website: http://www.nouspace.net/john

John F. Barber est professeur dans le programme des Médias créatifs et de la Culture numérique à l'Université de l'État de Washington à Vancouver. Ses travaux d'érudition, d'enseignement et de création sont issus des intersections de l'art, les humanités et la technologie, et se manifestent sous la forme d'un art littéraire médiatique où il estime que la recherche basée sur la pratique découvre et met en pratique de nouvelles connaissances. Ses œuvres radiophoniques et sonores sont diffusées et exposées dans le monde entier. Ses publications paraissent dans *Digital Humanities Quarterly, Digital Studies, ebr, Hyperrhiz: New Media Cultures, Leonardo, MATLIT (Materialities of Literature), Scholarly Research and Communication* et ailleurs. Barber est le conservateur du *Brautigan Library*, une collection de manuscrits non publiés, et a été présenté sur *This American Life*. Voir son site web, pour plus d'informations et pour accéder à son travail.
Site Web : http://www.nouspace.net/john

Biggs, Simon

Simon Biggs is a media artist, writer and curator with interests in digital poetics and interactive systems. His work has been widely presented, including at the Tate Modern, Tate Liverpool and Tate Britain, the Institute of Contemporary Arts London, the Centre for Contemporary Arts in Glasgow, the Georges Pompidou Centre in Paris, the Berlin Academy of Arts, the Kulturforum in Berlin, the Rijksmuseum Twenthe, the Bergen Kunsthall, the Maxxi in Rome, the Palazzo delle Arti in Naples, the Macau Museum of Art, the Oi Futuro in Rio de Janeiro, the Arizona State University Art Museum, SF Cameraworks, the Walker Art Center in Minneapolis and the Art Gallery of New South Wales. Publications include *Remediating the Social* (2012, editor), *Autopoeisis* (with James Leach, 2004), *Great Wall of China* (1999), *Halo* (1998), *Magnet* (1997) and *Book of Shadows* (1996). He has previously held lecturing posts at Middlesex University and Academy Minerva Groningen, a Research Fellowship at Cambridge University and Professorships at Sheffield Hallam University and the University of Edinburgh. He is currently Professor of Art at the University of South Australia.
Website: http://www.littlepig.org.uk

Simon Biggs est un artiste médiatique, écrivain et commissaire d'expositions qui s'intéresse à la poétique numérique et aux systèmes interactifs. Ses œuvres ont été exposées en de multiples endroits, dont au Tate Modern, au Tate Liverpool et au Tate Britain, à l'Institute of Contemporary Arts London, au Centre for Contemporary Arts de Glasgow, au Centre Georges Pompidou à Paris, à l'Académie des arts de Berlin, au Kulturforum à Berlin, au Rijksmuseum Twenthe, au Kunsthall de Bergen, au Maxxi à Rome, au Palazzo delle Arti à Naples, au Musée d'Art de Macao, Oi Futuro Rio de Janeiro, à l'Arizona State University Art Museum, au SF Camerawork à San Francisco, au Walker Art Center à Minneapolis et la Gallerie d'art de Nouvelles-Galles du Sud. Parmi ses publications, on note : *Remediating the Social* (2012, directeur), *Autopoeisis* (avec James Leach, 2004), *Great Wall of China* (1999), *Halo* (1998), *Magnet* (1997) et *Book of Shadows* (1996). Il a précédemment occupé des postes de professeur à l'Université du Middlesex et à l'Académie Minerva Groningen, de chercheur associé à l'Université de Cambridge et des postes de professeur à l'Université de Sheffield Hallam et à l'Université d'Édimbourg. Il est actuellement professeur d'art à l'Université d'Australie du Sud.
Site Web : http://www.littlepig.org.uk

Bizzocchi, Jim

Jim Bizzocchi is a professor emeritus in the School of Interactive Arts and Technology at Simon Fraser University. Bizzocchi's research interests include the evolving aesthetics of the digital moving image, the poetics of interactive narrative, the analysis of ambient video experience, and the creation of generative video systems. He has presented and published across a variety of academic conferences, journals and books, and is a recipient of Simon Fraser University's Excellence in Teaching Award. He is a practicing and widely exhibited video artist whose creative work complements and informs his scholarly writing. His art explores image, motion, time, and transition in both linear and computationally generative video forms. He has also built a generative video system that automatically sequences and presents in real time an ongoing constantly changing stream of moving images.

Jim Bizzocchi est professeur émérite à l'École des arts interactives et de technologie à l'Université Simon Fraser. Ses recherches portent sur l'esthétique évolutive de l'image numérique en mouvement, la poétique du récit interactif, l'analyse de l'expérience de la vidéo ambiante et la création des systèmes de vidéos génératifs. Il a présenté des conférences lors de nombreux congrès et et il a publié de nombreux textes dans des revues et livres. Il a reçu lé prix d'excellence en enseignement de l'Université Simon Fraser. En tant que vidéaste, son œuvre a été largement exposée; ce volet créatif complète son travail académique. Son art explore l'image, le mouvement, le temps et la transition dans des formes de vidéo linéaire et générative par calcul.

Booten, Kyle

Kyle Booten is an assistant professor in the Department of English at the University of Connecticut. Previously, he was a postdoctoral fellow in the Neukom Institute for Computational Science at Dartmouth College. His research has recently appeared in *electronic book review*, *Proceedings of the International Conference on Computational Creativity*, and *#Identity* (University of Michigan Press). His computationally-mediated and -generated poetic work has appeared in venues such as *Boston Review*, *Lana Turner Journal*, *Taper*, *Fence*, and *Tentacular*. In the fall of 2020, he will begin a position as assistant professor in the Department of English at the University of Connecticut, Storrs, and will be Nokturno.fi's poet-in-digital-residence.

Kyle Booten est professeur au Département d'anglais à l'Université du Connecticut. Auparavant, il était stagiaire postdoctoral à la Neukom Institute des Sciences computationnelles au Dartmouth College. Ses recherches ont récemment fait l'objet de publications dans *Electronic Book Review*, *Proceedings of the International Conference on Computational Creativity* et *#Identity* (Presses de l'Université du Michigan). Son travail de poésie générée par ordinateur a été publié dans des revues telles que *Boston Review*, *Lana Turner Journal*, *Taper*, *Fence* et *Tentacular*. À partir de l'automne 2020, il occupera un poste de professeur adjoint au Département d'anglais de l'Université du Connecticut à Storrs et sera le poète en résidence numérique de Nokturno.fi.

Borsuk, Amaranth

Amaranth Borsuk is a poet, scholar, and book artist working at the intersection of print and digital media. Her latest volume, *The Book*, published in the MIT Press Essential Knowledge Series, is a concise volume on the book's changing technologies that bridges book history, artists' books, and electronic literature. She is co-author with Brad Bouse of *Between Page and Screen* and a recipient of an NEA "Expanded Artists' Books" grant for the collaboration Abra, a limited-edition book and free iOS app that recently received the *Turn on Literature prize.* She has collaborated on installations, art bookmarklets, and interactive works and is the author of five books of poetry, most recently *Pomegranate Eater* (Kore Press, 2016). Borsuk is an Associate Professor in the School of Interdisciplinary Arts and Sciences at the University of Washington Bothell, where she also serves as Associate Director of the MFA in Creative Writing and Poetics.

Amaranth Borsuk est une poète, chercheuse et artiste de livre qui travaille à l'intersection des médias imprimés et numériques. Sa dernière publication, *The Book*, publié dans l'Essential Knowledge Series des Presses du MIT, est un court volume sur les technologies changeantes du livre qui couvre l'histoire du livre, des livres d'artiste et la littérature électronique. Elle est co-autrice, avec Brad Bouse, de *Between Page and Screen* et a reçu une bourse NEA « Expanded Artists' Books » pour la collaboration Abra, un livre à publication limitée et une application mobile iOS gratuite qui a récemment reçu le prix *Turn on Literature*. Elle a collaboré à des installations, des signapplets d'art et des œuvres interactives; elle est aussi autrice de cinq collections de poésie, la plus récente étant *Pomegranate Eater* (Kore Press, 2016). Borsuk est professeure agrégée à l'École des arts interdisciplinaires et des sciences à l'Université de Washington Bothell, où elle est également directrice associée de la maîtrise en beaux-arts et en écriture créative et poétique.

Bouchardon, Serge

Serge Bouchardon, specialist in Modern Languages, is currently a professor at the University of Technology in Compiègne. His research focuses on digital writing, more specifically digital literature. His publications include *The Heuristic Value of Digital Literature* (2014).
As an author of digital literature, he is particularly interested in the mise-en-scène of interactivity and the role of movement in interactive writing. His creations have been presented on many occasions in Europe, in the Americas, in African and in the Middle East, and have been published in online literary reviews (*bleuOrange, Hyperrhiz, SpringGun, The New River...*). His creative work *Déprise* received the New Media Writing Prize in 2011.
Websites: www.utc.fr/~bouchard/wordpress/home/ – www.sergebouchardon.com/

Serge Bouchardon, agrégé de lettres modernes, est actuellement professeur à l'Université de technologie de Compiègne. Son travail de recherche porte sur les écritures numériques, en particulier sur la littérature numérique.
Parmi ses publications figure *La valeur heuristique de la littérature numérique* (2014). En tant qu'auteur de littérature numérique, il s'intéresse notamment à la mise en scène de l'interactivité et au rôle du geste dans l'écriture interactive. Ses créations ont été présentées en diverses occasions en Europe, en Amérique, en Afrique et au Moyen-Orient. Elles ont fait l'objet de publications dans des revues en ligne (*bleuOrange, Hyperrhiz, SpringGun, The New River...*). La création *Déprise* a obtenu le New Media Writing Prize en 2011.
Sites Web : **www.utc.fr/~bouchard/wordpress/home/ – www.sergebouchardon.com/**

du Boullay, Boris

Boris du Boullay is an artist born in 1969. With a background in cinema, his creative work regroups and remixes the written word, analog film, digital videos and multimedia creations. His work traces a phenomenological pathway in the idea that cinema, as it manipulates time during filming and during viewing, reveals itself as a form of self-giveness (Michel Henry, 2005). He explores speed, improvisation, accumulation and profusion, developing a direct, ambiguous, emotional and ambivalent art where writing is realized in the burlesque.
He also collaborates with the AKL agency and teaches multimedia creation at the DSAA of Graphic design and multimedia narration in Boulogne-Billancourt and at Gobelins, l'école de l'image in Paris.

Boris du Boullay est artiste. Venu du cinéma, ses créations regroupent et recoupent écritures, films argentiques, vidéos numériques et créations multimédia. Il creuse un sillon phénoménologique avec l'idée que le cinéma, dans son travail de substitution du temps dans les champs du tournage et de la projection, s'approche d'une auto-donation (Michel Henry, 2005). Il joue sur la vitesse, l'improvisation, l'accumulation et la profusion, développant une œuvre directe et ambiguë, émotionnelle et ambivalente, où l'écriture trouve son achèvement dans le burlesque.
Il collabore également avec l'agence AKL et enseigne la création multimédia au DSAA Design graphique narration multimédia de Boulogne-Billancourt et à Gobelins, l'école de l'image à Paris.
Il termine un doctorat en esthétique sous la direction d'Anna Guilló à l'Université d'Aix-Marseille.

Brianza, Alejandro

Alejandro Brianza is a composer, researcher and teacher and has a Master's degree in Methodology of Scientific Research. He teaches at the University of Buenos Aires and the National University of Lanús, where he also participates in research related to sound technology, electronic music and contemporary languages.

Alejandro Brianza est compositeur, chercheur et enseignant. Il est titulaire d'une maîtrise en méthodologies de recherche scientifique. Il enseigne à l'Université de Buenos Aires et à l'Université Nationale de Lanús, où il participe à des recherches liées aux technologies du son, à la musique électronique et aux langues modernes.

Catrópa, Andréa

Andréa Catrópa holds a PhD. in Literary Theory from Universidade de São Paulo, Brazil (2013). She is a postdoctoral researcher in Design at Anhembi Morumbi University, where she researches Brazilian concrete poetry and digital literature. As a writer, she has published poetry, short stories and a novel. Her multimedia works include audiofictions and a radio program about contemporary literature. As an artist, she is currently conducting her first experiments in e-lit.

Andréa Catrópa détient un doctorat en théorie littéraire de l'Université de São Paulo, Brésil (2013). Elle est stagiaire postdoctorale en Design à l'Université d'Anhembi Morumbi, où elle effectue des recherches sur la poésie concrète brésilienne et la littérature numérique. En tant qu'écrivaine, elle a publié de la poésie, des nouvelles et un roman. Ses œuvres multimédia comprennent des audio-fictions et une émission de radio sur la littérature contemporaine. En tant qu'artiste, elle mène actuellement ces premières expériences en littérature électronique.

Cayley, John

John Cayley is a writer, theorist, and pioneering maker of language art in programmable media. Apart from more or less conventional poetry and translation (*Ink Bamboo*, Agenda, 1996 and *Image Generation*, Veer, 2015), he has explored dynamic and ambient poetics, text generation, transliteral morphing, aestheticized vectors of reading, and transactive synthetic language.
He now composes as much for reading in aurality as in visuality, and investigates the ontology of language in the context of philosophically informed practice-based research. Professor of Literary Arts at Brown University, Cayley directs a graduate MFA track in Digital & Cross-Disciplinary Language Arts. Selected essays are published in *Grammalepsy* (Bloomsbury, 2018).
Website: programmatology.shadoof.net
Twitter: @programmatology

John Cayley est un écrivain, théoricien et créateur pionnier de l'art du langage dans les médias programmables. À l'exception de la poésie et la traduction conventionnelle (*Ink Bamboo*, Agenda, 1996 et *Image Generation*, Veer, 2015), il a exploré la poésie dynamique et ambiante, la génération automatique de texte, le morphing transliteral, les vecteurs de lecture esthétisés et le langage synthétique transactif.
Il compose désormais autant pour la lecture orale que visuelle et il étudie l'ontologie du langage dans le contexte d'une recherche-création informée par la philosophie. En tant que professeur des arts littéraires à l'Université Brown, Cayley est directeur du programme de maîtrise en arts numériques et interdisciplinaires du langage. Des essais sélectionnés sont publiés dans *Grammalepsy* (Bloomsbury, 2018).
Site Web : **programmatology.shadoof.net**
Twitter : **@programmatology**

Chambefort, Françoise

Françoise Chambefort is an artist-researcher. She works with sound as well as fixed or moving images, and considers data as a material in its own right in her creations. After twenty years as a university library curator, she took up her university studies again in 2012. She was awarded a Master's degree in Multimedia with a focus on Music and Sound (2015) and a Doctorate in Information Science and Communications in 2020. She works on the flux of data and their potential narratives at the Center for Conception, Creation, and Mediation at the ELLIADD Laboratory at the University of Franche-Comté. Her research interests lie in different data sources: library loans (*Village Doc*, 2015), found objects (*Tout n'est pas perdu*, 2016), train schedules (*Lucette, Gare de Clichy*, 2018), tweets (*My Little Identity*, 2019), and the fight against the rat infestation in New York City (*Smart Rat City*, ongoing).

Françoise Chambefort est une artiste-chercheuse. Elle travaille aussi bien le son que l'image fixe ou animée et considère les données comme un matériau à part entière dans ses créations. Conservateur en bibliothèque universitaire depuis une vingtaine d'années, elle a repris ses études en 2012. Diplômée d'un Master en multimédia option Musique et son (2015) et d'un doctorat en sciences de l'information et de la communication (2020), elle travaille sur les flux de données et leurs potentialités narratives au sein du Pôle Conception, Création, Médiations du Laboratoire ELLIADD (Université de Franche-Comté). Elle s'est intéressée à différentes sources de données : les prêts des bibliothèques (*Village Doc*, 2015), les objets trouvés (*Tout n'est pas perdu*, 2016), les horaires de trains (*Lucette, Gare de Clichy*, 2018), les tweets (*My Little Identity*, 2019), la lutte contre les rats à New York (*Smart Rat City*, en cours).

Ciston, Sarah

Sarah Ciston (she/they) is a computational media artist and experimental writer of prose, poetry, and Python. Their practice-based research argues for embodied, embedded, and ethical approaches to "algorithmic intimacy." Named one of *San Francisco Weekly*'s "Best Writers Without a Book," their work appears in *Ada Journal*; *ZYZZYVA*; *Hobart*; and soon in *Leonardo Electronic Almanac*. They hold an MFA in Literature from UC San Diego and are an Annenberg Fellow in Media Arts + Practice at USC's School of Cinematic Arts, where they lead Creative Code Collective–a student community for artists to learn programming with an interdisciplinary, intersectional approach.

Sarah Ciston (ille) est un·e artiste en média informatique et un·e écrivain·e expériemental·e de prose, de poésie et de Python. Sa recherche-création soutient des approches incarnées, situées et éthiques de l'« intimité algorithmique ». Nommé·e l'un·e des « Meilleurs·es écrivain·es sans un livre » par le *San Francisco Weekly*, son travail figure dans *Ada Journal*; *ZYZZYVA*; *Hobart*; et bientôt dans *Leonardo Electronic Almanac*. Ille détient une maîtrise en littérature de l'Université de Californie San Diego et est boursier·ère Anneberg en arts et pratiques médiatiques à l'École des arts cinématographiques de l'Université de Californie du Sud, où elle dirige Creative Code Collective – une communauté étudiante pour les artistes souhaitant apprendre la programmation avec une approche interdisciplinaire et intersectionnelle.

Collard, Christophe

Christophe Collard has taught as a professor and guest professor at the universities of Brussels, Antwerp, Alicante, as well as at Beijing Normal University. Articles of his have appeared among others in *Adaptation, New Theatre Quarterly, Performance Research, Performing Arts Journal, Literature/Film Quarterly*, and *Re-Thinking History*. He is the author of the monograph *Artist on the Make: David Mamet's Work Across Media and Genres* (2012), which was shortlisted for the 2014 Young Scholar Book Award of the European Society for the Study of English (ESSE).

Christophe Collard a enseigné en tant que professeur titulaire et invité aux universités de Bruxelles, Anvers, Alicante ainsi qu'à l'Université normale de Pékin. Ses articles ont paru dans plusieurs publications, y compris *Adaptation, New Theatre Quarterly, Performance Research, Performing Arts Journal, Literature/Film Quarterly* et *Re-Thinking History*. Il est l'auteur de la monographie *Artist on the Make: David Mamet's Work Across Media and Genres* (2012), qui était sur la liste de présélection du prix Young Scholar Book Award of the European Society for the Study of English (ESSE) en 2014.

Colombo Machado, Gabriella

Gabriella Colombo Machado is a PhD candidate in English Studies at the University of Montreal. Her dissertation is on the politics of female friendship in contemporary speculative fiction across media. She has earned an MA in Comparative Literature from Western University, and an MA in Literatures in English from VU University Amsterdam. Her research interests are feminist theory, care ethics, science fiction, and graphic novels.

Gabriella Colombo Machado est candidate au Doctorat en anglais à l'Université de Montréal. Sa thèse porte sur la politique de l'amitié féminine dans la fiction spéculative contemporaine à travers les médias. Elle est titulaire d'une Maîtrise en littérature comparée de l'Université Western, en Ontario, et d'une Maîtrise en littératures anglaises de l'Université libre d'Amsterdam. Ses intérêts de recherche sont la théorie féministe, l'éthique de la sollicitude, la science fiction et les romans graphiques.

Costa, Cristiane

Cristiane Costa is a Brazilian writer, journalist, publishing and digital editor. She holds a PhD in Communication and Culture and is currently an associate professor in Journalism at Universidade Federal do Rio de Janeiro. "Love letters to strangers" is part of a post-doctoral research project on new narrative strategies for digital media completed at the Contemporary Culture Advanced Program (Pacc-UFRJ). A literary critic, with six fiction and non-fictions books published, she is also editor of the site Zona Digital.

Cristiane Costa est écrivaine, journaliste, éditrice et rédactrice numérique brésilienne. Elle détient un doctorat en communication et culture. Elle est professeure adjointe en journalisme à l'Université fédérale de Rio de Janeiro. « Love letters to strangers » fait partie d'un projet de recherche postdoctoral sur les nouvelles stratégies de narration pour les médias numériques complété au Contemporary Culture Advanced Program (Pacc-UFRJ). Critique littéraire, elle a fait paraître six ouvrages de fiction et essais. Elle est également rédactrice du site Zona Digital.

David, Sylvain

Sylvain David is a professor in the Department of French Studies at Concordia University, where he teaches 20th century and contemporary French literature. He has published the essay *Cioran. Un héroïsme à rebours* (2006) as well as the novels *Faire violence* (2013) and *Requiem en punk mineur* (2019). As a member of the group RADICAL, he contributed to the collection *Soif de réalité. Plongées dans l'imaginaire contemporain* (2018). Since the summer of 2016, he writes the "TV series" column for *L'Inconvénient.* In June 2019, he was named director of the academic journal *Captures.* His recent work focuses on the links between literature and media.

Sylvain David est professeur au Département d'études françaises de l'Université Concordia, où il enseigne la littérature française du XXe siècle et contemporaine. Il a publié l'essai *Cioran. Un héroïsme à rebours* (2006) ainsi que les romans *Faire violence* (2013) et *Requiem en punk mineur* (2019). Membre du groupe RADICAL, il a contribué à l'ouvrage collectif *Soif de réalité. Plongées dans l'imaginaire contemporain* (2018). Il tient, depuis l'été 2016, la chronique « Séries télé » de la revue *L'Inconvénient.* Depuis juin 2019, il est directeur de la revue *Captures.* Ses travaux récents portent sur les liens entre littérature et médias.

Ensslin, Astrid

Astrid Ensslin (she/her) is a professor in Digital Humanities and Game Studies at the University of Alberta, where she directs the BA Media Studies and the Faculty of Arts' "Digital Synergies" signature area. Her research examines electronic literature, digital fiction, cultural studies, gender and the body, as well as corpus-driven and sociolinguistic approaches to the language of gaming. Her latest books include *Digital Fiction and the Unnatural* (Ohio State UP, forthcoming 2021), *Approaches to Videogame Discourse* (Bloomsbury, 2019), and *Literary Gaming* (MIT Press, 2014). Her new monograph, *Pre-Web Digital Publishing and the Lore of Electronic Literature*, is under contract with Cambridge University Press. She is a Director of the Electronic Literature Organization and Project Director of the Electronic Literature Directory, and she leads the SSHRC-funded insight grant project, "Writing New Bodies: Critical Co-Design for 21st Century Digital-Born Bibliotherapy."

Astrid Ensslin (elle) est professeure en humanités numériques et en sciences du jeu à l'Université de l'Alberta, où elle est directrice du Baccalauréat en Sociologie des médias et du programme de recherche « Digital Synergies », qui fait partie des initiatives signature areas de la Faculté des arts. Ses recherches portent sur la littérature électronique, la fiction numérique, les études culturelles, le genre et le corps, ainsi que sur les approches sociolinguistiques ou basées sur des corpus pour le langage du jeu vidéo. Parmi ses dernières publications se trouvent *Digital Fiction and the Unnatural* (Ohio State UP, 2021), *Approaches to Videogame Discourse* (Bloomsbury, 2019) et *Literary Gaming* (MIT Press, 2014). Sa nouvelle monographie, *Pre-Web Digital Publishing and the Lore of Electronic Literature*, paraîtra aux Presses universitaires de Cambridge. Elle est directrice de la Electronic Literature Organization et du projet Electronic Literature Directory et elle dirige le projet « Écrire de nouveaux corps : co-conception critique pour la bibliothérapie numérique du 21e siècle », subventionné par le programme Savoir du CRSH.

Funkhouser, Christopher

Christopher Funkhouser is a writer, musician, and multimedia artist. He is author of two scholarly monographs, *Prehistoric Digital Poetry: An Archeology of Forms, 1959-1995* and *New Directions in Digital Poetry*; his poetry chapbooks include the titles *pressAgain*, *Subsoil Lutes*, and *Electro Perdix*. In 2009, he was commissioned by the Associated Press to prepare digital poems for the occasion of Barack Obama's inauguration; in 2016, he performed at the Whitney Museum's *Open Plan: Cecil Taylor* exhibition. Funkhouser teaches at New Jersey Institute of Technology, is a Contributing Editor at PennSound, and hosts POET RAY'D YO on WGXC in Hudson, NY.

Christopher Funkhouser est un écrivain, musicien et artiste multimédia. Il est l'auteur de deux monographies savantes, *Prehistoric Digital Poetry: An Archeology of Forms, 1959-1995* et *New Directions in Digital Poetry*, et de recueils de poésie, dont *pressAgain*, *Subsoil Lutes*, et *Electro Perdix*. En 2009, il a été chargé par l'Associated Press de préparer des poèmes numériques à l'occasion de l'inauguration de Barack Obama; en 2016, il a offert une performance dans le cadre de l'exposition *Open Plan: Cecil Taylor* du Whitney Museum of American Art. Il est professeur au New Jersey Institute of Technology, collaborateur à la rédaction à PennSound et il anime POET RAY'D YO sur WGXC à Hudson, NY.

Gervais, Bertrand

A professor in the Department of Literary Studies at the Université du Québec à Montréal, **Bertrand Gervais** holds the Canada Research Chair in Digital Art and Literature and is the director of the NT2 Laboratory, created in 2004. He was the founder (1999) and director (1999-2015) of Figura, the Center for Research on the Text and Imagination, and is the principal investigator for the CRSH partnership *Littérature québécoise mobile* (2019-2024). In 2018, he received the Excellence Award for Information Technology in Arts and Social Sciences from the Canadian Society for Digital Humanities and was elected to the Academy of Arts, Humanities and Sciences of the Royal Society of Canada. He conducts research on theories of the imagination, the contemporary, and the digital. His most recent publications are: *Architectures de mémoire* (co edited with Jean-Marie Dallet at the Presses du Réel, 2019), *Soif de réalité. Plongées dans l'imaginaire contemporain* (a collective publication from Nota Bene, 2018) and the novel *La dernière guerre* (XYZ, 2017).

Professeur titulaire au Département d'études littéraires de l'Université du Québec à Montréal, **Bertrand Gervais** est le titulaire de la Chaire de recherche du Canada sur les arts et les littératures numériques, ainsi que le directeur du NT2, créé en 2004. Fondateur et directeur (1999-2015) de Figura, le Centre de recherche sur le texte et l'imaginaire, il est le chercheur principal du partenariat CRSH *Littérature québécoise mobile* (2019-2024). En 2018, il a reçu le Prix d'excellence pour l'informatique dans les arts et les sciences humaines de la Société canadienne des Humanités numériques et il a été élu à l'académie des arts, des lettres et des sciences humaines de la Société royale du Canada. Il mène des recherches sur les théories de l'imaginaire, sur le contemporain et sur le numérique. Ses derniers titres sont : *Architectures de mémoire* (édité avec Jean-Marie Dallet aux Presses du Réel, 2019), *Soif de réalité. Plongées dans l'imaginaire contemporain* (un collectif paru aux éditions Nota Bene, 2018) et le roman *La dernière guerre* (éditions XYZ, 2017).

Goicoechea, María

María Goicoechea studied English Philology at the University Complutense of Madrid (UCM) and at the University of East Anglia (UEA), UK. She later obtained a MSc in Education (Secondary Education, English) at UCM and an MA in Intercultural Communication at the University of Maryland Baltimore County (UMBC), USA. Her doctoral dissertation is entitled *The Reader in Cyberspace: A Literary Ethnography of Cyberculture* (2004). Her research interests include literary theory, ethnography, and cyberculture. She is currently a teacher in the English Department at the University Complutense of Madrid (UCM) and Principal Investigator of the project eLITE-CM in Electronic Literary Edition. Goicoechea is part of LEETHI (UCM), and of HERMENEIA (Universitat de Barcelona), two research groups dedicated to the study of literature and computers.

María Goicoechea a étudié la philologie anglaise à l'Université Complutense de Madrid (UCM) et à l'Université de l'Est-Anglie (UEA) en Angleterre. Elle a ensuite obtenu une Maîtrise en éducation (éducation secondaire, anglais) à l'UCM ainsi qu'une Maîtrise en communication interculturelle à l'Université du Maryland Baltimore County (UMBC) aux États-Unis. Sa thèse s'intitule *The Reader in Cyberspace: A Literary Ethnography of Cyberculture* (2004). Ses intérêts de recherche incluent la théorie littéraire, l'ethnographie et la cyberculture. Elle est actuellement professeure au Département de littérature anglaise de l'UCM et chercheuse principale du projet eLITE-CM en édition littéraire électronique. Elle fait partie de LEETHI (UCM) et d'HERMENEIA (Universitat de Barcelona), deux groupes de recherche consacrés à l'étude de la littérature et des ordinateurs.

Guilet, Anaïs

Anaïs Guilet is an associate professor in Comparative Literature at the University of Savoy Mont Blanc – Chambery (France). She is affiliated with the LLSETI research lab where she codirects Team 3 of Research Area 2, dedicated to the "Body in question" («Corps en question»). She is an associated member of FIGURA – Center for Research on the Text and Imagination at the Université du Québec à Montréal. As a specialist in digital humanities, her research focuses on digital and transmedial aesthetics and poetics, the role of the book in contemporary culture, as well as representations of the body in a digital context.
Website: www.cyborglitteraire.com

Anaïs Guilet est maîtresse de conférences en Littératures comparées à l'Université Savoie Mont Blanc à Chambéry (France). Elle est rattachée au laboratoire de recherche LLSETI où elle codirige l'équipe 3 de l'axe 2 consacré au « Corps en question ». Elle est membre associée de FIGURA – Centre de recherche sur le texte et l'imaginaire, à l'Université du Québec à Montréal. Spécialisée dans les humanités numériques, ses recherches portent sur les esthétiques et poétiques numériques et transmédiatiques, sur la place du livre dans la culture contemporaine ainsi que sur les représentations du corps en contexte numérique.
Site Web : **www.cyborglitteraire.com**

Henrickson, Leah

Leah Henrickson is a recent doctoral graduate from Loughborough University. Her research has been published in such peer-reviewed journals as *Digital Creativity and Visual Communication*, as well as in popular outlets like *The Independent* and *3:AM Magazine*. Her monograph about reading computer-generated texts (Cambridge University Press) is forthcoming.
Twitter: @leahhenrickson

Leah Henrickson a récemment obtenu un doctorat de l'Université de Loughborough. Ses recherches ont été publiées dans des revues à comité de pairs telles que *Digital Creativity et Visual Communication*, ainsi que dans des revues populaires comme *The Independent* et *3:AM Magazine*. Sa monographie sur la lecture de textes générés par ordinateur paraîtra prochainement aux Presses de l'Université de Cambridge.
Twitter : **@leahhenrickson**

James, Kedrick

Kedrick James is Director of the Digital Literacy Centre, associate professor and Deputy Head of the Department of Language and Literacy Education at the University of British Columbia. He has published numerous articles utilizing digital arts based research and poetic inquiry to investigate automation of literacy, glitch pedagogy, transmediation, data visualization and sonification, and has published on network theory and critical media studies, as well as working extensively in curriculum studies of teacher education. Born in Vancouver, Canada, and based in the Boundary Country of British Columbia, he has worked as a professional poet, musician, and digital media artist, and has performed and presented his work internationally for more than 30 years. A specialist in English Language Arts education, he emphasizes the intersections of analogue and digital processes in creation of contemporary onto-epistemologies.
Website: www.kedrickjames.net

Kedrick James est directeur du Digital Literacy Centre, professeur agrégé et directeur adjoint du département d'enseignement des langues et de l'alphabétisation à l'Université de la Colombie-Britannique. Il a publié de nombreux articles employant des recherches basées sur les arts numériques et l'enquête poétique pour étudier l'automatisation de l'alphabétisation, la pédagogie des glitchs, la transmédiation, la visualisation des données et la sonification. Il a également publié sur la théorie des réseaux et les études critiques des médias, et a beaucoup travaillé sur les programmes de formation des enseignants. Né à Vancouver, au Canada et basé dans la province de la Colombie-Britannique, il a aussi travaillé en tant que poète, musicien et artiste numérique et a présenté ses œuvres à l'échelle internationale pendant plus de trente ans. En tant que spécialiste de l'enseignement de l'anglais, il met toujours l'emphase sur la rencontre des processus analogiques et numériques dans la création des onto-épistémologies contemporaines.
Site Web : **www.kedrickjames.net**

Kalinovski, Roman

Roman Kalinovski is an artist and art critic living and working in Brooklyn, NY. He received a Bachelor's of Fine Arts from Syracuse University's College of Visual and Performing Arts, and a Master's of Fine Arts from Pratt Institute. His paintings and digital artworks have been exhibited at galleries and venues in New York and abroad, and his writings on art have been published in *artcritical, Arcade Project, Quiet Lunch,* and *Hyperallergic*, among other outlets.

Roman Kalinovski est un artiste et un critique habitant et travaillant à Brooklyn, NY. Il détient un baccalauréat en beaux-arts de la Faculté des arts visuels et du spectacle de l'Université de Syracuse ainsi qu'une maîtrise en beaux-arts de l'Institut Pratt. Ses tableaux et ses œuvres numériques ont été exposés dans des galeries et d'autres lieux à New York et à l'étranger, et ses écrits sur l'art ont fait l'objet de publications dans *artcritical, Arcade Project, Quiet Lunch* et *Hyperallergic*, parmi d'autres.

Klobucar, Andrew

Andrew Klobucar, Associate Professor of English at New Jersey Institute of Technology in Newark, New Jersey is a literary theorist and teacher, specializing in internet research, electronic literature, and semantic technologies. His research on experimental literary forms and screen-based writing critically analyzes the transformative effect digital technology continues to have on the literary arts. He has worked on developing software for writing instruction and written on the use of programmable media in classroom instruction. Two books focusing on algorithmic culture and literature entitled *The Community and the Algorithm: A Digital Interactive Poetics from Vernon Press* and *The Algorithmic Impulse: Programmable Writing and the Aesthetics of Information are forthcoming.*

Andrew Klobucar, professeur agrégé au New Jersey Institute of Technology à Newark, New Jersey, est un théoricien et enseignant de littérature spécialisé dans la recherche sur Internet, la littérature électronique et les technologies sémantiques. Ses recherche sur les formes littéraires expérimentales et l'écriture à l'écran analysent de manière critique l'effet transformateur que la technologie numérique continue d'avoir sur les arts littéraires. Il a travaillé au développement de logiciels pour les cours de rédaction et il a écrit sur l'utilisation des médias programmables dans l'enseignement en classe. Ses deux ouvrages sur la culture et la littérature algorithmiques intitulés *The Company and the Algorithm: A Digital Interactive Poetics de Vernon Press* et *The Algorithmic Impulse: Programmable Writing and the Aesthetics of Information* paraîtront sous peu.

Lefebvre, Michel

Michel Lefebvre is a writer and cultural manager. He employs a multidisciplinary and collaborative practice in the field of digital arts. A pioneer of interactive fiction in Quebec, he pursues the exploration of new narrative forms as the director and cofounder of the artists' center TOPO. He has also created numerous websites for cultural organizations through his company, *Productions Sous le manteau.*

Michel Lefebvre, écrivain et gestionnaire culturel, a investi le champ des arts numériques avec une pratique multidisciplinaire et collaborative. Pionnier de la fiction interactive au Québec, il poursuit l'exploration de nouvelles formes narratives à titre de directeur et cofondateur du centre d'artistes TOPO. Il a aussi réalisé de nombreux sites web pour des organismes culturels avec sa compagnie *Productions Sous le manteau.*

Machado, Ana Maria

Ana Maria Machado holds a PhD in Medieval Hagiography from the University of Coimbra, where she is also currently teaching and member of the Portuguese Literature Centre. Her research has been focused on medieval literature (hagiography) and medievalism, comparative literature (imagology), teaching literature (reading comprehension abilities), and digital literature (reading). She is a professor at the bachelor, master and doctoral levels. She teaches subjects related to Portuguese Literature and Portuguese Literature Teaching. She is a member of the textbooks accreditation team within the Portuguese Ministry of Education and the coordinator of the following projects: *Inanimate Alice: Tradução de Literatura Digital em Contexto Educativo; Murais e Literatura: A Criação Digital em Contexto Educativo*; and "Literature in Portuguese as Foreign Language Teaching" and "Medievalism in Portuguese Language" (book upcoming). She has also coordinated the Portuguese Teaching cycle on "Literature and other Arts" (book upcoming). With A. Aguilar, she now coordinates the journal *MatLit*, vol. 8.1, on Teaching Digital Literature.

Ana Maria Machado détient un Doctorat en hagiographie médiévale de l'Université de Coimbra, où elle enseigne et est membre du Centre de littérature portugaise. Sa recherche s'est focalisée sur la littérature médiévale (hagiographie) et médiéviste, sur la littérature comparée (imagologie), sur l'enseignement de la littérature (habiletés de lecture et de compréhension), et sur la littérature numérique (lecture). Elle est professeure aux trois cycles et elle enseigne, plus spécifiquement, sur des sujets reliés à la littérature portugaise. Elle est membre de l'équipe d'accréditation des manuels scolaires pour le Ministre de l'éducation portugais ainsi que coordonnatrice pour les projets suivants : *Inanimate Alice: Tradução de Literatura Digital em Contexto Educativo; Murais e Literatura: A Criação Digital em Contexto Educativo*, "Literature in Portuguese as Foreign Language Teaching" et "Medievalism in Portuguese Language" (ouvrage à paraître). Elle a également coordonné le cycle d'enseignement portugais "Literature and other Arts" (ouvrage à paraître). Elle dirige actuellement, aux côtés d'A. Aguilar, la revue *MatLit*, vol. 8, no. 1, sur l'enseignement de la littérature numérique.

Magalhães, Cecília

Cecília Magalhães is a designer and doctoral candidate in Materialities of Literature at the University of Coimbra. Based on an ethnographic and participatory approach to analyse the experimental uses of the LdoD Archive: Collaborative Digital Archive of the Book of Disquiet (**https://ldod.uc.pt/**, CLP, 2017), she has organized workshops for scholarly and artistic audiences in Portugal and Brazil since 2017. Information about her "Fragments in Practice" PhD project can be found on its Facebook page and Youtube channel. Her research is funded by the Foundation for Science and Technology (FCT).
Facebook: **https://www.facebook.com/fragmentos.pratica/**
Youtube: **https://bit.ly/3eZUkBb**

Cecília Magalhães est designer et étudiante au Doctorat en Matérialités de littérature à l'Université de Coimbra. À partir d'une approche ethnographique et participative pour analyser les usages expérimentaux du LdoD Archive: Collaborative Digital Archive of the Book of Disquiet (**https://ldod.uc.pt/**, CLP, 2017), elle organise, depuis 2017, des ateliers pour des publics savants et artistiques au Portugal et au Brésil. Des informations sur son projet doctoral « Fragments in Practice » sont disponibles sur la page Facebook du projet et la chaîne Youtube. Ses recherches sont subventionnés par la Fondation des sciences et technologies (FCT).
Facebook : **https://www.facebook.com/fragmentos.pratica/**
Youtube : **https://bit.ly/3eZUkBb**

Marcotte, Sophie

Sophie Marcotte is a professor of literature in the Department of French Studies at Concordia University and is the director of Figura-NT2 Concordia. An expert in Quebec literature, her research interests in the last fifteen years focus on archives and electronic publication of literary manuscripts. She managed the HyperRoy project (**hyperroy.nt2.uqam.ca**) and edited the collection *Regards sur les archives d'écrivains francophones au Canada* (University of Ottawa Press, 2019). Her current research deals with representations and influence of digital culture and devices in the contemporary novel.

Sophie Marcotte est professeure de littérature au Département d'études françaises de l'Université Concordia et directrice de Figura-NT2 Concordia. Spécialiste de littérature québécoise, elle s'intéresse, depuis une quinzaine d'années, aux archives et à l'édition électronique de manuscrits d'écrivains. Elle a notamment mis sur pied le projet HyperRoy (**hyperroy.nt2.uqam.ca**) et dirigé le collectif *Regards sur les archives d'écrivains francophones au Canada* (Presses de l'Université d'Ottawa, 2019). Ses recherches actuelles portent sur les représentations du numérique dans le roman contemporain.

Marquet, Vinicius

Vinicius Marquet is a designer, an artist and a researcher. He holds a BA in Visual communication from the National Autonomous University of Mexico (UNAM); an MA in Interaction and Game design from the Utrecht School of the Arts (HKU) & The Open University and a postgraduate degree in Digital storytelling from the Royal Academy of Fine Arts of Ghent. He is currently a PhD student in Arts at KU Leuven with the LUCA School of Arts where he researches the remediation of collaborative storytelling workshops into the (information) network and programmable media. In 2017, the Centro de Cultura digital published his short story *Bucle: archivo de ficciones*, a hyperfiction based on Ulises Carrión's life and artwork. In 2009 his project *Anacron* was included in the *Electronic Literature Collection Volume 3*. Recently, under the context of COVID-19, he released **imaginaviral.net**, a platform that explores the online workshop experiences and brings people together.

Vinicius Marquet est designer, artiste et chercheur. Il détient un baccalauréat en communication visuelle de l'Université nationale autonome du Mexique (UNAM); une maîtrise en interaction et conception de jeux de l'École de Beaux-Arts d'Utrecht et de l'Université ouverte ainsi qu'un diplôme complémentaire en narration numérique de l'Académie Royale des Beaux-Arts de Gand. Il est actuellement étudiant au doctorat en art à la KU Leuven au LUCA School of Arts, où il s'intéresse à la remédiation des ateliers collaboratifs de narration en ligne (dans les réseaux informatiques) et aux médias programmables. En 2017, le Centro de Cultura digital a publié son récit *Bucle: archivo de ficciones*, une hyperfiction basée sur l'œuvre et la vie d'Ulises Carrión. En 2009 son œuvre *Anacron* est apparue dans le *Electronic Literature Collection Volume 3*. Dans le contexte de la COVID-19, il a récemment lancé **imaginaviral.net**, une plateforme qui explore l'expérience de l'atelier en ligne et qui réunit les gens.

Muntean, Reese

Reese Muntean is a professor of Interactive Media within the School of Media at the University of Quebec in Montreal (UQAM). His work is inspired from visual art, artificial intelligence, artificial life, biology and cognitive sciences. His computational artistic practice branches through multiple media including robotics, interactive installations, immersive environments, physical computing interventions, internet art, and electronic literature. He is currently working on a book about new media art in the age of machine learning. His work and research have been presented in multiple international events and venues around the world.

Reese Muntean est professeur en médias interactifs à l'Université du Québec à Montréal. Son travail s'inspire de l'art visuel, de l'intelligence artificielle, de la vie artificielle, de la biologie et des sciences cognitives. Sa pratique artistique computationnelle s'étend à de nombreux médias, notamment la robotique, les installations interactives, les environnements immersifs, les interventions informatiques physiques, l'art web et la littérature électronique. Il travaille actuellement sur un livre sur l'art des nouveaux médias à l'âge de l'apprentissage automatique. Ses œuvres et ses recherches ont été présentées à des nombreux événements internationaux.

Gómez, Verónica Paula

Verónica Gómez is an Argentinian doctoral candidate at Universidad Nacional del Litoral (viva voce: July 2020) and fellow researcher at CONICET (Council of Scientific and Technical Research of Argentina). She holds a BA in Modern Literature (Universidad de Buenos Aires, 2008) and an MA in Comparative Cultures and Literature (Universidad Nacional de Córdoba, 2015). Her research interest focuses on the relation between e-literature and its location(s), taking the Electronic Literature Organization as a case study. She investigates where e-literature locates itself when it abandons its national belonging. Nowadays, she is working on her postdoctoral project and on a collective project entitled "Archives in Transition" thanks to a grant from the European Union (RISE-Marie Curie, Horizon 2020-2024). She is a member of LiteLat (http://litelat.net/) and the Red de Cultura Digital (http://www.redculturadigital.net/) and was an Erasmus Mundus+ICM Fellow (Universitá Ca'Foscari UNIVE / Venice-Italy, 2018) and DAAD-Short-Term Grants Fellow (Goethe-Institut Frankfurt am Main, Universität Frankfurt / Germany, 2019).

Verónica Gómez est doctorante argentine de l'Université Nationale du Littoral (soutenance : juillet 2020) et chercheuse associée au CONICET (Council of Scientific and Technical Research of Argentina). Elle est diplômée d'un baccalauréat en littératures modernes (Université de Beunos Aires, 2008) et d'une maîtrise en littératures et cultures comparées (Université Nationale de Córdoba, 2015). Son intérêt de recherche porte sur le rapport entre la littérature électronique et ses emplacements, en prenant la Electronic Literature Organization comme étude de cas. Elle cherche à savoir où la littérature électronique se situe lorsqu'elle abandonne son appartenance nationale. Aujourd'hui, elle travaille sur son projet postdoctoral et sur un projet collectif intitulé « Archives en transition » avec une bourse de l'Union Européenne (RISE-Marie Curie, Horizon 2020-2024). Elle est membre du LiteLat (**http://litelat.net/**) et de la Red de Cultura Digital (**http://www.redculturadigital.net/**) et a été boursière Erasmus Mundus+ICM ((Universitá Ca'Foscari UNIVE / Venice-Italy, 2018) et DAAD (Goethe-Institut Frankfurt am Main, Universität Frankfurt / Germany, 2019).

Peña, Ernesto

Ernesto Peña holds a PhD in Language and Literacy Education from the University of British Columbia. Previous to graduate work, he acquired international experience as a professional designer and design educator. He is currently Director of Research in a Vancouver-based fintech startup and an Adjunct Professor in the Master in Educational Technology at the University of British Columbia. His doctoral research explored the mobilization and evolution of Visual Literacy across disciplines from its earliest occurrence in literature until the present day. His experience as both a producer and an analyst of visual discourses has been informed by classical design approaches such as Peircean semiotics and visual rhetoric. Ernesto's research work has been published in journals such as Visible Language, Design Issues and Leonardo.

Ernesto Peña est titulaire d'un Doctorat en langues et en alphabétisation de l'Université de la Colombie-Britannique. Avant d'obtenir son diplôme, il a acquis de l'expérience internationale en tant que designer professionnel et éducateur en design. Il est actuellement directeur de recherche dans une startup fintech basée à Vancouver ainsi que professeur titulaire à la Maîtrise en technologie éducative de l'Université de la Colombie-Britannique. Ses recherches doctorales ont porté sur la mobilisation et l'évolution de l'alphabétisation visuelle dans toutes les disciplines depuis sa première apparition dans la littérature jusqu'à nos jours. Son expérience en tant que producteur et analyste des discours visuels a été nourrie par les approches classiques du design telles que la sémiotique de Pierce et la rhétorique visuelle.

Portela, Manuel

Manuel Portela directs the PhD Program in Materialities of Literature at the University of Coimbra. He is the author of *Scripting Reading Motions: The Codex and the Computer as Self-Reflexive Machines* (MIT Press, 2013), the general editor of LdoD Archive: Collaborative Digital Archive of the Book of Disquiet (**https://ldod.uc.pt**, CLP, 2017), and one of the contributors to *The Bloomsbury Handbook of Electronic Literature* (2017). He has published widely on digital literature and digital editing.

Manuel Portela est directeur du programme doctoral de Matérialités de littérature à l'Université de Coimbra. Il est auteur de *Scripting Reading Motions: The Codex and the Computer as Self-Reflexive Machines* (MIT Press, 2013), rédacteur général du LdoD Archive: Collaborative Digital Archive of the Book of Disquiet (**https://ldod.uc.pt**, CLP, 2017) et l'un des contributeurs à *The Bloomsbury Handbook of Electronic Literature* (2017). Il a publié de nombreux ouvrages sur la littérature et l'édition numériques.

Prado, Gilbertto

Gilbertto Prado holds a PhD in Arts from the University of Paris 1 Panthéon-Sorbonne in France with a Post-Doctorate from the Polytechnic University of Valencia, Spain. He has also previously held the position of Lecturer-Professor at the Arts Institute of São Paulo State University (UNESP). He holds a degree in Engineering and Visual Arts at University of Campinas, where he later held the position of Professor at the Arts Institute. He has also held the position of Invited Professor at the University Paris 8 Vincennes-Saint-Denis in France. He is a retired Full Professor at the School of Communications and Arts at the University of São Paulo and coordinator of the group Poéticas Digitais. As an artist, he has held and participated in numerous exhibitions in Brazil and abroad. He received the 9th Prix Möbius International des Multimedia in Beijing, China in 2001; the Rumos Award in 2000 and the Transmídia in 2002 from the Itaú Cultural and the 6th Sergio Motta Award for Art and Technology in 2006. He is currently a professor in the Postgraduate Design Program at Anhembi Morumbi University.

Gilbertto Prado est titulaire d'un doctorat en art de l'Université Paris 1 Panthéon-Sorbonne en France et d'un diplôme postdoctoral de l'Université polytechnique de Valence en Espagne. Il fut également conférencier-professeur à l'Institut des arts de l'Université d'État de São Paulo (UNESP). Il est diplômé en ingénierie et arts visuels de l'Université de Campinas où plus tard il a été professeur à l'Institut d'art. Il a aussi été professeur invité à l'Université Paris 8 en France. Il est professeur retraité de l'École de Communications et arts à l'Université de São Paulo et coordonnateur du groupe Poéticas Digitais. En tant qu'artiste, il a organisé et participé à de nombreuses expositions au Brésil et à l'étranger. Il est lauréat du 9e Prix Möbius International des Multimédia au Beijing, Chine en 2001, le prix Rumos en 2000 et le prix Transmídia en 2002 du Itaú Cultural et le 6e Prix Sergio Motta pour Art et Technologie en 2006. Il est actuellement Professeur au programme du troisième cycle en Design à l'Université d'Anhembi Morumbi..

Quintas, Eva

Eva Quintas is a photographer and media artist. She is the cofounder of TOPO, where she serves as president of the artistic committee and secretary of the board of directors. She is the managing director of the ARTENSO center for research and innovation in art and social engagement in affiliation with the Cégep of Saint-Laurent in Montreal.

Eva Quintas, artiste en photographie et arts médiatiques, est cofondatrice de TOPO où elle agit à titre de présidente du comité artistique et de secrétaire du conseil d'administration. Elle est directrice générale du centre de recherche et de transfert en pratiques sociales novatrices ARTENSO, affilié au Cégep de Saint-Laurent, à Montréal.

Rodríguez, Jessica

Jessica Rodríguez is a visual/audio artist, designer and researcher currently completing a PhD in Communication, New Media and Cultural Studies at McMaster University in Canada. Her practice focuses on audiovisual practices, and live coding to produce a language for live visual music.

Jessica Rodríguez est artiste, conceptrice et chercheuse. Elle est actuellement étudiante au doctorat en communication, nouveaux médias et études culturelles à l'Université McMaster au Canada. Sa pratique se concentre sur les pratiques audiovisuelles et le codage en direct pour produire un langage pour la musique visuelle en direct.

Rodríguez, Rolando

Rolando Rodríguez holds a Master's degree in Contemporary Arts and is currently completing a Master's in Pedagogy. His work focuses on the exploration of three elements: image, text and sound. He leads research and production projects that use analog and digital technologies as tools to explore expanded possibilities through text.

Rolando Rodríguez est titulaire d'une maîtrise en arts contemporains et termine actuellement une maîtrise en pédagogie. Son travail se concentre sur l'exploration de trois éléments : l'image, le texte et le son. Il entreprend des projets de recherche et de production qui se servent des technologies analogiques et numériques afin d'explorer des possibilités élargies à travers le texte.

Saklofske, Jon

Jon Saklofske is a Literature Professor at Acadia University in Nova Scotia, Canada. His interest in the ways that William Blake's composite art illuminates the relationship between words and images on the printed page has inspired current research into alternative platforms for open social scholarship as well as larger correlations between media forms and cultural perceptions. In addition to experimenting with virtual environments and games as tools for academic research, communication and pedagogy, Jon's other research interests include virtuality and environmental storytelling in Disney theme parks, research creation experiments, and the relationship between networks and narratives in video games.

Jon Saklofske est professeur de littérature à l'Université Acadia en Nouvelle-Écosse. Son intérêt pour la façon dont l'art composite de William Blake met en lumière la relation entre les mots et les images sur la page imprimée a inspiré ses recherches actuelles sur les plateformes alternatives de recherche sociale ouverte ainsi que sur les corrélations plus vastes entre les formes médiatiques et les perceptions culturelles. Outre l'expérimentation d'environnements et de jeux virtuels comme outils de recherche universitaire, de communication et de pédagogie, Saklofske s'intéresse également à la virtualité et à la narration environnementale dans les parcs à thème Disney, aux expériences de recherche-création et à la relation entre les réseaux et les récits dans les jeux vidéo.

Silva Pereira, Paulo

Paulo Silva Pereira is Assistant Professor of the Department of Languages, Literatures and Cultures at the School of Arts and Humanities at the University of Coimbra and a Member of the Centre for Portuguese Literature. He holds a PhD from the University of Coimbra, teaches in the areas of Portuguese Literature; Interart Studies; Literature, Arts and Media, and Digital Humanities. He has published several works on Portuguese literature from the sixteenth to the eighteenth centuries and on digital media. He is a member of the project LdoD Archive, a collaborative digital archive of the Book of Disquiet. He co-edited an issue of *MATLIT* on "Arts, Media and Digital Culture," and has been working as thesis adviser on research projects in the fields of Digital Humanities, intermediality, and digital media. He is Director of the PhD Programme in Portuguese Language Literature and currently the principal investigator of the project "Ex Machina: Inscription and Literature." He is also a member of the COST Action "Distant Reading for European Literary History."

Paulo Silva Pereira est professeur titulaire au Département de langues, littératures et cultures à l'École des arts et lettres à l'Université de Coimbra et membre du Centre de littérature portugaise. Il détient un Doctorat de l'Université de Coimbra, enseigne dans les domaines de la littérature portugaise, des études inter-artistiques, de la littérature, des arts et des médias, et des humanités numériques. Il a publié sur de nombreuses œuvres de littérature portugaise du seizième au dix-huitième siècles et sur les médias numériques. Il est membre du project LdoD Archive, une archive numérique collaborative sur le Livre de l'intranquillité. Il a co-dirigé un numéro de *MATLIT* sur les « Arts, médias et culture numérique », et travaille comme directeur de mémoire sur des projets de recherches dans les domaines des humanités numériques, l'intermédialité et les médias numériques. Il est directeur du programme doctoral en littérature de langue portugaise et du projet de recherche « Ex Machina : Inscription et littérature ». Il est aussi membre du COST Action « La lecture à distance pour l'histoire littéraire européenne ».

Sondheim, Alan

Alan Sondheim is a new media artist, musician, writer, and performer concerned with issues of virtuality, and the stake that the real world has in the virtual. His writing is known for its "somatic grit" and skeletal codes that partially appear within and determine the surface. The textual body and body of text are deeply entangled. He has been writing his "Internet Text," a daily meditation on virtuality, daily for twenty-six Years.

Alan Sondheim est un artiste des nouveaux médias et de la performance, musicien et écrivain. Il s'intéresse à la virtualité et aux enjeux du monde réel dans l'univers virtuel. Son écriture est connue pour son « cran somatique » et son code squelettique qui apparaissent partiellement à l'intérieur et qui en détermine la surface. Le corps textuel et le corps du texte sont profondément enchevêtrés. Il écrit toujours son « Text Internet », une méditation quotidienne sur la virtualité, commencée il y a vingt-six ans.

Takeda, Yuya

Yuya Takeda is a PhD candidate in the Department of Language and Literacy Education at University of British Columbia. He studies conspiracy theories through an existentialist lens and explores how critical media literacy education can address the roles of desire in reading and writing of the world. He is also an experimental street photographer.
Twitter and Instagram: @yuyapecotakeda

Yuya Takeda est un étudiant en doctorat au Département d'enseignement des langues et de l'alphabétisation de l'Université de Colombie-Britannique. Il examine les théories du complot et explore comment l'éducation critique aux médias peut aborder les rôles du désir dans la lecture et l'écriture du monde d'un point de vue existentialiste. Il est également un photographe de rue expérimental.
Twitter et Instagram : **@yuyapecotakeda**

White, Melinda

Melinda M. White is a senior lecturer at the University of New Hampshire, where she teaches digital creative writing, electronic literature, and composition. She is a graduate of the interdisciplinary Media, Art, and Text PhD program at Virginia Commonwealth University and has been a member of the ELO since 2008. Intrigued by technology as a means of creative expression and ever-changing reader/author relationships, her research interests include postmodern and electronic literature, installation art, virtual reality, and immersive and embodied narratives. She has published and presented on digital composition and creative writing, digital feminist pedagogy, and immersive narratives. She also writes fiction, caters to two house bunnies, and is inexplicably obsessed with string theory. And elevators.

Melinda M. White est professeure à l'Université du New Hampshire, où elle enseigne la création littéraire numérique, la littérature électronique et la composition. Elle détient un doctorat en Médias, Arts et Textes interdisciplinaires de l'Université du Commonwealth de Virginie et est membre de ELO depuis 2008. Intriguée par la technologie en tant que moyen d'expression créative et par l'évolution constante des rapports lecteur/auteur, ses recherches portent sur la littérature postmoderne et électronique, l'art de l'installation, la réalité virtuelle et les récits immersifs et incarnés. Elle a publié des articles et présenté des conférences sur la composition et la création littéraire numérique, la pédagogie féministe numérique et les récits immersifs. Elle écrit également de la fiction, pourvoit aux besoins de deux lapins et est inexplicablement obsédée par la théorie des cordes. Et les ascenseurs.

ATTENTION À LA MARCHE MIND THE GAP

L'édition numérique multi supports est incluse, sans surcoût.

Pour y accéder :

**https://www.lespressesdelecureuil.net/
hm-attentionalamarche-mindthegap**

Une réalisation

Retrouvez-nous sur

www.lespressesdelecureuill.net